48.50

DOGS

A DICTIONARY
OF DOG BREEDS

DOGS

A DICTIONARY
OF DOG BREEDS

DESMOND MORRIS

EBURY PRESS
LONDON

√

Acknowledgements

Special thanks to the following: Julian Shuckburgh for his invaluable support in the early stages of this marathon project; Hannah MacDonald for her great enthusiasm in seeing it to fruition; Alison Wormleighton for her meticulous editing skills; and Philip Hood for completing his hundreds of drawings in record time.

First published in Great Britain in 2001

3 5 7 9 10 8 6 4 2

Ebury Press
Random House · 20 Vauxhall Bridge Road · London SW1V 2SA

Random House Australia Pty Limited
20 Alfred Street · Milsons Point · Sydney · New South Wales 2061 · Australia

Random House New Zealand Limited
18 Poland Road · Glenfield · Auckland 10 · New Zealand

Random House (Pty) Limited
Endulini · 5A Jubilee Road · Parktown 2193 · South Africa

The Random House Group Limited Reg. No. 954009

www.randomhouse.co.uk

Papers used by Ebury Press are natural, recyclable products made from wood grown in sustainable forests.

A CIP catalogue record for this book is available from the British Library.

ISBN 0 09 187091 7

Illustrations by Philip Hood

Edited by Alison Wormleighton

Typesetting by anizdamani@aol.com

Printed and bound by
Mackays of Chatham plc, Chatham, Kent

Contents

Introduction

This dictionary is the canine reference book I always wanted to have on my bookshelf. It was not there, so I had to write it myself. It has been a long journey through the byways of canine history, but it has been worth it because now, when any breed is mentioned, no matter how obscure, I should be able to turn up a brief account of it.

I have been fortunate in that my various activities have brought me in touch with a huge variety of dogs. Apart from my own family pets, I was able to study dingoes, wolves, jackals and coyotes in my role as Curator of Mammals at London Zoo in the 1960s. In the 1970s, when I lived in the Mediterranean region, I was able to take a closer look at many breeds I had never encountered before. In the 1980s, when I was a host on the television series *The Animals Roadshow* and *Animal Country*, I met new dog breeds and their owners almost every week, and also covered many major dog shows. In the 1990s my travels took me to over 70 different countries, where again I was able to make observations on more and more breeds.

I asked some canine experts how many breeds of dog there are in the world. One said about 200, another 300 and a third said there might be as many as 400. When I sat down to write this book I found that they had all underestimated and that my task was much bigger than I had realized. Even now, after investigating over 1,000 breeds, I feel sure that I must have missed some. I am haunted by the thought that, hidden somewhere in a country like Ecuador, or Burma, or Taiwan, there is a unique and fascinating breed, just waiting to be recorded. But for the moment, this volume presents all the ones that I have managed to uncover so far.

As this is a book solely about different breeds, it is important to define precisely what a breed is. According to my interpretation, a breed is a type of dog that differs from all others in some way, has a separate history and breed name, and has been breeding true for a number of generations. I include in this both the officially recognized and registered breeds that have been accepted by the major Kennel Clubs, and also the unrecognized ones that may never have entered a show-ring but have also played their part in the history of domestic dogs, no matter how small that part may have been.

It should be mentioned that all domestic dogs are descended from the wolf (*Canis lupus*).

Dogs have been in existence for at least 12,000 years, and probably much longer, and during that time there has been a progressive 'infantilizing' of the ancestral wolf species. That is to say, the wolf has, through domestication, become increasingly 'juvenile'. This process is called 'neoteny' and, whenever it occurs, it is accompanied by much greater variability in the anatomy and behaviour of the species concerned.

It is this variability that has helped so much in the creation of the different breeds. Curly tails, short legs, drooped ears, coat colour-patterns, and all the rest of the genetic variations that we now take for granted, began to appear thousands of years ago. Ancient artefacts show us just how varied dogs had become, even in the early civilizations of Egypt and the Middle East. Then, as the centuries passed, and dogs spread out around the globe, these variations increased dramatically. Dogs were asked to perform more and more tasks and they adapted brilliantly to our demands by changing in shape, size, colour and temperament. With the arrival of widespread field sports, the number of breeds multiplied yet again. And finally with the explosion of interest in companion dogs in recent centuries, the number of breeds rose once more.

Throughout this long history of the dog/man partnership, there have been six major types of dog breed, as follows:

FERAL BREEDS

Feral breeds are made up of populations of dogs that have been abandoned, or have left their human families, and have started to fend for themselves. They breed freely with one another, mixing together more and more until, after many years have passed, they start to develop a common type. This type may vary slightly from country to country, but it is surprising how similar the long-standing feral dogs are to one another. They all seem to be heading towards what could be called a 'dingo' condition. The Dingo itself is, of course, one of the most ancient of all feral dogs and has been in existence for thousands of years. In its long history it has stabilized its type to such an extent that it could almost join the carefully refined pedigree dogs in a major dog show.

ISOLATED BREEDS

Apart from the feral breeds (and the wild dogs), all others come under the control of man and each individual is associated with a particular person or family. In some cases, where isolated human communities are involved, a particular local breed may develop without any selective influence from its human companions, simply because it does not come into contact with other types of dog. Indigenous breeds that are isolated in this way for many years develop their own local type which is a pure-bred dog. This is not because its human companions have eliminated variants or are imposing selective breeding programmes, but because the native dogs have not suffered any dilution by random mixing with other breeds.

PROTECTED BREEDS

It is rare today for any breed to enjoy the luxury of complete genetic isolation. In most parts of the world, introduced dogs will soon inject their genetic qualities into the local population, and disrupt it. If the local dogs have, over the years, adapted well to their environment, or to the particular demands of their owners, then dilution from introduced dogs will have a detrimental effect and has to be resisted if the indigenous animals are to continue in their special relationship with their human families. In such cases, the local people, who may well be naive with regard to the subtleties of canine genetics, will seek to protect their old breeds from these new incursions. They may do no more than try to prevent cross-matings, or destroy mongrel litters, but it may be sufficient to keep their traditional breeds reasonably pure.

SPECIALIZED BREEDS

When a specific task requires a particular kind of dog, then the old indigenous breeds are subjected to selective breeding. Longer legs for faster runners, bigger bodies for imposing guardians, shorter legs for rapid diggers, thicker coats for northern sled-pullers, and many other such adaptations start to appear. To some extent these occur without human assistance. Thin-coated puppies in the frozen north do not have to be culled: they die out naturally. But in other cases, human selection does play a role. The individual dog that is the fastest runner, the one that can catch more game, is the one that is used for breeding the next generation. In this way, without applying any sophisticated genetic programmes, dog owners soon start to push their particular breed further and further in its specialized direction. This applies to personality as well as to anatomy. Hunting dogs must kill; sheep dogs must not.

REFINED BREEDS

Most of the breeds we know today have arisen as specialized breeds, modified for a particular function. They are working dogs, developed to be good at their given tasks. Sadly, for many of them, those tasks became obsolete during the 19th century, when industrialization dramatically altered human society. Cities grew bigger and became more densely populated, and even rural life became increasingly mechanized. A number of breeds became extinct as a result of these major changes, but human beings had become strongly attached to their canine partners and, even though these were no longer needed in their original capacities, there was a strong desire to keep them on, purely as companions. Many were kept as pets and, having no specialized duties, often lost their special features. Mongrels proliferated. But at the same time, competitive dog shows began and grew more and more popular as the 19th century drew to a close.

Throughout the 20th century, these dog shows flourished and, as a result, the old working breeds found themselves employed in a new role. All they had to do now was to look good, walk proudly and not bite the judges. In order for these competitions to work, each type of dog had to have a precise blueprint, a 'breed standard', against which all competitors could be assessed. This system exerted a new kind of pressure on the breeding of these show dogs, favouring rigid anatomical conformity and immaculate grooming. Working breeds that wore their scars with pride, like Foxhounds, were out in the cold. So too were Jack Russells and Lurchers, where personality had always been more important than anatomical conformity.

Most specialized breeds managed to adapt, however, and successfully made the switch from hard labour to beauty contest. In the process, three things happened to them. First, many differences in temperament had to be suppressed. The show dog was required to sparkle, even in a crowd of human strangers and surrounded by other dogs. If it was naturally shy of strangers, or aggressive to other dogs, those qualities had to be bred out of it. All show dogs had to become extroverts – good-natured, calm, friendly and outgoing – regardless of their past histories.

Second, anatomical variations had to be suppressed. Each breed had to become increasingly uniform. A splendid individual that happened to have one small feature which did not match the breed standard would be penalized.

Third, a creeping extremism overtook many breeds. If the breed standard called for a flat face, or short legs, or a long body, faces tended to get even flatter, legs even shorter and bodies even longer. In a few breeds this meant that the dogs began to suffer from various medical problems. Strictly speaking this type of exaggeration of special features should never have occurred, because the breed standard should have set down rules as to precisely how flat a face, or how short a leg, should be. But human nature being what it is, the competitive spirit often edges us towards extremes, as any body-builder or fashion model will confirm.

So, with hard labour in the field now only a distant memory, these new, refined breeds began to undergo progressive changes that set them apart from those dogs that still managed to fulfil a working role. 'Working-dog owners' were often critical of this split and referred disparagingly to the 'softness' of the 'showier' examples of the competition dogs. These criticisms were only justified, however, in a few cases. The vast majority of the competition breeds were actually improvements on their rough-and-ready ancestors. Refinement of a breed often meant perfecting it rather than weakening it. And, in any case, the function of these new show dogs was different, and it was unfair to overlook this fact when assessing them.

The great value of the refined breeds and the shows in which they compete is that they help to elevate the status of dogs generally. In some countries dogs are actively despised, and in many regions they have to endure a very low social status and all the abuses that go with it. Any country that has major dog shows and respected Kennel Clubs to organize them is a nation where some dogs, at least, are treated as highly valued members of society. Even for those not directly involved in the world of these refined breeds, there is a general feeling that they live in a culture where dogs are respected and, with luck, this attitude will spread far beyond the confines of the show-ring.

CREATED BREEDS

Finally, there is the controversial category of 'newly created breeds'. In these cases, somebody decides to invent a novel breed, either for fun or for profit, in order to add yet another name to the long list of approved dog breeds. Sometimes this starts out as a lucky accident, when an unplanned cross-mating occurs and the result is unusually appealing. Sometimes the cross-mating is deliberately contrived in order to combine two sets of good qualities to make an even better mixture out of them.

Most crosses lead to variable mongrels without a breed to call their own. Even when they are especially attractive, they fail to found a dynasty and their individual appeal dies with them. Once in a while, however, one of these crosses finds devoted enthusiasts to promote it. By back-crossing and inbreeding, they nudge it towards breeding true and eventually fix the type. At this point, if they can persuade enough other people to start breeding it, they can then form a small 'breed club', and begin campaigning to have their invention recognized by major canine organizations. This is not easy, because the well-established Kennel Clubs already have plenty of breeds on their lists and are resistant to modern novelties that may eventually prove to be no more than flash-in-the-pan fads.

Many traditionalists are openly hostile to these new dogs, claiming that they are often unstabilized, unhealthy or developed purely for commercial gain. These accusations may be justified in some cases, but not all. A number of new dogs do have special appeal and deserve their small place in the great rainbow of breeds.

Apart from stabilized crosses, there is one other kind of 'created breed' that deserves attention, and that is the distinctive variant of an existing breed. Many medium-sized dogs, for example, have been selectively bred down or up into dwarf or giant forms. Once these new size-types have become sufficiently extreme, they are then considered as separate breeds, and given their own classes at dog shows. Many toy breeds have been developed in this way.

These then are the six main breed types and all are included in the present work. Most dog books are selective and deal with only the best-known and most widely recognized breeds. I have taken the opposite approach and have included anything that has ever been seriously considered to be a true breed. Some traditionalists will be offended by this and will feel that some breeds are best forgotten. They will accuse me of promot-ing these 'dubious' breeds, merely by giving them a mention.

That is not my intention. I have set out to record the history of breeds, both ancient and modern, and it is not a historian's place to omit a breed simply because someone dislikes it. I would hate to think that, by describing the Pit Bull Terrier, I would encourage anyone to take up the disgusting sport of dog-fighting. But the fact remains that, for thousands of years, organized dog-fighting was a popular pastime; it is a part of canine history. It cannot be overlooked simply because we now deplore it. It is important that we know a little, at least, about every breed that has ever existed, if only to give us the chance to assess its value, or lack of value, in the scheme of things.

As a result, this dictionary includes more than 1,000 different breeds, which is two or three times as many as most other breed reference works. Instead of the usual random, alphabetical arrangement, I have set them out according to their original functions. Dogs have been used to perform so many tasks and adopt so many roles that this method does provide a classification system that has some historical meaning. Of course, many breeds are versatile and perform several tasks, in which case I have had to decide which was the principal one. This is not always entirely satisfactory but the alternatives are less so.

Some will complain that I have not followed the group classification employed by Kennel Clubs for their shows. Those groupings are excellent for dog shows, but they are too crude for a historical approach. They have grown up over the years as the best practical arrangement for big shows, but, although convenient, they result in some strange groupings that do not bear closer examination.

The quick way to find any dog is to use the Index of Breeds at the back of the book. There, every breed name is mentioned, including all the alternatives. Those given in capital letters are the ones I have chosen to represent each breed. But in almost every instance there are several alternative titles by which that particular dog has been called by someone, somewhere, at some time. This results in an extensive list of nearly 3,000 breed names.

At the front of the book, the table of contents shows the functional groupings. Within each functional grouping the breeds are arranged on a country-by-country basis. In the texts for each breed I have avoided abbreviations, with two exceptions: I have used FCI for the Fédération Cynologique Internationale and AKC for the American Kennel Club. Where the height of a breed is given, it is the traditional canine measurement of 'highest point of withers to the ground'.

Sporting Dogs

Most sporting dogs have been developed to accompany their masters on hunts of one kind or another. The canine hunting sequence consists of a number of distinct elements: sight-searching, scent-searching, flushing, digging, treeing, setting, pointing, decoying and retrieving. Many breeds of sporting dog have become specialized in one of these particular activities and now function only in that capacity. Others have one main activity, but are also useful in one or more additional, subsidiary capacities; they can, however, be classified by their principal specialization.

1   *SIGHTHOUNDS*: Sight-searching for prey by use of eyes

2   *SCENTHOUNDS*: Scent-searching for prey by use of nose

3   *SHORT-LEGGED SCENTHOUNDS*: Scent searching with small dogs

4   *FLUSHING DOGS*: Flushing prey from ground-level hiding

5   *EARTH DOGS*: Digging prey from below-ground hiding

6   *TREEING DOGS*: Treeing prey into above-ground hiding

7   *SETTING DOGS*: Setting to indicate presence of prey

8   *POINTING DOGS*: Pointing to position of detected prey

9   *DECOY DOGS*: Decoying prey into traps or gun range

10   *RETRIEVING DOGS*: Retrieving dead or helpless prey

11   *GENERAL HUNTING DOGS*: Other breeds, which have never become specialized, have remained general-purpose hunting dogs — opportunists that are capable of adapting to any challenge they encounter.

12   *FIGHTING DOGS*: Hunting is not the only sport for which dogs have been used in the past. They were also employed as fighting dogs, either against their own kind or against larger, tethered victims such as bears or bulls. The barbarous sports of dog-fighting, bear-baiting and bull-baiting have long been outlawed, but some of the specialized breeds they fostered have managed to survive in new roles as show dogs or household companions.

SIGHTHOUNDS

The members of this group are the slender, elongated, fast-running athletes that track their prey by sight rather than scent. This is the oldest type of pure-bred dogs, their ancestry stretching back at least 5,000 years to the earliest civilizations, where they were the most valued of all canine companions.

Collectively, they have been known by several names – sighthounds, gazehounds, windhounds and greyhounds. The last of these names, although once used to designate the whole group, is now usually restricted to certain breeds.

Sighthounds is the group name most widely used today and is the one chosen here. In Germany the sighthounds are called Windhunde, in Italy Labrelles, in Spain Lebreles, in France Lévriers and in Russia Borzaya. To a Russian, the title 'English Borzoi' refers to the English Greyhound.

They hunt in two different ways. The first is to chase, catch and kill the prey. The second is to chase, catch and secure the prey until the human hunter arrives. The second method is employed in cases where the local religious traditions require that if a game animal is to be eaten, it must first be killed in a ritual manner.

There are 53 breeds in this category, with Asia, Africa and the Mediterranean region accounting for half of these. Historically, it would appear that sighthounds began in the Middle East as high-status hunting dogs in ancient civilizations and then spread west to Europe, north to Russia and east to India.

BRITAIN

LONGDOG   BRITAIN

The name of this dog reflects the fact that it has 'a long head, a long neck, a long body, a long tail and long legs'. Originally it was simply a common name for any kind of sighthound, but then it became restricted to a special kind of cross-bred sighthound. In his study *Lurchers and Longdogs*, it was defined by Colonel Ted Walsh as 'a cross between two types of coursing dog (Greyhound to Deerhound, Greyhound to Saluki, etc) or the offspring of parents of such a cross'. This distinguished it from that other popular type of cross-breed, the Lurcher, which was created by mating a coursing dog with a working dog. To other recent authors, however, this distinction was outdated. They referred to both types of crosses as Lurchers, with the term Longdog being considered 'so rarely used these days as to be meaningless'.

References

1977. Walsh, Edward Geoffrey. *Lurchers and Longdogs*. Standfast Press, Gloucestershire.
1990. Walsh, Edward Geoffrey. *Longdogs by Day*. Boydell Press, Suffolk.
1993. Plummer, D. Brian. *Lurcher and Longdog Training*. Robinson.
1999. Sheardown, Frank. *The Working Longdog*. Swan Hill Press, Shrewsbury.

LURCHER   BRITAIN

The name of this dog is derived from the Romany word for a thief: 'lur'. Historically, it is a poacher's dog, ready to chase anything edible, especially rabbit and hare. It has also been recorded as the Didycoy Dog, or the Poacher's Dog.

The Lurcher is an anomaly. Known since the 17th century, it is one of the most popular dogs in rural Britain, with well over 5,000 examples in existence, and yet its status has never been formally recognized. This is because it has never been bred to a fixed type and is therefore excluded from the show-ring.

In general terms, a Lurcher is a dog that results from a mating between a sighthound and a working dog. Usually looking like a lanky, shaggy sighthound, the typical Lurcher is based on a cross between a male sighthound and a female sheepdog. One of the most popular crosses is between a Greyhound and a Rough Collie. There is also a smaller version based on a cross between a Whippet and a Border Collie, or between a Whippet and a Shetland Sheepdog. In Scotland a favoured cross is Greyhound and Golden Retriever. In the Midlands there is much interest in a Whippet and Bedlington cross.

Many breeders prefer to let the sighthound element become more dominant and make a back-cross to the sighthound, creating a dog that is three-quarters sighthound and one quarter sheepdog.

The thinking behind these crosses is to obtain a combination, in one animal, of the speed of the typical sighthound and the intelligence and stamina of the typical sheepdog. It is this magic mixture that gives the Lurcher its special appeal. Unfortunately, its precise appearance has been of less interest, and has never been stabilized, with the result that the show-dog world has studiously ignored it. To recognized dog judges, the Lurcher remain a mongrel, but this has not deterred the Lurcher enthusiasts, and in 1971 they began to organize Lurcher shows themselves at which their dogs could compete without bothering about fixed standards. In defiance of the show-dog world there are now over 50 such Lurcher contests held annually.

In personality, the Lurcher seems to have acquired the best of both its parent breeds, being described by modern authors as calm, dignified, friendly and affectionate. It would, however, be hard to guess this from descriptions of the dog recorded in earlier centuries, when it was looked upon as an 'illicit breed'. In 1790, Thomas Bewick, for example, refers to it in the following words: 'its aspect is sullen, and its habits, whence it derives its name, are dark and cunning.' But this is the type of comment that says more about the dog's owners than about the animal itself.

References

1975. Sheardown, Frank. *The Lurcher: Training and Hunting*. Swan Hill Press, Shrewsbury.

1977. Walsh, Edward Geoffrey. *Lurchers and Longdogs*. Standfast Press, Gloucestershire.

1979. Plummer, D. Brian. *Complete Lurcher*. Boydell Press, Suffolk.

1983. Tottenham, Katherine. *All About the Lurcher*. Pelham Books, London.

1985. Walker, Frank. *The Lurcher*. Dell, New York.

1993. Plummer, D. Brian. *Lurcher and Longdog Training*. Robinson.

1998. Plummer,D. Brian. *The New Complete Lurcher*. Swan Hill Press. Shrewsbury.

1999. Drakeford, J. *Understanding the Working Lurcher*. Crowood Press, Wiltshire.

Diprose, Tony (Editor). *Lurcher Ways and Lurcher Days*. Privately published.

Shaw, Michael. *The Modern Lurcher*.

ENGLAND

ENGLISH GREYHOUND   ENGLAND

Usually known simply as the Greyhound, this ancient breed, the ultimate canine athlete, has been used for chasing and coursing all kinds of prey for thousands of years. In more recent times it has become a racetrack animal in many different countries.

This is a dog of superlatives. It has the longest history of any breed, having been depicted in ancient art more than 6,000 years ago. It is the most aristocratic of dogs, having been owned by more royalty and nobility than any other breed. It is the fastest of dogs, reaching over 40 mph (64 kph). It has leapt further than any other dog, one having cleared 30 ft (9.14 m) in a single jump. It is the most prolific of dogs, one male having sired more than 3,000 pups. It is also the most expensive breed in the world, champion racing Greyhounds having changed hands for as much as $72,000.

But perhaps the most extraordinary record held by this amazing breed is that it has been given more names than any other dog. This fact reflects the vast number of historical references that have been made to the breed over the centuries, and sets it apart from all other dogs, in a class of its own. A survey of the English literature on the subject of Greyhounds reveals more than 50 different names. In alphabetical order they are as follows: Graihond, Graydog, Grayhound, Grayhownde, Grayhund, Greahound, Greahounde, Greahund, Grefhound, Grehound, Grehounde, Grehunde, Greihound, Gresehownd, Greund, Grew, Grewan, Grewand, Grewant, Grew-dog, Grewehound, Grewend, Grewhond, Grewhonde, Grewhound, Grewhounde, Grewhund, Grewin, Grewnd, Grewnt, Grewund, Grey, Grey-dog, Greyhound, Greyhounde, Greyhund, Griezhund, Grifhound, Grighund, Grihond, Grijphund, Grizhund, Grohund, Groond, Groo-und, Gruan, Gruand, Gruant, Grue-hound, Grune, Gryhond.

Inevitably there have been fierce arguments about the meaning of its name. The idea that 'grey' refers to its colour is rejected by most scholars. Some favour the idea that its correct name is Grewhound, the word 'grew' meaning 'Greek'. The dog was greatly favoured by the ancient Greeks, who frequently decorated their vases with its image, and the suggestion is that Greyhound is a modification of Greek Hound. Another school of thought sees it as meaning Badger Dog, because in the 17th century the word 'grey' meant 'badger'. However, this slow-moving animal was never the main quarry of the high-speed Greyhound. Others consider that it comes from the Saxon word 'grei', meaning 'beautiful'. Still others relate it to the Anglo-Saxon word 'grig', meaning 'bitch', but it is not clear why only the female gender should be involved. Finally, there is the idea that, so important was this dog, that it was the Great Hound of the nobility and that this title was later slurred in common speech to Greyhound. The truth is that we do not have a definite answer.

In earlier centuries this dog was so prized that 'common folk' were forbidden to own one. About a thousand years ago, a law was passed in England stating that only royalty and nobility could hunt with Greyhounds. Serfs could not own them at all, and freemen were required to have their dogs deliberately lamed if they lived within 10 miles (16 km) of a royal forest. Special dog-mutilators were despatched around the countryside by the king to enforce this brutal measure. In this way the exclusivity of royal sport was preserved for 400 years.

With the decline of the great forests, the Greyhound was found new occupations. First there was hare-coursing, organized in the form of controlled competitions. Then, for urban populations, there was the invention of the Greyhound racetrack complete with mechanical prey, prizes and gambling. This was done in imitation of thorough-bred horse-racing and, astonishingly, in some of the earliest races the dogs were provided with jockeys in the form of live monkeys fixed to their backs.

The very first Greyhound race using an artificial hare took place in 1876 near London, along a straight track, but it failed to catch on. This new sport was not taken seriously until the 1920s, when the first modern race was staged, using the now famil-iar oval track. This took place in Manchester in 1926, and the sport has since spread to many other countries around the world.

In recent times, both Greyhound-coursing and Greyhound-racing have been under attack from animal-rights groups who regard both activities, especially coursing, as sports involving cruelty to animals. In theory, racing should not involve cruelty. Indeed, it should, like drag-hunting, provide a useful, prey-free way of exercising hunting ani-mals. Unfortunately, commercial considerations are such that the dogs are not always treated as well as possible and they are often culled, even when perfectly healthy, sim-ply because they are past their racing best.

In temperament, the Greyhound is something of a surprise. It proves to be one of the most affectionate, relaxed, gentle and obedient of pets, although any small hairy animal that runs away from it (including small lapdogs) is liable to trigger its insatiable urge to chase. With proper precautions, retired racing Greyhounds make superb companions and there is no excuse for the widespread practice of slaughtering them as soon as their racing days are over. Most such dogs have at least another ten healthy years ahead of them, given a friendly home.

References

1853. 'Stonehenge'. *The Greyhound.* Longman, London.

1886. Dalziel, Hugh. *The Greyhound; its History, Points, Breeding, Rearing, Training and Running.* Upcott Gill, London.

1921. Dighton, Adair. *The Greyhound and Coursing.* Grant Richards, London.

1927. Smith, A. Croxton. *Greyhound Racing and Breeding.* Gay & Hancock, London.

1929. Matheson, James. *The Greyhound: Breeding, Coursing, Racing etc.* Hurst & Blackett.

1933. Ash, Edward C. *The Book of the Greyhound.* Hutchinson, London.

1934. Clarke, Mrs Carlo F. Culpeper. *Greyhounds and Greyhound Racing.* Methuen, London.

1937. McMichan, B. A. *The Greyhound: Training, Management, Diseases.* Angus & Robertson, London.

1945. 'The Rambler'. *The Complete Book of the Greyhound.* Parkside Press, Dublin.

1946. Genders, Roy. *Modern Greyhound Racing and Coursing.* Sporting Handbooks, London.

1947–9. Tartar. *The Greyhound Racing Encyclopedia.* 3 vols.

1949. Clarke, E. *The Modern Greyhound.*

1960. Genders, Roy. *Greyhounds.* Foyles, London.

1961. Wimhurst, C. G. E. *The Book of the Greyhound.* Frederick Muller, London.

1962. Montagu-Harrison, H. *The Greyhound Trainer.* Cashel Press, Co. Tipperary.

1963. Clarke, E. *A Complete Study of the Modern Greyhound.*

1965. Clarke, H. Edward. *The Greyhound.* Popular Dogs, London.

1965. Mueller, Georgiana. *How to Raise and Train a Greyhound.* TFH, New Jersey.

1969. Agostini, Mike G. *The Greyhound in Australia.* Cheshire Publishing, Melbourne.

1972. Bracht, William H. *Greyhounds and Mechanical Lure Racing.* Sydney.

1972. Hoffmann, Carl Timothy. *This is the Racing Greyhound.*

1973. Burnell, Roy B. *Racing Greyhounds: from Whelping Box to Starting Box.*

1974. Hoffmann, Carl Timothy. *Greyhound Racing – America's Fastest Growing Sport.*

1981. Genders, Roy. *The Encyclopedia of Greyhound Racing: a Complete History of the Sport.* Pelham Books, London.

1984. Burnell, Roy. *Selecting, Training & Racing Greyhounds.* Australia.

1987. Barnes, Julia. *George Curtis: Training Greyhounds.* Ringpress Books, Letchworth, Hertfordshire.

1988. Rolins, Anne. *All About the Greyhound.* Rigby, Adelaide.

1988. Tompkins, Barbara and Hearman, Pam. *All about the Racing Greyhound.* Pelham Books, London.

1990. Genders, Roy. *The National Greyhound Racing Club Book of Greyhound Racing.* Pelham Books. London.

1990. McBride, William F. *Greyhound Racing.* Carol.

1992. Branigan, Cynthia A. *Adopting the Racing Greyhound.* Howell, New York.

1993. Kohnke. *Veterinary Advice for Greyhound Owners.*

1994. Barnes, Julia (Editor). *The Complete Book of Greyhounds.*

1994. Blythe, Linda Lou. *Care of the Racing Greyhound: A Guide for Trainers, Breeders and Veterinarians.* National Greyhound Association.

1994. Thompson, L. *The Dogs: a Personal History of Greyhound Racing.*

1996. Coile, Caroline. *Greyhounds.* Barron, New York.

1997. Branigan, *The Reign of the Greyhound: a Popular History of the Oldest Family of Dogs.* Howell, New York.

1997. Raeke, Carolyn. *Guide to Adopting an Ex-Racing Greyhound.* TFH, New Jersey.

1998. LeMieux, Sue. *The Book of the Greyhound.* TFH, New Jersey.

1998. Stern, Daniel Braun. *The Greyhound: An Owner's Guide to a Happy Healthy Pet.* Howell, New York.

WHIPPET ENGLAND

In the past, this breed has also been called the Lightning Rag Dog and the Snap Dog. The present name appears to have originated from the word 'whappet', which used to mean 'a small dog that wapps [yaps]'. In the 17th century, the name Whippet was used to describe a 'little cur'. The Whippet as we know it today was developed in the 19th century as a rabbit-coursing dog.

The Whippet has been described as the 'Poor Man's Greyhound' and although many are now kept as prized and highly valued pets, this rather downbeat description does fit the origin of the breed. In Victorian times, the miners in the north of England could not afford to keep Greyhounds for coursing, so they invented their own miniature version and called it the Whippet after the 'small dogs' of earlier days. Detailed records were not kept at the time, but it is believed that the breed was created by either (1) breeding down in size from the Greyhound, mating runts with runts, until the animal's height had been reduced from roughly 30 to 20 in (75 to 50 cm); (2) crossing Greyhounds with Spaniels; or (3) crossing Italian Greyhounds with Terriers (especially Manchester Terriers). It is clear from the appearance of the modern Whippet, with its slender, streamlined shape, that if crosses were involved, the Greyhound elements were strengthened by back-crossing over a period of time.

When first developed, the Whippets were used for competitive rabbit-killing. These contests, in which rabbits were turned out into an enclosure and the dogs were released to see which one could make the quickest kill, permitted the northern miners to indulge in gambling without costly overheads. When their sport was condemned for its cruelty, they turned instead to 'rag racing' in which a cloth or fur lure was dragged down a straight track (often no more than a back alleyway) and the dogs were released from traps to hurtle after it. This again only involved modest running costs and their gambling urges could still be satisfied.

The Whippet is sometimes used today for competitive racing, still chasing a dummy prey down a straight track, but this is now usually done simply for pleasure and no longer involves serious gambling. Because of its lighter build, the Whippet has better acceleration than the Greyhound, but cannot reach quite such high speeds. Over very short distances, it could beat its bigger relative, but the Greyhound would soon overtake it.

References

1894. Lloyd, Freeman. *The Whippet & Race Dog.* Upcott Gill, London.

1947. Fitter, B. S. *The Show Whippet*. Fitter, Ipswich.

1957. Renwick, W. Lewis. *The Whippet Handbook*. Nicholson & Watson, London.

1961. Todd, C. H. Douglas. *The Popular Whippet*. Popular Dogs, London.

1964. Cormany, Christine. *How to Raise and Train a Whippet*. TFH, Jersey City.

1964. Daglish, E. Fitch. *Whippets*. Foyles, London.

1976. Pegram, Louis. *The Complete Whippet*. Howell, New York.

1979. Wilson, Pauline: *Whippets Rearing & Racing*. Faber & Faber, London.

1989. Cormany, Christine. *Whippets*. TFH, New Jersey.

1991. Rawlings. *An Owner's Companion to the Whippet*.

1994. Bengtson, Bo. *The Whippet*.

1994. Gilmour, Patsy. *Whippets Today*. Howell, New York.

1998. Coile, Caroline. *Whippets: Everything about Purchase, Adoption, Care, Nutrition, Behavior, and Training*. Barron, New York.

1999. Keppler, Dean. *Whippet: A Complete and Reliable Handbook*. TFH, New Jersey. Walsh, E. G. *The English Whippet*.

SCOTLAND

SCOTTISH DEERHOUND · SCOTLAND

This breed has had many names over the centuries, including Fleethound, Rough Highland Greyhound, Rough-coated Greyhound, Rough Greyhound, Scotch Greyhound, Scotch Deerhound, Highland Greyhound, Scottish Wolfhound, Wolfdog and Staghound. It was originally employed to hunt wolves but, when the wolves began to disappear, it was later developed as a deer-coursing breed. In France it is the Lévrier Écossais, in Germany the Schottischer Hirschhund, in Spain the Lebrel Escocés.

Large, shaggy greyhounds have been known in Scotland for at least 500 years. Early in its history, the breed now known as the Deerhound was essentially the same as the Irish Wolfhound, and was then called the Scottish Wolfhound. But over a period of time it grew slightly smaller, as its main quarry changed from the (now vanishing) wolf to the (still plentiful) deer.

The great, gangling, wire-haired Deerhound was immensely popular as a deer-courser in Scotland up until the 18th century, but when efficient firearms arrived in the Highlands, its usefulness was greatly diminished. It was kept on as a prized possession in some regions, but its numbers inevitably began to dwindle. Then, at the beginning of the Victorian period, in the early 19th century, it returned to favour with a number of breeders. Although it has never again been particularly common (because of its huge size and need for great running spaces), it is now safely preserved for the future by devoted enthusiasts and remains one of the most dramatic of all dog breeds.

When not hunting, this is said to be an unusually gentle dog – wistful, polite, graceful, elegant and gentlemanly in its behaviour towards its owners. Surprisingly, this glamorous breed is most common today, not in its native Scotland, but far away in South Africa.

References

1892. Bell, E. Weston. *The Scottish Deerhound*. David Douglas, Edinburgh.

1894. Cupples, George. *Scotch Deerhounds and their Masters*. Blackwood, Edinburgh.

1894. Graham, George Augustus. *Pedigrees of Scottish Deerhounds*.

1955. Hartley, A. N. *The Deerhound*. Privately published, Peterborough.

1965. Benbow, Audrey M. How to *Raise and Train a Scottish Deerhound*. TFH, New Jersey.

1993. Benbow, Audrey M. *Scottish Deerhounds*. TFH, New Jersey.

IRELAND

IRISH WOLFHOUND   IRELAND

This huge, rough-coated animal, sometimes known simply as the Wolfhound, or, in the past, as the Cu, the Wolf Dogge, the Rough Greyhound, the Irish Greyhound, the Irish Elk-hound, the Irish Wolf-dog, the Great Irish Greyhound Wolf-dog, or the Canis graius hibernicus, was developed to hunt down the wolves of Ireland, a task which it had completed so successfully by the end of the 18th century that it found itself out of work. In France it is the Lévrier Irlandais, in Germany the Irischer Wolfshund, in Spain the Lebrel Irlandés.

There is some disagreement over the origin of this impressive breed – the tallest dog in the world, weighing over 110 lb (50 kg). It is believed that, about 3,000 years ago, Phoenician traders brought Middle Eastern sighthounds (similar, no doubt, to today's Maltese Pharaoh Hound) to the British Isles, where they were crossed with the local mastiffs to produce what was, in effect, a giant greyhound. Others believe that the Irish Sheepdog was involved in its ancestry. Still others mention the Scottish Deerhound as a forerunner, but this is likely to have been a later addition.

So successful was this gigantic dog in defending livestock against the marauding wolves of Ireland that its importance grew and grew until it became a hero of mythic proportions. The most famous of all Wolfhound legends concerns a dog called Ailbé, who lived about 2,000 years ago, and whose fame as a protector was so great that a local ruler, the king of Connacht, offered 6,000 cows for him. The king of Ulster made a rival offer that was successful and, as a result, war broke out between the kings. Ailbé fought valiantly in battle and, in a moment of fearless folly, grabbed the axle of the Connacht king's chariot in his jaws and refused to let go. While he was still clinging on, his head was cut off and remained there, tightly clamped, as the chariot thundered off across the field of battle.

In the Middle Ages, the Wolfhound was widely used in wolf control and this much feared wild predator's numbers soon began to dwindle. By the 18th century the wolves had all been exterminated. It is usually accepted that the last Irish wolf was destroyed in 1770 in the Wicklow Mountains, although some believe that a few managed to hang on in County Carlow until 1786. After that, they were certainly all gone. The Wolfhound had proved too efficient for its own good and before long it, too, began to vanish, its great size making it unsuitable for other kinds of hunting.

By the middle of the 19th century there were only a few mongrel Wolfhounds left, but then a Scotsman, Captain George Augustus Graham, decided that such a majestic beast must somehow be preserved. He established a new breeding programme and set about reinstating the big hound. However, it has been argued that, in achieving this goal, the good captain was, in reality, creating a new breed. He introduced so much fresh blood that his programme was more of a reconstitution than a reinstatement. Among the breeds he is said to have brought in to cross with the mongrel remnants of the Wolfhound population were the Scottish Deerhound, the Great Dane, the Russian Wolfhound, the Pyrenean Mountain Dog and the Tibetan Mastiff.

Some authors insist that Graham's programme was even more radical — that the original Irish Wolfhound had become entirely extinct and that his modern version was merely a cleverly contrived counterfeit. Whatever the truth of the matter, the fact remains that he did manage to develop a magnificent breed — perhaps even more noble than the original version.

Like other very big dogs, this powerful breed is as docile and friendly when it is relaxing with its human family as it is fierce and relentless when hunting or guarding. It is as though, like a heavyweight champion, it has nothing to prove and leaves yappy belligerence to the minor breeds. It emanates a calm dignity that endears it to all those who come to know it well.

References

1885. Graham, G. A. *The Irish Wolfhound.* Whitmore & Son, Dursley.

1897. Hogan, Edmund. *The History of the Irish Wolfdog.* Sealy, Bryers & Walker, Dublin.

1908. Dawson, A. J. *Finn, the Wolfhound.* Grant Richards, London.

1915. Dunn, J. Allan. *Boru: The Story of an Irish Wolfhound.* Grosset & Dunlap.

1923. Byrne, Donn. *The Hound of Ireland.*

1931. Gardner. Phyllis. *The Irish Wolfhound.* The Dundalgan Press, Dundalk, Ireland.

1931. Martin, Nellie. *The Russian Wolfhound, its History, Breeding & Care.* Judy, Chicago.

1939. Hogan, Edmund and Graham, Capt. *The Irish Wolfdog and the Irish Wolfhound.* The Irish Wolfhound Club of Ireland, Dublin.

1943. Johnson, Margaret and Derry, Helen. *The Wolfhound*. Harcourt.

1959. Howe, Janet Rogers Star. *An Irish Wolfhound*. Westminster.

1964. Westover, Fredric and Westover, Margaret. *How to Raise and Train an Irish Wolfhound*. TFH, New Jersey.

1969. Starbuck, Alma J. *Complete Irish Wolfhound*. Howell, New York.

1974. Gordon, John. *The Irish Wolfhound*. Arco, New York.

1975. Sutton, Catherine G. *The Irish Wolfhound*. Dog Owner's Library.

1976. Donovan, John A. K. *You and Your Irish Wolfhound*. Denlinger's, Edgewater, Florida.

1976. Murphy. E. C. *Raising, Showing and Breeding the Irish Wolfhound*. Ireland.

1977. De Quoy, Alfred. *The Irish Wolfhound Guide*.

1980. De Quoy, Alfred. *The Irish Wolfhound in Competition*. McLean, Virginia.

1981. Samaha, Joel. *The New Complete Irish Wolfhound*. Howell, New York.

1986. Donovan, John A. *The Irish Wolfhound, Great Symbol of Ireland*. Alpine Publications.

1988. Pisano, Beverly. *Irish Wolfhounds*. TFH, New Jersey.

1996. Franklin, Kristine L. *The Wolfhound*. Lothrop, Lee & Shepard, New York.

1998. McBryde, Mary. *The Irish Wolfhound. Symbol of Celtic Splendor*.

FRANCE

MÂTIN   FRANCE

Sometimes called the French Mâtin, this is an extinct sighthound once employed for hunting wild boar and wolf. The French word 'mâtin' translates as 'mastiff', but this breed should not be confused with the Dogue de Bordeaux, which is sometimes also called the French Mastiff. That breed has a heavy, deep head, while the Mâtin described here had an elongated head.

Some 19th-century authors referred to this dog as being the French equivalent of the British Lurcher. It was a large dog with the typical sighthound head — long and tapering, with a flat forehead and semi-erect ears. In colour, the coat varied from white to fawn to red. Sometimes it was bicolour, in white and brown.

It was described as a fierce, muscular animal, but 'not remarkable for daring'. In height it was about 24 in (61 cm).

SPAIN

ANDALUSIAN PODENCO   SPAIN

Known locally as the Podenco Andaluz, this ancient Spanish breed has been employed for centuries in the pursuit of small game. There appears to be a naming confusion between this and a breed called the Spanish Podenco, or Podenco Español. In addition, there is mention of a Podenco Ibérico. These all appear to be varieties of the same general breed, which in English is sometimes called the Spanish Warren Hound.

This is one of a number of Mediterranean sighthounds that are all direct descendants of the early Egyptian dogs which were distributed around the region by the industrious Phoenician traders of the first millennium BC. This one appears to have begun its independent existence in the region of Cadiz and is still found today in the rural districts of Andalusia. In the past it was bred for its hunting skills rather than for its looks, with the result that it now exists in several varieties. There are three body sizes (small, medium and large) and three coat types (short, long and hard). In recent times it has attracted the attention of the Spanish show-dog world, which is giving it a new lease of life.

ANGLO-SPANISH GREYHOUND   SPAIN

Also known as the Spanish/English Greyhound, or the Galgo Inglés-Espagnol, this racing dog is a comparatively recent cross between the two ancient breeds of English Greyhound and Spanish Greyhound.

The Anglo-Spanish was created in Spain in the earlier part of the 20th century, to improve the racing speed of the smaller, local greyhounds. In modern Spain it is the recognized breed employed in professional greyhound-racing, although it is not yet accepted in the world of pedigree show dogs. Its popularity has meant that its Spanish ancestor has become increasingly rare. From the 1930s onwards, there have been more and more Anglo-Spanish dogs and fewer and fewer of the original, indigenous Spanish Greyhounds.

In recent years there have been serious complaints made against the organizers of Spanish greyhound-racing on the grounds of cruelty to the dogs, and a number of investigations have been carried out in attempts to improve their welfare.

CANARY ISLANDS PODENCO   SPAIN

Also known as the Canary Islands Hound, the Canarian Warren Hound, the Chien de Garenne des Canaries, and locally as the Podenco Canario, this ancient breed has been employed for centuries in the pursuit of small game, especially rabbits.

This is one of a number of greyhound-like sighthounds which are direct descendants of the early Egyptian dogs that were distributed across the Mediterranean and beyond by the ubiquitous Phoenician traders in the first millennium BC. In appearance it closely resembles the Ibizan Hound and the Pharaoh Hound, with its slender, athletic build, long face, tall, pricked ears and short, flat coat. It is a vigorous hunter, well adapted to working in the volcanic regions of the Canary Islands. In personality, it has been described as intelligent, stubborn and sometimes nervous.

IBIZAN HOUND   SPAIN

Also called the Ibizan Podenco, the Podenco Ibicenco, the Ivicene, the Balearic Hound, or the Balearic Dog, this breed has in the past spread to the Spanish mainland in the region of Catalonia, where it is known by the Catalan name of Ca Eivissenc or Ca Eibisenc. It also

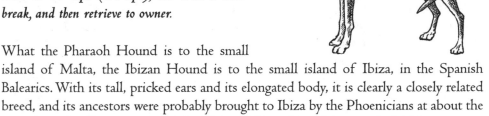

reached the south of France where it was christened the Charnique, Charnihue, Charneque, Charnegue, or Chien de Baléares. In Germany it is called the Balearen-laufhund. Its main function is rabbit-hunting, but it also pursues other small game. Its hunting sequence is: detect, flush, chase at 40 mph (64 kph), kill with a neck-break, and then retrieve to owner.

What the Pharaoh Hound is to the small island of Malta, the Ibizan Hound is to the small island of Ibiza, in the Spanish Balearics. With its tall, pricked ears and its elongated body, it is clearly a closely related breed, and its ancestors were probably brought to Ibiza by the Phoenicians at about the same time that they introduced the Pharaoh Hound to Malta, nearly 3,000 years ago.

In France, where it was used for hunting in the Provence and Roussillon regions, it became so strongly identified with poaching that it was eventually banned. Its special value to the poachers lay in the fact that it was unusually silent when engaged in hunting and therefore enabled them to work in secrecy.

In the 1950s, a famous Spanish dog judge and breeder, who lived on the island of Majorca, a short distance from Ibiza, took this breed under her wing and began a controlled breeding programme. (This is why it is sometimes referred to as the Podenco Mallorquin, or simply the Mallorquin.) From there it spread to the show-rings of Europe and later the United States. In 1958, some of these handsome dogs were imported into Egypt, the land of their ancient ancestors.

The typical Ibizan Hound is short-haired, but occasional wire-haired specimens are encountered. There is a characteristic white mark between the ears that is called the 'axe mark'. The most common colour form is white with red patches.

References

1980. Brearley, Joan McDonald. *Ibizan Hounds.* TFH, New Jersey.

SPANISH GREYHOUND   SPAIN

Also known as the Galgo Espagnol or the Seçoviano, this breed was originally used to hunt small game, but is today more likely to be encountered in the Spanish show-ring. In France it is the Lévrier Espagnol, in Germany the Spanischer Windhund.

The Spanish Greyhound is slightly smaller and lighter in build than its English counterpart. A shy, rather aloof dog, it is descended from Egyptian dogs brought to the Iberian peninsula by Phoenicians in the first millennium BC.

Some centuries after it first became established in ancient Spain, it is thought to have been modified by the introduction of the Sloughi, a breed brought from North Africa during the Moorish invasion of southern Spain. It is found today mostly in the regions of southern and central Spain, especially Castile and Andalusia.

According to Spanish experts, this breed is ancestral to the English Greyhound. They claim that it was exported in large numbers to other countries, like Ireland and England, during the 16th, 17th and 18th centuries.

PORTUGAL

LARGE PORTUGUESE PODENGO   PORTUGAL

Known locally as the Podengo Portuguesa Grande, this breed has also been described as the Portuguese Hound, the Large Portuguese Hound, the Large Portuguese Rabbit Dog, the Portuguese Rabbit Dog, or the Portuguese Warren Hound. It has been used for many years to hunt deer, hare, rabbit and other game, but is less common today than it has been in the past.

This large, prick-eared Portuguese sighthound is the result of ancient importations of greyhound-like dogs being crossed with local breeds. It is a strong animal capable of covering a great deal of ground in pursuit of its prey. Hunting is carried out either singly, in pairs, or in packs, usually over open ground. There are two coat types. One is short and hard and the other is wiry, shaggy and coarse.

MEDIUM PORTUGUESE PODENGO PORTUGAL

Sometimes called the Medium Portuguese Hound, or the Medium Portugese Rabbit Dog, and known locally as the Podengo Portuguesa Medio, this breed has been used for many years to hunt rabbits and other small game.

This reduced Podengo has been developed for speed and manoeuvrability when hunting over difficult, less open terrain. It is the fastest of the three Podengo types and has become the most popular in recent years. It is approximately 6 in (15 cm) shorter than its larger relative but in other respects is very similar. There are two coat types. One is short and hard and the other is wiry, shaggy and coarse.

A miniaturized version of this breed, called the Small Portuguese Podengo, was developed many years ago to go to ground and carry out the duties of a terrier. (It has therefore been placed with the terriers in the vermin-control group in this book.)

ITALY

SICILIAN GREYHOUND SICILY

Known locally as the Cirneco dell'Etna, and sometimes called the Sicilian Hound, this ancient breed has existed for centuries on the island of Sicily where it is employed to hunt rabbit, hare and ground-birds.

Looking like a smaller version of the Pharaoh Hound that inhabits the Maltese Islands 80 miles (130 km) to the south of Sicily, this pure breed has also enjoyed an existence free of outside interference. As a result, it is virtually unaltered since the time of its introduction by Phoenician traders some 3,000 years ago. It has the lean, streamlined shape of a greyhound, except for its huge, upright ears that stand as tall as its face. Its fawn-red coat is short and may show small of patches of white.

In height the Sicilian Greyhound stands at about 18 in (46 cm), compared with 23 in (58 cm) for the Pharaoh Hound. This lighter build may be related to the fact that it has been specialized for hill-coursing on the slopes of Mount Etna — hence its local name. Because of its smaller size, it has been suggested that it would make a more convenient pet dog for anyone who wanted an 'Egyptian-style' sighthound. But despite this, it has become an increasingly rare breed, proving far less popular abroad than the closely related, but much bigger Pharaoh Hound and Ibizan Hound.

POLAND

POLISH GREYHOUND   POLAND

Sometimes referred to as the Polish Sighthound, in its home country this breed is called the Chart Polski; in France the Lévrier Polonais; in Germany the Polnischer Windhund; and in Spain the Lebrel Polaco. It was originally developed to hunt wolf, deer, fox and rabbit.

Looking like a strongly built English Greyhound, this elegant, ancient Polish breed nearly became extinct, but local enthusiasts have recently revived it and today there are over 100 of them in existence. It was recognized locally by the Polish Kennel Club in 1981. A few have found their way to the United States, where the first litter was born in 1991, in Maryland.

The coat is short and hard, with some slight feathering on the tail and rear end. In personality it is said to be unusually intelligent, affectionate and obedient.

HUNGARY

HUNGARIAN GREYHOUND   HUNGARY

Also known as the Magyar Agar, the Magyarorszag, or the Magyar Greyhound, this breed was originally developed to course hare and fox. In France it is the Lévrier Hongrois, in Germany the Ungarischer Windhund, in Spain the Lebrel Hungaro.

The Hungarian or Magyar Greyhound is a smaller-than-average greyhound that was brought to its present homeland from the east, arriving with the Magyar people in the ninth century AD. Its first specific mention occurs between AD 895 and 907, in the writings of Count Arpad.

During the 19th century there was a great deal of interbreeding between this dog and the typical European greyhounds. The result is that today the Hungarian Greyhound looks much like the English version. The main difference is in the slightly shorter muzzle of the Hungarian breed. In Greece this animal has, like its English counterpart elsewhere, been co-opted for use on the racetrack. This is a dog with an intelligence that is as fast as its feet.

BOSNIA-HERZEGOVINA/CROATIA

OLD BOSNIAN SIGHTHOUND   BOSNIA-HERZEGOVINA/CROATIA

The Old Bosnian Sighthound and the Old Croatian Sighthound are one and the same. In Croatia it is known locally as the Starohrvatski Hrt (pronounced star-o-her-vat-ski her-tee). It is closely related to the Bosnian Rough-haired Hound, which is a large wire-haired hunting dog developed to chase hare, fox and even wild boar over rough and difficult terrain.

According to recent reports from that war-torn region, this ancient breed from the Balkans is on the verge of extinction, if it has not already disappeared completely. One estimate puts the present world population at between 10 and 20 individuals.

The breed is between 1,200 and 1,300 years old, as we know from the writings of early friars, and has remained largely unchanged over the centuries, with only an occasional injection of greyhound blood to freshen the line. Despite this, it has never been officially recognized or given a written set of breed standards. Recent efforts to promote it, preserve it, increase its numbers or improve the breed have failed through lack of interest. The last attempt to present it in public took place in 1993.

This sighthound, used for chasing all forms of local game, is similar in weight and appearance to the North Indian Rampur Hound – in other words, it is another 'overgrown' greyhound of powerful build. It is exclusively black-and-white in colour.

GREECE

CRETAN GREYHOUND   CRETE

An ancient sighthound found on the island of Crete in the Mediterranean, this rare breed is known locally as the Kritikos Ichnilatis. Its function is hunting hare and rabbit. It has remained on its small island, unaltered and undiluted, for centuries. In colour, it can be black, white, white with black markings, or white with red markings.

GREEK GREYHOUND   GREECE

This breed is also known as the Albanian Greyhound, the Greek Harehound, the Greek Saluki, the Greek Hound, the Hellenic Hound, the Hellenic Harehound or, in Greek, the Hellinikos Ichnilatis (somes given as Ellenikos Ichnilatis). The original function of the breed was to course hare or small deer, not only over open plains but also in the mountains. In earlier times it was hunted in packs but more recently it has been used in pairs.

An unusually large sighthound, standing almost 31 in (80 cm), this impressive black-and-tan dog, with fringed ears and tail, looks remarkably like an oversized Saluki. It is clearly descended from the sighthounds of the Middle East. In recent years it has become an increasingly rare breed.

An early record of an extinct breed called the Grecian Greyhound appears to refer to a different dog, as it was described as being 'somewhat smaller than the English dog'.

MALTA

PHARAOH HOUND

MALTA

This breed is known in its native Malta as the Kelb tal Fennec, which means Rabbit Dog. It was developed as a sighthound by Maltese farmers for hunting rabbits.

The Pharaoh Hound has been well known in Malta and Gozo for centuries as the local farmer's dog, employed in the more remote rural districts for hunting the elusive orange-coloured island rabbits. Until the late 1960s it had been largely scorned by the island's show-dog enthusiasts. It was so familiar to them that it was always passed over at local dog shows in favour of more exotic, imported pedigree dogs. Then, in 1968, a British enthusiast realized its potential and imported eight examples to England, where their striking appearance and proud demeanour soon attracted serious attention. It was felt that the traditional name of Maltese Rabbit Dog did not do it justice, so a more romantic title was sought.

It was known that the Phoenicians had visited the Maltese Islands in ancient times and had been active traders throughout the Mediterranean region. It had also been noted that the Rabbit Dog was remarkably similar to the depictions of houndlike dogs on the wall paintings and carvings of ancient Egypt. It was therefore decided to link the Maltese dog with the early Egyptian ones by giving it the more dignified title of Pharaoh Hound. There is no hard evidence to support this connection, but it makes an appealing story and may even be true, since the Maltese Dog is remarkably true-breeding and certainly appears to have been isolated on the islands over a very long period. When future DNA-analysis techniques are applied to dog breeds to settle matters of relationship, it will be interesting to see if DNA taken from mummified ancient Egyptian dogs matches closely with that taken from modern Pharaoh Hounds.

There are very similar breeds to be found on the nearby islands of Sicily and Ibiza and also on the Portuguese and Spanish mainlands. The existence of these four breeds

– the Sicilian Hound, the Ibizan Hound, the Portuguese Podengo and the Spanish Greyhound respectively – strongly supports the idea that the Phoenicians were actively trading in Egyptian dogs around this general region in ancient times.

With its huge, erect ears, its slender, elegant outline and its noble bearing, it is little wonder that this breed has graduated so quickly from a humble farmer's rabbiter to a glamorous show dog. In personality it is an alert, agile dog, affectionate and with high intelligence.

References

1977. Block and Sacks. *The Pharaoh Hound.*
1983. Black, Pauline. *Pharaoh Hound.* Denlinger's, Edgewater, Florida.
1985. Block. *Pharaoh Hound.* TFH, New Jersey.
1986. Camino, E. *Pharaoh Hound Champions, 1983–1986.* Camino Books.
1989. Sefscik. *Pharaoh Hounds.* TFH, New Jersey.
    Bullard, Randall A. and Martin, Joyce B. *The Ancient Egyptian Pharaoh Hound.*

MIDDLE EAST

SALUKI
MIDDLE EAST

Also known as the Persian Greyhound or the Gazelle Hound, this breed is revered by Muslims, who refer to it as El Hor, The Noble One. It has been used since ancient times to hunt hare, fox and gazelle.

The Saluki is one of the oldest pure breeds in the world, dating back thousands of years. It is claimed that it even pre-dates ancient Egypt, carvings of it from 7000 BC having been discovered during excavations in Sumer. In Egypt itself it was known as the Royal Dog and was depicted in carvings and on many painted walls, dating from as early as the third millennium BC. When one of these treasured hunting companions died, its Egyptian owners went into deep mourning and frequently had their beloved dogs mummified, wearing their ornate collars. In the tomb of Tutankhamun, the king is shown with his favourite hounds, which appear to be Salukis.

Like all sighthounds, this breed has the typical elongated greyhound shape, but its silhouette is distinctive because it is adorned with 'feathered' ears, legs and tail.

In temperament the Saluki is a loyal and courageous servant, affectionate without being demonstrative, vigilant but not aggressive. It has an independent spirit and is aloof with strangers. It enjoys the comforts of home when it is resting, but when working is prepared to hunt at high speed over rough and difficult terrain. It is an unusually intelligent breed and demands to be treated as such. If it is ill-treated it will retaliate.

Its intelligence and independence are essential because of the way it is used on the hunt. A small pack of the dogs (two to six individuals) is sent off against game and has to act with cunning and skill to effect a capture. The dogs are required to pursue the prey, racing at incredible speeds, take it by the throat and hold it down until their master arrives to perform the required ritual kill.

A frequent hunting method involves the combination of dogs and birds of prey. The dogs are carried on camels or horses by Arab hunters on whose wrists are perched hooded falcons. The falcons are released to fly high in the sky to search for prey. Once they have succeeded, they circle in the sky and this is the clue to the Salukis that a herd of gazelle has been located. The dogs are then released, whereupon they race towards the spot, often covering several miles (6–7 km) in the process. The human hunters follow on horseback or camel and eventually catch up with their swift hounds, who, by the time they have arrived, have caught and held their quarry.

References

1935. USA Club. *The Saluki Club of America Yearbook.*
1963. Burch, Virginia M. *How to Raise and Train a Saluki.* TFH, New Jersey.
1969. Waters, H. and D. *Saluki in History, Art and Sport.* David & Charles, Newton Abbot, Devon.
1974. Watkins, Vera H. *Saluki – Companion of Kings.* Fenrose, Tunbridge Wells, Kent.
1981. Birrell and Waters. *The Saluki Book of British Champions.*
1990. Burch, Virginia M. *Salukis.* TFH, New Jersey.
1991. Allan, Diana and Allan, Ken. *The Complete Saluki.* Howell, New York.
1995. Goodman, Gail. *The Saluqi: Coursing Hound of the East.* Midbar.

NORTH AFRICA

SLOUGHI
NORTH AFRICA

Also known as the Slughi, the Sloughui, the Slougui, the North African Gazelle Hound or the Arabian Greyhound, this breed is thought to have acquired its name from the Arabic word meaning 'fast as the wind'. Alternative theories suggest that the name comes either from the Yemeni towns of Saloug or Saluk, or from the Saharan settlement of Slouguia. (A different explanation, of course, is that these localities acquired their names from that of the dog.) It has been used since ancient times as a desert sighthound to hunt down hares, gazelles and even the small fennec foxes. In Germany it is the Arabischer Windhund, in Spain the Lebrel Arabe.

This ancient greyhound breed is viewed by some authorities as no more than a short-haired, North African desert version of the Middle Eastern Saluki. Sloughi enthusiasts disagree, regarding their favoured animal as a distinct breed in its own right. They point out that its body is heavier and bigger-boned than that of the Saluki, and that it has been known for thousands of years as a distinctive and separate entity.

The Sloughi's sandy-coloured coat helps to camouflage it in the arid environment in which it is traditionally used for hunting small game, and its long webbed toes give it a good grip when moving fast on the soft sands.

It almost certainly originated in the Middle East and then spread westwards across the Sahara and along the North African coast, in the service of nomadic Arab tribes. Today its main centre is in Morocco, but it is also found in Algeria, Tunisia and Libya.

Although dogs in general are despised by Moslems as unclean animals, an exception is made in the case of the Sloughi. It is revered by its male owners, who treat it as a family member and mourn its passing with due ritual. In some respects it is treated with more respect and given higher status than the female members of the tribe.

In temperament it is friendly and affectionate to the known members of its human group, but is usually hostile towards strangers. It has been described as a noble animal, independent, highly strung, vigilant and proud, and not suitable as a children's pet.

EGYPT

TESEM   EGYPT

Also known as the Egyptian Hunting Dog, this ancient breed was one of the first specialized sighthounds in the world.

Although described by some authors as an ancient Egyptian breed, in reality this dog is even older, being depicted in the rock paintings of East Africa that date back to the Neolithic period.

It appears in the tomb art of Egypt from about 3000 BC and is clearly shown as a short-coated, fawn-coloured, erect-eared, slender-bodied, greyhound-like dog. Its height is estimated to have been about 20 in (51 cm).

Described as the 'prototype greyhound', this ancestral dog can count among its descendants several other African breeds, such as the Basenji, the Manboutou, the Niam-Niam and the Shilluk. Courtesy of Phoenician traders of the first millennium BC, it is also the probable forerunner of the present-day Mediterranean breeds which we now refer to as the Sicilian Greyhound, the Pharaoh Hound and the Ibizan Hound.

Whether this breed is now extinct is debatable. It has been argued that it is unlikely to be found today in its original, undiluted form, but there are feral dogs in north-east

Africa that remain remarkably similar to the ancient form. And some of its descendants resemble the Egyptian tomb-art dogs so closely that one is inclined to think of them as surviving Tesems.

SUDAN

BISHARIN GREYHOUND   SUDAN

In the north-east of the Sudan, towards the Red Sea coast, the nomadic, pastoral Bisharin people have a strange type of greyhound with prick ears and a curly tail. It has been claimed that this breed is a direct descendant of the ancient Egyptian Tesem, but that is unlikely.

This tribe tends to feed its dogs largely on milk, with very little solid food, which is poor preparation for a strenuous chase in pursuit of fast-running game. As a result, the dogs are not strong enough to hunt singly and it usually takes a group of them to succeed in catching a hare.

DINKA GREYHOUND   SUDAN

The main Sudanese tribes each have their own, slightly different greyhound breed. The Dinka tribe, in the south-west of the country, hunt with one that is of a coarser type than the others. Its loss of quality is caused by mixed breeding with local Pariah Dogs. The degree of mixing is apparently so great that one explorer, on seeing the dogs, described them, not as greyhounds, but as 'greyhound-like pariahs'.

The Dinka Greyhound is very short-coated and light fawn in colour. The Dinka people castrate many of their male greyhounds, in the belief that it will increase their speed when on the chase, but this custom tends to limit the breeding gene pool of their dogs.

SHILLUK GREYHOUND   SUDAN

Also known as the Shilluk Dog, or simply the Shilluk, this rare, localized East African breed is used as a sighthound, by the Shilluk tribe, to run down medium-sized game.

The Nilotic Shilluk people, who inhabit the flat plains around the White Nile in south-east Sudan, possess 'well-bred' greyhounds of a special type. For a sighthound,

this breed has a rather robust body, and is usually fox-red in colour with a black muzzle. The colour pattern may vary a little and some dogs are grey, spotted with black. The ears try to be erect, but droop at the tips.

These Shilluk Greyhounds are set against antelope rather than against hare, a fact which may explain why this particular bred is more sturdily built than the better-known, typically lean and spindly sighthounds. Their speed and agility are exceptional.

MALI

AZAWAKH   MALI

Also known as the Azawakh Hound or the Tuareg Sloughi, this breed has been developed over hundreds of years as a sighthound to pursue gazelle, mouflon and hares.

Along the southern edge of the Sahara Desert, in Mali, this African breed of greyhound has for centuries been the prized possession of the nomadic Tuareg tribes. Valued as highly as a camel, the Azawakh has been developed for speed and staying power in an intensely hot climate.

A typical greyhound in shape, this short-coated breed is required by its owners to display some white in its colouring. It must also have black eye-rims and black nails and, rather oddly, five warts on its head. When a litter is born, only the strongest males are allowed to live, the weaker ones being culled. Females are kept for breeding purposes. This intense form of selection has resulted in the creation of an amazingly tough and hardy hunting animal.

When the Tuareg set off on a hunt, their dogs are carried with them on their saddles. Then, when the prey is sighted, they are released for the chase which may take up to five hours and reach speeds of 40 mph (64 kph).

The Tuareg tribesmen have always been extremely reluctant to allow any of their dogs to be sold or given to outsiders. As a result, few have ever been seen outside Mali. However, a Yugoslavian hunter called Dr Pecar recently managed to acquire a pair, in exchange for services rendered to the Tuareg, and these became the foundation stock for European breeding programmes. Examples

of this breed are now to be found not only in Yugoslavia but also in Germany and in Switzerland.

ZANZIBAR

ZANZIBAR GREYHOUND   ZANZIBAR

Also known as the Zanzibar Dog, this breed is named after the small island of Zanzibar lying off the Tanzanian coast of East Africa.

In the 19th century there was an unusual type of greyhound living on the tropical island of Zanzibar. This previously unknown breed aroused considerable interest and an example was taken to France in the late 19th century, where it was described and illustrated by Pierre Mégnin in 1897.

The Zanzibar Greyhound was a prick-eared dog, lacking the usual folded ear-tips of other, more typical greyhound breeds. A tall dog, it stood 27 in (68 cm) high and had a rough, red-and-white coat. It had a robust, powerful body, was remarkably intelligent and was keen-scented as well as keen-sighted. The German authority M. Siber in his work on African hounds, published in 1899, concluded that this breed was the result of a Saluki/Pariah crossing. It is not known whether a small population of these dogs still survives on the island today.

RUSSIA

BORZOI   RUSSIA

Also known as the Russian Greyhound, the Russian Wolfhound, the Siberian Wolfhound, the Fan-tailed Greyhound or the Psowaya Barsaya, this breed was originally developed for hunting wolves in the Russian forests. In the 19th century, in England, it was sometimes called by its French name, the Barzoi. In Germany it is the Russischer Windhund; in Spain the Lebrel Russo. In the Russian language the name of the breed is Borzaya, and Borzoi refers to the male dog. The names Borzoi, Barzoi and Borzaya are all derived from the Russian word 'borzyi', meaning 'swift'.

This exotic breed is the undisputed aristocrat of the canine world. Its haughty, elegant, graceful demeanour is instantly recognizable and is matched by a sensitive and aloof personality. Its long, silky, slightly wavy coat, its elongated body, and its narrow, domed

skull give it a unique silhouette. The small head has a characteristically convex top-line.

The origin of this tall, glamorous breed is disputed, but the most likely explanation is that greyhound-like dogs from ancient Egypt were taken north to Russia where they were later crossed with local, long-haired sheepdogs to produce the ancestor of the modern Borzoi. The breed became fixed by the 16th century and spent the next 400 years being refined as the ultimate wolf-catcher. Russian livestock was plagued by the many wolves resident in the vast northern forests, and hunting them down, although a colourful sport of the nobility, was also a case of practical predator-control.

The hunting technique was to use beaters to flush a wolf and then set a brace of perfectly matched Borzoi after it. Incredibly fast, they soon caught up with the fleeing animal and proceeded to attack it simultaneously, one from each side, seizing it by the neck and dragging it to the ground. When the huntsman caught up with them, he would despatch the pinned wolf with a dagger-thrust, or muzzle it and take it alive.

Hunting with Borzoi was a ceremonial affair. The horses and even the hounds themselves were often bedecked in brightly coloured hunting silks and the dogs were taken to the hunting grounds in a covered vehicle. The riders and the grooms were also elaborately attired and when the hunt was over there was extravagant feasting and celebration. This was one of the favourite pastimes of the czars of Russia, and gifts of Borzoi from them to the other crowned heads of Europe spread the fame of this noble dog far and wide. Some of the greatest of the Russian aristocrats could boast kennels containing as many as 150 of these exclusive dogs.

Following the Russian Revolution in 1917, this hound virtually vanished from its homeland, having been so closely associated with the hated nobility. Luckily, sufficient examples of the breed existed elsewhere in Europe by that time and it was later possible to return some to their place of origin.

References

1912. Thomas, Joseph B. *Observations on Borzoi.* Houghton, Mifflin, Boston.
1931. Craven, Arthur. *The Borzoi as I Know It.* Privately published, Manchester.
1931. Martin, Nellie. *The Russian Wolfhound.*
1952. Chadwick, Winifred E. *The Borzoi Handbook.* Nicholson & Watson, London.
1960. Hanks. *Borzoi, Most Noble Greyhound.*
1961. Plievier, Hildegard. *With my Dogs in Russia.* Hammond, London.
1964. McRae, Gail C. *How to Raise and Train a Borzoi.* TFH, New Jersey.
1968. Anon. *All About Borzois.* Borzoi Club, California.
1972. Chadwick, Winifred E. *Borzois.*
1976. Edlin, Alfred N. *Your Borzoi.*

1977. Gillette. *Life with Borzois.*
1977. Worthing. *Life and Legends of the Borzoi.*
1978. Gordon, John Frazer. *The Borzoi.* Bartholomew, Edinburgh.
1990. McRae, Gail C. *Borzois.*
     Groshans, Lorraine. *The Complete Borzoi.*

CHORTAI   RUSSIA

This breed is sometimes referred to as the Russian Greyhound or the Eastern Greyhound. The name 'Chortai' is sometimes spelled 'Chortaj'. It is still used today in its original role, as a sight-hunting hound of the Russian steppes.

Developed from two now-extinct Russian breeds, the Krymskaja and the Gorskaja, this streamlined dog looks like a cross between a typical greyhound and a short-coated Borzoi. It is employed in the traditional hunting style, with the huntsman on horseback accompanied by a brace of dogs and a falcon.

A little-known animal outside its homeland, the Chortai has been declared 'a breed worthy of preservation'. One was exhibited at the London Zoo in 1829, under the name of Russian Greyhound, but it does not appear to have been imported again after that early date.

CIRCASSIAN ORLOFF WOLFHOUND   RUSSIA

Also known simply as the Circassian Wolfhound, this large southern Russian breed was developed to pursue game in the mountainous regions of Circassia.

This elegant breed is similar to the more familiar Borzoi, but is faster, with even longer legs. It also has a flatter, less wavy coat and a slightly shorter head than the Borzoi, but is said to be a more intelligent dog.

In the 1880s a superb example of this breed, a reddish-coloured male called Domovoy, was seen at many European dogs shows, including one at the Crystal Palace in London. He made a great impression, being described as a handsome animal of aristocratic demeanour, belonging to a breed worthy of encouragement: 'a fine, upstanding dog, straight and strong in limbs'. Despite these admiring remarks, this breed does not seem to have caught on in the West.

In Russia it has a local relative called the Circassian Hare Hound, but it is not clear whether this is another name for the same breed or a different breed altogether.

SOUTH RUSSIAN STEPPE HOUND RUSSIA

Sometimes called the Steppe Borzoi, or South Russian Greyhound, this breed is known locally as the Ahk-Taz-eet, which translates as 'white Tasy dog'. It is used to course wolf, fox, hare and small deer.

This hound came into being following the Russian Revolution of 1917. After that upheaval, with its widespread destruction of the aristocratic hunting kennels, the noble Russian Greyhounds, or Chortai, were often abandoned to fend for themselves. They crossed with local dogs and the result was a slightly modified, new breed which was given the name of the South Russian Steppe Hound.

It is most common in the region of the Russian Caucasus Mountains, the Volga and the Don River, where it is kept for hunting by the Kirghiz tribes. It is renowned for its high speeds. In colour, it is white or cream, ideally without any darker markings.

TAIGAN RUSSIA

The name of this rare breed is sometimes written as Tajgan or Tagan (pronounced 'tie-gun') and means 'swift, fast'. It is also called the Kirghiz Greyhound, the Kirgizskaya Borzaya or the Kirghiz Borzoi, which means 'greyhound of Kyrgyzstan'. It is a large sighthound developed to hunt antelope, wild goat, wild sheep, fox, marmot, badger, wolf and wild cat, across difficult, mountainous terrain.

The main centre for this ancient but little-known breed is the Tien-Shan mountain range on the Russo-Chinese border. It has been specialized as a mountain hunter, possessing great speed and stamina, and capable of operating at altitudes of up to 10,000 ft (3,000 m). In recent years it has become increasingly scarce, and there are now thought to be only about 1,000 of them left alive.

As one might expect of a rugged mountain breed, the Taigan has a long, thick, double coat with heavy feathering on the ears, tail and upper legs. The long hair on the ears is referred to as the 'bourki'. The tail hangs like a sabre and has a spiral tip called a 'ring'.

In some respects, this breed is intermediate between the Tazi and the Afghan. Compared with the Tazi, it has a heavier build, a thicker coat and ears that hang lower. Compared with the Afghan, it has a shorter coat, a longer body, a ringed tail-tip and 'shoes' on its feet in the form of heavy-haired paws. Some authorities consider it to be no more than a cross between those two breeds, but others view it as a distinct, independent breed in its own right. It seems likely that the latter opinion is correct, but that in modern times its numbers have been so reduced that it has been crossed all too freely with the local Tazi dogs. This is thought to have happened most in the north of its range, in the Kirgizstan region of Chu Oblast.

In personality, the graceful, courageous Taigan is usually calm and relaxed, but as soon as it is on the hunt and sights its quarry, it becomes intensely excited.

TAZI   RUSSIA

This breed of Russian sighthound has many names. It is also called the Tazy, the Tasy, the Tadzi, the Taji, the Tasi, the Tazō, the Mid-Asiatic Tazi, the Mid-Asiatic Borzoi, the Mid-Asiatic Greyhound and the Sredneaziatskaya Borzoya. There are two local variants, the Khazakh Tazi and the Turkmenian Tazi. A courageous dog, it is used for hunting in the desert regions east of the Caspian Sea, where it is employed to pursue small game, including gazelle, hare, fox, wildcat and marmot. It is also prepared to tackle larger animals such as deer and even wolves. The main centre for this rare breed is the Kirhiz steppe country.

The Tazi is found in Kazakstan, Uzbekistan and Turkmenistan. It is similar to the Saluki, but is more strongly built. It is a hardy, fast and robust greyhound, with sharp reactions. Its coat is short, soft and straight and it has a fringed tail and long, fine hairs on its ears.

In the past, Tazi dogs have always been greatly prized, and their ability to obtain food has sometimes meant the difference between life and death for their owners. It is said that at one time a single pure-bred Tazi was worth 47 horses. However, modernization has meant that their role has been greatly reduced and their numbers have dwindled alarmingly. Furthermore, because the Tazi dogs were blamed for the disappearance of the local deer, they were severely persecuted in the 1970s, being pursued in jeeps and helicopters and ruthlessly culled. Now, only a few enthusiasts stand between them and extinction.

AFGHANISTAN

AFGHAN HOUND   AFGHANISTAN

This breed is also known as the Afghan Greyhound, or more simply as the Afghan. Among breeders it is usually referred to as the Affie. In Germany it is the Afghanischer Windhund; in France the Lévrier Afghan, in Spain the Lebrel Afgano. Earlier names for it include the Balkh Greyhound, the Baluchi Hound, the Barukzie Hound, the Barukhzy Greyhound, the Barukhzy Hound, the Barakzai Hound, the Kurram Valley Hound, the Kabuli Hound, the Kabul Hound and the Cabul Dog. In Russia they recognize two variants of the Afghan — the show dog, which they call the Afghan Decorative, and the working dog, which they call the Afghan Aboriginal. The latter is itself subdivided into two forms, the Bakhmul, Bakhmull, Bakmull or Makhmal, and the Khalag Tazy. The Afghan Hound was originally developed for chasing mammalian prey in the mountainous regions of its native Afghanistan.

This is without doubt the most spectacular of all the sighthounds. The greyhound may be the archetype, but the Afghan is the star performer. With its long, swishing coat, its thick 'trousers', and its lively, prancing gait, it is a dramatic show-stopper at any dog contest. In fact, its glamorous appearance has made it almost too popular, to the extent that it is often owned by people who, seduced by its looks, ignore its special needs.

In origin, this is probably a descendant of the Saluki, brought to Afghanistan from neighbouring Persia. Once there, it gradually developed a longer coat as a protection from the harsh environment of the mountains, where it was employed to pursue a variety of prey including everything from hare and fox, to deer and gazelle, to jackal and wolf, and even snow leopard. In a secondary role it also acted as a guard for the nomadic tribes and their livestock. These dogs were highly prized by the nomads and each year were brought down from the hills for a special festival at which they were decorated with traditional necklaces and flowers.

We have no idea concerning the antiquity of this breed. There are no reliable records of it before the 19th century, but this may mean only that Afghan nomads were poor record-keepers. The earliest certain picture of an Afghan Hound dates from 1813. Afghans first arrived in Britain in the 1920s and their rise to stardom was rapid. The breed was recognized by the Kennel Club in 1926.

In modern times, European-owned Afghans have been tried out on greyhound race-tracks, with mixed results. Unfortunately, some of the animals are too intelligent to bother racing around the track in pursuit of the mechanical hare and instead simply take a short cut across the central area to pounce on the hare as it comes round the bend towards them. This intelligent approach to the problem of high-speed chasing may well reflect the cunning that is needed by this breed when pursuing fleet-footed game on irregular mountain slopes.

With the recent arrival of the loathsome Taliban regime in Afghanistan, the future of this breed in its native home may well be at risk. One can only hope that enough of these magnificent dogs will be hidden away in such remote areas of the country that the breed as a whole will manage to survive the present cultural chaos. Fortunately, the range of the Afghan spreads slightly beyond the national boundaries of its home country and into parts of northern India, where it should be safe enough. In those regions it is referred to, not as the Afghan, but as the Barakzai (variants: Barukhzy, Barukzie) or the Kurram Valley Hound.

References

1951. Hubbard, Clifford, L. B. *The Afghan Hound Handbook*. Nicholson & Watson, London.

1958. Miller, Madeline. *Afghans*. TFH, New Jersey.

1958. Shay, Sunny and Barbaresi, Sara M. *How to Raise and Train an Afghan*. TFH, New Jersey.

1963. Brearley, Joan Macdonald. *This is the Afghan Hound*. TFH, New Jersey.

1965. Miller, Constance O. *The New Complete Afghan Hound*. Howell, New York.

1965. Miller, Constance O. and Gilbert, Edward M. *The Complete Afghan Hound*. Howell, New York.

1969. Kauffmann, Sue A. *Your Afghan Hound*. Denlinger's, Middleburg, Virginia.

1971. Hall, W. L. *The Afghan Hound*. John Gifford, London.

1972. Harrisson, Charles. *The Afghan Hound*. Arco, New York.

1976. Sutton, Catherine G. *The Afghan Hound. Its Care and Training*. K & R Books, Leicester.

1977. McCarty, E. *The Afghan Hound*. Bartholomew.

1979. Brearley, Joan Macdonald. *The Book of the Afghan Hound*. TFI I, New Jersey.

1980. Niblock, Margaret. *The Afghan Hound. A Definitive Study*. K & R Books, Lincolnshire.

1980. Pisano, Beverly. *Afghan Hounds*. TFH, New Jersey.

1997. Coile, Caroline D. *Afghan Hounds: Everything about Purchase, Care, Nutrition, Behavior, and Training*. Barron, New York.

1999. Race, Lynda. *Afghan Hounds*. TFH, New Jersey.

INDIA

BANJARA HOUND   INDIA

Sometimes referred to as the Banjara Greyhound, or simply as the Banjara, or the Vanjari, this breed is employed for general hunting duties.

The Banjara people are Indian nomads and their dogs accompany them as they move their camps from place to place. Their rough-coated greyhound, its black coat mottled with grey, has bred true for countless years but has recently been subjected to uncontrolled interbreeding with feral dogs and its purity is at risk. It has rarely been seen outside its homeland, although a few specimens have in the past been sent to the United States.

Said to have the speed of a greyhound and the stamina of a collie, this dog is thought to have originated from crosses between the Saluki and local Indian dogs. It is primarily a sighthound employed in the pursuit of game, but it is also used as a camp guard dog and even as a flock-control dog. According to Indian sources, when it is hunting

deer it attacks the quarry's hindquarters, unlike Deerhounds, which go for the throat. During the pursuit it utters a deep baying sound which is quite unlike any vocalization made by the Indian Pariah Dogs. A fearless attacker, the Banjara Hound is said to be 'sulky and treacherous with stronger dogs, though faithful to its master'.

CARAVAN HOUND   INDIA

A rare breed of Asiatic sighthound, employed to hunt both large and small game, including hare, monitor lizard and barking deer.

This is a dog from the borders of Maharashtra and Karnataka in central India, and is little known elsewhere. The local villagers have used these dogs for hunting since early times. It is thought that the ancestors of these hounds arrived on sailing ships from the Middle East centuries ago, landing at Karwar on the coast of Karnataka, just south of Goa, and spreading inland from there to the border with Maharashtra, where the landscape suited sight-hunting.

The elegant, racy, smooth-coated Caravan Hound resembles the Sloughi and the Azawakh, having the long body shape of the former and the graceful movement of the latter. A strong, fast dog, its gait is described as 'springy and flashy'. In personality it is said to be haughty, noble, brave, protective and reserved with strangers.

Its coat colour varies from light sandy, to fawn, to red sandy, often with patches of white or black. Its height is 28–30 in (71–76 cm). Today it has become the most popular indigenous breed at Indian dog shows.

CHIPPIPARAI HOUND   INDIA

This southern Indian breed was developed specifically for hare-hunting, although it now has other roles as well. Its name has sometimes been given as Chippirai.

In shape, the slender, white-coated Chippiparai is a typical greyhound, with very long legs and a streamlined body. Although its primary duties are associated with the hunt, in recent years the Madras police force has started training members of this breed as police dogs, with some success. This has the advantage of avoiding the expense of importing foreign police dogs.

In personality, this is a one-man dog. It does not like being touched or patted by strangers.

INDIAN HAIRLESS DOG INDIA

This extinct sighthound, which was once found in the hottest regions of India, was used for hunting small game.

Little is known about this breed, which had vanished by the middle of the 19th century. In appearance it was likened to a naked greyhound with pricked ears. It had grey or red skin, with tufts of hair on its head, legs, feet and tail-tip. Its thick, wrinkled skin was able to withstand the rigours of hunting, even in areas where it had to push its way through the undergrowth, although it was kept as much for its curiosity value as for its hunting ability.

KAIKADI DOG INDIA

This breed is named after the local people who keep them for hunting small animals.

A little-known breed of Indian sighthound, this dog is said to resemble the Whippet in appearance, but with a straight top-line. Some authorities believe that it is a close relative of the Caravan Hound. It is a type unique to the nomadic Kaikadi people from the region of Maharashtra, to the east of Bombay in central India. A smallish dog, it is skilled at hunting monkeys, jungle rats, rabbits and other small mammals. At night it is used as a camp watchdog.

This is a slender, long-legged, fast-moving dog with a lightning snap of its strong jaws, capable of snatching any unwary prey. The coat colour is variable, but is usually a mixture of white, black and tan.

MUDHOL HOUND INDIA

Described as the Greyhound of Maharashtra, this breed is sometimes referred to as the Maratha Hound, the Pashmi Hound or the Kathewar Dog. Its original function was hunting deer, rabbits and even jackals.

This Indian breed of sighthound is smaller than the English Greyhound but larger than the Whippet. It is found scattered over a wide range in the region of Maharashtra, to the east of Bombay, in central India. It is a slender, short-haired animal looking like a slighter, less elongated cousin of the greyhound. It is a graceful but hardy dog and is popular in its role as a hunting companion, although today it is more often employed as a watchdog.

In recent times, there has been much interbreeding with imported Salukis. The Saluki blood was used to strengthen the breed, but there are still pure-bred Mudhol dogs to be found in the more remote regions, especially in the more southerly parts of its range, in Karnataka. The Mudhol Hound is rated more highly than the other locally found sighthound, the Caravan Dog, because it is better able to withstand the fierce afternoon heat when hunting and because it is more nimble at making sudden turns during the chase.

POLIGAR HOUND INDIA

This breed is named after the military chieftains of southern India who originally developed the dog for hunting fox, deer, jackal and wild boar. It is sometimes referred to as the Greyhound of Southern India, or as the Polugar Dog or Polygar Dog.

The Poligar has been described as 'rather like a Lurcher, but with little coat of any kind, mere bristles, and the skin showing through of a purple colour'. A long-distance runner, it has for many generations been used as a companion on pig hunts which were carried out on foot and using only spears. It is most commonly encountered in the districts around Madras.

Writing in 1864, William Youatt mentions this breed, commenting: 'There is a dog in Dakhun [Deccan] with hair so short as to make him appear naked. It is called the Polugar Dog.'

RAMPUR HOUND INDIA

Also known as the Rampuri, the Rampuree, the Rampur Dog, the Rampur Greyhound, the North Indian Greyhound or the Northwest Indian Greyhound, this breed is mainly employed for hunting jackal, wild boar and deer. Its name is taken from its geographical location in northwest India. One was exhibited at the London Zoo in 1877, under the name of Rampoor Hound.

This Indian sighthound, once a great favourite of the Indian Maharajahs, looks like a slightly heavier, more powerful version of the greyhound. It has been aptly described as an 'overgrown greyhound of coarse build'. Its jaws are certainly more impressive than those of the ordinary greyhound and this is clearly a hunter who is both fast and fero-cious. It is claimed that its feet can stand hunting on hard ground better than those of the traditional greyhound. Its smooth coat is mouse-grey, or sometimes black, in colour. The rare black variety is said to be the best hunter. Some authorities believe that it is closely related to the Taigan breed found on the Russo–Chinese border.

Although it is friendly enough with its owners, it has a reputation of being 'queer tempered', to quote an early author, and ready to 'bite without barking' if any stranger comes too close. Many years ago some examples of this breed were brought to England, but they did not appear to arouse much interest and soon vanished. It has not been seen in the show-rings of Europe in recent times.

As with several of the Indian sighthound breeds, this one appears to have been sub-jected to a certain amount of cross-breeding in recent times, and some older hunters insist that the modern Rampur does not look much like the earlier, pure-bred Indian form they once knew.

TIBET

TIBETAN HOUND   TIBET

Sometimes known as the Sha-Kyi, this little-known breed is employed to hunt large game. It has also been called the Tibetan Hunting Dog.

This hound is unusual for a Himalayan dog, being a comparatively short-coated animal in a cold country, where every other local breed has long hair to protect it. But, presumably, for it to be fast-running in the hunt, it cannot be too heavy and has to sacrifice comfort to speed.

The only description of the dog that we have is as follows: The ears are drooped and hang forward, the coat is short but thick, and the tail is usually carried low but is raised up and curled over the back when the dog is active. In colour it is a creamy grey. The head is long and is smoky black in colour, shading gradually into the creamy grey of the body. The dog is about the same size as an Airedale.

It is used to hunt bharal (a kind of wild sheep), serow (a wild goat) and musk deer. With the bharal, it pursues the game towards cliffs, where the prey stops and defends itself, trying to butt the dog over the edge. Apparently this technique sometimes works with wolves that are rash enough to charge the prey and come within range of the dan-gerous horns, but the Tibetan Hound is trained to keep the animal at bay and not to make that final move. It continues harassing the animal and barking at it until the hunter arrives to shoot it at close quarters. (The guns used are so poor that a long-distance shot

would fail, so the assistance of the hound is crucial to the success of the hunt.) Sometimes the hound, which has very keen sight, will spot some game in the distance and strain to be let off the leash, but if there is no suitable place for the dog to corner the quarry, the hunter will hold it back.

A German visitor who encountered this hound described it as 'less hairy than ordinary Tibetan dogs, lean, swift as the wind, and indescribably ugly', a quality that is rare among sighthounds.

The most likely reason for the absence of more detailed information concerning this breed is that it is kept exclusively by tribal nomads and is therefore not often encountered by foreign visitors. The tribes said to be involved with this breed are the Khampas.

CHINA

CHINESE GREYHOUND   CHINA

Also known as the Kansu Greyhound, the Tschika, the Tsika or the Hsi Yang Min-tzu, this breed was used for coursing in China in earlier days.

The little-known Chinese Greyhound is probably extinct in modern China, a country now notorious for its ruthless treatment of domestic dogs. In its heyday this breed was most commonly found in the Shensi and Kansu districts.

In origin, this dog was probably developed long ago from Persian or Indian sighthounds imported as gifts to the ancient Chinese nobility. There is, for example, a greyhound-shaped dog clearly shown in a bas-relief from the Han dynasty, dating back about 2,000 years. Centuries later, these early hounds were mixed with imported English Greyhounds in an attempt to improve the stock. In the days of the East India Company, when trade in special forms of livestock was taking place between East and West, there are several records of specific requests from China for English Greyhounds.

The result of these crosses was an animal very similar to the English Greyhound, but reduced in size. It was about 20 in (50 cm) tall, against the English Greyhound's 27 in (69 cm). Another visible difference was the slight feathering on the tail of the Chinese animal, which is absent in the English version. Writing in 1927, the great canine historian Edward Ash is scathing about the breed, commenting: 'The Chinese Greyhound is a lank creature from which a strong hare would canter quietly away.'

In colour, the Chinese Greyhound's short, smooth coat was usually fawn or brown, though yellow and cream were also known. A white patch on the front of the body was sometimes present.

AUSTRALIA

KANGAROO DOG   AUSTRALIA

Also known as the Kangaroo Hound or the Australian Greyhound, this large sighthound was developed to pursue wallabies and kangaroos in the Australian outback. When an example arrived at the London Zoo in 1839, it was labelled as a Kangaroo Greyhound. It has also been recorded as the Kangoeroehond or the Australische Windhond.

Described as 'the great Australian hunter', this giant greyhound was created for the difficult task of chasing large marsupials. It was also used to catch emu and – in a case of canine treachery – to run down and kill native Dingoes. In order to produce a dog capable of these heavy duties, imported greyhounds were crossed with Deerhounds and Irish Wolfhounds. This helped to increase the breed's size and its strength. A typical greyhound registers 65 lb (29 kg), while a Kangaroo Dog weighs up to 80 lb (36 kg). The crosses also gave the Australian dog a rougher, more protective coat.

This impressive animal became a favourite with outback farmers. It gave them several important advantages: it controlled the 'farm pests', which was how they viewed the local fauna; it allowed them to hunt and kill without the use of guns, helping them to conserve their precious powder and shot; it provided them with delicious marsupial meat; and it allowed their imported sheep to graze without competition from the grass-eating marsupials.

Despite its popularity as a working breed, it was hardly ever introduced into the show-ring. An exception occurred in 1864, when the Prince of Wales exhibited a pair as a curiosity at the Second International Show in London. But, because it did not become established as a registered breed, the Kangaroo Dog eventually became a great rarity. When the killing of native marsupials became restricted by law, it inevitably began to vanish and is now almost extinct.

References

1978. Whyte, June. *Care and Training of the Australian Greyhound.* Rigby, Adelaide.

STRATHDOON DINGO KILLER   AUSTRALIA

Named after its stronghold, the Strathdoon Kennels in Blacktown, New South Wales, the Strathdoon Dingo Killer was developed specifically to pursue Dingoes.

This rare breed was developed to tackle Dingoes in the early days of settlement in Australia, when local animals were considered to be a serious threat to the livelihood of colonial farmers. The breed was created by crossing Deerhounds with Irish Wolfhounds.

The founding figure was Cecil Davies, a Deerhound breeder of New South Wales, who created the breed around the end of the 19th century, or the beginning of the 20th century.

UNITED STATES

AMERICAN STAGHOUND   UNITED STATES

A large sighthound, not to be confused with the extinct English Staghound (which in type was an overgrown Foxhound), it is sometimes referred to as the Cold-blooded Greyhound. This impressive breed was employed in the Wild West to hunt down marauding wolves and coyotes.

In appearance this dog is the American equivalent of the British Lurcher, but it is a much more powerful dog, built on a larger scale. Looking like a huge, rough-coated greyhound, it was created from crosses between English Greyhounds, Scottish Deerhounds, Irish Wolfhounds and Borzoi, all of which were imported into North America in the 19th century.

This tough, thick-skinned, athletic dog proved to be of great value to the early pioneers who were struggling to conquer the untamed lands of the West. Their livestock was constantly at risk from attacks by local predators, and they needed a canine defender capable of dealing with these formidable enemies. The Staghound was the answer to their prayers, accompanying hunters on sweeps through the countryside and defeating even the biggest wolves.

Once the West had been fully settled, the American Staghound was no longer needed as a wolf-hunter, but it was fast enough and strong enough to pull down even the most muscular deer. Deer-hunting became its new, exclusive role as a sporting dog, and remains so to this day.

SILKEN WINDHOUND   UNITED STATES

This is one of the newest breeds of dog in existence. The International Silken Windhound Society held its first meeting as recently as April 1999. The motivation behind the creation of this still experimental breed was the desire to find a dog that combined the athletic elegance of the typical sighthound, the aesthetically pleasing sight of a long, flowing coat, and the reduced size that would make it suitable for smaller houses.

The Silken Windhound was developed by Francie Stull of the Kristull Borzoi Kennels in Austin, Texas. She began in 1988 with Silken Windsprites from the Windsprite Kennels (see separate entry for Silken Windsprite), which were reputed to be pure-bred Whippets carrying long-haired genes. Over a ten-year period she then added Borzoi, to enhance the long coat, and normal, short-haired Whippet to broaden the gene pool. The breed is still in development but promises to be an attractive addition to the canine world, once it has started to breed true and is proven to be healthy and without defects. At present there is no indication of either of these problems, but some traditional breeders remain hostile to the project.

These dogs do not acquire their full coats until they are three years old. There is no colour restriction at present, Silkens appearing in a wide range, from black to white. It is said that a few of them have already found their way to Europe.

SILKEN WINDSPRITE   UNITED STATES

Sometimes referred to as the Longhaired Whippet, this very recent breed, developed largely in the 1980s, has caused considerable controversy since its creation by Walter Wheeler of the Windsprite Kennels in Massachusetts. Wheeler insists that he has developed the breed from individual, pure-bred Whippets that happened to be carrying a dormant long-haired gene. By selectively favouring this condition in a careful breeding programme he now claims to have created a new type of Whippet. A Longhaired Whippet Association has been formed.

This claim is hotly contested by the traditional Whippet breeders, who argue that Wheeler has exploited a breed 'fault'. Viewed dispassionately, however, the only serious objection, if he eventually stabilizes his new breed, will be if it proves to be either unhealthy or ugly. Since, at present, it appears to be neither, we must reserve judgement until it has been fully established as a pure-breeding line.

DUTCH ANTILLES

ARUBIAN CUNUCU DOG   ARUBA

This rare breed is named after its homeland, the small Caribbean island of Aruba in the Dutch

Antilles. The word 'Cunucu' means 'countryside' in the Arubian language of Papiamentu. In derivation, however, the word comes from the older language of the indigenous Arawak Indians. This is a medium-sized sighthound primarily employed in the pursuit of iguanas, to obtain their meat.

Modern research techniques have shown that this little-known breed has an interesting origin. DNA tests have revealed that its ancestors were probably introduced to Aruba by Portuguese slave-traders sometime in the 16th century. The dogs they took with them were probably very similar to the modern Iberian breed called the Medium Portuguese Podengo, known in its homeland as the Podengo Portuguesa Medio.

Once on the island, some of those imported dogs then came into the possession of the indigenous Arawak tribespeople, who crossed them with local dogs that were living on the island in a semi-wild, feral condition. Comparing the modern Podengo with the modern Cunucu, it is clear that there must have been some spitz genes present in the feral dogs, because the Cunucu has the typical upcurled tail of a spitz dog, a feature that is not present in the Podengo.

Once the Arawak Indians had developed their own breed of hunting dog, they employed it to pursue the island's iguanas, large lizards that offered a valuable source of protein. This would not have been difficult for a Podengo-type of dog, since the ancestral form in Portugal had been developed to chase rabbits and other fast-moving small game over rough terrain.

The Cunucu Dog is a medium-sized animal that appears in a variety of colour forms, especially brown-and-white and black-and-tan. It is athletic, courageous, loyal and intelligent. A very fast-moving dog, it is renowned for its amazing leaping ability. This is an adaptation to its lizard-chasing, when it must skilfully manoeuvre the rocky outcrops in the island's arid interior at high speed.

In 1999 the government of Aruba issued a special set of commemorative postage stamps depicting Arubian Cunucu Dogs, to honour this local breed.

BRAZIL

BRAZILIAN GREYHOUND   BRAZIL

Also referred to as the Brazilian Deerhound or the Veadeiro Catarinense, this little-known breed is said to have been created from crosses between imported greyhounds and foxhounds. Although essentially a sighthound, the Brazilian Greyhound can also track by scent if necessary. The short coat is grey or brown in colour and the ears are large, straight and pointed.

SCENTHOUNDS

The typical scenthound is a long-legged, droop-eared, smooth-coated, athletic dog, with a melodious voice. It frequently displays a tricolour, 'hound pattern' of white with black and brown patches on it. If the sighthounds are the sprinters of the canine world, the scenthounds are the long-distance runners. Their bodies are less extreme and less stiffly angular, more sturdily built and more flexible.

The scenthound's crowning glory, of course, is its amazingly sensitive nose, and the dog spends a great deal of time when hunting, dashing this way and that, with it thrust low to the ground, searching for the tiniest clues.

Scenthounds fall into three main categories:

1   *Large, heavy-bodied hounds* (eg, Bloodhound): These are hunted in small numbers on the leash, by huntsmen on foot, and are known as *leash-hounds*.

2   *Athletic, medium-built hounds* (eg, Foxhound): These are hunted as a pack, by huntsmen on horseback, and are known as *horse-hounds*.

3   *Small, short-legged hounds* (eg, Basset Hound): These are free-hunted off the leash, by huntsmen on foot, and are known as *foot-hounds*.

Another method of classifying scenthounds is by the type of hunting technique involved:

1   *Grande Vénerie – Chasse-à-Courre*: This is the hunting of large game – deer, wolf, wild boar – with a pack of hounds following scent and pursuing their quarry to the death.

2   *Petite Vénerie – Chasse-à-Tire*: This is the hunting of small game – hare, rabbit, fox, birds – with the hounds using scent to drive the quarry to the waiting huntsmen. In earlier days, the hunters would then have used birds of prey or nets to catch the game, and in later times, the sporting gun.

For centuries, Grande Vénerie was the sport of kings. But then the large game began to disappear. The forests shrank, weapons changed, society changed, people outside the nobility were allowed to hunt, and the whole fabric of the chase was transformed. Grande Vénerie fought a rearguard action in the form of fox-hunting. This was an anomaly because it employed the Chasse-à-Courre of the Great Hunt to run down and kill small game. Previously a 'Great Hunter' would not have given a mere fox a second glance, but there was no longer any alternative. The traditions of

Grande Vénerie could be kept alive, even if the quarry was a pathetically small and completely useless prize.

Petite Vénerie itself, on the other hand, went from strength to strength, as fields replaced forests, and as sporting guns became ever more efficient. Instead of a crude driving of quarry towards the hunters, there was now a whole series of specializations. Breeds became refined and developed for each of these tasks:

1 *Slow-driving dogs*: bassets

2 *Flushing dogs*: spaniels

3 *Treeing dogs*: coonhounds

4 *Setting dogs*: setters

5 *Pointing dogs*: pointers

6 *Decoy dogs*: tolling dogs

7 *Retrieving dogs*: retrievers

Many of the scenthound breeds can now be classified as belonging to one or other of these special activities (and can be found in this book under these various headings) but there remains to this day a large collection of general scenthound breeds that cannot be pigeonholed in that way, and they are the ones that make up the present section.

It is, perhaps, surprising that there are so very many of these scenthound breeds, but it is important to remember that, historically, these dogs were nearly always estate-controlled. Each big country estate would have its own inbred population of hunting dogs and would rarely mix these with dogs from nearby estates. So, each great house slowly created its own 'brand' of scenthound and then came to defend its 'type' against all others. This meant that, even though the dogs were all performing much the same tasks in the field, they each had their own slight differences in appearance and build. At one point, for example, there were no fewer than 300 separate estates breeding and hunting scenthounds in France alone. What is surprising is not that there are so many scenthound breeds today, but that there are not even more.

The present list comprises 98 breeds.

ENGLAND

ENGLISH FOXHOUND ENGLAND

Usually referred to simply as the Foxhound, this dog is given a more specific name to distinguish it from its relative the American Foxhound. As its title implies, it was developed exclusively to pursue the fox.

The Foxhound is the breed which pushes canine stamina to the limit. One early author asked the key question: 'What other breed of dog is there that could trot out a dozen or fourteen miles along the roads to a meet, then gallop about for five hours or so... all the time using his nose, intelligence and voice... and do it twice a week?'

This is a dog that has been bred, over hundreds of years, for endurance and for pack compatibility. It is friendly towards other dogs and docile and affectionate with human beings, but is potentially lethal with any small, furry, fox-sized animal and is hardly ever used as a household companion.

This breed became increasingly important in English hunting as the forests disappeared and the deer population dwindled. Stag-hunters, robbed of their traditional hunting rituals, had to look elsewhere for a suitable quarry to enable them to continue to display their prowess on horseback while enjoying the thrill of the chase.

It is sometimes claimed that fox-hunting has a long history and began as early as the 13th century, but this is not strictly true. In the Middle Ages foxes were treated strictly as vermin to be destroyed by any means available. This sometimes involved the use of dogs, but they did not belong to a specific breed.

It was not until the 17th century, in the reign of Charles II, that specialized fox-hunting began and hounds were bred whose exclusive role was to hunt and kill the English red fox. They were developed by combining the excellent nose of the old Southern Hound (a big, slow, stag-hunting dog) with the speed of some kind of 'northern gazehound' (although nobody is certain what these greyhound-like dogs really were). And it was not until the 18th century that fox-hunting replaced stag-hunting as the major sport of the English countryside. The Duke of Beaufort's hounds at Badminton, for example, were switched from stags to foxes in 1770.

It was during the 18th century that the true ancestors of the modern Foxhound emerged. As a 1735 poem put it: 'In thee alone... is bred the perfect hound, in scent and speed as yet unrivall'd.' This fast scenthound was gradually improved and refined over the next 200 years. Like thoroughbred horses, pedigree Foxhounds came from a narrow base. In 1930 it was claimed that all well-bred 20th-century Foxhounds were descendants of five ancestral dogs bred between 1748 and 1830.

By the end of the 20th century there were still 200 packs of these hounds in action on a regular basis. (To be precise, in 1984 there were 201 packs in England, Wales and Scotland.) Proposals, put forward in the late 20th century, to outlaw hunting with dogs altogether in the British Isles were viewed as the death knell of this breed, but as there were already a number of packs employed in drag-hunting, it was clear that it would manage to survive in that new role.

Although the Foxhound still exists in large numbers (an estimate in March 2000 put the total figure at 24,000) and is recognized by the Kennel Club in London, this breed uniquely never appears in the show-ring. It is also routinely missing from the annual Kennel Club registration lists. It lives in its own world – the world of hunts and huntsmen – where body scars are viewed as a badge of courage rather than as a show-ring disqualification.

The English Foxhound has a worldwide following. It has been exported to many countries including France, Germany, Sweden, Poland, Hungary, Italy, Spain, Canada, Africa, India, Australia and New Zealand. In France and the United States it has been crossed with local breeds and modified in the process (see Anglo-French Hound and the American Foxhound).

References

1848. Mills, John. *The Life of a Foxhound*. Hurst, London.

1914. Bensusan, R. B. *The Life-Story of a Foxhound*. Hutchinson, London.

1914. Bradley, Cuthbert. *The Foxhound of the Twentieth Century*. Routledge, London.

1922–1937. Wooldridge, S. L. *The International Fox Hunters' Stud Book*. Vol. I–Vol. XI. Chase Publishing, Kentucky.

1926. Bathhurst, Seymour Henry Earl. *The Breeding of Foxhounds*. Constable, London.

1935. Acton, C. R. *The Modern Foxhound*. Witherby, London.

1939. Acton, C. R. *Hounds: an Account of the Kennels of Great Britain*. Heath Cranton, London.

1947. Bell, Isaac. *A Huntsman's Log Book*. Eyre & Spottiswoode, London.

1947. Walker, Woods. *The International Fox Hunters' Stud Book*. Vol. 12. Chase Publishing, Kentucky.

1953. Acton, C. R. *The Foxhound of the Future*. Baylis, London.

1964. Moore, Daphne. *The Book of the Foxhound*. Allen, London.

1990. Ridley, Jane. *Fox Hunting*. Collins, London.

1998. Latimer, Emily. *The English Foxhound. A Complete and Reliable Handbook*. TFH, New Jersey.

Higginson, A. Henry. *Foxhunting Theory and Practice*.

Thomas, Joseph B. *MFH Hounds and Hunting Through the Ages*.

ENGLISH STAGHOUND   ENGLAND

The extinct English Staghound was the predecessor of the Foxhound. A big, heavy dog, it stood 27 in (69 cm) high and was used exclusively to hunt deer.

This early English breed was described as 'the first remove from the Bloodhound'. In other words, when the old-fashioned Bloodhounds and Talbots arrived in England with the Normans in the 11th century, they started to change as they adapted to life in their new environment. One of the new, slightly modified forms they took was called the Staghound, which remained an important breed as long as the great deer forests lasted. Then, as these began to dwindle and the hunters switched from deer to fox, the large, slow, old-style Staghounds began to disappear, to be replaced by the faster Foxhound.

The Epping Forest Staghound pack was hunting deer up until 1805, the Royal pack until 1814. After that, only one pack of old-fashioned Staghounds survived and that was the Devon and Somerset, which had been in existence since the days of Elizabeth I. This last pack was finally put up for sale at Tattersall's in 1825. The animals were moved to Hampshire for a few years but most of them were then shipped across the Channel, where they would soon be destroyed during a rabies scare. Their departure from England heralded the end of the breed.

The famous hunting parson, Jack Russell, was so upset by the sale of this last Staghound pack that, before they were dispersed, he acquired three of the bitches, in the hope that he could somehow save the breed and start up a new pack. When this did not happen, he gave the bitches to a friend of his who presented them to a kennels near Swansea. There they were used to improve the local breed of Welsh hounds (see Welsh Foxhound).

The so-called Staghound packs that existed long after the 1820s were in reality packs of the new Foxhounds co-opted to hunt deer in the old style.

FELL HOUND   ENGLAND

Sometimes referred to as the Fell Foxhound or the Lakeland Foxhound, this breed was used to hunt foxes in the fell counties of Cumberland and Westmorland in northern England.

In the early days of fox-hunting, several distinct types of foxhound, dogs which could be classified as separate breeds, developed in specific localities. The Fell Hound was one of these. It was a lighter-boned and lighter-coloured foxhound. The smaller body helped it in its chase after the fox in the difficult, hilly country of the Lake District, and the pale colouring made it more conspicuous at a great distance – an important consideration when the hunters so often had to follow the hounds on foot.

In the 1930s there were five Fell Hound packs still operating – the Blencathra, the Coniston, the Eskdale, the Ennerdale and the Ullswater. There were also several other packs working in the same countryside which were composed of part-Fell Hounds.

HARRIER   ENGLAND

This breed of scenthound was developed specifically for hare-hunting, and it is believed that its name is based on a combination of hare plus —ier. In some early works, it is referred to as the Hare-hound, or Heirer.

Advocates of stag-hunting looked down upon the hare-hunters, commenting that their sport with Harriers was 'an amusement better calculated for the initiation of juveniles, the entertainment of ladies and the enjoyment of gentlemen advanced in years, and replete with infirmities'. The hare-hunters dismissed these insults, retorting that 'to the contemplative naturalist, much more of the true spirit of hunting, and the instinct of animals, is to be observed and enjoyed' with Harriers than with Staghounds.

Known from at least as early as the 13th century, the Harrier is intermediate in size between the larger Foxhound and the smaller Beagle. It is traditionally followed on foot by the huntsmen, a practice that was adopted at least 700 years ago.

Some authorities are convinced that the Harrier is an even older breed that can be traced back far beyond the 13th century. In the 400 BC writings of Xenophon they have identified a small Greek hound that sounds exactly like the Harrier of the Middle Ages. They believe that this ancient Greek hound may have been brought to Britain by the Romans, where it then survived more or less unchanged over the centuries.

In 1825 the slow-moving, old-fashioned Harrier was upgraded by crossing it with Foxhounds to produce a faster, modern Harrier that could be used for both hare-hunting and fox-hunting. With these dogs, the hunters did not always confine themselves to travelling on foot, sometimes riding with the improved Harriers as they would with Foxhounds.

The 20th century saw a serious decline in the sport of Harrier hunting. In 1895 there were no fewer than 110 packs of Harriers working in England and

Wales. By 1902 there were 97 packs. By 1914 this figure had been reduced to 84 packs. World War I then caused a major setback. By 1930 there were only 41 packs left. After World War II the situation was even worse. By the 1960s there were only 28 packs remaining. Of those, 23 hunted the hare; one hunted both hare and fox; and four hunted only the fox. The average pack consisted of 22 couples, giving a total Harrier population (in 1964) of approximately 1,200 dogs.

References

1999. Auborn, John. *Harrier: a Complete and Reliable Handbook.* TFH, New Jersey.

LIMER   ENGLAND

The name of this breed has known many variants. To Chaucer in the 14th century it was the Lymer; in the 15th century it was the Lemor; in the 16th century it became the Lymmar; for Topsel in the 17th century it was the Lyemmer; in the 18th century it ended up as the Limer. By the 19th century it had vanished. It was also, at various times, called the Leymmer, the Lymmer, the Lymour, the Limmer, the Leviner, the Leamer and the Lemer. Of all these titles, the Oxford English Dictionary selects Limer as the most significant. In French, it was the Limier. It was also referred to as the Leash Hound. As regards its function, the only specific quarry mentioned were deer and wild boar.

In the earliest books on hounds and hunting, there is repeated reference to this mysterious dog. It was clearly a common breed in its day, but has long since disappeared, leaving little information behind it. From what records we do have, it was a lightly build scenthound, so light-bodied that it was also sometimes referred to as the 'Light Hound'. It is listed as a breed that is excellent for 'smelling and swift running' which will 'follow the game with more eagerness, and take the prey with a jolly swiftness'.

Reading the few comments that are available about this breed, it sounds as though it was a smaller, more athletic version of the Bloodhound. Some authors are of the opinion that the Limer and the Bloodhound were, in fact, one and the same. Thomas Pearce, for example, writing in 1872, states that sometimes Bloodhounds 'were described as Limehounds, Limiers, or Lyamhounds, because they were led in a leathern thong'. He goes on to say: 'The Leashhound, or Limier, was the "Rache", or guiding one of the pack, used for harbouring the deer. He was led for this purpose, and trained for this one thing.'

The relationship between the Limer and the Bloodhound was clearly close, and even today the French word Limier is used to mean Bloodhound. It is also the slang word for a French detective, meaning 'police bloodhound'. But the fact that the word Bloodhound was itself prominent in England throughout the centuries when the Limer was well known demonstrates that, although related, they must have differed in some way.

The few anatomical descriptions we have of the breed are contradictory. One author described it as being 'a breed betwixt the Greyhound and the Hound'; another called it 'a middle kind between the Harrier and the Greyhound'; yet another labelled it as being 'betwixt a Hound and a Mastiff.' Sadly, these descriptions are of little help in visualizing the breed, but they do make it clear that the dog in question was not a typical Bloodhound, which the authors in question described in quite different terms.

There were two theories concerning the meaning of its name. One suggests that it comes from the fact that the dog 'ran the line of scent' and that the Limer was a 'Liner'. The other proposes that it is derived from the practice of running the dog on a leash and then releasing it (an old word for a hound-leash being a 'lyme' or a 'lyam'). This second explanation seems more convincing.

Writing in 1790, Thomas Bewick comments that the breed 'is now unknown to us'. Another author, writing in 1829, says that, by that date, it was 'long extinct'.

OTTERHOUND

ENGLAND

In earlier days this breed was sometimes referred to simply as the Otter Dog, reflecting its sole purpose in life – the pursuit of the elusive river otter.

This ancient breed is a stocky, shaggy, usually fawn-coloured scenthound with a highly sensitive nose housed in a body that is amazingly insensitive to cold. In pursuit of river otters, this dog is prepared to plunge into even the most freezing waters. It has a shambling walk, large, webbed feet and strangely folded ears. Its coat, so important when hunting in water, is dense, rough and weatherproof.

Many ancestral breeds have been proposed as contributing to the origin of this appealing hound. Among the most important are the Griffon Nivernais from France and the Southern Hound, the Foxhound and the Bloodhound from England. Some authors also mention a Rough-haired Terrier as an important element, but this is probably overstated. The reason for the confusion is that, in its earliest days, the Otterhound was a much more terrier-like dog. In fact, it was not then a pure-bred form at all, but was rather a 'breed' made up of almost any tough, rough-and-tumble dogs that would hurl themselves into cold water. As time went on, the quality of the breed was improved until its original terrier element was all but eliminated and the newer, hound-based dog became dominant.

The history of this breed can be traced back to the 13th century, when King John hunted with a pack. In the 14th century, Edward II held among his many titles that of the first Master of Otterhounds. Elizabeth I was the first Lady Master of Otterhounds. Other British monarchs to hold the title of Master of Otterhounds were Henry VI, Edward IV, Richard III, Henry VII, Henry VIII and Charles II.

By the beginning of the 20th century there were as many as 20 or 30 Otterhound packs at work in the rivers of England, doing their best to reduce the number of otters in order to improve the fishing. They succeeded all too well, aided by extensive river pollution, and the otter population sank to a level of near-extinction. In 1978, to save the last otters from disappearing, a law was passed to protect these attractive carnivores. From a noble dog and the fisherman's champion, the unfortunate Otterhound was suddenly transformed into a national villain.

Devotees of the breed responded to this new situation by forming the Otterhound Club of Great Britain, in order to prevent the dog from vanishing like its prey. It was a close-fought battle because, following the ban on otter-hunting, many packs of Otterhounds had been destroyed by despairing owners. Eventually, only two packs remained – one in Kendal, in north-west England, and the other in Dumfries, in south-west Scotland. Together this amounted to about 100 dogs. The only hope now was to find them a new occupation, and the show-ring beckoned. Visually appealing, with a delightful, boisterous personality, these big shaggy dogs were an immediate dog-show favourite and the breed was rescued for the future, even if, as they sit patiently in their show-pens awaiting the judging, they have the expression of a dog dreaming of the dark, swirling waters of distant rivers.

References

1965. Mouat, Hugh. *How to Raise and Train an Otter Hound*. TFH, New Jersey.
1988. Anon. *The Otterhound: Recorded By Photograph and Pedigree*. The Otterhound Club of Great Britain.
1997. Mouat, Hugh and Conway, Elizabeth. *Otterhound: A Complete and Reliable Handbook*. TFH, New Jersey.

SOUTHERN HOUND   ENGLAND

Also known as the Old English Hound or the Heavy Finder, this extinct breed was developed primarily to hunt deer.

Described as a large, strong, long-bodied hound with a 'majestic solemnity of appearance', a tricoloured coat, a deep mellow cry and an exquisite sense of smell, this early breed was popular all over England. Its one drawback was that it was slow. When stag-hunting switched to fox-hunting, it inevitably fell out of favour. However, although its presence as a pure breed disappeared, its genetic influence survived when it was co-opted as one of the ancestors of the speedier, smaller, more athletic Foxhound. (The other ancestor was some kind of early sighthound.) It also contributed genetically to a now extinct dog called the Kibble Hound, which was created by crossing it with the Beagle. And some believe that it was the direct ancestor of the Otterhound.

The change from stag-hunting to fox-hunting came towards the end of the 18th century. One author, writing in 1801, recalled having hunted near Manchester with a pack of Southern Hounds as late as the year 1775. But he went on to say that, by the end of the 18th century: 'The breed... its size diminished by a mixture of other kinds, in order to increase its speed, is now almost extinct.'

One special claim made for this hound, which may or may not be justified, is that it was 'used by the ancient Britons in the chase of the larger types of game'. If this is true, the Southern Hound pre-dates the superior Norman hounds that were introduced to England in the 11th century. It also separates the Southern Hound from the very similar Staghound, which appears to have been an early descendant of the Norman Hounds.

TALBOT HOUND   ENGLAND

This ancient breed acquired its name from the de Talbot family who arrived in England with the Normans in the 11th century. It is recorded that these 'white hounds were brought to England by the head of the Talbot family, and rapidly gaining credit for their qualities in the chase of the stag... were known as Talbots'. Some authors refer to the breed as the Norman Hound.

The Talbot was descended from the St Hubert Hound. It was closely allied to the Bloodhound but was pure white in colour. Early authors often stress the importance of its colour, one describing the dog as being 'as white as Alpine snows'.

It figures in the heraldic crests of at least seven English families. Heraldic experts are in no doubt about its importance. To them: 'The original English dog, the hound of early days, is, of course, the Talbot.' The head of a Talbot also forms the crest of several princely houses in Germany.

In the *Oxford English Dictionary*, it is listed as a hound 'formerly used for tracking and hunting; a large white or light-coloured hound, having long hanging ears, heavy jaws, and great powers of scent'. Its name appears in English literature as an active breed from the 14th to the 18th century. Then it vanishes, while its close relative, the dark-bodied, black-and-tan Bloodhound, continues to find favour.

It seems likely that, when they arrived during the Norman Conquest, the Norman Hounds were at first of mixed colours. Some people called them Talbots, after the family that brought them to England, while others called them Bloodhounds. There was undoubtedly confusion between the names for some time, although Talbot seems to have been favoured early on. But then, somehow, the dark ones and the pale ones were kept apart, each with their own supporters, and bred as separate types. The name Bloodhound became attached to the dark ones, and Talbot to the pale ones. When they both became scarce, as fox-hunting increasingly replaced stag-hunting, it happened, probably by chance, that the dark ones managed to survive, while the pale ones disappeared for ever.

One lasting reminder of the Talbot today is in names such as The Talbot Arms or The Talbot Head, given to various English public houses in the glory days of the breed, and now outliving the dog itself by several centuries. There are, for example, five Talbot pubs in London alone.

WEST COUNTRY HARRIER ENGLAND

Sometimes called the Somerset Harrier, this breed is used for hunting fox and rabbit as well as hare. The title of Somerset Harrier is misleading, because these dogs are bred in Devon as well as Somerset, which is why the name of West Country Harrier is preferred.

It is sometimes claimed that this particular form of Harrier was created by crossing Foxhounds with the famous French royal dog, the Chien Blanc du Roi, or King's White Hound, but this seems unlikely. It is much more reasonable to suppose that this breed is simply a local – perhaps more original – form of the ordinary, typical Harrier.

The West Country Harrier is said by some to be closer to the old-fashioned type of Harrier, before Foxhound blood was introduced to 'improve' it. It is generally paler in colour, with much larger areas of white on its tricolour coat. Although it sometimes lacks the stamina of the typical modern Harrier, it more than makes up for this with its superior nose and more appealing voice. And it is said to be capable of out-hunting the common Harrier when working over rough ground.

The stud books of the official body that controls the activities of the Harrier packs – the Association of Masters of Harriers and Beagles, established in 1891 – keep a separate section for the West Country Harriers. By treating them in this way they are effectively classifying them as a distinct breed.

WALES

WELSH FOXHOUND   WALES

Sometimes referred to as the Welsh Wire-coated Hound, the Wire-coated Welsh Hound or sim-
ply the Welsh Hound, this dog has been bred exclusively to hunt the fox in the rugged, rocky and
mountainous countryside of Wales.

A relative of the English Foxhound, but smaller and with a rough coat, this breed has
three ancestral roots. The first was a pack of smooth-coated hounds that the monks of
Margam Abbey received from a continental monastery, believed to be that of St Hubert
in the Ardennes. They were black-and-tan dogs and were probably St Hubert Hounds
of the original kind. The second was a trio of bitches of the old, smooth-coated
English Staghound obtained from Parson Jack Russell in 1826. These two sources provided the Welsh Foxhound with its fine nose, its wonderful voice and its coat colouring. The third ancestor was the ancient, Celtic hound which had been indigenous to the
Welsh countryside since the fifth century. This source provided the rough, wiry coat
that was to remain a special feature of the Welsh Foxhound.

The smaller size and lighter bone of this hound make it more lively and active, and
therefore better suited to its role in pursuit of the fox in the difficult hill country of its
native Wales. It is also more independent in its hunting style, another feature which is
better adapted to the Welsh landscape.

By the 1930s there were only three or four packs of pure-bred Welsh Foxhounds that
were still active.

WELSH HARRIER   WALES

A local version of the Harrier, now extinct. In addition to hare-hunting it was said to be used
against otter and other game.

Little is known about this rare and long-vanished breed. Just as the Welsh Foxhound was
a rough-coated version of the English Foxhound, so the Welsh Harrier was a rough-
coated version of the English Harrier. This may be more than a coincidence, because one
early author suggested that Masters of Foxhounds in Wales were known to improve the
scenting ability of their packs by introducing Welsh Harrier blood, which may well have
bequeathed the Welsh Foxhounds their rough coat along with their better nose.

They were active in the 1870s, when they were referred to as 'rough Welsh Harriers…
of surpassing excellence'. With their shaggy appearance, they were recorded as 'more
resembling the Otterhound than our modern Harrier, in shape as well as in coat'. They
were, however, much smaller than the Otterhound.

In 1903 it was reported that they were 'still to be met with', but after that they disappeared from view, and probably became extinct sometime in the first half of the 20th century, possibly as a result of the deprivations stemming from the two World Wars.

Thomas Pearce, writing in 1972, waxed lyrical about this breed. No hound, he claimed, could 'be better suited to their difficult task than the genuine rough Harrier of Wales. He has a gift – a gift almost peculiar to him – of sticking to his game. His scolding voice rings and clangs through the mountain valleys. His dash and fling and the lash of his stern... and his resolute race for the first place, all these merits make us forget his somewhat rough yet thoroughly picturesque exterior, and we can forgive him for being coarse of the outside, when we witness his astonishing sense, honesty and zeal.'

IRELAND

KERRY BEAGLE   IRELAND

Also known as the Pocadan, this breed is from Kerry in the extreme south-west of Ireland, but despite its name it is certainly not a Beagle. A better name for it would be the Kerry Hound. It was originally developed for deer and hare-hunting, but in recent years has also pursued the fox.

This is a fast, well-balanced, fine-voiced pack-hound with an ancient lineage. It is hard to see how this hound acquired the name of 'Beagle', since it is nearly twice the height of that small dog. The Beagle stands at only 13–16 in (33–41 cm), while the Kerry dog at 22–26 in (56–66 cm) is as big as a Foxhound. One possible explanation is that, in the early days, when the Kerry Beagle was used in conjunction with the Irish Wolfhound, it was the smaller of the two and became known as 'the smaller hound'. The word for small in Irish is 'beag', the root from which the word beagle comes. So, although it was as big as a Foxhound, it was 'beagle' in relation to the huge Wolfhound. Its task on those early hunts, when, incidentally, the Kerry Beagle was known by the ancient name of 'gadhar', was to find the game by scent and set it running, so that it could then be chased at high speed by the massive Wolfhounds.

The Kerry Beagle has a long, unbroken history of active hunting. One particular pack, the Scarteen in County Limerick, has been kept by the Ryan family for well over 200 years, throughout most of the 18th, 19th and 20th centuries. It is said that the first Mr Ryan imported the foundation stock for this breed from the south-west of France some time before 1735. The most likely French ancestor is therefore the Ariège Hound from that region. The characteristic markings of that hound are black-and-white, with small pale tan markings on the head, a colour pattern sometimes seen in the Kerry hound. Black-and-tan is, however, the common colour form for the Kerry and it seems likely that there is also an element of early Bloodhound in its ancestry.

Irish immigrants to the United States sometimes took their Kerry Beagles with them and, once there, these dogs contributed to both the American Foxhound and the Black-and-Tan Coonhound. Some of these Irish hounds are thought to have arrived in North America as early as 1802.

FRANCE

ANGLO-FRENCH HOUND   FRANCE

The typical working pack-hounds of France are known as Anglo-French for the obvious reason that they were created by a series of crossings between French hounds and English hounds. The 'hybrid vigour' produced by these crossings results in robust, energetic hounds with few reproductive problems. To French breeders, their high level of fertility has been one of their special appeals. These are the scenthounds of the hunting field, not the show-ring, and they are rarely if ever seen in competitive dog shows.

When these crosses were first made, the dogs were named according to the locality in which the breeding first took place. Because they were not pure-bred, they were called 'bastard' breeds, and given titles such as 'Bâtards du Haut-Poitou'. These names did not do them any favours, and in 1957 it was decided to abandon that mode of nomenclature and replace it with a new one, based only on size and colour.

Three sizes – large, or 24–27 in (61–69 cm); medium, or 20 in (51 cm); and small, or 16–18 in (40–46 cm) – and three coat patterns (black-and-white, black-and-orange and tricolour) were recognized. Even this 'simplified' system resulted in nine different forms, and there has been the inevitable debate about whether each should be considered as a separate and distinct breed. Some authorities believe that there should be just three breeds – the Large Anglo-French, the Medium Anglo-French and the Small Anglo-French – each with three colour variants. Others insist that there is more than mere colour involved and that each of the nine forms is different in other, special ways that must be recognized. The solution here is to present them as nine sub-breeds, as follows:

Grand Anglo-Français Blanc et Noir

In English this type is known as the Large Anglo-French Black and White. It is one of the three forms of large Anglo-French hound, created by crossing large French hounds, such as Bleu de Gascogne and Gascon-Saintongeois, with bicolour Foxhounds imported from England. This type has a dramatic black-and-white coat. It is one of the

'Chiens d'Ordre' – hounds that hunt prey larger than themselves, in this case red deer, roe deer and wild boar. The most impressive of all the Anglo-French hounds, they have a splendidly bold appearance and a marvellous voice on the hunt. These are the 'glamour' hounds, with a devoted following of enthusiasts.

Grand Anglo-Français Blanc et Orange

In English this type is known as the Large Anglo-French Orange and White. It is one of the three forms of large Anglo-French hound, created by crossing large French hounds, especially the Billy, with bicolour, lemon-and-white Foxhounds imported from England. This type has a white-and-tan coat. It is one of the 'Chiens d'Ordre' (see above). This form was the last to be developed, is the least common, and still has some way to go.

Grand Anglo-Français Tricolore

In English this type is known as the Large Anglo-French Tricolour. It is one of the three forms of large Anglo-French hound, created by crossing large French hounds, especially the Poitevin, with tricolour Foxhounds imported from England. This type has the traditional hound coat pattern of white, black and tan. It is one of the 'Chiens d'Ordre' – hounds that hunt prey larger than themselves, in this case red deer, roe deer and wild boar. This is the most common of all large hound breeds in modern France. They are no-nonsense workers, appreciated for their ability as much as for their appearance.

Anglo-Français de Moyenne Vénerie, Blanc et Noir

This is the medium-sized Anglo-French hound, created by crossing French hounds, such as the Poitevin and the Porcelaine, with Harriers imported from England. This type has a dramatic black-and-white coat. It is a fast hound, suitable for work over a wide variety of terrain.

Anglo-Français de Moyenne Vénerie, Blanc et Orange

This is the medium-sized Anglo-French hound, created by crossing French hounds, such as the Poitevin and the Porcelaine, with Harriers imported from England. This type has a white-and-tan coat. It is a fast hound, suitable for work over a wide variety of terrain.

Anglo-Français de Moyenne Vénerie, Tricolore

This is the medium-sized Anglo-French hound, created by crossing French hounds, such as the Poitevin and the Porcelaine, with Harriers imported from England. This type has the traditional hound coat pattern of white, black and tan. It is a fast hound, suitable for work over a wide variety of terrain.

Anglo-Français de Petite Vénerie, Blanc et Noir

Originally known as the Petit Anglo-Français, this is the small Anglo-French hound, created by crossing French hounds, such as the Artois Hound or Beagle-Harrier, with Beagles imported from England. This type has a dramatic black-and-white coat. These small hounds were created in the 1970s specially to hunt rabbit, pheasant and quail. Unlike its larger relatives, this hound was the result of carefully planned breeding. It was given its first official standard in 1978.

Anglo-Français de Petite Vénerie, Blanc et Orange

Originally known as the Petit Anglo-Français, this is the small Anglo-French hound, created by crossing French hounds, such as the Artois Hound or Beagle-Harrier, with Beagles imported from England. This type has a white-and-tan coat. These small hounds were created in the 1970s specially to hunt rabbit, pheasant and quail. Unlike its larger relatives, this hound was the result of carefully planned breeding. It was given its first official standard in 1978.

Anglo-Français de Petite Vénerie, Tricolore

Originally known as the Petit Anglo-Français, this is the small Anglo-French hound, created by crossing French hounds, such as the Artois Hound or Beagle-Harrier, with Beagles imported

from England. This type has the traditional hound coat pattern of white, black and tan. These small hounds were created in the 1970s specially to hunt rabbit, pheasant and quail. Unlike its larger relatives, this hound was the result of carefully planned breeding. It was given its first official standard in 1978. Its little-used, anglicized name is the Small English-French Hound.

ARIÈGE HOUND   FRANCE

Known in France as the Ariégeois, this breed was developed specifically to hunt hare.

The elegant little scenthound makes its home in the dry, rocky hills of the extreme south-west of France, near the Spanish border in the Ariège district. Little is known about its existence before the beginning of the 20th century, but then, in 1908, the Gaston Phoebus Club was formed with the aim of promoting and developing it. Using a mixture of several other hounds, including the Grand Bleu de Gascogne and the Gascon-Saintongeois, and some smaller breeds, they created a 'bastard' hound of exceptional quality.

Although this is not a widely known or supported breed, those who work with it describe it in glowing terms as handsome, intelligent, vigorous, affectionate and serene, with a beautiful voice and a fine nose. Unusually for a pack-hound it has become popular locally as a devoted household companion. The characteristic markings of this hound are black and white, with small, pale tan markings on the head.

References

1940. Senac-Lagrange. *Le Braque Ariégeois.*

ARTOIS HOUND   FRANCE

Also known as the Chien d'Artois or the Briquet, this medium-sized hound was developed for hunting hare and other small game.

The correct French name for this dog should be the Briquet d'Artois, because it is a smaller version of the now extinct Grand Chien d'Artois. It is a typical, compact, tricolour pack-hound, developed for work with small game in thick undergrowth.

Packs of this kind of dog have been

known in northern France from as early as the 15th century and the fact that it is slightly smaller than average has helped it through hard times. When its bigger cousins were suffering so badly immediately after the French Revolution, in the late 18th century, the modest Artois Hound was able to muddle through with greater ease.

This breed became extremely popular in the 19th century, but suffered from the fashion for imported foreign dogs, being cross-bred rather too freely with English gun dogs. The type was being lost, but fortunately the packs of the Prince de Condé at Chantilly were kept pure. At the turn of the century a few specialist French breeders managed to salvage the original form and to rebuild it to recreate a dog closely resembling the traditional and ancient Artois Hound.

In the 20th century the two World Wars dealt the breed some severe blows, but it managed to struggle through those difficult periods and emerge with sufficient numbers for its population to be rebuilt once more. Today there are about 500 of these dogs listed in the stud books.

An oddity concerning this hound is that, despite its rebuilding in its original form, in the hunting field it still displays a tendency to pause and point, a legacy of its crossings with 19th-century gun dogs.

BEAGLE-HARRIER   FRANCE

A comparatively recent introduction, this breed was created not in England, but in France. In the 1920s and 1930s, Baron Gérard Grandin de l'Epriever and a group of his friends started a carefully planned breeding strategy to create a dog that would combine the best qualities of the two English hounds they most admired, the Beagle and the Harrier. They used the Beagle for its scenting ability and the Harrier for its extra speed. The result provided them with a scenthound that could be used like an ordinary Beagle, against hare, but with a more athletic bias in its favour. If you are an optimist, it is a super-Beagle; if you are a pessimist, it is a reduced Harrier.

BILLY   FRANCE

A French hound with an English-sounding name, this breed was called after the Château de Billy in Poitou, in the Atlantic Coast region of France. It is one of the 'Chiens d'Ordre', that is to say, one of the Grande Vénerie French hounds bred exclusively to hunt large prey, Chasse-à-Courre — scent-hunting ending with a kill. Its quarry are roe deer and wild boar.

The history of this rare breed begins in 1877, when Gaston Hublot de Rivault first formed a pack of hounds at his Château de Billy. He used three strains of French hound to establish his pack – mostly the Céris and the Montemboeuf (sometimes spelled Montainboeuf or Montaimboeuf), with a little addition of Larye (sometimes spelled Larrye). All three of these ancestral hounds have since become extinct.

After a decade of hunting, he decided to develop his own type and began selectively breeding for pale-coloured dogs. By 1914 he had fully established his own scenthound. These dogs were either white, or white with very pale markings – white and lemon or white and café-au-lait.

In 1927, when their creator was an old man, the pack was disbanded and dispersed all over France. During the ravages of World War II, most of them disappeared and the breed was almost extinct. But then, following the cessation of the war, Monsieur Hublot de Rivault's son, Anthony, set about reviving it. He was only able to locate two Billys, but used this pair as the foundation stock for rebuilding. Making careful crosses with other hound breeds – Poitevins, Porcelaines and Harriers – he gradually recreated his father's large-bodied, pale hound. By the 1970s he had been able to assemble several packs.

The Billy is a flat-sided, narrow-chested, fast-moving hound that is still hunting today in several regions of rural France. It remains a rare breed and is not found outside its native land.

GRAND BLEU DE GASCOGNE   FRANCE

Known in English as the Large Blue Gascony Hound, the Great Gascony Blue or the Grand Gascony, but better known internationally simply as the Grand Bleu, this huge hound was originally developed to hunt wolves, but was also used against wild boar and deer. More recently it has excelled at hare-hunting.

Described by one of its admirers as 'the most noble hound in the world', this impressive animal with its 'large, long and distinguished' head, hails from the Midi region in south-west France, near the Spanish border. It is an ancient breed, possible the oldest of all the scenthounds, descended from the now extinct Grand Chien Courant.

The Grand Bleu was well known in the Middle Ages, and at the end of the 16th century the French king, Henri IV, owned a pack of them. Later, when the wolf numbers declined, the breed declined with them, but managed to survive by being used to hunt other game.

Although hardy and with great stamina and staying power, it is essentially a lethargic hunter, pacing itself carefully in the often high temperatures of the south of France.

Its characteristic coat, with its mottled slate-blue colour, large patches of black, and tan extremities, sets it apart from the other French hounds. Words used to describe this hound have included majestic, elegant, formidable, regal and inspiring – a hound with a resonant, tuneful voice, an aristocratic melancholy, an archaic allure and an aspect without equal.

Early French settlers in the New World took a number of these great hounds with them and they made important contributions to the ancestry of the American coonhounds. At one time, George Washington owned a pack of seven of these hounds, one of which gave birth to a litter of 15 puppies. Today, it is claimed, there are more of these dogs in the United States than in its French homeland.

The Grand Bleu is the only large French scenthound to be recognized by the Kennel Club in London, although it remains one of the rarest of all the breeds on their registration lists.

PETIT BLEU DE GASCOGNE   FRANCE

Known in English as the Small Blue Gascony Hound, this ancient breed was created by breeding down from the Grand Bleu to create a faster dog more suitable for hunting small game, especially rabbit and hare. At a height of 20 in (51cm), it is 8 in (20 cm) shorter than the huge Grand Bleu, but in most other respects it is the same, including the characteristic mottled slate-blue colouring. It is not as common as its big relative.

PETIT GRIFFON BLEU DE GASCOGNE   FRANCE

Known in English as the Small Blue Gascony Griffon, this is the rarest of the Bleu de Gascogne breeds and, indeed, is probably the rarest of all French scenthounds. It was created in the 18th century by crossing the Petit

Bleu with wire-haired hounds, most probably the Wire-haired Pointing Griffon. It is only slightly smaller than its smooth-coated relative. The wiry coat means that it is well adapted for hunting in rough undergrowth.

CHAMBRAY   FRANCE

This little-known, ancient breed is closely related to the Billy, but is larger and more powerful. Its height is 28 in (71 cm), compared with the 23–26 in (58–66 cm) of the Billy. In addition to its larger size, it also has a deeper chest.

It is a predominantly white dog, although when young it also shows patches of fawn. These patches tend to fade as the animal grows older. In a younger animal there is often, in addition, a darker patch on the top of the head.

GRAND FAUVE DE BRETAGNE   FRANCE

Also known as the Fawn Hound of Brittany, or simply as the Breton or Bretagne, this hound was developed to hunt wolves in the sheep-grazing districts of north-west France.

This is an ancient French hound, with a history going back at least 500 years. Early in the 16th century, François I kept a royal pack of these dogs, and later in that same century Charles IX referred to it as one of the principal hounds of the day. But despite its elevated social status it gradually declined in importance. By the middle of the 19th century, when all the wolves had been destroyed, the great dog had almost vanished with them. In 1873 it was recorded that pure stock was hard to find and evidence could be found of 'only three packs as having any of the blood left'.

The Fauve de Bretagne tradition was saved by a few enthusiasts who transformed it into a smaller breed, the Griffon Fauve de Bretagne (see separate entry), more appropriate for modern times.

The strength of this dog lay in its courage and tenacity. It weakness was its fiery and headstrong personality. Its characteristic short, dense and harsh coat was a uniform, rich, pale golden brown.

GRIFFON FAUVE DE BRETAGNE   FRANCE

Also known as the Fawn or Tawny Brittany Griffon, this is the smaller, modified form of the now extinct Grand Fauve de Bretagne. Instead of attacking large prey, it concentrates mostly on hare, rabbit and fox.

Its large ancestor had been concerned exclusively with the elimination of the wolf packs that were attacking the herds of sheep in north-west France, but after all the wolves had been exterminated, there was nothing left for the big hound to do. It, too, was facing extinction, a victim of its own success.

By crossing the Grand Fauve de Bretagne with the smaller Briquet Griffon Vendéen, breeders created the Griffon Fauve de Bretagne, a more compact dog, better suited to hunting smaller game. In this revised and revitalized form, the centuries-long Fauve de Bretagne tradition was successfully kept alive by a few devoted enthusiasts. The future survival of this attractive hound now seems assured, although to this day it remains an extremely rare breed of dog.

As with its heavier ancestor, this breed's tousled, wiry coat is an all-over, solid fawn, tawny or wheaten colour.

FRENCH HOUND   FRANCE

Because of the confusion existing in the classification of the French pack-hounds, a special committee of canine experts was set up to investigate and revise the groupings. As a result of their 1957 pack surveys, it was decided to create two major types: the Anglo-French and the French. The French Hound – the Chien Français – is an elegant, obedient, affectionate dog descended mostly from the Gascon-Saintongeois and the Levesque. It is a hard-working pack-hound hunting all types of game, but specializing in deer.

The French Hound was subdivided into three colour forms, each of which was treated as a separate breed. However, because there is so little difference between them, it seems more appropriate to list them only as sub-breeds here. They are as follows:

Chien Français Blanc et Noir

This form, the French Black and White Hound, sometimes called the White and Black French Hound, displays a boldly dramatic black-and-white coat, but it may also have small tan markings on its head. It is the most common of the three colour variants and is a big hound standing at 26–29 in (66–74 cm). The French breeder Henri de Falandre, who played a major role in creating this breed, is said to have included some Bleu de Gascogne elements in his breeding lines.

Chien Français Blanc et Orange

This form, the French Orange and White Hound, sometimes called the White and Orange French Hound, displays a white-and-tan coat. It is the most recent of the colour forms and is the least common. Like the Black and White, it is a big hound standing at 26–29 in (66–74 cm).

Chien Français Tricolore

This form, the French Tricolour Hound, displays the typical tricolour hound coat pattern of white, black and tan. It is slightly smaller than its bicolour relative, standing at 25–28 in (63–71 cm). The French breeder Henri de Falandre played a major role in creating this breed and is said to have included some Billy and Poitevin elements in its development. It was officially recognized in 1965.

GRAND GASCON-SAINTONGEOIS
FRANCE

Also known as the Virelade after its creator, the Baron de Virelade, this powerful hound was developed to hunt large game, including deer and wild boar. Today it is used against fox as well. A hound listed as the Verelade appears to be a misspelling of Virelade.

In the south-western region of France, the old province of Saintonge was once famous for its wolf-hunting packs of hounds. Following the French Revolution, however, these packs were dispersed, and only scattered remnants remained. In the 1840s, the Baron Joseph de Carayon-la-Tour de Virelade was determined to salvage what he could of this historic line and gathered together the few remaining examples of the renowned Saintongeois Hounds.

He considered that they were insufficient to use alone as the foundation stock

for a revived breed, so decided to combine them with some Grand Bleu de Gascogne dogs from the kennels of Baron de Ruble. The crosses from these two breeds were strong and healthy and it was agreed to continue with this combination – the Gascon-Saintongeois hound. (A little Ariégeois blood was also introduced.)

In colour, this is a white-bodied dog, with small black spotting or ticking, and a largely black head with white and tan markings. The hounds are less glamorous than their Gascon parents, but faster and more determined on the hunt. At full tilt, they display an impressive 'elastic, reaching gallop'.

Despite their appeal, by the end of the 20th century only ten packs survived, and the future of the breed remains uncertain. This is particularly unfortunate because this dog is the only remaining Chien d'Ordre that is of pure French blood, without any contamination from English hound breeds.

PETIT GASCON-SAINTONGEOIS   FRANCE

This is simply a reduced form of the Grand Gascon-Saintongeois, created for hunting smaller game, such as hare and rabbit. It is 4 in (10 cm) shorter than its larger relative, but in other respects is much the same, with similar coat colours.

GRIFFON NIVERNAIS   FRANCE

Once known simply as the Chien de Pays, the Local Dog, this ancient breed was used to hunt wolves and wild boar in the central region of Nivernais, south of Paris. It has been given the nickname of Barbouillard because of its unkempt appearance. It has also been recorded as the Nivernais Griffon, or the Grey St Luis Dog, although this last title is more correctly applied to its ancestral breed, the St Louis' Grey Hound (see separate entry).

This is a big shaggy dog with a long, bearded head, a bushy face and a long-backed, heavy body built for stamina rather than speed. It is one of the great rustic dogs of Europe with a long and distinguished history. It can trace its ancestry back to the 13th century, when its forerunners were known as the King's Grey Dogs, the Chiens Gris de St Louis, the favourite hounds of Louis IX. In this ancestral form it retained its royal support for several centuries and was favoured by Louis XIV in the 17th century. But then, in the 18th century, it fell victim, as did so many French breeds, to the upheavals of the French Revolution.

By the end of the 18th century, there were only stragglers left in the central highlands of France, and marauding packs of wolves were causing problems with domestic live-stock. At the beginning of the 19th century, a group of 13 Grand Griffon Vendéen was brought in from the Vendée region to help. They were crossed with the surviving local dogs to create a breed called the Griffon Vendéen-Nivernais. They took on the wolves and defeated them. By the end of the 19th century, the predators had gone and the great dog had changed slightly, with the Vendéen element gradually reduced, so that the breed was now distinct enough to be known as the Griffon Nivernais. By 1925 the standard of this breed was officially recognized.

Although its original function of wolf control was gone, the great dog continued to enjoy a useful working life in pursuit of wild boar. It was renowned for its totally fear-less determination on the hunt, contrasting with a calm reserve at other times. It pur-sued its quarry relentlessly at a steady pace over any kind of terrain, no matter how rough, and, when the moment came, was prepared to throw itself into attack without hesitation.

Its colour varies today, but it is still essentially a grey dog, as of old, and the favoured coat is dark grey to off-black, with tan extremities.

GRAND GRIFFON VENDÉEN   FRANCE

The name of this breed tells us that it is a big, wire-haired hound from the Vendée region of western France, south of Brittany. Its title is sometimes anglicized as the Large Vendéen Griffon, but it is more usually known by its French name.
It was developed for hunting large game in the shape of wild boar, deer and wolf.

This impressive, shaggy-coated breed, active since at least the 15th century, is one of France's most ancient hounds. It is believed to have originated from the white Southern Hound and imported, rough-coated Italian hounds.

The name 'griffon', which today is understood as 'wire-haired', has an unusual origin. It comes from the French word 'greffier', meaning a clerk of the court. It was given to the ancestors of these dogs because the royal hounds were looked after by the king's clerk, and so they became known as the 'greffier's dogs'.

A famous, but now extinct breed called the Chien Blanc du Roi – the King's White Hound – played an important part in the Vendéen's ancestry and, to this day, white has remained its predominant colouring.

The Grand Griffon Vendéen has always been known as a hunter of courage, but despite its long and noble history, its numbers have remained small. Part of its problem seems to have been its 'riotous' character – it is so eager to hunt that it is hard to control. Also, it lacks the musical voice of the more typical, smooth-coated hound. But the main cause for its increasing rarity is the change in the nature of the French countryside. The large game traditionally hunted by this big breed has almost vanished and the hunting grounds over which it ranged so widely have become increasingly restricted in modern times. The grand hunts are fading into history and, like them, this great dog may also disappear if a few enthusiasts cannot be found to support it. A single breeder in the United States who recently imported some of them is attempting to set up a breeding group there. But the future of this appealing, historic breed is by no means certain.

BRIQUET GRIFFON VENDÉEN   FRANCE

This is the middle-sized Griffon Vendéen, and its name is sometimes anglicized to the Medium Vendéen Griffon, or the Medium Griffon Vendéen. The French word 'briquet' means 'beagle', although this French breed is much larger than the little English hound. It was developed, by reduction in size, from the Grand Griffon Vendéen to specialize in hunting all kinds of game, both large and small.

The Griffon Vendéen exists in four sizes. From large to small, they are: (1) the Grand; (2) the Briquet; (3) the Grand Basset; and (4) the Petit Basset. All share a rough coat and an origin in the Vendée region.

This version, the medium one, standing at 20–22 in (50–55 cm), is a shaggy-looking dog with a tough, waterproof coat that enables it to work in all weathers. It has become popular because of its versatility, being able to tackle both the larger game usually pursued by its big relative, the Grand Griffon Vendéen, and also the smaller game favoured by its diminutive cousin, the Basset Griffon Vendéen. One of its favourite game animals is the hare.

If the breed has a fault, it is that it is what the French call 'trop chasseur' – over-keen on the hunt. As a result, it is usually worked singly, or in very small packs of four to six dogs. It is a charming if somewhat gawky animal, lacking in graceful dignity but full of character. It is usually predominantly off-white in colour. Like so many French hounds, this one was nearly wiped out in World War II, but has managed to survive in small numbers, thanks to a small band of hunting enthusiasts.

KING'S WHITE HOUND
FRANCE

Known in France as the Chien Blanc du Roi, this breed was the pride and joy of a succession of French kings, who used them on royal staghunts. It was created in the 15th century and became extinct in the 18th.

In 1470, a poor squire of Poitou offered as a gift to his king, Louis XI, a pure white St Hubert's Hound by the name of Souillard. The dog was passed on to Louis's daughter Anne de Bourbon and was so much admired that he was used at stud. He produced such wonderful litters of white puppies that these dogs gradually replaced the older ones in the king's pack, until all the king's dogs were a dazzling white.

Later, in 1500, in the reign of Louis's son, Louis XII, the royal white dogs were crossed with an Italian Pointer called Greffier. Then, in 1520, in the reign of François I, another cross was made, this time with a Fawn Breton Hound – a powerful male called Miraud, who had the desired effect of strengthening the royal white pack, which was becoming delicate from inbreeding.

In 1560, Mary Queen of Scots sent the French king, by then François II, a beautiful white hound called Barraud and again this outbreeding improved the royal pack. Early in the 17th century, Henri IV despatched a pack of his white hounds to James I of England, as a special gift.

Louis XIV kept a large pack of 100 of these white hounds and displayed them grandly on his hunts. They were so fast that, as the king grew older, he found it hard to keep up with them, so they were crossed with Norman Hounds to slow them down a little.

At last, their lengthy royal journey was coming to an end. Louis XV abandoned the old white hounds and switched instead to a new pack based on Foxhound crosses. Louis XIV's white dogs were dispersed in 1725 and largely disappeared. A few of them did manage to survive long enough, however, to make major contributions to the ancestry of a number of other scenthounds, especially the modern Vendéen breeds, and also the Billy and the Porcelaine.

LEVESQUE
FRANCE

This rare French breed was named after its creator, Rogatien Levesque, of Pampoint in Brittany. It was developed as a pack-hound for hunting after a wide variety of game.

This hound was created, late in the 19th century, from a complex blending of other breeds. Possibly because there had been so much inbreeding of hound packs on the great estates, there was a concerted move to use 'hybrid vigour' to reinvigorate the French hunting dogs. Monsieur Levesque mixed together the Grand Bleu de Gascogne, the Grand Gascon-Saintongeois (sometimes called the Virelade), the Grand Griffon Vendéen and the English Foxhound and, in 1873, proudly named his new dog after himself. Today it is extremely rare, if not completely extinct, most of the surviving examples having been swallowed up in the creation of the Chien Blanc et Noir in 1957.

A thin, bony hound with a powerful, elongated head, it is described as having an exuberant, enthusiastic and affectionate nature. Its characteristic black-and-white coloration creates the impression of a white dog with a black rug thrown over its back.

NORMAN HOUND   FRANCE

The extinct Norman Hound was, to all intents and purposes, the old St Hubert Hound after it had left the Ardennes for the hunting fields of Normandy.

The importance of this breed lies in the fact that it was this version of the St Hubert Hound that was brought to England in the 11th century by William the Conqueror and his followers during the Norman Conquest. And it was the Norman Hound that gave rise to both the dark Bloodhound breed and the pale Talbot.

The colour of the Norman Hound was highly variable, ranging from black to milk-white. It was described as a huge hound, up to 30 in (76 cm) in height, with a magnificent voice, a sensitive nose and good stamina. Its weaknesses were that it lacked initiative and was rather unintelligent, slow-moving and dilatory. The pack usually took between six and eight hours to run down a stag. It is easy to see why it was superseded by the speedier Foxhound types.

In 1763, the Norman Hound was already becoming rare in Normandy itself, and local enthusiasts were complaining that their original hounds were being diluted and transformed by numerous crosses with the smaller, faster English hounds. In the 1830s there was, for certain, only one pack of the old Norman Hounds still surviving. By 1875, a French authority proclaimed the breed extinct except 'in England under the name of Bloodhound'. The Norman Hound now survives in France only as a genetic influence on various recent breeds that are faster and smaller.

POITEVIN   FRANCE

Known originally as the Chien du Haut-Poitou, or simply the Haut-Poitou, this ancient breed from the Poitiers region of western France was first developed for hunting wolves. Today it must make do with lesser game.

Looking rather like a mixture of Foxhound and Greyhound, this most elegant of pack-running scenthounds is, in reality, one of France's oldest and most respected hunting dogs. With its long, narrow, bony head, its slender neck, its deep chest and its tricolour coat, this distinguished dog has been described in glowing terms as a hound of 'immense stature', a 'masterpiece of breeding'. It is capable of travelling 35 miles (56 km) in a single day's hunting and has been known to follow a scent for up to seven hours.

The ancestors of this breed were three now-extinct lines of staghound – the Larye, the Montemboeuf and the Céris. The Larye Hounds were the most important, already being used against wolves and having a high reputation both for their power and for their attractive appearance. The mastermind behind the refinement of the Poitevin was the Marquis François de Larye, who began his campaign to create the perfect hound back in the 17th century.

The Poitevin pack was well established and greatly renowned when it met with disaster: in 1793 its owner was sent to the guillotine and the dogs were dispersed. Few survived. The stragglers were rescued by a family in Montmorillon and slowly the pack was rebuilt, only to face a new disaster when they were nearly all wiped out by rabies in the middle of the 19th century. Further inbreeding would have created severe problems and there was no choice but to outbreed. This was done by importing Foxhounds from England in 1844. The pack was once again reconstituted and it hunted successfully until meeting with a third massive setback, caused by the ravages of World War II. Foxhound blood was again introduced to strengthen what was left of the breed.

Since then it has happily avoided further catastrophe, although it remains a rare breed. It is claimed that the Foxhound influence is 'barely perceptible', thanks to carefully controlled breeding programmes, and that the Poitevin is once again its ancient, dignified self – a deep-voiced, sonorous, wonderfully balanced hound, enthusiastic on the hunt but docile at home.

POITEVIN-NORMAND   FRANCE

This breed has also been recorded as the Normand Poitevin.

This is a sturdy, little-known French scenthound created by mixing the ancient Poitevin from the district around Poitiers with the larger local hounds found in the region of Normandy. It has a finely chiselled head, like its Poitevin ancestor, but in some other respects resembles more closely the Billy. In colour it is either red and white or the typical hound tricolour.

PORCELAINE   FRANCE

This breed's popular name is derived from its pale, translucent coat which is reminiscent of the lustre of porcelain. In earlier days it was known as the Chien de Franche-Comté, the Franc Comptoise, or the Comptoise, from the district on the French/Swiss borders where it originated. It was developed to hunt roe deer and hare.

This useful French pack-hound, with its elegant, lightly mottled white coat, its musical voice and its excellent nose, has been active since at least the 17th century in the borderlands between France and Switzerland. It is said to have been descended from the Talbot via the Montemboeuf. Some authorities see it as a modern version of the old King's White Hound, the Chien Blanc du Roi.

Like so many French hounds, this one was decimated by the turmoil of the French Revolution at the end of the 18th century. Almost exterminated in the French countryside, it survived better across the border in western Switzerland, where local breeders did their best to revive its fortunes, boosting it with some of their own local Laufhunds, and eventually reintroducing it to France in the middle of the 19th century. Later in the 19th century further crosses, this time with other French breeds, took place. The final form of the Porcelaine was presented at a Paris dog show in 1889, but, for the purists, these 'rebuilt' hounds were not the real thing, one French author exclaiming: 'The true Porcelaine has effectively disappeared.' Supporters of the modern type respond by pointing out that the introduction of Billy and Harrier blood helped the seriously inbred hounds enormously, giving the breed extra stamina, extra speed and extra enthusiasm for the hunt.

At a much earlier date, a number of these dogs had travelled with their owners to the United States where they had become firmly established, especially in the southern states. Shortly before the American Civil War broke out in 1861 there were, for example, no fewer than 250 Porcelaines working on the Rousseau estates in Louisiana. After the South lost the war and the great plantations were broken up, the hounds were dispersed. They were absorbed by random crossing with other local dogs and, although they made important contributions to the canine bloodlines in the region, they failed to survive as a distinct, separate breed.

Said to be impetuous and fierce on the hunt, but serene and docile at home, the Porcelaine shows the familiar contrast in personality well known from many other scent-hound breeds. Aptly described as a quietly dignified, but 'unexaggerated' hound, it is unusually easy to manage, and is especially popular for hare-hunting. There are a number of packs still working today, not only in France but also in Switzerland and Italy.

St Louis' Grey Hound   FRANCE

Known in France as the Chien Gris de St Louis, this extinct breed played an important ances-
tral role in the creation of several modern French hounds. It was named after its patron, the
13th-century French monarch, Louis IX. It has also been called the Grey St Luis Dog.

It is claimed that, in 1248, Louis IX, who was canonized in 1297, brought back to France
from the Crusades the foundation stock from which this large, rough-haired, reddish-grey
breed was to develop. It is not clear precisely where he acquired them. With their thick
coats, it is unlikely that he discovered them in the heat of the Middle East. It is much
more probable that he collected them at some stopping point on his way home.

Once the foundation stock had arrived safely in France, the breed became firmly
established as the 'royal dog' and it is reported that 'the royal packs of France were composed, from about 1250 till 1470, exclusively of hounds of this type'.

The Abbot of Montemer is quoted as saying 'that the best ones were of a grizzled-
red colour, had rough coats and were full of fire and courage, and that they were capable of hunting any kind of animal regardless of weather conditions'.

After 1470 they were replaced in the royal kennels by the new favourite, the 'King's
White Hound', but they did not disappear altogether, having left their genetic imprint
on other local hounds, so that they were instrumental in the development of later
breeds such as the Griffon Nivernais.

Saintongeois Hound   FRANCE

An extinct French hound, from the region of Saintonge, in south-west France, the Saintongeois
Hound was developed for hunting wolf.

This breed was nearly wiped out by the French Revolution. Only one bitch, called
Minerve, and two males, called Mélanthe and Fouilloux, managed to survive. When their
owner, the Marquis de la Porte-aux-Loups was forced to flee the country, he left them
in the care of his agent at the Château of Beaumont. There they remained in safety until
they could be bred, both dogs being used to produce litters from the solitary bitch.

They passed into the hands of the Comte de Saint-Légier, who built them into a
pack for wolf-hunting. These dogs were described in glowing terms: 'Larger, handsomer,
nobler than all the other French breeds, free from all crosses for thirty generations…
Of gentle disposition… he hunts along without hurrying, trusting in his stamina and
his astonishing scenting powers.' The hounds were white with black spots and with tan
markings over the eyes. Large hounds, they measured 26–30 in (66–76 cm) in height.

It was, by all accounts, a magnificent pack, but because the Comte insisted on prolonged inbreeding they gradually became more and more delicate and difficult to breed.

By the time he was an old man, the pack was on its last legs, but was rescued by a great hound-breeder, the Baron Joseph de Carayon la Tour de Virelade, who, in the 1840s, took them over and began an urgent recovery programme. This consisted of invigorating them by breeding them with some Gascon hounds from the kennels of his friend the Baron de Ruble. This mixture produced a wonderful new breed which was called the Grand Gascon-Saintongeois (see separate entry).

BELGIUM

BLOODHOUND   BELGIUM

This ancient breed takes its name, not from the blood of its victims, but from its own. The name Bloodhound means a dog of the royal blood, a noble hound, a pedigree hound. In its native Ardennes, in Belgium, and also in France, it retains the name of its early ancestor, the Chien de St Hubert. In Scotland it used to be known as the Sleuth Hound. Alternative names were the Sleughhound, Sleuth Dog, Slot Hound, Slough Dog, Slough Hound, Slouth Hound, Slughound, Sluithound or Sluth Hound. Its original function was to track down wolves, deer and other large game.

This is the scenthound *par excellence*, the 'magic sniffer' of the dog world. Its direct ancestor, back in the seventh century, was the St Hubert's Hound. In those early days, that foundation breed existed in various colours, but later it was to be the dark, black-and-tan ones that took on the name of Bloodhound, while the pale, white ones became known as the Talbot Hound.

The Bloodhound was brought to Britain by William the Conqueror in the 11th century. Its main role was stag-hunting, when it was used to follow the scent of a wounded animal, if necessary over amazingly long distances. It soon became the most valued scent dog in the country. As the centuries passed, the deer population dwindled and, as the great deer-parks began to disappear, the huntsmen were driven to switch their attentions from deer to foxes. This required a much faster dog, and the Foxhound soon replaced the Bloodhound as the primary hunting dog. All the Bloodhound could be used for now was the minor role of tracking down poachers.

On the Continent it fared even worse, the original St Hubert's Hound becoming extinct during the French Revolution. At this point, in the late 18th century, only the British black-and-tan Bloodhound survived, and during the 19th century it was exported to many other parts of the world. This was just as well, because during World War II the British Bloodhounds almost disappeared, too. By the end of the war there were only about a dozen left in the country. Fortunately it was possible to import fresh stock from Canada and start to rebuild the population of this noble animal.

The scenting ability of this breed is almost beyond belief. It is capable of tracking a human being, even when that person is wearing wellington boots. It achieves this by detecting the tiny particles of human scent that fall to the ground as the person moves forward through the landscape. In field trails, a good Bloodhound can track a human scent that is 24 hours old, over a distance of 3 miles (5 km), in as little as 18 minutes. It will ignore other stronger scents that may criss-cross its path, a quality called being 'free from change'. This breed is so specialized as a tracker that, once it locates its quarry, it is more likely to lick it than bite it. It has been refined solely as a 'finder', not as a killer. In personality, this is an amiable, intelligent, solemn, almost overpoweringly friendly dog.

In the New World, the Bloodhound has historically been given three tasks. The first was to pursue Indians, the second to track down runaway slaves, and the third to aid in the capture of escaped criminals. One famous Kentucky Bloodhound was responsible for the recapture of more than 600 fugitives from justice. One trail was 104 hours old and one trail ran for 138 miles (222 km), but in both cases the hound was successful.

When James Earl Ray, the murderer of Martin Luther King, escaped from prison in 1977, it was a pack of Bloodhounds that tracked him down, several days later, in the Tennessee hills. This same ability had shown itself centuries before, during the Middle Ages, when the Bloodhound was employed after battles to track down fugitives from the ranks of the vanquished armies. And in the 17th century, the Duke of Monmouth was run to ground by these hounds after the disastrous battle of Sedgemoor. His subsequent execution was therefore directly due to the Bloodhound's infallible sense of smell.

References

1934. Mellor, J. E. M. *Hints On the First Stages in the Training of a Bloodhound Puppy to Hunt Man.*

1947. Whitney, Leon F. *Bloodhounds and How to Train Them.* Orange Judd, New York.

1959. Johnson-Ferguson, Edward. *Bloodhounds and Their Training.* Association of Bloodhound Breeders, London.

1960. Appleton, Douglas H. *The Bloodhound Handbook.* Nicholson & Watson, London.

1964. Owen, Hylda P. *How to Raise and Train a Bloodhound.* TFH, New Jersey.

1968. Harmer, Hilary. *The Bloodhound.* W & G Foyle, London.

1978. Brey, Catherine and Reed, Lena F. *The Complete Bloodhound.* Howell, New York.

1979. Caras, Roger. *Yankee. The Inside Story of a Champion Bloodhound.* Putnam, New York.

1981. Lowe, Brian. *Hunting the Clean Boot.* Blandford Press, Poole, Dorset.

1984. Tolhurst, William D. with Lena F. Reed. *Manhunters! Hounds of the Big T.* Hound Dog Press, Puyallup, Washington.

1991. Brey, Catherine and Reed, Lena F. *The New Complete Bloodhound.* Howell, New York.

1998. Thornton, Kim Campbell. *Bloodhounds: Everything about Purchase, Care, Nutrition, Breeding, Behavior, and Training.* Barron, New York.

1998. Tweedie, Jan. *A Practical Guide to the Working Bloodhound and Other Search and Rescue Dogs.*

St Hubert's Hound   BELGIUM

One of the most ancient breeds, this dog's ancestor was mentioned in second-century writings as the Segusium Hound. The breed was later championed by the seventh-century nobleman St Hubert. When he died in the year 727, his monks named the breed after him and continued to develop it. It is sometimes called the St Hubert Bloodhound, the St Hubert Hound, the St Hubert or the Chien de St Hubert.

This is the prototype of all scenthounds, developed by St Hubert, the bishop of Liège, whose priorities in life were hunting and the Church, probably in that order. He created a medium-sized, long-bodied, big-headed, heavy-boned hound with a scenting ability beyond anything that had existed before.

Each year, following St Hubert's death, the abbots of the monastery he had founded sent a birthday gift of six of their special dogs to the French king. At the French court these were treated as a great prize and tended by special servants. They may have been slow on the chase, but their scenting abilities were so outstanding that they were greatly valued.

It is claimed that this breed has exerted an ancestral influence on most modern scenthounds. It was brought to England in the 11th century by William the Conqueror and, once established there, developed into both the dark-coloured Bloodhound and the pale Talbot Hound. In the process, it changed. The modern Bloodhound is much bigger and heavier than the St Hubert, with a more massive head and much looser, more wrinkled skin, so that, although it is correct to say that the St Hubert is the 'father' of the Bloodhound, they nevertheless ended up as two rather different animals and should be considered separately as distinct breeds.

On the Continent, the original breed began to degenerate and eventually died out, failing to survive the French Revolution. But genetically its impact lingers on in many of the large French scenthounds.

SPAIN

Large Spanish Hound   SPAIN

Known in its homeland as the Sabueso Español de Monte (Spanish Mountain Hound), this breed was developed to track a variety of game in mountainous terrain.

This is a big, heavy-boned, cumbersome-looking hound with a large head, enormously long, drooping ears, and rather short legs. Its coat is either white with red patches, or white with black patches. The males are appreciably larger than the females.

Some authors believe that the ancestors of this dog arrived in Spain from the trading ships of the Phoenicians in the first millennium BC. Others say it was brought to Spain by the ancient Celts. Still others prefer the view that it is descended from the St Hubert's Hounds of the Ardennes. These widely differing opinions suggest that they are all guesses, but they do confirm that this is a very old breed with an extremely long pedigree. It is thought to have played an ancestral role in the creation of the Old Spanish Pointer, sometime before the 17th century.

Although it used to hunt in a pack, today this hound usually operates singly because of its temperamental and often unduly strong-willed personality. It is sometimes employed by the Spanish police for tracking duties, and is capable of working for long hours even in extreme heat.

SMALL SPANISH HOUND SPAIN

Known in its homeland as the Sabueso Español Lebrero (Spanish Hare-hunting Hound), this breed was developed to hunt smaller game.

Described as 'virtually extinct' at the end of the 20th century, this rare breed was simply a reduced version of the Large Spanish Hound, bred down in size for the pursuit of smaller prey. It also differs from its bigger cousin in its coat colour, which is nearly solid red, with only small patches of white, usually confined to the neck, muzzle and chest.

ITALY

ROUGH-HAIRED ITALIAN HOUND ITALY

Sometimes called the Italian Segugio, and known in its homeland as the Segugio Italiano a Pelo Forte, this breed not only tracks game but also captures and kills. Its usual quarry is boar, rabbit and hare.

This is the rough-haired version of the Italian Hound, with a coat that is coarse, but not more than 6 in (15 cm) long. Although this coat makes it look different from its

smooth-haired relative, the Short-haired Italian Hound, it is in other respects very similar. In recent years it has started to become popular outside its homeland.

The Italian Hound is an early breed, known since before the days of ancient Rome. It is thought to have been the result of a cross between the scenthounds of the Celts and the sighthounds of the Phoenician traders, some time in the first millennium BC. Others have suggested that it was a cross between the Phoenician sighthounds and the Roman Molossus, but this seems less likely.

In body shape, this dog could be said to have inherited its head from its Celtic scenthound ancestors and its long, athletic legs from its Phoenician sighthound ancestors. Its coat colour is usually black with tan extremities, and it has bushy eyebrows.

SHORT-HAIRED ITALIAN HOUND   ITALY

Sometimes called the Italian Segugio, and known in its homeland as the Segugio Italiano a Pelo Raso, this breed not only tracks game but also captures and kills. Its usual quarry is boar, rabbit and hare.

This is the short-haired version of the Italian Hound. Although its gleaming coat makes it look different from its rough-haired relative, it is in other respects very similar. In recent years it has started to become popular outside its homeland.

During the Renaissance the Italian Hounds were immensely popular, but in later centuries their numbers declined, due to a decreased interest in hunting. In the 20th century their fortunes took an upturn again because organizations, such as the Societa Italiana Pro Segugio, were formed that recognized their beauty and their unique place in Italian canine history.

Like its rough-haired relative, this dog could be said to have inherited its head from its Celtic scenthound ancestors and its long, athletic legs from its Phoenician sighthound ancestors. In many ways it remains an intermediate type between a typical scenthound and a typical sighthound. This smooth-haired version has a slightly more streamlined shape, which is not due solely to the shortness of its coat. One special feature is its long, tapering muzzle. Its coat colour is usually black with tan extremities.

In temperament the Italian Hounds are independent, slightly stubborn, untiring, and uncomplaining. Their stamina on the hunt is legendary, with 12 hours of pursuit a common event.

SWITZERLAND

BERNESE HOUND   SWITZERLAND

Also known as the Berner Laufhund, the Bernese Laufhund or the Bernese Scenthound, this breed was developed for hunting roe deer and small game in the mountain valleys in the region south of the Swiss capital, Berne.

This is an ancient breed, with a typical scenthound colouring of white with black and tan patches. It has been active in the mountainous landscape of its native homeland for at least a thousand years. There are representations of it in action in the artwork of the 11th-century cathedral in Zurich; and even earlier, from ancient Roman times, there exists a mosaic depicting a hunting scene with walking dogs of this type.

Before the 1880s all the Swiss walking hounds were called Swiss Beagles and were lumped together as a single, if highly variable type. Then, in 1881, a distinguished Swiss canine expert examined a large number of them and pronounced that, in future, they were to be divided into several distinct, local breeds, depending on the Alpine regions from which each came. At a local dog show, he identified four distinct colour types, as follows:

1   The Bernese: white, black and tan coat
2   The Lucernese: 'bluish' tricoloured with heavy ticking
3   The Jura: two-tone brown
4   The Schwyz: white with orange patches

At a later date (1933) it was officially decided to return to the earlier situation and classify all four types under a single standard. This decision appears to have been widely ignored by recent canine authors, who feel that the breeds are now visually distinct from one another and represent major regional variations. Following this trend, they are presented here as separate breeds.

Bruno Jura Hound   SWITZERLAND

Known locally as the Bruno Jura Laufhund or the Bruno du Jura type Bruno, this breed was developed for hunting deer, fox, hare and small game in the mountain valleys in the Jura region close to the French border, in north-west Switzerland.

The name 'laufhund', given locally to this breed and to its close relatives from the other regions of the Swiss mountains, means literally 'walking dog'. This title is used because, in the sloping mountain valleys, nearly all hunting is carried out on foot. This particular local breed has a rich, two-tone brown coat.

Some authors list this as a French breed, and there is a recently formed specialist club for the breed in France – the Club Français du Bruno du Jura – but it is more usually considered to be Swiss in origin. It has been described as an admirable breed with no faults, easy to manage, friendly and docile with humans and with an excellent voice and a keen nose. It has recently been gaining rapidly in popularity.

Lucernese Hound   SWITZERLAND

Also called the Lucerne Hound and known locally as the Luzerner Laufhund, this breed was developed for hunting wild boar, roe deer, hare and other small game in the mountain valleys in the region around the city of Lucerne in central Switzerland.

This local breed of Swiss hound is characterized by a tricoloured, heavily ticked, wire-haired coat. Its colour pattern is strongly reminiscent of the Bleu de Gascogne dogs of France, suggesting an ancestral relationship between them.

St Hubert Jura Hound   SWITZERLAND

Known locally as the St Hubert Jura Laufhund, or the Bruno du Jura type Saint-Hubert, this breed was developed for hunting deer, fox, hare and small game in the mountain valleys in the Jura region close to the French border, in north-west Switzerland.

This is a more heavily built version of the Bruno Jura Hound, with stronger bones, pendulous flews (the drooping upper lips) and pendulous dewlaps, giving it the appearance of having a much larger head. The largest of the Swiss walking hounds, it shares with the Bruno Jura Hound a rich, two-tone brown colouring.

SCHWYZ HOUND SWITZERLAND

Known locally as the Schwyzer Laufhund, this breed was developed for hunting deer, hare and small game in the mountain valleys of the region of Schwyz in eastern Switzerland. It is sometimes recorded as the Schweizerischer Laufhund, the Schweizer Laufhund, the Swiss Laufhund or the Swiss Hound.

A lean-bodied, lightly built hound specially adapted to the mountain valleys of its homeland, this breed is characterized by its bicolour, red-and-white coat pattern. Because of its restricted geographical range and the fact that it has never been exported to other countries, it inevitably remains a rare breed, supported only by a group of local enthusiasts.

AUSTRIA

AUSTRIAN HOUND AUSTRIA

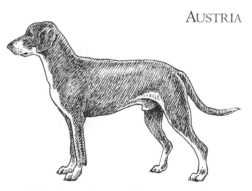

Well endowed with names, this breed is also known as the Austrian Smooth-coated Hound, the Austrian Smooth-haired Hound, the Austrian Black-and-tan Hound, the Austrian Brandlbracke, the Carinthian Brandlbracke, the Österreichischer Glatthaariger Bracke, or the Österreichischer Bracke-Brandlbracke. The 'Brand' in some of its titles means 'fire' and refers to the little patches of red hair on its otherwise black body. It is a scenthound used to track down a wide variety of game.

This smooth-coated, black-and-tan dog is descended from the ancient, local Celtic hounds, mixed with the Jura Hounds from nearby Switzerland, and possibly with the old St Hubert's Hounds from the Ardennes. A leggy, racy, lightly built hound, it was first officially recognized in 1884.

When following a cold scent the Austrian Hound trails its quarry in silence. However, when pursuing fox or hare it gives tongue. In personality it is sensitive, affectionate and obedient. This is exclusively an Austrian hunter's dog and the breed is little-known outside its native country.

STYRIAN ROUGH-HAIRED MOUNTAIN HOUND   AUSTRIA

This breed is also known as the Austrian Coarse-haired Hound, the Steirische Rauhhaarige Hochgebirgsbracke, the Peintinger Bracke, or, for short, simply the Peintinger (after its creator). Its role is to pursue a variety of game animals on the mountain slopes of its homeland.

Developed by Herr Peintinger in the 19th century from crosses between the Hanover Hound from Germany and the Istrian Wire-haired Hound from Yugoslavia, this tough, fawn-coloured scenthound is well adapted to working over difficult terrain in the Styrian Mountains. These mountains, in the south of Austria next to the Yugoslavian border, present any hunting dog with a major challenge in climate and altitude. The rugged, hard-working Styrian Hound has been carefully bred to meet these demands.

The first cross was made by Herr Peintinger in 1870 and he continued with a carefully planned breeding programme, which also included some of his native Austrian scenthounds, for the next 20 years before he was satisfied with his new breed. At first, it was named after him, as the Peintinger Bracke, but later, in 1889, when it was first formally recognized as a new breed, it was given the more descriptive, official title by which it is known today.

In personality, this is a calm, good-natured, intelligent, rather serious dog which appears to be immune to discomfort. A robust, well-built animal, it is highly valued by the mountain hunters of its homeland, but is rarely seen elsewhere.

TYROLEAN HOUND   AUSTRIA

Known in its native country as the Tyroler Bracke, this breed was developed for hunting rabbit and fox and for trailing wounded deer. Its name has also been recorded as the Tyrolese Hound.

This is a 19th-century breed, created in the 1860s by local hunters in western Austria, using ancestral stock that had been in the region since the Middle Ages. Early Alpine scenthounds had originally been brought to the region by the ancient Celts, but for centuries no attention was paid to developing pure lines. Then, in the second half of the 19th century, Tyrolean dog-breeders began controlled breeding programmes and by 1896 were able to exhibit their 'new breed' in Innsbruck. Soon afterwards the standard for the Tyrolean Hound was officially accepted.

This is primarily a black-and-tan dog, although several other colour forms do occur. It is of moderate size, well balanced and without exaggerated features. It has an excellent nose, a strong body and shortish legs suitable for work in the harsh Alpine terrain. It is especially efficient at high altitudes, where many other scenthounds would find it difficult to work. Today it exists in three coat types: smooth, hard and rough. In temperament, it is lively, intelligent, obedient and easily trained.

GERMANY

Bavarian Mountain Hound   Germany

Sometimes called the Bavarian Schweisshund, this breed is known in its homeland as the Bayrischer Gebirgsschweisshund. It has the reputation of being the champion Bavarian bloodtrailer, employed to track down wounded deer and other game.

This agile scenthound is lightly built and smallish, 20 in (51 cm) in height. It has a short glossy coat and is essentially a black-masked, brown-coloured dog, ranging from fawn, through red, to dark brindle.

The Bavarian is a breed especially designed to hunt on mountain slopes, where heavier dogs would find the going too hard. It was created from crosses between the Hanover Hound, the short-legged Tyrolean Hound and other unspecified breeds. In many respects it looks like a smaller, short-legged version of the Hanover Hound.

It is rarely seen outside Germany, although some are said to be at work in the nearby Czech Republic and Slovakia.

GERMAN HOUND

GERMANY

Known in its native land as the Deutsche Bracke or the Deutsche Sauerlandbracke, this breed of scenthound is used to hunt hare, rabbit, fox and wild boar. It has also been recorded as the Olpe Hound.

A beautifully balanced, smooth-coated, tricoloured hound, with a 'ram's nose' and an excellent scenting ability, it is worked in hilly country, where it moves quickly, giving tongue in pursuit of a hot scent. Occasionally it is also used for cold scent work, trailing injured quarry, when it works in silence. A medium-bodied hound, it is about the size of a Harrier.

In origin, this breed stems from the ancient Celtic hounds of Germany. In earlier days many varieties were recognized in the Sauerland and Westphalia regions of western Germany, and some of them, such as the Sauerlander Holzbracke and the Westphalian Bracke, were elevated to the level of full breeds. But at the end of the 19th century it was decided to merge them all and to recognize only one type of German Bracke. It was not given an official standard until as recently as 1955.

HANOVER HOUND

GERMANY

Sometimes called the Hanoverian Hound and known in its homeland as the Hannoverischer Schweisshund (Hanover Bloodhound), this breed was developed for tracking large game.

This is a heavy, robust, low-built hound with a melancholy expression, a large, sensitive nose and a short, thick coat. In colour it is usually red, often darkened towards black.

It was created in the 19th century by Hanoverian gamekeepers to assist them in tracking down wounded game, especially deer and wild boar. They crossed heavy hounds of the St Hubert's or Bloodhound type with lighter scenthounds, such as the Haidbracke and the Celtic hounds from the Harz mountains.

In the past this was an energetic pack-hound covering huge distances in the pursuit of injured game, but today it is also often worked in pairs, or even singly, on a long leash. These dogs are capable of following a trail that is as much as a week old, and of tracking it for as far as 30 miles (48 km).

This is a calm, intelligent, single-minded, obsessively persistent dog. It is rarely kept as a companion animal, almost all Hanovers being owned and worked today by game wardens and foresters, and is virtually unknown outside its native land.

NORWAY

BLACK NORWEGIAN ELKHOUND

NORWAY

*Also called the Black Elkhound, or the
Norwegian Black Elkhound, and known in
Norway as the Svart Norsk Alghund, or the
Norsk Elghund — Sort, this breed was developed
to hunt large game in the snowbound landscape
of its homeland.*

Apart from its all-black colouring, developed to make the dog conspicuous against the
white of the snow, this breed looks remarkably like the much more common Elkhound.
Despite its superficial similarity, however, Scandinavian canine experts believe that
this breed is of different ancestry. It has a shorter coat than its popular compatriot, a
slightly smaller body and proportionally longer legs. It is also tougher, more quarrel-
some and less affectionate.

This is a rare breed inside Norway and virtually unknown outside it. It was recognized as a distinct breed, completely separate from the Grey Elkhound, as long ago as
1877. Its main centre of activity is the border territory between Norway and Sweden.

DUNKER

NORWAY

*Also known as the Norwegian Hound, the Dunkerstovare or the Dunkerhund, this breed's
more popular title of Dunker refers to the man responsible for creating it. It was developed primarily to hunt rabbit and hare.*

Unique to Norway, this strongly built hound was created by dog-breeder Wilhelm
Dunker. Starting in the 1820s, he arranged carefully planned crosses between his traditional, indigenous Norwegian scenthounds and specially imported Russian
Harlequin Hounds. In this way he produced a dog with exceptional endurance and
stamina, well suited to the challenging
northern landscape. At one stage in its
development it was crossed with another
Norwegian scenthound, the Hygenhound,
but this experiment was not successful and
was abandoned in 1934.

The colour of this breed is one of its special features. Although it is basically a black-
and-tan dog, its most characteristic pattern

is the one in which its dark 'saddle' appears in a 'blue marbled' form – the desired legacy from its Russian ancestors.

An elegant, athletic-looking dog, with sleek, clean lines and a powerful, deep chest, the Norwegian Hound is able to track down rabbits or hares by scent alone and retrieve them. In personality, it is said to be confident, intelligent, unusually quick to learn, reliable and trustworthy.

HALDEN HOUND   NORWAY

Known in its homeland as the Haldenstövare or the Haldenstover, this breed is named after the town of Halden in south-eastern Norway, near the Swedish border. It was developed to hunt a wide variety of game, especially hare.

A comparatively recent breed, this is a predominantly white, tricoloured scenthound, from the southernmost parts of Norway. It was created in the middle of the 20th century by mixing local hounds with imported breeds. Some authorities believe that the mixture was a complex one involving foreign hounds from Sweden, Russia, Germany, Britain and France. Others mention only one imported ancestor – the Foxhound.

This is a lightweight hound, a compact, muscular athlete, that hunts singly rather than in a pack. It is bred for speed and, with its short coat, is less suitable for the more frozen, northern parts of the country. It remains a rare breed with a very limited range and is virtually unknown in the rest of the world.

HYGENHOUND   NORWAY

Also known as the Hygenhund or the Hygenstövare, this breed was named by its creator after himself. It was developed for hunting small game in the northern wilds.

Like the Norwegian Hound bred by Wilhelm Dunker, this scenthound was the result of planned crosses masterminded by a Norwegian dog-breeder in the 19th century. In this case the breeder in question was F. Hygen and his foundation stock consisted of imported German Hölsteiner Hounds mixed with various Scandinavian breeds.

The dog he produced had smaller ears and a more pointed muzzle than the other Norwegian scenthounds. A compact, solidly built dog, the Hygenhound has great staying power, even in the harshest of northern conditions. Although it is a strong, active, lively and trustworthy hunter, it has for some reason never proved very popular and has remained a rare breed.

NORWEGIAN ELKHOUND   NORWAY

This is also known as the Dyrehund, the Grey Elkhound, the Grey Norwegian Elkhound, the Grey Elk Dog or the Swedish Grey Dog, and, in Norway, as the Norsk Elghund — Gra, the Grahund or the Graa Dyrehund. The breed was originally used for tracking elk (moose), reindeer, bear, wolf, lynx and badger, not to mention a variety of smaller game. It has also sometimes been trained to hunt ground-dwelling birds such as black grouse and capercaillie.

A typical northern spitz dog, this is one of the oldest of all known breeds. Archaeological excavations in Norway have revealed skeletons of hounds of this type dating from 6,000 to 7,000 years ago. Its remains have also been found buried with those of its Viking masters. It appears to have remained almost unchanged over the centuries. It is now looked upon as the National Dog of Norway.

Until comparatively recently this bold and energetic hound was used for hunting all over Norway and also in neighbouring Sweden. It was renowned for its fearless character and its impressive stamina. However, as the 20th century wore on and the game became more and more scarce, the Elkhound's hunting role became increasingly restricted. It found a new role, however, as one of the most common of all breeds at Scandinavian dog shows and its popularity has since spread to many other countries. As a pedigree show dog it was officially recognized as long ago as the 1870s.

In its hunting days there were two ways in which this breed was employed: as a *löshund*, or as a *lurhund* or *bandhund*. The *löshund* is a 'loose dog' – one that is allowed to roam freely to track the scent of the game, follow it and then keep the quarry at bay until the hunter arrives to kill it. This method is employed in thick woodlands. The *lurhund* or *bandhund* is kept on a leash at all times and used only to track the quarry. This method of hunting is used in more open country.

Outside the hunting season, the Elkhound is usually employed as a watchdog and is often kept outside, even in the coldest weather. For this reason, it requires an exceptionally heavy coat, with a thick, woolly undercoat and a protective neck-ruff. Its hairs are black-tipped grey in colour, giving its fur a wolf-like quality.

Like all spitz dogs, it carries its tail tightly curled, high up over its back. It has been suggested that selection for this type of tail was originally governed by the ancient hunters' need to tell their domestic dogs from the wild ancestors, the wolves, which carry their tails horizontally behind them. This difference in tail posture, creating two contrasting silhouettes, enabled the hunters to distinguish between dog and wolf even at a great distance.

References

1936. Ritson, Kitty. *Elkhounds and Finsk Spets and All About Them.* Idle, Bradford, Watmoughs, London.
1941. Johnson, Rolf. *An Elkhound of Norway.*
1957. Wallo, Olav O. and Thomson, William C. *The Complete Norwegian Elkhound.* Denlinger's, USA.
1961. *The Elkhound Club Handbook.*
1964. Crafts, Glenna Clark. *How to Raise and Train a Nowegian Elkhound.* TFH, New Jersey.
1970. Wallo, Olav O. *The New Complete Norwegian Elkhound.* Howell, New York.
1973. Franciose, Helen E. and Swanson, Nancy C. *Your Norwegian Elkhound.* Denlinger's, USA.
1983. Nicholas, Anna Katherine. *Norwegian Elkhounds.* TFH, New Jersey.
1993. Roslin-Williams, Anne. *The Elkhound in the British Isles.* Privately published.
1995. Ross, Nina P. *The Norwegian Elkhound.*

SWEDEN

HAMILTON HOUND   SWEDEN

Known in its homeland as the Hamiltonstövare, this breed is named after its creator, Count Adolf Patrik Hamilton, who founded the Svenska Kennelklub in 1889. Before 1921 it was called simply the Swedish Hound, but a more precise title was felt to be needed, to distinguish it from the other Swedish scenthounds. The breed was developed to hunt a variety of game, including deer, wild boar, fox and hare.

This breed has the look of a typical tricoloured Foxhound, but is specially adapted to hunting in the frozen wilds of Sweden. It is employed singly rather than in a pack.

According to one source, it was created from a mixture of East European Hounds that were brought to Sweden back in the 15th and 16th centuries, Swiss Hounds and English Foxhounds. Another authority lists its ancestors as the Hölstein Hound and the Hanover Hound from Germany, the Curland Hound from Latvia, and the English Foxhound. A third view sees it simply as a cross between the Hanover Hound and the Foxhound.

The Hamilton is a rare breed and is restricted almost entirely to Scandinavia, although a few were exported to Britain, where they became prized show dogs. Those British examples were originally given the name of Swedish Foxhound, but today the Kennel Club in London recognizes this breed under its Scandinavian title of Hamiltonstövare. In Sweden it was first entered at a dog show as early as 1886.

This is a beautifully proportioned hound, attractively marked with a large black 'saddle', tan legs and head, and white on the face, chest, feet and tail-tip. Like most scenthounds, it is friendly and cheerfully relaxed as a companion, but determined and courageous on the hunt.

SCHILLER HOUND

SWEDEN

Known in its homeland as the Schillerstövare, this breed was developed to hunt fox and snow hare. It was named after its creator, a farmer called Per Schiller.

In the 19th century, a Swedish farmer and dog-breeder was seeking a fast, lightweight scenthound that could hunt efficiently in the snow. Unable to find what he wanted among local breeds, he decided to import some German hounds. He crossed these with indigenous Swedish dogs and created a new breed of his own that would be quick enough and agile enough to track down quarry as fleet-footed as the snow hare and the northern fox. Some authorities believe that he also used Swiss and Austrian hounds in his breeding programme, but this is not certain.

The result of his breeding programme was an energetic tracking hound that specialized in locating, pursuing and then cornering the game, but not killing it. Once the quarry was at bay the hound would call to its master and wait for him to arrive and despatch it.

Some critics have stressed that very similar hounds have been hunting in the cold Swedish forests since the 15th century and that Per Schiller did no more than refine those early dogs, rather than 'inventing' a completely new breed. The truth probably lies somewhere between these two views.

The Schiller Hound is a black-and-tan dog with a large black 'saddle' marking. An athletic-looking, muscular, well-balanced dog, it was first shown at a Swedish dog show as long ago as 1886. Two of Schiller's dogs, called Ralla I and Tamburini, exhibited on that occasion, were destined to become the foundation stock for the breed.

Despite this early activity in the show-ring, the Schiller Hound was not officially recognized as a pedigree breed until 1952. Even after that date, equipped with its new, official status, it remained predominantly a hunter's working companion, rather than a show dog. Towards the end of the 20th century, however, it did start to become more popular in the show-ring, partly because of its cooperative, steady temperament.

SMALANDS HOUND   SWEDEN

Known in its homeland as the Smalandsstövare, this breed was developed to hunt fox, hare, rabbit and other game. It is named after the southern region of Sweden which was its stronghold.

This is an old breed of Swedish scenthound, known to have been hunting in the forests of central and southern Sweden since the Middle Ages. It was bred for stamina rather than speed and its short, compact and stocky body is ideally adapted for tracking and locating game in dense forest. It has an excellent nose.

A smallish, light-footed hound, with a height of only 17–20 in (43–50 cm), it is nevertheless a sturdy, powerfully built animal with a thick, smooth coat. Its black-and-tan pattern is predominantly black, with tan colouring on the muzzle, eyebrows and lower legs.

Unusually for a scenthound, this breed typically (but not always) displays a very short tail. This is the result of selective breeding, rather than tail-docking, since surgical tail removal is viewed as an illegal mutilation by Swedish authorities.

In personality it is steady, affectionate and intelligent. It was accepted as a pedigree dog by the Svenska Kennelklub in 1921, and its standard was revised and updated in 1952.

SWEDISH ELKHOUND   SWEDEN

Known in its homeland as the Jämthund, this breed was originally bred to hunt elk (moose), bear, wolf and lynx. Later, it was also pitted against smaller game, such as marten, ermine and grouse. Its Scandinavian name is derived from the district of Jämtland in central Sweden. It has also been recorded as the Greater Swedish Elkhound.

This ancient breed is the biggest of the Elkhounds. At 24 in (61 cm), it stands 4 in (10 cm) taller than its better-known Scandinavian neighbour, the Norwegian Elkhound.

Its hunting method is to pursue its quarry, often through deep snow, until it has the animal cornered. Then it holds it at bay until the hunters arrive to make the kill. In Sweden it has also acquired secondary duties as a sled dog, a property guard and an army dog. In modern times, it has become popular as a companion animal, not only in Sweden but also abroad, in both northern Europe and North America. It is now regarded as Sweden's National Dog.

Like the Norwegian Elkhound, it has a wolf-like colouring of greyish-black and a tightly curled-up tail. Its coat, which has to protect it from extremes of cold, is thick and dense, and its body is stocky, sturdy and powerful. It is not suited to life in hot climates and, if taken there, may suffer from skin problems.

In earlier times, there was some variation in the form of this breed, but then, as happened with many ancient breeds, it came under stricter breeding control and was finally recognized as a pedigree animal by the Svenska Kennelklub in 1946.

In personality it is very calm, composed and steady, which helps its cause when competing in the show-ring, where it stands defiant and proud, challenging the judge to ignore it. When on the hunt it is agile, determined and courageous.

FINLAND

FINNISH HOUND   FINLAND

Known in its native country as the Suomenajokoira, the Ajokoira, or the Finsk Stövare, this breed was developed primarily to hunt fox and hare. It is also sometimes used against deer.

Looking like a big, rangy, leggy Foxhound, with huge, hanging ears, this northern scenthound was created by mixing together local dogs with imported hounds from various countries. England, France, Germany, Switzerland and Russia have all been mentioned as contributing to this mixture. It displays the typical hound tricolour coat pattern, with a black 'saddle' marking. It is very similar in appearance to the Swedish Hamilton Hound, but a little taller and more rectangular in shape.

Known since at least the 18th century, it was originally a variable hound. Then, in the 19th century, it was subjected to planned breeding 'improvements' and, by the 1930s, was fixed and breeding pure in its present form. Throughout the 20th century it was common and widespread inside Finland, with 3,000 puppies registered each year. Despite this, it has always been extremely rare outside the country.

A hunter's dog, the Finnish Hound is not commonly exhibited at dog shows. In the field it follows trails brilliantly and leads the hunters to the game, but it does not kill or retrieve, leaving that to its human companions.

The annual cycle for this breed is to undertake the energetic hunting of small game throughout the summer months and then, during the freezing Finnish winters, to stay snugly indoors, near the fire, with its owners. Although determined and active on the hunt, it is calm, placid, gentle and friendly when at home in human company. For this reason it does not make a good watchdog or property guard.

ESTONIA

ESTONIAN HOUND
ESTONIA

Also known as the Estland Hound or the Gontchaja Estonskaja, this breed was specifically developed to hunt fox and hare.

This is one of the smaller, short-coated scenthounds, standing only 18–21 in (46–53 cm) high. It was originally created by crossing the large local hounds with Beagles, small Swiss scenthounds and English Foxhounds, to reduce its size and increase its stamina. This was done by Estonian hunters at the start of the 20th century. By 1954 it had been officially accepted and a breed standard established.

In colour it is essentially a black dog with tan extremities. It is popular in Estonia as a hunting companion and, in a secondary role, as a house guard. In recent years it has spread its range into Russia, but it is little known outside eastern Europe. Regarded as the only Estonian pedigree dog, it was exhibited at the Tampere Dog Show in southern Finland in the 1990s.

LATVIA

CURLAND HOUND
LATVIA

This is a long-legged scenthound used for the pursuit of deer and wild boar in the forests of the small Baltic country of Latvia.

The Latvian hunters created this breed from a mixture of English hounds, Polish Hounds and Lucernese Hounds from Switzerland. Curland Hounds were popular in the 19th century, when they were employed to drive the quarry from the dense forests into open country, where it could be shot by the waiting guns.

The Latvian forests were artificially divided up into square units with open spaces cut between them, and the hunters were forbidden to enter the dense forests with their guns. They had to wait in the open patches between the forests and rely on their hounds to drive the deer or boar out to them. For this reason, obedience rather than stamina was the special quality required in these dogs.

This special type of hunting continued until 1920, when the Forestry Department decided that extra protection was needed for the game animals. To provide this, they banned the large Curland Hounds and since then the breed, in its original, long-legged form, has more or less vanished.

The authorities insisted that, from 1920 onwards, the hounds used by the local hunters must measure 20 in (51 cm) or less in height, and this meant developing a new, reduced breed that would conform with these new regulations. The result was the creation of the Latvian Hound (see separate entry).

LATVIAN HOUND   LATVIA

This compact scenthound was developed after 1920 to hunt deer and wild boar in the Latvian forests.

When Latvian hunters were banned from using their long-legged, Curland Hounds in the local forests, and were forced to employ dogs with a height of only 20 in (51 cm) or less, they had to undertake an urgent new breeding programme. They solved the problem by crossing the existing Curland Hounds with Dachshunds and Beagles, which resulted in a much shorter-legged dog with a height of 16–19 in (41–48 cm).

This reduction process began in 1920 but it was not until 1947 that the Latvian authorities decided to make a serious attempt to fix the type of this new hound and develop it into a separate breed. They obtained 40 of the smallest of the reduced hounds and used them as the foundation stock for a carefully planned breeding programme. By 1971 they had a true-breeding dog and its official standard was registered. Although it is described as a 'basset-like' dog, its height is just above that of the typical 'short-legged hounds', which I have classified as having a height of 16 in (41 cm) or less (see section on Short-legged Scenthounds). Had the breeders taken these scenthounds just a little lower, they might have been given the name of the Latvian Basset.

The Latvian Hound is a black-and-tan dog with a dense, hard coat, short, straight legs and cat feet.

LITHUANIA

LITHUANIAN HOUND   LITHUANIA

A recently developed scenthound originally created for hunting wild boar. Unfortunately the boar proved too strong an opponent, and killed so many of these newly introduced dogs that they were switched to the less dangerous sport of pursuing fox and hare.

This little-known breed is rarely if ever encountered outside its native land. It was not developed until the 20th century, when it was established from a complex mixture of

local Lithuanian hounds and imported Bloodhounds, Polish Hounds, Beagles and Russian Hounds. This was not a casual breeding programme, but rather a concerted effort on the part of Lithuanian hunters to reconstruct the big Curland Hound which had recently vanished from neighbouring Latvia. The Curland had been a powerful, long-legged breed, which was outlawed as an active hunting dog by new Latvian Forestry regulations imposed in the 1920s.

At first there was some success with the Lithuanian Hound, but by the 1970s its numbers had dwindled to a dangerously low level. Local canine authorities then took matters in hand. They made a concerted effort to prevent it from becoming extinct and began an officially supported programme of breed development. Although it remains rare, its protected status means that it is probably safe for the future.

This breed is a large, strong hound with a fine voice, good speed and a stubbornly energetic personality. In colour it is essentially a black dog with tan extremities.

POLAND

POLISH HOUND   POLAND

Known in its homeland as the Ogar Polski, or the Polski Oyan, this breed is employed for tracking a wide variety of game.

Little is known about the origin of this breed, but it has an uncanny resemblance to the old St Hubert's Hound from the Ardennes, before it became exaggerated into the form of the modern Bloodhound. It has been used in the hunting fields of Poland for centuries and has always been renowned for its trailing abilities. It is a slow and methodical worker, but is amazingly persistent when in pursuit of game.

Since it is virtually unknown outside Poland, it was inevitable that the ravages of World War II in its native country would nearly destroy the breed. Fortunately a few did manage to survive in the more remote rural districts and, from these, the breed was rebuilt in the second half of the 20th century. Even so, it remains a comparatively rare dog. Its smaller relative, the Gonczy Polski, was not so lucky, being completely destroyed by the upheavals and deprivations of World War II.

The Polish Hound has been described as 'massive and ponderous', with a heavy, well-balanced body and a short, hard, black-and-tan coat, often with a black 'saddle' marking.

SLOVAKIA

BLACK FOREST HOUND   SLOVAKIA

This breed, sometimes called the Slovakian Hound, and known in its native country as the Slovensky Kopov, was developed primarily to hunt wild boar.

Before Czechoslovakia split into two, this was the national dog of the country and was widely popular there. It is the only indigenous scenthound of the region and has been known for many centuries.

Its precise ancestors are unidentified, but it is similar to the Polish Hound and may well be closely related to that breed. Hungarian breeds may also have been involved in its creation. Although the Black Forest Hound was known from ancient times, it was not until the 1950s that local breeders cooperated to refine and standardize this impressive hound, after which time it was subjected to carefully planned and selective breeding programmes.

A tough, powerful, intelligent, black-and-tan dog (predominantly black with tan extremities), possessing a strong personality, the Black Forest Hound is less docile and obedient than most scenthounds and requires a firm hand in training. Compensating for this is its ability to hunt well in difficult, mountainous terrain.

In recent times, this breed has acquired secondary roles as a guard dog and as a police dog. It has also been seen in the show-ring more frequently than most other working scenthounds, its official show standard having been established in 1963.

HUNGARY

SHORT TRANSYLVANIAN HOUND   HUNGARY

Also known as the Hungarian Hound, the Short Hungarian Hound or, in its native country, the Erdelyi Kopo, this breed was developed to hunt fox and hare.

In the ninth century, the Magyars invading Hungary brought with them their faithful hounds. Once installed, the invaders crossed these hounds with local dogs and the result was what we today call the Transylvanian Hound. Two versions were developed, a taller

one to hunt bigger game and this one, a shorter dog, more suited to smaller game. The difference in height was about 4 in (10 cm).

After more than a thousand years of history, this smaller version of the Transylvanian Hound is facing extinction in its native Hungary, another victim of World War II. Those that lived across the border, in the Transylvanian forests of Romania, might have been luckier, but were struck down by another catastrophe. In 1947 the Romanian government ordered a complete extermination of the breed (in both its short and tall forms) for no other reason than that it reminded them of a past occupation of the region by Hungary, further proof that the stupidity of politicians is worldwide.

This is a smooth-coated, red-and-tan or tricoloured scenthound, well built and with no exaggerated features. In temperament it is obedient, easy to train and good-natured with its human companions.

TALL TRANSYLVANIAN HOUND   HUNGARY

Also known as the Hungarian Hound, the Tall Hungarian Hound or, in its native country, the Erdelyi Kopo, this breed was developed to hunt large game such as wolf, bear, lynx, boar and deer.

This larger version of the Transylvanian Hound is a rare breed, but is in less danger of disappearing altogether than its shorter cousin. Both were decimated by the upheavals of World War II, but this taller breed was later revitalized by adding other bloodlines, mostly from Swiss Laufhunds. Care was taken, however, not to swamp out the original Hungarian Hound and such crosses were soon abandoned.

In earlier days this bigger scenthound was a favourite hunting companion of the Hungarian nobility. It would often accompany Hungarian kings into the mountain forests in search of bears and wolf-packs. Later in its history it was used more against boar and deer.

A heavily built but well-proportioned dog, it has a smooth coat, usually with typical hound markings in either black-and-tan or a tricolour pattern of black, tan and white. Like its smaller relative it is a friendly hound that is easy to train.

CROATIA

ISTRIAN SMOOTH-HAIRED HOUND CROATIA

Also known as the Smooth-haired Istrian Hound, the Istrian Smooth-coated Hound, the Istrian Hound — Kratkodlaki, or the Istrian Setter and, in its native country, as the Istarksi Gonic, the Kratkodlaki Istarski Gonic or the Istarski Kratkodlaki Gonic, this breed was originally used to trail wild boar and deer, but in more recent times has also been widely used against fox and hare.

The region of Istria, which gives the dog its name, is a peninsula protruding into the Adriatic Sea in the north-west corner of what used to be Yugoslavia, but which is now shared by the separate states of Slovenia and Croatia. Both these states have laid claim to this breed as one of their 'five indigenous breeds', but the Croatian Kennel Society appears finally to have won the struggle with the Slovenian Kennel Club and gained international recognition as the rightful 'owner'.

This attractive, distinguished-looking dog is identifiable by its white coat marked with a few small orange patches. These patches occur mostly on the head, especially the ears. To the purist, the paler the orange patches are, the better the specimen. A thin tail is also favoured.

An ancient hound, it is believed to be descended from crosses between the indigenous scenthounds of Europe and the sighthounds brought to the region in the first millennium BC by Phoenician traders. As a result, it has a rather racy build for a scent-trailer.

When tracking game, which it does 'with a passion', it is said to have an excellent nose and an appealing voice. Since the disastrous war in the region in the late 20th century, the numbers of these dogs have fallen dramatically in most districts. Only in Slovenia and Croatia does it appear to be safe and it is now thought of as a Croatian dog (or, in Slovenia, as a Slovenian dog) rather than a Yugoslavian dog.

ISTRIAN WIRE-HAIRED HOUND CROATIA

Also known as the Wire-haired Istrian Hound, the Istrian Rough-coated Hound, or the Istrian Hound — Resasti, and, in its native country, as the Istarksi Gonic, the Resasti Istarski Gonic or the Istarski Ostrodlaki Gonic, this breed was originally set on the trail of wild boar and deer, but in more recent times has also been widely used against fox and hare. As with its smooth-haired relative, this breed is today claimed by both Croatia and Slovenia, but Croatia has now been recognized internationally as the parent country.

This is the rough-coated version of the Istrian Smooth-haired Hound, with hair that is up to 4 in (10 cm) long, and a woolly undercoat. It is better protected in foul weather than its smooth relative. The two breeds are similar in almost every respect other than their hair type, and both display the same colour pattern of white coats with small patches of orange, mostly on the head. One other small difference is that the wire-haired breed is slightly larger than the smooth – it is 2 in (5 cm) higher and 3 lb (about 1.5 kg) heavier.

This breed is a more recent offshoot of the ancient smooth-coated type. In the middle of the 19th century, Istrian Smooth-coated Hounds were deliberately crossed with the rough-haired Griffon Vendéen from France. The aim of this crossing was to improve the voice of the Istrian Hound, but it had the added bonus of providing it with a more protective coat.

Today, following growing interest from the world of dog shows, the appearance of these dogs is taken more seriously than in earlier times, when it was selected solely on its hunting merits. As a result, interbreeding between the rough and the smooth types is now forbidden. As a show dog, this hound was first put on display in Vienna in 1866. Its docile, friendly personality has served it well in this new role.

BOSNIA-HERZEGOVINA

BOSNIAN ROUGH-HAIRED HOUND

BOSNIA-HERZEGOVINA

Also known as the Bosnian Coarse-haired Hound, the Bosnian Rough-coated Hound or the Bosnian Brack, in its native country it is called the Bosanski Barak or the Bosanski Ostrodlaki Gonic-Barak. It has also been recorded as the Bosanski Ostradlaki. It was developed to hunt wild boar, fox and hare. (Note: Bosanski has sometimes been spelled Basanski or Bonanski.)

A big, shaggy, rather ungainly hound, little-known outside its homeland, it was created from unidentified ancestors in the 19th century by Bosnian hunters for work in difficult, mountainous country. Its thick, wire-haired coat protects it from the harsh climate. It ranges from grey to yellow and may appear in both bicolour and tricolour patterns.

Essentially a combination of sighthound and scenthound, this versatile dog is said to be brave and determined on the hunt, but friendly and tranquil at home. A robust, consistent, ingenious and adaptable hunter, it possesses great stamina, and perseveres on the hunt even in the foullest of weather conditions. It is therefore surprising that it is still so little-known outside its native land.

During the hostilities in the region at the end of the 20th century, its numbers inevitably fell, but local enthusiasts ensured its survival.

It should be pointed out that considerable confusion has existed recently concerning the relationship between this breed and a dog called the Illyrian Hound. Most major canine reference works list the two breeds as though they are separate and distinct from one another. They are even given different local names: Bosanski Ostrodlaki Gonic-Barak for the Bosnian Hound and Keltski Gonic for the Illyrian Hound. One major work, for no apparent reason, calls the Illyrian Hound by its French title of Chien Courant de Bosnie à Poil Dur. However, according to the FCI, they are one and the same breed: 'This breed was registered with the FCI on the 19th June 1965, under... the name of Illyrian Hound. In the present standard... the name of the breed is changed to "Bosnian Coarse-Haired Hound — Barak".'

YUGOSLAVIA

BALKAN HOUND   YUGOSLAVIA

Also known as the Yugoslavian Balkan Hound or the Balkan Harrier, and called in its homeland the Balkanski Gonic, this breed has been developed to hunt wild boar, deer, fox and hare.

This powerful breed is found in the borderland between Yugoslavia and Bulgaria. It is an excellent tracker, with a distinctive, high-pitched voice. Like all the scenthounds from this general region, it is untiring over even the roughest terrain.

Its short, dense coat has been described as being 'coloured like that of a red fox', but with a black area on the upper part of the body, like a typical hound 'saddle' marking. In personality it is energetic, tenacious and lively.

POSAVAC HOUND   YUGOSLAVIA

Also known as the Posavatz Hound, the Yugoslavian Posavatz Hound, the Jugoslovenski Posavski Gonic, or the Posavaski Gonic, this breed was developed to hunt deer and hare. It has also been recorded as the Sava Valley Hound. Following the break-up of former Yugoslavia, the breed was claimed by the Slovenian Kennel Club as a 'Slovene indigenous breed', and referred to by them as the Posavec Hound. The Croatian Kennel Club refer to it as the Posavina Hound.

This is an excellent tracking hound with a strong, high voice. It has been worked for centuries on the fertile plains that border the Sava River. Like the other scenthound breeds from this part of Europe, it is restricted to one special locality and is little-known outside it.

A typical scenthound in body shape, but rather short in the leg, this is a vigorous, but obedient and friendly dog. Its short coat is either red, wheaten or fawn, with white markings. These markings usually consist of a white collar, a white patch on the breast, a white marking down the middle of the head, a white tail-tip, and white feet. The dog's ears are dropped and rounded. Its height is 18–23 in (46–58 cm) and its weight is 71–88 lb (16–24 kg).

YUGOSLAVIAN MOUNTAIN HOUND YUGOSLAVIA

Known in its homeland as the Jugoslavenski Planinski Gonic, this breed is used to hunt varied game including wild boar, fox and hare. Following the disintegration of the former Yugoslavia, there has been some confusion over this breed. In Slovenia, the dog called the Slovene Mountain Hound appears to be the same animal.

This powerful, robust breed hunts in the Planina Range of mountains in the south-west of Yugoslavia. It is an ancient breed, highly valued and known in its homeland for centuries.

It is similar to the Tricolour Hound but slightly heavier in build. The coat is essentially black-and-tan, but there may be a small amount of white.

A persistent, persevering hunter, with an excellent nose and a fine voice, it is always enthusiastic, even when working in hazardous conditions in the mountains. It has been described as 'audacious, intelligent, and resistant'. When at home, it is, like so many of these working scenthounds, calm and good-natured. A local breed, it is now considered to be extremely rare.

YUGOSLAVIAN TRICOLOUR HOUND

YUGOSLAVIA

Known in its homeland as the Jugoslavenski Tribarvni Gonic, the Jugoslavaneski Trobojni Gonic, or the Jugoslavaneski Drobojni Gonic, this breed has been developed to hunt wild boar, deer, fox and hare.

A well-proportioned, short-coated dog, very similar to the Yugoslavian Mountain Hound, but of lighter build, this hound is black with fawn markings and a white blaze and extremities. Like its heavier cousin, it is considered to be a tough, weather-resistant, steadily determined hunter, ready to face any terrain, no matter how difficult.

This is an ancient breed from the south of Yugoslavia. Always a local dog, it is now considered to be extremely rare.

SOUTHERN AFRICA

HOTTENTOT DOG

SOUTHERN AFRICA

Sometimes called the Kaffir Dog or the Khoi, or referred to simply as the Ridged Dog, this breed was used by the Hottentot tribesmen for hunting. An extinct, ridgebacked native dog called the Mha Kon Klab appears to be the same breed.

This old tribal breed is the vanished ancestor of the modern Rhodesian Ridgeback. When, many centuries ago, the Hottentots retreated from their ancient homeland in East Africa to the less hospitable regions of south-west Africa, they took with them their slender hunting dogs. Then, much later, when Europeans colonized southern Africa, they too brought their dogs with them and matings occurred between these pedigreed newcomers and the indigenous tribal dogs. One of the results of this mixing was the now well-known Rhodesian Ridgeback (see separate entry). But some of the original, tribal dogs managed to survive in pure form long after the arrival of the white settlers. In fact, a few living specimens were still recorded as recently as the 1950s.

These dogs were said to look like a cross between the typical African Pariah Dog and a leaner form of sighthound. They had small heads, with a sharp, pointed muzzle, pointed ears (sometimes erect and sometimes drooping) and rough, bristling hair. The coat colour was typically ash grey, but occasional individuals were sandy red with a black muzzle, or dirty cream with a dark stripe down the back.

According to one eye witness, 'it was an ugly creature, its body being shaped like a jackal and the hair on the spine turned forward; but a faithful and serviceable animal of its kind'. This comment about the direction of the spine-hair reveals that the Hottentot Dogs possessed the ridgeback gene, and it was this unusual feature that they passed on to the much larger Rhodesian breed.

When the Hottentot people moved southwards they encountered their close relatives, the Bushmen. There were exchanges of goods, and the Bushmen, who traditionally had no dogs of their own, acquired some of the Hottentot ridgebacked dogs. Writing in 1936, a European visitor found that 'the finest type of Bushman hunting dog, a light brown ridgeback mongrel with a dark brown stripe and a trace of greyhound in its appearance', had a broad head, a sharp muzzle, upright ears and a long, drooping tail. He also noted that it was on the verge of extinction. The main reason for this decline was that the dogs were being shot as pests. The last record we have of them is when a game warden in the Etosha Game Reserve in south-western Africa reported shooting two Bushman ridgebacks in 1955.

Note: Some recent authors have identified the Hottentot Dog as the Basenji, but this is an error.

RHODESIAN RIDGEBACK SOUTHERN AFRICA

Also known in the past as the Rhodesian Lion Dog, the African Lion Dog, the African Lion Hound, the African Bull-Dog or the Ridgehound, this breed was originally developed as a scent-hound to track a variety of South African game. When it was later taken north to Rhodesia it was employed there to hunt lion, but this was not its primary role. At one stage in Rhodesia it was given the title of the Van Rooyen Dog, after one of the big-game hunters who championed the breed there. It has sometimes been referred to informally as 'the dog with a snake on its back'.

This is one of the most formidable of all the scenthounds. It works in packs, tracking and pursuing the game fearlessly and driving it in panic towards the waiting guns. Alternatively, it may corner the quarry and keep it at bay until hunters on horseback can arrive to make the kill.

Its ancestors were ancient ridgebacked hunting dogs from the southern regions of Africa, belonging to the Hottentot people. These unusual hounds have been traced back to at least the beginning of the 16th century, and were probably there long before that. When European settlers arrived in southern Africa in the 17th century, they brought with them some of their large dogs, to protect their farms, and for many years looked upon the local dogs, which were semi-wild, as marauders to be shot on sight. Eventually, however, the Boer farmers realized that the Hottentot dogs were well adapted to the difficult African climate and, instead of killing them, they started to cross them with their own dogs, to develop a new, improved breed. The first man to do this was Gert Pienaar, who, in the mid-19th century, obtained two Hottentot dogs, which he called Rogers and Rinkhals, and used them as his foundation stock.

The imported dogs included various kinds of scenthound, mastiff and, in particular, the Great Dane. Interbreeding between these dogs and the indigenous ridgebacked dogs resulted in the creation of a big, powerful scenthound that was ideal for the pursuit of African game animals. It combined the size, fine nose and strong character of the European dogs with the speed and tropical-disease resistance of the Hottentot dogs.

In the latter half of the 19th century, the Pienaar family was visited by a missionary, the Revd Charles Helm, who acquired two of their dogs and took them north to Rhodesia (now Zimbabwe). There they bred successfully and the Ridgeback dog became popular with the local big-game hunters, who used small packs of them as an aid in the horseback pursuit of lions and leopards. Amazingly, a typical pack usually consisted of no more than three dogs, and these were prepared to face up to a pride of as many as five lions. It was from this dramatic role that the dogs acquired some of their local names.

In the 1920s a specialist club was formed to help standardize the breed which, at that stage, was still showing some variability. This went from strength to strength and by the 1930s Rhodesian Ridgebacks were being exported as far afield as India and Canada. An impressive animal, typically with a plain fawn or tan coat that was probably inherited from its Great Dane ancestry, it was soon becoming a favourite at dog shows on several continents.

The unusual anatomical feature for which this breed is famous is the curious ridge of hair that grows down the centre of its back. This ridge is formed by a reversal of the direction of hair growth along the dog's spinal region, creating a visible, but flattened 'crest'. Many canine reference books refer to this ridge as a 'unique feature' of the breed, but we now know that it is not. It is shared with the lesser-known Thai Ridgebacks and closely related Phu Quoc Dogs (see separate entries). Some authorities believe that these Thai dogs were brought to Africa by early sea-traders and that they are the primary source of the back-ridge gene. The evidence for this is slim, however, and it is possible that a back-ridge gene occurred independently in the two cases.

Although fierce in the hunting field, it is a good-natured dog at home and many are kept today simply as family pets. Words that have been used to describe the breed's personality have included brave, faithful, obedient, vigorous, affectionate (towards its owners), stand-offish (to strangers) and possessing a wonderfully intimidating, low growl when faced with an intruder.

References

1940s Dry, G. C. and Hawley, Thomas C. *The Rhodesian Ridgeback; its Origin, Development and Treatment*. Caxton, Pretoria.

1966. Lutman, Frank C. M. D. *How to Raise and Train a Rhodesian Ridgeback*. TFH, New Jersey.

1975. Hawley, T. C. *The Rhodesian Ridgeback. The Origin, History & Standard of the Breed*. Privately published, Johannesburg.

1981. Pata, Jan L. *Rhodesian Ridgeback Champions, 1955–1980*.

1986. Woodrow. *The Rhodesian Ridgeback*.

1988. Anon. *Rhodesian Ridgeback Champions 1981–1986*.

1991. Nicholson, Peter and Parker, Janet. *The Complete Rhodesian Ridgeback*. Howell, New York.

1993. Camino E.E. Staff. *Rhodesian Ridgeback Champions 1987–1991*. Camino Book Company.

2000. Bailey, Eileen M. *Rhodesian Ridgeback: An Owner's Guide to a Happy Healthy Pet*.

2000. Carlson, Stig G. *The Rhodesian Ridgeback Today*.

RUSSIA

RUSSIAN HARLEQUIN HOUND   RUSSIA

Also known as the Russian Piebald Hound, or, in its native home, as the Gontchaja Russkaja Pegaja, this breed was originally called the Anglo-Russian Hound. It was given its new name in 1951. It is sometimes referred to simply as the 'Harl'. In the hunting field it is used to pursue wolf and fox.

This Russian scenthound was created by crossing the ordinary Russian Hound with imported English Foxhounds. The result was a sturdy, well-balanced, tricoloured dog that was smaller than the Foxhounds but slightly larger than the typical Russian Hounds. Its distinctive coat pattern is considered of value in the hunting field because it makes the dogs visually distinct from their quarry.

This breed was employed as one of the ancestors of the Norwegian Dunker and it shares with that hound the occasional merle-coloured (blue-marbled) saddle marking.

RUSSIAN HOUND   RUSSIA

Also known as the Kostroma Hound or the Russian Drab Yellow Hound, or, in its homeland, as the Gontchaja Russkaja, this breed was used most against hare, but was also employed to hunt fox and badger.

This is a popular and common scenthound in Russia, with thousands of new puppies being registered each year. It has been working in its native country from at least the 16th century and there is a widely held view that it was originally developed from the Russian Laikas. The czars maintained packs of these dogs for their royal hunts.

In its earlier days, when hunters cared little for a fixed type, it was highly variable and this applied right up to the early 20th century. Then, in 1925, pure-breeding was begun in earnest and the many local variations were eliminated.

A stolid scenthound, the Russian Hound has an expressive, melodious voice, a sensitive nose and a good-natured personality. It is still variable in colour, but a dull, pale fawn colour, sometimes called 'drab yellow', is the most popular tone.

Although in the past Russian Hounds were nearly always hunted in packs, today they are more likely to be employed singly. In their historical role they were worked in conjunction with the Russian Borzoi, the sighthounds being slipped to chase the game that had been discovered by the scenthounds. Later, this kind of hunt fell out of favour and was replaced by one in which all the work was done by the scenthounds.

UNITED STATES

AMERICAN FOXHOUND   UNITED STATES

This breed, developed from imported English Foxhounds, was at first used to hunt the indigenous grey fox, but was later pitted against the faster, imported English red fox.

The American Foxhound is a taller, slimmer version of its English ancestor, with lighter bones and less rounded ears. Its story begins in 1650, when Robert Brooke imported the first pack of English Foxhounds and established them in Maryland. He became the first Master of Hounds in America and his family kept the tradition going for many years after his death. His dogs were of black-and-tan colouring, rather than the more usual tricolour, and at one stage in their history were used as the ancestral stock in the creation of the Black-and-Tan Coonhound (see separate entry).

Early in the 18th century, more packs were imported, this time to Virginia. The local grey fox was found to be rather slow for good hunting, and the American red fox did not extend its range into the eastern states where foxhunting was gaining a foothold. So the speedy English red fox was imported and released, giving the hounds a much better run for their money. (Later on, the imported and indigenous red foxes met and interbred.)

In 1770 George Washington imported his own pack from England. Then, in 1785, his friend the French Marquis de Lafayette sent him some French hounds which were crossed with the English ones to produce bigger dogs. In the 1830s Irish hounds arrived, this time to increase the speed of the pack. These three ancestral types — English, French and Irish — together comprised the foundation stock that was ultimately to lead to the highly efficient, modern American Foxhound. From Maryland and Virginia, it spread outwards to Kentucky, Tennessee, Ohio, Illinois, Missouri and Arkansas.

Like all foxhounds, the American breed excelled at keeping to its allotted task. Even if deer, raccoon, rabbits, or other kinds of game presented themselves as easy targets while the pack was on the hunt, the dogs were trained to ignore them and seek out only the fox. And if a hound was lost at the end of a long hunt, it was expected to be able to find its own way home to its kennels, without any help.

References

1967. Hart, Ernest H. *How to Raise and Train an American Foxhound.* TFH, New Jersey.

1970. Mackay-Smith, Alexander. *American Foxhunting; An Anthology.* American Foxhound Club, Millwood, Virginia.

2000. Hart, Ernest H. *American Foxhound: A Complete and Reliable Handbook.* TFH, New Jersey.

JULY HOUND   UNITED STATES

In the early days of the American Foxhound the huge size of their New World home meant that many localized forms started to develop and to diverge from one another in various details. In modern times, with greater social mobility, most of these differences have disappeared, but three of the old strains have managed to survive with sufficient independence to be worth treating as separate types. They are the July Hound, the Trigg Hound and the Walker Hound.

The July Hound is famous for its exceptional speed and unswerving determination. It owes its origin to a wealthy plantation owner in Georgia called Miles Harris. In 1860 he obtained two 'Irish Hound' puppies from kennels in Maryland. He gave them the names June and July, and the July Hound astonished everyone with its amazing efficiency. It was even claimed that this dog could catch a fox single-handed without the aid of a pack.

July's fame spread and he was eventually acquired by another famous breeder in Georgia, George Birdsong. Birdsong mated July back to other 'Irish Hounds' in his kennels and set about creating an outstandingly fast foxhound which was soon to spread to

Missouri, Mississippi, Louisiana and all across the southern states. It is still to be found there today, enjoyed by enthusiasts, but never bred commercially.

TRIGG HOUND   UNITED STATES

The Trigg Hound is a rangy, powerful, rugged breed that owes its continued existence to the foresight of one man, the expert Kentucky huntsman Colonel Haiden Trigg. In the 1840s he had hunted the local grey fox with a pack of rather slow, black-and-tan hounds. When the cunning red fox appeared on the scene, his hounds were unable to cope with it and he vowed to improve his stock.

After the Civil War had ended he purchased a group of hounds from the kennels of the Georgian breeder, George Birdsong. The first five arrived in 1866 and two more followed in 1868. Trigg devised a breeding programme that involved mixing these Birdsong dogs with some special hounds he had already obtained from General Maupin and John Walker. These matings created the foundation stock for the new, improved foxhound that would eventually carry his name.

The colonel cared little for the colour-pattern of his dogs, being interested solely in their performance against the red fox. In modern times, however, there has been a tendency to standardize the Trigg Hound colours, and today these dogs are usually seen only in red-and-white, or solid black.

WALKER HOUND   UNITED STATES

This breed is also occasionally referred to as the Walker Foxhound.

The Walker hound is probably unique in the world of dogs for being a breed founded on a criminal act. An amazing black hound, with a tan spot over each eye and a rat-tail, was stolen by a livestock-dealer during a visit to the mountains of Tennessee. He presented it to General Maupin, a well-known Kentucky huntsman, who immediately recognized it as an outstanding hound and used it as the foundation animal of a new strain.

This super-hound was given the name of Tennessee Lead and the General also allowed it to be used to improve the stock at the kennels of his friend, John Walker. When both Maupin and Walker died, the improved strain was taken over by Walker's two sons. They continued to refine and develop the strain, adding occasional injections of English Foxhound to the bloodline. Soon, many other American huntsmen were acquiring examples of these impressive dogs and the Walker Hound, as it was now called, began to spread all across the United States.

A traditionally tricoloured hound, its outstanding quality is its tireless energy. It was this type of hound that was used as the basis for the development of the Treeing Walker Coonhound (see separate entry).

BRAZIL

BRAZILIAN TRACKER   BRAZIL

Also known as the Rastreador Brasiliero, this breed was developed specifically to track the jaguar.

This dog is the creation of one man, the Brazilian hunter Oswalde Aranha Filho. He combined several scenthound breeds, including the American Foxhound, the Treeing Walker Coonhound and the Bluetick Coonhound. The German Shepherd Dog is also rumoured to have been used.

The result of his complex breeding programme was a powerful, fearless scenthound with a fine nose and great stamina. Its typical coloration is described as white with blue, chestnut or black markings. The coat is short and harsh. Its muscular body has a deep chest and a sabre tail. The ears are long and drooping. Its height is 25–27 in (63–69 cm).

Because the jaguar is now extremely rare and is a protected species, this dog has inevitably faded into obscurity and some believe that it may already be extinct.

SHORT-LEGGED SCENTHOUNDS

Short-legged scenthounds have been popular for centuries for the task of trailing small game, accompanied by hunters on foot. They have several advantages over their larger cousins:

1   With no horses involved, the hunts are comparatively inexpensive.
2   With low-slung bodies these dogs can penetrate close cover and work over terrain unsuitable for hunters on horseback.
3   Their short legs make them slow and this means that the game is driven forward at a steadier pace and not panicked out of the hunters' range.

Hunting with these hounds takes two forms. In the first, the dogs find and noisily trail the quarry, driving it towards hunters waiting with guns. In the second, they trail, eventually catch the quarry, and then kill it themselves.

Geographically the main centre for this type of hunting has always been France. The short-legged hounds were first developed there and have since spread out across Europe and eventually to the New World.

I am defining a short-legged breed as a scenthound with a body height of 16 in (40 cm) or less. The typical members of this group are the beagles and the bassets. Eighteen breeds are considered here. Some other scenthounds are used by hunters working on foot, but as they are larger dogs with longer legs, they have been classified with the general scenthound group. Only those that are either small or low-slung are included here.

Some authorities will expect to find the Dachshunds included here, but functionally they are clearly earth dogs and have therefore been placed in that group, along with the more typical terriers.

There are 19 breeds in this category.

ENGLAND

FRANCE

AUSTRIA

GERMANY

SWITZERLAND

DENMARK

SWEDEN

CANADA

ENGLAND

BEAGLE

This is the smallest of the British pack-hounds, developed for hunting hare, with the huntsmen on foot. The origin of the name is not clear, but there is a Gaelic word, 'beag', meaning 'little', which may have been involved. In later years, if hares were scarce, Beagles were also used to hunt rabbits, but historically this was always a secondary activity for them. At one time they were called Jelly Dogs, because they caught the hares which were later served at table with red-currant jelly.

The attractive black-white-and-tan Beagle is a compact, wonderfully balanced little scent-hound, renowned for its 'merry' personality. Enthusiasts claim that it also possesses the finest tones in the canine world, with its haunting, bell-like voice echoing across the countryside as the pack goes off in full cry. It is a sturdy, lively little dog, with a very even temperament. It is so highly sociable that it is happiest when kept with a companion of its own kind.

The Beagle has been popular for over a century as a show dog but it has an even longer history covering many more centuries as a sporting breed. An early British author described the Beagle as 'the foot hound of our country, indigenous to the soil' and it found favour among royalty time after time, so much so that it was once called the 'Regal Beagle'.

As a foot hound it was also popular, of course, with those who could not ride to hunt. To enjoy the pleasures of hunting on horseback with a pack of scenthounds, it has always been necessary to be both rich and, above all, fit and healthy. But Beagles appealed to a wider audience. To quote a countryman of the Georgian period: 'Hunting with the Beagle was admirably adapted for ladies and gentlemen up in years; and, besides, affording such amusement to rustics, and other pedestrian hunters; for there were few male persons of any activity who could not keep up with them.'

There was little standardization of size in the earlier centuries. Beagles were bred to be small, but the degree of miniaturization varied a great deal, to the extent that a sep-arate form was created — a dwarf animal usually called the Pocket Beagle (see separate entry). These tiny dogs were later to fall out of favour and disappear, but the bigger animal has remained an immensely popular hound, both as an enthusiastic working dog and as a cheerful household companion.

Beagles were first exported to the United States in 1876 and were accepted there as a new breed by the AKC in 1884. The National Beagle Club was formed in 1888.

The fact that the Beagle is such a compact, healthy, genetically stable and physically uniform breed has in one respect been its undoing, for this has made it the ideal dog for use in medical research, for which, sadly, it is factory-farmed in large numbers.

References

1920. Prentice, H. W. *Beagle in America and England.*

1923. Paget, J. Otho. *Beagles and Beagling.* Hutchinson, London.

1926. Smith, Carl E. *Training the Rabbit Hound: Bassets and Beagles.* Wilcox, Chicago.

1933. Barker, K. F. *Bellman. The Story of a Beagle.* A & C Black, London.

1940. Colville, Robert. *Beagling and Otter Hunting.* A & C Black, London.

1946. Free, Roger. *Beagle and Terrier: Their Training & Management at Home & in the Field.* Chapman & Hall, London,

1950. Bellman, Barker. *The Story of a Beagle.*

1954. Lloyd, J. Ivester. *Beagling.*

1955. Miller, Madeline. *Beagles as Pets.* TFH, New Jersey.

1955. Whitney, George D. *This is the Beagle.* TFH, New Jersey.

1955. Williams, Courtney. *Beagles, Their History and Breeding.* Baylis, London.

1956. Denlinger, William. *The Complete Beagle.* Denlinger's, USA.

1956. Holcombe, A. D. *Pet Beagle.* All-Pet Books, Fond du Lac, Wisconsin.

1958. Ward, Mary Alice and Barbaresi, Sara M. *How to Raise and Train a Beagle.* TFH, New Jersey.

1959. Appleton, Douglas, H. *The Beagle Handbook.* Nicholson & Watson, London.

1960. Hewitt, W. Lovell. *Beagling.* Faber & Faber, London.

1961. Daglish, E. Fitch. *Beagles.* Foyles, London,

1963. Gray, Thelma. *The Popular Beagle.* Arco, New York.

1966. Colombo, Henry J. et al. *The New Complete Beagle.* Howell, New York.

1967. Schneider, Earl. *Enjoy Your Beagle.*

1968. Gordon. *Beagle Guide.* Pets Library.

1970. Appleton. *Beagles and Beagling.*

1973. Priestley, Heather. *All About the Beagle.* Pelham, London.

1973. Scharnberg, James Fagan. *Beagling and Basseting.*

1976. Berndt, Robert J. *Your Beagle.*

1977. Sutton, Catherine. *The Beagle.* Bartholomew.

1985. Foy, Marcia A. and Nicholas, Anna Katherine (Editor). *The Beagle.* TFH, New Jersey.

1987. Hobson. *Beagling.*

1990. Musladin, Judith M. *The New Beagle. A Dog for All Seasons.* Howell, New York.

1995. Bennett, Bill. *Beagle Training Basics: The Care, Training and Hunting of the Beagle.*

1995. Vriends-Parent, Lucia. *Beagles: Everything About Purchase, Care, Nutrition, Breeding, Behavior, and Training.* Complete Pet Owner's Manual. Barron, New York.

1996. Arnn, Barbara. *Beagles.*

1996. Roth, Richard. *The Beagle. An Owner's Guide to a Happy Healthy Pet.* Howell, New York.

1996. Vallila, Andrew. *The Guide to Owning a Beagle.* Popular Dog Library.

1997. Mason, Robert L. *The Ultimate Beagle. The Natural Born Rabbit Dog.*

1998. Kallen, Stuart A. *Beagles.*

1998. Wilcox, Charlotte. *The Beagle.*

1999. Dunbar, Ian (Editor). *The Essential Beagle.* Howell, New York.

2000. Mulvany, Martha. *The Story of the Beagle.* Dogs Throughout History.

2000. Palika, Liz. *How to Train Your Beagle.*

2000. Thornton, Kim Campbell. *Your Beagle's Life: Your Complete Guide to Raising Your Pet from Puppy to Companion.*

Carrel, Ike. *The Beagle Handbook.*

Sanford, William. *The Beagle.* Top Dog Series.

KIBBLE HOUND ENGLAND

This short-legged hunting breed was known as early as the 16th century, but has since disappeared.

In his *Treatise of Hunting*, published in London in 1590, Sir Thomas Cockaine advised young gentlemen to 'breed fourteen or fifteen couple of small Kibble Hounds, low and swift, and two couple of terriers'. There are occasional references to this type of dog in the centuries that follow, but little is known about it and it appears to have vanished by the early years of the 20th century.

There were two views concerning its origin. Thomas Bewick, writing in 1793, described it as 'a mixture of the Beagle and the Old English Hound', while W. D. Drury, in 1903, said that it came into being when 'the Southern, or Talbot, was rendered short-er in the leg... by crossing', adding that these crosses probably involved 'Edward II's Welsh Harriers'.

It was also recorded that, in the reign of James I, the working Kibble Hounds 'ran together in a lump' and hunted both by scent and by 'view'. It seems likely that this breed was a prototype of the modern Short-legged Scenthounds and eventually became obsolete, having been replaced by them.

POCKET BEAGLE ENGLAND

This extinct breed was known by many names during its day, including the Glove Beagle, the Mitten Beagle, the Sleeve Beagle, the Dwarf Beagle, the Toy Beagle, the Lap Beagle, the Lapdog Beagle, the Singing Beagle, the Rabbit Beagle and the Elizabethan Beagle.

A miniature version of the Beagle we know today, this breed was developed by royal hunters to fit into their saddlebags. It could then be transported to the hunting grounds, where it could be released and followed on foot in difficult terrain unsuitable for the larger hounds. Some were said to be so small that they would even fit in a pocket. Typical Beagles are usually 14–15 in (35–38 cm) in height, whereas this reduced version measured only 8–10 in (20–25 cm).

Early records show that Elizabeth I of England kept a pack of these little dogs. There exists a portrait of the Queen with one of her miniature beagles in the year 1575. She kept her pack for hunting and it was said that each of her animals was so small that it 'could be carried in a man's glove'. (It should be added that the gloves in question were huge gauntlets.) Later, in the 18th century, one famous pack of 'ten or eleven couple' was 'always carried to and from the field in a large pair of panniers slung across a horse'. In the early 19th century, George III and George IV also owned packs, so there was a royal connection that spanned at least four centuries.

Later, in a report on gentlemen's sporting pursuits published in 1615, the author advises would-be hunters who can only walk on foot with their dogs to 'keep the little small Mitten-Beagle which may be companion for a ladies kirtle, and in the field will hunt as cunningly as any hound whatsoever'.

It is not clear precisely when this attractive little dog started to go into the decline from which it never recovered. We know that a Colonel Thornton was still hunting a pack of them in the middle of the 19th century, and a Mr Crane in the 1850s, but after that date little more is heard. The fashion changed and bigger beagles were increasingly in favour. There was a brief resurgence in interest in late Victorian times, but this appears to have been ruined by ruthless commercial breeders who simply took the tiniest runts they could find, interbred them without regard for defects and sold the puppies on as appealing little pets. As a result, Victorian Pocket Beagles began to experience more and more problems with reproduction. Bitches often had great difficulty in giving birth. The breed began to acquire a bad name and numbers fell rapidly. In 1890 the Beagle Club was formed and they included special rules for Pocket Beagles, demanding that they be 'of true Beagle type and show great quality and breeding'.

World War I led to the disbanding of the remaining Pocket Beagle packs and by the 1920s there were only a few isolated animals left alive. Early in the 1930s a serious attempt was made to save the breed, but only a single bitch could be located. When she herself finally died, in 1935, this historic dog finally became extinct. There was later talk of recreating it, but nothing appears to have come of it.

WIRE-HAIRED BEAGLE   ENGLAND

In earlier centuries there were two forms of Beagle, the wire-haired Northern and the smooth-haired Southern. The rough-coated Northern animal was thought to have been the result of introducing some wire-haired terrier blood into the pure Beagle strain. In its heavier coat, the Northern dog was more suited to a tougher, colder climate. It was also said to be faster and stronger than the short-coated Southern form and had greater stamina. Despite this it was the Wire-haired Beagle, also known as the Rough Beagle, that vanished and the other that survived to become the favoured form of modern times.

In 1903 a Beagle enthusiast wrote of the rough-haired Beagle: 'He is now seldom seen at shows or in the hare-hunting packs. A revival is urgently needed if the variety is to be rescued from oblivion, and it is well worth the attention of the breeders.' Apparently this advice was not taken and the breed soon faded into canine history.

There is also a reference to an extinct, rough-coated Beagle found in Wales and sometimes called the Welsh Beagle, but it is not clear whether this was the same breed, or a separate, independent development of a rough-haired variety.

FRANCE

BASSET ARTÉSIEN NORMAND   FRANCE

Sometimes called the Artesian Norman Basset, the Norman Artesian Basset or the Normandy Basset, this breed acquired its name from a merging of two related hounds, the Basset d'Artois and the Basset Normand, in 1911. In France it is usually referred to simply as the B.A.N. It was originally developed for use on rabbit hunts.

In north-west France two breeds of large hound, the Artois and the Normandy, both became extinct, but their dwarf forms, the Basset d'Artois and the Basset Normand, managed to survive. The two breeds differed only slightly from one another and in the early part of the 20th century they were merged to create a new, improved breed, the Basset Artésien Normand. At first, this was an unwieldy and slothful dog, but through selective breeding it was made more streamlined and more lively. In the process, it is said, it lost some of its stamina, but it was certainly a more popular dog and was soon being exported to England, Belgium, Holland and Scandinavia.

This low-slung hound has straight legs and a short coat which is either bicolour or tricolour. This is a less 'extreme' form than the more familiar Basset Hound and, in general appearance, looks rather like a short-legged Foxhound. It is more athletic and vigorously hunts through thick cover. In personality it is brave and headstrong when hunting, but friendly, obedient and patient in the family home.

References
Browne, A. Gondrexon-Ives. *De Franse Basset: Artâesien Normand.*

BASSET BLEU DE GASCOGNE   FRANCE

Sometimes known as the Blue Gascony Basset, this is more usually recorded under its original French name.

Towards the end of the 19th century, this little dog from the south-west of France, near the Pyrenees, was on the verge of extinction. By 1911, a survey revealed that it had disappeared completely from its homeland and was virtually unknown elsewhere. In the years that followed, an enthusiastic breeder and sportsman called Alain Bourbon, of Les-Agets-St- Brice in Mayenne, set to work to recreate it.

He started by crossing short-legged males of other Basset breeds with the smallest bitches he could find of the Bleu de Gascogne hounds. At first, the results were highly variable, but little by little he managed to stabilize a true-breeding short-legged form, and the old Basset Bleu de Gascogne type was reborn. Even so, it remains a rare breed to this day.

This type of Basset has been described as wise, affectionate, musical, slow and reserved. According to Monsieur Bourbon they are highly suitable 'for the old huntsman riddled with gout… with a few couples of these little hounds he will rediscover his youth'.

References

1997. Limouzy, Christian. *Le Basset Bleu de Gascogne.* Éditions de Vecchi, Paris.

BASSET FAUVE DE BRETAGNE   FRANCE

Also sometimes called the Tawny Brittany Basset or the Fawn Brittany Basset, this uniformly coloured breed was developed to run in packs of four against rabbit, hare and wild boar.

This rough-coated breed from the north-west of France was created in the 19th century by crossing the larger Griffon Fauve de Bretagne (originally used for hunting wolves in that region) with a smaller Basset breed – probably brought up from further south in the form of the Basset Griffon Vendéen.

The coarse, tough coat of this dog makes it the ideal hunter for working in dense coverts, hedge-banks, briars and heaths. In recent years, its golden colouring has appealed to pet-keepers as well as to hunters, and although it remains a rare breed, it is now finding increasing favour as an affectionate household companion.

BASSET HOUND   FRANCE

This breed derives its name from the French word 'basset', meaning short or low. It was developed in northern France for trailing hare, rabbit and deer.

In origin this breed appears to have sprung from a chance, short-leg mutation in an otherwise normal litter of scenthounds. Back-crossing to this abnormal dwarf dog then led to the creation of stunted hounds which could easily have been rejected as freaks, but which were retained because they had special uses. Their main advantage was that, being slower than the typical long-legged hounds, they could be followed by hunters on foot instead of on horseback. There were two reasons why this situation could have arisen. In some regions there was good hunting in close cover where horses could not move with ease. Also, after the French Revolution, with the aristocracy in disarray, there were many hunters who were horseless. For them, a pack of Bassets was a perfect solution. A special niche therefore arose for the strange little dog that was once rudely described as a 'legless bloodhound'.

The first Basset Hounds to arrive in England crossed the Channel in 1866, acquired from the Comte de Tournon by Lord Galway. Another English breeder, Sir Everett Millais, added a little more Bloodhound to the breed and, in so doing, altered the shape of the dog slightly, making the English version longer-headed and heavier-bodied than the original French type. Some of this English type were sent to America, where they were crossed with other, lighter, French-type bassets that had arrived from Russia. The result was that the American Basset was intermediate in size and shape between the original French and the more recent English version.

Today the show-dog Basset and the working field Basset have diverged slightly. The facial skin of the show dog is looser and more easily wrinkled.

In personality the Basset is a solemn, friendly dog not given to frantic displays of excitement. With its human companions it is polite, gentle, benign and reserved. Once on the hunt, however, it is stubbornly single-minded and relentless in pursuit of its quarry. It has a beautiful voice, deep and resonant, and a golden nose — the latter always, inevitably, being close to the trail. In colour, it is like a typical Foxhound — black, white and tan, or any two of these three colours.

Commercial exploitation of this breed – with Hush Puppies shoes, for example, and the cartoon character Fred Basset – has led to its increased popularity as a household pet, much to the disgust of the hunting fraternity, who wish to see the less extreme form of field-working Basset as the only surviving form, and to see the breed treated exclusively as a serious working hound.

References

1944. Smith, Carl E. *Training the Rabbit Hound: Bassets and Beagles.* Wilcox & Follett, Chicago.
1956. Look, Mrs Travis. *Pet Basset.* All-Pets, Fond du Lac, Wisconsin.
1958. Miller, Evelyn. *Basset Hounds.* TFH, New Jersey.
1959. Johnson, Margaret S. *Jamie, a Basset Hound.* William Morrow, New York.
1959. Liebers, Arthur and Hardy, Dorothy. *How to Raise and Train a Basset Hound.* TFH, New Jersey.
1960. Appleton, Douglas H. *The Basset Hound Handbook.* Nicholson & Watson, London.
1961. Sherwood, Basil. *The Basset Hound.* Rupert Hart-Davis, London.
1964. Daglish, E. Fitch. *The Basset Hound.* Foyles, London.
1965. Braun, Mercedes. *The Complete Basset Hound.* Howell, New York.
1968. Johnston, George. *The Basset Hound.* Popular Dogs, London.
1972. Borland, Hal. *Penny, The Story of a Free-Soul Basset Hound.* Lippincott, Philadelphia.
1973. Johns, Jeanne Rowett. *All about the Basset Hound.* Pelham Books, London.
1973. Scharnberg, James Fagan. *Beagling and Basseting.*
1974. Hart, Ernest. *This is the Basset Hound,* TFH, New Jersey.
1979. McCarty, Diane. *Basset Hounds.*
1985. Nicholas, Anna Katherine. *The Basset Hound.* TFH, New Jersey.
1988. Braun, Mercedes. *The New Complete Basset Hound.* Howell, New York.
1990. McCarty,Diane. *Basset Hounds.* TFH, New Jersey.
1993. Walton, Margaret S. *The New Basset Hound.* Howell, New York.
1996. Wicklund, Barbara. *The Basset Hound: An Owner's Guide to a Happy Healthy Pet.*
1997. Mars, Julie. *Basset Hounds.*
1998. Morgan, Diane. *The Basset Hound Owner's Survival Guide.*
1999. Booth, Robert E. *The Official Book of the Basset Hound.*
Schneider, Earl. *Know Your Basset Hound.* Pet Library, New York.
Browne, A. Gondrexon-Ives. *De Franse Basset: Artâesien Normand.*
Stahlkuppe, Joe. *Basset Hounds.* Barron, New York.

GRAND BASSET GRIFFON VENDÉEN FRANCE

Occasionally given the anglicized title of the Large Vendéen Griffon Basset, or the Large Vendéen Basset, this breed is more usually known by its original French name. It owes part of this name to the Vendée region of western France. And the word 'griffon' means wire-haired. So its full title translates as 'the large, low-slung, wire-haired hound from the Vendée region'. It was developed for hunting hare and rabbit in the Vendée countryside, where it was extremely difficult for huntsmen to operate on horseback, and where the efficient pursuit of game could only be carried out on foot.

Originally this breed occurred in variable litters, with some puppies being much smaller than others. At first, these different-sized dogs were allowed to interbreed freely, but later it was decided to separate the smaller ones and treat them as a distinct breed (see next entry).

One dynasty of breeders has stood at the centre of this breed's history for over a century. The Desamy family of La Chaize-le-Vicomte in the Vendée has become so closely associated with this particular hound that the dogs they breed are usually referred to simply as '42 Desamys'. The figure '42' (the animals' height in centimetres) reflects the fact that their breeding line is so carefully standardized that the dogs are all exactly the same height.

PETIT BASSET GRIFFON VENDÉEN   FRANCE

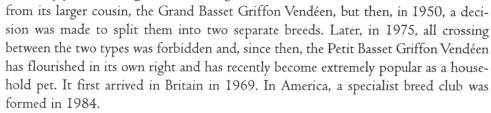

Occasionally given the anglicized title of the Small Vendéen Griffon Basset, or the Small Vendéen Basset, this breed is more usually known by its original French name. In Britain and America, for convenience, its name is often shortened to the PBGV, or PeeBee-GeeVee.

For many years this dog was not distinguished from its larger cousin, the Grand Basset Griffon Vendéen, but then, in 1950, a decision was made to split them into two separate breeds. Later, in 1975, all crossing between the two types was forbidden and, since then, the Petit Basset Griffon Vendéen has flourished in its own right and has recently become extremely popular as a household pet. It first arrived in Britain in 1969. In America, a specialist breed club was formed in 1984.

In personality, it is a lively extrovert, full of energy. On the hunt it is tenacious and headstrong, with a high level of curiosity, but in the home it is known simply as 'the happy breed'. The coat, which is never trimmed, is rough and wiry, and some owners in Britain refer to PBGVs as 'Roughies'. Its height is 15 in (38 cm), compared with 17 in (42 cm) for the Grand version.

References

1987. Steidel, Kitty. *Understanding the Petit Basset Griffon Vendéen: Rustic French Hound*. Orient Publications.

1993. Pepper, Jeffrey. *Petit Bassett Griffen Vendéen*. TFH, New Jersey.

2000. Link, Valerie and Skerritt, Linda. *Petit Basset Griffon Vendéen, A Definitive Study*.

AUSTRIA

ALPINE BASSET   AUSTRIA

Sometimes referred to as the Alpine Basset Hound, the Alpine Dachsbracke, or the Montano-Alpine Dachsbracke, and known in its homeland as the Alpenlandischer Dachsbracke, this breed has been developed as a specialized trailer of wounded game.

This tough, hardy scenthound was developed for use in the woodlands of the Austrian Alps. When deer are wounded, the local hunters refuse to allow them to escape to suffer a long and painful death. Instead they laboriously track them down by their blood-trail, with the help of these short-legged hounds.

The Alpine breed was created by crossing local Austrian hounds with Dachshunds. It is characteristically stag-red in colour, or black-and-tan. Throughout its existence it has remained almost exclusively a local hunter's dog, having rarely travelled abroad or been adopted as a family pet.

GERMANY

WESTPHALIAN BASSET   GERMANY

Sometimes called the Westphalian Dachsbracke or the Sauerland Basset Hound, and known in its homeland as the Westfälische Dachsbracke or the Sauerlander Dachsbracke, this breed was developed to hunt rabbit, hare, fox and wild boar. In recent times it has been used for blood-trailing work in pursuit of larger, wounded game. In Holland it is called the Bonte Westfaalse Dasbrak.

Several centuries ago, German hunters in the region of Westphalia and Sauerland created what is effectively a short-legged foxhound by crossing fox-hounds with Dachshunds. This combination produced a tough, short-legged dog ideal for hunting parties travelling on foot in the mountain woodlands.

We know little about the breed's history in the Middle Ages, except that it appears in works of art of the time. The 19th century was the period when it grew in prominence. Its popularity increased dramatically after the year 1848, when changes in the law permitted common people to hunt for the first time. The smaller landowners, having restricted hunting grounds available to them, preferred a slower hound than those previously favoured by the nobility.

This short-legged German hound was first given an official name in 1886 and was formally recognized by the German Kennel Club in 1935.

SWITZERLAND

BERNESE BASSET   SWITZERLAND

Sometimes referred to as the Small Bernese Hound and known in its homeland as the Berner Niederlaufhund, this breed was developed for tracking small game in mountain valleys. It is named after the Swiss Alpine region in which it hunts, the district around the capital, Berne.

This is the short-legged version of the Berner Laufhund, or Bernese Scenthound. It is the only Swiss breed of hound to exist in both smooth- and rough-haired versions. At 13–16 in (33–41 cm), it is 6 in (15 cm) shorter than its relative.

This and the other three Bassets from the Swiss mountain valleys (the Jura, Lucerne and Schwyz) were developed at the beginning of the 20th century, when a system of hunting in preserves was started in several Swiss cantons. The existing, larger Swiss hounds, with longer legs, were thought to be too fast for this, and a careful breeding programme was introduced to reduce their speed by selecting for shorter and shorter legs. This was done essentially to impair the efficiency of the hunts, for the controlled protection of the game. Included in the breeding programme was the important step of introducing Basset crosses with the older Swiss walking hounds, to lower their body height more rapidly. The first club formed to support these new breeds was established in 1905.

JURA BASSET   SWITZERLAND

Sometimes referred to as the Small Jura Hound, this breed was developed to pursue all kinds of small game over difficult terrain. It is named after the Alpine region in which it hunts, in the north-west of Switzerland, near the French border.

This is one of four short-legged sighthounds (the others being the Lucerne, the Schwyz and the Bernese) developed locally in different districts of Switzerland and showing only minor differences from one another – largely in coat colour. They are all descended from the larger Swiss hounds. These bigger versions have been hard at work in the mountain valleys of Switzerland for centuries, but their shorter-legged relatives are of more recent origin. These breeds have seldom been seen outside their country of origin. The height of the Jura Basset is 13–16 in (33–41 cm), 6 in (15 cm) shorter than its close relative, the Jura Hound.

LUCERNE BASSET   SWITZERLAND

Sometimes referred to as the Small Lucernese Hound and known in its homeland as the Luzerner Niederlaufhund, this breed was developed to track small game in the mountain valleys. It is named after the Alpine region in which it hunts, in central Switzerland.

This is a smaller version of the Lucernese Hound, bred down in size to adapt it to work with smaller quarry in enclosed preserves. Its height is 13–16 in (33–41 cm), 6 in (15 cm) shorter than its big relative. It has a tricoloured, heavily ticked, wire coat.

Because of the complex, mountainous nature of the Swiss landscape, each region tends to be isolated to an unusual degree from its neighbours. If this were not the case, there would probably be only one single type of basset for the whole country. Instead, there are four separate types, each so limited geographically that it is, of necessity, a rare breed. Although protected by local enthusiasts, these breeds are always vulnerable, especially as they have not been exported to other countries for working or show purposes.

SCHWYZ BASSET   SWITZERLAND

Sometimes referred to as the Smaller Schwyz Hound and known in its homeland as the Schwyzer Niederlaufhund, this breed was developed to track small game in the mountain valleys in the region around Schwyz, in the east of the country. It is sometimes recorded as the Schweizer Niederlaufhund, or the Small Swiss Hound.

Distinguished from its close relatives by its white-and-red colouring, this breed originates from early French scenthounds. These were modified to adapt them to working in the Swiss Alpine landscape, their bodies being made lighter and less cumbersome. Then at the beginning of the 20th century, a Basset version of the Schwyz Hound was developed. The extra shortening of its legs helped to slow it down in terrain where faster dogs would have been a problem. Its height is 13–16 in (33–41 cm), 6 in (15 cm) shorter than its big relative. The wire-haired version of this breed no longer exists. Like the other basset breeds from Switzerland, this one survives only in very small numbers.

DENMARK

DANISH BASSET DENMARK

Also referred to as the Danish Dachsbracke and known in its homeland as the Strellufstover, a title which honours its creator's kennels, this breed specializes in tracking hare, fox and deer.

This small but powerful breed was developed by the Danish breeder Frands Christian Frandsen, of Holsted in Jutland, in the early part of the 20th century. It was designed by him as the ideal dog to work slowly across big estates, baying loudly and driving the game to the waiting hunters. He lived to see his creation recognized by the FCI in 1937, by which time there was a small but enthusiastic breed club to support it in Denmark.

Frandsen created the breed by mixing together the Westphalian Basset from Germany, the Smalands Hound from Sweden, and the Bernese Hound from Switzerland. In its turn, the Danish Basset was used in the creation of the Swedish Drever, which ultimately came to be more popular and overshadowed it. By the end of the 20th century, for example, a survey revealed that, although there were only about 500 Danish Bassets, there were as many as 11,000 Swedish Drevers. In the 1960s Scandinavian canine authorities decided that there was too little difference between the Danish and Swedish dogs to warrant separate breed status and decided to lump them together, a move unpopular with local enthusiasts who, predictably, continued to call them by their separate local names of Strellufstover and Drever.

SWEDEN

DREVER SWEDEN

Also known as the Swedish Drever, the Swedish Dachsbracke or the Swedish Beagle, this northernmost representative of the short-legged scenthound is used to hunt hare, fox, roe deer and even wild boar. The name 'Drever', which means 'hunter' in Swedish, was formally given to the breed in 1947.

Looking rather like a cross between a Dachshund and a Foxhound (others have described it as a cross between a Basset and a Beagle), this tough little dog with its loud, musical voice has become immensely popular inside its native country. Despite this, it

remains surprisingly little-known outside Scandinavia. An exception is Canada, where it was recognized by the Canadian Kennel Club in 1956.

In origin, its most important ancestors were the Westphalian Bassets or Dachsbrackes. These were used as a major element in the creation of the Danish Basset, and it was the Danish Basset that was the precursor of the Drever. The first litter was recorded in 1913.

The popularity of the Drever increased dramatically in Sweden in the late 1930s when there was a rapid growth of the local roe deer population. It was officially recognized as a new breed by the Swedish Kennel Club in 1949. By the 1980s it was reported that about 2,000 were being registered each year.

Despite its small size, the courageous Drever is prepared to challenge a cornered wild boar. Unable to take too many risks with physical assaults on such a well-armed animal, its technique is to circle it and harass it, barking furiously until the hunters arrive to despatch the quarry.

It is said that, when encountering deep snow, the determined little Drever will 'swim' through it, using its short legs and big feet to 'paddle' its long body forward.

In personality this is a determined, friendly, energetic, non-aggressive little dog which enjoys life to the full and which, inevitably, has become a favourite family pet in addition to its working role in the hunting field. It has not, as yet, featured importantly in the world of the show-ring.

CANADA

TAHLTAN BEAR DOG   CANADA

Also known as the Chien d'Ours de Tahltan, this is a small Indian dog with no close relatives, descended from prehistoric Pariah Dogs, and developed to track grizzly bear, black bear and Canadian lynx.

Kept as a hunting companion by the Tahltan Indians of northern British Columbia, this small scenthound experienced an unusual lifestyle. The unfortunate dog was subjected to special rituals before being allowed to set off in search of game. These rituals varied according to the nature of the quarry.

If the little animal was being taken out to track lynx, it was first marked in a special ceremony. The claw of a lynx was used to make small cuts on the dog's face, presumably to provide a kind of magical protection from a real attack. If the quarry was to be

a bear, the sharpened leg-bone of a wolf was used to stab the dog in its hindquarters.

Surprisingly, despite this bizarre treatment, the dogs were still very keen to undertake the hunt. To conserve their energies they were carried to the hunting grounds in small sacks, slung over their owners' shoulders. As soon as game tracks were spotted, the dogs were released and the pursuit began. Yapping wildly, they harassed the lumbering bear or fleeing lynx, rather like small birds mobbing an owl. Eventually, the quarry would give up the chase, unable to outpace the fast little dogs. Then, once it was at bay, having been confused and circled by the snapping, yelping dogs, the Indian hunters were able to approach and make the kill, using arrows or spears.

The object of these hunts was primarily to obtain bearskins for trade, but when the demand for these pelts dried up, the little Bear Dogs found themselves out of work and their numbers dwindled rapidly. By the 1980s there was only a handful left and it is now widely believed that they have become extinct. With luck, however, a few pure-bred individuals may still be clinging on in the more remote regions of the far north of Canada. Only a careful search by canine experts will finally settle this matter.

Described as looking like a 'foxy terrier', this diminutive terror stood only 15 in (38 cm) high. Typically it displayed an attractive, black-and-white, piebald coat, with a thick, bushy 'shaving-brush' tail. Despite the fact that it was a showy little animal, affectionate and gentle at home in the Indian encampments, it is odd that it was not adopted for the show-ring in Canada before it became so rare. One explanation sometimes given is that it could not adapt to warmer climates, but there are plenty of northern countries where it could presumably have flourished, if anyone had gone to the trouble of taking special precautions. If this breed really has vanished now, its demise will be a sad loss for the world of dogs.

FLUSHING DOGS

The role of a flushing dog is to search the undergrowth in front of the guns, panic game birds from cover, wait for them to be shot and to drop and then, on command, locate the bodies and retrieve them to the hunters. In the era before sporting guns existed, the flushing dog's duty was much the same as it is today, except that when it drove the birds into the air they were killed by the hunters' hawks. An alternative method was to drive them into large nets, where they were trapped.

The typical flushing dog is the spaniel. The earliest reference to one is in Chaucer (1383), who says of a woman: 'as a spaynel, she wol on him lepe.' This early spelling of the word spaniel gives the clue to the geographical origin of the dog, for at that time a Spaniard was also called a 'Spaynell', and there is little doubt that the earliest form of this type of dog was being called a 'Spanish Dog'. A rival theory that derives the word 'spaniel' from the Carthaginian term 'span', meaning a rabbit, has little supporting evidence.

The prototype spaniel was soon divided into three types – the Land Spaniel, the Water Spaniel and the Spaniel Gentle. The Water Spaniels (see section on Retrieving Dogs) became specialized as aquatic retrievers, while the miniaturized Spaniel Gentles became high-status pets. Only the Land Spaniels were out-and-out flushing dogs, and they themselves eventually became split up into a number of breeds, depending largely on their size. Arranged in order of body weight, from the heaviest to the lightest, the main flushing breeds are the Clumber, the English Springer, the Sussex, the Field, the Welsh Springer, the English Cocker and the American Cocker.

Although all the flushing dogs are called spaniels, not all spaniels are flushing dogs. Some, like the King Charles Spaniel, are small breeds employed solely as household companions. Others, like the Tibetan Spaniel, are completely unrelated. And there are several French 'spaniels' which are, in reality, general-purpose hunting dogs.

There are 11 breeds in this category.

ENGLAND

CLUMBER SPANIEL
ENGLAND

This large spaniel takes its name from the Clumber estate of the Duke of Newcastle, where it has been bred since the late 18th century.

The Clumber has been described as 'the aristocrat of the spaniel family'. A heavy-bodied spaniel, with a massive head and shortish legs, the Clumber is reputed to have begun its existence as a noble refugee from the French Revolution. According to popular legend, the Duc de Noailles, fearing that his favourite dogs might be slaughtered, moved his whole kennel of spaniels to England. He presented them to the Second Duke of Newcastle, who kept and bred them on his huge Nottingham estate, Clumber Park, near Sherwood Forest. In 1788 the Duke had his portrait painted proudly surrounded by six descendants of those original dogs.

Unfortunately for this appealing story (repeated time and again in the canine literature), the spaniels were sent as a gift to the Duke of Newcastle from the French Duc around 1770, long before the French Revolution, which did not occur until 1789. Sadly, no detailed records exist to tell us the precise circumstances of the gift, but it is clear that the imported dogs were gratefully accepted, and were soon being developed at Clumber Park as a valuable new type of spaniel.

In later years the breed became extremely popular in England, especially among the nobility. Indeed, it was difficult for others to obtain examples of them, as this comment from the year 1888 reveals: 'The breed of Clumbers has been guarded with great jealousy by several of the noble families in whose kennels it has long held a place; of these the principal are the Dukes of Newcastle, Norfolk, and Portland, and Earl Spencer.' The names of the Duke of Westminster and the Earl of Abingdon are also mentioned by other authors.

The breed retained its popularity right through the Victorian period and on into the early 20th century. It lost favour, however, following World War II and has since become a minority interest. (According to Kennel Club registration figures, the Springer Spaniel is 100 times more popular than the Clumber, and the Cocker is well over 100 times more favoured.)

In the hunting-field, Clumbers used to work as a pack, slowly and systematically moving through the undergrowth and flushing the game towards the hunters' guns. Today they are more likely to operate singly or in small groups. They are silent workers, so much so that they are 'frequently worked with bells attached to their collars'. In this way the hunters can keep track of their dogs as they move through the undergrowth.

In personality, the Clumber is considered to be the most reserved of the spaniels. Matching its heavier build, its character is avuncular, strong, dependable, steady, friendly, intelligent and lacking in aggression. Other words used to describe it include dignified, solemn, proud, patrician and docile.

It has been suggested that, at some remote time in its history, a drop of French Basset blood was added to the Clumber Spaniel line. Were this to be true, it would explain both the Clumber's unusually calm personality and its heavy, low-slung body.

References

1912. Farrow, James. *The Clumber Spaniel.* Illustrated Kennel News, London.
1965. Meyer, Mr and Mrs R. Wilton. *How to Raise and Train a Clumber Spaniel.* TFH, New Jersey.
1991. Grayson, P. and Furness, R. *The Clumber Spaniel.*
1997. Meyer. *Clumber Spaniel. A Complete and Reliable Handbook.* TFH, New Jersey.
1999. Irving, Jan. *Clumber Spaniels.*

ENGLISH COCKER SPANIEL   ENGLAND

Known in England simply as the Cocker Spaniel, or Cocker, and in earlier times as the Cocking Spaniel or Woodcock Spaniel, this breed acquired its name from the birds which were its main quarry: the woodcock, the moorcook (red grouse) and the heathcock (black grouse).

Today this is the most popular of all the spaniel breeds. Originally it was lumped with the Springer Spaniel as a single breed, called the Land Spaniel (to distinguish it from the Water Spaniel). But, as time passed, certain hunters favoured smaller and smaller dogs and a separate, compact type was developed. This was most commonly seen in Wales and in Devon. Some early authors suggested that this size reduction was assisted by crossing the Springer Spaniel with a 'Small Water Spaniel', but this is not certain. Others believe that the Dukes of Marlborough, who favoured the Cocker, crossed in the diminutive King Charles Spaniel at one point to improve the breed.

Eventually the two sizes of Land Spaniel each became recognized in their own right and were given different names. As early as 1803, a leading canine authority observed: 'The large Springing Spaniel and the diminutive Cocker, although they vary in size, differ but little in their qualifications.' The fact that only body size differentiated them meant that more conservative opinion was against classifying them as two full breeds, and throughout much of the 19th century the matter remained unsettled. Finally, however, the split was too great to ignore, and in 1893 the Springer Spaniel and the Cocker Spaniel were both formally registered as separate, distinct breeds by the Kennel Club in London.

The advantage of this smaller spaniel was that it was faster and could push more easily into hedgerows and dense thickets. These benefits more than made up for its slight loss of power. In addition to its tireless, energetic flushing, it is also a brilliant retriever.

In personality the Cocker is desperate to please, gentle, playful, friendly and affectionate. An appealing dog that is fastidious, highly intelligent, curious and devoted, it is little wonder that in recent years it has become such a favourite household pet and always features in the lists of 'top ten' dogs of all kinds.

References

1915. Glass, Eugene. *The Cocker Spaniel*. Dog Fancier, Battle Creek, Michigan.

1929. Lloyd, H. S. *The Popular Cocker Spaniel*. Our Dogs, Manchester.

1932. Johns, Rowland (Editor). *Our Friend the Cocker Spaniel*. Methuen, London.

1935. Ash, Edward C. *The Cocker Spaniel as a Champion, Show Dog and Working Dog*. Cassell, London.

1935. Moffit, Ella B. *The Cocker Spaniel: Companion, Shooting Dog and Show Dog*. Orange Judd, New York.

1937. Bruette, William. *The Cocker Spaniel: Breeding, Breaking and Handling*. Stackpole, New York.

1938. Woodward, John. *The Cocker Spaniel*. Arthur Pearson, London.

1942. Dodge, Gerlandine R. *The English Cocker Spaniel in America*. English Cocker Club of America, New York.

1944. Mangrum, Marion. *Who's Who in Cocker Spaniels*. University of Oklahoma, Norman, Oklahoma.

1946. Denlinger, Milo G. *The Complete Cocker Spaniel*. Denlinger's, Washington, DC.

1947. Denlinger, Milo G. *Your Cocker Puppy: Care and Training*. Denlinger's, Washington, DC.

1947. King, Bart. *Dogs as an Avocation, Emphasizing the Cocker Spaniel*. Des Moines, Iowa.

1950. Daly, Macdonald. *The Cocker Spaniel*. Findon, London.

1950. Harman, Ian. *Cocker Spaniels*. Williams & Norgate, London.

1950. Mathews, V. A. H. *The Cocker Spaniel: Standard, Care, Showing and Breeding*. Oxford University Press, Oxford.

1951. Broughall, Nesta M. Basnett. *The Cocker Spaniel Handbook*. Nicholson & Watson, London.

1952. Ghent, Brian and Gillibrand, Eric. *The Cocker Spaniel Book*. Seeley Service, London.

1953. Lucas-Lucas, Veronica. *The Popular Cocker Spaniel*. Popular Dogs, London.

1955. Miller, Madeline. *Cocker Spaniels as Pets*. TFH, New Jersey.

1956. De Casembroot, Judy. *The Merry Cocker*. Rockliff, London.

1956. Whitney, Leon F. *This is the Cocker Spaniel*. TFH, New York.

1957. Lloyd, H. S. *Cocker Spaniels*. Foyles, London.

1957. Miller, Evelyn. *How to Raise and Train a Cocker Spaniel*. TFH, New Jersey.

1958. King, Bart. *Pet Cocker Spaniel*. All-Pets, Fond du Lac, Wisconsin.

1962. Gannon, Robert. *How to Raise and Train an English Cocker Spaniel*. TFH, New Jersey.

1968. Hart, Ernest H. *The Cocker Spaniel Handbook*. TFH, New Jersey.

1969. Harmar, Hilary. *Cocker Spaniel Guide*. Pet Library, New York.

1970. Lucas-Lucas, Veronica. *The Cocker Spaniel*. Arco, New York.

1974. Cartledge, Joe and Cartledge, Liz. *The Complete Illustrated Cocker Spaniel*. Ebury Press, London.

1979. Doxford, Kay. *The Cocker Spaniel: its Care and Training.* K & R Books, Edlington, Lincolnshire.

1979. King, Bart. *Cocker Spaniels.* TFH, New Jersey.

1980. Jenkins. C. C. *The Cocker Spaniel.*

1980. McCarthy. *The Cocker Spaniel.*

1981. Kraeuchi, Ruth M. *The New Cocker Spaniel.* Howell, New York.

1982. Brearley, Joan McDonald. *The Book of the Cocker Spaniel.* TFH, New Jersey.

1983. Greer, Frances and Austin, Norman. *Cocker Champions in Story and Pedigree.* Frances Greer Books. 2 vols.

1986. McKinney and Romanski. *English Cocker Spaniel. Vols. I & II.*

1987. Knapper and Zabawa. *Beginner's Guide to Cocker Spaniels.*

1988. Balfour, Judith and Kemp, Rosemary. *Cocker Spaniels in Australia.*

1990. Gannon, Robert. *English Cocker Spaniels.* TFH, New Jersey.

1992. Carey. *Owner's Companion to the English Cocker Spaniel.*

1995. Caddy. *English Cocker Spaniel Today.*

1995. Judith, P. *The Cocker Spaniel.* Howell, New York.

1996. Fogle, Bruce. *Cocker Spaniel, American and English.* Dorling Kindersley, New York.

1998. Smith, Mike. *Working Springers and Cockers.*

Schneider, Earl (Editor). *Know Your Cocker Spaniel.* The Pet Library, New York.

Vanacore, Connie. *The Complete English Cocker Spaniel.*

ENGLISH SPRINGER SPANIEL ENGLAND

Known in England simply as the Springer Spaniel or the Springer, this breed acquired its name from its primary function, namely to make the game 'spring' up out of hiding and expose itself to the hunters' guns. In earlier days it was sometimes called the Wood Spaniel, the Norfolk Spaniel or the Springing Spaniel.

This popular breed of spaniel, second only in numbers to the Cocker, remains to this day very close to the original, prototype Land Spaniel, before it was subdivided into different forms. It is described by enthusiasts as the perfect gun dog for flushing and retrieving work. It has strength and stamina, boundless enthusiasm and, with its longish legs, great athleticism.

In recent years the Springer has developed in two different directions – as a field worker and as a show dog. The former have been repeatedly bred for character and the latter for appearance, with the result that there has been some divergence between the two, but without any great detriment to the breed as a whole. In fact, the show-dog/household-pet Springers still possess so much of their ancestors' love of field work that, if they are denied vigorous daily activity, they are liable to become a problem. If kept in restricted spaces with little to occupy them, they are likely to develop behaviour difficulties and, in extreme cases, to become destructive.

From the 17th century onwards, this kind of spaniel is to be seen accurately portrayed in many great paintings, and it is clear that it has changed little over the centuries. In personality it is cheerful, energetic, affectionate and, like other spaniel breeds, singularly lacking in aggression. Compared with many other modern dogs, it is a long-lived breed.

In some early dog books, the Springer Spaniel was given the title of Norfolk Spaniel; the breed was reported to have gained this name because it had been fostered by the Duke of Norfolk. Then a Mr James Farrow took the trouble to write to the Duke to obtain confirmation of this, only to be told by His Grace that 'my family has never owned such a strain'. After this, the title of Norfolk Spaniel discreetly disappeared.

References

1932. Ferguson, Henry Lee. *The English Springer Spaniel in America.* Derrydale Books, New York.

1934. Johns, Rowland (Editor). *Our Friend the English Springer.* Methuen, London.

1939. Riddle, Maxwell. *The Springer Spaniel.* Judy, Chicago.

1943. Meek, S. P. *Dignity, A Springer Spaniel.* Knopf, New York.

1954. Henneberry, Janet H. *Pet English Springer Spaniel.* All-Pets, Fond du Lac, Wisconsin.

1957. Riddle, Maxwell. *The Springer Spaniel for Show and Field.*

1958. Goodall, Charles S. *The Complete English Springer Spaniel.* Denlinger's, USA.

1960. Miller, Evelyn. *English Springer Spaniels as Pets.* TFH, New Jersey.

1960. Scott, Mary C. *The English Springer Spaniel Handbook.* Nicholson & Watson, London.

1961. Gannon, Robert. *How to Raise and Train an English Springer Spaniel.* TFH, New Jersey.

1963. Hooper, Dorothy Morland. *The Popular Springer Spaniel.* Popular Dogs, London.

1970. Smith, Beatrice P. (Editor). *The English Springer Spaniel in North America.* English Springer Spaniel Field Trial Club.

1973. Hankwitz, Reed F. *Your English Springer Spaniel.* Denlinger's, USA.

1973. Hill, Frank Warner. *English Springer Spaniels.* Foyles, London.

1974. Goodall, Charles S. and Gasow, Julia. *The New English Springer Spaniel.* Howell, New York.

1980. Gasow, Julia and Roggenkamp, Edward K, III. *The New Complete English Springer Spaniel.* Howell, New York.

1980. Hampton, O. *All About the English Springer Spaniel.*

1983. Nicholas. *The Book of the English Springer Spaniel.* TFH, New Jersey.

1995. Erlandson, Keith. *The Working Springer Spaniel.* Excellent Press, Ludlow, Shropshire.

1995. Wood. *English Springer Spaniels.*

1996. Muirhead. *The Complete English Springer Spaniel.*

1996. Ritter. *An Owner's Guide to the Pet English Springer Spaniel.* Howell, New York.

1998. Smith, Mike. *Working Springers and Cockers.*

Callahan, Carol and Don. *The English Springer Spaniel. An Owner's Guide to a Happy Healthy Pet.*

McCarty, Diane. *English Springer Spaniels.* TFH, New Jersey.

Nicholas, Anna Katherine. *Book of the English Springer Spaniel.* TFH, New York.

FIELD SPANIEL   ENGLAND

This breed has had two lives — as an active, game-flushing gun dog and as a carefully presented show dog. In its latter role it came to look quite different for a while and often appeared under the title of 'Black Field Spaniel' or simply 'Black Spaniel', this being the favoured colour for the show-ring version.

The Field Spaniel is a longer-bodied and slightly larger version of the Cocker Spaniel. At first it had been a valuable hunting companion and had proved itself a worthy member of the spaniel family. Then, in the second half of the 19th century, it underwent a major change of direction, when it was accepted as a pedigree breed for the show-ring and taken up as a show dog.

Competition breeders, or 'show-bench fanciers' as the hunting fraternity called them, immediately began to modify the breed and exaggerate its shape, to improve its 'type' for showing. What was called 'an extremist craze' developed for producing 'the longest and lowest of the ultra-show type'. Instead of improving it, however, this trend nearly ruined it, giving it a 'weak, long body, sagging underbelly, cumbersome head and crooked leg'. One critic suggested that the show dog's only hope of survival was for it to sprout a third pair of legs in the middle of its hammock-slung body.

As the years passed, it became increasingly clear that this new-style Field Spaniel would be hopeless if it were once again asked to go to work in the hunting field. By the end of the 19th century attempts were being made to restore it to its original form, but the breed had lost so much support that this proved an uphill struggle.

By 1945, with a progressive loss of interest in the breed and with the ravages of two World Wars, it was nearly extinct. But there were still those who thought that the old hunting version of the breed was worth saving, and they laid plans to rescue it and reconstitute it. They started this process in the 1960s by introducing Cocker and Springer crosses. This rebuilt the original working Field Spaniel and the breed was safe once more, although it has to be admitted that it is still a great rarity, completely overshadowed by the immensely popular Cocker Spaniel.

In character it is said to be the most docile of the spaniels, with a personality that has been described as 'sweet, mild, affectionate and tranquil'.

References

1997. Wolkenheim. *The Field Spaniel, a Complete and Reliable Handbook.* TFH, New Jersey.

OLD ENGLISH SPANIEL   ENGLAND

This old-fashioned type of spaniel may now be extinct.

The last examples of this early breed were seen in the Norfolk Broads and other parts of East Anglia. According to Clifford Hubbard, writing in the 1940s: 'It is directly related to the Aqualate Spaniel through the Old English Water Spaniel, but no longer has the curly coat of the latter.'

This was a slim, lightweight spaniel of the kind so often portrayed in 17th-century sporting pictures. It was fast and active and able to travel long distances but light enough to be picked up and carried under the arm. It weighed only 18 lb (8 kg), compared with the 30 lb (14 kg) of the Cocker Spaniel or the 45 lb (20 kg) of the Springer.

The coat was white with bold red markings. The head was red with a white blaze. The coat was described as 'flat, silky and abundant'. The ears were well feathered and the long, plumed tail was left undocked. The height was 14 in (36 cm).

SUSSEX SPANIEL   ENGLAND

This breed takes its name from the English county where it was created. It was developed specifically for flushing work in thick, heavy undergrowth.

Described by one early author as 'grave and somewhat weird', the slow-moving, long-bodied, heavy-headed, low-slung Sussex is today the rarest of all the English spaniels. In a recent year, only 58 new examples were registered with the Kennel Club, compared with over 12,000 Springers and over 14,000 Cockers.

This powerfully built breed, with its characteristic rolling gait, was developed in the late 18th and early 19th century by a Mr A. E. Fuller of Rosehill Park, Brightling, near

Hastings in Sussex. He was seeking a slower, tougher breed of spaniel, one he could follow with ease through the local hunting grounds, which included an unusual amount of dense cover. He is thought to have created it from carefully planned crosses involving other spaniel breeds, including the Springer, and possibly with the addition of a little hound blood.

Two adaptations to its specialization as a dense-cover flushing dog are its thick, protective skin and its informative voice. Unlike other spaniels, it gives tongue while searching through dense thickets. This helps to keep the men in touch with their animals, and it is even said that an expert hunter can tell the kind of quarry being flushed by listening to the precise tonality of the dog's calls. An early Sussex devotee described the dog's voice in a colourful way: 'He is a noisy, babbling sort, that will rouse a cock from the densest covert. So natural does this babbling seem... that no matter how young, down go their heads and out comes the music.'

When the breed's creator died in 1847 his dogs were dispersed and the breed became scarce. Later enthusiasts set about reviving it in 1870, but, although they succeeded, it has never become a popular breed and its numbers have always remained low, largely because most spaniel men prefer a faster dog on the hunt.

Like all spaniels, this breed is exceptionally friendly and unaggressive. In personality it is said to be exceptionally laid-back and completely devoted to its family. Its coat is a characteristic rich, dark red colour.

References

1987. Orton. *A History of the Sussex Spaniel.* Privately published.
1989. Grayson. *The Sussex Spaniel.*

WALES

WELSH SPRINGER SPANIEL   WALES

In the past this breed has been called variously the Starter, the Tarfgi, the Red-and-White Spaniel, the Welsh Spaniel or the Welsh Cocker. Like all the other Land Spaniels, its gun-dog role is to locate, flush out and then retrieve small game. To many of its friends it is known simply as the Welshie. The name 'Tarfgi' means, literally, 'the dispersing dog'.

There is some evidence that this may be the oldest surviving breed of spaniel. Welsh Spaniels are mentioned in the Laws of Howel Dda which date from the early part of the tenth century. In these laws it is stated that 'the Spaniel of the King is a pound in value'. This is many years before there is any mention of this type of dog in England and suggests that it began as a Celtic dog and only later started to move east across the border.

Those very early Welsh dogs were not specified as being one particular type of spaniel or another. Sometimes they were called simply Welsh Spaniels; at other times, Welsh Cockers. At the end of the 19th century, when the breed was accepted by the Kennel Club in London, the name was changed from Welsh Cocker to Welsh Springer, but since its body weight is intermediate between the large English Springer and the smaller English Cocker, the choice of precise name appears to have been almost arbitrary.

What is puzzling about the origin of the Welsh Springer Spaniel is how a Spanish dog made the journey to Wales, there having been little direct connection between these two countries prior to the tenth century. Two theories have been put forward. One sees an early migration from Spain to Ireland and then from Ireland to Wales. The other envisages a shorter journey from Brittany to south Wales, with the Brittany Spaniel and the Welsh Spaniel sharing a common ancestor.

In addition to being smaller than the English Springer, the Welsh dog also has a more tapering head and a characteristic red-and-white coat pattern. No other colour form is permitted. It was rarely encountered outside its homeland until the 20th century, but because of its attractive appearance has in recent years gained some popularity as a show dog. Its ability to withstand extremes of temperature has also meant that it has been exported across the globe to work as a gun dog in such countries as Australia, Thailand and India.

References

1977. Pferd. *The Welsh Springer Spaniel.*

GERMANY

GERMAN SPANIEL   GERMANY

Also called the German Quail Dog, the Deutscher Wachtelhund or the Stober, this breed is little known outside its homeland. Although, as its German title suggests, its speciality is locating and flushing quail, its range of game birds is much wider than that.

With its wavy coat, its general body shape and its eager personality, this breed is a typical spaniel, most reminiscent of the Springer. There are some who believe that it is closer than any of today's better-known spaniels to the prototype Land Spaniel of earlier years, before that type started splitting up into the various modern forms.

This dog has been hard at work in the

German countryside for at least three centuries, and even though it has not successfully travelled abroad like so many other German breeds, it has nearly always been popular among the local hunters. Having an excellent nose, it has been especially useful for dense woodland hunting. Its only crisis, as a breed, occurred at the very end of the 19th century, when its numbers were in serious decline. Happily, a group of enthusiastic German hunters combined forces to introduce a planned breeding programme and to save it for the future. It has been suggested that to achieve this they introduced some new blood from several of the modern spaniel breeds, including the Cocker.

According to one authority, the German Spaniel was used in crosses with Smooth-haired Dachshunds, when creating the Long-haired Dachshund breed.

RUSSIA

RUSSIAN SPANIEL
RUSSIA

This has also been recorded as the Russkaja Spaniel.

This is a small breed of spaniel, similar in appearance to the Springer Spaniel. It was created by Russian hunters following World War II, and was developed from a mixture of Western European spaniels for use in finding, flushing and retrieving in the Russian countryside. Although this breed lacks stamina and is not suited to very rough work, it is highly efficient in game-rich areas and has been used in hunting for quail, corncrake, sandpiper and hare. The Russian Spaniel was officially recognized as a distinct breed by the Soviet canine authorities in 1951 and some were exported to Soviet satellite countries in the 1970s, but it remains virtually unknown in other parts of the world.

UNITED STATES

AMERICAN COCKER SPANIEL
UNITED STATES

There is some confusion over names between this breed and the English Cocker Spaniel. To Americans, this is simply THE Cocker Spaniel. To English enthusiasts, the English Cocker Spaniel is THE Cocker Spaniel. For clarity, the only solution is to add the country prefix in both cases. The original function of this breed was to flush and retrieve game birds.

Towards the end of the 19th century, mostly in the 1870s, English Cocker Spaniels were being imported into North America to hunt birds – usually woodcock, grouse or pheasant. By 1881 there was already an established American Cocker Spaniel Club, but until the 1930s there was no marked difference between the New World and Old World examples of the breed. Then, those breeders with a special interest in show dogs began to shrink the breed to a more petite scale, suitable for modern households. The result was an increasingly popular show-breed that was soon to become the Number One pet dog in the United States.

Those still employing the dog as a hunting field-worker were not happy about this new trend. They wanted to keep the breed as it had always been, and decided to split away from the dog-show breeders. In 1935 they formed a separate club and inter-breeding between the small show dog and the larger field dog was forbidden. By 1946, the existence of these two separate breeds of Cocker was formally accepted by the American Kennel Club.

So successful was the little American Cocker Spaniel that it started to attract the unwelcome attentions of commercial puppy-farmers. For a while, the breed looked as though it would sink into medical chaos as a result of this, but gradually the serious breeders and more scholarly enthusiasts intervened and saved the breed in its high-quality form. The future of this wonderfully lively and appealing little dog now looks bright again.

References

1956. Kraeuchi, Ruth M. *The Cocker Spaniel, a Complete Work on the American Cocker Spaniel.* Judy, Chicago.

1988. Grossman, Alvin. *American Cocker Spaniel* (The Pure-Bred Series). Doral Publishing, California.

1993. Austin, Norman A. and Austin, Jean S. *The Complete American Cocker Spaniel.* Howell, New York.

1994. Gorodner and Alton. *World of the Cocker Spaniel.* TFH, New Jersey.

1995. Iby. *An Owner's Guide to the Pet Cocker Spaniel.* Howell, New York.

1995. Teasley. *Guide to Owning a Cocker Spaniel.* TFH, New Jersey.

1996. Ackerman, Lowell. *Dr Ackerman's Book of the American Cocker Spaniel.* TFH, New Jersey.

1996. Fogle, Bruce. *Cocker Spaniel, American and English.* Dorling Kindersley, New York.

1996. Zervas (Editor). *Basic Guide to the American Cocker Spaniel.*

BOYKIN SPANIEL   UNITED STATES

This 20th-century breed of spaniel is named after the Boykin community near Camden, South Carolina, where it was developed for flushing and retrieving wild turkeys in the Wateree River swamp region.

In the early years of the 20th century, a small stray dog — some kind of brown spaniel — was found outside a church in Spartanburg, South Carolina. Alexander White, a member of the congregation, took pity on it and gave it a home. The dog was a young male and was given the name of 'Dumpy'. Later, when White took it out hunting with his retrievers, he found that, to his surprise, it showed  a great enthusiasm for the sport and outclassed his other dogs. So he sent the young animal to his hunting partner, Whitaker Boykin, for training. It turned out to be a superb turkey-dog and was crossed with other hunting dogs to create a new breed, which soon became known as the Boykin Spaniel. The other breeds involved were the Cocker Spaniel, the English Springer Spaniel, the American Water Spaniel and the Chesapeake Bay Retriever, but it was 'Dumpy' that was the true founding father.

At first, hunting with this attractive new type of spaniel was confined to the rural districts of Camden, Sumter and Boykin, but it later became popular across much of the United States, especially the eastern-seaboard regions. In addition to its turkey-work, it has become a favoured breed for both dove-hunts and duck-hunts.

This small spaniel has a dark, liver-brown coat and is slightly rangier than a Cocker. It has a docked tail, not for aesthetic reasons but because, if left undocked, the long tail was wagged so furiously when the animal scented a turkey that it rustled the leaves and alerted the quarry too soon.

But the most characteristic feature of this dog is its personality. Devotees of the breed insist that it has a uniquely cheerful, energetic, enthusiastic nature that endears it to all those who work with it. Because of this, it has also enjoyed a new career as a well-loved household pet. It is a 'gentle and tender' dog that responds rapidly to kindly training, but cannot stand harsh treatment.

The Boykin Spaniel Society was formed in 1977 to promote the breed and within one year could boast over 300 members from 25 states. In 1979 the society started a registry to keep accurate records of all existing Boykin Spaniels. Within a few years there were over 4,000 dogs on their list. Before the end of the century, the Boykin had been named as the official State Dog of South Carolina.

References

1997. Creel, Mike and Kelley, Lynn Russell. *The Boykin Spaniel — South Carolina's Dog*.

EARTH DOGS

The members of this group of dogs have been carrying out the important function of pest control for at least a thousand years. Their task is to destroy small mammals that make their homes below ground. They achieve this end in one of three ways:

1   They enter the burrows of their prey, confront them and kill them.
2   They enter the burrows of their prey and force them to bolt, to be killed above ground by others.
3   They kill their prey when the animals come above ground.

Historically, for dogs, burrowing vermin have consisted of five main types of quarry, namely rats, rabbits, badgers, foxes and otters. Since these five offer such different challenges, there has been a degree of specialization in the dogs which have been bred to attack them. Canine vermin-controllers fall into six main categories:

1   General-purpose earth dogs (eg, Irish Terriers)
2   Dogs specialized to destroy rats (eg, Manchester Terriers)
3   Dogs specialized to dig out badgers (eg, Dachshunds)
4   Dogs specialized to dig out rabbits (eg, Miniature Dachshunds)
5   Dogs specialized to join the hunt for foxes (eg, Fox Terriers)
6   Dogs specialized to join the hunt for otters (eg, Airedale Terriers)

In some classifications, these dogs are referred to collectively as the 'Terrier Group', but this is misleading. Most terriers are vermin-controlling earth dogs, but not all. Some, like the Bull Terrier, were created as fighting dogs. Others, like the Japanese Terrier, have never been working dogs and were created purely as companion dogs.

Furthermore, although most vermin-controlling earth dogs are terriers, not all of them are. Dachshunds and some Pinschers, Griffons and Schnauzers belong to this functional category.

There is a total of 65 breeds in this category, with the British Isles as the geographical stronghold, accounting for no fewer than 37. Of the remainder, 20 originate from continental Europe and 8 from the rest of the world.

ENGLAND

AIREDALE TERRIER   ENGLAND

Earlier names for this breed were the Waterside Terrier, Yorkshire Waterside Terrier, Bingley Terrier, Warfedale (or Wharfedale) Terrier, Broken-haired Terrier and Working Terrier. The name Airedale refers to a small otter-river (the Aire) near Leeds in northern England. The breed was originally used for destroying otters to protect the interests of fishermen.

The Airedale is a hardy, water-loving dog, often referred to as the 'King of Terriers', with an all-weather, wire-haired, black-and-tan coat. This, the largest of all the terriers, was developed in the Valley of Aire in Yorkshire, supposedly from crosses between the now extinct Black and Tan Terrier (for its rough coat); the Otterhound (for its sensitive nose); and the Bull Terrier (for its tenacity). Although its primary function was to hunt otter, it soon became a multi-purpose terrier and has been variously employed as a duck-catcher, ratter, deer-tracker, guard dog, gun dog, army messenger-dog and railway-police patrol dog. In the early days it was also used in dog fights, although it was always said to be peaceful with other dogs unless provoked. But if attacked, it was a fearless opponent and could kill a bull terrier with ease.

A 19th-century breed, the Airedale was first developed in 1853 by Wilfred Holme. It was first shown competitively in 1876, at Shipley, in the Valley of Aire, and became officially recognized soon afterwards. The Airedale arrived in the United States in 1881. In 1902 there was a move to delete the word 'terrier' from the breed's name because the dog was too big to be classed with other, more typical terriers, but it did not succeed.

Expressions used to describe this breed include loyal, bold, resolute, reliable, stubborn, plucky, curious, fun-loving, eager and tireless. It is kind and docile with children, but will fight to the death to protect its home or its family. It never starts a fight but always finishes one.

References

1905. Buckley, Holland. *The Airedale Terrier.* Our Dogs, Manchester.

1911. Palmer, R. M. *All about the Airedale.*

1913. Jowett, F. M. *The Complete Story of the Airedale.* Our Dogs, Manchester.

1916. Jowett, F. M. *The Airedale Terrier.* W. Glass.

1917. Lingo and Lytle. *Your Airedale.*

1921. Baker, W. E. *The Airedale Terrier.* Field and Fancy, New York.

1921. Hochwalt, A. F. *The Airedale for Work and Show.* Sportsman's Review.

1921. Phillips, W. J. *The Modern Airedale.* Buttles, Kansas City.

1922. Haynes, William. *The Airedale.* Macmillan, New York.

1929. Saunders, James. *The Modern Airedale.* Watmoughs, Bradford.

1948. Aspinall, J. L. *The Airedale Terrier.* Dog World, Bradford.

1950. Bowen, Aylwin. *Airedales.* Williams & Norgate, London.

1953. Johns, Rowland. *Our Friend the Airedale.* Methuen, London.

1960. Hayes, Irene E. *The Airedale Terrier.* Foyles, London.

1962. Edwards, Gladys Brown. *The Complete Airedale Terrier.* Howell, New York.

1963. Strebeigh, Barbara. *Pet Airedale Terrier.* All-Pets, Fond du Lac, Wisconsin.

1977. Strebeigh, Barbara and McCready, Pauline. *Your Airedale Terrier.* Denlinger's, USA.

1978. Miller, Evelyn. *How to Raise and Train an Airedale.* TFH, New Jersey.

1987. Clark, Steve H. *Airedale Terrier Champions: 1952–1986.* Camino Books.

1991. Dutcher, June and Franke, Janet. *The New Airedale Terrier.* Howell, New York.

1991. Swash, Mary. *Airedale Terriers.* Crowood Press, Wiltshire.

1994. Cummins, Brian. *The Working Airedale.* OTR Publications.

1996. Miller, Evelyn. *Airedale Terriers.* TFH, New Jersey.

1998. Miner, Dorothy M. *Airedale Terriers.* Barron, New York.

1999. Huxley, Janet. *Pet Owner's Guide to Airedale Terriers.* Ringpress Books, Lydney, Gloucestershire.

BEDLINGTON TERRIER   ENGLAND

Earlier names of this breed include Rothbury Terrier, Rodberry Terrier, Northumberland Fox Terrier, Northumberland Terrier, North Counties Terrier, Northern Counties Fox Terrier and Gypsy Dog. The name Bedlington refers to a small mining village in Northumberland. This was originally a poacher's or tinker's dog, sometimes used for pit-fighting.

With its poodle-like coat, its pear-shaped head and its arched back, this is a unique form of terrier, once seen never forgotten. It is a deceptive breed – a wolf in sheep's clothing. Although today, when immaculately groomed for the show-ring, it looks remarkably like a docile little lamb, it is in reality far from meek. Despite its fragile appearance, it is extremely tough, with a working history of having hunted rats, rabbits, otters, polecats, foxes and badgers. It was also used in the brutal sport of dog-fighting. Its forebears were the vermin-controlling Rothbury Terriers. These were crossed with Whippets to give them longer legs and greater speed, so that they could be used for coursing as well as for going to ground. The Dandie Dinmont was also probably involved in its creation.

Its ancestors existed in Northumberland in the late 18th century, and the first dog of its type, a male called Old Flint, was said to have belonged to a Squire Trevelyan in 1782. It is, however, impossible to prove beyond doubt that this is the founding father of the Bedlington. The first hard evidence we have of the origin of this breed dates from 1820, at the village of Bedlington, when a local stone mason, Joseph Ainsley,

acquired a dog called Peachem from nearby Rothbury and mated him to a bitch called Phoebe. Their off-spring, named Piper, was then mated to a bitch called Coate's Phoebe, producing a dog called Ainsley's Piper – and this was the first animal to bear the name of Bedlington Terrier.

The breed first entered the competitive show-ring in 1870 and since then has undergone a gradual change in appearance to reach its present extreme form. It has also lost some of its early pugnacity. In recent years the breed has suffered from copper-toxicosis, a severe liver disease that affects a significant proportion of the modern population. When obtaining a puppy it is important to ensure that it stems from stock that has been proved free of this inherited condition.

Today, as a companion dog, it is described as affectionate, loyal and full of fun. But, because of its ancestry, it is also said to be stubborn and sometimes aggressive to other dogs. At the end of the 19th century it was described as 'the smartest and quickest of our Terriers'.

References

1935. 'Red Marshall' (T. F. Carlisle) et al. *The Bedlington Terrier, comprising a short account of the early history and the origin of the breed.* Bedlington Terrier Association.

1964. Young, Elinore W. *How to Raise and Train a Bedlington Terrier.* TFH, New Jersey.

1990. Glover J. *The Working Bedlington.*

1991. Young, Elinore W. *Bedlington Terriers.* TFH, New Jersey.

1997. Phillips, Ian James. *Centenary Book of the National Bedlington Club, 1898–1998.* Published by the Club.

BLACK AND TAN TERRIER   ENGLAND

Also known as the Old English Black and Tan Terrier, the Old English Terrier or simply the English Terrier, this breed was developed as an urban rat-killing specialist. It was eventually replaced by its more refined descendant, the sleeker Manchester Terrier.

The Black and Tan was one of the earliest of all terriers and was used for centuries as a working vermin-killer. It was also employed in the rat pits for sport, where much gambling occurred, based on the estimated speed of rat-killing. One famous Black and Tan

Terrier called Billy was credited with having killed nearly 4,000 rats in one day. Referred to modestly as 'the Phenomenon of the Canine Race', he was (at 7.30 pm on 1st March 1825) 'matched to kill 100 Rats against any two dogs in England, for 100 Sovereigns'. On one occasion there was a wager that Billy could kill 100 rats in less than 8½ minutes. Bets were taken and Billy went to work. Such was his speed that he had completed the task and won the bet in a staggering 6 minutes 35 seconds. Billy broke his own record later, with a time of 6 minutes 13 seconds.

The Black and Tan became obsolete when it was crossed with Whippets in the middle of the 19th century, to create the more athletic Manchester Terrier. Some breeders wished to keep the old name of Black and Tan for this new breed, but despite their efforts at the turn of the century, the new name took hold and the old one was lost, to fade into canine history.

References

1880. Lamb, Louisa Mary Caroline. *The Veracious History of a Black and Tan Terrier.* Newman, London.

BORDER TERRIER   ENGLAND

Earlier names for this breed were the Reedwater Terrier, the Ullswater Terrier and the Coquetdale Terrier, titles taken from the local districts in the North of England where they worked. Their present name came about because of their close association with the Border Foxhounds. The Border Terrier was bred to be fast enough to run with the hounds but small enough to flush the fox out of its den.

Although it was not officially recognized as a distinct breed until 1920, the Border gives the impression of being close to the ancestral form of terrier from which all the others have descended. One of the first descriptions of this breed, written in 1891, refers to it as 'the original terrier of the hills' which 'still retains its pristine purity'. Another author called it a terrier 'unspoiled by fads and fancies'. Its homeland is along the borders of England and Scotland, especially in the region of Northumberland, where it is sent out to hunt with the hounds. Its legs are long enough for it to be able to keep up with the pack and its body is compact and flexible enough for it to squeeze into small crevices to bolt a hiding fox. It has a characteristically short muzzle and broad head, sometimes described as 'otter-shaped', and a remarkably harsh, dense, weatherproof coat with which it is able to withstand the rigours of the northern climate and the difficult terrain. Its tough skin is loose-fitting and very thick, protecting it from bites.

The Border type has been known since the 17th century, but written records of the breed under its modern name do not appear until towards the end of the 19th century. It was already well established as pure-breeding stock long before it became a show dog in the 1920s. Some feared that its adoption as a pedigree show dog would soften the breed, but this has not happened. The breed nevertheless had its critics, one famous terrier man remarking that the Border was 'slow to start and indifferent to work'. Few would agree with him, however, and passionate supporters of the breed insist that, once you have worked with a Border, no other breed will do. At one point, they started a campaign based on the slogan 'champions can still be workers'.

Because it has been bred to act closely with hounds, the Border Terrier is more friendly than usual when meeting other kinds of dogs. It makes an excellent companion, has a lively intelligence, and is good with children, but must always be given ample daily exercise.

References

1936. Johns, Rowland. *Our Friends the Lakeland and Border Terriers.* Methuen, London.
1948. Lazonby, T. *Border Lines.* Shiach, Carlisle, Cumberland.
1960. Orme, H. Garnett. *Border Tales.* Southern Border Terrier Club.
1967. Horn, Montagu H. *The Border Terrier.* Catherall, Hexham, Northumberland.
1969. Jackson, Frank and Irving, W. Ronald. *Border Terriers.* Foyles, London.
1976. Roslin-Williams, Anne. *The Border Terrier.* Witherby, London.
1992. Gardner, Walter J. F. *About the Border Terrier; a View of its History and Breeding.* Seven Hills Books.
1995. Kline, David Vangordon. *The Border Terrier.* Doral Publishing.
1996. Roslin-Williams, Anne. *Border Terriers Today.* Howell, New York.
1997. Jackson, Frank and Jackson, Jean. *Border Terriers, an Owner's Companion.*
1998. Collins, Verite Reily. *About the Border Terrier.* TFH, New Jersey.
Weiss, Seymour N. *How to Raise and Train a Border Terrier.*

CHESHIRE TERRIER   ENGLAND

A lost breed described as 'a kind of small white Bull Terrier', this was about 20 lb (9 kg) in weight. Its importance lay in its involvement in the creation of the Sealyham Terrier in the 19th century by Captain John Edwardes. He used the Cheshire in crosses to introduce gameness and a white coat. The pale colour was important to him because he had observed one of his brown terriers, emerging from below ground and stinking of fox or badger, being mistakenly attacked by his hounds.

It is not clear precisely when the Cheshire Terrier became extinct, but it is said that a small version of the Bull Terrier was still being bred in Cheshire until the 1920s.

ENGLISH TOY TERRIER

ENGLAND

There is no final agreement about the official name of this breed. In 1926 the American Kennel Club recognized it as the Toy Black and Tan Terrier, changing this to the Toy Manchester Terrier in 1934. More recently they have styled it as the Manchester Terrier (Toy). In 1938 the Kennel Club in London called it the Miniature Black and Tan Terrier, changing this in 1960 to the English Toy Terrier (Black and Tan). The Canadian Kennel Club calls it the Toy Manchester Terrier. To confuse matters further, it is sometimes recorded as the Black and Tan Toy Terrier. It was developed as a smaller version of the Manchester Terrier for use as a pit-contest rat-killer.

This tiny breed has lost none of its fire and can still give a good account of itself against even the largest rat, although it must be admitted that today it is kept almost exclusively as a house pet or a show dog. It is clear, however, that in origin it was a working dog, despite its small size. In the 19th century, pit contests between terriers and rats provided a popular source of gambling. The full-sized Manchester Terrier was the champion of all rat-killers, but then, as a new fashion developed, miniaturized versions of this breed were employed to make the outcome of contests more uncertain. Could a tiny runt of a terrier, weighing no more than 5 lb (2 kg), really despatch 300 rats in three hours? Surely it was too tiny to accomplish such a feat? Because it looked so puny, reckless gamblers were persuaded to wager large sums against its success. But they were wrong. In 1848, for example, a toy dog called Tiny the Wonder managed it in less than an hour. The gamblers had made the mistake of assuming that the little terrier was too feeble to complete the task, and therein lay the appeal of breeding minute dogs – they looked less likely winners and therefore won more money for their owners.

The result of this trend was that the English Toy Terriers became more and more reduced in size until, eventually, medical problems began to arise and the toy breed started to lose favour. By the end of the 19th century they were almost extinct, but a few enthusiasts took matters in hand and started to breed them in a more responsible way, eliminating the defects and strengthening the breed, so that today it now has more and more supporters and its future as a show dog appears to be in safe hands.

The small size of this breed has been obtained in two ways – first, by selecting Manchester Terrier litter runts and mating runt to runt; and second, by crossing with diminutive breeds such as the Italian Greyhound. The result, for the ordinary pet-owner, is a delightfully lively little dog, intelligent and faithful, and ideally suited to the restricted spaces of urban living.

References

1937. Clark, Russell D. *Russell's Famous Strain, Toy Manchester Terriers.* Virginia.
1950. Dempsey, Dixie. *The Complete Manchester Toy Terrier.* Denlinger's, USA.
1957. Miller, Evelyn. *Manchester Terriers as Pets.* TFH, New Jersey.
1958. Mack, Janet. *Pet Manchester.* All-Pets, Fond du Lac, Wisconsin.
1981. *The English Toy Terrier Club Handbook.*

ENGLISH WHITE TERRIER ENGLAND

This is sometimes referred to as the Old English White Terrier, the White English Terrier, or simply the White Terrier. Little is known about this early form of terrier, but it was suggested in 1894 that it came into being essentially as an urban rat-killer and not as a hunting dog.

Basically, this was a pure white form of the old English Black and Tan Terrier, there being little other difference between the two breeds. Now extinct, the English White Terrier was known to have been popular from at least the 1860s until the end of the 19th century. According to some reports, it was present in England even as early as the 15th century, but it never seems to have played a major role, partly because it was said to lack typical terrier bravery, and partly because it was rather delicate and often suffered from deafness. It was even said to be 'not celebrated for its intelligence', a rare criticism for any dog breed.

It was, however, a much fancied show dog at the early exhibitions and was, indeed, an elegant, well-proportioned dog that must have looked striking in the show-ring. Some showed a few small patches of dark colouring, but the ideal ones were all white. A smallish dog, weighing only about 14 lb (6 kg), it was thought to have arisen from a cross between a Smooth Fox Terrier and a white Italian Greyhound, but it is just as likely to have been developed by inbreeding white mutations of the Black and Tan Terrier, with no other breeds involved.

The best examples of this attractive breed were said to come from London, Manchester, Bolton, Rochdale and Birmingham. Rather appropriately, their main champion was a Mr White of Clapham Common, south-west of London. He is credited with having launched the breed as a serious contestant at early dog shows and it was rumoured that he wanted them to be known as White's Terrier.

For a while, this dog had its own specialist breed club, but this was disbanded in 1902. By 1927 the dog too had gone, its demise reported by Edward Ash in the following words: 'The elimination of the English White Terrier is accounted for on the following ground: To keep it in show form considerable care and attention, and no little trimming, were necessary, and it is probably because of this, and in consequence of the "little money in the breed", that it came to an abrupt end.' It did, however, leave its mark on the history of British dogs, because it played a major role in the development of certain other breeds, notably the Bull Terriers.

Jack Russell Terrier   England

Sometimes called the Working Terrier or the Jack Russell Working Terrier, this breed was named after its originator, the Reverend John (Jack) Russell, a 19th-century English parson. Its role was to accompany the hunt and go to earth to bolt foxes.

This breed was born on an afternoon in May in 1819, when an Oxford undergraduate who was shortly due to face an examination for which he was ill-prepared, was taking a stroll in the sunshine. The young Mr Russell had spent several years at Oxford, supposedly studying to take holy orders, but in reality spending most of his time shooting, fishing, hunting, boating, fighting, drinking and singing. He was walking from the centre of Oxford towards the village of Marston when he encountered a milkman, going on his rounds accompanied by an unusual terrier bitch. Russell fell in love with the animal at first sight and, after much persuasion, managed to purchase it on the spot. Her name was Trump and she became the foundation figure of the breed that was to give Russell his greatest claim to fame. A public house called The Jack Russell exists today in Marston, near the spot where the famous transaction took place.

Russell obtained his university degree, was ordained and took up a post as curate in a rural parish where he could devote as much time as possible to the hunting field, and as little time as possible to his human flock (who loved him dearly, perhaps because of this). His terrier Trump, which appeared to be a cross between a Fox Terrier and a Black and Tan Terrier, formed the basis of his special terrier pack. She looked similar to a Wire Fox Terrier, but with slightly shorter legs and a wider skull. In improving this breed, Russell was at pains to create a terrier that would be tall enough to keep up with his hounds, but small enough to go to earth and bolt a fox. He avoided introducing any killer blood as he wanted the terrier to set the fox running again, rather than attack it and kill it below ground, which would spoil the thrill of the chase.

After Russell's death (when 'a thousand followed him to his grave... nearly all of them sportsmen') the descendants of his terriers spread far and wide, often becoming modified in the process. Later crosses, supposedly with Dachshunds, Corgis and various toy dogs and terriers, were reputed to have been made and there was considerable variation in body size and shape. This was because the dogs were being bred for temperament, not looks. They were consistent in personality, but too variable in form to be accepted by the Kennel Club for competitive showing. There is an amusing irony in the fact that the Reverend Russell was himself a founding member of the Kennel Club and yet, even after the breed had become one of the most popular in the British Isles, the lively, intensely curious, endlessly entertaining Jack Russell Terrier was forbidden official recognition. (See separate entry for the Parson Jack Russell Terrier.)

This breed holds a unique record. A Jack Russell is the only dog ever to have set paw on both the North Pole and the South Pole. Explorers Sir Ranulph Fiennes and his wife, Ginnie, took their pet dog Bothie with them on their Transglobal Expedition, from 1979 to 1982.

References

1962. Smith, Betty. *The Jack Russell or Working Terrier.* Countrywise Books, London.

1979. Russell, Dan. *Jack Russell and His Terriers.*

1980. Plummer, David Brian. *The Complete Jack Russell Terrier.* Boydell Press, Suffolk.

1981. Huxham, Mona. *All about the Jack Russell Terrier.* Pelham, London.

1982. Tottenham, Katherine. *The Jack Russell Terrier.* David & Charles, Newton Abbott.

1985. Massey. *The Jack Russell Terrier, Above & Below Ground.*

1993. Chapman. *The Real Jack Russell Terrier.*

1995. Atten, Sheila. *Jack Russell Terriers Today.* Howell, New York.

1996. Brown, Catherine Romaine. *The Jack Russell Terrier: An Owner's Guide to a Happy Healthy Pet.* Howell, New York.

1996. Coile, D. Caroline. *Jack Russell Terriers: Everything About Purchase, Care, Nutrition, Behavior, and Training.* Barron, New York.

1996. Kosloff, George. *Guide to Owning a Jack Russell Terrier.* TFH, New Jersey.

1997. Valentine, John. *Pet Owner's Guide to the Jack Russell Terrier.* Ringpress Books, Lydney, Gloucestershire.

1998. Brown, Catherine Romaine. *The Jack Russell Terrier: Courageous Companion.* Howell, New York.

1998. Stockdale, Renee, et al. *The Essential Jack Russell Terrier.* Howell, New York.

1999. Britt-Hay, Deborah. *The Complete Idiot's Guide to Jack Russell Terriers.* Howell, New York.

1999. Strom, Mary (Editor). *Ultimate Jack Russell Terrier.* Howell, New York.

2000. McKay, James. *The Complete Jack Russell.* Swan Hill Press, Shrewsbury.

LAKELAND TERRIER   ENGLAND

In earlier days this breed was known by several other names, including Cumberland Terrier, Westmorland Terrier, Coloured Working Terrier, Fell Terrier and Patterdale Terrier. Its main task was to take part in horseless hunts with packs of hounds, over difficult, rocky terrain, with the aim of protecting lambs from foxes.

Developed in the Lake District in Cumberland in north-west England, this breed is thought by some to be the old Black and Tan Terrier in modern form. Others believe that it was created by crossing several different terriers, but these authorities vary in their opinion as to which precise breeds were involved. Those usually mentioned include the Bedlington (for gameness), the Welsh Terrier (for a smarter appearance), the Border, the Dandie Dinmont and the Wire-haired Fox Terrier. Whatever the truth might be, the result was an animal looking very much like a smaller version of the Airedale. Its principal duty on the hunt was that it should be able to keep up with the hounds – hence its rather long legs – and that it should be eager to crawl into rocky crevices and brave enough to bolt or attack hiding foxes. Because they must be able to squirm and slither though small gaps in the rocks, the Lakeland has been bred with a deep, narrow chest. It is claimed that, if it can get its head through a crevice, its body can follow.

A breed club was formed in 1912, and by 1928 the Lakeland Terrier had become a show dog, appearing for the first time at Crufts. It proved extremely popular in the ring and one of its champions holds the distinction of being the only dog ever to have achieved a 'double crown' – a Lakeland called Stingray having won best-in-show at both Crufts in London and the Westminster in New York. A special trophy commemorating this unique double is kept at the Kennel Club in London.

This breed has been described as an ideal family dog, affectionate with children, a useful guard dog, and suitable for both town and country. It is smart, sensitive, lively, tireless and courageous. But it has also been called 'rascally' because of its terrier tendencies. If you possess an immaculate garden and do not wish to see holes dug in your neatly mown lawn, choose another breed.

References

1936. Johns, Rowland. *Our Friends the Lakeland and Border Terriers.* Methuen, London.
1937. Spence, A. *The Lakeland Terrier.* Dog World, Bradford.
1946. Morris, Irene. *Line Breeding with Lakeland Terriers.* Privately published.
1964. Kirk, Archie Paton. *The Lakeland Terrier.* Privately published.
1991. Ehmer, Cheryl. *Lakeland Terrier Champions (1934–1990).*
1993. Weiss, Seymour N. *Lakeland Terriers.* TFH, New Jersey.

LUCAS TERRIER   ENGLAND

Named after its creator, this rare, local breed was used to destroy rats, badgers and otters.

Sir Jocelyn Lucas was a World War II hero (famous for having amputated his own toes when they became infected) who became an expert with working terriers. His pack of Sealyham Terriers was well known and he considered that breed to be one of the best and most versatile of all earth dogs. He was not happy, however, about the way in which the world of show dogs was modifying and exaggerating the Sealyham, creating a dog that was, in his opinion, much too large and too heavy to go to earth efficiently. As a

Member of Parliament, he stood up in the House of Commons one day to ask the curious question: 'Is it legal to have a type of terrier named after me?' The answer must have been in the affirmative because his improved working terriers subsequently became known as Lucas Terriers.

It was Lucas's aim to keep to the smaller size of the original, working Sealyhams, in defiance of the growing bulk of the show champions, and in addition to make them more agile. He achieved this by introducing crosses between his Sealyhams and some little Norfolk Terriers. It was the result of these crosses that became known as the Lucas Terrier. A Lucas Terrier Club was formed, and in 1988 it issued a breed standard that emphasized this dog's affectionate and unaggressive nature. It also mentioned that the Lucas Terrier should have a smaller head than the Sealyham and that it could appear in any colour, from light to dark. Few of these small terriers are alive today.

MANCHESTER TERRIER ENGLAND

Named after the city of Manchester in north-west England, which was its stronghold during its early development, this breed was developed specifically as an efficient ratter/rabbiter. It was sometimes referred to as the English Gentleman's Terrier, or, more simply, as the Gentleman's Terrier.

Appearing at first glance to be a miniature form of the Doberman Pinscher, this slender little terrier is in reality an improved version of the coarser, heavier Black and Tan Terrier of earlier days. Unlike most terrier breeds, which are dogs of the countryside, this one is descended from city dwellers, bred specially to seek out and kill the rats that infested the old city buildings and the areas of wasteland nearby.

As a descendant and close relative of the old Black and Tan Terrier, it shares many of that breed's features and characteristics. The main difference is that it is a more streamlined, athletic animal, as a result of crosses made with Whippets. The founding fathers of the modified breed were a small group of Manchester enthusiasts who, during the 1850s and 1860s, were attempting to create a dual-purpose ratter/rabbiter. At the beginning, their Manchester Terrier (first named as such in print in 1879) was immensely successful. Rat-pit contests were at the height of their popularity and everyone wanted to own the most efficient killer. But then the sport went into a decline and the terrier went with it.

A second blow was to follow, when the cropping of ears was forbidden in 1898 (thanks to the efforts of the Prince of Wales, later Edward VII). The cropped, early Manchesters had displayed little pointed ears that suited their general body shape and aggressive demeanour. When cropping ceased, their 'natural' ears were floppy and ungainly. It took some years to breed them into a better shape and by this time the breed had lost ground and was becoming a rarity. At the end of World War II, it was almost extinct, with only 11 registered pedigree dogs of this breed left in the whole of England. Determined to save it, its supporters rallied round and formed the British Manchester Terrier Club. Its numbers began to increase again and by the 1970s it was once more a popular breed, but now largely for the show-ring.

Having originated as an urban dog, it is an ideal pet for city-dwellers and enjoys the company of children. Its lean body and very short, dark coat do not, however, do it any favours in the 'cuddly' stakes.

References

1956. Mack, Janet. *The Pet Manchester.* All-Pets, Fond du Lac, Wisconsin.
1960. Cassels, K. A. H. *The Manchester Terrier.* British Manchester Terrier Club.
1998. Dresser, Pat. *Manchester Terrier: A Complete and Reliable Handbook.* TFH, New Jersey.

MINIATURE BULL TERRIER   ENGLAND

Known to enthusiasts simply as the MiniBull, the small version of the Bull Terrier was originally used for competitive rat-killing rather than dog-fighting.

This breed is what its name suggests, a reduced Bull Terrier. It retains the fiery, courageous personality of its larger cousin but is small enough to adapt easily to a modern city apartment. In other words it is an urban Bull Terrier and is becoming popular as a companion dog for modern city-dwellers.

It was first developed in the 19th century by those who sought a nimble killer for the gamblers' rat pits. It was created from litter runts that were inbred to produce smaller and smaller specimens. Later, during attempts to reduce its size still further, to the level of what could be called a Toy Bull Terrier, deformities arose and the MiniBulls lost favour. Then, in the 1930s, they were taken up seriously again and special efforts were made to produce an attractive, compact animal, but without any of the common dwarfing distortions.

The main weakness of the Miniature Bull Terrier is its susceptibility to blindness (caused by lens dislocation), a defect which is at present under investigation by a genetics committee set up by the Miniature Bull Terrier Club of America. A minor weakness is its tendency to fall asleep on your lap and snore loudly. Despite these drawbacks, these are dogs that seem to inspire as much devoted loyalty in their owners as their owners receive from them.

References

1973. Rosenblum, Edwin E. *How to Raise and Train a Bull Terrier (Standard & Miniature)*. TFH, New Jersey.

Andrews, B J. *Miniature Bull Terrier — a Complete and Reliable Handbook*. TFH, New Jersey.

NORFOLK TERRIER   ENGLAND

This was originally called the Drop-eared Norwich Terrier, until the two variants of the Norwich were given separate breed status. The primary role of the breed was that of a fox-bolter.

This terrier did not come into being as a distinct breed until September 1964. Prior to that it had been no more than a minor variant of the Norwich. Its story begins in the 1930s, when it was discovered that crossing a prick-eared Norwich with a drop-eared one could produce an intermediate ear that was unappealing. As a result, breeders began to keep the two ear types separate. During World War II the drop-eared Norwich strain nearly died out, but just managed to survive until peace returned. They then increased in numbers again, but always had to play second fiddle to the more popular prick ears. In 1957 Norwich breeders decided, by an overwhelming majority, to treat the two types as separate breeds, so that they would not have to compete against one another at dog shows. The Kennel Club felt that the difference was too trivial and refused to accept the proposal. (Skye Terriers, for example, were accepted with either pricked or drooped ears.) The Norwich breeders persevered, however, and eventually, in 1964, the Kennel Club relented and the new breed of Norfolk Terrier was officially recognized.

In all respects except its ear posture, the Norfolk is so similar to the Norwich that, for non-specialists, it is sometimes difficult to remember which is which. The simple trick used by some people is to remember that Norwich Cathedral has a spire that sticks up in the air, like the ears of the Norwich Terrier. Or, the Nor-wich has ears that stick up like a witch's hat.

In North America, both the American and the Canadian Kennel Clubs held out against the separation into two breeds and continued to classify both ear types under the heading of Norwich Terrier. As the years passed, however, it was clear that, following the 1964 separation in England, subtle differences in the general conformation of the two breeds were beginning to develop, and eventually, in 1977, the Canadians officially recognized both breeds. Two years later, in 1979, the AKC followed suit.

References

1965. Fournier, B. S. *How to Raise and Train Norfolk and Norwich Terriers.* TFH, New Jersey.

1989. Read, Joan R. *The Norfolk Terrier.* Privately published.

1997. Nicholas, Anna Katherine. *The Complete Handbook of the Norfolk Terrier.* TFH, New Jersey.

NORWICH TERRIER   ENGLAND

The ancestral form of this breed was called a Trumpington Terrier or a Cantab Terrier, because of its connection with Cambridge University. In America it was originally known as the Jones Terrier, after the owner of the first example to go there. The primary role of the breed was that of a fox-bolter.

The story of the Norwich Terrier begins at Cambridge University in the 1870s and 1880s, where it was the fashion among young varsity sportsmen to own a small, rough-haired terrier of a particular type. These dogs were obtained from a livery stable in Trumpington Street, which ran past several of the colleges in the centre of Cambridge. They were at this time referred to as Trumpington Terriers and were popular as college ratters. Some undergraduates wanted to rename them Cantab Terriers, but this never caught on.

Around 1900, a tough, sandy-coloured male called Rags was given to the owner of a stableyard near Norwich. There he became established as the prolific sire of a string of litters, and is generally accepted as the founding father of the Norwich Terrier as we know it today. Other kinds of terrier were crossed with Rags and out of this sequence there arose a fixed type of small, compact, harsh-haired, working breed that became renowned as a superb earth dog. Unlike some other terriers, it was willing to work in a pack and was soon in great demand. It was this new breed that was given the official title of the Norwich Terrier.

In 1914, one of Rags's descendants, named Willum, bred by a horse-breaker called Roughrider Jones, was sent to Philadelphia where he, in his turn, became the founding father of the Norwich breed in the United States. Because of his connection with Jones, he and his relatives were given the local name of the Jones Terrier. In 1932 the Norwich was officially recognized by the Kennel Club in London and four years later the American Kennel Club followed suit. At this point the title of Jones Terrier was dropped in favour of Norwich, although many American breeders ignored this and continued, for many years, to call their dogs Jones Terriers.

Like most terriers this breed is intelligent, tough and tenacious, but its supporters point out that it is also unusually cheerful as a companion dog, lacking the rather dour attitude of some others. One of the smallest of the terriers, it is a bossy little dog, but despite this is excellent with children.

References

1960. Monckton, Sheila. *The Norwich Terrier.* Privately published.
1965. Fournier, B. S. *How to Raise and Train Norfolk and Norwich Terriers.* TFH, New Jersey.
1985. Bunting, Marjorie. *The Norwich Terrier.* Norwich Terrier Club.
1994. Nicholas, Anna Katherine. *Norwich Terrier.* TFH, New Jersey.

PARSON JACK RUSSELL TERRIER   ENGLAND

This name was given to one type of Jack Russell Terrier, to distinguish it from all the other varieties of this variable breed. Its role was to accompany the hunt and go to earth to bolt foxes.

Because the Jack Russell Terrier (see separate entry for details) was always bred for temperament, rather than for a fixed appearance, it was for many years refused recognition by the Kennel Club. As it was by far the most popular terrier in Great Britain, this created an anomaly. Jack Russell enthusiasts responded by forming an independent Jack Russell Terrier Club. This was established in 1974 and organized its own competitive shows.

A conflict soon arose between those members who wished to see a fixed type of dog recognized and those who wished to judge more by temperament. The first group wished to impose a rigid standard on the breed and then seek acceptance by the Kennel Club. The second group wanted nothing to do with the world of the pedigree show dog and gave priority to the working qualities of their terriers. The matter was settled in the early 1980s when the first group split away and formed what they called the Parson Jack Russell Terrier Club, for the promotion of the 'Genuine Jack Russell'. They drew up their own breed standard and then applied to the Kennel Club for recognition. This was granted in 1989 because, for the first time with this dog, judges could operate on the basis of a set of precise breed points.

The Parson Jack Russell differs from the more popular, but defiantly variable, Jack Russell in that the former, the 'official Kennel Club breed', has longer legs and is considered to be much closer to the Reverend Russell's original, preferred form of terrier – one that could keep up with his hounds, but was small enough to go to earth.

References

1986. Jackson, Jean and Jackson, Frank. *The Making of the Parson Jack Russell Terrier.* Boydell Press, Suffolk.

1991. Jackson, Frank. *An Owner's Companion to the Parson Jack Russell Terrier.*
(See also entry for the Jack Russell Terrier.)

PATTERDALE TERRIER   ENGLAND

The word Patterdale refers to a village in Cumbria, but it is an unfortunate misnomer, because the breed that has been given this name did not develop there. Some authorities have insisted that the breed's title should be changed to Black Fell Terrier, or more simply to Fell Terrier, but the name Patterdale has become so widely accepted that to abandon it now would only add further confusion. The breed was developed for going to earth to attack rats, rabbits and foxes.

In the past the Lakeland and the Patterdale Terriers have often been considered to be one and the same, but it is clear from modern illustrations that today they exist as two distinct types. The explanation for this is that originally, the tough, working terriers of the Lake District, in north-west England, were known collectively as Fell Terriers. These little dogs had always shown considerable variation in form because they were bred for specific personality rather than for specific appearance. But then, in 1912, one particular variation was given the name of Lakeland Terrier, and certain breeders concentrated on developing and exaggerating this strain. By 1928 it had been exhibited under Kennel Club rules and was on its way to becoming a showy competition dog. By now it differed markedly from the more basic, working Fell Terrier, not only in appearance but also in its hunting ability.

Two Lake District breeders decided to develop, as an alternative, a fixed type of Fell Terrier that would still be a good working dog and would not be led astray by 'show business'. By the early 1950s, Cyril Breay and Frank Buck had created a Black Fell Terrier of a distinct type. In the 1960s this was further developed by a gamekeeper called Brian Nuttall and for some mistaken reason was given the name of Patterdale Terrier. The name of Patterdale stuck, despite the fact that the village in question was some distance from the centres where the breed was created. But whatever confusion over names existed, the fact remains that there are now two quite distinct breeds of Fell Terrier, the showy Lakeland and the more workmanlike Patterdale.

To understand the special role of the working Patterdale it is important to recognize the practical attitude of the Lake District hunters. For them, the fox is not a 'worthy opponent' to provide an afternoon's gentlemanly sport. Like the rat, it is dirty vermin to be destroyed by whatever means are at hand. The fearless little Patterdale is sent to earth and, if the fox bolts, it will be pursued by hounds. But if it resists, the terrier is brave enough to attack it and usually manages to kill it. This quick killing spells success for the local hunters, but would ruin a more leisurely afternoon's sport. So the role of this terrier in the traditional fox-hunting field has been severely limited, and to this day it has remained a lesser-known local breed. It did not reach America until the late 1970s but once there became a favourite companion on expeditions to destroy groundhog, raccoon, fox or badger.

In personality, this is a brave, stubborn, tenacious and determined breed.

PLUMMER TERRIER ENGLAND

This terrier was originally known as a variant of the Jack Russell Terrier, and was then sometimes referred to as the Huddlesford Working Terrier. After 1976 it was no longer accepted for registration in the Jack Russell Club and was later given full recognition as a separate breed. It was then renamed after its main sponsor, the author and dog-breeder Dr David Brian Plummer. As a working dog, it is used in small packs against rats, rabbits and foxes.

This is a distinctive new terrier breed with an attractive tan-and-white coat. Its markings are arranged in such a way that it looks as though someone has thrown a reddish-brown blanket over a white dog. It is similar to a Jack Russell, but taller and sturdier. The forerunners of this breed were brave but rather quiet terriers from south Wales. They were given more voice by the introduction of some Wiltshire blood. At a later

date, several crosses took place to improve the breed, including Beagle, for stronger voice and better nose, Bull Terrier for more powerful head, Fell Terrier to reduce aggression, and Jack Russell to correct shoulders. Careful, selective breeding is continuing to perfect this terrier, and when its development has been completed it is intended to apply for Kennel Club recognition.

ROTHBURY TERRIER ENGLAND

The name Rothbury refers to a village in Northumberland. The breed was employed by miners to clear their tunnels of rats.

The now extinct Rothbury Terrier was popular in 18th-century England in the mining districts of the north-east, where it worked underground as a vermin-controller and was also employed as a rodent-killer in local factories. In addition it was a favourite terrier of the local gypsies and tinkers, and was invaluable to them on their poaching expeditions, or when seeking out otters and badgers. In the early 19th century the Rothbury was crossed with Whippets, creating a more slender-bodied, longer-legged breed that was eventually to become the Bedlington Terrier. The Rothbury then died out.

SHROPSHIRE TERRIER ENGLAND

Also known as the Shropshire Fox-terrier, this is an extinct, localized breed, named after the English county in which it originated and was developed.

This old breed was a special type of Fox Terrier. It was known to be flourishing in the middle of the 19th century, but then appears to have gone into a decline, partly because it was too inbred and partly because it was too aggressive.

Domville Poole, a Shropshire squire who was its main champion, is said to have introduced bulldogs into his breeding programme with the idea of increasing the tenacity of his working terriers. His goal was to 'get his dogs with as much as possible of the exterior of the pure Fox-terriers and the internal temper and character of the Bull-terrier'. They were apparently too keen on killing the fox, rather than bolting it for the hounds to chase, and soon lost favour.

According to another report, an additional weakness of the Shropshire was a tendency to suffer from deafness, caused by a loss of cochlear hair cells, a condition also found in Dobermanns.

The Shropshire was closely related to the Cheshire Terrier (see separate entry), and some authors have suggested that they were virtually the same breed. Since both are extinct, it is impossible to be certain.

SMOOTH FOX TERRIER ENGLAND

This breed used to be known simply as the Fox Terrier (before the separation of the wire-haired form). It was later known as the Smooth-haired Fox Terrier, or Smooth-coated Fox Terrier, until, in recent times, this was shortened to the modern wording. As its name implies, the original function of this breed was to bolt the fox from its earth.

This breed has been called the 'gentleman of the terrier world'. It is the 'professional' fox-hunting terrier, specializing in going to earth to rout out the hidden quarry, for the hounds to pursue. It has remained close to the early terrier type, but has been improved slightly along the way. Starting from the old Black and Tan Terriers, it was refined by small additions of the old English White Terrier, the Bull Terrier, the Greyhound and the Beagle.

The form of the Smooth Fox Terrier had become fixed by about the middle of the 19th century and since then has undergone remarkably little modification. The earliest examples of this breed were dark-haired dogs, but after emerging from working below ground, smelling of fox, terriers with this coloration were sometimes mistaken for the quarry and accidentally attacked by the hounds. To prevent this, more and more pale colouring was added, to make the hunt terriers distinctive until, by the 1860s, the typical Fox Terrier could be described as being 'predominantly white with a few small dark patches'.

The year 1862 saw the first class devoted to this breed at a dog show. This was held at the Islington Agricultural Hall in London. The following year, at Birmingham, the three founding fathers of the modern breed, called Old Jock, Old Tartar and Old Trap, appeared in the show-ring, and a new career for the hunting terrier had begun in earnest. Ten years later the Fox Terrier class was huge, with no fewer than 276 entries. In a single decade, it had risen to become one of the most popular terriers in England. The year 1876 saw the formation in England of the first Fox Terrier Club, and the breed soon had its own journal, the *Fox Terrier Chronicle*. The first American club followed in 1885. By the early part of the 20th century, the Smooth Fox Terrier had risen to become the most popular of all dog breeds in England. It was to be overtaken, however, by its wire-haired counterpart in the 1920s. Later, the popularity of both types waned and they were overtaken by many other breeds, including a number of other terrier breeds. In 1998, for example, the West Highland White Terrier was 70 times as popular as the Smooth Fox Terrier, in terms of Kennel Club registrations.

This breed is so devoted to its hunting duties that, despite its great success in the field and the show-ring, it has been less popular than some other terriers as an ordinary family pet. Its personality has remained tenacious and strong-willed, and various authors described it as being 'stubborn, obstinate, wilful, undemonstrative, snappy, and obsessed with digging'. Even so, its lively, alert spirit have won it many friends and, for some, its fiery, intelligent, rugged character has its own special appeal. It is also, incidentally, the breed that has enjoyed lasting fame as the logo for the music company HMV.

References

1888. Dalziel, Hugh. *The Fox Terrier.* Upcott Gill, London.

1897. Harrison, T. H. *The Breeding of Show Fox Terriers.* Stock-keeper, London.

1899. Dalziel, Hugh. *The Fox Terrier and All About It.* Upcott Gill, London.

1902. Lee, Rawdon B. *Fox Terrier.* Horace Cox, London.

1910. Astley, L. P. C. *The Perfect Fox Terrier in Word and Picture.* Illustrated Kennel News, London.

1910. Castle, Sidney. *A Monograph on the Fox Terrier.* Our Dogs, Manchester.

1923. Haynes, Williams. *The Fox Terrier.* Macmillan, New York.

1926. Skinner, A. J. *The Popular Fox Terrier.* Popular Dogs, London.

1927. Castle, Sidney. *Breeding Fox Terriers.* Underhill, Plymouth.

1932. Johns, Rowland. *Our Friend the Fox Terrier.* Methuen, London.

1933. Naylor, L. E. *The Modern Fox Terrier.*

1935. Bruce, Rosslyn. *Fox Terrier Breeding, Smooth and Wire.* Strange, Eastbourne.

1938. Ackerman, Irving C. *The Complete Fox Terrier, Wire Haired and Smooth Coated.* Kegan Paul, London.

1938. Woodward, John. *The Fox Terrier.* Pearson, London.

1948. Skelly, George. *All About Fox Terriers.* Orange Judd, New York.

1949. Pardoe, J. H. *Fox Terriers.* Williams & Norgate, London.

1950. Bruce, Rosslyn. *The Popular Fox Terrier.* Popular Dogs, London.

1950. Holdsworth, M. J. *The Smooth Fox Terrier.* Dog World, Bradford.

1954. Daly, Macdonald. *Fox Terriers.* Chambers, London.

1955. Miller, Madeline. *Fox Terriers as Pets.* TFH, New Jersey.

1958. Beyer, Tilly. *Pet Fox Terrier.* All-Pets, Fond du Lac, Wisconsin.

1960. Wood, E. Lindley. *Smooth Fox Terriers.* Foyles, London.

1961. Miller, Evelyn. *How to Raise and Train a Fox Terrier.* Sterling, New York.

1961. Silvernail, Evelyn L. *The Complete Fox Terrier (Smooth and Wire).* Howell, New York.

1965. Williams, Elsie. *The Popular Fox Terrier.* Popular Dogs, London.

1997. Chads, Diana. *The World of Dogs: Fox Terrier.* TFH, New Jersey.

1998. Hearn, Ann D. *Smooth Fox Terrier: A Complete and Reliable Handbook.* TFH, New Jersey.

WIRE FOX TERRIER   ENGLAND

This breed used to be known by the longer title of Wire-haired Fox Terrier, or Broken-haired Fox Terrier. As its name implies, the primary function of this breed was to bolt the fox from its earth.

Apart from its rough coat, this breed is virtually identical with the Smooth Fox Terrier. It had the same early history and the same function in the hunting field; indeed, the two breeds were not considered separately until the 1870s. The Wire Fox Terrier was given its first separate class at a dog show in 1873. After that, the two forms were awarded different classes, and crosses between them were discouraged. As the years passed they vied with one another for popularity, sometimes one being in favour, sometimes the other. Today, the Wire Fox Terrier is the more numerous of the two, with three times as many annual registrations at the Kennel Club as its rival.

The fame of this breed was given a major boost in the 1930s by Hollywood's *Thin Man* films starring William Powell and Myrna Loy. Their lively pet dog, a male Wire Fox Terrier called Asta, played a prominent role in these immensely successful detective thrillers, of which there was a series of six, running from 1934 to 1947.

References

1888. Dalziel, Hugh. *The Fox Terrier.* Upcott Gill, London.

1897. Harrison, T. H. *The Breeding of Show Fox Terriers.* Stock-keeper, London.

1899. Dalziel, Hugh. *The Fox Terrier and All About It.* Upcott Gill, London.

1902. Lee, Rawdon B. *Fox Terrier.* Horace Cox, London.

1910. Astley, L. P. C. *The Perfect Fox Terrier in Word and Picture.* Illustrated Kennel News, London.

1910. Castle, Sidney. *A Monograph on the Fox Terrier.* Our Dogs, Manchester.

1923. Haynes, Williams. *The Fox Terrier.* Macmillan, New York.

1926. Skinner, A. J. *The Popular Fox Terrier.* Popular Dogs, London.

1927. Castle, Sidney. *Breeding Fox Terriers.* Underhill, Plymouth.

1932. Johns, Rowland. *Our Friend the Fox Terrier.* Methuen, London.

1933. Naylor, L. E. *The Modern Fox Terrier.*

1934. Ackerman, Irving C. *The Wire-Haired Fox Terrier.* Howard Watt, New York.

1935. Bruce, Rosslyn. *Fox Terrier Breeding, Smooth and Wire.* Strange, Eastbourne.

1938. Ackerman, Irving C. *The Complete Fox Terrier, Wire Haired and Smooth Coated.* Kegan Paul, London.

1938. Woodward, John. *The Fox Terrier.* Pearson, London.

1948. Skelly, George. *All About Fox Terriers.* Orange Judd, New York.

1949. Pardoe, J. H. *Fox Terriers.* Williams & Norgate, London.

1950. Bruce, Rosslyn. *The Popular Fox Terrier.* Popular Dogs, London.

1954. Daly, Macdonald. *Fox Terriers.* Chambers, London.

1955. Miller, Madeline. *Fox Terriers as Pets.* TFH, New Jersey.

1958. Beyer, Tilly. *Pet Fox Terrier.* All-Pets, Fond du Lac, Wisconsin.

1958. Dangerfield, Stanley. *The Wire-Haired Fox Terrier.* Nicholson & Watson, London.

1961. Miller, Evelyn. *How to Raise and Train a Fox Terrier.* Sterling, New York.

1961. Silvernail, Evelyn L. *The Complete Fox Terrier (Smooth and Wire).* Howell, New York.

1965. Williams, Elsie. *The Popular Fox Terrier.* Popular Dogs, London.

1970. Beak, Linda G. *Wire Fox Terriers.* Foyles, London.

1997. Diana Chads. *The World of Dogs: Fox Terrier.* TFH, New Jersey.

1998. Hearn, Ann D. *Wire Fox Terrier: A Complete and Reliable Handbook.* TFH, New Jersey.

YORKSHIRE TERRIER   ENGLAND

This breed was originally called the Broken-haired Scotch Terrier, before being recognized as a distinct breed. It was given its present name in 1870 and in modern times has acquired the nickname of Yorkie. It has also been recorded as the Halifax Blue and Tan Terrier, or the Yorkshire Blue and Tan Terrier. Although now exclusively a companion dog, its original function was to kill rats in the Yorkshire mines and cotton mills and to be small enough to carry in its owner's pocket.

At the height of the Industrial Revolution, in the Victorian era, when Scottish labourers came south of the border in search of work, they often brought with them their small Scottish terriers. In Yorkshire, these dogs crossed with local terriers and produced a new breed, called the Broken-haired Scotch Terrier. This small ratter became popular as a vermin-controller in the factories and mining centres. It was further improved with additional crosses involving other breeds. No two authors can agree on precisely which breeds were used. The following have all been mentioned at one time or another: the long-haired Leeds Terrier; the Black and Tan Terrier; the Skye Terrier; the Paisley Terrier; the Clydesdale Terrier; the Dandie Dinmont Terrier; the Manchester Terrier; and even the little Maltese. Out of this complex mixture came a diminutive, long-haired super-ratter, which was given the obvious name of the Yorkshire Terrier. Although small, it was larger than the modern Yorkie and well able to tackle even the fiercest of rodents.

The founding father of the breed was a dog named Huddersfield Ben, who was born in 1865. Within 20 years his offspring had helped to establish the new breed, which was recognized by the Kennel Club in 1886. Its appeal as a ladies' companion dog grew rapidly and with this new interest, selective breeding soon began to make the breed smaller and smaller, until its miniature condition eventually became its most characteristic feature. For some reason, its shiny, soft, straight hair, in its appealing colour mixture of grey and tan, did not shrink at the same rate as its body, and the final result was a minute dog with a dramatically, abnormally lengthy coat. In prize show dogs, the hair is so long that it has to be tied up in curlers when the little terriers are waiting to enter the ring.

Despite its small size, this dog is fearless, bossy, dynamic, tenacious, intelligent and lively. Because of its small size, it is better suited to urban life than are many other breeds.

References

1958. Miller, Evelyn. *Yorkshire Terriers as Pets.* TFH, New Jersey.

1958. Munday, Ethel. *The Popular Yorkshire Terrier.* Popular Dogs, London.

1958. Swan, Annie. *The Yorkshire Terrier Handbook, giving the origin and history of the breed, its show career, its points and breeding.* Dog Lover's Library, Nicholson & Watson, London.

1961. Whitehead, Hector F. *The Yorkshire Terrier.* Foyles, London.

1971. Huxham, Mona. *All about the Yorkshire Terrier.* Pelham, London.

1971. Martello, Aileen Markley. *The Yorkshire Terrier.* Arco, New York.

1975. Eikeland, Jessie. *Bogen om Yorkshire Terrier.* Clausen, Copenhagen. (Danish text)

1977. Bulgin, Gwen. *The Yorkshire Terrier.* Bartholomew, Edinburgh.

1978. Howard, Morris. *Your Yorkshire Terrier.* Denlinger's, USA.

1979. Donnelly, Kerry. *Yorkshire Terriers.* TFH, New Jersey.

1984. Brearley, Joan McDonald. *Book of the Yorkshire Terrier.* TFH, New Jersey.

1985. Kolbe, A. *Der Yorkshire Terrier.* (German text)

1986. Beuttler, Susan. *Das Buch vom Yorkie.* (German text)

1988. Ransom, Jackie. *A Dog Owner's Guide to Yorkshire Terriers.* Salamander, London.

1988. Sayer, Angela and Bunting, Edward. *Yorkshire Terriers.* Hamlyn, London.

1992. Fisher, Anne. *Yorkies Today.* Ringpress Books, Letchworth, Hertfordshire.

1992. Sameja, Osman A. *Yorkshire Terriers.* Crowood Press, Wiltshire.

1993. Gordon, Joan B. *The New Complete Yorkshire Terrier.* Howell, New York.

1994. McKay, Douglas. *Pet Owner's Guide to the Yorkshire Terrier.* Ringpress Books, Lydney, Gloucestershire.

1996. Ackerman, Lowell. *Dr Ackerman's Book of the Yorkshire Terrier.* TFH, New Jersey.

1996. Downing, Elizabeth. *Guide to Owning a Yorkshire Terrier.* TFH, New Jersey.

1996. Kriechbaumer, Armin, et al. *Yorkshire Terriers.* Barron, New York.

1996. Lane, Marion. *Yorkshire Terrier; an Owner's Guide to a Happy Healthy Pet.* Howell, New York.

1998. Kallen, Stuart A. *Yorkshire Terriers.*

1999. Downing, Elizabeth. *Yorkshire Terrier.* Popular Dog Library. Chelsea House Publishing.

1999. Dunbar, Ian (Editor). *Essential Yorkshire Terrier.* Howell, New York.

1999. Killick, Robert. *Yorkshire Terrier.* HarperCollins, London.

SCOTLAND

ABERDEEN TERRIER   SCOTLAND

This breed from the north-east of Scotland has often been confused with the Scottish Terrier. It was developed in the city of Aberdeen for the destruction of vermin. It has sometimes been recorded as the Aberdeenshire Terrier or simply as the Aberdeen.

The patron of the Aberdeen Terrier was a Dr Van Best of Aberdeen, who mated his dog – the founding father of the breed – with a variety of local terrier bitches. Some authorities have described the results of these crosses as no more than an early form of the more famous Scottish Terrier, but it differed from that breed in several respects and appears to have been a distinct type – a rival of the Scottie rather than its prototype.

The Aberdeen was said to be shorter in the leg and not so nimble as the Hard-coated Scotch Terrier. One author described it as 'a Skye Terrier in the rough'. Another said: 'In general appearance it resembles the Scottish Terrier, but is a rougher dog with a mixed coat.' It also had a much longer body than the Scottie.

The breed had its supporters and there was an early move to gain official recognition for it as a show dog. It first appeared in the ring in 1877, but despite the attempts to promote it, it failed to gain acceptance. In the 1880s further efforts were made to establish it, but it soon lost out to the Scottie. Its name vanished and it sank from view as the Scottie rose to new heights.

This victory pleased the early supporters of the Scottish Terrier who had been very critical of the 'rival' Aberdeen, belittling it by describing it as a local mongrel, a 'broken-haired, prick-eared terrier that haunts the streets of Aberdeen' and which, if put to work, was revealed as 'an arrant coward'. There is little evidence to back these remarks and they smack of the breed bigotry that was common in the terrier world at the time, when competing groups were trying to establish fixed breeding lines from the many unidentified and highly variable working terriers of the British Isles – dogs which had nearly always been bred for their digging ability and their tenacity, rather than their body shape, colour or form.

Those who liked the Aberdeen wrote in more glowing terms about it. It was said by them to be a rugged working dog, a 'rough-and-tumble varmint', strong, dour, hardy, plucky and full of terrier fire, ready and eager to work in all weathers. It was low on the leg, long in the back, with prick ears and a rough coat. This sounds closer to the truth, but now that the breed has gone, we can never be certain.

CAIRN TERRIER   SCOTLAND

Originally confused with other terriers and known by such names as Scotch Terrier, Highland Terrier, Tod-hunter, Skye Otter Terrier or Short-haired Skye Terrier, it did not appear in print as the Cairn Terrier until 1887. Its primary duty was vermin control in the bleak, rocky Highlands.

Its ancestors have been known since the 17th century in the Western Highlands of Scotland, especially on the Isle of Skye, where it was developed as a killer of the rodents that infested the cairns, or piles of stones, that were found on the game moors. These rodents were a threat to the game and it was the special task of the Cairn Terrier to reduce that threat. Packs of them were also used to rout out foxes, badgers and otters.

Although it is one of the smallest of the working terriers, it was game enough to deal with any mammal that had gone to ground.

A tough, plucky little dog with a thick, shaggy coat to protect it against the extreme weather conditions in the north of Scotland, the Cairn has remained remarkably faithful to its original form despite exposure to nearly a century of pedigree dog shows. While some other terriers have become beautified and exaggerated for the show-ring, the Cairn has stubbornly resisted change. It still looks remarkably like early portraits of the unnamed terriers of the Highlands that existed long before the various breeds became separated and labelled. It is close to the ancestral type that gave rise to the modern Scottish Terrier, the West Highland White, the Long-haired Skye, the Kyle and the Clydesdale.

The Cairn was first exhibited at a dog show in 1909, had its first breed club in 1910, was recognized by the Kennel Club in 1912, arrived on the dog-show scene in the United States in 1913 and grew steadily in popularity during the 1920s and '30s. In personality, it is noted for its spirited curiosity and its active alertness. It has also been praised for its hardiness and its intelligence.

References

1922. Rogers, Mrs Byron. *Cairn and Sealyham Terriers.* McBride, New York.

1926. Ross, Florence M. *The Cairn Terrier.* Our Dogs, Manchester.

1930. Beynon, J. H. *The Popular Cairn Terrier.* Popular Dogs, London.

1933. Johns, Rowland (Editor). *Our Friend the Cairn.* Methuen, London.

1936. Ash, Edward C. *The Cairn Terrier: its Care, Management and Exhibition.* Cassell, London.

1938. Woodward, John. *The Cairn Terrier.* Arthur Pearson, London.

1957. Casparsz, T. W. L. *The Cairn Terrier Handbook.* Nicholson & Watson, London.

1959. Whitehead, Hector. *Cairn Terriers.* Foyles, London.

1961. Beynon, J. H. and Fisher, Alex. *The Popular Cairn Terrier.* Popular Dogs, London.

1965. McCormack, Erliss. *How to Raise and Train a Cairn Terrier.* TFH, New Jersey.

1976. Jacobi, Girard A. *Your Cairn Terrier.* Denlinger's, USA.

1986. Anon. *The New Complete Cairn Terrier.* Howell, New York.

1987. Camino. *Cairn Terrier Champions: 1952–1986.* Camino Books.

1995. Marcum, Betty. *The New Cairn Terrier.* Howell, New York.

1996. Carter, Christine. *The Cairn Terrier.* TFH, New Jersey.

1999. Lehman, Patricia F. *Cairn Terriers: Everything about Purchase, Care, Nutrition, Grooming, Behavior, and Training.* Barron, New York.

CLYDESDALE TERRIER   SCOTLAND

The Clydesdale was originally called the Silk-coated Skye Terrier, the Glasgow Skye, the Glasgow Fancy Skye Terrier, the Glasgow Terrier, the Paisley Skye or the Paisley Terrier. The breed, though descended from a working terrier, was created specifically for the show-ring.

This now extinct breed was a silk-haired variety of the Skye Terrier, or, to put it another way, was a Skye Terrier with a Yorkshire Terrier coat. In early dog shows it was entered simply as a Skye, but then in the 1880s it was treated as a separate breed. Its supporters saw it as a more appealing form of the Skye, but the Skye enthusiasts referred to it disparagingly as a fancy terrier or a Skye 'reject'.

When these new silky Skyes started winning the prizes at the early dog shows, the traditional Skye owners angrily insisted that silky coats should be outlawed in their breed. And so it came about that a new breed of dog, now called the Paisley Terrier, was established, distinct and separate from its ancestral Skyes. There was still a great deal of snarling and growling between the rivals (the owners, not the dogs) but once the traditionalists had won the day and established that their non-silky Skye was the true Skye, matters settled down.

The Paisley soon lost ground and was on the verge of extinction, but towards the end of the 19th century a small band of enthusiasts started showing them as a special class at local dog shows. Soon, most of the Scottish shows included them, and their popularity, purely as show dogs, was on the increase again. At about this point their name was changed from Paisley to Clydesdale (to give the breed a new lease of life and distance it from the earlier disputes) and it was under this new title that it even managed to spread south and to be given a class by the Kennel Club in London. Eventually more squabbles about the true form of the dog broke out among breeders, and support for the breed waned. By the 1930s it was in rapid decline and never recovered. By the time World War II had ended, it had vanished for ever.

Most authorities accept that the Clydesdale was simply a modified Skye, bred from individuals with unusually soft, silky coats, but some feel that it was the result of crosses between Skye and Yorkshire Terriers. Two features favour the latter view: the colour and texture of the long coat of the Clydesdale was almost exactly the same as that of the Yorkie, and the size of the Clydesdale was slightly reduced, compared with the traditional pure-bred Skye.

DANDIE DINMONT TERRIER   SCOTLAND

It was originally known as Dandie Dinmont's Terrier, but this name was later condensed to its present form. Other early names for this breed were Charlie's Hope Terrier and the Mustard and Pepper Terrier (or Pepper and Mustard Terrier). As a working terrier it was a vermin-destroyer, specializing in rodents, but later extended its activities to include rabbits, otters and badgers.

This is a dog with a name as unusual as its appearance. Like so many terriers, its ancestors could boast no specific breed name. The earliest dog books refer to all terriers simply as 'the terrier', as if they constituted a single breed, like the Foxhound. But each locality bred its own version of the ancestral terrier and these began to differ from

region to region. Eventually they were so different from one another that they had to be given separate names and treated as distinct breeds.

The Dandie Dinmont, the ancestors of which, since at least the 17th century, had been popular along the southern borders of Scotland, was one of the very first to be given a special name, and acquired it in an unusual way. In the year 1800, a border farmer called James Davidson obtained a pair of this type of terrier and called them Tarr (short for Mustard) and Pepper, the first being sandy and the second grey in colour. When Sir Walter Scott was writing his famous novel *Guy Mannering* (published in 1814), he based one of his characters on Davidson and gave him the fictional name of Dandie Dinmont. Although Scott claimed he never knew Davidson, there is little doubt that Dandie was based on him because, in the book, Dandie Dinmont owned a pack of terriers called Auld Pepper, Auld Mustard, Young Pepper, Young Mustard, Little Pepper and Little Mustard. After the novel was published, Davidson's friends started teasing him by calling him Dandie Dinmont, and soon his dogs were known as Dandie Dinmont's dogs. Other farmers with similar terriers took up this name and the old, nameless working dog became transformed into an identified breed. By 1876 it has acquired its own breed club.

The unusual appearance of the breed is largely thanks to the fact that its very long, low-slung body is surmounted by a head wearing what looks like a white fur crash-helmet. This strange topknot, although present in early examples of the breed, has been increasingly exaggerated in modern show dogs, as have the length of the body and the length of the ears, to create one of the most distinctive of all terriers. The origin of the breed is not known, which has inevitably led to many theories. Some feel that the breed is simply a local descendant of the 'primitive' terriers of Scotland and only terrier blood runs in its veins. Others think that the only way it could have acquired such a long, low body and such long ears would have been if some Dachshund crosses were introduced. They suggest that Dachshunds could have arrived on the scene via travelling gypsies returning from trips across the English Channel. There have many other suggestions, but the true facts will never be known for certain.

In personality the Dandie Dinmont is dignified, reserved, independent and, like all terriers, highly intelligent. It is tolerant of quite cramped living conditions and is playful and friendly with children. It is an excellent guard dog because its unusually loud, deep bark gives the impression that a house is occupied by a much larger animal.

References

1885. Cook, Charles. *The Dandie Dinmont Terrier: its History and Characteristics.* Douglas, Edinburgh.

1938. Johns, Rowland (Editor). *Our Friends the Dandie Dinmont and Skye Terriers.* Methuen, London.

1959. Gordon, John F. *The Dandie Dinmont Terrier.* Nicholson & Watson, London.

1964. Kirby, Mrs William M. *How to Raise and Train a Dandie Dinmont.* TFH, New Jersey.

1998. Kirby, William M. *The Dandie Dinmont Terrier. A Complete and Reliable Handbook.* TFH, New Jersey.

PITTENWEEM TERRIER   SCOTLAND

A conspicuous white terrier from Fyfeshire, the Pittenweem was developed for going to ground against vermin.

This extinct dog was a white form of the Scottish Terrier, bred by a Dr Flaxman of Pittenweem. White puppies kept appearing among his Scottish Terrier litters and he decided to cross these with one another to create a pure-breeding white strain. This he did with some success, until he had reached the point where he considered his Pittenweems to be a distinct breed in their own right.

However, when these animals were inspected by Colonel Malcolm of Poltalloch, who was developing his own white strain (which he called the Poltalloch Terrier and which was eventually to become the popular West Highland White Terrier), they did not appeal to him. There was too much Scottie in them for his taste and he declined to introduce them into his breeding programme, which was based more on the Cairn Terrier type. His rejection led to the Pittenweem's decline and ultimately to its becoming extinct.

POLTALLOCH TERRIER   SCOTLAND

This breed takes its name from a small town in Argyllshire. It was developed to go to earth for fox and otter, but was also a good ratter.

Originally described as a 'yellowish-white variant' of the small, brown working terriers so common in Scotland, this breed was created by a Colonel Malcolm of Poltalloch, back in Victorian times. The Colonel wrote of it: 'A good one at his best looks like a handsome deerhound, reduced in some marvellous way... As for wisdom, make one your friend and he will know everything and do it.'

The Poltalloch had a bristly coat, pricked ears, short straight legs and unusually large teeth. In the late 19th century, the Colonel recorded its colour as follows: 'They are not invariably white, but run between creamy-white and sandy.' This was eventually to change. Colonel Malcolm continued to improve his terrier breed and to lighten its coat until it was, finally, a pure white dog, at which point it ceased to be the Poltalloch and became transformed into the West Highland White Terrier.

SCOTTISH TERRIER   SCOTLAND

Originally referred to as the Hard-coated Scotch Terrier, the Die-Hard or the Wire-haired Terrier, this breed was called the Scottish Terrier for the first time in 1879 and has retained this official title ever since. Its popular nickname today is the Scottie. Although it is now primarily a show dog, its original function was vermin control.

Descended from the ancestral Highland Terrier, this rough-coated breed was developed in Perthshire as a tough, muscular, compact, short-legged working dog that would go to earth to attack any kind of farm pest. In 1879 Captain Gordon Murray gave it its present name and started a careful breeding improvement plan. In 1882 it acquired its first breed club and very soon the Scottie's type was fixed. It arrived in the United States in 1883 and became even more popular there than in Britain. The modern show version sports a dramatic amount of facial hair including excessively bushy eyebrows and a prominent beard, appendages that were much more modest in earlier examples of the breed. One minor weakness of the breed is that it has a tendency to develop muscle cramps, so much so that they are referred to as 'Scottie cramps'.

In personality, this rugged, hardy little breed has been called lion-hearted, conceited, aloof, dour, bold, headstrong, businesslike, loyal and reserved. One author summed up its temperament by describing it as 'not a gushing breed' and another likened it to a sergeant major carrying out an inspection. In its working days it was said to be exceptionally efficient at disposing of its quarry, especially rats. One Scottie called Billy, put in a room with 100 live rats for a wager concerning how long he would take to kill them all, is reputed to have managed his task in the astonishing time of only seven minutes. In the 1930s, as a pet, the Scottie became popular with national leaders. Hitler gave two to his mistress, Eva Braun, and President Roosevelt kept one called Fala in the White House.

References

1894. Green, James E. *The Scottish Terrier and the Irish Terrier.*
1899. Robertson, James. *Historical Sketches of The Scottish Terrier.* Robertson, Leeds.
1906. Davies, C. J. *The Scottish Terrier.* Everett, London.
1909. McCandlish, W. L. *The Scottish Terrier.* Our Dogs, Manchester.
1913. Buckley, Holland. *The Scottish Terrier.* Illustrated Kennel News, London.
1922. Haynes, William. *The Scottish and Irish Terriers.* Macmillan, New York.
1923. Maxtee, J. *Scotch and Irish Terriers.*
1928. Gabriel, Dorothy. *The Scottish Terrier; its Breeding and Management.* Dog World, London.

1932. Ewing, Fayette C. *The Book of The Scottish Terrier.* Orange Judd, New York.

1932. Johns, Rowland (Editor). *Our Friend the Scottish Terrier.* Methuen, London.

1934. Bruette, William A. *The Scottish Terrier.* Howard Watt, New York.

1934. Caspersz, Dorothy (Editor). *Scottish Terrier Pedigrees.* Higgs, Henley-on-Thames, Oxfordshire.

1936. Ash, Edward. *The Scottish Terrier.* Dog Owner's Handbook.

1938. Woodward, John. *The Scottish Terrier.* Arthur Pearson, London.

1949. Daly, Macdonald. *The Scottish Terrier.* Findon Publications, London.

1951. Caspersz, Dorothy. *The Scottish Terrier Handbook.* Nicholson & Watson, London.

1958. Snethen, Mr and Mrs T. H. *Pet Scottish Terrier.* All-Pets, Fond du Lac, Wisconsin.

1959. Miller, Evelyn. *Scotties as Pets.* TFH, New Jersey.

1970. Kirk, Thomas Allen. *This is the Scottish Terrier.* TFH, New Jersey.

1976. Caspersz, Dorothy. *The Scottish Terrier.* Popular Dogs, London.

1978. Marvin, John T. *The New Complete Scottish Terrier.* Howell, New York.

1995. Lee. *The Official Book of the Scottish Terrier.*

1996. Cooke, Cindy. *The New Scottish Terrier.* Howell, New York.

1998. Snethen, T. H. *Scottish Terriers.* TFH, New Jersey.

SKYE TERRIER   SCOTLAND

This breed was originally called the Isle of Skye Terrier. Its primary role was to go to earth to kill vermin.

In its working days, the Skye Terrier, from the rugged Western Isles in the north of Scotland, was a tough, hard-coated earth dog renowned for its courage in pursuing its quarry into underground burrows, and equipped with the short legs appropriate for such a task. The modern Skye has been modified more than most terriers for its new role as a show dog. Its body has been enlarged and elongated and its striking, bat-like ears have become even more imposing.

In 1842 a Skye Terrier was acquired by Queen Victoria, who became so attached to this type of terrier that she began to breed them in the royal kennels. As a result of this royal patronage, word soon spread about the breed, and its popularity widened. Later, Queen Alexandria also owned Skyes. The first image of a Skye appeared in Volume XIX of Jardine's Naturalist's Library in 1843. The dog shown there displayed the huge prick ears so characteristic of the breed, indicating that these were already impressive even in the early days of this terrier.

The most famous of the Skyes was a dog called Greyfriars Bobby. When its owner, John Gray, died and was buried in Greyfriars Churchyard in Edinburgh, the dog refused to leave his grave. It was turned away but each day it came back. Eventually people took pity on it and began to feed it. It continued to keep vigil at the grave every day for 14 years (from 1858 to 1872) until it, too, finally died and was laid to rest next to its master. Its astonishing devotion was honoured by the erection of a bronze statue which stands in Edinburgh to this day.

The Skye Terrier was one of the breeds to compete at the first major dog show, held in Birmingham in 1860. Its own breed club was formed in 1876. The official breed standard for the Skye calls for a hard coat, but in recent years this has become softer, presumably because it looks more glamorous. This has annoyed the working-terrier enthusiasts, who see the change not as an improvement but as a decline. One of them recently complained that the modern Skye's coat is 'the most unsuitable jacket ever to cover a working terrier', pointing out that it quickly balls up in snow, mud or clay.

In show dogs, the ears may be erect or drooped, but the famous prick ears are generally more favoured. In personality the Skye is said to be wary of strangers, and has been described as a one-man dog. It is always completely devoted to its family and is rarely aggressive.

References

1903. Hutton, Henry T. *The True Story of Greyfriars Bobby*. Oliver & Boyd, Edinburgh.
1907. Wilmer, Agnes. *The Skye Terrier*. Illustrated Kennel News, London.
1912. Atkinson, Eleanor. *Greyfriars Bobby*. Harper, New York.
1938. Johns, Rowland (Editor). *Our Friends the Dandie Dinmont and Skye Terriers*. Methuen, London.
1951. Miles, Lady Marcia. *The Skye Terrier*. Privately published.
1960. Nicholas, Anna K. *The Skye Terrier*.
1962. Atkinson, Eleanor. *Greyfriars Bobby*. Penguin, London.
1962. Montgomery, E. S. *The Complete Skye Terrier*. Howell, New York.
1965. Weiss, Seymour N. *How to Raise and Train a Skye Terrier*. TFH, New Jersey.
1975. Brearley, Joan McDonald and Nicholas, Anna Katherine. *This is the Skye Terrier*. TFH, New Jersey.
1980. MacGregor, Forbes. *The Story of Greyfriars Bobby*. Ampersand, Edinburgh.
1997. Threlfall, Sue. *The Skye Terrier*. TFH, New Jersey.

WEST HIGHLAND WHITE TERRIER   SCOTLAND

Originally known as the Highlander or the West Highlander, this breed was given its present title when it became a show dog in the early years of the 20th century. Today it is usually referred to simply as the Westie. It began life as a working terrier, sent to earth against rats, rabbits, badgers or foxes.

The Westie owes it existence to an unfortunate accident. A certain Colonel Malcolm was out hunting one day with his brown-coloured terriers – dogs close in type to the Cairn Terrier. He aimed at what he thought was a fox and killed it, only to discover that

it was his favourite terrier. He vowed that he would never make such a mistake again and set about creating a white breed of dog that could never be confused with a brown-furred fox. As luck would have it, there were often whitish puppies in Cairn litters. In the past, these had usually been rejected as unsuitable. He reversed this process, removing only the coloured offspring and keeping the white ones. Before long he had produced a true-breeding near-white terrier and called it the Poltalloch, after the Argyllshire estate where he hunted.

As the years passed, he improved the colour of the Poltalloch's coat until it was virtually pure white. Similar white dogs were being bred elsewhere, but the Colonel preferred not to incorporate those into his bloodlines. The Roseneath was one of these other white terriers and it was this that was first sent to dog shows, appearing under that name at the Crystal Palace show in 1899. At this point there was confusion between the very similar Roseneaths and Poltallochs, and the problem was solved by introducing the general title of West Highland White Terrier.

Terriers were first shown under this new name at Edinburgh in 1904 and at the LKA in 1906. The Kennel Club in London formally accepted them in 1907, when they were first shown at Crufts. From that point onwards the Westie became more and more favoured as a show dog, until, by the end of the 20th century, it had risen to a point where it was more popular than any other terrier breed, and was, indeed, the third most popular of all dog breeds — something Colonel Malcolm could never have imagined.

As a working dog the Westie was renowned for its courage. It was said that 'no water was too cold, no earth too deep' for this tenacious breed. Its one weakness was that it was too independent to work in a pack. Later, as a show dog, it had the great advantage of an appealingly broad head, an unusually bouncy gait and a jaunty, lively spirit that showed it off especially well when parading in the ring.

In personality, the Westie shows great adaptability to different kinds of home environment, and this is obviously the secret of its huge success. It has been described by one enthusiast as being 'as Scotch as a bagpipe'.

References

1911. Buckley, Holland. *The West Highland White Terrier; a Monograph*. Illustrated Kennel News, London.

1930. Beynon, J. W. H. *The Popular West Highland White Terrier*.

1935. Johns, Rowland (Editor). *Our Friend the West Highland White Terrier*. Methuen, London.

1961. Marvin, John T. *The Complete West Highland White Terrier*. Howell, New York.

1963. Pacey, May. *West Highland White Terriers*. Foyles, London.

1964. Sherman, Florence J. *How to Raise and Train a West Highland White Terrier*. TFH, New Jersey.

1967. Dennis, Mary. *The West Highland White Terrier*. Popular Dogs, London.

1972. Cartledge, J. and Cartledge, L. *The Complete and Illustrated West Highland White Terrier.*

1972. Hands, Barbara. *The West Highland White Terrier.* Bartholemew, Edinburgh.

1982. Sherman, Florence. *How to Raise and Train a West Highland White Terrier.* TFH, New Jersey.

1989. Faherty. *Westies from Head to Tail.*

1992. Tattersall, Derek. *Westies Today.* Howell, New York.

1993. Nicholas, Anna Katherine. *The Book of the West Highland White Terrier.* Thomasson, Grant & Howell.

1994. Bolle-Kleinbub, Ingrid and Metzger, Christine. *West Highland White Terriers.* Barron, New York.

1995. Cleland, Sheila. *Pet Owner's Guide to the West Highland White Terrier.* Ringpress Books, Lydney, Gloucestershire.

1996. Ackerman, Lowell. *Dr Ackerman's Book of the West Highland White Terrier.* TFH, New Jersey.

1996. Wallace, Martin. *Guide to Owning a West Highland White Terrier.* TFH, New Jersey.

1996. Weiss, Seymour. *The West Highland White Terrier; An Owner's Guide to a Happy Healthy Pet.* Howell, New York.

1998. Barnes, Julia. *All About Your West Highland White Terrier.* Ringpress Books, Lydney, Gloucestershire.

1998. Gentry, Daphne S. *The New West Highland White Terrier.* Macmillan.

1999. Dunbar, Ian (Editor). *The Essential West Highland White Terrier.* Howell, New York.

1999. Killick, Robert. *West Highland White Terrier.* HarperCollins, London.

WALES

SEALYHAM TERRIER WALES

This breed, which was originally also known as the Pembrokeshire Terrier or the Sealy Ham Terrier, is named after the Welsh estate where it was first developed. Its primary role was to go to earth for otters, as support to a pack of Otterhounds.

The origin of this Welsh breed is reasonably clear. It was created by an eccentric hunter, a retired army captain called John Edwardes, who developed it in the middle of the 19th century to work alongside his pack of Otterhounds. His estate at Sealy Ham on the Seal River, in the south-west corner of Wales, was rich with game and he wanted to develop a terrier more courageous, more assertive and more fearless than any other. In his search for the perfect terrier, he mixed together several breeds, including, it is thought, Bull Terriers, Cheshire Terriers, Staffordshire Bull Terriers, West Highland Whites, Wire-haired Fox Terriers, Dandie Dinmonts and even Corgis. No two authorities can agree about the exact mixture he employed and the Captain kept no records to help us. Whatever its precise pedigree, there is no doubt that he managed to produce a delightful, rough-haired, predominantly white little terrier that was game for anything. In addition to otters, it went to earth for foxes, badgers and polecats. Nothing was too difficult for it. The manner in which the Captain improved his strain was, to say the least, blunt. If any young terrier showed a reluctance to stand its ground or to kill, he shot it on the spot.

The Sealyham first appeared at a local dog show in 1903. A specialist breed club followed in 1908, and by 1911 it was officially recognized by the Kennel Club in London and also by the American Kennel Club in the United States. As a show dog it displayed a gradual tendency to become heavier and more docile. By the 1920s and 1930s it had become a great favourite as a companion dog and, despite its early history, had grown into one of the most friendly of all terriers and was excellent with children. Working-terrier men, however, felt that it was being softened and spoiled and some went to great lengths to maintain the original, smaller and more aggressive version.

References

1922. Lucas, Jocelyn. *The Sealyham Terrier.* Crumbie, Leicester.

1922. Marples, Theo. *The Sealyham Terrier.* Our Dogs, Manchester.

1922. Rogers, Mrs Byron. *Cairn and Sealyham Terriers.* McBride, New York.

1929. Lucas, Jocelyn. *The New Book of the Sealyham.* Simpkin & Marshall, London.

1933. Johns, Rowland (Editor). *Our Friend the Sealyham.* Methuen, London.

1938. Barber, Winifred. *The Sealyham Terrier.* Our Dogs, Manchester.

1956. Chenuz, Frida J. *Sealyhams.* Benn, London.

1960. Chenuz, Frida J. *Sealyham Terriers.* Foyles, London.

1965. Weiss, Seymour. *How to Raise and Train a Sealyham Terrier.* TFH, New Jersey.

1988. Camino. *Sealyham Terrier Champions: 1911–1987.* Camino.

1997. Weiss, Seymour. *Sealyham Terrier, a Complete and Reliable Handbook.* TFH, New Jersey.

WELSH TERRIER   WALES

This breed was originally shown under the cumbersome name of the Welsh Black-and-Tan Rough-coated Terrier. Its primary function was to go to earth in the hunt for foxes, badgers, otters and martens.

The Welsh Terrier of today looks rather like a smaller version of the Airedale. Descended from the old broken-coated Black and Tan Terrier, with minor additions of Airedale, Lakeland and Irish Terrier, this long-legged breed was developed in the 18th century to hunt over the rough country of the Welsh mountains. Its predecessors, of which few details are known, were present in the Welsh

mountains for several centuries before this. There are records of a similar type ('a black, red-bellied terrier') dating from as early as 1450. Three centuries later, in 1750, a portrait of a Welsh farmer depicts an accompanying dog that is clearly a Welsh Terrier. The legs of this breed were long enough for it to be able to keep up with the hounds and there are hunting documents, also from the 18th century, recording the use of such dogs alongside the hound packs.

A specialist breed club was formed for this terrier as early as 1885. By 1898 it was being shown in North America and by 1900 the Welsh Terrier Club of America was already established. The show-dog version of this working terrier has the same tenacious, rugged temperament as its ancestors, but has been improved visually, becoming more elegant in profile, with hairier legs, bigger whiskers and a bushy beard.

In personality, the wiry-haired Welsh Terrier has been described as courageous, intelligent and eager to please, with the advantage of being easier to handle than some of its close terrier relatives. Despite this, for some reason it has never become one of the most popular breeds of terrier.

References

1959. Thomas, I. Morlais. *The Welsh Terrier Handbook*. Nicholson & Watson, London.
1968. Schneider, Earl. *Know Your Welsh Terrier*. Pet Library, New York.
1993. McLennan, Bardi. *The Welsh Terrier Leads the Way*. TFH, New Jersey.
Maxtee, J. *English and Welsh Terriers*.

IRELAND

GLEN OF IMAAL TERRIER   IRELAND

This terrier is named after the locality where it originated, south of Dublin, in County Wicklow. Although it is universally known as the Glen of Imaal Terrier, there was a recent move by the Irish Kennel Club to have this altered to the cumbersome title of Irish Glen of Imaal Terrier. Since everyone familiar with this ancient breed knows full well that it hails from Ireland, this alteration has the hallmark of bureaucratic overkill. But although it has been ignored in Britain, it is only fair to point out that the title has been formally accepted by the FCI (in 1994) and the AKC (in 1997). To lovers of the breed it is, in any case, known simply as the Glen. A low-slung dog, it was originally developed to go to earth for badgers.

This is one of the earliest of the terrier breeds that are native to Ireland, having been known from at least the 17th century. It has changed little during the passing years and even today's carefully groomed show champions remain very close in type to their early working ancestors, both in appearance and in temperament. It has been aptly described by one author as a dog that is 'endearing rather than handsome'.

The Glen was first recognized as a distinct breed by the Irish Kennel Club in 1933 and in the same year it gained its first specialist breed club and appeared competitively in the show-ring. It thrived for a while, but then began to lose favour and its club was eventually disbanded. By the 1950s it was nearly extinct, but survived thanks to a handful of devoted breeders. In 1971 a new association was formed to foster the breed. Their endeavours succeeded and there are now examples in a number of different countries in Europe and North America, especially Germany, Italy, Sweden and the United States. Even today, however, it remains an uncommon breed compared with most other terriers. In 1998 the Kennel Club in London recorded only 58 new registrations, making it one of the rarest of all their officially recognized terriers.

In personality it was always a fearless attacker and, in addition to its badger-hunting duties, was also frequently used in locally staged dog fights. These took place weekly, on Saturdays, and were accompanied by much gambling and drinking. Around the home, when it was not out hunting or fighting, it proved to be a useful ratter and in early times was also employed as a kitchen turnspit. When out and about in the wild countryside, it became what was described as a typical 'devil-may-care Irishman', full of mischief and lively curiosity. Although a short-legged breed, it was extremely athletic when circumstances demanded it. As a family dog, however, it remained remarkably gentle with its owners and tolerant of their children.

The locality in the Wicklow Mountains that gave the dog its name has always been a rugged, desolate place which has demanded rugged inhabitants, both human and canine. Today, it is uninhabited and impossible to visit because it has become a military zone, owned by the Irish Ministry of Defence.

IRISH TERRIER   IRELAND

This has sometimes been called the Irish Red Terrier because, since the 1880s, its coat colour has become diagnostic of the breed. A versatile terrier, it has been used against rats, rabbits, foxes, otters and badgers.

Once described as 'the poor man's sentinel, the farmer's friend and the gentleman's favourite', this is the oldest of the four Irish terrier breeds. It was first shown in 1870, but at this stage there was some variability in the dog's appearance. Then two early champions called Killiney Boy and Erin appeared on the scene and effectively became the founders of the modern breed. One of their offspring, a bitch called Poppy, had a

bright red coat and it is she who appears to have endowed the modern Irish Terrier with its characteristic colour. All her puppies displayed the same attractive hue and, by the end of the 19th century, all other colours had been eliminated from the breed.

The wiry-coated Irish Terrier's development as a pedigree dog had been organized by a specialist breed club set up in Dublin as early as 1879, with a branch in London. Some English terrier specialists poured scorn on this Irish cousin of their beloved dogs, but the hostility soon faded, helped by the courageous role the dogs played as messengers in the carnage of the front lines of World War I.

It is a lanky dog for a terrier, built as much for speed as for digging, and easily capable of keeping up with the hounds. A fiery, spirited dog, sometimes referred to as the 'daredevil' of terriers, it is said to be reckless in its fearlessness when attacking prey or enemy, but tender and affectionate with its owners. Its extraordinary bravery is epitomised by an anecdote from Africa, where an Irish Terrier was accompanying big-game hunters and was seen to bolt a lion by hanging on to the great cat's tail with its teeth.

References

1894. Green, James E. *The Scottish Terrier and the Irish Terrier.*
1907. Jowett, F. M. *The Irish Terrier.* Our Dogs, Manchester.
1922. Haynes, William. *The Scottish and Irish Terriers.* Macmillan, New York.
1923. Maxtee, J. *Scotch and Irish Terriers.*
1925. Thorndike, John R. *The Irish Terrier Standard Simplified.* Field & Fancy, New York.
1935. Johns, Rowland (Editor). *Our Friends the Irish and Kerry Blue Terriers.* Methuen, London.
1937. Large. *The Kind Companion (Irish Terrier).*
1948. Irish Terrier Club of America. *A Book of the Breed.* Published by the Club, Battleboro', Vermont.
1959. Jones, Edna Howard. *Irish Terriers.* Our Dogs, Manchester.
1965. Kidd, Drusilla and Kidd, George. *How to Raise and Train an Irish Terrier.* TFH, New Jersey.

KERRY BLUE TERRIER   IRELAND

Officially named as the National Dog of Ireland, this breed from County Kerry in the southwest of Ireland is also known as the Irish Blue Terrier. Its original function was to kill rats and to take to the water in the hunt for otters.

For some reason, pedigree dogs and cats that display an attractive grey coat colour are optimistically referred to as 'blue'. This applies to the Kerry Blue, which displays an attractive pale grey coat with dark, almost black extremities. The puppies are born black and their colour gradually fades until, by the time they are one or two years old, the adult colouring has arrived. The coat has a 'silky-woolly', astrakhan quality reminiscent of the coat of the Bedlington Terrier, and it has been suggested that the breed was created by crossing the indigenous Irish Terrier with imported Bedlingtons. But the truth is that nobody is certain about the beginnings of this handsome dog, which is no doubt why the legend about its ancestor swimming ashore from a shipwreck in the Bay of Tralee remains popular to this day.

In origin, this is a versatile, hard-working farmer's dog, not only able to assist with vermin-control and hunting, but also a reliable house guard. It existed as a working dog for centuries before its striking appearance attracted the attention of the pedigree show-dog world. A few examples appeared in local Irish dog shows in the late 19th century, but then, in 1920, the Dublin Blue Terrier Club was formed and its fame began to spread beyond Irish shores. The breed was officially recognized in 1922 by the then new Irish Kennel Club. In the same year, a specialist breed club was formed in England and the dog's breed standard was established. The Kerry Blue reached its peak of popularity during the interwar years, but for some reason has remained a minority interest in the post-war period. The Kennel Club in London records fewer than 300 registrations in 1998 (compared, for example, with over 15,000 registrations for the West Highland White Terrier).

In temperament this has been described as a fierce, even surly dog, but one who is also highly intelligent, charming and trustworthy. It does not, however, mix well with cats, a 1922 report stating: 'His disposition seems well nigh faultless, if a slight tendency to diminish the cat population is excepted.'

References

1928. Clarke, Egerton. *The Popular Kerry Blue Terrier.* Popular Dogs, London.

1933. Handy, Violet E. *The Modern Kerry Blue Terrier.* Our Dogs, Manchester.

1935. Johns, Rowland (Editor). *Our Friends the Irish and Kerry Blue Terriers.* Methuen, London.

1950. Montgomery, E. S. *The Complete Kerry Blue Terrier.* Denlinger's, Fairfax, Virginia.

1964. Schweppe, Frederick. *How to Raise and Train a Kerry Blue Terrier.* TFH, New Jersey.

1976. U.S. Kerry Blue Terrier Club. *U.S. Kerry Blue Terrier Club. 50th Anniversary Edition.*

1982. Izant, Edith. *The Kerry Blue Terrier.* Denlinger's, Fairfax, Virginia.

Schneider, Earl (Editor). *Know Your Kerry Blue Terrier.* Pet Library, New York.

SOFT-COATED WHEATEN TERRIER   IRELAND

Previously known as the Irish Wheaten Terrier, or the Wheaten Irish Terrier, this breed was originally developed for going to earth against badgers and foxes.

The soft and silky coat of this breed, which should be the colour of ripening wheat, is its crowning glory and endows it with its modern title. In other respects it is a typical working terrier, tough and fearless in the field and friendly and loyal in the home. Although it is an old breed that has been present in Ireland for centuries, its early owners paid little attention to a precise breed standard. As a result, there was too much variability for it to be taken seriously as a show dog. For this reason it was late arriving in the competitive show-ring and it was not officially recognized by the Irish Kennel Club until 1937. It was first exhibited in a dog show in Ireland in 1938. It was not fully recognized by the AKC until 1973 and in England it was not awarded Challenge Certificates until as recently as 1975. To this day it remains one of the less common terrier breeds.

Wheaten enthusiasts claim that it is their breed that was ancestral to the other Irish terriers, its coat colour being turned blue to create the Kerry Blue, and red to create the Irish (Red) Terrier, and its legs being shortened to produce a badger specialist, the Glen of Imaal Terrier. This may well be true, but it should be remembered that all breed enthusiasts like to envisage their own particular type of dog as being the ancestral form from which others have sprung, so caution is needed. But in their favour is the fact that the Wheaten is a versatile dog which, when not out hunting and going to earth, could be found taking on secondary roles such as guarding the house, destroying vermin, driving cattle or even herding sheep. In others words, it was the perfect all-rounder from which the more specialized breeds could easily have been developed.

References

1965. O'Connor, Margaret A. *Raise, Train, a Soft-Coated Wheaten Terrier.*

1977. Holmes, Maureen. *The Wheaten Years.* Alpha Beta Press, Orland Park, Illinois.

1990. O'Connor, Margaret A. *Soft Coated Wheaten Terriers.* TFH, New Jersey.

1991. Vesley, Roberta A. *The Complete Soft Coated Wheaten Terrier.*

1992. Holmes, Maureen. *The Softcoated Wheaten Terrier.* Racmo, Meppel.

1997. Wyatt, Glenda. *Trimming the Soft Coated Wheaten Terrier.*

1999. Vesley, Roberta A. *The Soft Coated Wheaten Terrier, Coat of Honey — Heart of Gold.* Howell, New York.

2000. Bonham, Margaret H. *Soft Coated Wheaten Terriers: Everything About Purchase, Care, Feeding and Housing.* Barron, New York.

Shoemaker, Marjorie C. *Soft Coated Wheaten Terrier.*

BELGIUM

BRUSSELS GRIFFON

BELGIUM

Also known as the Griffon Bruxellois, this little dog was first developed as a rat-killer for stables where horse-drawn carriages were kept.

The ancestors of these small, reddish-brown dogs were the terrier-like pest-controllers of the Belgian cities of earlier centuries. Their main role was to destroy the vermin that infested the urban stables, and because of this they were sometimes referred to as the Stable Griffon, or Griffon d'Ecurie. During the day they could often be seen perched on cab-drivers' seats, attracting attention as their owners plied for business.

These tiny dogs appear in Flemish art from a very early date and it is clear that, in their original form, they had a less flattened face than they do today. The best-known example appears in the famous 1434 painting of the Arnolfini Couple, in which Van Eyck has placed a small Griffon in the foreground (symbolizing faithfulness). This dog has a longer coat and a longer face than those of the modern Griffon and this would appear to have been the norm during the centuries when the dogs were humble ratters.

In the 1870s their fortune was to change because it was at this point that they acquired royal patronage, becoming the favourites of the Belgian queen, Henrietta Maria. With their elevated social status they soon became the darlings of the upper classes, and much greater care was taken with their breeding. Attempts were made to increase their appeal and they were crossed with several other breeds to modify their appearance. In the process, their bodies shrank in size and their faces became flatter and more human.

Authors fail to agree about the details of the crosses that brought about these changes. Germans claim that their monkey-faced Affenpinscher was the main influence. (Inevitably, Belgians prefer to think that it was their Griffon that helped to create the Affenpinscher.) Others claim that the flattened face came from the Pug. Yorkshire Terriers, King Charles Spaniels and the Dutch Smoushond have all been cited as possible crosses. We will probably never know the whole truth, but the result was an immensely appealing little dog which remained a favourite high-status companion long after the horse-drawn cabs had disappeared and its original role as a lowly ratter had vanished.

At first sight, it is mysterious that such an appealing breed has not become more popular worldwide. Why, for example, is the Cavalier King Charles Spaniel 70 times more numerous in Britain than the Griffon? The answer, sadly, is that because of its genetic history it has accumulated major reproductive problems. The bitches often fail to conceive and, when they do, they have serious difficulties giving birth. Caesarean deliveries have become commonplace. Puppies that are born are often delicate and the litters are unusually small. Often there is only a single puppy, and mortality is high (60 per cent in the first few weeks). This makes the breeding of the Griffon a hazardous business and many people, despite their love of the breed, prefer to turn elsewhere. (It is hard to see how these problems have arisen, because in the 1920s, at the peak of the breed's popularity, it was reported that there were 5,000 brood bitches in Brussels alone, each producing litters of five to seven puppies.)

References

1926. Rhodes, Mabel Parker. *The Cult of the Griffon Bruxellois.* Watmough, London.

1960. Cousens, Marjorie. *Griffon Bruxellois.* Foyles, London.

1962. Cousens, Marjorie. *The Second Book of the Griffon Bruxellois.* Sharp, Evesham, Worcester.

1962. Pucci, Ilde. *Il Griffone di Bruxelles e le sue Varietà.* Italy.

1969. Weiss, Seymour N. *How to Raise and Train a Brussels Griffon.* TFH, New Jersey.

1984. Ball, Richard A. *The Brussels Griffon Primer.* National Brussels Griffon Club, USA.

1985. Raynham, L. C. *The History and Management of the Griffon Bruxellois.* Scan, London.

1989. Pucci, Ilde and Braun, E. Villemot. *Griffon Bruxellois, Griffon Belge, Petit Brabançon.* Flamina Editrice, Rome.

1992. Grocott, Molly. *The Griffon Bruxellois Handbook.* New Zealand.

1997. Weiss, Seymour N. *Brussels Griffon, a Complete and Reliable Handbook.* TFH, New Jersey.

1999. Vickers-Smith, Lorene. *The Brussels Griffon: An Owner's Guide to a Happy Healthy Pet.* IDG Books Worldwide.

BELGIAN GRIFFON   BELGIUM

Also known as the Griffon Belge, this is a dark colour variant of the Brussels Griffon.

Among the reddish-brown Brussels Griffon puppies there were often some with black markings, or even a completely black coat. In Belgium these are now considered as a separate breed and are called the Belgian Griffon. In all other respects they are similar to the Brussels breed, having the same inquisitive, 'impertinent', watchful personality and lively, vivacious spirit. In some countries no distinction is made between the two types. Where this occurs they are lumped together, for competition purposes, under the name of Brussels Griffon.

References

1989. Pucci, Ilde and Braun, E. Villemot. *Griffon Bruxellois, Griffon Belge, Petit Brabançon.* Flamina Editrice, Rome.

PETIT BRABANÇON   BELGIUM

This smooth-haired breed was originally known as the Griffon Brabançon, the Smooth Griffon or the Smooth-haired Griffon, but these names were abandoned as confusing because the word 'griffon' means literally 'rough-haired'. It is sometimes called simply the Brabançon and is also referred to as the Piccolo Brabantino.

Both the Brussels and the Belgian Griffon are rough-haired dogs, but when they were occasionally crossed with Pugs (presumably to flatten their faces a little more) there were a number of smooth-haired puppies among the offspring. At first these were rejected as being of bad type, but then it was decided to retain them and develop them separately as a distinct breed. This smooth-coated form was called the Petit Brabançon and soon acquired a devoted following of its own.

References

1989. Pucci, Ilde and Braun, E. Villemot. *Griffon Bruxellois, Griffon Belge, Petit Brabançon.* Flamina Editrice, Rome.

HOLLAND

DUTCH SMOUSHOND   HOLLAND

Also known as the Smousbart, the Dutch Smous, the Dutch Terrier or, in its native country, the Hollandse Smoushond or Heerrenstalhond (Gentleman's Stable Dog), the breed was originally employed as a rat-killer.

This rare breed was created in the 19th century by a Dutch merchant who discovered that German breeders of Coarse-haired Pinschers were discarding all the fawn-coloured puppies from their litters. They preferred their dogs to have a darker colouring. The Dutchman obtained the rejects cheaply and began offering them in Holland as an exciting new breed that would control the numerous rats infesting the Dutch stable-yards. They proved both endearing dogs and efficient pest-controllers and were soon breeding true as a distinct type.

With gradual improvements over the generations, these ratters developed into the Smoushond, and during the early part of the 20th century they were popular and thriving. Then World War II dealt them a cruel blow and almost succeeded in exterminating them. In 1949 the entire breed was reduced to two families, and it soon vanished and was removed from the lists of the Dutch Kennel Club and the FCI.

There were those who remembered this friendly, shaggy, straggly-coated dog with great affection and who were unhappy about its disappearance. One such enthusiast, a Dutch woman with the appropriate name of Mrs Barkman, began a campaign to reinstate it. In the early 1970s she began by scouring Holland for mongrels that resembled the breed. When she had found a number of likely candidates, she started a breeding programme in which she mated Smous-like with Smous-like. Before the end of the decade she had achieved her dream of recreating the Smoushond — or at least something very close to it. She was soon to see her new Smoushond accepted by the Dutch Kennel Club and the FCI, but she was still not satisfied and kept working to improve the breed further, personally inspecting every new litter that was born. Even today, however, it remains a rare dog, little known outside its native Holland.

PORTUGAL

SMALL PORTUGUESE PODENGO PORTUGAL

Known locally as the Podengo Portuguesa Pequeno, or simply the Podengo Pequeno, it has been used for many years to go to ground to flush out small game. It was specialized as a rabbit-hunter in rocky countryside. Alternative names include the Small Portuguese Hound, the Small Portuguese Rabbit Dog, or the Small Portuguese Warren Hound.

Because it is a miniaturized version of the typical Portuguese sighthounds, the Large Portuguese Podengo and the Medium Portuguese Podengo, this little dog is often classified alongside them as a hound, but its hunting role is clearly that of a typical terrier. Although it is a sighthound by ancestry, it has been reduced so much in size that it can no longer carry out its original chasing duties above ground and is now used exclusively as an earth dog. It goes to ground to flush out the prey — usually rabbits — while its bigger cousins wait above to pursue them as they break cover.

This tiny Podengo was developed by 'shrinking' the Medium Portuguese breed. Its height is only 12 in (30 cm) or less. Lacking the longer legs of its close relatives – it is 15 in (38 cm) shorter than the Large Podengo – this compact little dog has become a popular house pet, and has been seen on city streets in Portugal for at least three centuries. It exists in two coat types. One is short and hard and the other is wiry, shaggy and coarse.

AUSTRIA

AUSTRIAN SHORT-HAIRED PINSCHER   AUSTRIA

*Known in its native country as the Österreichis-
cher Kurzhaariger Pinscher, or to others simply as
the Austrian Pinscher, this breed was developed as
a general farm worker, being used as a watchdog,
a guard dog, a pest-controller and a livestock
driver, and also to go to earth.*

A heavier, broader version of the Standard
Pinscher, this breed was the result of matings
between German Pinschers and local Austrian hounds. It was first recognized in 1928 but has remained a rare dog, restricted almost entirely to its homeland. It is typically a black-and-tan dog, but often shows a few small white patches, especially on the throat and chest. Its weakness is a tendency to bark louder and longer than most other dogs.

GERMANY

AFFENPINSCHER   GERMANY

*Also known as the Monkey Pinscher, the Monkey Dog, the Monkey Terrier, the Black Devil or
simply the Affen, this tiny German breed was originally developed as a vermin-controller.*

This small, shaggy, monkey-headed dog, with its flattened face, its bushy eyebrows, moustache and beard, and its exuberant personality, soon graduated from its role as a hard-working rat-killer to become a much loved household pet. Its lively, playful char-acter won it many devoted friends but, for some strange reason, it has never become widely popular. According to Kennel Club records, there were only 87 new registrations in Britain in 1998, which puts it into the category of a rare breed.

The Affen has been known in Germany for several centuries, although claims that it

appears in Dürer woodcuts in the early 16th century seem to be incorrect. (The little dog he depicts is clearly a Lowchen.) Nobody knows for certain how this small Pinscher acquired its flattened face, but it has been suggested that ordinary German Pinschers were probably mated with imported, flat-faced oriental breeds. What is clear, however, is that when the breed was nearly extermin-ated as a result of the ravages of World War II, it was decided to improve the remnant stock that managed to survive by crossing it with the Griffon Bruxellois. This gave the Affen an even flatter face and created the appealing Monkey Dog we know today.

It was after this injection of Brussels blood that it began to gain favour with breed-ers in a number of countries. In addition to the increased flattening of its face, during its development as a pedigree show dog its weight has gradually been reduced, until it has reached its modern level of only 7–8 lb (3–3.5 kg).

In personality, the Affenpinscher is said to be one of the most entertaining of all breeds, exhibiting endless curiosity and a territorial fearlessness out of all proportion to its physical strength. One Affen was seen to face up to an angry stallion and, on a memorable trip to Alaska, was even observed to confront and see off an intruding grizzly bear.

References

1969. Gibbs, D. V. and Tobin, Jackson. *How to Raise and Train an Affenpinscher.* TFH, New Jersey.

SMOOTH-HAIRED DACHSHUND   GERMANY

This is also known as the Dachel, the Teckel, the Normalgrosse Teckel or the Dachslein. In England in earlier days it was sometimes referred to as the Beagle Terrier. It has occasionally been recorded as the Smooth-haired Standard Dachshund, or the Standard Smooth-haired Dachshund, to distinguish it from the Miniature version. Sometimes it is given the nickname of Sausage Dog. In America it is often called the Daxie. In France it was sometimes called the Basset à Jambes Torses or the Chien Rouge. Its original function was to go to earth to attack badgers and other burrowing mammals.

An unfortunate translation error has resulted in the Dachshund being misclassified for many years as a hound. Its German name means Badger Dog, not Badger Hound as many authors wrongly call it. Despite the way it sounds, the German word 'hund' means 'dog' and not hound. The error dates back to 1874 when Dachshunds were recorded in the English stud book as German Badger Hounds. Functionally, the Dachshund is not a hound but a terrier and the fact that it has to compete with hounds rather than other terriers at dog shows is a curious anomaly that has become hallowed by years of tradition. This has occurred despite repeated reference in the canine literature to its true affinities. As long ago as 1906 James Watson commented: 'That it is used occasionally as a hound in the sense that it follows rabbits and hares by scent as does a beagle, does not alter the fact that it is essentially a dog that goes to earth and is therefore a terrier.' In 1927, Edward Ash, one of the greatest of all dog historians, remarked that a Dachshund 'is, in fact, a terrier with very crooked legs, but possessing in a very great degree both the appearance and fine nose of the beagle'.

Those who have defended the status of this breed as a hound and are reluctant to see it classified as an earth dog have stressed that it is merely a dwarf hound with a gene for abbreviated legs. This may explain its origin, but ignores its primary function. Perhaps the best way to settle this argument is to say that the Dachshund is a hound that became a terrier and that it displays the qualities of both.

Attempts to trace the origin of this intriguing breed have focused on images from ancient Egypt, especially a 2000 BC depiction of a domestic dog that the Egyptians called Tekal. It has been suggested that this could explain the origin of the word Teckel – the popular German name for the Dachshund. Unfortunately, an examination of the image in question reveals that Tekal was in reality a long-legged mastiff guard dog. There is a short-legged dog depicted on a tomb wall at Beni Hassan, dating from roughly the same period, but this looks more like a Corgi. What it does prove, however, is that the deliberate shortening of the legs of domestic dogs had occurred at least 4,000 years ago.

In Germany itself the earliest specific record of the breed dates from 1735, although this type of dog had been known for several centuries before that date. It is thought that an important influence on the form of the breed occurred in the 18th century when French noblemen, fleeing from the French Revolution, arrived in Germany with their low-slung bassets and introduced these into the bloodline. Certainly, the 18th-century Dachshunds were more basset-like than their modern equivalents.

The earliest working Dachshunds to arrive in England were said to be 'clumsy and inelegant', but selective breeding soon improved their appearance and they became increasingly popular as companion and show dogs. Their bodies became longer and lower and more streamlined. Queen Victoria owned Dachshunds as early as the 1840s (a gift from one of her German relatives). Rather surprisingly, the English were ahead of their German counterparts in establishing a specialist breed club – in England the Dachshund Club was formed in 1881; in Germany the Deutscher Teckelklub was not set up until 1888.

In personality, the breed has been described as clever, mischievous, energetic, affectionate, good-humoured and a show-off who trains its owner with great cunning. The use of the name 'hot dog' for a sausage-in-a-roll stems from a 1903 cartoon showing a Dachshund in a bread roll.

References

1896. Ugner, Emil. *Der Dachshund.* J. Neumann, Germany.
1898. Woodiwiss, E. Sydney and Allen, E. Whatlock (Editors). *Dachshund Pedigrees.* Crowther, London.
1934. Johns, Rowland (Editor). *Our Friend the Dachshund.* Methuen, London.
1935. Greenburg, Grayce. *The Dachshund.* Judy, Chicago.
1937. Daglish, E. Fitch. *The Book of the Dachshund.* Our Dogs, Manchester.
1937. Sanborn, Herbert C. *The Dachshund or Teckel.* Orange Judd, New York.
1937. Sawyer, Mary J. *Modern Dachshund Breeding.* Dog World, Bradford.
1945. Naylor, Leonard. *Dachshunds.* Williams & Norgate, London.
1947. Denlinger, Milo G. *The Complete Dachshund.* Denlinger's, Washington, DC.
1949. Sawyer, Mary J. *The Dachshund Reference Book.*
1950. Hubbard, Clifford. *The Dachshund Handbook.* Nicholson & Watson, London.
1952. Daglish, E. Fitch. *The Popular Dachshund.* Popular Dogs, London.
1952. Lister-Kaye, Charles. *Dachshunds.* Chambers, London.
1954. Horswell, Mr and Mrs Laurence Alden. *Pet Dachshund.* All-Pets, Fond du Lac, Wisconsin.
1955. Miller, Madeline. *Dachshunds as Pets.* TFH, New Jersey.
1956. Daglish, E. Fitch. *Dachshunds.* Foyles, London.
1958. Engelmann, Fritz. *Der Dachshund.* Melsungen, Neumann-Neudamm.
1958. Meistrell, Lois and Barbaresi, Sara M. *How to Raise and Train a Dachshund.* Sterling, New York.
1960. Biss, Amyas. *Dachshunds.* Batsford, London.
1961. Dolan, Sheila and Triefus, Michael (Editors). *The Dachshund Club Handbook and Records, 1946–1960.* Published by the Club.
1965. Lawley. *Your First Dachshund Litter.* Privately published.
1966. Adler, Leonore Leob. *This Is the Dachshund.* TFH, New Jersey.
1966. Cox, Herman G. *Your Dachshund.* Hawthorn Books, New York.
1969. Brunotte, Hans. *Dachshund Guide.* All-Pets Books, Fond du Lac, Wisconsin.
1972. Raine, Katharine. *All about the Dachshund.* Pelham Books.
1976. Meistrell, Lois, et al. *The New Dachshund.* Howell, New York.
1985. Fiedelmeier, Leni. *Dachshunds; A Complete Pet Owner's Manual.* Barron, New York.
1988. Nicholas, Anna Katherine. *The Dachshund.* TFH, New Jersey.
1991. Heesom, Elizabeth, *Dachshunds.* Crowood Press, Wiltshire.
1995. Carey, Ann. *The Dachshund; An Owner's Guide to a Happy Healthy Pet.* Howell, New York.
1996. Ackerman, Lowell. *Dr Ackerman's Book of Dachshunds.* TFH, New Jersey.
1996. Schopell, M. William. *Guide to Owning a Dachshund.* TFH, New Jersey.
1996. Ladd, Kaye. *New Owner's Guide to Dachshunds.* TFH, New Jersey.
1997. Fogle, Bruce. *Dachshund.* Dorling Kindersley, London.
1997. Hutchinson, Dee. *The Complete Dachshund.* Howell, New York.
1998. Lyn, Edita Van Der. *Dachshunds.* TFH, New Jersey.
1999. Hutchinson, Robert. *Dachshunds.* Brown Trout Publications.

1999. Douglas, Eileen Falconer. *Contemporary Dachshund*. Kingdom Books, Waterlooville, Hampshire.
1999. Dunbar, Ian. *Essential Dachshund*. Howell, New York.
Migliorini, Mario. *Dachshunds*.
Sanford, William R. and Green, Carl R. *The Dachshund* (Top Dog Series).
Schneider, Earl (Editor). *Know Your Dachshund*. Pet Library, New York.

LONG-HAIRED DACHSHUND GERMANY

This is also known as the Langhaariger Teckel. Its original function was to go to earth to attack badgers and other burrowing mammals.

An attractive variant of the traditional, Smooth-haired Dachshund, with a beautifully feathered coat. One theory concerning its origin is that it was created by crossing typical Dachshunds with either setters or spaniels. According to one view, the spaniel breed involved was either the Field or the Sussex; according to another it was the German Spaniel.

A rival theory sees the Long-haired Dachshund as being no more than a minor variant of the Smooth-haired. In this view, the prototype Dachshund had a variable coat, sometimes shorter, sometimes longer, and the two versions were separated out by breeders and exaggerated away from one another to create two distinct breeds. Either way, it is believed that the Long-haired Dachshund has been present in Germany for over two centuries.

WIRE-HAIRED DACHSHUND GERMANY

Its original function was to go to earth to attack badgers and other burrowing mammals.

It is sometimes said that this second variant of the Dachshund is more recent than the other two and was not created until the 1880s. German records seem to suggest that this is incorrect and that this breed is also over two centuries old. From the latter part of the 18th century we have a report of the existence of a Rough-coated Teckel, and a few years later, in 1911, another author remarks that 'there is also a wire-haired Dachsel'. A year later, there was a comment that this type of wire-haired

Dachshund was especially useful as a working dog – presumably because its rough coat protected it so well.

It is thought to have been created when a Smooth-haired Dachshund was crossed with a wire-haired breed. Precisely which wire-haired breed was involved has been the subject of much debate. Suggestions have included the Irish Terrier, Scottish Terrier, Wire-haired German Pinscher, Rough-coated Basset Hound and Dandie Dinmont Terrier.

The Wire-haired Dachshund was first exhibited in its own, named class in 1888 in Berlin.

MINIATURE SMOOTH-HAIRED DACHSHUND GERMANY

In Germany this small breed is known as the Zwergteckel, the Kaninchenteckel, the Kurzhaariger Kaninchenteckel or the Kaninchen Dachshund. Its primary function was as an earth dog used against rabbits, and it has occasionally been referred to as the Rabbit Dachshund or the Smooth-haired Rabbit Dachshund.

The need for a smaller variety of Dachshund to be put to earth after rabbits led to the development of a miniature form at the end of the 19th century. The essential feature of this small dog was that it should have a reduced chest measurement to enable it to enter narrow burrows. This was achieved by breeding from the smallest members of normal litters until the body weight had been reduced from a typical 16–26 lb (7–12 kg) to around 8–11 lb (3.5–5 kg). It has been suggested by one author that perhaps the 'bantamization' of the Dachshund was aided by introducing crosses with 'Dwarf Pinschers' or with Toy Terriers, but other authorities refute this, insisting that the Miniature is simply a very small version of the pure-bred Dachshund.

By 1905 the popularity of these small dogs in Germany had led to the formation of a specialist breed club – the Kaninchenteckelklub. The first Miniatures to arrive in England from Germany appeared in 1909, but they made little impact. The breed did not take off fully as an international show dog until the 1920s.

MINIATURE LONG-HAIRED DACHSHUND GERMANY

This has also been called the Long-haired Rabbit Dachshund, or the Langhaariger Kaninchenteckel. Its primary function was as an earth dog used against rabbits.

The long-haired version of the Miniature Dachshund did not arrive in England until the 1930s. These little dogs immediately found a ready audience and rose rapidly in popularity. However, among the ardent supporters of the larger, traditional Dachshunds there was considerable opposition to these appealing midgets. The traditionalists described the new imports as freaks and degenerates and would have nothing to do with them. But they were overlooking the fact that, far from being pampered weaklings, these miniatures had been carefully bred as tough, small-scale working dogs. Their lively, spirited personality, which contrasted with their tiny size, eventually won everyone over and by 1935 a Miniature Dachshund Club had been formed and was soon flourishing. Although it catered for both the Smooth-haired Miniature and the Wire-haired Miniature, it was the latter that attracted most attention.

MINIATURE WIRE-HAIRED DACHSHUND   GERMANY

This was also known as the Wire-haired Rabbit Dachshund, or the Rauhaariger Kaninchenteckel. Its primary function was as an earth dog used against rabbits.

In the period following World War II a sixth type of Dachshund, the Miniature Wire-haired, was imported into England and soon had its own devoted followers. It is said that this breed arose from crosses between a small Wire-haired Dachshund bitch and a Miniature Smooth-haired Dachshund. Another source was litter-runts from full-sized Wire-haired parents.

References

1980. Kartye. *Roots: Miniature Wirehaired Dachshund.*

GERMAN HUNT TERRIER   GERMANY

Also known as the Jagd Terrier or, in its native country, as the Deutscher Jagdterrier, this rugged breed was developed as a general-purpose hunting terrier.

This is that rare thing, a dog designed by a committee. After World War I was over, four German hunters broke away from the main Fox Terrier Club in Germany and formed a splinter group dedicated to manufacturing a new, improved hunt terrier. Their names were Rudolf Friess, Carl-Erich Grunewald, Herbert Lackner and Walter Zangenberg. With the help of German zoo director Lutz Heck, they started a breeding programme in which carefully selected terrier types were crossed with one another in a special way, bringing out the best qualities of each of them and combining them to create an ultra-efficient new breed.

Authors differ as to the precise terrier breeds involved, but there is general agreement that Fox Terriers and Black and Tan Terriers provided the main ingredients, and that perhaps German Pinschers and Welsh Terriers were also involved to some extent. The result was an unusually aggressive all-rounder which would hunt game birds, fox, badger, deer and even wild boar, and would not only go to earth, but also track and retrieve. This terrier was so fearless and assertive that it became what one owner described as the 'perfect hunting machine'.

According to some authors, the main drawback of this breed is that it is exclusively a working dog and is so belligerent that it is quite unsuitable as a pet or a household companion. For this reason, they say, it remains a rare breed. Others disagree, stating that although it may be stubborn and may indeed be aggressive towards other dogs, it is extremely friendly with its owners and affectionate towards their children.

The four hunters who originated the breed were able, through ruthless selection, to stabilize it very quickly and by 1926 had established a German Hunt Terrier Breed Club. It has since been recognized as a distinct form of pedigree dog by the FCI. In the United States a Jagdterrier Club was formed in 1956, and 30 years later there were estimated to be about 500 Jagds in the country.

PINSCHER   GERMANY

Sometimes referred to as the German Pinscher, the Medium Pinscher or the Standard Pinscher, it used to be known in its native country as the Reh Pinscher. 'Pinscher' appears to be a Germanic form of the French word 'pincer', meaning 'to seize' or 'to nip'. In origin, this small working dog is the equivalent of England's Manchester Terrier — a devout vermin-controller and rat-killer.

Cropped and docked, bright and alert, this sleek, smooth-coated breed has been a popular ratter in Germany and Switzerland for centuries. This is the archetypal, original Pinscher, from which several other forms have been developed, including the larger and nowadays more popular Doberman Pinscher. (Dobermann owners have been heard to

refer to the Pinscher as the 'little Dobie', but it would actually be more correct to call the Dobermann the 'Big Pinscher'.)

Although an ancient breed, the Pinscher was not subjected to controlled breeding until the 19th century and did not receive official recognition as a pedigree dog until the year 1879. The first Pinscher Club was formed in 1895.

Today the Pinscher is kept mainly as a companion dog, rather than a working ratter and has proved itself to be an efficient watchdog. It is an elegant, athletic little animal, with an appealingly streamlined body. Hardy and healthy and desperately keen to please its master, it makes an ideal urban pet. But despite its attractive personality, the Pinscher has for some reason remained a comparatively rare breed and is still far less common than its descendants, the Miniature Pinscher and the Dobermann. The latest Kennel Club registration figures show that the Miniature is nearly eight times as popular, while the Dobermann is 138 times more popular.

MINIATURE PINSCHER   GERMANY

Best known in the English-speaking world by its nickname of Min Pin, but more correctly called by its German name of Zwergpinscher, this version of the ancient German Pinscher is, like its bigger relative, a highly efficient ratter. Because of its appearance it is sometimes incorrectly referred to as a 'Miniature Doberman Pinscher'.

As with many very small breeds, the Min Pin secretly believes that it is a fully grown wolf and will square up to all-comers, showing amazing courage that often leaves larger dogs confused and bewildered. It may look delicate, but in reality it is extremely tough and always seems to be fighting-fit.

It has been in existence for several centuries, but in its early days, when it was required to work hard for its living, it was heavier-bodied that it is today. Since its principal role has switched from rat-killer to that of family companion dog and pedigree show dog, it has been further reduced in size until today it weighs less than 10 lb (4.5 kg).

This pocket-sized dog, with its sprightly, prancing gait, has become increasingly popular in recent years. It was first officially recognized in Germany in 1895, but did not arrive in the United States until 1920. A specialist breed club was established there in 1929, well ahead of its English counterpart, which did not appear until the 1950s.

References

1956. Bagshaw, Margaret R. *Pet Miniature Pinscher.* All-Pets, Fond du Lac, Wisconsin.
1957. Ricketts, Viva Leone. *The Complete Miniature Pinscher.* Denlinger's, USA.
1958. Miller, Madeline. *Miniature Pinschers as Pets.* TFH, New Jersey.
1961. Miller, Evelyn. *How to Raise and Train a Miniature Pinscher.* TFH, New Jersey.
1969. Boshall, Boris R. *Your Miniature Pinscher.* Denlinger's, USA.
1969. Jones, Chips. *The Miniature Pinscher You May Know.* Lund, Wisconsin.
1971. Krogh, David M. *Miniature Pinschers in America.* AMDS.
1988. Tietjen, Sari Brewster. *The New Miniature Pinscher.* Howell, New York.
1989. Miller, Evelyn. *Miniature Pinschers.* TFH, New Jersey.
1996. Coile, Caroline. *Miniature Pinscher.*
1997. O'Neil, Jackie. *Guide to Owning a Miniature Pinscher.*

STANDARD SCHNAUZER GERMANY

This breed is known in its homeland as the Mittelschnauzer (Medium Schnauzer), to distinguish it from the Giant and Miniature Schnauzers, but is sometimes referred to simply as the Schnauzer, because it was the original form from which the other two were later developed. It originally worked as a farm rat-killer, but was soon given additional tasks and became a general, working farm dog.

The grizzled, rough-coated, bearded, be-whiskered Schnauzer has the striking appearance that was bound to make it a favourite in the show-ring, but long before it arrived there it was a popular German working dog with a long pedigree. From early works of art it is clear that this breed was active in Germany from at least the 14th century. The great German artist Dürer owned one in the 15th century and it was painted by both Cranach and Rembrandt.

It first appeared at a dog show in 1879, in Hanover, when it was called a Wire-haired Pinscher. The winner of that contest was a dog with the pet name of 'Schnauzer' (which means 'whiskered snout'), and from that date onwards the rough-coated Pinschers adopted its name and were viewed as belonging to a separate breed. While the favoured colour for the smooth-coated Pinschers was black-and-tan, the most popular Schnauzer colouring was pepper-and-salt — in other words, mixed greys.

The standard for the Schnauzer was drawn up in 1880 and five years later its first specialist breed club had been established in Germany. Much later, in 1925, the Schnauzer Club of America was established in the United States.

Like the Pinschers, the Schnauzers were

typical fearless working terriers, primarily concerned with vermin control on farm properties, but they were co-opted to carry out other chores, including flock-guarding, house-guarding, driving cattle and even pulling carts to market. Although they are clearly terriers, they are not classified as such, presumably because they are not used by hunters to go to earth. But when one thinks of rat-killing breeds such as the Manchester Terrier, this is clearly illogical.

References

1930. Schwabacher, Joseph. *History of the Schnauzer and Miniature Schnauzer.* Popular Dogs, London.

1932. Fitzgerald, Anne (Editor). *The Schnauzer Book, Past and Present of the Breed.* Popular Dogs, Philadelphia.

1938. Nash, Cyril. *Yours Faithfully; the Autobiography of a Schnauzer.* Longmans, Green, London.

1965. Hertz, Hamilton and Hertz, Joan. *How to Raise and Train a Standard Schnauzer.* TFH, New Jersey.

1981. Fiorone, F. *Le Schnauzer — Schnauzer Moyen, Schnauzer Géant, Schnauzer Nain.* Éditions de Vecchi, Paris.

1996. Gallant. *World of Schnauzers: Standard, Giant, Miniature.*

1997. Dille, Barbara M. *Standard Schnauzer, a Complete and Reliable Handbook.* TFH, New Jersey.

MINIATURE SCHNAUZER   GERMANY

Known in its homeland as the Zwergschnauzer, this smaller version of the Standard Schnauzer was originally developed as a small ratter and then later became a popular household companion dog.

It is claimed that this breed was created by crossing the larger, Standard Schnauzer with the little Affenpinscher. Both these breeds had been present in Germany from at least the 17th century, and such crosses would have been easy to arrange.

At the end of the 19th century, two Frankfurt breeders, Georg Riehl and Heinrich Schott, were active with both Schnauzers and Affenpinschers and it is thought that the process of miniaturization, already started by selecting the smallest members of Schnauzer litters, was taken further by them. The earliest recorded example of a Miniature Schnauzer in a stud book dates from 1888, and the breed's first appearance at a dog show from 1899.

Some authorities have cited Miniature Pinschers, Miniature Poodles, Pomeranians, Fox Terriers and Scottish Terriers as possible contributors to the ancestry of the Miniature Schnauzer, but these claims have not been substantiated.

Looking like a dwarf version of the larger Schnauzers, the Miniature displays the typical bushy eyebrows, moustache and whiskers, and the wiry, black or 'pepper-and-salt' coat typical of all Schnauzers. Its height is 14 in (36 cm) or less, compared with 18–20 in (45–50 cm) for the Standard breed. Its tail is traditionally closely docked and its ears have often been cropped to create erect points. Today ear-cropping is widely condemned in the veterinary world and, when left in their natural state in this breed, they fold over and downwards.

This is a hardy, playful, intelligent little dog that has gained greatly in popularity in recent years as a companion animal, rather than as an active, terrier-like ratter.

References

1930. Schwabacher, Joseph. *History of the Schnauzer and Miniature Schnauzer.* Popular Dogs, London.

1935. Fitzgerald, Anne. *The Miniature Schnauzer.* Orange Judd, New York.

1938. Nash, Cyril. *Yours Faithfully: The Autobiography of a Schnauzer.* Longmans, Green, London.

1956. Slattery, Mary. *Pet Miniature Schnauzer.* All-Pets, Fond du Lac, Wisconsin.

1958. Anon. *Miniature Schnauzers... as Pets.* TFH, New Jersey.

1958. Martin, Leda and Barbaresi, Sara M. *How to Raise and Train a Miniature Schnauzer.* Sterling, New York.

1959. Doud, Mildred L. *Your Miniature Schnauzer.* Denlinger's, USA.

1959. Paramoure, Anne Fitzgerald. *The Complete Miniature Schnauzer.* Denlinger's, USA.

1960s. Kiedrowski, Daniel. *You and your Schnauzer.* Privately published, La Honda, California.

1963. Spirer, Louise Ziegler and Spirer, Herbert F. *This is the Miniature Schnauzer.* TFH, New Jersey.

1966. Gordon, John F. *Miniature Schnauzers.* Foyles, London.

1967. Schneider, Earl (Editor). *Know Your Miniature Schnauzer.* The Pet Library, New York.

1968. Eskrigge, Anne Paramoure. *The Complete Miniature Schnauzer.* Howell, New York.

1971. Martin, Leda B. and Barbaresi, Sara M. *How to Raise and Train a Miniature Schnauzer.* TFH, New Jersey.

1976. Migliorini, Mario. *Miniature Schnauzers.* Arco.

1979. Pisano, Beverly and Lewis, Gloria. *Miniature Schnauzers.* TFH, New Jersey.

1981. Fiorone, F. *Le Schnauzer – Schnauzer Moyen, Schnauzer Géant, Schnauzer Nain.* Éditions de Vecchi, Paris.

1990. Newman, Peter. *The Miniature Schnauzer.* The Miniature Schnauzer Club.

1996. Gallant. *World of Schnauzers: Standard, Giant, Miniature.*

1996. Janish, Anton. *Guide to Owning a Miniature Schnauzer.* TFH, New Jersey.

1996. Stark, Jeannette. *An Owner's Guide to the Pet Miniature Schnauzer.* Howell, New York.

1997. Kiedrowski, Dan. *The New Miniature Schnauzer.* Howell, New York.

1997. Rugh, Karla S. *Miniature Schnauzers: Everything about Purchase, Care, Nutrition, Breeding, Behavior, and Training.* Barron, New York.

1998. Newman, Peter. *Miniature Schnauzers Today.*

1998. Schwartz, Charlotte. *A New Owner's Guide to Miniature Schnauzers.*

1999. Dunbar, Ian (Editor), et al. *The Essential Miniature Schnauzer.*

Migliorini Mario. *Schnauzer Grooming Made Easy.*

Nicholas, Anna K. *Book of the Miniature Schnauzer.*

DENMARK

DANISH FARM DOG   DENMARK

Sometimes known as the Danish Chicken Dog, this versatile breed has recently been saved from obscurity. In its working days, its main task was vermin control, but in addition to killing rats, it was also employed to drive livestock and act as a farmyard watchdog.

This breed was nearing extinction when it was rediscovered and given a new lease of life by interested breeders. Its ancestors, which had been bigger dogs, had operated as cart-pullers, but this smaller cousin was employed as a farmer's versatile working dog.

It is a medium-sized dog with a short coat that is basically white, with large dark patches. The ears fold forward and downward. The tail is severely docked. It is as yet unregistered, but there is growing interest in it as a show-dog. Its maximum height is 18 in (46 cm) and maximum weight 30 lb (14 kg).

In addition to its native Denmark, it is also found in the southernmost parts of neighbouring Sweden, a legacy of the time when the Danes occupied that region. At present it does not seem to have travelled very far from its ancient homeland, but it may do so in the near future if it becomes popular in the show-ring.

CZECH REPUBLIC

CESKY TERRIER   CZECH REPUBLIC

This breed has also been known as the Bohemian Terrier, the Czech Terrier, the Czesky Terrier or, more simply, the Seski. It original role was as a ratter and mole-catcher.

This attractive, short-legged breed, with its bushy beard and eyebrows, was deliberately created by the Czech geneticist Dr Frantisek Horak, of Klanovice, following World War II. Before the war he had been a keen hunter and had then favoured Scottish Terriers, but in the late 1940s he decided to experiment with a new cross, to produce a terrier that would be a winner both in the field and in the show-ring. In 1949, he started a ten-year breeding plan, crossing Scotties with Sealyhams. To improve its type, the Cesky (pronounced ses-ki) was again crossed with Sealyhams in the 1980s.

Judging by the appearance of the modern Cesky breed, it is thought that Dr Horak must also, at some point, have introduced some Dandie Dinmont and Wire-haired Dachshund blood, but this is not certain. What is clear is that his breeding strategy created a unique terrier which is both handsome and workmanlike. Unusual features for a terrier include its remarkably long neck and its undocked tail.

In personality it is described as being a fearless, inquisitive, vigorous hunter, but also gentle, obedient and patient with people. If properly trained, it is excellent with children. Its breed name was formally accepted by the FCI in 1963 and the Cesky is now officially recognized as the National Dog of the Czech Republic. It was first registered in England in 1990.

SOUTH AFRICA

SEALYDALE TERRIER   SOUTH AFRICA

The Sealydale was a recent breed specially created to control vermin on South African farms.

During the 1930s and 1940s an English resident in South Africa, a Miss Bodmer, made careful crosses between Sealyham Terriers and Airedale Terriers. Her breeding activities were based in Grahamstown and her goal was to develop a breed that would be a good ratter and would also be suited to local climatic conditions. The result, looking rather like a rough-haired Jack Russell, was a great success for a while, but did not appear to survive the century. Its first mention in the canine literature was in the 1940s and its last in the 1960s.

In addition to being put to work as a rodent controller, the Sealydale was also employed as a watchdog and a companion. Its harsh coat was basically white, with black, brown or fawn patches. Its height was 12–13 in (31–33 cm). It was breeding true surprisingly quickly after the initial crosses, and there is always the faint possibility that the breed still survives on some of the more remote farmsteads.

AUSTRALIA

AUSTRALIAN TERRIER

AUSTRALIA

This breed was known originally as the Blue-and-Tan Terrier, the Blue Terrier, the Broken-coated Terrier or the Australian Rough Coated Terrier, and today affectionately as the Aussie. It was developed to control the vermin, such as rats and rabbits, that were becoming major pests in Australia, after being introduced by early European settlers. In addition to its normal duties, this fearless little dog also attacked the local poisonous snakes, employing a special — if somewhat risky — leap-twist-and-pounce technique to take them from behind.

In origin, this small, shaggy, short-legged breed of terrier is said to have been created from a mixture of Yorkshire, Norwich, Cairn, Scottish, Dandie Dinmont, Skye and Irish Terriers. Out of this complex blending of types, a uniquely Australian dog eventually emerged and was soon breeding true. We know that it was already firmly established by the end of the 1870s and that, by 1889, the Australian Rough Coated Terrier Club had been formed to preserve it. They drew up a breed standard and organized club shows, but interest waned and the club 'was allowed to lapse'.

Towards the end of the 19th century, there arose, rather surprisingly, some considerable hostility towards the breed. In 1897 an authoritative book on *The Dog in Australasia* was published and its author, Walter Beilby, mounted a savage attack, calling it an 'arrant nondescript' and an 'unmitigated mongrel'. He and others seemed to be especially incensed by the suggestion that the dog should be called an Australian breed, insisting that a local society was correct not to allow 'the name Australian to be prostituted to such vile uses and hung around the neck of a wretched mongrel'.

Despite these verbal assaults, the breed was becoming more and more popular and eventually, in the early years of the 20th century, a new effort was made to promote it as a true-breeding pedigree dog, suitable for competition in the show-ring. This time its supporters met with great success and its future was assured. In England, the Kennel Club recognized it in 1933. In recent years it has been exported all over the world and is becoming a familiar figure at many major dog shows. It was recognized by the American Kennel Club in 1960.

References

1963. Young, Betty. *How to Raise and Train an Australian Terrier*. TFH, New Jersey.

1964. Wheatland, W. A. *The Australian Terrier and the Australian Silky Terrier.* Hawthorne Press, Melbourne.

1965. Fox, Mrs Milton: *How to Raise and Train an Australian Terrier.* TFH, New Jersey.

1965. Ireland, Joan M. *The Book of the Australian Terrier.* Privately published.

1965. Hamilton-Wilkes, Monty. *The Australian Terrier.* Angus & Robertson, Sydney.

1969. Anon. *The Show Australian Terrier.* Australian Terrier Club of Great Britain and Ireland, London.

1974. Christian, Ray, et al. *The Australian Terrier.*

1997. Fox, Nell and Fox, Milton. *Australian Terrier.* TFH, New Jersey.

TENTERFIELD TERRIER   AUSTRALIA

This breed was originally known as the Mini Foxie, but takes its modern name from the location in New South Wales where it was first developed.

Early settlers in Australia, including the famous bushranger Ben Hall, first brought dogs of this type out to Australia, but the founding father of the breed is generally recognized to be the man known as the 'Tenterfield Saddler'.

This small working terrier is thought to be related to the Toy Fox Terrier, the Jack Russell, the American Rat Terrier, the Teddy Roosevelt Terrier and the Patterdale Terrier. They all have similar histories and look superficially like one another, but a specialist can easily tell them apart.

The Tenterfield originated in England in the 1800s, created largely from crosses between the Manchester Terrier and litter runts of the Smooth-haired Fox Terrier. Some authors believe that Whippet and Jack Russell Terrier crosses were also made and that even the Chihuahua was involved at some stage. All such crosses are now forbidden.

The Tenterfield Terrier Club of Australia has now been formed and is working towards gaining full recognition for this recently stabilized breed.

CANADA/UNITED STATES

SHORT-LEGGED INDIAN DOG   CANADA/UNITED STATES

This is an extinct breed of dog which is the closest approximation to a terrier that we find among the early Native American tribes. It was said to look very similar to the little Turnspit Dog of Europe, with a large head, a long body and a medium coat that was either white or white spotted with brown. Its short legs were thought to have been developed as an adaptation to canoe travel. The canoe was the favoured form of transport for the forest-dwelling tribes of the northern regions, and a short-legged dog was much easier to control on these low-slung craft. The short legs also helped the dogs to become expert hunters of small, ground-living mammals such as the beaver, the groundhog and other burrowing rodents.

The first person to write about this breed was the explorer John Richardson, who described it in 1829 as having 'a good deal of intelligence in its countenance mixed with wildness'. It was noted that when it was not working it was a favourite pet of the women and children of the tribes. The last eyewitness report of this dog dates from 1877, and it seems that, by the end of the 19th century, it had vanished for ever – like most of the tribes that enjoyed its company.

UNITED STATES

RAT TERRIER   UNITED STATES

A small working terrier, it is sometimes known as the American Rat Terrier, the Squirrel Terrier or the Feist. It was originally developed as a breed specializing in vermin control.

In a broad sense this little terrier is the United States counterpart of England's Jack Russell Terrier. But although it is essentially an American dog today, it was first developed in England in the 1820s by crossing Smooth-haired Fox Terriers with Manchester Terriers. The goal was to create the ultimate rat-killer and this certainly seems to have been achieved: one Rat Terrier broke all records by dispatching no fewer than 2,501 rats in a large barn in a period of seven hours. In the rat-infested farms of the 19th century, such a breed was clearly of great value and the Rat Terrier was eventually transported to the United States in the 1890s to carry on the good work on the other side of the Atlantic.

Once in America, the breed gained a boost in popularity when President Theodore Roosevelt decided to take three Rat Terriers along with him on some of his highly publicized hunting trips. He also used them to hunt down rats in the White House. Indeed, it was he who gave the breed its present name. Later, there were attempts to improve the quality of the breed by crossing it with the Whippet, to increase its agility; the Beagle, to increase its scenting ability and to add weight; and additional Smooth-haired Fox Terriers, to produce a lighter coat. In the end, two basic types were created, the long-legged and the short-legged. To avoid confusion and to keep the two types distinct, the short-legged version has recently been awarded separate breed status and has been given the name of Teddy Roosevelt Terrier, or Teddy Terrier. This will help to give both breeds a better chance of being recognized by the world of pedigree show dogs. Recently a Rat Terrier Club of America (RTCA) has been formed and has prepared official breed standards to this end.

In America, the role of this breed in sport hunting and as a family pet has become increasingly important. It is especially adept at treeing its quarry and then keeping it

treed by circling the trunk and barking loudly. Renowned for its combination of a good eye, a good ear and a good nose, this little terrier reached its peak of popularity in the interwar period of the 1920s and 1930s. Since then it has been on the decline, but the activities of the RTCA are designed to reverse this trend. With an animal as versatile as this one, combining the attributes of a hound, a spaniel and a terrier, the task should not prove to be too difficult.

References

1998. Hibbard, Linda. *Rat Terrier: A Complete and Reliable Handbook.* TFH, New Jersey.

SHELBURNE TERRIER   UNITED STATES

A compact working terrier developed for digging and holding the quarry in small tunnels. It takes its name from the location of its originator, who lived in Shelburne, Vermont.

This little-known breed was developed by a hunter called J. Watson Webb. Realizing that the foxholes of the New World were generally smaller than those of Europe, he set about creating a smaller terrier, more suited to restricted digging space. He started out in 1911 with a Sealyham bitch, imported from England, which he crossed with a Wire Fox Terrier. The offspring from this mating were then, in turn, put with the result of a cross between a Norfolk Terrier male and a West Highland White bitch. The result of this mixture was a small, short-legged, short-headed dog, weighing about 12 lb (5.5 kg), which formed the foundation stock for the new breed. It was improved from time to time by being put back to Sealyhams, until it was exactly what Mr Webb wanted. This working terrier was not intended to run with the hounds, but was a 'digging and holding' specialist.

TEDDY ROOSEVELT TERRIER   UNITED STATES

When the Rat Terrier was developed and modified in the United States, two types emerged – the long-legged (A-type) and the short-legged (B-type). For some time they were allowed to mix together, but then it was decided to keep them separate and let them become two distinct breeds. The long-legged version retained the original title of Rat Terrier, while the short-legged version was given the name of Teddy Roosevelt Terrier, or simply the Teddy Terrier. 'No mixing of the types' became the golden rule.

This short-legged breed is thought by some to have resulted from crosses of the Rat Terrier with Dachshunds or Corgis, but there is no certain proof of this. In personality it has been described as energetic, alert, curious, intelligent and easy to train, with a strong protective nature and well-developed pack instinct.

The United Kennel Club in America announced the recognition of this new breed of pure-bred dog in November 1998 and it was admitted to full UKC privileges as from 1st January 1999.

BRAZIL

BRAZILIAN TERRIER   BRAZIL

Known in its homeland as the Terrier Brasiliero or the Fox Paulistinha, this breed is a general-purpose terrier, used for both ratting and hunting.

Although it has only recently been officially recognized, this little terrier has been a common sight on Brazilian ranches for over 100 years. In the late 19th century many wealthy young Brazilians travelled to Europe to complete their education and frequently returned home with 'a wife, a horse and a dog'. The dogs in question were usually small terriers and the most popular choice was the lively little Jack Russell Terrier (in its original form, similar to today's Parson Jack Russell Terrier). These energetic working dogs proved to be a great success on the South American estates where they found themselves and were soon breeding and spreading across Brazil. During this process they often interbred with other small dogs that were present locally. No detailed records were kept, of course, but it is thought that the main crosses involved Pinschers and Chihuahuas.

Out of these casual beginnings there gradually developed a new type of terrier and as the decades passed it started to breed true. Brazilian canine enthusiasts decided to take a close interest in it and in the 1981 they formed a specialist breed club, the Clube do Fox Paulistinha. A founding member, Marina Vicari Lerario, made a special effort to gain international recognition for the breed, and her persistence was rewarded when it was finally accepted by the FCI in 1995. Following this, a small number of these dogs were exported to European countries such as France, Austria, Spain, Portugal and Finland, but even today it remains rare outside its native Brazil.

This breed of terrier is said to be a superb ratter, a keen hunter and a useful watchdog. In this last role, it works in combination with Brazil's other local breed, the huge and ferocious Fila Brasiliero. The Filas are heavy sleepers, but the barking of the little terriers wakes them up and they are then able to deal effectively with any intruder. When accompanying a hunt, the terriers work in packs, chasing, surrounding and exhausting the prey, which includes armadillos, guinea pigs and quail.

In personality, the Brazilian Terrier is agile, fearless, loyal, intelligent and a quick learner, and can often be seen performing circus tricks. Its height is 14–16 in (36–41 cm), it weighs less than 20 lb (9 kg), and its short, tricolour coat is white with black and tan markings. Its tail is traditionally docked.

TREEING DOGS

This is a category of North American hounds that contains breeds specially developed to hunt arboreal prey. In Europe, the usual prey species were those that went to ground when pursued, such as the badger, fox, otter, rabbit and rat, or which stayed at ground level, such as the hare, boar, deer and wolf. But in the United States and Canada, the presence of animals such as the raccoon and the opossum, which take to the trees when pursued, led to the creation of a new type of scenthound. Usually referred to as treeing dogs or coonhounds, these breeds were improved in one important respect. The dogs had to be prepared to remain at the foot of a tree when the quarry had climbed up into it and to continue barking up at the cornered animal for as long as it took for the hunters to arrive and make the kill.

The ancestors of these treeing dogs were mostly the ordinary scenthounds that had been taken to America for pack-hunting. When the hounds were set against a raccoon or an opossum, they were efficient enough for the ground-level pursuit when the prey was running away, but as soon as it took to the trees they lost interest and wandered off in search of other quarry. They may have barked up a few times at their lost prize, but they did not persist long enough for the hunters to catch up with them.

Starting with these breeds, hunters began to select for those individuals that showed a stubborn refusal to give up once the quarry had been treed. The classic action photograph of these hounds shows them surrounding a tree with their front paws on the trunk, staring intently upwards and giving voice.

Once the hunters have caught up with their treeing dogs, they either shoot the treed prey or climb up and dislodge it, allowing the hounds below to kill it. This type of hunting generally takes place at night, because both the raccoon and the opossum are nocturnal animals and only become active at dusk.

In recent years competitive coonhound field trials have become increasingly popular. These are of three types. The first is the 'night-hunt', in which rival dogs are sent after wild raccoons, with the best performers given the title of 'Night Champions'. The second is the drag-hunt, in which the hounds pursue a scent-stick over dry land. And the third is the water-race, in which the dogs have to pursue the scent across a river. At the peak of the field trials' popularity, thousands of people attended them, and there was big prize-money and a great deal of unofficial gambling. In some districts these activities have fallen foul of the authorities and been outlawed.

In addition to the coonhounds there is a group of slightly smaller treeing breeds called 'squirrel dogs'. Although these specialize in trailing and treeing squirrels, they are also capable of hunting larger prey and, despite their modest size, have been known to tree quarry as large as bears or pumas.

The development of a treeing specialist could have led to the creation of no more than one or two North American breeds, but local differences in the choice of ancestral dogs have resulted in regional variations. Today as many as 23 different forms have been named.

UNITED STATES

AMERICAN BLUE GASCON HOUND   UNITED STATES

Not to be confused with the Bluetick Coonhound, this heavy breed has been used to tree not only raccoon, but also bobcat, puma and even bear. It has sometimes been called the Big 'n Blue.

This dramatic treeing dog, one of the less well known of the coonhounds, is an unusually large animal with a heavy head, a massive torso and long ears. It has a thunderous voice to match its massive size.

Because this dog has a similar coat-colouring to the Bluetick, these two have sometimes been viewed as a single breed, with the Blue Gascon being dismissed as no more than an overgrown Bluetick. However, enthusiasts insist that this is not the case. Despite the fact that the breed has not been granted official recognition, they still contend that it is a separate entity and should be considered as a unique type worthy of special interest. The American Blue Gascon Hound Association has been formed in Louisiana to support the breed.

This dog, which can be traced back to the early 1900s, has been described as powerful, agile and athletic, with great stamina, a 'thundering bawl mouth' and a pleasant disposition. Unlike some of the better-known coonhounds, which have been modified to suit modern tastes, the Blue Gascon has remained true to its origins and is still very close to the ancestral American treeing dog.

BLACK MOUTH CUR   UNITED STATES

Also known as the Southern Black Mouth Cur, the Southern Cur or the Yellow Black Mouth Cur, this breed was developed to hunt a wide variety of game, from squirrel, opossum and raccoon to bear.

This is a powerful dog, well known for its characteristic loping gait. A fast, relentless, courageous hunter, widely used in the southern states of America, it is also employed in secondary roles as a property guard and a cattle-herder.

According to one theory, the breed originated in southern Mississippi, where European settlers had brought with them their Belgian Malinois dogs. In their new environment, these imported dogs began to change and to develop into the Black Mouth treeing breed. In its modified form, it later became popular in the mountains of Tennessee, Missouri and North Carolina, and eventually spread westwards from there, into the Big Thicket region of the state of Texas. In 1987 the Southern Black

Mouth Cur Breeders Association was formed to support it, and it remains a favoured hunting breed today.

This ferocious hunter often fails to tree the game, for the simple reason that it is so efficient at catching and killing its prey on the ground before the animal has managed to reach the temporary refuge of the branches. While tracking, the Black Mouth Cur is usually silent, giving voice only when the game has been driven up into a tree, at which point it gives vent to a 'hard chopping bark'.

This is a short-haired breed, typically fawn or pale brown in colour, with a black muzzle and other small dark markings. Some individuals may be much darker, right through to solid black, and brindles may also occur. The dome of the head is broad and flat and the jaws are powerful. The chest is deep and wide, the ears are drooping, the body is athletic and sturdy, and the tail is undocked. The height varies considerably, from 16 to 28 in (41–71 cm).

References

1996. Anon. *First Annual Yearbook of the Southern Black Mouth Cur Dogs.* Howell Print and Graphics, Hot Springs, Arkansas.
1999. Osborn, David A. *Squirrel Dog Basics. A Guide to Hunting Squirrels with Dogs.* Treetop Publications, Watkinsville, Georgia.

BLACK AND TAN COONHOUND UNITED STATES

Also known as the 'Cooner', this is the oldest of the coonhound breeds. Although primarily used against raccoon, it is occasionally employed on puma and bear hunts. Its original, official title, when it was first registered with the United Kennel Club back in 1900, was the American Black and Tan Fox and Coonhound. This was later abbreviated to the American Black and Tan Coonhound.

In the 17th century, Bloodhounds and Foxhounds were brought from England to the British colony in Virginia. The Bloodhounds were employed to defend the colonists from attacks by the local Indian tribes. The Foxhounds were for sport, the wealthier European settlers enjoying pack-hunting on horseback. This expensive leisure pursuit was, however, out of the reach of poorer farmers. For them, the chase had to be on foot, and by the 18th century they had created their own breed of hunting dog by crossing the Bloodhounds with the Foxhounds. These new dogs were specialized for night-hunting after raccoon and opossum and soon acquired the name of coonhound.

The Black and Tan is similar in appearance to a Bloodhound, but more streamlined and lacks any wrinkling of the skin on the head. Enthusiasts claim that this is the most efficient treer of all the various coonhound breeds. It has a loud 'bawl', a highly sensitive nose, and an ability to solve with great speed problems it encounters in the field.

This breed was recognized by the AKC in 1945 and is the most common of all the coonhounds. In personality it is described as brave, confident, intelligent, obedient, aggressive, active and fast.

References

1990. Nicholas, Anna Katherine. *Black and Tan Coonhounds.* TFH, New Jersey.

BLUETICK COONHOUND   UNITED STATES

Sometimes referred to as the Bluetick-English, or simply the Blue Tick, this breed exists in two sizes. The original form, known as the Big Blue, was a large dog specialized for treeing powerful game such as puma and bear. A later version, more compact and streamlined, was developed for faster work against raccoon.

The Bluetick originated in Louisiana at the beginning of the 20th century. It was developed from crosses between the English Coonhound, the Foxhound and the French Grand Bleu de Gascogne. Its tricoloured, blue-speckled coat sets it apart from other coonhound breeds. Originally it was registered as a variant of the English Coonhound, but in 1946 it was given separate recognition as a distinct breed in its own right (by the United Kennel Club). Today the English Coonhound is sometimes referred to as the Redtick.

The original, old-fashioned Bluetick dog, which was larger and slower than the modern type, began to lose ground because it did less well in the increasingly popular field competitions and night trials. The smaller, faster version began to eclipse it and became one of the most popular and numerous of all coonhound breeds. This upset the

traditionalists, who preferred the old-style 'Big Blue', and some of them reacted by switching their allegiance to other large-bodied breeds, such as the Blue Gascon and the Majestic.

A competitive, fearless, dedicated hunter, the Bluetick is described as 'a very dignified looking animal' with a 'good hound bawl'.

CAMUS CUR   UNITED STATES

A rare, localized breed, the Camus Cur originated in South Carolina. It is employed to hunt squirrel and raccoon.

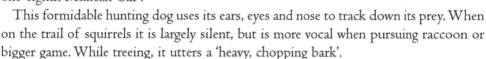

This is a recent breed, created in 1985 by J. Richard McDuffie of Aiken, South Carolina. He developed it by carefully crossing other treeing breeds and then stabilizing the crosses to retain the most desirable qualities of the founding dogs – breeding 'the best to the best'. The Camus Cur has been described as 'one-half Leopard Cur, three-eighths Canadian Cur, and one-eighth Mexican Cur'.

This formidable hunting dog uses its ears, eyes and nose to track down its prey. When on the trail of squirrels it is largely silent, but is more vocal when pursuing raccoon or bigger game. While treeing, it utters a 'heavy, chopping bark'.

It is a laid-back dog, which is easy to train and makes a delightfully cooperative companion. Its coat is short and thick, in various shades of red or brindled red. The ears are drooped and the tail is undocked.

In 1998, the Camus Cur Breeders Association was founded to support the breed.

References

1999. Osborn, David A. *Squirrel Dog Basics. A Guide to Hunting Squirrels with Dogs.* Treetop Publications, Watkinsville, Georgia.

DENMARK FEIST   UNITED STATES

This recent treeing breed takes its title from the first parts of the names of its creators, Dennis Willis and Mark Slade. It is a primarily a squirrel dog, but has also been used against raccoons, bobcats and occasionally hogs.

The history of this breed began in 1917 when the Slade family of Chatham, Virginia, acquired an exceptional dog from a travelling-wagon salesman. He bartered the dog for 'three opossum hides, one large raccoon, and a wagon round'. The Slades were so impressed by the hunting abilities of their little feist dog

that they used him as the founding father of a new line of treeing dogs. In 1984, Mark Slade, along with Dennis Willis of Danville, Virginia, formally introduced the breed as the DenMark Feist, and two years later, in 1986, the DenMark Treeing Feist Association was formed.

These are silent-trailing dogs that kill prey on the ground as well as treeing them for the hunters to dispatch. They are fearless when facing a threat to the farms where they live, but are immensely friendly with their owners, to whom they become strongly attached.

This breed has a short, rough coat that is usually yellow or red in colour, but is also occasionally red-and-white. It has a broad muzzle, an athletic body and longer legs than its closest relatives. Its ears are drooped and its tail is short. It is said that 70 per cent of puppies are born with naturally bobbed tails.

References

1999. Osborn, David A. *Squirrel Dog Basics. A Guide to Hunting Squirrels with Dogs.* Treetop Publications, Watkinsville, Georgia.

ENGLISH COONHOUND   UNITED STATES

Sometimes called the Redtick Coonhound, this rather variable breed is the fastest of the coonhounds and does well in field-trial competitions. When it was first registered with the United Kennel Club it was given the official name of the English Fox and Coonhound, but as it became more and more of a raccoon specialist, this cumbersome title was shortened to its present, more appropriate form.

Despite its name, this is an exclusively American breed. It is called the English Coonhound because of its ancestors – it is descended from English Foxhounds imported into the Americas back in the 19th century. These original dogs were modified by selective breeding to create an efficient treeing dog that was eventually officially recognized as a new breed in 1900.

Up until the end of World War II, this breed was not officially distinguished from the Treeing Walker Coonhound or the Bluetick Coonhound, but then, in 1945 and 1946 respectively, these dogs were separated and treated as distinct breeds in their own right. After this, breeders of the traditional English Coonhound began to favour redtick coat colours, as a way of contrasting their old breed with its more modern offshoots. Some authorities went so far as to rename the English Coonhound the 'Redtick Coonhound'.

KEMMER STOCK MOUNTAIN CUR UNITED STATES

Also known as the Kemmer Stock Cur or the Kemmer Cur, this modern variant of the old Mountain Cur was developed by Robert Kemmer and has been named after him. Although it is primarily used as a treeing dog, it is versatile enough to be co-opted for other duties.

This breed originated in Tennessee, where Robert Kemmer grew up on his father's farm in Grassy Cove, south of Crossville. His family had bred Mountain Curs for many years and, as a child, Robert knew them well. In 1965 he was drafted into the army and when he returned in the 1970s he began to develop his own, improved strain of Mountain Cur. He worked as a guide for wild-boar hunters, went raccoon-hunting by night and started his own stock farm. He needed a new type of dog that could excel as an aid in all three of these activities. With this in mind, Kemmer carefully selected foundation animals from the available Mountain Curs and began a selective breeding programme. He concentrated more on hunting ability than on precise appearance.

By 1991, enough people had acquired Kemmer Stock Mountain Curs to make it possible to establish a Kemmer Stock Breeders Association, and to formulate an official breed standard.

This is a well-built, muscular, medium-sized dog, with a height of 18–26 in (46–66 cm). In colour it is typically yellow, but black, brindle, blue and variations of these colours are also accepted. The coat may be smooth or rough. The dome of its wide head is flat and it has a heavy muzzle. Its ears are short and set high. The neck is strong and muscular. The tail may be naturally short, bobbed or long.

A fast-learning, intelligent breed, it is alert and quick-moving when on the hunt. In addition to its usual quarry, it is brave enough to take on either boar or bear, snapping at them and circling to keep them at bay. When this versatile animal is not hunting, it can guard the farm livestock, protect the farmer's children, heel cattle like a stock dog, catch groundhogs and even track snakes. Despite this it appears to be little-known outside the American deep south.

LEOPARD TREE DOG UNITED STATES

Also known as the Leopard Cur or the American Leopard Cur, this breed was originally a dual-purpose hound that could act as a livestock-controller as well as a treeing dog. Its main function, however, was to hunt game such as raccoon, bear and puma.

On first hearing the name of this breed, one could be forgiven for thinking that the animal had been developed in Africa for the dangerous sport of treeing leopards, but this is not the case. Instead it gains its title from its spotted coat, and is in reality a typical American coonhound.

Its history has been traced back to the eastern region of North Carolina in the early 18th century. Its earlier ancestry is not clear, but it is known that the Spanish, French, English, Scottish and Irish settlers had all brought dogs with them to this region and that these had been allowed to mix together rather freely. It is thought that from their various hounds and herding dogs, the first spotted Leopard Tree Dogs were created by this mixing and eventually became fixed as a specialized hunting breed.

As the years passed and coonhunting with these early treeing dogs became increasingly popular, they spread out to Tennessee, Kentucky, Texas and Oklahoma. They remained a favoured breed until the 20th century, when their numbers began to fall. By the 1950s they had been allowed to interbreed to such an extent that pure-bred examples were hard to find. At this point, three enthusiasts, Richard McDuffie, Leroy Smith and A.W. Carter, set up mating programmes to save the breed. Scouring the more remote regions for surviving undiluted examples, they established a register and began to keep proper records. In 1959 they formed the American Leopard Cur Breeders Association. McDuffie became the central figure and later, in 1977, he opened a Leopard Tree Dog Registration Office where he recorded all dogs that could trace their ancestry back to the original North Carolina pedigrees.

A frequent comment on the personality of these dogs concerns their unusual readiness to please their owners. This obedience and ease of training is said to be stronger than in typical scenthounds, and it is thought to have been contributed by the herding-dog element in their mixed ancestry. They are also highly regarded for their courage, their stamina and their ability to work in extremes of temperature. When cornering larger prey, they exhibit great skill in 'ducking and dodging' to avoid injury.

Their 'leopard' title is slightly misleading because close examination reveals that their coats are 'splotched', rather than truly spotted. Technically it is called a 'merle' pattern (blue-grey flecked with black).

MAJESTIC TREE HOUND   UNITED STATES

This large coonhound was developed as a specialist in treeing larger prey, such as bear, bobcat, puma and even jaguar.

This is a recent coonhound breed, although it is based on an early type. The original 'raccoon dogs' of the southern states were essentially modified forms of scenthounds that were descended from imported English Foxhounds. These Foxhounds were mixed with imported Bloodhounds to create the treeing breeds. The earliest treeing dogs were rather heavy and tended to favour the Bloodhound element. Later developments saw many coonhounds made faster and more streamlined, but some breeders mourned the passing of the earlier, slower types, with their ability to pick up the scent of even the faintest trail.

In 1979 Lee Newhart, Jnr, decided to reconstitute this early type in the form of the Majestic. After a carefully organized programme of ruthlessly selective breeding, he was able to have this 'new-old' breed accepted by the National Kennel Club in America in April 1980. A National Majestic Tree Hound Association has been formed in Ithaca to support and promote the breed.

In personality this is a noble and dignified dog, easy to train, affectionate and good-natured. It has been designed to have a 'keen scenting ability, even temperament, beautiful voice, natural treeing ability and extra houndy appearance'. It displays the facial wrinkling and the dewlaps that reflect the Bloodhound element in its ancestry.

MOUNTAIN TREEING FEIST   UNITED STATES

Originally the term Treeing Feist was applied to any small dog that showed treeing ability in the hunting field. But some of these dogs were carefully selectively bred to improve their quality and these were given the title of Mountain Treeing Feist, or American Treeing Feist, to distinguish them as a special breed. As this is exclusively an American phenomenon, the word American in the title is superfluous, and Mountain Treeing Feist is preferable. This dog specializes in treeing squirrels and raccoons, but has also been used against bear, bobcat, puma and opossum.

Back in the 19th century, American country folk in the mountains of the south-eastern states were making good use of their small hunting dogs. Living conditions were often hard for these mountain people, and their dogs were important to them. But towards the end of the 20th century, circumstances had changed and living conditions had improved to the point where these working dogs were becoming increasingly obsolete and ultimately quite rare.

At the beginning of the 1980s, a number of enthusiasts realized that the Treeing Feists could disappear altogether and started to rally support for them. There was a strong response and in 1984 the Mountain Feist Association was formed. In 1985 this was replaced by the American Treeing Feist Association, and in 1986 the Mountain Feist Breeders Club was formed to establish a registry. In 1992 the Mountain Treeing Feist Organization appeared on the scene and in 1999 the Traditional Treeing Feist Club was founded.

For a small, rural working dog this would appear to be a case of 'committee overkill', but it is better to have a surfeit of organizational control than it is to see a complete lack of interest leading to extinction. In the future, no doubt, these various rival groups will cooperate to establish a single, central regulatory body. In the meantime the breed remains rather variable. Treeing-dog expert David Osborn comments: 'There are many widely recognized strains of Treeing Feist... most do not yet have organized, strain-specific registries, and cross-breeding of strains is common.'

For the present, the characteristics of the Mountain Treeing Feist remain rather vague. The height varies from 10–22 in (25–55 cm) and the weight from 10 to 35 lb (5–16 kg). Any colour or colour-pattern is acceptable. The tail may be docked, or of any length. The ears should be pricked, but semi-pricked ears, in which the tips fold over, are often seen. On a more precise note, a specific rule states that the coat must be short and that long-haired or shaggy dogs are not acceptable.

References

1999. Osborn, David A. *Squirrel Dog Basics. A Guide to Hunting Squirrels with Dogs.* Treetop Publications, Watkinsville, Georgia.

MOUNTAIN VIEW CUR   UNITED STATES

This recent breed was developed in New York State as an improved, all-round treeing dog.

In the 1980s Michael Bloodgood of Afton, New York, started a carefully planned breeding programme with the aim of producing an exceptional treeing breed. It was a major undertaking involving the acquisition of no fewer than 56 Mountain Curs. Half of these were Original Mountain Curs and half were Kemmer Stock Mountain Curs. By studying them carefully he was able to select the best two individuals as his first foundation pair. Later, he added a second pair and from these four animals he started to develop his breed. In 1997 the Mountain View Cur Registry was formed and he was able to start recording dogs as examples of his new breed.

It has proved to be a versatile hunting dog. In addition to treeing the traditional quarry — squirrels, raccoons and opossums — it has also been used against puma, coyote, bear, boar, turkey, grouse, pheasant and rabbit. In addition, on the farm, it has been co-opted for herding livestock.

This is a fast-moving tracker. It is silent when in pursuit of squirrels, but calls out with a distinctive 'clear ringing chop' when treeing the quarry. A short-coated dog, it has drooped ears, and a tail that is either naturally bobbed or moderately docked — 'long enough to serve as a handle'. In colour it may be black, black-and-brindle, brindle, red, yellow, or off-white.

References

1999. Osborn, David A. *Squirrel Dog Basics. A Guide to Hunting Squirrels with Dogs.* Treetop Publications, Watkinsville, Georgia.

MULLINS' FEIST   UNITED STATES

This recent breed was named after its creator, Jody Mullins. Its main function is treeing squirrels, raccoons and opossums, but it is also occasionally used against wild boar. The word 'feist' is a variant of 'fist' and is a 20th-century slang term, from the deep South of the United States, for a small but fierce dog. It is the source of the word 'feisty', now often applied to a truculent or assertive person.

Standing at only 15–18 in (38–45 cm), this is a smaller dog than the typical coonhounds, which have a minimum height of at least 20 in (51 cm).

This breed began in the 1970s when Jody Mullins discovered a local strain of Treeing Feist that had been developed by a family living in Tennessee. Impressed by their dogs, Mullins acquired a male and two females and used these as the foundation stock for the new breed. The breed was developed at the Mullins family home at Bearden, Arkansas.

An agile, active animal, its movement is described as effortless, fast and smooth. Its head is wide and strangely flat-topped, its ears are drooped and its straight tail may be long or naturally bobbed. The coat is short, dense and smooth. In colour it is either solid yellow (light or dark yellow), solid black, yellow with white points, or black with white points.

A breed registry was established in 1997 and a breed club formed in 1998. There are biannual gatherings of supporters of this breed at which 'Bench Shows, Treeing Contests, Roll Cage Contests, and Buddy Hunts' are staged.

This breed and its close relatives, the DenMark Feist, the Thornburg Feist, the Mountain Treeing Feist and the Original Cajun Squirrel Dog, are jointly referred to as 'squirrel dogs'.

References

1998. Osborn, David A. *Squirrel Dog Basics; a Guide to Hunting Squirrels with Dogs.* Treetop Publications, Watkinsville, Georgia.

ORIGINAL CAJUN SQUIRREL DOG   UNITED STATES

Of all the treeing dog breeds, this is the most specialized as a squirrel-hunter, showing little interest in other kinds of game.

The Original Cajun Squirrel Dog is a recent breed, not having been developed until the late 1980s, when Calvin Boutee of St Martinville, Louisiana, and Robert Kemmer of Crossville, Tennessee, started line-breeding carefully selected crosses between curs and feists. The complex mixture of foundation breeds that was involved in the creation of the Cajun Squirrel Dog is recorded as including 'five Mullins Feists, one Mountain Treeing Feist, three Kemmer Feists, and six Kemmer Stock Mountain Curs'. The new breed was gradually stabilized, and pedigree records were started in 1985; by 1996 it was possible to establish the Original Cajun Squirrel Dog Register.

The coat is short and may be yellow, red, red-and-white, or brindle. The head is flat-domed, the ears are drooped and the tail is either naturally bobbed or severely docked.

References

1998. Osborn, David A. *Squirrel Dog Basics. A Guide to Hunting Squirrels with Dogs.* Treetop Publications, Watkinsville, Georgia.

ORIGINAL MOUNTAIN CUR   UNITED STATES

Sometimes called simply the Mountain Cur, this breed once included a variant called the Treeing Tennessee Brindle, but the latter has now been given its own, separate breed status. A rugged, powerfully built dog, the Mountain Cur is capable of fearlessly treeing large prey.

Closely related to the Leopard Tree Dog, this old breed had as its original stronghold the Ohio River Valley. Its ancestors consisted of imported Foxhounds, imported herding dogs, and native Indian dogs. The Indian element has given this particular dog a less 'houndy' quality than the other, related coonhound breeds. Its head is wider and its body stockier. Some are born tailless, others are docked and still others are allowed to remain fully tailed. They are quieter hunters than the more typical coonhound and are usually less efficient at scent-trailing. But they excel at treeing, once the prey is cornered.

The popularity of this breed waned during the 20th century, and by the end of World War II there were few pure-bred specimens left. Then a group of enthusiasts came to the rescue, founded the Original Mountain Cur Breeders Association and did their best to revive its fortunes, with some success.

The famous book *Old Yeller* was based on the exploits of a boy and his Mountain Cur, but unfortunately for the breed, the Hollywood film version of the story incorrectly featured a Golden Labrador.

References

1980. Ledbetter, D. and Ledbetter, V. *The History and Stories of the Original Mountain Cur.* Privately published.
1999. Osborn, David A. *Squirrel Dog Basics. A Guide to Hunting Squirrels with Dogs.* Treetop Publications, Watkinsville, Georgia.

PLOTT HOUND   UNITED STATES

This breed was named after the German immigrant Jonathan Plott, who brought his favourite German hounds with him when he moved from his homeland to settle in the mountains of western North Carolina. In this new environment, faced with novel game species, his animals developed into efficient treeing dogs.

Jonathan Plott moved to America in 1750 and settled just to the west of the town of Asheville. The brindle dogs that accompanied him had been used in their original homeland for hunting wild boar. When these powerful hounds began to explore their new mountain home, they discovered a different form of quarry – the American black bear. Over the years they became increasingly expert at treeing these bears and later turned their attention to the treeing of other, smaller game, changing in the process from boarhounds to coonhounds.

Plott guarded his breed carefully, protecting them from any unwanted crosses and pure-breeding them for over 30 years. It is said that there was only one official out-cross in their 200-year history. This was to a 'Leopard Spotted Bear Dog' from Georgia, at the beginning of the 19th century. The story goes that Henry Plott, who had inher-ited the family pack, was visited by a proud huntsman from Georgia who believed that his own dogs were the best in the land. The two men hunted together, each with his own dogs, and became close. Plott agreed to loan a stud dog to his Georgian friend. Later, when the man came back to return the dog, he also brought with him a fine young male puppy that it had sired. Plott was so impressed by this cross that he kept the animal and uniquely allowed it to breed with his other pure-breds. This is the only 'outside impurity' to which the Plott clan is prepared to admit. Others have suggested that Bloodhounds, Black and Tan Coonhounds and various other breeds have been introduced to strengthen the stock, but this is hotly denied.

Although Plott Hounds became well known in their new territory – the Great Smoky Mountains of North Carolina and Tennessee – their fame did not spread further afield. This was largely because the Plott family were so resistant to dispersing them.

Eventually, the fame of the Plott Hounds did manage to spread outside their restric-ted homeland and, little by little, good specimens were allowed to pass into the hands of other hunters and breeders. But, even so, this remains one of the purest strains in the coonhound world. In 1946 the breed was formally recognized by the United Kennel Club. In temperament, it is described as an alert, intelligent, confident dog, with great stamina and fearless aggression when on the hunt.

REDBONE COONHOUND UNITED STATES

Sometimes referred to as the Redbone, the Redbone Hound or the Red-coon Dog, this breed was developed to hunt and 'tree' not only raccoon but also wildcat, puma and even bear. There are two theories about the origin of its name. Some believe it commemorates the Tennessee breeder Peter Redbone; others think that it simply reflects this dog's red coat colour.

It is recorded that, in the later years of the 18th century, red scenthounds were brought to North America by Scottish immigrants. In addition there were importations of red Irish hounds, so that there were plenty of individual red-coated dogs present to form the foundation stock of what would later become the true-breeding Redbone Coonhound. No attempt was made to breed true from the early red hounds. Then, in the 1920s, a group of enthusiasts decided to start a serious breeding programme to fix a stable line. The very first ones were called Saddlebacks because they often had a black saddle-patch on their backs, but this was gradually eliminated by selective breeding until the dogs were all solid red. This is now the only solid-coloured member of the coon-hound group.

Today this handsome breed has become increasingly popular and has spread outside its original homeland in the southern states. It is now to be found not only in the United States, Canada and Mexico, but also in South America and even Japan. A good-tempered, intelligent, obedient dog, the Redbone is energetic, fearless, tenacious and tireless on the hunt.

STEPHENS STOCK   UNITED STATES

Sometimes called the Stephens Stock Mountain Cur or the Stephens Cur, this breed was named after the family that created it. A smallish coonhound, it was specialized for hunting squirrel and raccoon.

The Stephens family from south-eastern Kentucky developed their own strain of Mountain Cur for over a century until eventually it was so distinctive that, in 1970, it was accepted as a separate breed and given their name. Hugh Stephens is now recognized as the founder of the modern, standardized breed.

The Stephens Stock is a short-coated, black dog, often with a few small white markings on the extremities. Known affectionately as the 'Little Black', and standing only 16–23 in (40–59 cm) tall, it is too small to be used singly against bigger game but, if hunted in a pack, will have the courage to take on either puma or bear. What it lacks in power it makes up for in speed.

This is a short-coated breed. The dome of the head is flat and wide, the ears are drooped and the tail is left undocked.

THORNBURG FEIST

UNITED STATES

This breed takes its name from its creators, the Thornburgs of North Carolina. It was bred as a treeing dog specializing in hunting squirrel, opossum and raccoon.

In origin, this breed can be traced back to the 1940s, when three North Carolina hunting men starting a breeding programme by crossing their little feist dogs. A male feist owned by John Little of Farmer, North Carolina, was mated with a female belonging to his neighbour, Marshall Thornburg, and to another female belonging to Holton Thornburg of Asheboro, North Carolina. Their aim was to create a small treeing dog which would be inexpensive to maintain but which would, despite its small size, prove to be a vigorous and determined hunter. By the 1980s the line had passed down to Holton Thornburg's son Farrell, and his dog Buck became a key animal in the furthering of the breed.

The Thornburg Feist is only 13–17 in (33–43 cm) in height, but is a persistent hunter and exceptionally intelligent. It follows a trail silently until it has treed its quarry, when it barks noisily. In colour, the short coat is usually red-and-white, but may also be black-and-white, tricolour, red, blue-ticked or black-and-tan. The ears are nearly always erect, although there are exceptions to this rule. Six out of ten puppies are born with naturally bobbed tails. The others may be docked or may retain their full tail.

TREEING CUR

UNITED STATES

Originally this name was given to any cross-bred dog that was created as a treeing specialist. In hunting trials such animals were labelled as Grade Dogs, but today they are now regarded as belonging to a distinct breed of their own. They were developed to hunt squirrel, raccoon, puma or bear.

In origin this type of dog was the result of crosses between curs and hounds, between curs and feists, or between one type of cur and another. Out of this mixture there gradually grew a new kind of treeing dog with improved hunting abilities and, in 1993, it was sufficiently distinctive to be given a breed name and to see the foundation of a National Treeing Cur Association to support it.

As a hunter, this dog combines the best qualities of its parent breeds. It uses vision, scent and sound in the pursuit of its prey, silently after squirrel, but vocal after raccoon. It is a sturdy, muscular dog with drooped ears. Its tail may be of any length and its coat of any colour.

References

1998. Osborn, David A. *Squirrel Dog Basics. A Guide to Hunting Squirrels with Dogs.* Treetop Publications, Watkinsville, Georgia.

TREEING TENNESSEE BRINDLE UNITED STATES

This dog was once lumped with the Mountain Cur as a single form but is now given separate breed status. It has been used on raccoon and squirrel hunts for many years, and will also tree both bears and large felines such as bobcats and pumas.

The TTB is more 'houndy' than its close relative, the Mountain Cur. The foundation stock for this breed was a mixed bag of brindle tree dogs from many regions. In 1959 the Revd Earl Phillips of Flora, Illinois, began a search for treeing dogs that would give voice both on the trail and when treeing. His search took him, in his own words, to 'the coves of the rough mountains of North Carolina, southern Virginia, eastern Kentucky, eastern Tennessee, and north-eastern Georgia', where he found breeds by the name of Brindle Cur Stock, Hunting Bull, Tennessee Brindled Cur, Old Brindle Bear Dog, Cherokee Brindle Cur and Plott Cur. In his opinion the ancestors of these localized breeds included the Old English Brindle Bull Dog and the Old Saddleback Virginia Hound, or High Tan Hound.

The Revd Phillips purchased the best examples he could find and used them as the foundation stock for a new, improved breed of hunting dog. In 1967, under his leadership, a group of enthusiasts got together and formed the Tennessee Brindle Breeders Association. They gave their dogs a formal title, the Treeing Tennessee Brindle, and set about stabilizing and registering the breed. The success of their campaign has resulted in the TTB spreading across much of the United States.

This is a small, fast-moving coonhound which is as friendly and relaxed with its human owners as it is fearless and courageous when on the hunt. It has a smooth coat, a flat-domed head, drooped ears, and a medium-length tail. Its height varies from 16 to 24 in (41–61 cm).

TREEING WALKER COONHOUND UNITED STATES

Originally thought to be no more than a variant of the English Coonhound, this breed was not officially recognized (by the United Kennel Club) as a distinct entity until 1945. It is a fast-moving nocturnal hunter that specializes in treeing raccoon and opossum.

In 1742 Thomas Walker imported English Foxhounds into Virginia, where his local strain later became known as Walker Hounds. Later still, in Kentucky, some of these dogs were selectively bred to improve their treeing ability. It is known that in the 19th century there was a significant out-cross to some unidentified dog from Tennessee, which helped to modify the hound and alter its character. Anatomically, these 'improved' Treeing Walker Coonhounds still looked very much like their fox-hunting ancestors, but in behaviour they showed a marked change, being much more persistent in keeping a treed quarry aloft with prolonged barking, until the hunters arrived on the scene.

   In personality they are described as confident, fearless, graceful, energetic and sensible. Being very fast, they have proved unusually successful in field-trial competitions. There is disagreement about their temperament, some experts describing them as composed, while others consider them to be highly strung.

   There is a smaller, faster version of this dog, called the Running Walker Coonhound, or the Running Treeing Walker (see separate entry).

CANADA

CANADIAN CUR CANADA

This is a recent breed with a complex origin. It was specifically developed to hunt raccoon.

This northern representative of the Treeing Dog group was created in Ontario in the 1980s by David Rogers and Larry Smith, whose stated aim was to 'develop a hunting dog with tracking power, treeing ability, stamina and intelligence, while maintaining such intangibles as dedication, loyalty and a friendly disposition'. To achieve this goal they began a carefully controlled breeding programme involving the Border Collie, the English Pointer, the Original Mountain Cur, the Kemmer Stock Mountain Cur and the Leopard Tree Dog.

Once the new breed had been stabilized it was discovered that, in addition to its specialization of treeing raccoons, it was extremely useful for the pursuit of squirrel and bigger game such as bear, boar, coyote, deer and puma. As a sideline, it was also a valuable stock-herder, and it was adaptable enough to become an affectionate household pet. In support of this versatile breed, the Canadian Cur Breeders Association was founded in 1995.

When trailing, the Canadian Cur usually works in the 'head-up' position. Unlike some other treeing dogs, it is often vocal while following the scent. Some individuals are silent trailers by day, but vocal by night.

This is a well-balanced, athletic dog, with drooped ears and a naturally short tail. It is said that 80 per cent of puppies are born with a bobbed tail. The colour of the short coat is highly variable.

References

1998. Osborn, David A. *Squirrel Dog Basics. A Guide to Hunting Squirrels with Dogs.* Treetop Publications, Watkinsville, Georgia.

SETTING DOGS

The setters were once referred to as the 'setting spaniels' or the 'crouching spaniels', and it seems certain that they were originally developed from some of the ancient spaniel lines.

The first person to train a spaniel-like dog to act as a setter is usually recorded as being the Duke of Northumberland. This event is supposed to have occurred at the beginning of the 16th century, and an early document describes the Duke as 'noted for... being the first of all that taught a dog to sit in order to catch partridge'.

Others feel that 'setting' first began in France. In the 1620s the French king, Louis XIII, sent the English king, James I, some setting dogs as a royal gift. William Arkwright, the canine historian, comments: 'It seems pretty sure that the setting-spaniels... were from an early period naturalised in France, and conferred upon us by the latter country.'

Anatomically, the typical setter could be described as a lanky, long-legged spaniel. Behaviourally, it is a cautious, self-disciplined spaniel. The major change in personality centres on the fact that, at the very moment when the searching dog detects its quarry, instead of moving forward to flush it out into the open, it freezes, 'sets' its body in the direction of the hiding prey, and then remains stock still until given permission by the hunter to move again. This self-imposed inhibition at the very moment of discovery might seem extraordinary, but it is no more than a modified form of wolf behaviour, borrowed from the repertoire of the dog's wild ancestor. 'Setting' in wolves occurs at the moment the hunting pack has surrounded its prey and is preparing for a final rush to make the kill. For the setter, the human hunters are its 'pack', and it is therefore genetically programmed to await their orders. Thus, its behaviour is more natural than it might at first appear.

The actions of the hunting setter are best described by the 18th-century poet, William Somerville, who wrote that it 'cautious creeps, low-cow'ring, step by step; at last attains his proper distance; there he stops at once, and points with his instructive nose upon the trembling prey'.

In medieval England, the setters worked to nets or falcons, but with the arrival and steady improvement in sporting guns, they came into their own. In the 19th century their showy gait and appealing shape made them early favourites on the show bench, and a new role opened up for them. During the 20th century this new role more or less eclipsed the old one and today they are seldom seen in the hunting field.

Ten breeds fall into this category.

ENGLAND

ANGLESEA SETTER   ENGLAND

This was an extinct breed of setter created by and named after the Marquis of Anglesea. It had no connection with the island of Anglesea, being developed at his residence at Beaudesert in Staffordshire.

The dog was a black, white and tan colour, less smooth than a typical English Setter, but less curly than a Welsh Setter (see entry for Llanidloes Setter). An active, leggy dog with a narrow body, it was fast but delicate, gaining in pace what it lacked in stamina.

ENGLISH SETTER   ENGLAND

This breed was developed as the English refinement of the old 'setting-spaniel', a dog that would sit quietly as soon as it had located game-birds and wait for the hunter to make the next move.

In the 19th century, many local strains of English Setter were being developed, each with its own slight variation on the main theme, but few of these forms merit the distinction of being called separate breeds. Among the named ones were the Anglesea Setter (see separate entry), the Featherstone Setter, the Laverack Setter, the Llewellin Setter, the Newcastle Setter, the Old Hemlock Setter and the Ryman Setter.

The English Setter's early champions vied with one another to produce the best dogs. In the end, it was generally agreed that it was Sir Edward Laverack who did most to establish the modern form of the breed. He began in 1825 with a pair of dogs obtained from kennels in Carlisle and spent the next half-century refining and improving his strain.

Such was the hostility between competing breeders, however, that one of Laverack's rivals, Thomas Pearce, refused to mention him by name, referring to him only as 'the Manchester Gentleman' and dismissing his dogs as too much like retrievers, heavy in the shoulder and too wide in the chest. Despite this, Laverack is today generally regarded as the father of the modern English Setter. Another important breeder was Purcell Llewellin, who focused on field trials. His role with working setters was so significant that, for a while, people spoke of the Llewellin Setter as if it were a breed in its own right.

This is a beautifully formed dog, with a characteristically long and silky, speckled white coat. The flecking is technically referred to as 'belton'. It has a calm, gentle, warmly affectionate personality and its elegant stride as it sets off across a field is a pleasure to behold. Compared with the other two main breeds – the Irish and the Gordon – it is slightly shorter in the leg, not having to contend, as one early author put it, with 'bog or heather'.

An amusing story is told of an early poaching technique employed with the aid of this breed. Back in Georgian times, at Castle Howard, an English Setter with a lantern strapped to its head was observed moving about in a field at dead of night. When it stopped and sat down, three men rushed forward with nets and threw these over the roosting birds the dog had discovered. Unfortunately for the poachers, the strangely moving light was easily spotted by the estate's gamekeepers. The interest in this story lies in the extent to which this breed is prepared to go to aid its human companions. Many other dogs would have spent the night trying to shake the head-lamp free.

References

1872. Laverack, Edward, *The Setter.* (Reprinted 1999)
1937. Bepler, M. Ingle and Ryan, C. W. *Setters: Irish, English and Gordon.*
1948. Rechnitzer, F. E. *Raff, The Story of an English Setter.* John C. Winston.
1951. Tuck, Davis. *The Complete English Setter.* Denlinger's, USA.
1958. Hubbard, Clifford L. B. *The English Setter Handbook.* Nicholson & Watson, London.
1964. Maire, Susan S. *How to Raise and Train an English Setter.* TFH, New Jersey.
1975. Allan-Scott, Lesley. *The English Setter.* K & R Books, Leicestershire.
1976. Foss, Valerie. *The English Setter.* Foyles, London.
1986. Tuck, Davis. *The New Complete English Setter.* Howell, New York.
1988. Pisano, Beverly. *English Setters.* TFH, New Jersey.

DROPPER   ENGLAND

This is an extinct breed that was developed from crosses between setters and pointers. The idea was to intensify the hunting abilities of this new field dog by giving it the best of the two 'freezing' specialists. The fact that it was given the name of Dropper reveals that, when it inherited both the standing 'point' and the lying 'set', it was the latter that dominated, causing the dog to 'drop' to the ground on discovering game.

Apparently, although some of these dogs did indeed display the best features of both parents, there was too much variability in the breed. As one early observer put it: 'His talents are uncertain, his temper is capricious.' As a result, interest waned and, as a serious breed, the Dropper was eventually dropped.

SCOTLAND

BALLOCH SETTER   SCOTLAND

An extinct breed that takes its name from the small town of Balloch, 18 miles north-west of Glasgow.

Once a greatly admired type of setter, those dogs were described as 'carrying their head high, and working for the body scent in beautiful style'. They had a long, low form with strong bones and rather short heads.

In colour they were 'red marbled' or 'blue marbled', and their distinguishing feature was the presence of a thick, woolly undercoat, a protective 'fur' that helped them adapt to the extremely cold countryside in which they had to hunt at all times of the year. It is not clear why these excellent setters eventually vanished. They were last discussed at the end of the 19th century and do not seem to have been heard of since then.

GORDON SETTER   SCOTLAND

Also known as the Black-and-Tan Setter or the Scottish Setter, this northern breed was developed especially for hunting woodcock, pheasant and partridge. It owes its name to the Duke of Richmond and Gordon whose Banffshire kennels were famous for the breed.

Setters existed in Scotland from the early 1600s, but it was not until the end of that century that the Duke of Gordon set about fixing the type that was ultimately to bear his name. He concentrated on creating a stronger, more powerful version of the ordinary setter, one that would be more suited to the rugged northern countryside and that would be prepared to work long hours under harsh conditions. In the process he had to forfeit some speed, but the added power of his breed more than compensated for this.

It is thought that, at some stage, the Duke must have introduced a little Collie blood into his breeding programme, because early examples of the Gordon Setter were observed to circle the game before setting at it, as if they were trying to 'herd' their quarry like a sheepdog. This tendency was eventually removed by selective breeding.

During the Victorian period, this breed reached its peak of popularity, but lost ground in the 20th century.

The Gordon's coat, largely black but with tan extremities, is soft and silky. Its only weakness is that, being so dark, it is less conspicuous in the hunting field than that of the English Setter. Although it is usually assumed that it was the Duke himself who favoured the black-and-tan coloration, the truth is that his kennels contained Setters with several different coat patterns, including both black-and-white and red-and-white, and also tricolours. It seems that it was slightly later in the breed's history that the coat colour became fixed as exclusively black-and-tan, probably in connection with the Gordon's early success in the show-ring.

In temperament, the dog is gentle and affectionate and often becomes a much loved family pet.

References

1934. Schilbred, Cornelius. *The Gordon Setter, or the Scottish Setter.* Fraser, Aberdeen. (Translated from *Pointer og Setter,* Oslo, 1927.)

1937. Bepler, M. Ingle and Ryan, C. W. *Setters: Irish, English and Gordon.*

1965. King, Bart. *How to Raise and Train a Gordon Setter.* TFH, New Jersey.

1984. Look, Jean Sanger and Lustenberger, Anita. *The Complete Gordon Setter.* Howell, New York.

1990. Schweppe, Frederick. *Gordon Setters.* TFH, New Jersey.

1994. Baddeley, Jose. *Gordon Setters Today.* Howell, New York.

Gompertz, G. St G. M. *The Gordon Setter: History and Character.*

WALES

LLANIDLOES SETTER   WALES

This breed appears to be the same as the one designated the Welsh Setter in early dog books.

An extinct breed of setter, this was, at one time, sufficiently distinctive for a special class to be provided for it at a Welsh dog show in 1889. The main centre for the breed appears to have been at Kingston, Hereford.

The dog was very similar to the English Setter, but had a 'coarse, hard, curly coat and a thick, though long, head'. Its coat was said to be 'as curly as the jacket of a Cotswold Sheep… as unlike that of a modern fashionable Setter as it is possible to imagine'. It was chalk-white in colour, with an occasional lemon patch.

It had an excellent nose, but was said to be a rather slow, methodical worker in the field, and slightly more spaniel-like than its more favoured English counterpart. A hardy dog, it was better suited to working over rough ground.

IRELAND

AHASCRAGH SETTER   IRELAND

This is an extinct breed of Irish setter about which little is known. It was an all-red dog and appears to have been a precursor of the modern Irish (Red) Setter. In the 18th century almost all Irish setters were of the red-and-white type, and all-red ones were extremely rare. Examples did exist, however, sometimes in the form of a restricted, local breed. One of these was the Ahascragh.

The only report available on this rare breed comes from Irish dog expert W. C. Bennett of Dublin in the 1890s. It reads as follows:

> The Ahascragh breed (kept in the Mahon family of Galway) were highly prized, but which from being bred in and by the gamekeeper, Jemmy Fury, degenerated into weeds... Mr Mahon mentions one... a big bitch, beautifully feathered, very enduring and staunch, and with her he hoped to resuscitate the Ahascragh strain. Owing, however, to the death of his father, he abandoned the attempt.

It would seem, therefore, that this particular breed of red dogs vanished, but other examples did exist elsewhere in Ireland, and it must have been from some of these that the modern Irish (Red) Setter was eventually developed.

IRISH RED AND WHITE SETTER   IRELAND

Also known as the Particoloured Setter, this breed was originally developed to work with falcons, and in medieval times was known as the Falconer Dog. It was also used with nets. The fact that it lay down when it located the game made it easier for the hunters to throw their nets over the crouching birds. Later, when firearms were more advanced, it became a useful gun dog.

This is the traditional Irish Setter, the favourite breed in Ireland before the Red Setter swept all before it. Apart from its coat colour, it differs very little from the more famous Red Setter, although close inspection does reveal that it has a higher-set ear, a slightly shorter, wider, heavier body, and less extreme feathering. In other words it remains closer to the original working setter, than the glamorized 'show-business' Red Setter.

In 18th-century Ireland there were three colour types of Irish Setter: (1) the Red and White; (2) the Solid Red; and (3) the Shower of Hail. This last type, sometimes known simply as the 'Hail', was found in the extreme north-west of the country and displayed a red coat sprinkled with small white spots. It was always rare and many believe that it has long since vanished altogether, but as recently as 1998 one of these Hail Setters appeared in a litter of all-reds.

The Red and White was preferred to the Solid Red Irish Setter because hunters felt that, with its conspicuous white patches, it was easier to see in the field. There was a fear that the Solid Red Irish Setter, crouching in the long grass, might not be seen clearly and could accidentally be shot. However, in the 19th century, when dog shows began, the Solid Red animal became an instant success and soon overshadowed its more traditional relative. The Red and Whites started to disappear all over Ireland and only a few survived in the more remote corners.

By the 1940s, interest in this now rare breed had started to swell again and its numbers slowly increased. A specialist breed club was formed and, by the 1970s, a special committee was formed to monitor the breed's progress. By 1987 the Kennel Club in London had conferred championship status on the Red and White, and its future, at last, seemed assured. Today there are about 200 new registrations at the Kennel Club each year. Some Red and Whites have crossed the Atlantic and there is now also a specialist breed club in the United States.

References

1990. Brigden. *The Irish Red & White Setter*.

IRISH (RED) SETTER   IRELAND

Also known as the Red Dog or the Red Setter, or, in Gaelic, as the Modder Rhu, this impressive breed was first developed as a net and falcon setter, later became a gun dog and finally moved into the centre of the show-ring. In earlier days it was sometimes given the ill-fitting name of the Red Spaniel.

This is perhaps the most glamorous of all modern dog breeds. The extraordinary, solid-red coloration is unique and unforgettable, and it is easy to see how, once setters entered the show-ring, this breed would surpass the others. The bright, glossy top-coat and the lighter undercoat, with its copper sheen, together create the look of a star attraction.

Once the Red Setters had started to gain attention in the show-ring, some breeders decided to improve their appearance by crossing them with other glamorous breeds. They introduced a little Borzoi blood, giving the Red Setter a rangier, lankier look. Traditionalists were horrified because their efficient working animal was being turned into a fashion-model of a dog, and these out-breedings were quickly stopped. Nevertheless, the modern show dog does have a more streamlined, elongated look to it than any of the ancestral Red Setters we see in early paintings and engravings.

The Red Setter was always revered as an amazingly efficient hunting dog. It is fast, thorough and endlessly enthusiastic, trawling energetically to left and to right to cover as much ground as possible. It is used against woodcock, grouse, partridge, pheasant, wild duck and teal, and can be trained to operate as a pointer as well as a setter.

As an urban companion dog it occasionally causes trouble. Described by harassed owners as restless, highly strung, excitable or even 'crazy', it is sometimes unfairly viewed as a 'difficult pet'. But the truth is that there is nothing wrong with such an animal. It is the owners who are at fault. The dog is simply being forced to endure an inappropriate lifestyle. What it demands, as a breed, are long hours of exercise, either in the hunting field or, at the very least, in the city park. This is a high-energy dog. Lazy owners beware.

References

1924. Millner, J. K. *The Irish Setter. Its History & Training*. Witherby, London.

1932. Johns, Rowland (Editor). *Our Friend the Irish Setter*. Methuen, London.

1932. Naylor, L. E. *The Irish Setter: Its History, Temperament and Training*. Witherby, London.

1937. Bepler, M. Ingle and Ryan. C. W. *Setters: Irish, English and Gordon*.

1949. Denlinger, Milo. *Complete Irish Setter*. Denlinger's, USA.

1949. Schilbred, Major Corn. *Irish Setter History*. Denlinger's, USA. (Translated from *Pointer og Setter*, Oslo, 1929)

1954. Baird, Jack. *Pet Irish Setter*. All-Pets, Fond du Lac, Wisconsin.

1954. Thompson, William C. *The Irish Setter in Word and Picture*. Denlinger's, USA.

1961. Gannon, Robert. *How to Raise and Train an Irish Setter*. TFH, New Jersey.

1967. Thompson, William C. *The New Irish Setter*. Howell, New York.

1970s. Schneider, Earl. *Know Your Irish Setter*. Pet Library.

1973. Baird, Jack. *Irish Setters*. TFH, New Jersey.

1973. Leighton-Boyce, Gilbert. *Irish Setters*. Arthur Barker, London.

1975. Allan-Scott, Lesley. *The English Setter*. K & R Books.

1975. Baron, Bernard and Baron, Wilma. *Official National Pictorial of the Irish Setter Club of America*.

1975. Brearley, Joan McDonald. *This is the Irish Setter*. TFH, New Jersey.

1976. Migliorini, Mario. *Irish Setters*. Arco, New York.

1977. Hobbs, H. Von. *Irish Setter: a Complete Guide*. Arco, New York.

1978. Holvenstot. *Irish Setters*. TFH, New Jersey.

1978. Roberts, Janice. *The Irish Setter*. Popular Dogs, London.

1981. Sutton, Catherine G. *The Irish Setter*.

1992. Stahlkuppe, Joe. *Irish Setters: Everything About Purchase, Care, Nutrition, Breeding, Behavior, and Training*.

1998. Gardner, Eve. *Irish Setters Today*.

1998. Wilcox, Charlotte. *The Irish Setter*. Learning About Dogs Series.

Barnes, Margaret. *English Setters Ancient and Modern: Their History in the Field and on the Bench and their General Care*.

Hurden, Lil. *My Love, the Irish Setter*.

Irving, E. *The New Complete Irish Setter*.

RUSSIA

RUSSIAN SETTER   RUSSIA

In earlier works this now extinct breed was sometimes called the Russian Braque or the Russian Pointer, but most of those who encountered it in the flesh agreed that it was, in fact, a setter.

This rare and little-known breed is described, rather surprisingly, as looking 'like a big warm Bedlington Terrier'. It existed in two coat forms, one curly and deep brown and the other straight and fawn. The body shape of the curly variety is 'almost entirely concealed by a long woolly coat, which is matted together in the most extraordinary manner'. It had the bearded muzzle of a Scottie.

In his famous canine monograph of 1801, Sydenham Edwards (referring to this breed as the Russian Pointer) comments:

> ...in size and form like the Spanish; coat not unlike a drover's dog, rough and shaggy, rough about the eyes and bearded, colour like the Spanish, but often grizzle and white... this is probably a cross between the Spanish Pointer and the Barbet, or rough water dog; he has an excellent nose, sagacious, tractable, and easily made staunch... is not incommoded by the most cold and wet weather; he will frequently prefer laying in a hole formed in the snow to the shelter of his kennel; his whole frame is loose, and his travelling slow.

A small number of these dogs were brought to England, where a few local hunters found them 'wilful and savage' or 'obstinate and bad-tempered'. This probably said more about these particular hunters, who admitted being used to whipping their dogs into shape, than it did about the strong-willed Russian dogs themselves. Other English hunters were more impressed. The good qualities of the breed were said to be that it was 'determined and courageous' and 'a magnificent type... buried in a coat of very long floss silky texture... by far the greatest profusion of coat of any dog'.

An English sportsman, writing in 1841, praised his Russian Setters with the words: 'For all kinds of shooting there is nothing equal to the Russian, or half-bred Russian Setter, in nose, sagacity and every other necessary qualification that a dog ought to possess.' Another English hunter agreed: 'They were the best dogs I ever had, and never varied.' Those who worked with them urged that Russian blood should be added to the English Setter to improve its field abilities. It was felt that, although the English dog's handsome appearance might suffer, improvements in its field performance would more than compensate for this: 'What he [the Russian Setter] wants in dash and ranging propensities, he makes up for in unwearied assiduity, extreme carefulness, and extraordinary scenting powers.'

With comments like these, it is extraordinary that this breed has vanished. The only explanation appears to be that too few specimens were ever imported to avoid serious inbreeding. They were first introduced into English kennels in the 1830s, but by 1860, according to the leading canine expert of the day, 'are now almost lost sight of again'. By the early 20th century, the breed had vanished.

POINTING DOGS

The ancestor of the modern pointers was first developed as a specialized breed in the 17th century in Southern Europe – in the hunting fields of Italy, the south of France and Spain. The primitive field guns in use in those days, with their very slow-loading, flintlock action, required a perfected form of silent restraint on the part of the flushing dog. At the precise moment when the location of the hidden quarry was detected, the animal had to freeze like a statue, its head held high, one foreleg raised as if about to take another step but unable to do so, its tail held out stiffly behind, and with the whole of its rigid body pointing precisely at the spot where the scent had just been detected. In this way, if the hunters had not yet had time to reload since the previous shot, they would have plenty of time to do so before the quarry would be panicked by the further advance of the dog.

The pointer would 'hold' the game in this way for as long as was needed and would never release its frozen pose until instructed to do so by the hunter's command, such was its astonishing self-discipline.

With advances in the quality of sporting guns and the gradual loss of the larger game animals, both of which occurred in the 18th century, these early pointers had to be modified. With the introduction of new blood, they were transformed into smaller, quicker breeds, more appropriate for the new style of hunting.

Today there are two types of pointer: the specialists that only point and do not retrieve, and the more general-purpose breeds that will hunt, point and retrieve. The latter are often referred to as the HPR breeds.

The French word for a pointer is 'braque'; the Italian is 'bracco'. Some of the breeds in this functional category are pure pointers and have no other function; others will also retrieve and carry out various subsidiary duties. There are 33 breeds in the category.

ENGLAND

ENGLISH POINTER ENGLAND

Often referred to simply as the Pointer, this breed is the quintessential gun dog, specializing in game birds such as partridge, woodcock and snipe.

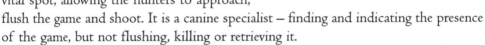

With the muscular body of a powerful athlete and the physical self-control of a Zen Master, the Pointer is an impressive dog, combining strength with grace. When hunting, it sniffs the air, head held high, and explores the territory systematically, until its fine nose detects hidden prey. It then rapidly slows to a halt, pointing like an arrow at the vital spot, allowing the hunters to approach, flush the game and shoot. It is a canine specialist — finding and indicating the presence of the game, but not flushing, killing or retrieving it.

Great controversy surrounds the ancestry of this breed, so much so that there is, uniquely, a whole book devoted to the subject *(The Pointer and His Predecessors* by William Arkwright). Simplifying the situation, there are two main views. The most popular one is that the breed's forebears were to be found among the southern European pointers, from Spain, Portugal, France and Italy. The Spanish Pointer is the most favoured of these, and this school of thought visualizes these dogs being brought back to England by soldiers returning from war-zones. The principal date given for this influx of foreign dogs is 1713, when Spanish Pointers were known to have made such a journey. Once in England, these slower, heavier dogs were crossed with Foxhounds and perhaps, to a lesser extent, with Greyhounds. This created the modern form of the English Pointer, a smaller, quicker kind of dog, better suited to the new type of hunting that was becoming fashionable with the introduction of efficient sporting guns in the 18th century. In support of this view is the fact that the earliest English reference to a dog specifically called a Pointer is from the year 1717.

Some voices have been raised in protest against this view, claiming that an early form of the Pointer was already well established in England long before the introduction of Spanish blood. They see the English Pointer as an ancient, indigenous breed, influenced by the later arrival of Spanish Pointers but not descended from them. They describe the old form of Pointer as having preceded the sporting guns of the 18th century, it being used to point at game such as hare, which was then pursued and killed by Greyhounds or hawks. Either way, the fact remains that, in the 18th and 19th centuries, the faster, more agile, modern English Pointer was perfected and eventually replaced the older, bigger, slower Spanish type.

In personality the English Pointer is an earnest, sensitive, intelligent, obedient, friendly and even-tempered dog. Although there are a number of colour variations in this short-coated breed, the typical Pointer is a white dog with dark patches.

References

1819. Johnson, T. B. *Shooter's Companion: Directions for the Breeding, Training, and Management of Setters and Pointers.* Edwards & Knibb, London.

1902. Arkwright, William. *The Pointer and His Predecessors.* Humphreys, London.

1917. Hochwalt, A. F. *The Modern Pointer.* Privately published, Dayton, Ohio.

1939. Daly, Lola Macdonald. *The Pointer as a Showdog.* Our Dogs, Manchester.

1940. Antunano, J. A. Sanchez. *Practical Education of the Pointing Dog.* Chicago.

1946. Willoughby. *The Cream Of Pointerdom 1900–1945.* Privately published.

1954. Lytle, Horace J. *Point.* The Stackpole Company, Pennsylvania.

1960. Brown, W. F. *Know your Setters and Pointers.* Pet Library, Canada.

1965. Stetson, J. *Hunting with Pointing Dogs.* TFH, New Jersey.

1966. Hart, Ernest H. *How to Raise and Train a Pointer.* TFH, New Jersey.

1973. Beazley, John Manners, et al. *Training Setters and Pointers for Field Trials.* Faber & Faber, London.

1974. Long, Paul. *Training Pointing Dogs.* Lyons & Burford, New York.

1974. Webb. *Practical Pointer Training.*

1975. de Wailly, Philippe. *Les Pointers.* Solarama, Paris.

1980. Bissell, Nicky. *Pointing Dog Training.* Privately published.

1983. Brander. *Training the Pointer-Retriever Gun Dog.* Pelham, London.

1987. Sutsos, Mike. *Training Your Pointer and Spaniel.* Putnam.

1990. Hart, Ernest H. *Pointers.* TFH, New Jersey.

1993. Villa, M. Le. *Pointer.* Éditions de Vecchi, Paris.

Craveri, Eugenio. *El Pointer: câomo se crâia, câomo se adiestra.*

FRANCE

ARIÈGE POINTER

FRANCE

Known in France as the Braque d'Ariège or the Braque de Toulouse, this breed was developed for hunting game in rough country.

The origin of this breed is uncertain, but it has been suggested that, long ago, crosses were made between Spanish Pointers and Italian Pointers, which gave rise to its foundation stock. Some authors believe that a French scenthound, the Chien Blanc du Roi – the King's White Hound – was also involved in its ancestry.

In its original form, this was a slow, tireless, methodical hunter with a powerful and yet graceful body. It had a docked tail, a deep chest and a heavy muzzle. It was a white dog with dark patches and speckling.

When hunting styles changed in the 20th century and faster dogs were required, it was necessary to modify this ancient breed. The required changes were achieved by making new crosses, this time with French Pointers and Saint-Germain Pointers. This gave it extra speed without reducing its massive size or its physical strength.

AUVERGNE POINTER   FRANCE

Known in France as the Braque d'Auvergne or the Bleu d'Auvergne, this breed is named after the mountainous region in central France where it was developed.

One of the early pointers, this heavy animal is yet another with a disputed origin. One theory sees it as a direct descendant of the old French Pointer, and another claims that it originated in Malta and was brought back to France by the Knights of the Order of St John when their base (including the Auberge d'Auvergne) on the small Mediterranean island was closed down by Napoleon in 1798. He gave them only four days in which to vacate the island, but permitted them to take their movable belongings with them, which presumably included their dogs, so there may be some truth in this story.

Originally the Auvergne existed in two size forms, the smaller, more elegant one being called the Braque Bleu and the larger, more cumbersome one the Grand Braque.

It is a slow, steady hunter, and what it lacks in speed it makes up for in stamina. The coat pattern is basically white but with so many black speckles that it may appear grey. In personality it is an intelligent, quiet, obedient dog. It is little-known outside its homeland.

BOURBONNAIS POINTER   FRANCE

Known in its homeland as the Braque du Bourbonnais, this breed originated in the Bourbon district of Central France.

Long-established in central France, but little-known elsewhere, this breed is a descendant of the older types of French Pointer. A medium-sized dog with a 'humpy back' and a tail that is either genetically absent or is docked to 2 in (5 cm), this is a less elegant breed than some of its close relatives. Its short, waterproof coat is typically white with brown ticking. In personality it is docile, gentle, slow and careful.

It was first noted by a foreign traveller as early as the start of the 17th century, and recorded as an interesting, local 'strain' of French Pointer, but it was not officially recognized as a distinct breed until the end of the 19th century. In modern times it has not proved popular, probably because of its clumsy appearance, and its numbers have dwindled. Extinction is said to be a serious possibility, although the breed still does have a few devoted supporters.

CHARLES X POINTER   FRANCE

Known in its native land as the Braque Charles X, this breed was named after the King of France. (It should not be confused with the Saint-Germain Pointer which, for a while, was also given this name.)

This is an extinct breed of French gun dog which was the ancestral form from which the two modern dogs now known as the Gascony Pointer, or Large French Pointer, and the Pyrenees Pointer, or Small French Pointer, were descended.

Some recent authors have confused this breed with the Saint-Germain Pointer because, for a brief period, that breed was given the same title. This was unfortunate because, although the two breeds were both pointers, they were markedly different in appearance. For example, in 1907, the Charles X was described as 'a coarse, inelegant dog to look upon', while the Saint-Germain was 'a fine, upstanding lemon-and-white dog... elegant in shape and showing admirable quality'.

Little is known about the Charles X Pointer, except that it was a heavy dog and rather slow, and it had a liver-and-white coat, a keen nose and a remarkable steadiness on point. Its tail was traditionally docked to half its length. (The tail of the Saint-Germain was undocked.) Its ears were unusually long which, it was said, 'did not add to its beauty'.

DUPUY POINTER   FRANCE

Known in France as the Braque Dupuy, this breed owes it name to the Frenchman who created it. It is sometimes called the Greyhound Pointer, the Greyhound Braque or the Braque Lévrier.

A tall dog, combining power with elegance, this breed was more strongly influenced than the other French pointers by the introduction of English Pointer blood. It has been suggested that there may even have been a minor addition of Greyhound or Sloughi in its ancestry, probably because of the 'sighthound shape' of its long, narrow head, its narrow chest and its generally racy shape.

Amazingly, there are five completely different theories concerning the origin of this breed:

1   It was a local variant of the French Pointer (Braque Français), with a white-and-chestnut coat, which had been pure-bred for 200 years at the estate of the Marquis of Rochelambert, where it was refined and perfected by a Poitou stock-breeder by the name of Dupuy.

2   It was an ancient French breed that was nearly exterminated during the ravages of the French Revolution, at the end of the 18th century, and it only survived that turbulent period because a few dogs were secretly hidden in the Abbey of Argensois, where they were protected by a devoted game warden called Dupuy.

3   It was created at the beginning of the 19th century, in Poitou, where it was developed by two gamekeeper brothers called Homère and Narcisse Dupuy. They mated their own liver-and-white bitch French Pointer (Braque Français) with a Sloughi, called Zidar, imported from North Africa by a Lieutenant Roy of the 33rd Artillery Regiment.

4   The breed was created at the beginning of the 19th century by a French huntsman called Pierre Dupuy, who owned a wonderful pointer bitch called Leda which he mated with a dog of unknown ancestry called Mylord, to producethe litter of puppies which were to become the foundation stock of the Dupuy breed.

5   The breed was created from a cross between an exceptional Poitou Pointer and an imported Greyhound.

It is not unusual to have several vague theories about the origin of a little-known breed of dog, but in this case, the contrasting stories are all so specific and the surfeit of Dupuys is embarrassing. It is perhaps not surprising that, with such a confusing and contradictory history, an official breed standard did not appear until the 1960s.

The Dupuy Pointer's height is 26–27 in (65–69 cm). The coat pattern is basically white, with dark brown patches and some ticking. The tail is undocked. This lively, intelligent, dignified breed is little-known outside France, and is extremely rare even inside the country. Some authors believe that it may now be extinct, although this is not certain. One author insists that it had 'disappeared completely' by 1940, but in that case why did the FCI grant it official recognition as a breed on 21st June 1963?

GASCONY POINTER FRANCE

Also known as the Large French Pointer, the French Gascony Pointer, the French Braque or the French Pointer – Gascony Type. In its homeland, it is called the Braque Français de Grande Taille. This breed from the Gascony region of southern France was developed to hunt a variety of game.

One of the oldest of all French breeds, this is believed to have descended from the early Spanish Pointer, and possibly the Italian Pointer. It has been involved in the ancestry of most other French gun dogs but has somehow also managed to survive in its original form, as its own breed.

This is a noble, powerful dog, up to 27 in (69 cm) in height. It is the larger of two size forms which exist today, descendants of a single earlier breed. Before these two size forms had split into separate, distinct entities, their immediate ancestor was known as the Charles X Pointer (see separate entry) or simply as the French Pointer (Braque Français).

By the end of the 19th century the Gascony's numbers were dwindling, due to an increasing fashion among French huntsmen for importing English Pointers and other foreign breeds. By the early part of the 20th century it was in danger of disappearing. However, three energetic enthusiasts took up its cause before this could happen and managed to established a firm breeding base. It now appears to be safe for the future.

The short coat is white with brown patches and speckles. The back is slightly arched. The tail may be docked or entire. Like its close relatives, it is a friendly, tranquil, loyal dog around the home.

Note: In two major canine reference works published recently, there is an unfortunate error in which the Gascony Pointer is incorrectly referred to as the Small French Pointer.

PYRENEES POINTER FRANCE

This breed is also known as the Small French Pointer, the French Pyrenean Pointer or the French Pointer – Pyrenees Type. In its homeland, it is called the Braque Français de Petite Taille, or the Petit Braque Français.

This is the smaller form of the French Pointer, with a shorter and smoother coat, a broader head, lips slightly less pendulous and ears set higher. It was originally bred down in size from the Gascony, but is now considered to be a distinct breed in its own right. It is 4–5 in (10–13 cm) shorter than its large cousin, measuring no more than 22 in (56 cm) in height. Its white coat tends to show more extensive brown markings.

This is essentially a more agile, more refined and more graceful version of the Gascony and was developed in the Pyrenean region of southern France. It is described as being 'fiery and fast' in the field. Like its large relative, it is very steady on point, always alert, highly intelligent, rather sensitive, and unsuited to harsh training methods. It is said to be 'born trained'. At home it is mild-mannered and relaxed.

Note: In two major canine reference works published recently, there is an unfortunate error in which the Pyrenees Pointer is incorrectly referred to as the Large French Pointer.

SAINT-GERMAIN POINTER   FRANCE

Known in France as the Braque Saint-Germain, this breed owes its name to the place where it was developed, the forest of Saint-Germain, near Paris. It is also sometimes called the Compiègne Pointer, because that is the name of the forest where it was first created. It was used to hunt rather larger game than that targeted by its close pointer relatives.

This breed was created in 1830 or thereabouts, as a result of a gift received by the French king, Charles X. His chief huntsman, Monsieur de Girardin, had been on a visit to England, where he acquired a pair of English Pointers. On his return, he presented these dogs to his monarch, who passed them on to the Inspector of the Forest of Compiègne, the Baron de Larminat.

Unfortunately the male dog, called Stop, died, so the Baron decided to cross the bitch, known as Miss, with a French Pointer, a dog known as Zamor. The result was a litter of seven white-and-orange puppies, which were destined to form the basis of a new breed.

The Compiègne Forest wardens who reared the puppies were so impressed with them that, when staff were transferred to the Saint-Germain Forest near Paris, they took their dogs with them. It was there that this new type of pointer found fame. Parisian hunters took them up and they soon acquired a new title – the Braque Saint-Germain. Unfortunately, because of their close association with the king, they were also sometimes referred to as the Braque Charles X. This name already belonged to another, older breed (see entry for Charles X Pointer) and for a time there was some confusion between the two. In 1909 the confusion was ended by dropping the name of Charles X for the Saint-Germain Pointer.

This is a tall, leggy, handsome gun dog, which, as its shape would suggest, is a fast hunter. It is athletic, elegant and well balanced. The typical colouring of this breed is predominantly white, with orange patches, a legacy from the foundation pair. Unlike some of its docked relatives, it displays a long, tapering tail. A hard-working, easily trained, quietly intelligent and gentle dog, it will retrieve as well as point.

BELGIUM

BELGIAN SHORT-HAIRED POINTER   BELGIUM

This breed is sometimes referred to simply as the Belgian Pointer. In its homeland it is known as the Braque Belge.

Little is known of this rare breed of pointer, which may by now be completely extinct. It was popular enough in the 19th century, but became less and less common during the 20th, when Belgian hunting territories were greatly reduced and imported French and German pointers became increasingly favoured. By the 1960s it was registered as 'very rare' in Belgium, and was unknown elsewhere. By 1984 the Belgian Kennel Club listed it as 'completely disappeared'.

Despite these official comments, one must always allow for the possibility that, in some remote corner of its homeland, a few isolated specimens still exist, their owners unaware that they are the guardians of the last remnants of a once well-established breed.

The Grand Bleu de Gascon and the Old Danish Pointer are thought to have been involved in its ancestry. This was a pointing breed that emphasized power rather than speed. Traditionally its tail was docked. The colour of the short coat was white, with large brown patches and possible ticking.

HOLLAND

WIRE-HAIRED POINTING GRIFFON HOLLAND

Also known as the Pointing Wire-haired Griffon, the Wire-haired Continental Pointer, the Korthals Griffon, the Griffon Korthals, the Griffon d'Arrêt Korthals or the Griffon d'Arrêt à Poil Dur, this breed was developed as an all-purpose gun dog, capable of retrieving as well as pointing. Among those close to the breed, it is often called simply 'the Griff'.

A young Dutchman, Eduard Korthals, the son of a banker from Schooten, near Haarlem, created this versatile breed in the Netherlands, starting with a grey-and-brown wire-haired bitch called Mouche. Purchased for a small sum in Amsterdam in April 1874, her precise ancestry is unknown, but she proved to be so rewarding in the hunting field that she was used as the founding female of Korthal's new breed.

The Dutchman's breeding programme involved a complex mixture of dogs, the details of which are not clearly known, although many guesses have been made. It seems likely that he used various griffon breeds, mixed with different kinds of pointer. Several other diverse breeds are also mentioned as part of its ancestral mixture, but the truth is that these are all speculations.

Korthals's aim was to create the ideal all-round gun dog, a breed that would trail, point and retrieve in all weathers and over all terrains. After a furious argument with his wealthy father, who was also an expert cattle-breeder and who considered dogs to be of no significance, he left his native land, taking some of his dogs with him. Moving to Biebesheim in Germany, he continued to develop and refine his stock. By 1887 a breed standard had been established and in 1890 he was awarded a special medal by the German emperor for his breeding successes.

Later, when working for a ducal estate in France, Korthals made further progress with his gradually improving breed, with the result that the dog was later claimed as a French breed by some authorities. However, despite this rival claim it has to be accepted that, in origin, it is a truly Dutch creation.

This was one of the first European gun dogs to be officially accepted in the United States, having been imported in 1901 by an enthusiast in New Jersey. Unpopular at first, because it was too slow for local hunters and did not do well in field trials, it later gained a wider following, although it has always remained a comparatively rare breed.

The Griff has an exceptionally wiry, bristly coat which protects it well in the field but gives it a somewhat unkempt appearance. In colour it is either chestnut or chestnut-and-white, and may be roan-marked with grey. The tail is traditionally docked. Like all pointers, it is a friendly, intelligent, affectionate dog with its owners, but does demand a great deal of physical activity on a daily basis if it is to thrive.

References

1994. Harmand, André. *Les Griffons et le Korthals.* Éditions de Vecchi, Paris.
1996. Bailey. *Griffon, Gun Dog Supreme.*

SPAIN

OLD SPANISH POINTER   SPAIN

Referred to in early works simply as the Spanish Pointer, this is also called the Navarra Pointer, the Navarro Pointer, the Perdiguero Navarro, the Bracco Navarro, the Bracco Navarone, the Pachon de Vitoria or the Bracco Carlos VIII. Its original function was to aid in the hunt for larger types of game but today it is used mostly for game birds.

This breed is the 'founding father' of many of the gun dogs of Europe. It was mentioned in 1644 by Alonzo de Espinar in his *Arte de Ballesteria* ('The Art of the Crossbow'), but is certainly much older than that. Its own ancestors are thought to include the ancient Spanish breeds called the Sabueso Hound (the Large Spanish Hound) and the Pachon Iberico.

Although the Old Spanish Pointer was used to create the more modern version of the Spanish Pointer (see next entry), it has also managed to survive, albeit in very small numbers, in its original form. This ancient type became so rare, however, that on several occasions it was falsely reported to have become extinct. Luckily, there were always a few local devotees ready to come to its aid and ensure its survival in an unaltered form. Its main supporters are in the Basque region of northern Spain, in the districts of Alava and Navarra.

A unique feature of this breed is its split or double nose, there being a deep groove where the bridge of the nose should be. This groove separates the left nostril from the right, giving the dog's face a strangely primeval quality.

The coat, which is usually smooth, but which may also be long, is white with extensive brown patches and/or ticking. Its tail is traditionally docked. It is a rather heavily built animal with a workmanlike rather than an elegant silhouette, and is renowned for its methodical searching and its stamina, rather than its speed.

SPANISH POINTER   SPAIN

Known in its homeland as the Burgos Pointer, the Spanish Perdiguero, the Perdiguero De Burgos or the Perdiguero Burgalés, this breed was once used on heavier kinds of game, especially deer, but today is more likely to be employed against hare and game birds such as partridge. In addition to pointing, it will also retrieve.

This breed was created by crossing the Old Spanish Pointer with the English Pointer. Its numbers were greatly reduced during the first half of the 20th century, but made slight gains in the second half of that century. The main centre for this breed is in the north of Spain, in the districts of Leon, Vitoria and Burgos.

The speciality of this gun dog today is as an aid to hunters seeking the elusive Spanish Red-Legged Partridge, known locally as the Perdiz. The Spanish government supports these Perdiz hunts to the extent of subsidizing farmers to ensure that they leave enough cover for the game birds to thrive.

A large dog, up to 30 in (76 cm) in height, it is popular at Spanish dog shows but has rarely been seen outside its homeland. The coat colour is white with dark brown patches or ticking. The tail is traditionally docked. In personality it is docile and affectionate with its owners, and is so good with children that, when not hunting, it is frequently kept in the home as a household pet.

PORTUGAL

PORTUGUESE POINTER   PORTUGAL

Known in its homeland as the Perdigueiro Portugueso, this breed was developed especially for hunting game birds. The word 'perdigueiro' is Portuguese for 'partridge'.

Descended from Spanish ancestors, and possibly from the now extinct Portuguese breed called the Podengo de Mastra, this is one of the smaller pointers, being only 22 in (56 cm) high, compared with 30 in (76 cm) for its neighbour, the Spanish Pointer.

It is an ancient breed, pure-bred for centuries, with records dating back to the 14th century. Some authorities believe that it can even be traced back as far as the fifth century, making it one of the earliest fixed breeds in European history. It is thought to have been exported in the early 1600s to England, where it influenced the form of several local breeds, including the English Pointer.

In its earliest days it was used as an aid to hawking, pointing to the quarry which was then pursued and killed by a bird of prey flown from the glove. As a modern gun dog, it not only points but will also retrieve. It is capable of working in almost any environmental conditions. With such a long pedigree it is not surprising that pointing is in its blood. It is said that a puppy only eight weeks old will display the pointing action without any training.

This deep-chested breed has a well-proportioned body with a rather broad head. The coat is short and smooth, with a light brown colour, usually showing small patches of white, especially on the extremities. The tail is traditionally docked.

ITALY

ITALIAN POINTER   ITALY

Known in its homeland as the Bracco Italiano, this all-purpose breed not only points, but also retrieves from both land and water.

Some Italian authorities believe that this breed is one of the most ancient of all hunting dogs, having been created in ancient times from matings between lighter sighthounds imported by the Phoenicians in the first millennium BC and heavier Molossus breeds that were already indigenous to the country. It is easy enough to envisage a Mastiff x Greyhound cross producing a compromise body shape not unlike that of the Italian Pointer, but there must have been other influences over the centuries.

Others describe a different origin. They see the breed arising much more recently, at the end of the 17th century, from a mixture of hound and gun dog. They point out that it has the heavy head of a hound and the body of a gun dog. Its temperament, they say, is also a mixture of the two types. Whichever theory is correct, the fact remains that this breed has changed remarkably little over the last few hundred years and retains an impressive 'primal' quality and bearing.

As the 19th century was coming to a close, and Italian hunters turned increasingly to imported breeds, their own Italian Pointer nearly vanished. Numbers dwindled alarmingly, but thanks to the efforts of an enthusiastic Italian breeder, Fernindando Delor, who was also instrumental in the foundation of the Italian Kennel Club, it was saved from extinction. His efforts in the 1880s established serious breeding programmes which began to rebuild the breed. In the 20th century, the dog slowly gained more support until, today, it is present in reasonable numbers, in both Italy and other European countries.

The short coat is predominantly white, with pale brown patches. Two local colour varieties are recognized today: the orange and white Piedmont Bianco Arrancio, and the chestnut roan Lombardy Roano Marrone. The tail is traditionally docked.

In personality, this sober, pensive-looking dog has a reputation for being obedient, responsive, vigorous and powerful on the hunt, and gentle, sensitive, docile and faithful in the home.

SPINONE ITALY

In English, this breed has been called the Italian Coarse-haired Pointer and the Italian Griffon, but it is universally better known by its original Italian name of Spinone. Its full title, rarely used today, is the Italian Spinone or the Spinone Italiano. Its name is derived from that of a formidably prickly bush, into which only a Spinone would risk pushing itself. Like most of the pointers of continental Europe, this breed will also retrieve.

This is a big, friendly, shaggy dog with a lively, rowdy personality – once met, never forgotten. It has been voted Italy's favourite gun dog and is becoming increasingly popular in other countries.

Its origin is uncertain. According to one theory, its original ancestors were various early French hounds (such as Barbets and Griffons) that were mixed together to create this heavy-headed gun dog. Others see the influence going in the other direction, with the Spinone the founding father. This second, more popular view depicts it as an indigenous Italian breed, descended from the ancient Italian Hound, the Segugio Italiano. It is certainly a very old breed and has been traced back to at least the 13th century. Some Italian authorities take it even further back, regarding its ancestors as hunting dogs imported from Greece into ancient Rome and there crossed with indigenous mastiffs to create the precursor of the modern Spinone.

In the field it is slower than the English Pointer, but excellent at systematic searching and good at pointing. Thanks to its rugged, protective outer covering, it will work in any terrain, no matter how rough, and can face any climate. It will retrieve from both land and water, being equally at home in 'field, swamp or forest'.

Because of its appealing, slightly comical appearance, and its ambling gait, it has become more prominent in the ring in recent years and is now seen in competitive shows in many parts of the world. In England, the Kennel Club gave it full Championship status in 1994. Its colour is variable, although predominantly white dogs are favoured. Its bushy face, with sprouting eyebrows, long whiskers and beard, is expressive and appealing. The tail is traditionally docked. The Spinone's temperament is ideal for a dog that has a double life — tireless running in the field and playful relaxing in the home. One author has made the bold assertion that 'nobody has ever been bitten by a Spinone'.

References

1999. Frye, Carolyn H. *The Italian Spinone.* TFH, New Jersey.

GERMANY

GERMAN BROKEN-COATED POINTER   GERMANY

This breed is known in Germany as the Stichelhaar or the Deutscher Stichelhaariger Vorstehhund — the literal translation of the name is 'prick-haired'. In the struggle to find the best way of describing its harsh coat, it was also sometimes called the Straufhaarig, or Hard-haired Pointer. An earlier German name for the breed was the Hessischen Rauhbart.

This breed is very similar to the much more common German Wire-haired Pointer. Its numbers are very low and it may well become extinct. It differs from its popular relative especially in the shape of the head, which is heavier and broader, thanks to an injection of German Shepherd Dog blood at some point in his history. Its coat is brown-and-white, in a speckled or grizzled, roan pattern.

In the 19th century there were several varieties of rough-haired pointers, with little attempt made to separate them or standardize their forms. Then in the second half of that century, serious breeding plans were made and each type was isolated and bred true. One of the new, fixed types to emerge was this one, the Broken-coated, and by the end of the 19th century it was fully accepted as a distinct pure-bred dog in its own right. It should be added that, despite this, it is easy to confuse it with the German Wire-haired Pointer.

GERMAN LONG-HAIRED POINTER   GERMANY

Known in Germany as the Langhaar, or the Deutscher Langhaariger Vorstehhund, this breed was originally developed to assist with hawking and falconry. In dog circles it is often referred to simply as the GLP.

Because of its long, shiny, wavy coat, this breed looks more like a typical setter than a pointer, but its appearance is deceptive. This is a true pointer like its close German

relatives, the Shorthair and Wirehair. It is large, with a height of 25–28 in (63–70 cm).

The early ancestry of this powerful dog is similar to that of the other German pointers, consisting of early German gun dogs. At later dates, however, a number of other bloodlines were introduced, some deliberately and others rather more haphazardly. These latter additions are believed to have included the old Water Spaniel, the Gordon Setter, the Irish Setter, the Newfoundland and French spaniels.

Ideally, the coat is solid liver, but may also be liver and white. The attractive, feathered tail should remain entire, although it has sometimes been docked.

The rarest of the German pointers, this is a dog that has never known great popularity, but has always enjoyed a moderate following. It remains little-known outside its homeland, although some have been exported to Canada, where it is officially recognized by the Canadian Kennel Club.

GERMAN SHORT-HAIRED POINTER   GERMANY

Known in Germany as the Kurzhaar or, more formally, as the Deutscher Kurzhaariger Vorstehhund, this breed is used to hunt a wide variety of game, especially pheasant, partridge and snipe. In dog circles it is often referred to simply as the GSP.

Described by enthusiasts as a dog that combines power and serenity, this aristocratic dog is multi-faceted. Although primarily a pointing dog, it is far less specialized than the English Pointer, since it also retrieves game from both land and water, and trails and holds at bay larger quarry. To its supporters it is the perfect, all-round gun dog.

The breed was created in the 17th century by combining the old Spanish Pointer, ancestor of so many pointing dogs, with early German bird dogs. This produced a heavy, rather slow animal and later on, in the 19th century, it was modified by crosses with the English Pointer, itself a mixture of Spanish Pointer and Foxhound. This led to a slightly smaller, more agile dog but, even in this new improved form, the possession of a personality that stressed thoroughness in searching was considered more important than speed. The Kurzhaar Stud Book was begun in 1870, when serious attempts were begun to standardize the breed.

Because of its dramatic, sculptured body and its calmly composed nature, this dog soon became popular in the show-ring, and some individuals achieved the rare distinction of becoming champions in both field trials and dog shows. As often happens, however, the type of dog favoured in these two arenas started to diverge, with the show dogs being bred for greater size and the field dogs for slightly smaller size, making dual-championship status increasingly difficult to achieve.

The popularity of the breed has seen it exported to many foreign countries. In some it has retained its multi-purpose role, but in others, such as the United States, it has become more and more specialized as a pure pointer, like its English counterpart.

In colour this breed is strictly limited to liver or liver-and-white, often with speckling. The tail is docked. In character it is described as methodical, businesslike, vigorous, obedient and efficient. This is summed up by the hunter's saying: If you can't find anything with a Shorthair, there's nothing there.

References

1951. Seiger, H. F. and Dewitz-Colpin, F. von.
The Complete German Shorthaired Pointer. Denlinger's, USA.

1956. Johns, Richard S. *Pet German Short-haired Pointer.*
All-Pets, Fond du Lac, Wisconsin.

1961. Leibers, Arthur. *How to Raise and Train a German Shorthaired Pointer.* TFH, New Jersey.

1962. Hardy, Michael Meredith. *An Account of the Origins and History of the German Shorthaired Pointer.* Hive Printers, Letchworth, Hertfordshire.

1963. Maxwell, C. Bede. *The New German Shorthaired Pointer.* Howell, New York.

1970. Spirer. *This is the German Pointer: Shorthaired & Wirehaired.* TFH, New Jersey.

1975. Dapper, Gertrude. *Your German Shorthaired Pointer.* Denlinger's, USA.

1980. McCarty, Diane (Editor). *German Shorthaired Pointer.* TFH, New Jersey.

1994. Layton, David. *German Shorthaired Pointers Today.* IDG Books Worldwide.

1998. McKowen, Robert H. *The New Complete German Shorthaired Pointer.* IDG Books Worldwide.

1998. Pinney, Chris C. *German Shorthaired Pointers: Everything About Purchase, Care, Nutrition, Breeding Behavior, and Training.* Barron, New York.

1998. Tabor, Joan S. *New Owner's Guide to German Shorthaired Pointers.* TFH, New Jersey.

1999. Campbell, Nancy C. *The German Shorthaired Pointer. An Owner's Guide to a Happy Healthy Pet.* IDG Books Worldwide.

Migliorini, Mario. *German Shorthaired Pointers.*

Nicholas, Anna K. *The German Pointer: Shorthaired and Wirehaired.*

GERMAN WIRE-HAIRED POINTER GERMANY

Also called the German Rough-haired Pointer and known in Germany as the Drahthaar, the Deutscher Drahthaariger Vorstehhund, or the Deutsch Stichelhaar Vorstehhund, this is an old breed that was developed specifically for hunting game birds. In dog circles it is often referred to simply as the GWP.

The tough, bristly coat of this large gun dog makes it a resilient, all-weather hunter. Like the other German pointer breeds, it is an all-purpose dog. A tall, tough, robust dog, it flushes and retrieves in addition to acting as a pointer. Compared with its nearest relatives, it is more rugged but less speedy.

Back in the 19th century, there were several varieties of large, rough-haired gun dogs in Germany, and little care was taken in keeping them distinct from one another and breeding true. Then, in the second half of that century, efforts were made to separate them and treat them as individual breeds. This form, with its rough, wiry coat, was not particularly popular and, at one stage, was facing extinction. But in 1865 a local breeder set out to save it and, by 1970, it was officially recognized.

Some authors claim that its ancestry, during its formative years, included the German Short-haired Pointer and the Airedale. Others insist that its foreign blood came, not from the Airedale, but from French Griffons.

Like its Long-haired cousin, its coat colour must always be liver or liver-and-white. Its tail is traditionally docked. In personality, this breed is said to be obedient but aloof, although sometimes capable of clowning. Its appealing, bearded, bushy face can, in turn, be impish, stern or noble. This is a dog that demands hard work. If left unoccupied, it soon becomes bored and can then become rather destructive.

For many years this German dog was virtually unknown in the rest of the world, but then, in the 20th century, it was exported to several other countries, including the United States, where it was officially recognized by the AKC in 1959.

References

1970. Spirer. *This is the German Pointer: Shorthaired & Wirehaired.* TFH, New Jersey.

1975. Anon. *The German Wired Haired Pointer In America 1973–1975.*

1990. Compere, Newton L. *German Wirehaired Pointers.* TFH, New Jersey.

1994. Pinkerton, Sharon. *German Wirehaired Pointers Today.* IDG Books Worldwide.

Nicholas, Anna K. *The German Pointer: Shorthaired and Wirehaired.*

LARGE MÜNSTERLÄNDER GERMANY

Known in its homeland as the Grosser Münsterländer, this is a typical continental gun dog that not only points but also tracks and retrieves. Among its friends it is usually referred to simply as the Münster.

This is a close relative of the German Long-haired Pointer. When, in the late 19th century, there was an attempt to introduce pure breeding lines into the rather haphazardly interbreeding German gun dogs, the club that was formed to support the German Long-haired Pointer insisted on a rigid standard for that breed. This standard demanded either liver or liver-and-white colouring. Such a rule meant that many black-and-white pointers were excluded. In the region of Münster, breeders ignored this strict new code and continued to produce black-and-white dogs, basing their breeding decisions on performance rather than appearance. In 1919 they formed their own club for their defiantly black-and-white dogs and gave them a new breed name of their own – the Münsterländer.

This is a long-coated dog with a long, feathered tail. It is a typical HPR (hunt, point and retrieve) breed and performs well in field trials. It has recently become increasingly popular overseas, especially in Britain and Canada, where it has adapted well to life as a companion dog, largely because of its strong desire to please its owners at every opportunity. It is obedient, resourceful, alert, and good with children, dogs and other animals.

SMALL MÜNSTERLÄNDER   GERMANY

Also sometimes called the Moorland Spaniel, and known in its homeland as the Kleiner Münsterländer Vorstehhund or the Heidewachtel, this is simply a smaller relative of the Large Münsterländer. In Germany it is often referred to as the Spion.

The height of the Small Münsterländer is about 3 in (7.5 cm) less than that of its larger cousin. Apart from its size, there is also a colour difference, this breed being brown-and-white instead of black-and-white.

This is a more recent breed. The Small Münsterländer was created in the early part of the 20th century by crossing the Large Münsterländer with continental spaniels. Despite this introduction of 'flushing' blood, it remains a pointer in the field. In appearance, as might be expected bearing in mind its ancestry, it looks intermediate between a setter and a spaniel. Because of its smaller size, it has in recent years become even more popular as a household companion, and its deeply ingrained urge to retrieve can find an outlet in fetching newspapers and slippers.

PUDELPOINTER   GERMANY

Although its name is rarely anglicized, if it were to be translated, this dog would be called the Poodle Pointer. It was developed to hunt game in a variety of environments, including grassland, marshland and woods.

This dog was created in the late 19th century by Baron von Zedlitz, who succeeded in combining the hunting qualities of the Pointer and the Poodle in a single breed. It has the gun-dog restraint of the Pointer, with the lively intelligence and protective coat of the Poodle.

It is usually stated that this was a simple cross between the Poodle and the English Pointer, but more careful studies have indicated that, in reality, it was the Barbet – the ancestor of the Poodle – that was involved, and that this was first crossed with several indigenous types of German pointer. It was the offspring from these matings that were then crossed with English Pointers, to produce what was hoped would prove to be the ideal all-round gun dog. The original gene pool consisted of 90 German Pointers and seven Barbets.

This multi-purpose German hunting dog was able to point partridge in open country, but was also prepared to work in marshy country and even thick cover in woodland. It was also able to retrieve after the kill, making it a jack-of-all-trades when compared with the refined specialization of the English Pointer, which performed only its one designated task.

The Pudelpointer is a strong, sturdily built, rough-haired breed, with a docked tail and a brown-coloured coat. Despite its great stamina and the ability to work in almost any climate over almost any kind of terrain, it has, for some unknown reason, never been popular, either in Germany or abroad. A few have been exported to the United States and Canada, and it was officially recognized by the Canadian Kennel Club in the 1960s, but it has rarely been shown there.

WEIMARANER

GERMANY

Originally known as the Weimar Pointer or the Weimaraner Vorstehhund, this breed was developed as a hunting dog capable of dealing with both small and large prey. It is also referred to as the Greydog.

The unique feature of this distinctive breed, which renders it immediately recognizable, is its glamorous, unmarked, silvery-grey coat, giving the dog a strange, metallic sheen as it moves. It is an aristocratic dog, often referred to as the Grey Ghost, with a muscular, compact, athletic body that makes it stand out in a crowd. Indeed, it is so striking that it was, for many years, jealously guarded from the attentions of the outside world.

It was created at the court of the Grand Duke Karl August of Weimar, in Germany, in the early years of the 19th century. The year 1810 is usually given as the starting point for the pure breed, although its early precursors had been around for several centuries before that. It is thought that Bloodhounds, various German pointers and some

French hounds were mixed together with the aim of producing the perfect hunting dog. Its first role was to hunt bigger game such as deer, wolf, bear and boar, but when the numbers of these wild mammals began to dwindle, the dog was further improved to make it an efficient bird dog as well.

This was a pointer specifically designed for the nobility. In 1897 a meeting was held at Erfort to protect the breed and to prevent its use by the general public. The Weimaraner Club of Germany was formed at that meeting and it was agreed that only the select members of the club would be permitted to own one of these exclusive dogs. When, occasionally, they were forced by the rules of etiquette to part with one of their coveted animals, the dog was always secretly sterilized before it was handed over, so that nobody outside the club could start breeding from it.

The rules of the club were strictly enforced by a Major Herber. Even among club members, no Weimaraner mating could take place without the prior approval of a breed master or a breed committee. Litters considered unsuitable were ruthlessly destroyed. Into this strictly controlled atmosphere came an American hunter and dog-breeder called Howard Knight, from Providence, Rhode Island. He hunted in Germany with club members and, realizing that they possessed an exceptional gun dog, decided that he must take some home with him to the United States, to develop the breed there. In 1929, club members broke with tradition and he was allowed to take a pair home with him.

When he arrived back in America he discovered that both animals had been sterilized and his plans were thwarted, but he did not give up. It took him another nine years before he managed to obtain breeding stock. Then, just before the outbreak of World War II, he acquired a male called Mars and two bitches called Dorle and Aura. From these he was, at last, able to found his American dynasty of Weimaraners. In 1941 he established the American Weimaraner Club and in 1943 the AKC officially recognized the breed.

Like his German predecessors, Knight applied rigid breeding rules to preserve the dog in its true form. He followed Major Herber's strict regulations: no sale of animals to non-members and the destruction of all unsuitable puppies. However, as the years passed and his club grew and grew, he found it impossible to keep complete control of the situation. Non-members began to acquire and breed these exciting new dogs which, at the time, were among the most expensive canines in the world.

Inevitably, with its floating gait and its shimmering body, this breed was destined to become a popular show dog. Its days of exclusivity were rapidly coming to an end. But those times had stood the breed in good stead. The many years of highly selective breeding had produced a strong, unique dog. By the 1950s it had reached Britain and was soon to be seen at dog shows all over the world.

In its working role, this is a dog that, in addition to pointing, will also track and retrieve. In personality it is obedient, trainable, friendly and protective with its owners, but completely fearless when on the hunt.

References

1882. *Die Deutsche Bühne deren geschichtliche Entwickelung in Bild und Wort. Dargestellt von einem Weimaraner.* Wilhelm Streit, Dresden.

1953. Scott, Jack Denton. *The Weimaraner.*

1954. Baird, Jack. *Pet Weimaraner.* All-Pets, Fond du Lac, Wisconsin.

1954. Denlinger, William W. *The Complete Weimaraner.* Denlinger's, USA.

1958. Miller, Evelyn. *Weimaraner.* TFH, New Jersey.

1959. Liebers, Arthur and Jeffries, Paul. *How to Raise and Train a Weimaraner.* TFH, New Jersey.

1960. Reifenberg, Benno and Staiger, Emil. *Weltbewohner und Weimaraner.* Ernst Beutler, Zürich/Stuttgart.

1960s. Schneider, Earl. *Know Your Weimaraner.* Pet Library, New York.

1965. Hart, Ernest H. *This is the Weimaraner.* TFH, New Jersey.

1983. Nicholas, Anna Katherine. *The Weimaraner.* TFH, New Jersey.

1992. Hollings, Patsy. *All About the Weimaraner.* Pelham Books.

1985. Burgoin, Gillian. *Guide to the Weimaraner.* Howell, London.

1991. Bambridge, Vicky. *The Weimaraner Today.* Ringpress Books, Letchworth, Hertfordshire.

1996. Hollings, Patsy. *The Essential Weimaraner.* Howell, New York.

2000. Fox, Susan. *Weimaraners.* Barron, New York.

2000. Riley, Patricia. *The Weimaraner: An Owner's Guide to a Happy Healthy Pet.* IDG Books Worldwide.

2000. Wilcox, Charlotte. *The Weimaraner.* Capstone Press.

LONG-HAIRED WEIMARANER   GERMANY

In recent times, an attractive new, long-haired breed has been developed from the short-haired Weimaraner. Its flowing, silky coat makes it look more like a setter, but it is still a pointer at heart and is a good hunting dog.

This breed is accepted by some European canine organizations, but is still outlawed in America by the AKC. Despite this, some American breeders have imported German Long-haired Weimaraners and are campaigning to have them recognized for competition. Because the tail of this new breed is attractively feathered, it is not docked, unlike that of the short-haired breed, which is traditionally reduced to about half its natural length.

WÜRTEMBERG POINTER   GERMANY

Little is known about this extinct German pointer from the Würtemberg region, now part of southern Germany. It appears to have survived at least until the early part of the 20th century, but then fades from view. It was a heavy, thickset dog with unusually large ears. A tall animal, reaching 27 in (69 cm) in height, it was also used to retrieve both hare and game birds.

Its colour was described as 'brown, brindle about the back and head, with light tan-and-white markings, the white being plentifully ticked with brown, which reminds one of a speckled trout'. In general appearance it was one of the more 'houndlike' pointers.

DENMARK

HERTHA POINTER

DENMARK

The closeness between this breed, originally known as the Hertha Dog or the Hertha Hound, and the English Pointer eventually led to its name being changed to the Hertha Pointer. The word Hertha in its title comes from the nick-name of the foundation bitch.

This breed is unusual in that we know the exact year of its creation – 1864. It was in that year that defeated Danish troops were wending their way home from a war against Germany. As often happens, war zones beget starving dogs that see in passing soldiers the chance of a free meal. One such dog, a handsome, light red pointer bitch, attached herself to a group of weary Danes and followed them eagerly. They called her Hertha and, when they finally reached home, sold her to a local sportsman who gave her to an expert hunter in the Jutland forests.

The Duke of Austenborg, whose estates were nearby, possessed a kennel of superb, imported English Pointers which, by chance, also happened to be light red in colour, with a few small white markings. One of these, a male called Sport, was acquired and was mated with Hertha. Their offspring formed the foundation stock that was to become the Hertha Pointer Breed.

Towards the end of the 19th century a specialist breed club was formed for the Hertha Pointer, and in 1897 a breed standard was established. The dog was similar to the English Pointer, but clearly distinct enough to be considered as a separate breed. And, inside Denmark at least, it had a longer and better pedigree. This was because, although the Hertha Pointers were kept completely pure and free of injections from other breeds, the English Pointers in Denmark were frequently 'refreshed' with a shot of Hertha.

With a clean pedigree stretching back well over a hundred years, it is not surprising that the supporters of this breed were angry at the official refusal by the Danish Kennel

Club, as recently as 1982, to give it official recognition.. The Kennel Club saw the Hertha as merely a variant of the English Pointer, but it is obviously more than that and will one day receive the recognition it deserves.

The Hertha continues to increase in popularity inside Denmark, although it is little-known elsewhere. Although its rich tan colouring is part of its appeal, it is also liked for its robust athleticism, its lively intelligence and its exceptional trainability in the field.

OLD DANISH POINTER   DENMARK

This is also known as the Old Danish Bird Dog, the Old Danish Honsehund or the Old Danish Pointing Dog, and in its homeland as the Gammel Dansk Hønsehund. At one time it was also referred to in Denmark as the Bakhund, because of the major role played in its development by local breeder Morten Bak. In addition to its pointing abilities, it is also used to track injured game and to retrieve.

Dating back to the 17th century, this long-established Danish Pointer is descended from the early Spanish Pointer. It has retained a great deal of its ancient ancestor, including the thick neck and heavy, broad head. Some authorities look upon this breed as a living representative of the ancestral form of all pointing gun dogs.

In addition to the Spanish Pointer, a little Bloodhound is thought to have been added to the early breeding programmes. Also, local farm dogs of no fixed pedigree are believed to have made their own contribution, long before the modern type was fixed.

Like many European hunting dogs, it suffered badly from the ravages of war and nearly vanished, but was saved by local enthusiasts and was eventually fully reinstated and finally recognized by the Danish Kennel Club in 1962.

The coat is basically white, with brown patches and some speckling. The tail is never docked. In personality, it is said to be calm and affectionate with its owners, but tenacious and determined on the hunt.

A breed characteristic mentioned in connection with its pointing action is that, instead of holding its tail rigidly out behind it when it scents game, it stops wagging it and starts to rotate it. As with many of the older European pointing breeds, it has hardly ever travelled outside its native country, but with increasing popularity in recent times, this situation is likely to change.

CZECH REPUBLIC

CZECH POINTER   CZECH REPUBLIC

Before Czechoslovakia broke up into the Czech Republic and Slovakia in 1993, this breed used to be known throughout the region as the Rough-coated Bohemian Pointer, the Rough-haired Bohemian Pointer, the Bohemian Griffon, the Czechoslovakian Pointer or the Böhmisch Rauhbart. It is now known as the Czech Pointer, the Czech Coarse-haired Pointer or the Cesky Fousek (sometimes spelled Czesky Fousek). Some authors misleadingly refer to it as the Czech Coarse-haired Setter, but it is a true pointer.

This is an ancient breed whose ancestors have been known in the region since the 15th century. In its early days it was highly variable, but then, in the late 19th century, its type was fixed and its future looked assured. An unforeseen setback in the 20th century occurred when the breed was nearly exterminated by the ravages of two World Wars, but a few enthusiasts managed to save it.

With few examples of the breed surviving, its supporters took special steps to establish sufficient breeding stock for it to survive into modern times. They did this by strengthening the remnants of the old breed with crosses involving the German Wirehaired Pointer and the German Short-haired Pointer. This effectively created a new breed, but one that still owed a great deal to the ancient Czech Pointer. Official breed standards were accepted by the FCI in 1963.

A tall, long-legged, distinctively bristly or shaggy-looking dog, it displays a coat that is either brown-and-white or plain brown. Traditionally, the tail is docked. Today, like its close German relatives, it acts as both a pointer and a retriever, and has become increasingly popular in its homeland.

SLOVAKIA

SLOVENSKY POINTER   SLOVAKIA

This breed is also known as the Slovakian Wire-haired Pointer, the Slovakian Pointing Griffon or, in its homeland, the Slovensky Hruborsty Stavac or the Slovensky Hruborsty Ohar.

A recent breed, dating from the 1950s, it was created by crossing the Czech Pointer with the German Wire-haired Pointer. The offspring of these matings were then

themselves crossed with the German Weimaraner. The result, first recognized as a distinct breed in its homeland in 1975, is an attractive, wiry-coated pointer with a distinctive colouring reminiscent of its Weimaraner ancestor. It was officially accepted by the FCI in 1983.

This is a tough hunter, ready to face any terrain in all weathers, with an appealing, bushy, bearded face and a well-balanced body form. It is little-known outside its homeland, though a few have been exported to Switzerland.

HUNGARY

VIZSLA

HUNGARY

This breed is sometimes called the Hungarian Pointer, the Hungarian Vizsla, the Magyar Vizsla, the Yellow Pointer, or (when it is being compared with its Wire-haired relative) the Smooth-coated Vizsla, the Short-haired Hungarian Vizsla, or the Vizsla Korthaar. It may have been named after a 12th-century settlement called Vizsla, which was located in the Danube Valley. Some authors, however, interpret the name as meaning 'alert and responsive'. In function, this is one of the continental pointers that will also act as a retriever.

In many respects, this is the Hungarian counterpart of the popular German gun dog the Weimaraner, and some canine authorities have argued that it was created by crossing the Weimaraner with various Pointers as recently as the 20th century.

This view angers Hungarian dog experts, who believe that it is the Weimaraner that is the later of the two breeds. They insist that, long before the silvery-grey Weimaraner appeared, there were reliable records of the rust-gold Vizsla. According to them, the earliest of these records date from the 11th and 12th centuries, when the Vizsla played an important hunting role for the Magyars, who used it as an aid to falconry. And they point out that, in a 14th-century Hungarian codex, the Vienna Chronicle, the image of a Vizsla appears in the chapter dealing with the falconry exploits of the nobility.

There seems to be no reason to reject these claims, and the Vizsla can therefore be accepted as an indigenous Hungarian dog with an impressively long pedigree. Despite this, it did not always fare too well. Towards the end of the 19th century this ancient breed was in serious decline and few examples were left. To ascertain just how serious the position was, a careful survey of hunting establishments was undertaken and it was found that there were only about a dozen of the dogs remaining alive in the entire country. This discovery led to a salvage operation and a gradual rebuilding of the breed.

Some have argued that it was shortly after this, in the early part of the 20th century, that the few surviving Vizslas were mated with various pointers to strengthen the stock, and that the modern Vizsla is this 'improved' stock, rather than the original Magyar dog. If this is true, it could provide a reason for the heated argument between the Hungarian breeders and the others. It becomes a moot point as to whether an improved Vizsla is a true Vizsla. But so many other breeds have been enhanced by occasional crosses during their long histories that it seems churlish to call the modern Vizsla a '20th century' breed, and its ancient status should therefore be accepted.

The breed was to suffer further setbacks as a result of the upheavals of World Wars I and II, with most of the Vizslas remaining in Hungary being destroyed. Fortunately, however, many refugees from the wars fled with their much loved dogs to neighbouring countries, where the scattered remnants of the breed managed to survive. Later, when peace was restored, it was possible to return enough of these to Hungary to safely re-establish the dog in its homeland.

Geographically, this breed's traditional hunting activities have always been located on the hot central plains of Hungary, the game-rich region called the Puszta. This is the reason for the development of the dog's very short coat, a feature which assists it when hunting in high temperatures. Hunting in cold winter weather is left to its thicker-coated, wire-haired cousin (see separate entry).

The Vizsla is the pointer breed that becomes strongly attached to its owners and shows a preference for a place near the hearth, rather than a bed in the kennels. It is a gentle, sensitive dog with an excellent disposition. Abroad, it has become a popular household companion, and an elegant show dog. In the United States it was given official recognition by the AKC in 1960.

References

1958. Hart, Ernest H. *How to Raise and Train a Vizsla.* TFH, New Jersey.

1973. Boggs, B. C. *The Vizsla.* Glenbrier Publishing, Jackson, Ohio.

1973. Strauz, John and Cunningham, Joseph. *Your Vizsla.* Denlinger's, USA.

1985. Gottlieb, Gay. *The Hungarian Vizsla.* Nimrod Book Services, Liss, Hampshire.

1990. Hart. Ernest H. *Vizslas.* TFH, New Jersey.

1991. Coffman. Marion I. *Versatile Vizsla.* Alpine Publications, Loveland, CO.

1992. Gottlieb, Gay. *The Complete Vizsla.*

1998. Pinney, Chris C. *Vizslas: Everthing About Purchase, Care, Nutrition, Grooming, Behavior, and Training.* Barron, New York.

1999. Gottlieb, Gay. *The Hungarian Vizsla.*

WIRE-HAIRED VIZSLA HUNGARY

This breed has also been recorded as the Hungarian Wire-haired Vizsla, or the Vizsla Draadhaar. It is very similar to the Smooth-coated Vizsla, but is more than a mere variety of it, since it was created from crosses between that dog and the German Wire-haired Pointer. In its homeland it is referred to as the Drótszörü Magyar Vizsla.

The first cross took place in Hungary, in 1904, by accident rather than design. A Wire-haired Pointer mated with a Vizsla bitch and two of the puppies from the subsequent litter were put on display at a dog show in Budapest. They appealed to a Czechoslovakian breeder by the name of Ladislaus Gresnarik, who acquired them and made them the foundation stock of a new breed.

Within ten years Gresnarik was able to create a pure-breeding stock which retained the golden colour of the Vizsla, but had the wiry hair texture of the German Pointer. By 1950, this breed had been accepted by the Hungarian Association of Canine Affairs. In the 1970s it attracted the attention of a visiting dog judge from America, who was impressed by the high quality of the dogs. Because its thicker coat made it better suited to rough and cold hunting conditions, some of these dogs were exported to Canada, where hunters found them an excellent breed for local conditions. Although the Wire-haired Vizsla was prepared to retrieve from both land and water, its main claim to fame was its pointing, an activity at which it excelled.

By 1978 the Wire-haired Vizsla had become sufficiently established in Canada for it to graduate from the hunting field to the show-ring, and in that year it was given official recognition by the Canadian Kennel Club.

UNITED STATES

CESKY WIRE-HAIRED POINTING GRIFFON UNITED STATES

When the Wire-haired Pointing Griffon, the Dutch gun dog developed by Eduard Korthals, was first imported into the United States by a New Jersey breeder in 1901, it did not prove very popular with American hunters. It did, however, survive in small numbers and a specialist breed club was eventually established to promote it.

This organization, the Wire-haired Pointing Griffon Club of America (the WPGCA), continued to support the breed for many years, but in 1984 took the controversial decision to improve their dogs by introducing crosses with the Czech Pointer, the Cesky Fousek. This decision split the breed enthusiasts into two rival camps, those who thought this step would 'restore' and revitalize the breed, and those who felt that the crosses would destroy the purity and long-standing heritage of the breed.

The second group broke away and formed their own organization, called the American Wire-haired Pointing Griffon Association (the AWPGA). They began using the term 'Fullblood Griffons' for their dogs, to distinguish them from the Cesky/Griffon crosses. And they objected strongly to the latter being called Wire-haired Pointing Griffons, insisting that these new dogs, a strictly American creation, should be called by some other name. Their hope, to quote them, was that 'some time in the future, the two breeds will have separate names... The Cesky Fousek x Griffon should take his place in the world of hunting dogs and be awarded his own name'.

This seems a reasonable request, and the title given here to the new, 'improved' American version is a start in that direction. It remains to be seen which of the two types eventually becomes the more popular breed.

DECOY DOGS

Looking rather like spaniels, but with smaller heads and slightly longer legs, the decoy dogs are used to entice waterfowl into a position where they can be netted or shot. They do this by behaving in an unusual way that arouses the curiosity of the birds, who approach to investigate and are then at the hunters' mercy. In cases where guns are used, if the birds are successfully downed, the decoy dogs then act as retrievers.

One now extinct dog, the Tumbler, was also used to lure other kinds of game, especially rabbits. This breed more closely resembled a Whippet.

There are four breeds in this minor category.

ENGLAND

RED DECOY DOG   ENGLAND

This is an extinct breed about which little is known. Sometimes listed as the English Red Decoy Dog, it was used to lure waterfowl into nets.

Old records show that, long ago, there existed in England a small, rufous dog employed to decoy wildfowl into large nets. These nets were strung up across a stream and the little dog would then run up and down until it had attracted the attention of the inquisitive birds. It continued to make eye-catching, irregular movements until it had lured them into the area of the nets, where they were then trapped by waiting hunters.

This specialized breed of dog had been developed as a result of field observations made by early hunters. They had noticed that a pair of foxes would sometimes use clever subterfuges to lure their prey close enough for a sudden, killing pounce. One fox would dash back and forth making erratic movements (an activity known as 'protean behaviour'), while its mate hid in ambush. When puzzled ducks approached to see what was going on, the hidden fox was then able to leap out and grab them.

It was seeing this ingenious behaviour of foxes that led to the idea of creating a sporting dog that would also make erratic movements which would entice wildfowl in a similar way. So, although the fox was not genetically involved in the creation of the decoy dog (as some have suggested), it was fox behaviour that inspired it. (Foxes have also been known to 'play dead' in order to attract curious birds and then suddenly leap up and snatch them before they can fly away. This behaviour was originally thought to be no more than an old folktale, but it has recently been filmed and is now fully authenticated.)

It is not clear precisely when the Red Decoy Dog became extinct, but its disappearance probably coincided with the arrival of efficient sporting guns. When shooting replaced netting, other types of hunting dog became more popular and the decoy technique faded into history. It did, however, manage to survive in at least two regions (see separate entries under Holland and Canada).

TUMBLER   ENGLAND

This is an extinct breed of which little is known. It was used to lure and kill rabbits and other small game.

Early dog books sometimes include in their breed lists a dog called the Tumbler, occasionally with the added Latin name of *Canis saltator* (literally, the jumping dog) or *Canis vertagus* (literally, the whirling dog). This animal was clearly employed as a decoy dog, but mostly against rabbits, rather than wildfowl. It was released by the hunter near a rabbit warren and proceeded to behave in a strangely playful, erratic manner, lulling the rabbits into a false sense of security, before suddenly pouncing on one, killing it and then carrying it back to its master.

The colourful words of the early authors describe this procedure in the following way: 'This sort of dogs, which compasseth all by crafts, frauds, subtilties and conceits, we Englishmen call "Tumblers" [1576].' 'For in hunting they turn and tumble, winding their bodies about circularly, and then fiercely and violently venturing on the beast [1721].' 'He does not directly run at the game, but scampers about in a careless and apparently inattentive manner, tumbling himself over until he comes within reach of it, and then seizes it by a sudden spring [1829].'

In appearance, the Tumbler was described as 'somewhat lesser than the hounds, and they be lancker, leaner, beside that they be somewhat prick-eared. A man that shall marke the form and fashion of their bodies, may well call them mungrel Gray-hounds if they were somewhat bigger [1658].' Another source described it as looking like 'a small lurcher'.

In 1829, this breed was said to be 'nearly extinct'. It probably disappeared at about the same time as the Red Decoy Dog, for much the same reason, namely the introduction of increasingly efficient sporting guns.

HOLLAND

Dutch Decoy Spaniel

HOLLAND

Sometimes called the Kooiker Dog or Kooikerhond and known in its homeland as the Kooikerhondje, this breed was originally developed to decoy waterfowl into nets or to entice them within range of hunters' guns. The word 'kooiker' is the Dutch name for the main type of duck involved.

This attractive little red-and-white dog has been known since at least the 17th century, when it became famous for having been responsible for a royal rescue. According to Dutch historians, it was a Kooiker Dog that on one occasion saved the life of Prince William of Orange. When intruders broke in, his little dog barked at them so loudly that he awoke and was able to escape.

This breed appeared in paintings by several 17th-century Dutch masters, including Vermeer and Jan Steen. Its fortunes changed in the 20th century, however, when the ravages of two World Wars nearly eliminated it.

One person was largely responsible for the recovery of this appealing breed. In the early 1940s Baroness Hardenbrock van Ammerstol, alarmed at its near disappearence, and wishing to start an emergency breeding programme, scoured the Netherlands for surviving specimens. She managed to locate a male and two bitches in the north of the country, and these were used as the foundation stock from which the breed could be revived and rebuilt. The first litter appeared in 1943, and at the close of World War II, in 1945, the world population stood at 25 dogs.

Although it did not become widely known outside the Netherlands, inside the country its popularity increased greatly in the second half of the 20th century, with many new breeders becoming interested. A special breed club was founded in 1967. Towards the end of the 20th century, it is reported that 500 puppies were being born each year. Thanks to the baroness, the breed is now safe for the future.

In recent times the expert services of this decoy dog have been employed by hunters who are also conservationists. About 100 of these specialized dogs are active in Dutch nature reserves, where they are trained to entice mixed wildfowl into nets. Once trapped, the common birds are taken, but the rare species are banded for identification and then released.

This intelligent, industrious dog attracts the birds by waving its heavily fringed, long white tail.

CANADA

Nova Scotia Duck Tolling Retriever   CANADA

Also known as the American Duck Retriever, the Little River Duck Dog, the Yarmouth Toller or simply the Toller, this breed has been used as a decoy dog since the 19th century. The word 'toll' is an antique term for 'entice' which has been in use since the 13th century.

Duck-hunters work this breed at the water's edge. They throw a stick (called a tolling stick) or a ball for the dog to fetch. It scampers along in a highly conspicuous way, jumping, playing and leaping, but without barking. It may do this repeatedly – often disappearing from sight and then suddenly reappearing – until the watching wildfowl, curious at these strange activities, approach more closely to investigate. From his cover nearby, the hunter waits until they are close enough for a shot, emerges and, as they panic up into the sky, makes his kill. His dog then acts as a retriever and brings him the shot birds.

This is a breed of very mixed ancestry. It is said that spaniels, setters, collies and several retrievers were all involved in its creation, in a long series of matings that began in 1860. Out of these crosses, a special type developed, but it was not until 1945 that formal breed standards were introduced and the dog was officially recognized by the Canadian Kennel Club. International acceptance was not gained until the 1980s.

There is a fanciful old claim that the ancestry of this breed also included the fox. Genetically there is no truth in this, but it is easy to see how the story arose, bearing in mind the way in which the cunning ambush behaviour of wild foxes originally inspired the creation of domestic decoy dogs.

Inevitably, this is a highly intelligent dog, easy to train and with good swimming ability for water retrieving. Above all, this is a breed with a playful personality, whose lively actions and sudden, unexpected movements are an essential part of the strategy of luring and enticement.

References

1996. Strang, Alison. *The Nova Scotia Duck Tolling Retriever.*
1998. MacMillan, Gail. *A Breed Apart: Nova Scotia's Duck Tolling Retriever.*

RETRIEVING DOGS

Most gun dogs – spaniels, setters and pointers – are capable of bringing back shot game, but as the different breeds became more clearly defined in their separate tasks, a need arose for a specialized category of sporting dog for which the act of finding the downed game and carrying it back to the hunter would become its central role. These dogs were given the group name of 'retrievers' and their origin is neatly summed up by a Victorian authority, writing in the 1890s: 'Our retriever was produced when the British sportsman found out that it was not good for his pointer or setter to fetch his game, and that his spaniel would not do this so well and quickly as a bigger dog; so the retriever became a necessity.'

An important feature of the successful retriever's fieldwork is the possession of a 'soft mouth'. The hard-mouthed dog holds the game too tightly in its jaws while carrying it to the hunter and damages it. The soft-mouthed dog holds it firmly but gently and leaves no tooth-marks on its body. Some hunters train their retrievers to work with a softer mouth by throwing prickly objects for them to fetch.

All retrievers will bring back downed game from both land and water, but most breeds have become specialized essentially as water dogs for retrieving dead or injured waterfowl.

A few retrieving breeds are unusual in that they are able to find and collect prey that are neither dead nor injured. These dogs are sent off to catch and bring back living quarry. The quarry has to be vulnerable in some way. Nesting seabirds fall into this category, and certain dogs have become specialists in finding and retrieving either nesting birds or their eggs.

There are 16 breeds in this special category.

ENGLAND

CURLY-COATED RETRIEVER

In its early days this breed was sometimes called simply the Curly Retriever. It was developed as a specialist waterfowl retriever.

This breed is the oldest of the surviving English retrievers. It is descended from the now extinct English Water Spaniel. At the beginning of the 19th century, the old water dog was crossed with newly imported Labrador Retrievers (or St John's Dogs, as they were then known) to create an improved wildfowl retriever. Some authorities believe that the Irish Water Spaniel may also have been involved in its creation. Certainly, at a later date, the Poodle was briefly introduced to tighten the curl of its coat. In colour it is nearly always solid black, but very dark brown also occurs.

Because of its highly characteristic hair type, with its mass of close, crisp curls, the breed soon attracted the attention of the show-dog world. This type of 'astrakhan' coat had originally been created as a waterproof, thorn-resistant protection for the working dog, but the breed's strange visual appeal led to its being taken into the show-ring at some of the first dog shows. There were special classes for it as early as 1859.

By the beginning of the 20th century, the breed's popularity was decreasing. Its followers deserted it in favour of the Flat-coated Retriever, which was said to be softer-mouthed when retrieving waterfowl, and to have a gentler, more docile temperament. The Curly-coated Retriever had, however, already been exported around the world, especially to Australia, New Zealand and the United States, and even today retains a wide, international presence, although its numbers are always small.

In personality this old-fashioned retriever is affectionate, faithful, trainable and intelligent, with a good memory, but is also said to be proud and sometimes aloof.

References

1953. Johns, Rowland (Editor). *Our Friend the Retriever. Curly-coated, Flat-coated, and Golden.* Methuen, London.

ENGLISH WATER SPANIEL

This extinct breed was known by various names. In the 16th century it was called the Water Spaniel or Fynder. In the 17th century it was recorded as the Water Dogge. In the 18th century it was split into two breeds, the Large Water Spaniel and the Small Water Spaniel. It was developed to retrieve waterfowl.

The old English Water Spaniel was the forerunner of the modern retrievers. It had a thick, oily coat which with one shake was dry again, even when the dog had been working in the water for hours. Much bigger than typical land spaniels, it was liver-and-white in colour, with a curly coat, and in many respects similar to the Curly-coated Retriever.

An 18th-century description of the breed says: 'Its form is elegant, its hair beautifully curled or crisped, its ears long, and its aspect mild and sagacious.' It was also praised for its swimming ability, faithfulness, obedience, trainability and docility. It is mentioned that there were two types, the Large and the Small, which differed only in size.

During the 19th century the breed appears to have been eclipsed by its improved descendants – the Curly-coated and Flat-coated Retrievers. It was still present in the 1870s, but was clearly being superseded. A statement from 1875 reflects this: 'Although a class of this variety of the spaniel is often included in the prize lists of our shows, the exhibits are generally of a most miscellaneous character.'

By the 1890s the breed was said to be 'almost, if not entirely extinct', although in 1893 its existence was still being formally acknowledged by the Spaniel Club. Examples of this breed did appear in the earliest Victorian dog shows, but the numbers soon began to dwindle and the classes set aside for them were discontinued. The last example to be registered with the Kennel Club was in 1886. After that they disappeared completely from the show-dog scene, although a few stragglers may well have survived for a while in the more remote corners of the country, as working field dogs.

FLAT-COATED RETRIEVER ENGLAND

Also known in the past as the Wavy-coated Retriever, the Black Wavy Retriever or the Smooth-coated Retriever, this breed was once called 'the Gamekeeper's Dog' because of its widespread use as a retriever on large estates in England. It works well on both land and water.

This dog appeared in England in the second half of the 19th century, probably some time in the 1860s, and was soon overshadowing the earlier Curly-coated Retriever. It had a softer mouth and a more docile temperament, and was increasingly popular until it was itself overtaken by the Golden Retriever and the improved Labrador. In origin, it was the result of crosses between the early version of the Labrador – the St John's Dog – and unidentified British setters. Some say that there may also have been a minor addition of Collie blood.

The setters gave the breed its wavy coat and its original name of Wavy-coated Retriever. But then, as the years passed, the waviness was reduced more and more until it was necessary to change the dog's name to Flat-coated Retriever. It remained popular until World War I, both as a hunting dog and in the show-ring. Then its star started to fade. After World War II it was in serious decline and was saved from extinction only because of the efforts of a few devoted supporters. Today, although not common, it is once again reasonably safe, with over a thousand registrations at the Kennel Club each year.

This is a strong, intelligent dog, appealing to the eye in its glowing, shiny black coat, calm and restrained in the show-ring, and one of the finest gun dogs in the hunting field. It is a breed which has been revered by some of the canine world's greatest experts, and it is no accident that the portrait of the founder of the Kennel Club in London depicts him, not with one of the top favourite breeds, but in the company of a favourite Flat-coated Retriever. Had he been around a century later, he would have enjoyed the moment when a member of this breed was awarded Best in Show at the 1980 Crufts.

References

1953. Johns, Rowland (Editor). *Our Friend The Retriever. Curly-coated, Flat-coated, and Golden.* Methuen, London.
1968. Laughton, Nancy. *A Review of the Flat Coated Retriever.*
1980. Petch, Paddy. *The Flat-Coated Retriever.* K & R Books, Edlington, Lincolnshire.
1988. Petch, Paddy. *The Complete Flat-Coated Retriever.* Boydell Press, Suffolk.
1996. Mason, Joan. *The Flat-Coated Retriever Today.* Howell, New York.
1996. Phillips. *The World of the Flat-Coated Retriever.* TFH, New Jersey.

SCOTLAND

GOLDEN RETRIEVER   SCOTLAND

The original function of this breed was to retrieve waterfowl, but in modern times it has also found fame as a field-trial dog, a show dog, a companion dog and a guide dog for the blind, making it one of the most widespread and popular canines in the world.

To its army of admirers this is the perfect dog. It is a kindly, sensible, affectionate, gentle, willing and obedient companion. First exhibited at a dog show in 1908, it has been popular in the show-ring ever since, consistently holding a place among the 'top ten' favourite breeds. It has changed little over the years, except that lighter shades of gold have been more and more favoured.

In origin this breed is descended from the Flat-coated Retriever, a breed which it came to overshadow and largely replace. It was originally called the 'Flat-coated

Retriever, Golden', and it was registered with the Kennel Club under that name in 1903. By 1911, the year in which the Golden Retriever Club was formed, it was classed as a separate breed and was then called the Yellow or Golden Retriever. Later, the 'Yellow or' was dropped from its title.

There have been conflicting views about the ancestry of this breed. For many years there was support for a romantic tale about a troupe of Russian circus dogs performing in Brighton, which were supposed to have become the foundation stock for the Golden Retriever breed. Detailed modern research into early stud books has, however, failed to find any backing for this story. What is now confirmed is the following:

In 1865 Sir Dudley Marjoribanks (later to become Lord Tweedmouth) set out to create the ideal gun dog on his Scottish estate at Guisachan, near Inverness. His breeding plan was complicated. He began by purchasing a one-year-old yellow retriever called Nous, which had been the only yellow puppy in a litter of black Wavy-coated Retrievers, belonging to a Brighton cobbler. In 1868 he mated this dog with a Tweed Water Spaniel bitch called Belle. Their litter consisted of four yellow puppies. The best bitch from this litter, called Cowslip, was crossed first with a Red Setter and then with a Tweed Water Spaniel. Offspring from both these litters were then crossed back to black Wavy-coated Retrievers. The puppies created in this way varied greatly in colour from intense black to light cream. From these, the golden coloured ones were selected and mated together, producing what was to be the foundation stock of the breed that would later come to be known as the Golden Retriever.

A small puzzle remaining in this history is the source of Nous, the founding father of the breed. According to the original legend, he was purchased from a Russian circus trainer in Brighton. In another version the owner was a Brighton cobbler. In yet another, he was a gypsy. Finally, there was the report that the dog was obtained from Lord Chichester. Considering its importance in the creation of a major breed, it would be good to know a little more about the background of this particular animal, but the surviving records give little hope of this.

The Golden Retriever first arrived in North America at the end of the 19th century – in Canada in 1881 and the United States in 1890 – but it was not exhibited at dog shows there until 1930, and was not registered with the Canadian Kennel Club until 1927 or the AKC until 1932. The first to be registered in France was in 1934. During the rest of the 20th century, this breed spread far and wide around the globe and is now one of the most internationally recognized of all dogs.

References

1933. Charlesworth, W. M. *The Book of the Golden Retriever.* The Field, London.

1952. Charlesworth, W. M. *Golden Retrievers.* Williams & Norgate, London.

1953. Johns, Rowland (Editor). *Our Friend the Retriever, Curly-coated, Flat-coated and Golden.* Methuen, London.

1953. Stonex, Elma. *The Golden Retriever.* Nicholson & Watson, London.

1954. Shaul, H. Edwin. *The Golden Retriever.* Indian Springs Press, Boston.

1959. Cofield, Thomas R. *Training the Hunting Retriever: Labrador, Chesapeake and Golden.* Van Nostrand, Princeton.

1960. Hubbard, Clifford L. B. *The Golden Retriever Handbook.* Nicholson & Watson, London.

1960. Miller, Evelyn. *How To Raise and Train a Golden Retriever.* Sterling, New York.

1962. Gill, Joan. *Golden Retrievers.* Foyles, London.

1963. Coykendall, Ralf W., Jnr. *You and Your Retriever.* Doubleday, New York.

1970. Tudor, Joan. *The Golden Retriever.* Popular Dogs, London.

1974. Sawtell, Lucille. *All about the Golden Retriever.* Pelham Books, London.

1976. Fischer, Gertrude. *The Complete Golden Retriever.* Howell, NewYork.

1979. Kersley, J. A. *Training the Retriever.* Howell, New York.

1980. Free, James Lamb. *Training Your Retriever.* Coward, McCann & Geoghegan, New York.

1980. Walsh, James. *Golden Retrievers.* TFH, New Jersey.

1983. Nicholas, Anna Katherine. *The Book of the Golden Retriever.* TFH, New York.

1983. Quinn, Tom. *The Working Retrievers. The Training Care and Handling of Retrievers for Hunting and Field Trials.* Dutton, New York.

1984. Fischer, Gertrude. *The New Complete Golden Retriever.* Howell, New York.

1984. Pepper, Jeffrey. *The Golden Retriever.* TFH, New Jersey.

1986. Schneider, Evelyn. *The Golden Retriever.* Denlinger's, USA.

1986. Tudor, Joan. *The Golden Retriever Puppy Book.* Medea, Washington, DC.

1988. Denis, Paula. *Vous et Votre Golden Retriever.* Les Éditions de l'Homme, Canada.

1988. Sayer and Bunting. *Labrador & Golden Retrievers.* Hamlyn, London.

1988. Twist, Michael. *The Complete Guide to the Golden Retriever.* Boydell Press, Suffolk.

1993. Bargh, Bernard. *Pet Owner's Guide to the Golden Retriever.* Howell, New York.

1993. Bauer, Nona Kilgore. *The World of the Golden Retriever.* TFH, New Jersey.

1994. Foss, Valerie. *Golden Retrievers Today.* Howell, New York.

1994. O'Driscoll, C. *The Golden Retriever Companion.*

1994. Titterington, Albert J. and Gaffney, Michael. *The Golden Retriever in Ireland.* Privately published, Dundonald, Northern Ireland.

1995. Cairns, Julie. *The Golden Retriever; an Owner's Guide to a Happy Healthy Pet.* Howell, New York.

1996. Ackerman, Lowell. *Dr Ackerman's Book of the Golden Retriever.* TFH, New Jersey.

1996. Fogle, Bruce. *Dog Breed Handbooks: Golden Retriever.* Dorling Kindersley, London.

1996. Huxley, Joanne P. *Guide to Owning a Golden Retriever.*

1996. Schlehr, Marcia. *The New Golden Retriever.* Howell, New York.

1996. Siegal, Mordecai and Margolis, M. *The Golden Years: A Pet Owner's Guide to the Golden Retriever.* Little, Brown, New York.

1996. Wilcox, Charlotte. *The Golden Retriever.*

1997. Bauer, Nona Kilgore. *The Proper Care of Golden Retrievers.* TFH, New Jersey.

1998. Vanderbilt, Arthur. *Golden Days: Memories of a Golden Retriever.* Bantam, New York.

1999. Hubbard, Coleen. *One Golden Year: A Story of a Golden Retriever.*

1999. Siino, Betsy Sikora. *Your Golden Retriever's Life: Your Complete Guide to Raising Your Pet from Puppy to Companion.*

Foss, Valerie. *The Ultimate Golden Retriever.* IDG Books Worldwide.

TWEED WATER SPANIEL   SCOTLAND

Also known as the Tweed-side Spaniel or simply the Tweed Spaniel, this breed was once commonly seen working as a water retriever along the banks of the River Tweed.

As with its close relative, the English Water Spaniel, the information about this extinct breed is scanty. Its importance lies in the ancestral role it played in the development of the Golden Retriever.

The breed originated in the region of the River Tweed in the extreme south-east of Scotland, and was said to be rare except in the Border country. In appearance, it looked more like a Curly-coated Retriever than a true spaniel, and its colour varied from yellow to brown (unlike its bicoloured English relative, which was brown-and-white).

It was an unusually resourceful dog, and an anecdote dating from 1848 is of particular interest. The author, General Hutchinson, recalls: 'When recently salmon-fishing on the upper part of the Tweed, I occasionally met on its banks a totally blind man... led about by a large brown Tweed-side Spaniel, of whose intelligence wonderful stories are told.' He goes on to explain that the blind man travelled around the country with his dog, which understood a whole series of verbal commands, and appears to have been one of the first fully trained guide dogs in history. The significance of this story is that the descendants of this breed, the modern Golden Retrievers, have in recent years proved themselves to be the best of all modern guide dogs.

IRELAND

IRISH WATER SPANIEL   IRELAND

In Ireland this breed is sometimes fondly referred to as the Bogdog. It was developed from the old Southern Irish Water Spaniel, or Southern Water Spaniel, primarily as a waterfowl retriever, but it can also be trained to point. At one stage in the 19th century it was known as McCarthy's Breed, and it has also been called the Shannon Spaniel.

This is the largest of the dogs called 'spaniels' — 23 in (58 cm) in height — but unlike true spaniels, which are specialized for flushing, this is, first and foremost, a dog that leaps into the cold waters of Ireland to bring back dead or wounded wildfowl. It must therefore be classed as a retriever, despite its name. Perhaps the most unbiased title for it would be the simple name used for it long ago by certain authors – the Irish Water Dog.

Its dark brown, almost black coat is thick, dense, curly and waterproof. It has a prominent 'topknot' and its characteristic tail is thin and stiff. In personality it has a boundless sense of fun when it is not working, but can become headstrong if it is allowed to get out of control.

A descendant of the ancient French Barbet, the now extinct English Water Spaniel, and possibly the Poodle, this breed was not fully developed until the 19th century. And yet there was some kind of water spaniel working in Ireland many years before. The Irish Bishop of Armagh, writing as early as 1600, makes reference to 'water dogs that pursue water fowl', but there is no evidence that this was a separate Irish breed, distinct from its ancestors. The earliest specific references to the Irish Water Spaniel are found in works dating from the 1840s and 1850s.

By the 1850s there were two forms of this breed. The Northern one had a white-and-liver-coloured coat which was very curly, and short ears with very little feathering. The Southern one had a pure liver-coloured coat with short crisp curls, and long, feathered ears. It also had a tail that was 'round and carried slightly down, but straight, without any approach to feather'. From these descriptions it is clear that the modern Irish Water Spaniel was developed from the Southern form. The tail is especially significant here, because a special feature of the modern breed, which distinguishes it from all other related water dogs, is the unusual 'rat tail'.

The development of the Southern form owed a great deal to one man, Justin McCarthy. His dog Boatswain, born in 1834, has been described as the founding father of the entire breed. He produced excellent dogs for many years and was largely responsible for establishing the breed. The Irish Water Spaniel Club was formed in 1890, and many examples were exported to America, Scandinavia and elsewhere in Europe, where they attracted great attention.

The Irish Water Spaniel has been described by one enthusiastic owner as 'a bundle of rags in a cyclone', by another as a 'buccaneer and a glutton' who stands 'shivering with excitement' when a hunt begins, and yet another as 'a lamb at home and a lion in the chase'. It clearly wins the hearts of all those who work with it or come to know it well.

References

1966. Hutzmann, Erwin. *How to Raise and Train an Irish Water Spaniel.* TFH, New Jersey.

1982. Waters, Nick. *A Bundle of Rags in a Cyclone. The Irish Water Spaniel.* Waters, Rodington, Shropshire.

FRANCE

BARBET FRANCE

Also known as the Griffon d'Arrêt à Poil Laineux, this breed was developed centuries ago to retrieve waterfowl. It was given the name Barbet, meaning 'bearded', in the 16th century. It was known in England in the 18th century, where it was called the Large Rough Water-Dog. In addition to its main task of retrieving from water, it has also been trained, at various times, to point and to flush game.

This is the original water dog of Europe, known since the Middle Ages. It was once common and widespread, but is now comparatively rare. It is thought to have been the principal ancestor of many other breeds, including the Poodle, the Irish Water Spaniel, the Newfoundland, the Briard and the Bichon.

The Barbet is a shaggy, curly-coated dog, well protected from the often icy water into which it has to plunge to retrieve downed waterfowl. After early hunts, before the age of sporting guns, it would adapt its skills to retrieving arrows that had fallen in the water, or onto swampy land, and which could not be reached by human hand. It was a favourite hunting companion of a number of French monarchs, especially Henri IV and Louis XV.

Its feet are webbed and it is a seemingly tireless swimmer. Coat colours include black, brown and grey, with or without white markings. Working Barbets are unclipped, but show-dog examples of this breed are sometimes given the 'lion-clip', in imitation of the show Poodle.

The Barbet is a faithful, obedient, amiable and intelligent dog, with an appealing appearance and a passion for water, which makes its rarity surprising. Having lost ground to its descendants, the Poodles, during the 19th century, the breed never regained its position, and by the end of the 20th century there were only a few hundred Barbets left alive.

SPAIN

SPANISH WATER DOG SPAIN

Known in its homeland as El Perro de Agua de Espagnol, La Mesta or La Medera, this ancient breed was not only employed as a waterfowl retriever, but was also required to carry out an important annual sheep-herding task.

This is an excessively shaggy dog, reminiscent of the French Barbet and probably an ancient relative of it. Its coat is so heavy that it would seem highly unsuitable for a swimming breed but despite this, with its webbed feet, it is said to be able to progress efficiently under water. It has even been known to descend to a depth of 10 ft (3 m).

In its special, occasional role as a herding dog, this breed was required, each spring, to shepherd large flocks of sheep from the hot south of Spain to the cooler north and then, at the end of the scorching summer months, to guide them back south again for the winter. As with so many traditional working animals, these once important duties were eventually overtaken by modern technological advances in the transportation of livestock.

The thick, curly coat, with a tendency to cord, like some Hungarian breeds, is seen in solid colours, either black, brown or pale fawn. Standing at only 16–19 in (41–48 cm) high, this is a rather small dog for the water-retrieving and herding tasks it must perform. Although it has occasionally appeared at European dog shows, it remains a rare breed.

GERMANY

CORDED POODLE

GERMANY

Also known as the Koordenpoedel, this was once treated as a separate breed, but is now viewed as merely a variation of the Standard Poodle, the Corded Poodle was originally developed as a rugged water retriever.

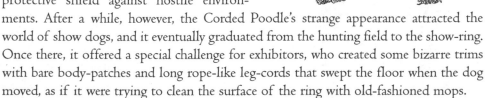

This breed once had a strong following because of its dramatic visual impact. In its early, working days, the interweaving of the top-coat and the undercoat, which created the heavy, hanging cords of hair, had a practical purpose, providing the dog with a thick, protective shield against hostile environments. After a while, however, the Corded Poodle's strange appearance attracted the world of show dogs, and it eventually graduated from the hunting field to the show-ring. Once there, it offered a special challenge for exhibitors, who created some bizarre trims with bare body-patches and long rope-like leg-cords that swept the floor when the dog moved, as if it were trying to clean the surface of the ring with old-fashioned mops.

When these show dogs were not being exhibited, their leg-cords were tied up in unsightly bundles on the dogs' backs. The cords had to be oiled regularly to prevent them from snapping and, since they could not be combed or brushed, the dogs were often dirty and smelly. The task of washing the coat was both laborious and time-consuming. Despite these drawbacks, however, they still had their ardent supporters.

In its earlier heyday the Corded Poodle was confidently separated as a distinct breed in its own right. This was done because of the striking difference in appearance between the 'Curly Poodle' and the Corded Poodle. But this difference was so superficial that certain distinguished dog judges rebelled. The Poodle owners fought back and eventually it was necessary to hold a special committee meeting at the Kennel Club in London to settle the matter. The meeting took place on 1st February 1898, when both sides of the case were put. The exhibitors demanded separate classes for the two types of Poodle, while the chairman of the Committee insisted that this separation be abandoned, because, in his own words: 'If the coat be cut, or brushed, combed or fluffed, the Poodle is Curly; whereas, if it be uncut and untouched by comb or brush, and simply be kept from getting matted, its natural tendency is to form cords, and the dog is Corded.'

The chairman presented a petition to support his view, signed by 80 of the most prominent dog judges in Europe, and won the day. Officially the Corded Poodle breed ceased to exist. After that, only a few dedicated enthusiasts continued to favour them and today they are extremely rare.

STANDARD POODLE   GERMANY

The name of this breed is German, indicating its place of origin, not French, despite its long association with France. To the Germans it is the Pudel (from Low German, puddeln, meaning 'to splash in water'), to the French it is the Caniche (meaning 'duck dog') or the Chien Canne (meaning 'reed dog'), and to the Italians it is the Barbone (which means it is 'barbered'). In France it has also been recorded as the Caniche de Grande Taille.

The modern Poodle, displaying the most elaborate and meticulous coat trim known to the canine show world, would appear to be a far cry from its ancient, working ancestor. In reality, however, the fancy grooming of the champion pedigree dog of today is only a refinement of a style that has been known for centuries. There is a woodcut dating from 1665 that shows a 'Water Dogge' wearing a very similar coat-clipping pattern. This was not a deranged hair-stylist's fantasy, it was a practical, down-to-earth adaptation to life as a rough, tough water retriever. The rear half of the body was closely shorn in order to reduce drag when the dog was struggling through the water with a duck in its jaws. Tufts of longer hair were left on the legs and the tip of the tail to protect those parts of the body from chilling.

The ancestors of the Poodle were the old water dogs of Europe, renowned for their intelligence, skill and daring. Their canine cleverness became so admired that they were frequently co-opted for work in the circus, where their acrobatic skill and trainability often led to them becoming star performers. Their natural exuberance also meant that, with the arrival of competitive dog-showing in the 19th century, it was easy for them to make the transition from circus-ring to show-ring. They have remained favourites there ever since and their original, hard-working lives as hunting dogs in marsh, swamp and lake have long been forgotten.

The favourite style for show Poodles today is the 'Continental clip', in which the shearing of the rear end of the body leaves 'bracelets' at the hocks (supposedly to protect the joints against rheumatism), rosettes or 'pompons' on the hips (a feature borrowed from clowns when the dogs worked in the circus) and a 'pompon' on the tip of the tail. The face is also sheared. An accepted alternative is the 'English saddle clip', which lacks the hip rosettes, but has two bracelets on each hind leg. An entire book has been written about alternative Poodle clips, with no fewer than 50 variations depicted.

From its earliest days, the Poodle has usually appeared in solid colours. It was said that German Poodles were brown, Russian Poodles were black and French Poodles were white. Today, in the show-ring, these three basic colours have been modified, using dilution genes, to produce a variety of appealing pastel shades.

There are two smaller versions of this breed, the Miniature and the Toy Poodle (see separate entries). It was the fashion at one time to give the Standard Poodle the title of Giant Poodle (in French, the Caniche Grand), to identify it as the largest of the three types.

References

1949. Bischoff, Ilse. *The Wonderful Poodle.* Thomas Y. Crowell, New York.

1949. Naylor, Leonard E. *Poodles.* Williams & Norgate, London.

1950. Tracy, T. H. *The Book of the Poodle.* Viking Press, New York.

1951. Hopkins, Lydia. *The Complete Poodle.* Denlinger's, USA.

1951. Rogers, Alice Lang. *Poodles in Particular.* Orange Judd, New York.

1952. Hoyt, Hayes Blake. *Your Poodle.* Popular Dogs, London.

1953. Bowring, Clara and Monro, Alida. *The Popular Poodle.* Popular Dogs, London.

1955. Miller, Madeline. *Poodles as Pets.* TFH, New Jersey.

1957. Dangerfield, Stanley. *Your Poodle and Mine.* Denlinger's, USA.

1957. Johns, Rowland (Editor). *Our Friend the Poodle, Miniature and Standard.* Methuen, London.

1957. Miller, Evelyn. *How to Raise and Train a Poodle.* TFH, New Jersey.

1958. Erlanger, Alene. *Pet Poodle.* All-Pets, Fond du Lac, Wisconsin.

1958. Reimlinger. *Der Pudel.*

1960. Bowring, Clara. *Poodles.* Batsford, London.

1960. Ivens, William H. (Editor). *Poodles in America: A Comprehensive Record from 1929 to 1959.* Poodle Club of America, Doylestown, Pennsylvania.

1960. Martin, Lester H. *This is the Poodle.* TFH, New Jersey.

1960. Price. *The Miniature Poodle.*

1960. Sheldon, Margaret Rotery and Lockwood, Barbara. *Clipping Your Poodle.* Foyles, London.

1960. Walne, Shirley. *A to Z of Poodles.* Max Parrish, London.

1962. Cameo, Miss. *Poodle Clipping Book.* TFH, New Jersey.

1962. Sherwood, Basil. *The French Poodle.* Rupert Hart-Davis, London.

1963. Hart, Ernest H. *How to Clip Your Own Poodle.* TFH, New Jersey.

1963. Robin, R. A. *Le Caniche.* Editions Bornemann, Paris.

1963. Sheldon, Margaret Rothery and Lockwood, Barbara. *Breeding from Your Poodle.* Foyles, London.

1964. Hallgren, Rae. *Poodles in Your Home.* TFH, New Jersey.

1964. Hopkins, Lydia. *The New Complete Poodle.* Howell, New York.

1965. Daly, Macdonald. *Our Pal the Poodle.* Chambers, London.

1965. Rosenblum, Edwin E. *The Poodle Primer.* TFH, New Jersey.

1965. Sheldon, Margaret Rothery and Lockwood, Barbara. *The Poodle Owner's Encyclopaedia.* Pelham Books, London.

1965. Stone, Pearl. *Clipping and Grooming Your Poodle.* Arco, New York.

1966. Hart, Ernest H. *The Poodle Handbook.* TFH, New Jersey.

1966. Skelton, Mollie. *You and Your Poodle.* TFH, New Jersey.

1968. Griffen, Jeff. *The Poodle Book.* Doubleday, New York.

1968. Kalstone, Shirlee. *The Complete Poodle Clipping & Grooming Book.* Howell, New York.

1968. Lockwood, Barbara. *Pet Library's Poodle Guide.* Pet Library, London.

1969. Sabella, Frank T. *Your Poodle, Standard, Miniature, and Toy.* Denlinger's, USA.

1970s. Schneider, Earl (Editor). *Enjoy Your Poodle.* The Pet Library, New Jersey.

1970. Fretwell, Francis P. (Editor). *Poodles in America, a Comprehensive Record from 1965 thru 1969.* The Poodle Club of America.

1970. Monro, Alida. *The Family Poodle.* Popular Dogs, London.

1970. Sheldon and Lockwood. *All About Poodles.*

1972. LaFetra, William. *Clip and Groom Your Own Poodle.* TFH, New Jersey.

1974. Glover, Harry. *The Book of the Poodle.* Batsford, London.

1979. Donnelly, Kerry. *Poodles.* TFH, New Jersey.

1980. Meadows, Faye. *Fifty New Creative Poodle Grooming Styles.* Arco, New York.

1984. Martin, Lester H. *This is the Poodle.* TFH, New Jersey.

1985. Anon. *Votre Caniche.* Fernand Nathan, Paris.

1987. Kalstone, Shirlee. *The Complete Poodle Clipping and Grooming Book.* Howell, New York.

1987. Nicholas, Anna Katherine. *A Complete Introduction to Poodles.* TFH, New Jersey.

1994. Dahl, Del. *The Complete Poodle.*

1995. Guidry, Virginia Parker. *The Poodle.* Howell, New York.

1996. Ackerman, Lowell. *Dr Ackerman's Book of the Poodle.* TFH, New Jersey.

1996. Donnelly, Kerry. *Poodles.*

1996. Kallen, Stuart A. *Poodles.*

1997. Arnn, Barbara. *Poodles.*

1997. Fogle, Bruce. *Dog Breed Handbooks – Poodle – Standard, Miniature, & Toy.* Dorling Kindersley, London.

1997. Stahlkuppe, Joe. *Poodles: Everything About Purchase, Care, Nutrition, Breeding, Behavior, and Training.* Barron, New York.

1998. Geeson, Eileen. *The Complete Standard Poodle.* IDG Books Worldwide.

1999. Dib, Pierre. *Poodle.* Popular Dog Library.

1999. Dunbar, Ian (Editor). *The Essential Poodle.* Howell, New York.

Cherry, Barbara. *Pet Owner's Guide to The Poodle.* Howell, New York.

Mackey, Irick J. *The New Poodle.* Macmillan.

Miller, Dana. *Know how to Clip A Poodle.* Pet Library, New York.

Schneider, Earl (Editor). *Know Your Poodle.* Pet Library, New York.

Telford, Helen. *Beginner's Guide to Poodles.*

Ullmann, H. J. and Ullmann, E. *Poodles. A Complete Pet Owner's Manual.*

NORWAY

NORWEGIAN PUFFIN DOG NORWAY

Sometimes called the Norwegian Lundehund, and known in its homeland as the Norsk Lundehund, or simply as the Lundehund, this breed was developed specifically for climbing cliff pathways in search of a fledgling puffin, capturing it and then carrying the bird back to the hunters. It is referred to informally as the Lundie.

This highly unusual dog from the remote Arctic islands off the coast of northern Norway has four strange anatomical features. It has an additional toe on each of its large paws, giving it an improved grip when climbing; it has ears which it can fold over, providing protection from freezing rain; it has forelegs that can move sideways through a 90-degree angle, giving it incredible flexibility; and it has a double-jointed neck, enabling it to wriggle into narrow crevices in pursuit of hiding puffins.

It was important for the Norwegian farmers who owned these dogs to understand the breeding cycle of the puffins. The adult birds, with their powerful beaks, were able to defend themselves with savage pecks and had to be avoided. But once their nestlings had grown and were about to leave the nest in August, the parental urge to protect them from all-comers waned and the plump, 40-day-old fledglings were vulnerable, just before they were ready to fly away. It was during this brief 'window of opportunity' that the hunters had to act and send in their dogs.

The dogs had to clamber up the cliffs, crawl into the rocky crevices and start digging into the puffin tunnels. This often involved lying on their sides and twisting this way and that in the tiny dark spaces, before they could reach their quarry. The fledgling was finally grabbed and carried back alive and undamaged to the dog's owners. Each dog caught between 20 and 40, sometimes as many as 80, birds in a single hunting session. The islanders made full use of the puffins – the feathers were plucked and used to stuff pillows; the entrails were removed and fed to the dogs; and the meat was eaten or salted and preserved for later consumption.

These agile little dogs dutifully carried out their difficult search-and-retrieve task every puffin breeding season from the 16th to the 19th century. We know this from reports of explorers, dating from 1591, which recorded observations of Puffin Dogs already in action in those early days. But then, in the middle of the 19th century, the breed suffered a serious setback when new puffin-trapping techniques were introduced, using nets. The population of these unique dogs dwindled rapidly, but luckily a small number did manage to cling on in the more remote island areas. One such place was the island of Vaeröy in the Lofoten archipelago.

In the 1930s, canine enthusiast Eleanor Christie, of Hamar in southern Norway, acquired a few of these Vaeröy dogs and began breeding from them. This proved to be the breed's salvation because in 1943 an epidemic of distemper nearly wiped out the island population, with only one dog surviving. Mrs Christie was able to send some of her kennel dogs back to the island and they resumed work there. This too was a lucky move because the following year distemper hit her own dogs and wiped out her entire breeding stock. This time the island came to *her* rescue, sending her a group of their working dogs. From this stock she was able, after the end of World War II, to start building up their numbers and to ensure the safety of this fascinating breed.

By the 1970s there were enough Puffin Dogs in existence for some to be exported to other countries, including Sweden, Denmark, Germany and Finland. In the 1980s they crossed the Atlantic to the United States. By the end of the 20th century there was a Norwegian population of 350 and a world population of between 700 and 800. In modern times, with the puffins now protected by Norwegian law, the exclusive role of this attractive, brown-and-white hunting dog has become that of a friendly household companion and a show dog.

RUSSIA

MOSCOW RETRIEVER   RUSSIA

This breed is also known as the Moscow Water Dog.

This little-known Moscow Retriever was descended from a mixture of Newfoundlands, Caucasian Sheepdogs and Eastern European Sheepdogs. It was employed in the early stages of the creation of the Red Army military guard dog called the Black Russian Terrier. Several Moscow Retriever bitches were mated with the founding father of that breed, a Giant Schnauzer called Roi, in the late 1940s. It seems that, soon afterwards, the Moscow Retriever was allowed to disappear and must now be considered as almost certainly extinct.

CANADA

LABRADOR RETRIEVER   CANADA

In its original form, this breed was known as the Small Water Dog, the Lesser Newfoundland, the St John's Dog, the Lesser St John's Dog, or the Short-coated St John's Dog. Today it is usually referred to simply as the Labrador. It began life as a Canadian fisherman's dog, retrieving fish-laden nets.

This is currently the world's most popular dog breed, with the Kennel Club in London recording over 30,000 new registrations each year. Although it is normally listed as an English breed, the truth is that it had been busy working along the shoreline of Newfoundland long before it arrived in the Old World. Some worked from land, swimming out to retrieve the cork floats of the nets; others worked from the fishing boats, leaping overboard to grab the nets and swim ashore with them, so that the fishermen could empty out the fish. In the water, the dogs used their characteristic 'otter-tails' as rudders to guide them. They were immensely popular with the Canadian fishermen, but when the boats visited English ports, the fishermen were occasionally persuaded to sell a few to local sportsmen, and the Labrador gradually became established as an English gun dog. It was especially prized for its soft mouth, which meant that shot game could be recovered without suffering damage from clamped canine jaws. It was said to deliver the game to its master 'like a well-trained butler'.

Throughout the 19th century, England received a steady trickle of these well-built, patient, hard-working retrievers. The Canadian fishermen had discovered that their dogs would fetch good prices among the English gentry and, instead of struggling to keep hold of them, were now actively offering them for sale. Soon there were enough of these dogs in England for their new, hunting owners to start breeding them themselves, and they became more and more firmly established as important gun dogs. It was one of the early sporting owners of this breed, the Earl of Malmesbury, who gave them their new name of Labradors. Then, late in the century, new British quarantine laws were introduced that put an end to their importation, and new dog taxes in Canada (stemming from the Newfoundland Sheep Act) conspired against them at home. In Canada they soon went into decline, and in England, without new blood, their numbers began to dwindle.

At this point in their history they were crossed with several other breeds of gun dog – the Curly-coated Retriever, the Flat-coated Retriever and the Tweed Water Spaniel have all been mentioned. This did little to alter the Labrador's appearance, but the result was an even more valuable gun dog, with an excellent nose and a delightful temperament. Throughout the 20th century its popularity rose and rose and eventually it was exported all over the world, to become a global favourite. Socially, it has also become a 'high status' dog. One famous French politician, when asked why he owned a Labrador replied: 'If you wish to get on in politics, you simply must have one.' It certainly worked for him – he later became the president of his country.

There are two traditional colour forms, the typical black and the attractive golden (technically known as the 'yellow'). The latter is sometimes confused with the Golden

Retriever. This is not surprising as they have two common ancestors – the Flat-coated Retriever and the Tweed Water Spaniel. But they are easy to tell apart by their coats, the Golden Labrador's being much shorter. (Its hair was short, incidentally, to stop it clogging with ice, during its ancestors' early days in the freezing waters of Canada – a measure of just how tough it is.) In modern times, a third colour form has also found favour, a rich brown usually referred to as 'liver' or 'chocolate'. In the early days, both yellow and liver-coloured puppies were culled and only black was allowed.

The steady temperament of the Labrador has meant that it has frequently been chosen to carry out arduous tasks for human beings, from guiding the blind, to sniffing out drugs at airports and detecting mines for the army. As a show dog, it was recognized by the Kennel Club in 1903.

References

1933. Johns, Rowland (Editor). *Our Friend the Labrador*. Methuen, London.

1933. Sprake, Leslie C. *The Labrador Retriever*. Witherby, London.

1936. Scott, Lord John and Middleton, Sir John. *The Labrador Dog: its Home and History*. Witherby, London.

1947. Henry, Clarence. *Training Your Labrador*. Methuen, London.

1949. Mackay, Sanderson. *The Labrador Retriever Club Stud Book*.

1952. Naylor, Leonard E. *Labradors*. Barnes, New York.

1954. Griscom, Frances and Ivens, W. H. *Pet Labrador Retriever*. All-Pets, Fond du Lac, Wisconsin.

1957. Lorna, Countess Howe. *The Popular Labrador Retriever*. Popular Dogs, London.

1958. Brewer, Mrs Frances Griscom. *Labrador Retriever*. All-Pets, Fond du Lac, Wisconsin.

1963. Bowtell, Kevin. *The Labrador Retriever in Australia*. Labrador Retriever Club of Victoria.

1964. Henshel, Stan. *How to Raise and Train a Labrador Retriever*. TFH, New Jersey.

1965. Beck, Elizabeth. *Train Your Own Labrador*. Country Life, London.

1965. Warwick, Helen. *The Complete Labrador Retriever*. Howell, New York.

1970. Free, James Lamb. *Training Your Retriever*. Coward, McCann & Geoghegan, New York.

1970. Hill, F. Warner. *Labradors*. Foyles, London.

1970. Shoemaker, Paul E. *Training Retrievers for Field Trials and Hunting*. Superior, Seattle.

1970. Waring, Geoffrey. *Labrador Retriever*. Popular Dogs, London.

1972. Howe, Dorothy. *This is the Labrador Retriever*. TFH, New Jersey.

1974. Cartledge, Joe and Cartledge, Liz (Editors). *The Complete Illustrated Labrador*. Ebury Press, London.

1975. Howe, Lorna and Waring, Geoffrey. *The Labrador Retriever*. Arco, New York.

1976. Farrington, S. Kip, Jnr. *Labrador Retriever, Friend & Worker*. Hastings House, New York.

1977. Darlington, Katya. *The Labrador Retriever*. Bartholomew.

1979. Satterthwaite, Marjorie. *The Labrador Retriever*. K & R Books.

1980. Martin, Nancy. *Legends in Labradors*. Spring House, Pennsylvania.

1981. Wolters, Richard A. *The Labrador Retriever. The History, the People*. Petersen, Los Angeles.

1983. Berndt, R. J. and Myers, R. L. *The Labrador Retriever*. Denlinger's, Fairfax, Virginia.

1983. Nicholas, Anna Katherine. *The Book of the Labrador Retriever*. TFH, New Jersey.

1983. Roslyn-Williams, Mary. *All About the Labrador Retriever*. Pelham, London.

1984. Howe, D. *Labrador Retriever*. TFH, New Jersey.

1985. Tottenham, K. *The Labrador Retriever*. PSL.

1986. Warwick, Helen. *The New Complete Labrador Retriever*. Howell, New York.

1987. Satterthwaite, Marjorie. *A Dog Owner's Guide to Labrador Retrievers*. Tetra Press, New Jersey.

1988. Roslyn-Williams, Mary. *Advanced Labrador Breeding*.

1988. Sayer and Bunting. *Labrador & Golden Retrievers*. Hamlyn Dog Breed Handbook. Hamlyn, London.

1988. Twist, Michael. *The Complete Guide to the Golden Retriever*. Boydell.

1992. Wolters, Richard A. *The Labrador Retriever. The History, the People, Revisited*.

1993. Coode, Carole. *Labrador Retrievers Today*. Howell, New York.

1994. Beckett, Diana. *Pet Owner's Guide To The Labrador Retriever*. Howell, New York.

1994. Martin, Nancy A. *The Versatile Labrador Retriever*. Doral, Wilsonville, Oregon.

1995. Agresta, Lisa. *An Owner's Guide to the Pet Labrador Retriever*. Howell, New York.

1995. Anon. *The Basic Guide to the Labrador Retriever*. Dace Publishing, Ruckersville, Virginia.

1995. Burrows, Richard T. *Guide to Owning a Labrador Retriever*. TFH, New Jersey.

1995. Churchill, Janet I. *The New Labrador Retriever*. Howell, New York.

1995. Kern, Kerry V. *Labrador Retrievers: Everything About Purchase, Care, Nutrition, Diseases, Breeding, and Behavior*. Barron, New York.

1995. Livesay, Dennis. *The Proper Care of Labrador Retrievers*.

1995. McCarty, Diane. *Labrador Retrievers*. TFH, New Jersey.

1995. Ziessow, Bernard W. (Editor). *Official Book of the Labrador*. TFH, New Jersey.

1996. Ackerman, Lowell. *Dr Ackerman's Book of the Labrador Retriever*. TFH, New Jersey.

1996. Feazell, Mary. *A New Owner's Guide to Labrador Retrievers*.

1996. Fogle, Bruce. *Labrador Retriever*. Dorling Kindersley, London.

1996. Jury, Anthony W. *Labrador Retrievers, an Owner's Companion*.

1996. Kallen, Stuart A. *Labrador Retrievers*.

1996. Mars, Julie. *Labrador Retrievers*.

1997. Barnes. *The Ultimate Labrador Retriever*. Howell, New York.

1997. Smith, Steve. *Just Labs*. Willow Creek Press, Wisconsin.

1997. Wiles-Fone, Heather. *The Ultimate Labrador Retriever*. Howell, New York.

1997. Zervas, Michael R. (Editor). *The Basic Guide to the Labrador Retriever*. Dace.

1998. Dunbar, Ian. *The Essential Labrador Retriever*. Howell, New York.

1998. Hutchinson, Robert, et al. *For the Love of Labrador Retrievers*.

1998. Palika, Liz. *How to Train Your Labrador Retriever*.

1998. Stockdale, Renee. *The Essential Labrador Retriever*.

1999. Burrows, Richard T. *Labrador Retriever*. Popular Dog Library.

1999. Gould, Mike, et al. *The Labrador Shooting Dog*.

1999. Walton, Joel. *The Complete Idiot's Guide to Labrador Retrievers*.

1999. Wiles-Fone, Heather. *All About Your Labrador Retriever*. Barron, New York.

1999. Yow, John Sibley (Editor). *In Praise of Labs: An Illustrated Treasury*.

2000. Berger, Todd R. (Editor). *Love of Labs: the Ultimate Tribute to Labrador Retrievers*. Petlife Library.

2000. Coulson, Jo. *Living With a Labrador Retriever*.

2000. Guidry, Virginia Parker, et al. *Your Lab's Life: Your Complete Guide to Raising Your Pet from Puppy to Companion*.

2000. Morn, September B. *Training Your Labrador Retriever*.

2000. Pavia, Audrey. *The Labrador Retriever Handbook*. Barron, New York.

2000. Smith. Steve. *The Labrador Retriever: A Comprehensive Guide to Buying, Owning, and Training*.

2000. Walton, Joel. *Labrador Retrievers for Dummies*. IDG Books.

Cowie, James. *Know Your Labroador Retriever*. Pet Library, New York.

ST JOHN'S WATER DOG   CANADA

This is the old Lesser St John's Dog, from which the Labrador was created, but which has now reappeared in its original form. It was developed to retrieve from icy, northern waters, and is sometimes referred to as the St John's Retriever.

This is a rediscovered breed. During their 1979–1982 Transglobal Expedition, explorers Ranulph and Virginia Fiennes took with them their Jack Russell pet, Bothie. When they stopped at the Eskimo settlement of Tuktoyaktuk, Bothie discovered a two-month-old black puppy bitch, called Toulouguk, meaning 'Black as a Raven'. Known to the explorers simply as Black Dog, she was brought back to England where she later became the foundation figure of Virginia Fiennes's attempt to re-establish the old St John's Water Dog, of which the puppy was a surviving example.

At the time of writing, the Fiennes dogs have extended to three generations and a total of 39 animals, of which 26 are still living. Examples from England have now gone to Ireland and Scotland. One of them, living on a Scottish island, is reported to spend a great deal of its time in the water, playing with the local seals.

This breed of St John's Water Dog is thought to have been the result, centuries ago, of crosses between spaniels, taken to Canada by early settlers, and native Newfoundlands. The dogs have webbed feet and stocky, heavy bodies weighing 120–170 lb (54–77 kg). They are good-natured, docile and gentle with children, and have very soft mouths when retrieving. As might be expected, bearing in mind that their ancestors swam in the Arctic Ocean off the north-west coast of Canada, they plunge into even the coldest water without hesitation.

Essentially, this is the undiluted, ancestral form of the Labrador Retriever, unmodified by later cross-breeding and by a century of selective fine-tuning. It differs from modern Labradors in several ways. Its double coat is thicker and its tail is feathered. Its head is wider and of a slightly different shape. Its feet are fully webbed, whereas the feet of the Labrador are only one-third webbed.

In 1993 it was reported that a few dedicated Canadian breeders were also, independently, trying their best to salvage the old breed. It remains to be seen whether they, or Ranulph and Virginia Fiennes, or both, are successful in achieving their goals.

UNITED STATES

AMERICAN WATER SPANIEL   UNITED STATES

Originally called the Brown Water Spaniel, this breed was developed primarily as a duck retriever, but it was also used to flush waterfowl. In many respects it is intermediate between the true spaniels and the retrievers.

This dark brown, woolly-coated dog looks like a smaller version of the Irish Water Spaniel, except that its legs are less hairy and its tail is more hairy. Its suggested ancestors include the now extinct English Water Spaniel, the Irish Water Spaniel, the Curly-coated Retriever, the Field Spaniel and the Poodle, but these are little more than informed guesses.

The history of the breed begins in the Midwest of the United States, and is centred in Wisconsin, although the dog was also popular in both Michigan and Minnesota. It first appeared in the 1860s and was fully established by the end of the 19th century. In the 1920s further refinements were made to the breeding of this dog, by a Wisconsin doctor called F. J. Pfeifer. Despite his efforts, however, the breed was gradually over-shadowed by the more specialized gun dogs imported from abroad. As a result it remained a localized favourite.

A common hunting method employed with this breed is for the hunter to take his dog out with him in a canoe or other small boat, from which the dog leaps to retrieve the downed waterfowl, swimming 'like a seal'. Because of its small size, compared with other water retrievers – it is 5 in (12 cm) shorter than the Irish Water Spaniel – this dog's activities are restricted to inland regions, away from the rougher coastal waters.

A specialist breed club, the American Water Spaniel Club, was formed in 1937, and the dog was first formally recognized by the AKC in 1940. Today it remains a uniquely American gun dog, little-known outside its homeland. Devotees of the breed insist that it is an overlooked, underestimated dog.

CHESAPEAKE BAY RETRIEVER UNITED STATES

This retriever owes its name to the large inlet on the Atlantic coast of the United States, just to the south of Washington, DC. In earlier days it was sometimes referred to as the Red Chester, the Brown Winchester, the American Duck Retriever or simply the Ducking Dog. Its primary role is as a cold-water retriever of game birds. It is known to its friends as the Chessie.

This is a tough, workmanlike dog, sturdy rather than elegant, with a thick, oily coat that protects it 'like a duck's plumage' from the often icy waters in which it works. Its stamina, energy and feats of endurance under terrible conditions are legendary, and there are claims that a single dog was once capable of retrieving as many as 300 downed ducks in a single day, from waters at near freezing temperatures.

Even heavy seas do not deter it. One author described the spartan nature of the breed when he commented that 'he cannot be enticed into a kennel, but must sit out on the frozen shore, rain or shine'. Another praised it as 'the greatest heavy-duty water dog

America has ever seen… a steam-roller of a dog'. It is such a remarkable retriever that the only explanation for its lack of success as a modern breed must be that, in appearance, it is a rather plain, homely dog. For those who have worked with it, however, this has never been a problem.

Unusually, we know the precise date of origin of this breed. It is the result of crosses made at the beginning of the 19th century between a pair of Newfoundland dogs, a light brown male called Sailor and a black bitch called Canton, and local Maryland retrievers. In 1807 a British vessel was shipwrecked off the Maryland coast and two Newfoundland puppies on board were rescued and taken ashore. There they were kept until adult, when they were mated with local retrievers. The offspring of these crosses inherited the aquatic abilities of the Newfoundlands and the retrieving skills of the local dogs. This combination proved so successful that hunters in the region of Chesapeake Bay reared more and more of them, and a new breed was born. It was improved and refined throughout the 19th century and by the 1880s had been more or less perfected in its modern form. Its fame spread across the United States and a national breed society, the American Chesapeake Club, was formed in 1918.

It is not clear exactly which breed of retriever was involved. One early author referred to them as 'English Water Poodles', but it is more likely that several breeds were involved. Flat-coated and Curly-coated Retrievers, and even coonhounds, have been suggested as possible ancestors.

The Chesapeake Bay Retriever is a heavily built, tan to dark brown dog of indomitable character, with a massive head, muscular neck and exceptionally powerful hindquarters – the powerhouse of its amazing swimming strength. In personality it is intelligent and brave, and there are several cases of these dogs saving drowning children.

References

1933. Bliss, Anthony A. (Editor). *The Chesapeake Bay Retriever.* The American Chesapeake Club, New York.

1965. Henschel, Stan. *How to Raise and Train a Chesapeake Bay Retriever.* TFH, New Jersey.

1994. Horn, Janet, *The New Complete Chesapeake Bay Retriever.* Howell, New York.

1997. Henschel, Stan. *Chesapeake Bay Retrievers.*

1999. Kennedy, Stacy. *Chesapeake Bay Retriever: A Complete and Reliable Handbook.*

1999. Rice, Dan. *Chesapeake Bay Retrievers: Everything About Purchase, Care, Nutrition, Behavior, and Training.* Complete Pet Owner's Manual.

1999. Sarnoff, Lolo. *Dara: Autobiography of a Chesapeake Bay Retriever.*

Cherry, E. H. *The Complete Chesapeake Bay Retriever.*

GENERAL HUNTING DOGS

Most breeds of sporting dog have become specialized in one particular activity and now function only in that capacity. Others have one main activity, but are also useful in one or more additional, subsidiary capacities. In both these categories the dogs can be classified by their principal specialization.

There are, however, other breeds that have never become specialized. They have remained general-purpose hunting dogs – opportunists that are capable of adapting to any challenge they encounter.

Yet other breeds have descended from specialized breeds but have lost their specializations. Many continental European hunters prefer the company of an all-purpose gun dog, for example, and expect their canine companions to find, point, set, or flush, and then retrieve. In France there is a small group of six breeds that are sometimes called spaniels and sometimes setters. Physically they are intermediate between these two types. All of them look like lanky, long-legged, light-bodied spaniels, but in the field they also act as expert retrievers, so it is impossible to place them in one specific category or another.

There are 43 breeds in this general-purpose category.

FRANCE

BLUE PICARDY SPANIEL   FRANCE

Known in its homeland as the Épagneul Bleu de Picardie, this breed was developed to hunt snipe in marshy land.

Very similar to the brown-and-white coloured Picardy Spaniel, but now treated as a separate breed, this northern French dog was created by crossing Picardy Spaniels with English Setters some time in the late 19th or early 20th century. In colour, it is black with patches of ticked-white that give it a bluish tinge.

It is a docile breed, very good with children, but of little use as a guard dog. Looking like a cross between a spaniel and a setter, it has great stamina when working and is equally good at finding, flushing and retrieving game.

BRITTANY SPANIEL   FRANCE

Sometimes called the Breton Spaniel or simply the Brittany, and, in its homeland, the Épagneul Breton, this breed is a general-purpose gun dog. When it first appeared in the show-ring, in 1896, it was called the Short-tailed Brittany.

This dog works in all seasons over any kind of land. As a gun companion it can be trained to do anything – it is capable of being a tracker, a flusher, a setter, a pointer or a retriever.

Although widespread today, back in the 18th century its ancestors were restricted largely to the Argoat forests in the region between the Monts d'Arrée and the Montagnes Noires in the western part of Brittany. Originally it was more spaniel-like than it is today and was used primarily for flushing and retrieving, but then in the 19th century it was modified by matings with imported English Setters and English Pointers. In its new form it was transformed into a dog that could perform whatever task was demanded of it.

It has a fine nose, a tenacious personality and the readiness to work on land or in water. Its favourite quarry is woodcock but it also hunts pheasant, duck, partridge and almost anything else that happens to be available. Its early, deeply ingrained, spaniel tendency is to flush out game but, on command, it can easily be switched to setting or pointing.

Traditionally, its tail is docked brutally short, which is unusual for this type of dog. It is claimed that, as with the Old English Sheepdog, some puppies are born naturally short-tailed. In colour this breed is brown-and-white, black-and-white or tricoloured.

At the beginning of the 20th century, its numbers were dwindling, and its quality declining, but it was then taken in hand by a devoted enthusiast, Arthur Enaud, who instigated a strict breeding programme to redevelop it and return it to its former glory. The first breed standard for this reconstituted dog was introduced in 1907. In the 1930s, examples of this breed were exported to the United States where they became immensely popular and soon diverged into a slightly different breed (see entry for American Brittany Spaniel). The Brittany was not recognized in England until 1986.

References

1956. Monte, Evelyn. *Pet Brittany Spaniel.* All-Pets, Fond du Lac, Wisconsin.
1963. Gagniard. *L'Épagneul Breton.*
1965. Rosenblum, Edwin E. *How To Raise and Train a Brittany Spaniel.* TFH, New Jersey.
1971. Hammond, Ralph B. and Hammond, Robert D. *Training & Hunting the Brittany Spaniel.* Barnes, New York.
1974. Riddle, Maxwell. *The Complete Brittany Spaniel.* Howell, New York.
1980. Pisano, Beverly. *Brittany Spaniels.* TFH, New Jersey.
1987. Riddle, Maxwell. *The New Complete Brittany.* Howell, New York.
1998. Rice, Dan. *Brittanys: Everything About Purchase, Care, Nutrition, Behavior, and Training.* Barron, New York.
2000. Webb, David A. (Editor). *A Feisty Little Pointing Dog: A Celebration and Tribute to the Brittany.*

ÉCOSSAIS SPANIEL   FRANCE

Known in its homeland as the Épagneul Écossais, this breed appears to have vanished.

References have been made by some authors to a variety of French Spaniel called the Épagneul Écossais, which translates literally as the Scottish Spaniel. Little is known about it other than that there were classes for it at early French dog shows.

Some authors believe that it was no more than an alternative name for the breed we now call the French Spaniel. Others report that it was a closely related breed which has since become extinct. One, writing in 1907, suggests that, despite its name, it may have been a French version of the Irish Red and White Setter and that 'it is conceivable that this Irish variety has been resuscitated in France'.

FRENCH SPANIEL

FRANCE

Known in its homeland as the Épagneul Français, and sometimes called the French Setter, this breed is an all-purpose gun dog.

In appearance, this tall, leggy dog is regarded as the most attractive and well balanced of the French spaniel group. Like most of its French relatives, it has been trained as a multi-functional dog. In addition to flushing and retrieving, it can also be trained to stand at point.

Known since the Middle Ages, it has changed little over the years. In the 16th century its popularity grew and it spread out across Europe. It retained its importance through the 17th and 18th centuries, but then, in the 19th, it went into a decline due to the new fashion for imported English gun dogs. As its numbers dwindled, so did the quality of the survivors.

The future of this ancient dog looked bleak, but help was at hand. It was saved from extinction by the efforts of a priest, a hunting enthusiast by the name of Abbot Fournier, who assembled a group of stragglers from the last remnants of the breed. Using these dogs as his foundation stock, he began a selective breeding programme with the aim of re-establishing the French Spaniel and rebuilding it in its true, original form. He achieved his goal and during the 20th century the breed once again found widespread favour in France.

It is a calm, sensitive dog that needs gentle handling. As a family pet it has become increasingly popular in recent years, because of its affectionate and docile nature in the home and the gentle way in which it interacts with children. Despite its great appeal, it has remained largely confined to its home country and is rarely seen abroad.

PICARDY SPANIEL

FRANCE

Known in its homeland as the Épagneul Picard, and sometimes called the Picardy Setter, this breed was developed primarily to hunt for ducks in marshy land.

The Picardy is a versatile breed, capable of retrieving ducks as well as flushing them, and also useful in the fields, away from the water, for both furred and feathered game. In appearance, it is intermediate between a spaniel and a setter. Its coat is brown, white and tan, with brown ticking in the white areas, and with the tan markings being confined to the extremities.

It is said to be a courageous hunter but a docile companion at home. Although very businesslike when working, it is unduly friendly in the house and does not like to be kennelled or kept apart from its owners.

An ancient breed from northern France, known since the 14th century, it was at serious risk of becoming extinct at the end of the 19th century, but was saved by a small band of enthusiasts. They had to fight against the almost random crossing that was taking place at the time and which was threatening to dilute the breed beyond recognition. Led by a devotee called Rattel, they initiated a planned series of carefully controlled selective breeding programmes and had considerable success in re-establishing the breed in its pure form. However, despite their efforts, it has always remained an extremely rare breed.

This dog was once considered to be no more than a variety of the French Spaniel, but is now classed as a separate breed. It was first exhibited in its own right in 1904, and a specialist breed club was formed in 1907.

PONT-AUDEMER SPANIEL FRANCE

Known in its homeland as the Épagneul Pont-Audemer, and sometimes called the Pont-Audemer Setter, this breed was developed as an all-round gun dog.

This rare breed of gun dog from Normandy in north-west France is characterized by an unusually thick, woolly, curly coat. In colour it is brown, brown and white, or brown and ticked white. Its ancestry is thought to have included local French spaniels, Irish Water Spaniels, Poodles and/or Barbets. With these breeds in its background, its strong affinity for working in water was inevitable. Marshland is its favourite habitat. In addition to flushing the game, it can also be trained to point and to retrieve. Its tail is traditionally docked to one-third of its length.

It is barely known outside its homeland and, even there, so few pure-bred specimens are left that it is at serious risk of disappearing altogether. Recently a club, the Société Havraise, has been formed in an attempt to save it from extinction. The society has taken under its wing all three of the rare northern spaniel breeds – the Picardy, the Blue Picardy and the Pont-Audemer – and is determined to keep them pure-bred and separate for the future.

HOLLAND

DUTCH PARTRIDGE DOG   HOLLAND

Also known as the Dutch Setter, the Drentse Partridge Dog or the Drentsch Partridge Dog, and in its homeland as the Drentse Patrijshond, this is an all-purpose breed employed as a general hunting companion, capable of searching, setting, pointing and retrieving from both water and land, and also used as a watchdog and household pet. Colloquially it is called the Drent.

This is an early breed from the province of Drenthe in north-east Holland, near the German border. It has been known for at least four centuries and was depicted in Dutch art of the 16th century. Intermediate in appearance between a setter and a spaniel, it has a long, bushy tail that is left undocked. The slightly wavy coat is white with patches of light to dark brown.

An intelligent, obedient, sensitive dog, with an easy-going, friendly disposition, it was originally employed to hunt partridge, grouse and quail. Recently it has more often been used for pheasant, rabbit and hare.

The combination of a good nose and a spirit of initiative has made this breed a favourite among Dutch hunters. However, although well known inside Holland, where the current population of Partridge Dogs is put at about 6,000, it is rarely encountered outside that country.

References

1947. Quartero. *Over de Drentse Patrijshond.*

MARKIESJE   HOLLAND

Also known as the Hollandse Tulphond, this small, general-purpose hunting dog is a recent development.

This is a slightly built dog, weighing only 20–22 lb (9–10 kg), with a height of no more than 14 in (35 cm). Looking rather like a slender spaniel, it has a long, smooth, silky coat, with well-feathered ears, legs and tail. It is a jet black dog, but may have a small white marking, usually on the chest.

In origin, it appears to have been created from crosses between the Miniature Poodle, the Continental Toy Spaniel and the Brittany Spaniel. It is reputed to be an excellent retriever and a good all-round hunting dog. According to one authority, it has been developed in an attempt to recreate a small hunting dog of the mid-18th century, which is known from the art of that period in Holland.

It is an ever-alert breed, intelligent, well balanced and attentive, sometimes independent and often shy with strangers. In Holland it is becoming popular with hunters of small game and also in the show-ring, but it is little-known elsewhere and must still, at this early stage, be considered a rare breed.

STABYHOUN   HOLLAND

A general-purpose Dutch gun dog which is used for pointing, flushing and retrieving from both water and land. Nearer home it acts as a mole-catcher, a farm guard and a household pet. In the past it has also been employed as a draught dog. It is known colloquially as the Bijke.

This ancient breed has a long, slightly wavy coat that is basically white but with large black, brown or tan patches. The long, undocked tail is heavily feathered. The Stabyhoun comes from the district of Friesland, in north-west Holland, where it has been active since the 17th century.

In personality it has been described as the perfect domestic companion, being affectionate, calm, good-natured, reliable, and excellent with children. Despite this, it remains an uncommon breed even in its homeland and is rarely encountered outside it. In recent years Dutch breeders have made a concerted effort to protect this long-established, indigenous breed and have introduced strict breeding programmes to ensure its future.

WETTERHOUN   HOLLAND

This breed has sometimes been called the Otterhoun, because one of its duties was as a hunter and killer of otters, but when the otters were conquered and that role became obsolete, the breed was developed as a general-purpose hunting dog. It is sometimes called the Dutch Spaniel, the Dutch Water Spaniel or the Friesian Water Dog. Some authors believe that the name Wetterhoun means 'Water-dog', but others consider it to be a corruption of the German words 'wittern' (meaning 'scent') and 'hund' ('dog').

This is a rare breed from the north-western corner of Holland where, in Friesland, it has long been a favourite hunting companion with local farmers. In earlier centuries it was highly variable and had no fixed breed type. It is thought to have been created by a mixing of local farm dogs with water spaniels and with spitz dogs from the north. The result was an all-purpose dog that acted partly as a terrier – digging out vermin such as moles, polecats and otters; partly as a land spaniel – flushing out game animals for hunters; partly as a water retriever – collecting shot game from the water; and partly as a guard dog – useful around the farmsteads. In other words, it was a general hunter's/farmer's dog.

In the 1940s, attempts were made to fix the breed and standardize its appearance, and this had largely been achieved by the 1960s. Although it is still rare and little-known outside Holland, its supporters now feel that they have managed to salvage this interesting dog and secure its future.

In appearance, it is a stolid, heavily built, wide-bodied animal with a broad, powerful head and a tightly curled tail twisted up over its back in the spitz tradition. It is protected by a thick, oily coat that is either black or dark brown, often with extensive white patches. Although the face and legs are smooth-haired, the rest of the body is covered in tight curls, rather like those of the Irish Water Spaniel or the Curly-coated Retriever. Rugged and tough, it is ready to thrust itself through even the densest cover, and thinks nothing of plunging into freezing water to retrieve a bird that has been downed and is floating there.

Although friendly enough with its owners, in other respects it is said to be rather reserved and cautious. Its personality has been described as obstinate but loyal, reticent but lovable, 'like the Friesian people for whom it works'.

GERMANY

BULLENBEISSER   GERMANY

The name of this dog means, literally, 'bull-biter'. When it was set against bears rather than bulls, it was called the Bärenbeisser. During the Middle Ages this was the only native hunting hound known in Germany. It was also occasionally used for baiting and guarding.

The earliest-known records of this breed date back to the 16th century. A medium-sized dog which traditionally had both its ears cropped and its tail docked, it looked like an intermediate between a mastiff and an old-fashioned bulldog. Its hunting role

was to attack the cornered game, whether bull, bear, deer or boar, and hold it until the hunters arrived to kill it. To achieve this end, the Bullenbeisser would leap up and clamp its jaws on either the victim's nose or its ears. It then had to hang on and refuse to let go, while trying to avoid injury.

Eventually, there was a tendency to breed for slightly smaller dogs, because they were faster. These small Bullenbeissers were called Brabanters. It was the Brabanters that were crossed with English Bulldogs in the late 19th century to create the well-known Boxer breed.

With the passage of time, German hunting for large game declined and the Bullenbeisser became increasingly rare. It disappeared during the 19th century, to be replaced by the modern Boxer.

SWEDEN

NORDIC SPITZ   SWEDEN

Also known as the Norbottenspets or the Norbottensskollandehund, and in Finland as the Pohjanpystykorva, this almost unpronounceable little dog was developed as a general hunting and farm dog and is also encountered today as a popular household pet.

This small spitz breed is unusual in that it lacks the long, thick coat commonly associated with life in the frozen north. Also, its curled-over tail is less tightly twisted than the more typical spitz tail.

This was once a common dog, but then in the early part of the 20th century importing foreign breeds became fashionable, and as a native dog it fell out of favour. By the middle of the 20th century it was becoming extremely rare and there were fears that it would soon be facing extinction.

The Swedish Kennel Club removed its name from their lists in 1948. Luckily, after that, local breeders began to take more pride in it as an indigenous dog and started to protect its numbers. Today its popularity has risen again, although now its main occupation is not in the field, but to act as a companion in the comfort of the home. Some Nordic Spitzes are still employed to hunt game birds

and in bird-hunting trials, but the breed's role as a working dog has been greatly reduced.

Following the Nordic Spitz's return to favour, it was reinstated by the Swedish Kennel Club in 1967. It is a calm, relaxed and friendly dog in the home, and good with children, but it is always ready to be a businesslike and briskly alert hunting dog when the occasion calls for it. The coat is basically white, but with patches of cream, tan, brown or black.

FINLAND

FINNISH SPITZ   FINLAND

In Finland this breed is called the Suomenpystykorva, or Suomalainen Pistykorven, which translates as the Finnish Cock-eared Dog. It is also known as the Finnish Hunting Dog, the Finnish Spets, the Finsk Spets or the Loulou Finois. In England it has the colloquial name of the Finkie or Finsky, and in its homeland it is sometimes referred to as the Barking Bird Dog. It was originally used to hunt all kinds of game, from squirrels to bears, but later it was employed more against birds.

This ancient, golden-coloured breed, the most popular dog in its native Finland, began its existence in the far north of Scandinavia. It then spread gradually south and became so common in southern Finland that it suffered from widespread cross-breeding and started to lose its pure-bred quality. In the second half of the 19th century the situation was becoming so serious that a Finnish sportsman, Hugo Roos, set off on expeditions to the more remote corners of the far north to search for dogs that were untainted examples of the genuine Finnish Spitz.

He was successful and was able to collect together some high-quality dogs that he brought south to form the foundation stock for a controlled revival of the breed. He continued careful line-breeding with these dogs for 30 years, and most modern examples of the Finnish Spitz are descendants of his dogs.

In 1892 a formal standard for the breed was established and it was soon on the way to recovery. By the 1920s it had been accepted by the Finnish Kennel Club. Its fame then spread to other countries and in 1935 it was recognized by the Kennel Club in London. In 1974 the Canadian Kennel Club followed suit, and in the United States the AKC did so in 1987.

In the field, its oddity is that, when it pinpoints a bird in a tree, it yodels at it until the hunter arrives. The yodelling is, in reality, very fast barking and there are claims that the Finnish Spitz can reach a speed of 160 barks per minute, hence its nickname of the

Barking Bird Dog. It is also said to wave its tail slowly back and forth as it yodels, which has a strangely mesmeric effect on its victim in the tree, as if the bird feels it is being confronted by a swaying serpent, and conveniently responds by remaining immobile on the branch as the hunter approaches to shoot it. The most experienced dogs then add one further trick to their repertoire. They move around the tree in such a way that, as the mesmerized bird follows them with its transfixed gaze, the unfortunate victim has to turn its back on the approaching hunter, who can then get much closer before taking his shot. To refer to this dog as an intelligent breed is clearly an understatement.

In modern times it has also become a popular household companion and a prized show dog, and there is a special annual contest to find the champion Finnish Spitz in its native country. Indeed, the breed is now recognized as the National Dog of Finland.

In personality the breed has been dubbed 'a big dog in a small dog's body'. It has also been described as having a strangely feline quality, and was once called 'the ideal dog for people who like cats'. Characterized as sensitive, cautious, strong-willed and independent, with a strong urge to be the 'top dog' in any human family, it is an animal that does not take kindly to being fussed over or fondled.

References

1936. Ritson, Kitty. *Elkhounds and Finnish Spets and All About Them.* Watmoughs, London.
1990. Nicholas, Anna Katherine. *Finnish Spitz.* TFH, New Jersey.

KARELIAN BEAR DOG   FINLAND

Also sometimes called the Karelian Bearhound, in Germany it is known as the Karelischer Barenhund, in Holland the Karelische Berenhond, in Sweden the Karelsk Bjornhund, and in Finland the Karjalankarhukoira, the Karjalan Karkuloirat or the Karjalankarhukoira Karelsk Bjornhund. This breed was developed to hunt a wide variety of game, from bear, wolf, lynx and deer to squirrel, rabbit and marten. In a secondary role, when not in the field, it acted as a watchdog and property guard.

This is a large, powerful and robust hunting dog with a characteristic black-and-white coat and a typical, tightly curled, spitz tail. Its hunting method is different from that of hounds. It does not undertake long chases but works close to the hunter and makes a short, fast chase when the quarry is encountered, trying to corner it. Once this has been done, it keeps it at bay until the hunter has killed it. The conspicuous black-and-white coat makes it easy for the hunters to spot.

Bears have almost vanished from Finland in recent times, so these dogs, despite their proud name, must now content themselves with smaller prey. Some of the game animals that have now become their main quarry tend to climb trees to escape, with the result that this breed has become a good 'treeing' dog. And some of those that have been exported to the United States have now been hailed as an exciting new kind of 'coonhound'.

The ancestors of this hunting dog inhabited the northern lands of Scandinavia and north-east Europe since the Neolithic era. The distribution of those early dogs ignored national boundaries, but in recent times their modern descendants have fallen foul of political divisions. The two main areas of interest in the breed have been Finland and north-western Russia. The Finns called the dog the Karelian Bear Dog, while the Russians insisted that it was the Russo-European Laika. It was the same animal, but the two countries refused to accept this. The conflict led to a separation, not only of titles, but also of dog populations, with the inevitable result that the breed started to split into two different types. These remain almost identical, but because they did not interbreed, they did begin to diverge slightly and today are treated as distinct breeds. This one, the Karelian Bear Dog, living in Finland, is slightly less powerful and less aggressive than its close Russian cousin (see separate entry).

During the 1800s and early 1900s, many imported breeds were allowed to mate indiscriminately with these indigenous hunting dogs. As a result, the pure type was being lost. This decline was halted in Finland in 1936, when local enthusiasts began breeding to a fixed standard. It was at this point that they introduced the official name of Karelian Bear Dog, and opposed any further crossings. (Inconveniently, Karelia switched from Finnish to Russian control in 1941, but despite this the word Karelian was retained in the Finnish name of the dog.) In 1946, after a decade of proper control, the FCI and the Scandinavian Kennel Club formally accepted this breed. In 1980 the Canadian Kennel Club followed suit.

As regards the personality of this breed, there are strongly conflicting views. It has recently been described as 'not an easy dog to have as a companion', but many of its supporters would disagree with that. They insist that it 'loves everyone in the family, and is absolutely reliable with children'. Again, it has been said that 'extensive training is necessary' if it is to be kept as a household companion, but supporters say it is 'very easy to train and teach to tolerate other animals in the house, including chickens and cats'. One feature which everyone seems to agree on, however, is that, no matter how friendly it may be inside the home, it is intensely hostile to strange dogs. Presumably, it has a genetic disposition to treat any large furry object that is unfamiliar to it as if it were a bear.

AFRICA

AFRICAN SAND DOG   AFRICA

This breed is also known as the Abyssinian Sand Terrier, the Abyssinian Sand Dog, the Abessijnse Zandterrier, the African Hairless Dog or the Zulu Sand Dog. It is said to be semi-wild, 'following rather than living with the cattle-breeders', but occasionally being employed by them as useful companions on hunting trips. In the past it has also been called the Egyptian Hairless Dog, or the Hairless Egyptian Dog, but this is confusing because there is a separate, extinct breed with this name, from ancient Egypt (see separate entry).

This is the hairless dog of Africa. Little is known about it and it must be considered a rare breed. Some authors even believe that it may be extinct, but it is doubtful if a thorough search has been made of its entire African habitat to establish this with certainty.

All that has been recorded of the behaviour of this animal is that it has a short, sharp bark, is fast-moving and is used for hunting purposes and as a companion animal. According to one author, it has a sandy-coloured body with a small crest of hair on the head and a tuft on the tail. Early photographs fail to confirm this, showing little or no visible hair, and a naked, rat-like tail. There is a preserved specimen, dating from 1903, on display at Tring Zoological Museum in Hertfordshire, England, which shows a dark-coloured skin with small, irregular, pale markings. Its long, bat-like ears are fully erect.

The first three examples of it to be seen in Europe arrived at the London Zoo in 1833, where they were labelled as 'Egyptian Hairless'. One died before the year was out, and its skull was examined. It was found to be as deficient in teeth as it was in hair, 'there being neither incisors nor canines in either jaw, and the molars being reduced to one on each side'. The teeth of the two living specimens were then examined and were also found to be deficient. The implication was that the gene which reduced the dog's hair also reduced its dentition. How animals of this type, if running wild in Africa, managed to kill and eat is hard to say. As domestic dogs they could have survived on a diet of slop, but were clearly at a grave disadvantage if forced to fend for themselves.

Since some of these naked African dogs do seem to thrive as feral animals, a more likely explanation is that the early London Zoo specimens were not typical. It may well be that there are several different genetic forms of African Hairless Dog, some with strong teeth and some with weak. The fact that, among the names of this 'breed' are the words Egyptian, Abyssinian and Zulu, suggests that genes for hairlessness have cropped up independently in several parts of the continent, wherever great heat has favoured naked skin as a cooling system. In other words, the name African Sand Dog should be considered as a temporary label for what may turn out to be several convergent forms. The Chinese Crested Dog and the Mexican Hairless Dog are also most likely to be independently naked types and not, as was once believed, scattered representatives of a single hairless breed.

BASENJI   AFRICA

This unusual breed is also known as the Congo Dog, the Belgian Congo Dog, the Congo Bush Dog, the Congo Hunting Terrier, the Congo Terrier, the African Bush Dog, the African Barkless Dog or simply the Barkless Dog. The African word Basenji means 'Little Thing of the Bush'. The breed also rejoices in the native name of M'bwa M'kubwa M'bwa Wanwitu, which means 'The Jumping-up-and-down Dog'.

This small African dog, with its athletic body, its short, silky coat, its prick ears and its tightly twisted tail, has been an all-purpose hunting dog for thousands of years. It is both a sighthound and a scenthound – it can pick up a scent 250 ft (75 m) away – and it can be trained both to point and to retrieve. Also, with bells attached to its body, it can be despatched into the bush to flush out game and drive it into waiting nets. Back home in the villages it can act as a watchdog. About the only thing it cannot do is to bark.

This is one of the strangest of all domestic dogs and has several features which set it apart from other breeds. These include the following:

1   Whenever the dog becomes alert, the skin on its forehead wrinkles up into unusual furrows that give it a 'worried' look, like a human being with knitted eyebrows.
2   As already mentioned, it does not bark; instead it yodels, chortles, howls, growls and crows.
3   Like the wolf, it has only one breeding season a year.
4   It grooms itself fastidiously, like a cat.
5   Also like a cat, it will sit for ages gazing out of the window.
6   It trots like a horse.

The Basenji is as old as the Pyramids. It appears in art of ancient Egypt from the 4th dynasty, some 4,500 years ago. Precise images appear again in relief carvings of the 11th dynasty, about 4,000 years ago. The Egyptian artists captured the exact form of the Basenji, even in those very early periods. The same type of dog reappears time and again for hundreds of years in the funerary art of that early civilization. Clearly these were important animals to the Egyptians and were already breeding true to type. What

is more, they have outlasted the ancient Egyptian civilization by over two thousand years, because they are still with us today, almost unaltered.

As the great days of Egypt faded into history, these little dogs managed to survive as the prized possessions of African tribesmen. They were so highly valued that they were said to be 'worth more than a wife'. The breed's range extended from Egypt and the Sudan in the north-east, right across to the Congo basin in the west. It was there that Europeans first encountered them, during the 19th-century explorations of the 'dark continent'.

Several of these Victorian explorers commented on dogs of this type, and mentioned that the natives used them for hunting, but it was not until 1895 that a pair was shipped to England. They were exhibited at Crufts as African Bush Dogs, but died from distemper shortly afterwards. Later, in 1923, a group of six was brought back from the Congo, but these too died, and it was not until the 1930s that there was a successful introduction.

In 1936 dog-breeder Olivia Burn was visiting the Belgian Congo with her husband and saw to her surprise that the local dogs were not the usual stray mongrels, but instead were remarkable, true-breeding dogs of high quality. She acquired some of these from tribal chieftains and undertook the laborious task of bringing them back to England. Because of her expert knowledge as a breeder, she chose excellent examples and was able to care for them on the arduous journey. As a result they survived and went on to become the foundation stock of the breed in the West. They were registered with the Kennel Club as Basenjis, and a pair was shown at Crufts in 1937. They attracted such attention that police had to be brought in to control the crowds. After this, more dogs were successfully collected from Africa, notably by Veronica Tudor-Williams. In 1939 the Basenji Club of Great Britain was formed. Soon they crossed the Atlantic, and in 1945 the Basenji Club of America was established. The breed was now on its way to an assured future both as a household companion and as a show dog. It reached its peak in 2001, when, to everyone's surprise, a Basenji was judged Best in Show at Crufts.

This is a poised, graceful, alert, tireless, swift-moving dog that has become a 'cult breed' – not widely popular but fanatically supported by those who know it. Its coat colour is black, black-and-tan, tan, or brindle, all with white areas on the feet, tail-tip, chest and, often, face and neck as well. It is only 16–17 in (41–43 cm) high and, being barkless, appears to be the ideal urban dog, but it must be remembered that it is such a bundle of energy that it requires a huge amount of exercise.

References

1954. Tudor-Williams. *Basenjis, the Barkless Dogs.* Watmoughs, London.
1958. Anon. *The Basenji: a Handbook.* Basenji Owners' and Breeders' Association, St Helens, Lancs.

1962. Pickering, B. and Brach, R. J. *The Barkless Dog. A Handbook for the Basenji Owner.* Exposition Press, New York.

1976. Green, Evelyn M. *Your Basenji.* Denlinger's, USA.

1978. Johnson, Forrest Bryant. *Basenji — Dog from the Past.* Privately published.

1979. Cardew, Mirrie. *A Basenji for Me.* Midland Counties Publications.

1992. Anon. *Basenji Owners Manual.* Evergreen Basenji Club.

1993. Ford, Elspet. *The Complete Basenji.* Ringpress Books, Lydney, Gloucestershire.

1994. Coe, Susan. *The Basenji — Out of Africa to You — A New Look.*

Wylie, Jill. *Call of-the-Marsh: Life with a Basenji.*

NIAM-NIAM   AFRICA

Also known as the Nyam-Nyam, the Nyam Nyam Terrier, or the Haute-Agooue Terrier, this little hunting dog from central Africa takes its name from the tribe that breeds it. The tribe is also known as the Azande or Zande, and the breed itself has occasionally been referred to as the Zande Dog. A neighbouring tribe called the Manboutou (or Mangbattu) also has this type of dog; though sometimes called the Manboutou Dog, it belongs to the same breed.

This 'mute' breed was first described by the 19th-century German explorer Georg August Schweinfurth. He had encountered it when he was travelling in southern Sudan in the 1860s, studying the tropical flora and fauna. Although it was only a domestic animal, kept by local tribespeople, he was impressed enough to record his observations of it:

> The dogs belong to a small breed resembling the wolf-dog, but with short, sleek hair. They have ears that are large and always erect, and a short, curly tail, like that of a young pig. They are usually a bright yellowish tan in colour, and very often have a white stripe upon the neck. They are made to wear little wooden bells round the neck so they should not be lost in the long steppe-grass.

Some of these dogs were acquired by Europeans living in Cairo and sent to England in 1925. Others were exhibited in Geneva in 1934. After this, little more seems to have been heard of the breed, unlike the Basenji, which was successfully developed in the West. It seems probable that the Niam-Niam is a close relative of the Basenji, and it would appear that the Niam-Niam is employed in a similar manner as a tribal hunting dog.

RUSSIA

EAST SIBERIAN LAIKA SIBERIA

Also known as the Vostotchno-Sibirskaia Laika, or the Laika Wastatchno-Sibirskaia, this breed is used to hunt large game such as bear and deer. The word 'laika' is Russian for 'barker'.

The original forebears of this Arctic breed were sled dogs. They were later adapted to hunt large game in the frozen north, and the result was this tough, powerful breed, always ready to take on all-comers. Its type was standardized 1947.

Those who hunt with this dog are more concerned with performance than appearance, with the result that there has been some variability in the breed. In the 1980s, however, there was a concerted effort to stabilize the type and introduce pure-breeding programmes. The habit of occasionally crossing them with wolves, to strengthen the breed, does not seem to have continued much after the middle of the 20th century.

The colour of the thick, plush coat is still highly variable, but the size and other features of its well-muscled body are more standardized. There is a thick, powerful neck and, as with all Laikas, a curled, bushy tail.

Unlike some other northern dogs, this one adapts well to life as a household companion, and has a reputation for being a calm, good-natured dog. It is said to be obedient and trainable, and many can now be seen on city streets, as companion dogs. It is the largest of the four Russian Laikas, having a height of up to 25 in (64 cm), compared with 24 in (61 cm) for the West Siberian and the Russo-European, and 19 in (48 cm) for the Karelo-Finnish (see separate entries).

WEST SIBERIAN LAIKA SIBERIA

This breed, known in Russia as the Zapadno Sibirskaia Laika, was developed to hunt large game such as deer and bear, but it can be trained to pursue small game, both fur and feather. It is also sometimes employed to pull sledges. Older reference works sometimes call it the West Siberian Husky, the Ostiak, the Ostiah Laika or the Laika Ostjazkaja.

This powerful, rugged hunting dog is thought to have been developed by hunters in the Ural Mountains, in the regions of Khantu and Mansi. It has a thick, wolf-like coat with grizzled markings that often make it look more like a wild dog than a domesticated breed. Today it is more common and more pure-bred than the East Siberian Laika and is the most widespread of all the Russian Laikas. It can be distinguished from the East Siberian breed by its longer, narrower head and its longer body.

It works well over icy terrain, its long legs helping it to move well over difficult, snowy ground. The local tribesmen use it when hunting both bear and deer, but its speciality is the pursuit of the valuable sable or ermine. It is probably true to say that these tribal people in the far north would not be able to survive without the help of their Laikas. It is little-known outside its homeland.

KARELO-FINNISH LAIKA   RUSSIA

Also known as the Karelskaja, this is one of the smaller Russian hunting dogs. It is employed in many different ways in the hunting field, being used against grouse, pheasant, duck, squirrel, hare, fox, marten and even bear.

This is the Russian version of the Finnish Spitz and is a very similar dog. For centuries the range of the Finnish Spitz had extended across eastern Finland and into the adjacent Karelia district of north-western Russia. Following the Russian Revolution, there was a change of attitude that led to the Russian population of these dogs being renamed the Karelo-Finnish Laika.

After that date they seem to have diverged slightly from the Finnish original. The thick, ruffed coat, for example, instead of always being solid red, may be fawn or black, and may show small white markings on the head, chest, legs and tail.

This Laika has a very foxy head and a fanciful legend suggests that it began life as a cross between a fox and a Nordic dog. It has a thick neck ruff, a heavy protective coat and a typically curled-up, spitz tail.

The Russian hunters, among whom it is so respected, describe it as a cheerful, energetic dog, desperate to please its human companions, bursting with enthusiasm for the hunt and capable of working even in deep snow. Any form of punishment quickly destroys its spirit. Although popular in its homeland, it remains virtually unknown outside Russia.

RUSSO-EUROPEAN LAIKA   RUSSIA

Also called the Russian-European Laika, the European-Russian Laika, the Karelian Bear Laika, the Karelian Laika, the Laika Ruissisch Europaisch, the Laika Roussko-Europaiskaia, or the Russko-Europaiskaia Laika, this powerful breed was developed to hunt large game such as wolf, bear and deer.

The Russian Laika breeds were created long ago by crossing old wolf-hunting dogs from Finland with sheepdogs from Russia. Originally, this particular Laika breed was indistinguishable from the Karelian Bear Dog of Scandinavia. Indeed, they were treated as one and the same dog. But then, in the 1940s, the Russians decided to separate the Scandinavian from the Russian dog population – a kind of canine apartheid. In future, they said, only true Russian dogs can be called Laikas.

As a result, this breed became the Karelian Bear Laika, while the Scandinavian version could only be called the Karelian Bear Dog (see separate entry). This was confusing, so a new name was applied to the Russian breed, and it was called the Russo-European Laika instead – a name with all the hallmarks of having been designed by a committee.

The result of the geographical separation of the two groups is that the two dog populations started to grow apart. And so, today, there are two recognized breeds instead of one. This one, in Russia, was bred to become bigger and more aggressive and, although it is fearless when tackling even the most daunting adversary in the hunting field, there is a downside in that it is no longer suitable as a household companion. It is said that, as part of the campaign to make the dog more powerful and more belligerent, it was deliberately crossed with the notoriously aggressive Utchak Sheepdog. Additional crosses with the West Siberian Laika are also reported to have been made as part of the breed's modification.

Like its Finnish equivalent, this dog has a boldly black-and-white thick coat, making it highly conspicuous in the hunting field. Its only colour variation is in the proportion of black to white.

MEDELAN   RUSSIA

A giant Russian molossian breed, now extinct, the Medelan was once used on royal hunts in pursuit of bears.

These huge, ferocious dogs were favoured by the last czar of Russia and kept at his summer palace at Gatchina. Described as 'the last descendants of the original dogs of war', they were capable of killing a man single-handedly. Even as puppies they were known to have torn a nine-year-old boy to pieces in less than a minute. It was claimed that the puppies were the size of Great Danes and that the adults were as big as calves.

During the summer, they were employed to drive brown bears out of thickets and even in the dead of winter they were taken into the freezing forests to rouse the slumbering bears from their hibernating quarters deep in the snow.

This dramatic breed had been kept by successive czars over a long period of time, but when the Revolution came, all the existing dogs were destroyed and the breed came to as sudden an end as its master.

INDIA

ALANGU   INDIA

This is a general hunting dog from the extreme south-east of India, in the Tanjore district. It has been described as a dog 'of magnificent proportions with noble carriage'. It is a big dog, about 27 in (69 cm) tall, with heavy, well-muscled limbs. Its ears are pricked, its back long, and its tail tapers to a fine point. When moving, it takes long strides. The coat colour varies from red to fawn to black. There may be some white markings in the chest region, and the muzzle is nearly always black. When it is not employed on its hunting duties, it is also enlisted as a fearsome watchdog.

KOMBAI   INDIA

This southern Indian breed is employed for hunting wild animals. (The name of this dog is sometimes incorrectly given as Kombia.)

The Kombai is a general hunting dog kept by the Zaminders and certain other Indian tribes. It is lean, long, fast, muscular, powerful and athletic, and is well known for its ability to overcome almost any obstacle in its path. Its coat is usually reddish brown, with a paler underside. The long tapering tail is normally held up and over its back.

Its original home was the Ramnad district, but its popularity saw it spread to other regions as well. In addition to hunting, it is also favoured both as a pet and as a guard dog. Despite its ferocity on the hunt, with its owners it is sweet-tempered and tolerant of their children.

There is some confusion about the status of this breed. According to one report in the 1960s, it was then popular and its range was spreading, but others claim that it is on the verge of extinction. Still others have reported that it is now extinct. Clearly this is a breed that would repay a field study to assess its current position.

KUCHI   INDIA

A small breed from the extreme south-east of India, the Kuchi is used for hunting animals such as squirrels, rats and other modestly sized mammals.

The Kuchi is found in the Tanjore district, where it is the smallest of the local breeds, but it is said to be very fast for its size. A long-haired dog, measuring only 10 in (25 cm) and weighing no more than 15 lb (7 kg), it is slender in build and is rather foxlike in appearance. Its bushy tail is carried in a characteristic way, curled up and, towards the tip, looking 'like a ball of hair gaily turned over the short back'. It has recently become a popular companion dog.

RAJAPALAYAM   INDIA

A large, southern Indian dog, named after its location, the Rajapalayam is employed principally for hunting wild boar, but is also used for other tasks.

This handsome, ancient breed is a big dog similar in general appearance to the Great Dane, but with a slightly lighter, more 'racy' body. Typically, it has a white or ivory coat, but it may also be in black, red, grey or a combination of these. It is an intelligent, affectionate, noble animal that, in addition to its main function as a hunting dog, is popular as a watchdog or a companion dog, although it is said not to take kindly to an indoor life.

SHENKOTTAH DOG   INDIA

A breed of Indian dog named after its location in southern India and used for hunting big game.

The Shenkottah was popular in the days of big-game hunting in the extreme south of India, in the Trivandrum district, where it was employed as a valued companion in the pursuit of the most dangerous animals in the jungle. It was said that a pair of these dogs could even pull down an adult tiger, although they sometimes lost their lives in the process. They are now on the verge of extinction, presumably because of the decline in big-game hunting itself, and the increasing rarity of the large prey they were usually set against. Their nearest living relative is another Indian hunting dog called the Kombai (see separate entry).

TRIPURI DOG   INDIA

This breed takes its name from the Tripura hills in north-eastern India, where it has been traditionally employed by local tribesmen in the hunt for wild boar and deer. It is also found in the nearby Lushai hills of Assam.

This is an intelligent, alert, spitz-type dog of medium size, with a foxy muzzle, small, pricked ears, a tightly curled, bushy tail, and a short, thick coat of variable colour. It is seen in black, brown, white and particolour forms.

Sadly, the Tripuri Dog is a rare local breed facing extinction, thanks to social changes in the region. In earlier days the breed was kept pure by its isolation. Now, however, its tribal owners are increasingly coming into contact with urban areas, and the dog's pedigree is being swamped out through casual matings with itinerant mongrels. With luck, a few pure specimens may have managed to survive in the remoter corners of its range, but it still requires a dedicated enthusiast to locate them and start a serious breeding programme.

TIBET

KONGBO DOG   TIBET

Also known as the Kong-Kyi, or Kongkyi, this little-known breed is most probably used as a general hunting dog, although hardly any information is available.

Kongbo is a region in south-eastern Tibet. When Mrs Eric Bailey was visiting the area in the 1930s she encountered a 'very distinctive breed' that she described in the following way: 'This dog is on the lines of a Schnauzer, with small, prick ears… reddish in colour. When in Tibet, I kept Finnish Spitz, and Tibetans, on seeing these, would always point with surprise and say "Kongkyi". The Kongkyis I have seen are much heavier in build than the Finnish Spitz, with coarse hair like a Schnauzer and the ears are shorter.' She adds that this breed has never been exported from Tibet.

That is the sum total of knowledge we have of this breed, which, despite the appalling slaughter of Tibetan dogs instituted by the Chinese Communists, may still exist in small numbers in the more remote regions.

CHINA

CHINESE HOUND   CHINA

An early hunting dog known by the Chinese name of Ma-Chu-Gou, this hound was used to pursue both wild boar and deer.

This little-known breed was said to be disappearing by the early part of the 20th century and may now be extinct. It was described as a heavily built version of a greyhound, with ears that were pricked or semi-pricked, and a dense, short coat that was a shaded, dark brown. There was said to be a suspicion of a ridge of hair along the back, reminiscent of that seen on the Rhodesian and Thai Ridgeback breeds.

An intelligent, powerful hunter, with a very good nose, it was said to be keen and persistent in the pursuit of boar and deer, which it hunted in packs. When the pack had cornered the game, the dogs did not attack it, but held it at bay until the hunters arrived to kill it.

JAPAN

AINU DOG   JAPAN

Also known as the Ainu, the Ainou, the Ainu-Ken, the Hokkaido-Ken, the Hokkaido Inu, the Hokkaido Dog or simply the Hokkaido, this breed was developed to hunt a wide variety of game, from bear downwards. It is named Ainu after the ancient Ainu people of Japan, and Hokkaido after the island where the dogs live. Other names attached to this breed are the Japanese Bear Hound and the Choken.

This is one of the medium-sized spitz-type dogs that are indigenous to Japan, others being the Kai, the Kishu and the Shikoku. It has smaller ears than the other breeds, a broader face and a fierce expression. In the field it is ferocious, brave and fearless, even when faced with a large bear, but in the home it is obedient and friendly. Apart from its main duty of hunting, it also has a secondary role as a village guardian.

Thousands of years ago, a strange, white, hairy-bodied race, the Ainu, arrived on the islands we now call Japan and settled there. They brought with them a northern type of dog and colonized all four of the main islands. Much later, the Yamato people arrived and, little by little, pushed the Ainu hunter-gatherers out. Their tribes survived only on the northern island of Hokkaido, where they managed to cling on, although their numbers grew ever smaller. (Today there are only a few hundred full-blooded Ainu left.) From the earliest times they had hunting dogs with them and, on Hokkaido, these animals adapted to the rugged, often freezing conditions and developed into the tough, thick-coated breed which today we call either the

Ainu or the Hokkaido. Ainu was its original name, but the Japanese government formally changed this to Hokkaido in 1937, when it declared the breed a Natural Monument and instituted a special protection programme for it. Most canine authorities, however, have ignored this official change of title and still insist on calling the dog by its earlier, better-known, traditional name.

One oddity of this breed is that a blue-black tongue sometimes occurs, suggesting an ancestral genetic link with the Chinese Chow Chow. This fact fits well with the theory that the Ainu people originally migrated south from Siberia.

KAI DOG   JAPAN

Also known as the Kai Shika Inu, the Kai Inu, the Tora Inu, the Kai Ken, the Kai Tora-Ken, the Kohshu-Tora, the Tora Dog or the Tiger Dog, this breed was developed in medieval times for hunting large game, such as wild boar and deer. The Japanese words 'shika inu' means 'medium-sized dog'.

Like several other native Japanese dogs, this one was overshadowed by exotic imported breeds in the period following World War I. Then, in the 1930s, an attempt was made to revive the ancient breeds and arrange them into some sort of ordered classification. This was done largely by canine expert Haruo Isogai, using size distinctions as his main criterion. The Kai Dog was one of the medium-sized breeds, and in 1934 it was declared a Natural Monument.

A general-purpose hunting dog, it was named after the mountainous Kai district of the Yamanashi Prefecture where it originated. Its alternative name of Tiger Dog is not meant to indicate that it once pursued tigers, but is probably derived from its typically dark, brindled coat that, with a little imagination, can be said to show a few striped markings.

There are three brindled coat colours – red, called Aka-Tora; red-black, called Chu-Tora; and black, called Kuro-Tora. The puppies are all born solid black, and do not develop their brindled colours for some months.

The Kai can be distinguished from other medium-sized Japanese breeds by its more tapered head and narrower skull. It is a stocky, spitz-type dog with a thick neck, pricked ears and a tightly curled tail. It is still little-known outside its native homeland, although a few examples have reached North America.

KISHU   JAPAN

Also known as the Kishi Shika Inu, the Kishu Ken or the Kyushu, this breed was developed as a general-purpose hunting dog. It was used mainly against deer and wild boar, assisting the Matagi, or local hunters.

This is one of the medium-sized dogs (Shika Inu) that were officially named and classified in the 1930s. As an indigenous Japanese breed, it was designated a Natural Monument in 1934.

Renowned for its bravery, the Kishu was known to rush to protect its master from the charge of an angry, wounded wild boar, giving the hunter sufficient time to reload and fire again.

It originated in the mountainous regions of Kishu in the Mie and Wakayama districts, south of Osaka. In its earlier days it had extremely varied colour-patterns, including red, sesame and brindle. Later, after its formal recognition in 1934, only solid colours could be accepted, and today Kishus with all-white coats seem to be the most popular.

With large-game hunting dramatically reduced in recent years, many Kishus are now kept as companion dogs. In the home they are clean, quiet, contented and docile. Their height is 17–22 in (43–56 cm), and their coat is short, straight and coarse. In the typical spitz tradition, the pointed ears are pricked, the neck is thick and muscular, the body well balanced and the tail twisted in a tight curl.

SHIBA INU   JAPAN

The name of this breed translates as 'small dog'. It is sometimes called the Japanese Shiba Inu, the Shiba Ken or simply the Shiba. It has also been given the English title of Brushwood Dog, Japanese Turf Dog or Little Turf Dog. The use of the word 'brushwood' is said to refer either to the kind of bushes in which it hunted, or to the similarity between the dog's coat colour and that of autumn brushwood leaves. This breed was originally developed to hunt small game.

Of Japan's indigenous breeds, this is the most popular as a companion animal. Looking like a small version of the Akita, with a height of only 14–16 in (35–41 cm), it has a permanently alert expression, as if anticipating some activity which it eagerly awaits.

This is believed to be one of Japan's most ancient breeds. Bones matching its modern skeleton have been found at an archaeological site from the Jomon period, dating from at least 500 BC. Later, in the 3rd century AD, those Jomon Dogs were refined by matings with new, immigrant dogs to create a typical spitz animal with pricked ears and a tightly curled tail. By the 7th century these dogs were already recognized as part of Japanese culture and a special 'dogkeeper's office' was established to foster them.

In three separate regions, local varieties of Shiba began to develop their own characteristics. In the Nagano district there was the Shinshu Shiba, in the Gifu district the Mino Shiba, and in the north-eastern part of the country the Sanin Shiba.

Although, in its hunting heyday, this

compact little dog's main quarry was small game such as ground-breeding birds, it was also capable of helping occasionally in the hunt for bigger game such as wild boar, deer and even bear. A sturdily built dog, with a muscular body, pricked ears and a typically curled, spitz tail, the Shiba Inu has the look of a tough survivor. Its thick coat is typically pale brown, but may also appear in darker shades. It rarely barks – instead, it utters a strange, shrieking call.

By the 1920s this breed had become extremely rare, thanks to the fashion for importing exotic foreign dogs. Hunters became so concerned that in 1928 they started a planned survival programme to preserve their ancient, native breed. By 1934 the breed standard had been fixed and in 1937 the Shiba Inu was declared a Natural Monument. After that, the breed grew steadily in numbers until the outbreak of World War II. It suffered heavily during that period and, even after the war was over, its problems continued when there was a massive outbreak of distemper which killed most of the surviving Shibas. The Mino Shiba and the Sanin Shiba varieties were nearly extinct. Only the Shinshu Shibas remained in sufficient numbers to rebuild the breed. These were combined with the last remnants of the other two varieties – those that had managed to survive in remote rural districts – to create the modern breed. Careful breeding plans were undertaken and soon the little dog was well on the road to recovery. In the second half of the 20th century it went from strength to strength, until it became the most numerous of all the native Japanese breeds. Today it is also becoming increasingly popular outside Japan, in Australia, North America and Europe.

References

1990. Lane. *Shiba Inu*. Australia.
1992. Tomita. *Shiba Inu*. TFH, New Jersey.
1993. Hoflin. *Shiba Inu Annual*.
1997. Haskett, Gretchen and Houser, Susan. *The Total Shiba*. Alpine Publications.
1998. Atkinson, Maureen. *The Complete Shiba Inu*. IDG Books Worldwide.

SHIKOKU   JAPAN

Also referred to as the Shikoku Shika Inu, meaning 'the medium-sized dog from Shikoku', this breed has been used for centuries to hunt game. Shikoku is a large island off the coast of mainland Japan, south-west of Osaka. In ancient times, in the more remote rural areas of the island, the local people used this dog to help them in the hunt for game. The breed was centred in the Kochi region, and is sometimes called the Kochi-ken, or Kochi Dog.

In appearance, this is a typical Japanese breed, with a dense, harsh coat in various shades of brown. It has a muscular neck and body, pricked ears and a typical, tightly curled spitz tail. In size, it is intermediate between the large Akita and the small Shiba Inu, with a height of 18–22 in (46–55 cm). In personality, this is one of those breeds that stubbornly attempts to dominate other dogs, but is pleasant enough with its owners. It is a tough and agile dog, well adapted to hunting in difficult mountain terrain.

Three kinds of Shikoku have been identified in the past – the Awa, the Hongawa and the Hata. Each of these was named after a particular locality within the general breed range. The Hongawa was considered to be the best variety, with the greatest level of breed purity, thanks to its isolation.

This is an extremely rare breed and there have been fears for its future survival. Fortunately there is now a Society for the preservation of Japanese Breeds, which is doing its best to protect this breed and prevent it from disappearing altogether. It was declared a Natural Monument in 1937.

KOREA

JINDO   SOUTH KOREA

This breed is sometimes called the Jindo Gae or the Jindo Dog. Alternative spellings are Chindogae, Chindo Dog or Chin-Do Dog. It is named after the island on which it has managed to survive. It was originally developed as a general hunting dog, with secondary duties as a ratter, a watchdog and a property guardian.

In a country that is still beating millions of dogs to death each year, supposedly to improve the taste of their flesh when they are served as favourite dishes in restaurants, it is a miracle that any pure breed can have survived at all. The Jindo Dog is such an animal. On the island of Jindo, to the south-west of the mainland, it was isolated enough to survive in a pure form.

It is not clear how a northern spitz dog first appeared in Korea, but there is a legend concerning its arrival on a Mongolian 'turtle' ship. Another legend describes how a scholar took his red Korean bitch into the mountains of Jindo Island, where it mated with a Korean wolf and produced three puppies, one white, one red and one black. These were the foundation dogs for the Jindo breed.

This is a typical spitz breed, with a strong, compact body, prick ears and a tail that is either tightly curled or long and bushy. Its height is 18–22 in (45–55 cm). The colour of its dense coat was originally red, white, black or grey, but today only red or white is permitted.

The Jindo is amazingly agile, almost catlike in its ability to climb walls or jump over fences 6 ft (1.8 m) high. On flat ground it has been timed doing a steady 35 mph

(56 kph). It is intelligent, proud and independent, with a remarkable homing ability. If it sets off on its own, it is capable of finding its way home again over distances of many miles. Unlike most other hunting dogs, this one prefers to go into action on its own. It is a hunting dog, but it is not a gun dog. With a Jindo, no guns are necessary. It will take off and return later carrying the game it has killed and present it to its master. The quarry may be a pheasant, a hare or some other small animal. If the Jindo has managed to kill something that is too big to carry, such as a deer, it will return home and then lead its master to the place of the kill. If several Jindos make such a kill together, only one of them goes to fetch its master, while the others stand guard over their prize.

Nobody is indifferent to this breed – you either love it or hate it. It is courageous and highly protective of its human family, but does not tolerate strangers. In fact, it is not an easy dog to deal with. Even its most ardent defenders describe it as 'naturally beautiful, ridiculously loyal, but stubborn as an ox'. They admit that Jindos are never to be trusted 'near an open door'.

At some stage in their past, these dogs have been employed in the debased sport of pit-contests, and some of their fighting spirit remains lodged deep inside them to this day. They will think nothing of subduing a Mastiff, but their goal is to dominate, not to kill. Once other dogs have submitted to the Jindo, it will leave them alone.

In 1938, at the insistence of a visiting Japanese professor, the government of South Korea declared this dog to be a National Treasure. It was designated the 53rd Natural Monument of Korea. When Japanese troops slaughtered all the dogs of Korea during World War II, to use their pelts to make fur coats for their soldiers fighting in Manchuria, only the Jindo dogs were spared.

Recently there has been another threat to these dogs. In 1984 a new bridge joining Jindo Island to the mainland was opened. A pair of Jindo dog statues stand guard at each end of this bridge, but they are incapable of stopping the much freer movement of mainland dogs to the island and vice versa. After thousands of years of isolation, this threatens the purity of the Jindo in a serious way.

Despite the fact that exporting Jindos from Korea is prohibited, from the 1980s onwards a number have found their way to the United States with many of the Korean immigrants who have moved there. In America, the breed has developed a new lease of life as a pedigree dog and is being treated with care and respect by a small band of devoted enthusiasts who are now trying to obtain official recognition for it.

POONGSAN   NORTH KOREA

Also known as the Poongsan Dog, the Poongsan-Gae or the Poong-San, this breed takes its name from the region where it originated. It was developed as a general hunting dog, but also has a secondary role as a property guard.

This is a little-known North Korean breed from the Poongsan district of South Hamkyong Province, where it is found working in the mountainous landscape. It is a large, agile dog capable of running fast even up mountain slopes. It has a reputation as a fierce hunter and is the largest and toughest of all the indigenous Korean breeds.

The Poongsan is a spitz-type dog, with prick ears and a thick, dense coat. It is 22–26 in (55-65 cm) in height and weighs 55–77 lb (25–35 kg). Its coat colour varies, being white, red-brown, grey, black or brindled.

On the hunt it is used to pursue tiger, deer and wild boar. It has amazing stamina and can withstand severe cold, working enthusiastically even in deep snow. Some Russian hunters are reputed to have employed small packs of no more than three Poongsans to hunt Siberian Tigers.

Apart from those Russian-owned dogs, the breed was apparently not seen outside North Korea until 1994. Then, in March of that year, 18 of these rare dogs were imported into South Korea, via China, by a South Korean farm manager called Lee Hee-hoon from Koyang in Kyonggi Province. He was quoted as saying that he was motivated by 'the hope that the traditional Korean dog will not be exterminated but preserved long into the future'. The fact that he was charging one million won (about $1,290) for each puppy may also have been a consideration, especially as the Poongsan has been declared the 35th Precious Natural Resource of North Korea.

According to the latest reports from Korea, there is now a Poongsan Dog Research Centre, established to foster the breed.

UNITED STATES

AMERICAN BRITTANY SPANIEL   UNITED STATES

Sometimes called simply the Brittany, this breed is an all-purpose gun dog, similar in its working details to the Brittany Spaniel from France.

This dog is basically the same as its French counterpart, except for its colour-patterns and certain minor differences in the breed standards. French Brittany Spaniels were first imported into the United States in 1931 and soon became extremely popular, both as working gun dogs and as show dogs. In 1934 the breed was recognized by the AKC and in 1942 the American Brittany Club was formed.

This club immediately set about clarifying and improving the dog's breed standard, and restricting its colour forms. As a result, unlike its French counterpart, the American breed is only permitted in brown and white. Technically, the permitted coat colours are orange-and-white or liver-and-white, in clear or roan patterns.

In recent times, some American devotees of this breed have objected to the use of the word 'spaniel' in its name, and certain organizations have dropped it from the title. The

AKC, for example, introduced this change in 1982. The owners of these dogs have pointed out that it is much more than a flushing spaniel. It could, with equal justification, be called a setter, a pointer or a retriever, but since it is any of these, its supporters have given up all specialization qualifiers and reduced its name to the simple, non-specific 'Brittany'.

HAITI/DOMINICAN REPUBLIC

GOSCHI   HAITI/DOMINICAN REPUBLIC

This breed has also been called the Gasque and both names are thought to be contractions of Guarachay. Little is known about its function except that it was used for general hunting purposes.

This small breed, now almost certainly extinct, was used as a hunting dog by the native population of the Caribbean island they called Hayti (meaning 'the mountainous country'), before the arrival of the Spanish explorers in 1492. The island is now split up into two modern states: Haiti and the Dominican Republic.

According to Charles Hamilton Smith, writing in 1840, these small dogs were 'absolutely mute, with downy, or silky hair of different, and often bright colours'. He believes that they 'must have been imported from the Southern continent; most likely by the conquering Caribs'. Little more is known about them.

BRAZIL

FILA BRASILIERO   BRAZIL

Also known as the Brazilian Guard Dog, the Brazilian Fila, the Brazilian Mastiff, the Brazilian Molosser, the Dogue Brasiliero or the Cão de Fila, this breed was originally developed to hunt big game such as wild boar and jaguar.

The original ancestors of this powerful dog were the mastiffs brought to the new World by the Conquistadors. Later these were crossed with bulldogs and Bloodhounds, to create a fearless, all-round hunting dog of enormous strength and stamina. The mastiff element gave it size and power, the bulldog element gave it a fearless tenacity, and the Bloodhound element gave it a great scenting ability. This awesome combination made it into a formidable hunter's aid. It was employed to track, attack, grasp its prey and hold it firm until the hunter arrived to make the kill. The word 'fila' in its title is derived from a Portuguese word meaning 'to hold' or 'to secure'.

Because of its success at this type of hunting, it was at one time employed to track down and capture runaway slaves, but without hurting them. It was also used on ranches to capture runaway cattle, pursuing them and then leaping up to grab them by the ear.

Later it became a popular guard dog for both livestock and property. Formal breeding to a fixed standard did not begin until the 1950s.

These dogs were bred to be deeply suspicious of strangers, and this quality has never left them, making them something of a liability in a modern setting. When they are entered in dog shows, for example, the judges are instructed never to touch them. If they forget this warning, they are liable to lose some of their fingers. With its own human family, however, it is calm and faithful, and gentle with the children. It has been described by one enthusiast as 'the security system that loves you'. It is certainly true that, with one of these huge, fearless, stranger-hating dogs in your house, you would have no need of any sophisticated electronic device to protect you from intruders.

Visually, this dog is exactly as one would expect a cross between a mastiff, a bulldog and a Bloodhound to look. One strange feature of its body-shape is that its hind legs are longer than its front legs, giving it a 'going downhill' appearance, and a strange rock-and-roll, camel-gait. Its short coat is either brindle or a solid colour, but never white or grey.

In the 1970s this breed developed a following in the United States and in 1984 the Fila Brasiliero Club of America was formed. This was followed in 1992 by the Fila Brasiliero Association, based in Texas. The breed is now recognized by the FCI.

TARUMA HUNTING DOG   BRAZIL

Also known as the Woyawai Dog, this native South American breed is used to hunt all forms of indigenous game.

These highly valued Indian dogs, belonging to the Taruma and Woyawai tribes on the borders of Brazil and Guiana, are such expert hunting companions that they have proved useful for bartering (through Indian agents) for such commodities as guns and canoes. The dogs are so prized that the women of the tribe take extra care of them, providing them with sleeping quarters and a special diet.

Their bodies are described as being of the 'greyhound type', with short, black-and-white coats.

CHILE/ARGENTINA

PATAGONIAN DOG   CHILE/ARGENTINA

This dog was used by Patagonian Indians to hunt and kill large prey.

At the southern end of South America, in a savagely hostile environment, the Tehuelche Indians barely managed to scrape a living. To obtain sufficient protein they needed to

kill the wild Guanaco and the ostrich-like Rheas that inhabited the region, but these animals were too swift for human capture. They were not, however, able to outrun the packs of Indian dogs, which were trained to chase them, pull them down and kill them. So, from the Indians' point of view, the assistance of their dogs was a matter of tribal survival.

The Patagonian Dog was about the size of a Foxhound, but with a tapering muzzle, prick ears, a wiry, dark coat, a slender body, a bushy tail and long legs. It was an alert, energetic animal, looking rather like a small wolf. Only one sketch of it exists. This was made by Philip King, a member of Charles Darwin's party when HMS *Beagle* stopped in Patagonia for repairs in 1834. Before the end of that century, both the Patagonian Dog and the Tehuelche Indians had vanished for ever, defeated by the harsh land in which they lived, and we have no more information concerning this hard-working hunting dog.

ARGENTINA

DOGO ARGENTINO   ARGENTINA

Also known as the Argentine Dogo or the Argentinean Mastiff, this breed was developed as the ideal big-game hunter, to pursue wild boar, puma and jaguar. It was expected to track in silence, corner, attack and hold the quarry for the arrival of the hunter, who would himself make the kill.

Described as the dog with 'Coat of White Satin, Body of Steel, Heart of Gold', this imposing breed has an unusual origin. It was planned by two schoolboy brothers called Antonio and Augustin Nores Martinez. In 1925, when Antonio was 18 and Augustin was 17, they started a breeding programme that would preoccupy them for the rest of their lives. Beginning with ten bitches of a fearsome fighting breed, now extinct, called the Cordoba Dog, they set about creating the ideal animal for hunting wild boar across the great expanses of the Argentinean pampas.

In order to reduce the aggression of the Cordoba Dog and improve its hunting qualities, they arranged a series of crosses involving no fewer than nine other breeds. They added: (1) Pointer, to improve the sense of smell, for tracking the game; (2) Boxer, to add vivacity and gentleness; (3) Great Dane, for increased size; (4) Bull Terrier, for fearlessness and insensitivity to pain; (5) Bulldog, for its broad chest and its courage; (6) Irish Wolfhound, for hunting ability; (7) Dogue de Bordeaux, for its powerful jaws;

(8) Pyrenean Mountain Dog, for its pure white coat; and (9) Spanish Mastiff, for power.

There can hardly be another breed in the world that can boast such a complex origin. After 20 years of careful selective breeding, the brothers were ready to present their perfected dog to the world and, in 1947, Antonio, now a successful surgeon, published the first breed standard.

Nine years later Antonio was murdered while on a wild-boar hunt, and it was left to his brother Augustin to continue to promote and support the breed. Augustin had risen to become an Argentinean ambassador, and his travels to distant embassies helped to spread the word about their impressive dog.

This pure white dog, looking remarkably like a white Pit Bull Terrier, was more than just a hunting dog. It was also employed in a wide variety of subsidiary roles, including property guarding, drug detection, guide-dog work for the blind, bomb detection, police work, therapy-dog work with retarded children, and search-and-rescue.

In personality it has been described as intelligent, loyal, docile, faithful, patient, tolerant, obedient and willing to please. When in action as a hunter, however, it is brave, determined and tireless. As a guardian, it is prepared to fight any intruder to the death, regardless of injury to itself. Its one weakness is that ten per cent of its puppies are born deaf.

This breed was first recognized by the Federación Cynologique Argentina in 1964 and by the Argentina Kennel Club in 1973. It has also been accepted by the FCI. In 1985, the Dogo Argentino Club of America was formed. Despite this wide acceptance, it remains a banned breed in Britain, where, like the Pit Bull Terrier, government authorities consider it to be a 'dangerous dog'.

References

1974. Nores Martinez, Augustin. *El Dogo Argentino.* Albatros, Buenos Aires.

FIGHTING DOGS

In earlier centuries powerful dogs have often been employed as combatants in staged fighting matches, sometimes to satisfy the curiosity and blood-lust of onlookers, but more usually to provide an outlet for serious gambling. This has been a savage spectacle for several thousand years. Huge dogs were pitted against one another, against larger animals and even against captive humans on many occasions in the Roman arena. In medieval Europe special kinds of dogs were widely employed to bait bears and bulls, and this was a spectacle enjoyed, not only by the peasantry, but also on festive occasions by royalty. Elizabeth I staged many such events for her court.

To provide the most violent forms of encounter, special breeds of dog were developed, with massive jaws and a fearless temperament. When public baiting displays were outlawed early in the 19th century, these dogs then had to be modified to adapt them to the clandestine alternative of pit-fighting, dog against dog. New breeds arose to satisfy this demand, and organized dog-fighting flourished for many years until that, too, was banned. At this point, some fighting breeds inevitably became extinct, but others managed to survive as pets or show dogs. It is a surprising fact that even the most aggressive dog-fighting dog can remain gentle and friendly with the members of its human family, and it was found that a number of these ex-fighters made excellent companions.

In some parts of the world staged dog fights still occur, usually as undercover events, but without a great deal of interference from the local authorities. Inevitably, the breeds that are specialized for this brutal work are still surviving in those regions. Some of these breeds have now been completely banned from being imported into certain other countries. The importers' defence – that the dogs are required as pets – is not believed by the police, and the animals are confiscated.

Dog-fighting is a dark chapter in the history of man's long relationship with the canine world, and there may be some who feel that those breeds that were exclusively developed for fighting should not be included in a modern reference work such as this one. But the fact is that they were part of dog history and cannot be ignored.

There are 27 breeds in this category.

ENGLAND

ENGLISH BULLDOG

This breed was developed exclusively for the sport of bull-baiting. When this activity became illegal in Britain in 1835, the Bulldog found a new role as a companion animal and later as a show dog. Earlier names included the Bull-baiting Dog, the Old English Bulldog and the British Bulldog.

The public entertainment called bull-baiting was introduced into England by the Normans in the 12th century. When they conquered the country, their street entertainers accompanied them. The Norman jugglers brought with them their bulls and bears and a primitive kind of mastiff. The dogs were allowed to torment the tethered bulls and bears as a crude sideshow. These pastimes became more and more popular, and by the time of Henry II's accession, in 1154, they were widespread.

These early travelling entertainments were not as brutal as later displays. The bears and bulls were too valuable to be killed and had to perform time and again. As the years passed, however, the baiting of bulls grew more savage, and torturing them to death became routine. It was discovered that the flesh of tortured bulls tasted better than that of swiftly killed ones, and butchers were sometimes castigated for not improving their meat in this way.

By the 16th century, bull-baiting had risen from a peasant pastime to a royal entertainment, and Elizabeth I frequently offered it as a spectacle for visiting ambassadors. It was at this point that serious attempts were made to improve the quality of the dogs that were used. Their mode of attack was to leap at the bull's head and cling on to its nose, ears or tongue with their powerful jaws. Once they were clamped on tightly, they had to keep hold firmly as the enraged bull tried to shake them loose. To achieve this feat, the dogs had to have massive jaws and had to be able to continue breathing freely. This required a change in the anatomy of the dog's skull. A broader, heavier head was needed. Also, the mastiff's body had to be reduced in size to enable the dogs to approach the bull without falling easy prey to its horns. So the development of the specialized bull-baiting dog, which was eventually to become the pure-bred English Bulldog, involved the primeval mastiff becoming smaller, wider-mouthed, heavier-jawed and with its nose pulled back from its jawline.

This refined Bulldog (if one can use such a term in this brutal context) was perfected by the 1600s and continued its bloody sport for the next two centuries until, in 1835, all cruel animal sports were banned in England. At this point the Bulldog was out of work and looked set to vanish. However, enough were kept on as companion dogs to prevent its extinction. As the 19th century wore on, competitive dog shows began in earnest, providing a major new role for this highly distinctive breed. The Kennel Club officially recognized the Bulldog in 1873.

Over the next hundred years, the pet Bulldog changed its shape dramatically, with its specially exaggerated features becoming more and more extreme, its short legs growing shorter, and its broad, flattened face becoming wider and even flatter. Those who enjoy the dramatic appearance of this modern Bulldog, and continue to support the breed, insist that, as a companion dog, it has a most delightful personality, being gentle, loyal and good-natured. It also retains its tenacity and its courage, even though its physical shape means that it would now stand little chance against a lively bull. The veterinary world, however, is highly critical of it, claiming that the breed now suffers from 'distressing eye problems, incapacitating respiratory conditions, congenital heart conditions, dental and skin problems and vertebrae deformities.' Inevitably, Bulldog enthusiasts insist that these criticisms are unjustified and that they are doing their utmost to improve the breed and eliminate any weaknesses that may have developed. The proof of this will lie in the future success of the breed.

References

1892–8. Jackson and Bowers. *Bulldog Pedigrees.*

1899. Farman, Edgar. *The Bulldog A Monograph.* The Stock Keeper Co., London.

1905. Cooper, Henry St John. *Bulldogs and Bulldog Breeding.* Jarrolds, London.

1908. Cooper, Henry St John. *Bulldogs and Bulldog Men.* Jarrolds, London.

1908. Hutchison, J. Hay. *The Perfect Bull Dog.* Kennel News, London.

1910. Thomas, Mary E. *British Bull Dogs.* Our Dogs, Manchester.

1925. Cooper, Henry St John and Fowler, F. Barrett. *Bulldogs and All About Them.* Jarrolds, London.

1926. Deacon, Sidney H. *Show Bulldogs.* Our Dogs, Manchester.

1926. Simmonds, Walter E. *The Complete Bulldog.* Judy Publishing, Chicago.

1926. Sturgeon, A. G. *Bulldogdom.* Heywood, Manchester.

1932. Berger-Wheeler. *The International Bulldog Yearbook.*

1934. Johns, Rowland. *Our Friend the Bulldog.* Methuen, London.

1934. Nugent, J. Ross. *The Gorgeous Sourmug: A Treatise on Bulldogs.* Orange Judd, New York.

1948. Meyer, Enno. *The Bulldog: an Illustrated Standard of the Breed. A Picture Study of Good Points and Faults.* Orange Judd, New York.

1954. Forbush, A. R. and Forbush, G. E. *Pet English Bulldog.* All-Pets, Fond du Lac, Wisconsin.

1956. Hanes, Bailey C. *The Complete Bulldog.* Denlinger's, USA.

1957. Gordon, John. *The Bull-Dog Handbook; Giving the Origin and History of the Breed, its Show Career, its Points and Breeding.* Nicholson & Watson, London.

1959. Miller, Evelyn. *Bulldogs as Pets.* TFH, New Jersey.

1960. Miller, Evelyn. *How to Raise and Train a Bulldog.* TFH, New Jersey.

1966. Hanes, Bailey C. *The New Complete Bulldog.* Howell, New York.

1976. Berndt. *Your Bulldog.* Denlinger's, USA.

1985. Brearly, Joan McDonald. *The Book of the Bulldog.* TFH, New Jersey.

1987. Fulton. *The Bulldog.*

1988. Barnard, M. *The 20th Century Bulldog.*

1988. Forbush, Gabrielle E. *Bulldogs.* TFH, New Jersey.

1995. Thomas, Chris. *Bulldogs Today.* Ringpress Books, Lydney, Gloucestershire.

1997. Andree, Marie. *The Bulldog: An Owner's Guide to a Happy Healthy Pet.*

1997. Grebe and Eltinge. *The Flat Faced Encyclopedia.*

1997. Maggitti, Phil, et al. *Bulldogs: Everything About Purchase, Care, Nutrition, Breeding, Behavior, and Training.*

1996. McGibbon. *Bulldogs – Yesterday, Today and Tomorrow.* Howell, New York.

1998. Bruton, Christian. *Bulldogs.* Crowood Press, Wiltshire.

1998. Williams, Hank and Williams, Carol. *A New Owner's Guide to Bulldogs.*

1999. Wilcox, Charlotte. *The Bulldog.*

Schneider, Earl (Editor). *Know Your Bulldog.* The Pet Library, New York.

BULL TERRIER   ENGLAND

The first recorded name for this dog was the Bull-and-terrier. It was also referred to as the Bull-dog Terrier or the White Cavalier. It was created specifically as a fighting dog to be set against others in pit contests, for purposes of 'sport'.

The ancestor of the modern Bull Terrier was a deliberate cross between a Bulldog and a large, smooth Black and Tan Terrier. It came into being following the ban on cruel sports that was imposed in England in 1835. The men who enjoyed such spectacles were forced to go undercover. Their most popular sport had been bull-baiting with Bulldogs, but this was too public a spectacle to be concealed, so they turned their attention to less conspicuous events – to fights between one Bulldog and another, staged in special pits. However, set against one another, the Bulldogs proved to be too slow and cumbersome, and it was argued that, by crossing them with terriers, a better fighting breed might be created. And indeed it was. The early Bulldog-terrier cross, although an ugly-looking animal, proved to be 'the most determined and savage race known'. It was the ultimate fighting dog, and the popularity of these contests grew rapidly, especially in the cities of London and Birmingham. The Bull Terrier possessed the stamina, power and solidity of the Bulldog and the intelligence, tenacity and speed of the Terrier. In the 1850s James Hinks of Birmingham improved the breed by crossing it with White English Terriers. He also added a dash of Dalmatian, and the result was a much more handsome dog with a white coat, sometimes showing a few black patches.

By 1880 the Bull Terrier had become a breed 'noted for its beautiful form'. An early depiction of this improved version shows a handsome, well-balanced dog, but one that still differs from the modern type. Further selective breeding gave it a longer muzzle, its now famous egg-shaped head with its 'Roman nose', and slightly shorter legs. Although, like bull-baiting, dog fights were eventually also banned, the Bull Terrier managed to survive as a successful pedigree show dog and, with further breeding to calm its temperament, as a much loved family dog. Today, coloured examples are much more common, because of medical problems – especially deafness – associated with the white dogs.

Despite its ferocious origins, this breed has many ardent supporters in its role as a companion dog. They sing its praises as a devoted, faithful and intelligent friend. Sir Walter Scott described it as 'the wisest dog I ever had', and President Teddy Roosevelt even shared the White House with one.

References

1912. Haynes, William. *The Bull Terrier*. Macmillan, New York.

1915. Glass, Eugene. *The Sporting Bull Terrier*. The Dog Fancier, Michigan.

1916. Mendel, Rosalie G. *Spark, The Story of a Bull Terrier & His Dog Friends*.

1920. Dighton, Adair. *The Bull Terrier and All About It*. Our Dogs, Manchester.

1926. Robbs, Mrs D. H. *The Bull Terrier Handbook*. Perivale Press.

1930. Hogarth, T. W. *The Bull Terrier*. Our Dogs, Manchester.

1934. Hollender, V. C. *The Bull Terrier and All About It*. Dog World, Bradford, Yorkshire.

1934. Johns, Rowland (Editor). *Our Friend the Bull Terrier*. Methuen, London.

1936. Barker, K. F. *Champion: The Story of a Bull Terrier*. Country Life, London.

1936. Glyn, Richard H. *Bull Terriers and How to Breed Them*. Hall, Oxford.

1939. Meader, Stephen W. *Bat, The Story of a Bull Terrier*. Grosset & Dunlap, New York.

1940. Briggs, L. Cabot. *Bull Terriers, the Biography of the Breed*. Derrydale, New York.

1946. Montgomery, E. S. *The Bull Terrier*. Orange Judd, New York.

1951. Hollender, V. C. (Editor). *Bull Terriers*. Williams & Norgate, London.

1952. Adlam, Gladys M. *Forty Years of Bull Terriers*. Dog World, Bradford, Yorkshire.

1957. Gordon, John F. *The Bull Terrier Handbook*. Nicholson & Watson, London.

1959. Eberhart, Ernest. *The Complete Bull Terrier*. Howell, New York.

1961. Sweeten, Margaret O. *The Bull Terrier Book*.

1964. Oppenheim, Raymond H. *A Bull Terrier History*. Dog World, Bradford, Yorkshire.

1965. Rosenblum, Edwin E. *How to Raise and Train a Bull Terrier*. TFH, New Jersey.

1967. Sweeten, Margaret O. *The Second Bull Terrier Book*.

1968. Oppenheimer, R. H. *McGuffin & Co. A Bull Terrier History*. Dog World, Ashford, Kent.

1970. Sweeten, Margaret O. (Editor). *The Third Bull Terrier Book*. Bull Terrier Club.

1971. Drewes, M. *The Bull Terrier*. Denlinger's, Middleburg, Virginia.

1971. Eberhard, Ernest. *The New Complete Bull Terrier*. Howell, New York.

1973. Horner, Tom. *All About the Bull Terrier*. Pelham, London.

1975. Horner, Tom. *The Standard of the Bull Terrier*.

1975. Sweeten, Margaret O. (Editor). *The Fourth Bull Terrier Book*. Bull Terrier Club.

1983. Morse, Cynthia and Vargo, Allan. *Buying and Rearing a Bull Terrier*.

1983. Weil, Martin. *Bull Terriers*. TFH, New Jersey.

1989. Remer, John H., Jnr. *The New Bull Terrier*. Howell, New York.

1989. Salyn, Robin. *Bull Terriers: An Owner's Companion*. Crowood Press, Wiltshire.

1993. Anon. *The Second Australian Bull Terrier Book*. National Bull Terrier Council (Australia).

1998. Desmond, Betty. *A New Owner's Guide to Bull Terriers*.

1998. Harris, David. *Bull Terriers Today*. Ringpress Books, Lydney, Gloucestershire.

Gordon, John Frazer. *The Bull Terrier: Giving the Origin and History of the Breed, its Show Career, its Points and Breeding*.

Hogarth, T. W. *The Bull-Terrier*. Our Dogs, Manchester.

Horner, Tom. *All About the Bull Terrier*.

Lee, Muriel P. *Guide to Owning a Bull Terrier*.

Oppenheimer, Raymond Harry. *McGuffin & Co: a Bull Terrier History*.

STAFFORDSHIRE BULL TERRIER

ENGLAND

The first recorded name of this dog was the Bull-and-terrier. It has also been referred to as the Bull-dog Terrier, the Pit-dog, the Brindle Bull, the Patched Fighting Terrier, the Staffordshire Terrier and the Staffordshire Pit-Dog. Its modern name replaced all these in the 1930s. Today it is best known by its nickname of Staffie. It was originally created specifically as a fighting dog to be set against others in pit contests, for purposes of 'sport'.

The early history of this breed is the same as that of the Bull Terrier. Both were created by crossing Bulldogs with Black and Tan Terriers. The result was a dog with the muscle power of the Bulldog and the intelligence and agility of the Terrier. This made it the perfect combatant for the staged dog fights that were so popular following the 1835 ban that had wiped out bull-baiting.

In the middle of the 19th century, James Hinks of Birmingham began a breeding programme to create a modified form of this early Bull Terrier. He crossed it with the English White Terrier and produced a more streamlined animal with a pointed head, prick ears and a predominantly white coat. This, he said, was *the* Bull Terrier and began entering it at dog shows under that name as early as 1862. Those who supported the unmodified form of the original Bull Terrier and who, as one of them put it, preferred a dog with a head like a mastiff rather than one with a head like a polar bear, were upset that the name Bull Terrier had been officially registered for this new, fancy breed, rather than kept for the old established one. Unfortunately there was nothing they could do about it because the 'new' Bull Terrier was becoming firmly established at dog shows, and their own, much loved dog was still carrying the taint of being linked to the illegal dog-fighting that had managed to survive in several regions, even late into the 19th century.

This situation delayed the Kennel Club acceptance of the old-style Bull Terrier for many years. Eventually, in the 1930s it was agreed to admit it, providing that another name could be found. It was decided to add the location which had long been a stronghold of the breed, and call it the Staffordshire Bull Terrier. The other Bull Terrier faction objected and wanted it to be called simply the Staffordshire Terrier, to avoid confusion, but they were overruled because the Staffie was, after all, the *real* Bull Terrier of olden times.

And so it came about that the Staffordshire Bull Terrier Club was established in 1935 and that in the same year the breed was officially recognized by the Kennel Club in London. (The breed standard was revised in 1949, to keep the dog nearer to its original form and prevent it from becoming 'softened' for the show-ring.) It says a great deal for the Staffie that, despite its dubious beginnings, by the end of the 20th century it was consistently among the Kennel Club's 'top ten' most popular breeds. Across the Atlantic, it was recognized by the Canadian Kennel Club in 1952 and the American Kennel Club in 1974.

As a modern show dog, the Staffie has a split personality. Without proper control, it may still display its ancient tendency to be aggressive to other dogs ('getting its retaliation in first', as the Kennel Club puts it), but with people, especially children, it has proved itself to be a delightfully trustworthy, intelligent and friendly companion.

References

1935. Barnard, Jack W. *The Staffordshire Bull Terrier*. Privately published.

1943. Beilby, H. N. *The Staffordshire Bull Terrier*. Blackie, Glasgow.

1950. Dunn, Joseph. *The Staffordshire Bull Terrier*. Privately published.

1951. Gordon, John F. *The Staffordshire Bull Terrier Handbook*. Nicholson & Watson, London.

1951. Ivester-Lloyd, Ginger. *The Staffordshire Bull Terrier*.

1952. Hollender, V. C. (Editor). *Staffordshire Bull Terriers*. Williams & Norgate, London.

1956. Ormsby, Clifford A. (Editor). *The Staffordshire Terrier*. Owen, New York.

1960. Gordon, John F. *Feeding, Training, Welfare and Maintenance of the Staffordshire Bull*.

1964. Gordon, John F. *Staffordshire Bull Terriers*. Foyles, London.

1964. Rosenblum, Edwin E. *How to Raise and Train a Staffordshire Terrier*. TFH, New Jersey.

1972. Gordon, John F. *The Staffordshire Bull Terrier*. Popular Dogs, London.

1977. Gordon, John F. *The Staffordshire Bull Terrier Owner's Encyclopedia*. Pelham Books, London.

1982. Morley, W. N. *This is the Staffordshire Bull Terrier*. TFH, New Jersey.

1984. Gordon, John F. *All about the Staffordshire Bull Terrier*. Pelham Books, London.

1986. Eltinge, Steve. *The Staffordshire Bull Terrier in America*. Santa Barbara, California.

1988. Camino. *Staffordshire Bull Terrier Champions 1975–1986*. Camino Books.

1988. Homan. *Staffordshire Bull Terrier in History and Sport*. Nimrod Press, Hampshire.

1989. Nicholas, Anna Katherine. *Staffordshire Bull Terrier*. TFH, New Jersey.

1990. Barnard, Jack. *Staffordshire Bull Terrier*. Nimrod Press, Hampshire.

1990. Fleig, Dieter. *Staffordshire Bull Terrier*. Denlinger's, USA.

1991. Nicholas, Anna Katherine. *Staffordshire Terriers: American Staffordshire Bull Terrier and Staffordshire Bull Terrier*. TFH, New Jersey.

1993. Pounds, V. H. and Rant, Lilian V. *Staffordshire Bull Terriers: An Owner's Companion*. Crowood Press, Wiltshire.

1994. Gilmour, Danny. *The Complete Staffordshire Bull Terrier*. Ringpress Books, Lydney, Gloucestershire.

1996. Camino. *Staffordshire Bull Terrier Champions 1988–1994*. Camino Books.

1998. Lane, Marion and Tomback, Jeffrey. *Guide to Owning a Staffordshire Bull Terrier*. TFH, New Jersey.

1999. Lee, Clare. *Pet Owner's Guide to the Staffordshire Bull Terrier*. Welsh Academic Press.

VICTORIAN BULLDOG

This breed is a recent attempt to recreate the form of the original working Bulldog, before it was modified for the show-ring. The breeding programme was undertaken by Ken Mollett who, over a period of two decades, has bred back to the longer-leg version that was popular in the days before bull-baiting was banned.

The height of the Victorian Bulldog is 20 in (51 cm), compared with only 12–14 in (31–36 cm) for the modern English Bulldog. Its weight is 80–90 lb (36–41 kg), compared with 50–55 lb (23–25 kg).

An owner of one of these dogs comments: 'My Victorian Bulldog can run miles, lay in the sun and suffer no wrinkle sores or breathing problems. He looks identical to the Bulldog of the 19th century.' Mollett himself describes it as 'the Real Bulldog… athletic, healthy and sweet-natured'… doesn't snort and snore… can run a country mile… doesn't sleep and slobber away a perfectly fine day… the bulldog has come home'.

It is no surprise that breeders of the modern English Bulldog refer to the Victorian Bulldog dismissively as 'a mixed breed dog'.

SCOTLAND

BLUE PAUL

Also known as the Blue Poll, the Blue-and-Tan Terrier, or the Blue Paul Bull-terrier, this was a Scottish version of the English Bull Terrier. It is supposed to have acquired its name from the pirate Paul Jones, who is said to have first brought the breed to Scotland in 1770. This is a dog that was created specifically for staged dog-fighting.

According to the most popular theory of its origin, Scottish gypsies acquired English Bull Terriers (possibly from pirates, as some claim) and then increased their size by selective breeding, to improve their fighting power in the pit. There are, however, two rival theories. One view sees it as the result of a cross between the Bulldog and a blue greyhound. Another opinion regards it, rather mysteriously, as a descendant of the powerful Poligar Hound of India, with the name Paul or Poll being taken from its first syllable.

This impressively large fighting dog was described as 'leggy and all muscle and bone'. It was said that no other breed of dog would stand a chance if pitted against it. The bluish colour of the coat gave it the first part of its local name.

This fearsome dog was popular, especially in the Glasgow region, around the middle of the 19th century, but towards the end of that century, when dog-fighting was finally suppressed, it became extinct. In personality it was said to combine nimbleness with tenacity, and courage with great intelligence. It was said to fight in silence. Its supporters felt that, had it survived, it would have become an important show dog.

BOWSY TERRIER   SCOTLAND

Little is known of this extinct fighting breed. In local Scottish dialects, the word Bowsy can mean either 'crooked' or 'bushy'.

This ancient Scottish breed appears to have been created by crossing household Turnspits with local terriers. Richardson, writing in 1874, remarks: 'I have seen dogs in Scotland, resembling the Turnspit, called Bowsy Terriers, that were remarkable for their combative powers; I conceived them to be a cross between the old Turnspit and the low-legged Scotch terrier.' If he is correct, the name Bowsy probably refers to the well-known crooked front legs of the typical Turnspit.

FRANCE

FRENCH MASTIFF   FRANCE

Sometimes called the Bordeaux Mastiff, the Bordeaux Bulldog or the Bordeaux Dog, and known in its homeland as the Dogue de Bordeaux, this massive breed was originally developed to fight bulls, bears and its own kind. In France in the 18th century it was referred to simply as the Dogue.

This dog is one of the magnificent grotesques of the canine world. Its blunt, broad head, claimed to be the largest on any breed of dog, is covered in deep furrows that give it the sinister appeal of an ancient gargoyle. Its fine, strongly athletic, fawn-coloured body looks as though it has been borrowed from a lion.

The precise origin of this breed is unknown, but there is no shortage of theories. They include the following suggestions:

1   Like the Bullmastiff, this is a cross between a bulldog and a mastiff.

2   It is an ancient Roman breed and is a close cousin of the Neapolitan Mastiff.

3   It is descended from the early Mastiff via the Spanish Alano.

4   It is descended from the Tibetan Mastiff and the Greek Molossus.

5   It is an indigenous French breed that has developed slowly there over a period of 2,000 years.

Clearly this is all guesswork, but whichever theory is correct, the fact remains that for many years there existed in France a huge, powerful dog that was capable of attacking any animal that was placed in front of it. On one occasion it was even pitted against a jaguar.

In its fighting days the breed was available in two sizes, the large Dogue and the slightly smaller Doguin. The former would fight anything, but the latter specialized more in bull-baiting and donkey-baiting. The Doguin appeared in Buffon's *Natural History* in the 18th century, but after that it seems to have faded out of sight, while its larger cousin has continued to prosper.

The Dogue has passed through several phases in its long history. It began as a ruthless fighter, but at one time or another was also used as a war dog, a hunting dog and a guard dog. At one stage it was known as 'the Butcher's Dog' because it was employed to drive cattle to market. In more recent times it has become both a devoted companion dog and a show dog.

Its role as a guardian on aristocratic estates in France saw it suffer a major setback during the French Revolution at the end of the 18th century, when many noble dogs were slaughtered along with their noble masters. The breed barely managed to survive, but some of those acting the more lowly role of butcher's dogs did escape and from these it was later possible to rebuild the breed. It is said that, to do this, it was at some point crossed with the Bulldog and reduced in size, although it is still a very large dog, standing 27 in (69 cm) high and weighing up to 110 lb (50 kg).

One of these dogs achieved international fame as Tom Hanks's unruly, slobbering partner in the 1989 film *Turner and Hooch*. Its massive, heavily wrinkled face gave it star appeal and attracted a great deal of attention to a breed that was unknown in many countries.

SPAIN

CA DE BOU   BALAEARIC ISLANDS

This rare breed is also known by its Spanish name of Perro de Presa Mallorquin, which means, literally, 'the dog from Majorca that grips or seizes'. It was also sometimes called the Mallorquin Bulldog. Ca de Bou is its local name in the Catalan language. Its primary function was to compete in staged dog fights.

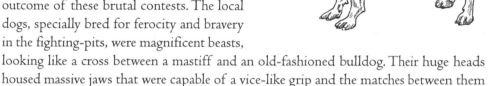

In earlier centuries, dog-fighting contests were a popular sport in the ports and harbours of the Mediterranean island of Majorca. No doubt many visiting mariners lost their hard-earned cash gambling on the outcome of these brutal contests. The local dogs, specially bred for ferocity and bravery in the fighting-pits, were magnificent beasts, looking like a cross between a mastiff and an old-fashioned bulldog. Their huge heads housed massive jaws that were capable of a vice-like grip and the matches between them must have been savage in the extreme.

The ancestors of these dogs had been used since the earliest days for controlling the cattle on the island farms. From this they graduated to the spectator sport of bull-baiting and then to dog-fighting. It was in this final role that the present, ferocious breed was developed and improved as a refined assault machine. When dog-fighting was outlawed, the Ca de Bou nearly vanished, but Spanish breeders from the mainland rescued it and began exhibiting it at dog shows. In its new role it was subjected to further selective breeding, which softened its aggressiveness without damaging its formidable appearance.

CANARY DOG   CANARY ISLANDS

Known in its native home of the Canary Islands as the Perro de Presa Canario, this powerful dog was originally developed for use in dog-fighting competitions.

In earlier centuries the Canary Islands were famous for its dogs, to such an extent that they were named after them. The Spanish word 'canario' means 'of dogs', not 'of birds', as some believe. (The canary was named after the islands, but the islands were named after the dogs.)

The ancient, indigenous dog on the Canary Islands was called the Bardino Majero, but this disappeared as a pure breed in the 19th century when English Mastiffs and Bulldogs were imported and crossed with it. The result was a fearsome fighter used in the brutal sport of competitive dog contests. When these were eventually outlawed in 1940, the Canary Dog numbers declined rapidly, and by the 1960s the breed was on its way towards complete extinction. Fortunately a few pure-bred examples were still kept by farmers in the more remote corners of Tenerife and Gran Canaria. In the 1970s, when there was greater interest in Spanish breeds, these surviving specimens were used to start a new breeding programme and, thanks to the efforts of a handful of enthusiasts, its numbers started to rise again, although it still remains a rare breed. At a later date, Dr Carl Semencic introduced the breed to the United States, where it now has a number of devoted followers.

In appearance the Canary Dog is a sturdy, well-muscled dog with a thick neck and a wide head. Like all fighting dogs, it has a short, tough coat. Typically this is brindled, but there are also red and fawn forms. There is always a black mask from the muzzle to the eyes. In personality it has been described as impetuous and aggressive when encountering strangers, but loyal, subdued and trustworthy with its owners. For this reason it has managed to find a new working role as a formidable guard dog, used to protect people, property and live-stock. A single glance from this impressive dog would be enough to terrify any intruder.

CORDOBA DOG   SPAIN

The now extinct Cordoba Dog was one of the early forms of Spanish fighting dog, used in brutal pit contests.

In origin this breed was said to be a mixture of Spanish Mastiff, Bull Terrier and the early type of Bulldog. Described as 'large, white and ferocious', the Cordoba was exported to Spanish colonies in South America where, in the Argentine, it became the ancestor of the Dogo Argentino, a breed which still exists today. In Spain it became extinct following the banning of dog-fighting.

In personality this breed was developed to be so aggressive to any other dog which came close to it that males were said to attack their bitches even while they were mating with them. It was so totally dedicated to fighting that its demise in modern times is not surprising. With the disappearance of dog-fighting contests there was simply nothing left for it to do.

SPANISH BULLDOG   SPAIN

The Spanish Bulldog was one of the early forms of Spanish fighting dog, used in brutal pit contests. Its Spanish name was Perro de Presa España.

This dog has been confused with the Spanish Mastiff by some authors, but was a distinct breed in its own right. Its role was similar to that of the Cordoba Dog, but whereas that breed was white in colour, the Spanish Bulldog was typically dark-coated.

From its name, it would appear to have been a bull-baiting dog, but old records seem to suggest that, although it may well have been set against bulls, it was primarily a pit-fighter, dog on dog. In appearance it was like a taller, heavier version of the English Bulldog (before that animal's legs were shortened by selective breeding).

According to one recent author, this ancient breed 'has long been extinct'. However, Robert Leighton published a photograph of an impressive example of it in 1907 and wrote of it at the time as though it was still very much alive. He makes the intriguing comment that 'some writers doubt the existence of a genuine Spanish Bulldog' but then goes on to insist that not only does it exist, but one was actually exhibited at an English dog show in 1896. Several others were apparently brought to England to strengthen the English Bulldog lines, but the experiment seems to have been abandoned. It is, of course, possible that the Spanish Bulldog did eventually become extinct at a later date in the 20th century.

ITALY

NEAPOLITAN MASTIFF   ITALY

Also known as the Italian Mastiff, the Italian Bull, the Neo, the Molosso Italiano, the Mastino Napoletano, or simply the Mastino, this ancient breed was developed as a fighting dog for use in the Roman arena, taking on all-comers, including both lions and Christians. It is little wonder that the Romans gave these dogs the name 'pugnaces'.

In appearance, this is perhaps the most terrifying of all dogs, with a face so ugly that it is strangely appealing. At first glance, it gives the impression of being a Shar Pei crossed with a Great Dane. In reality it is no hybrid, but a pure breed that can trace its ancestry back more than 2,000 years. The skin around its massive head is loose and hangs in heavy folds, creating a large dewlap, long pendulous lips and a deeply furrowed brow. It has been rudely described by one author as being the only dog that looks like a hippopotamus.

The ancestral form of this dog was a favourite breed of Alexander the Great, who was given a pair by a defeated Asian king (King Porus) in northern India, in the year 326 BC. It seems likely that he sent these rare dogs back to Greece, along with other booty, and that they contributed to the foundation stock for the molossian fighting dogs that

would eventually pass from the ancient Greeks to the Romans. His dogs were not the only ancestors, however, because the image of this breed appears on many works of art dating back to even earlier periods. They are, for instance, known from Assyrian reliefs and Persian plaques of the seventh century BC. Whether these Middle Eastern dogs also stemmed originally from northern India, with the Tibetan Mastiff acting as the primal source for all of them, is hard to say, but it is certain that, throughout the ancient civilizations, the forebears of the Neapolitan Mastiff were highly valued fighting dogs of the early courts, palaces and warrior leaders. They fought anything, guarded everything and, in suitable armour, even went to war.

As time passed and weapons became more sophisticated, the importance of these huge dogs declined, but they did not disappear completely. They may have lacked uniformity of type, having been bred for action rather than for looks, but the ancestral form was still there, waiting to be developed. The patron of the modern breed is generally accepted to be the Italian artist Piero Scanziani, who devoted years to improving and stabilizing it. He drew up the modern standard and was instrumental in gaining official recognition of the breed by the Italian Kennel Club (Ente Nazionale della Cinafilia Italiana). It was exhibited at the first dog show to be held in Naples, in 1946.

Although this breed began as a fighting dog and owes its fearsome appearance to that occupation, it has since been employed in several other major roles, as a much feared house guard, as a police dog, and even as a draught dog. The modern pedigree version is reputed to have a steady temperament, which in practice means that it will only attack on command and is safe and reliable at other times. Owners swear by it as a dramatic and loyal companion, proud, watchful, serious and dignified. It does, however, have one minor weakness, namely a tendency to drool and slobber. Indoor feeding is not advised. Nor is playful wrestling with pups a good idea because, when they eventually grow up, they may wish to continue these games, with overpowering results.

References

1974. Imbimbo, Nicola. *Il Mastino Napoletano.* Olimpia, Florence.

1975. Cesarino, Felice. *Il Molosso – Viaggio Intorno al Mastino Napoletano.* Fiorentino, Naples.

1983. Zacchi, Mario. *Il Molosso Italiano: Mastino Napoletano.* Calderini, Bologna.

1987. Zacchi, Mario. *The Neapolitan Mastiff.* La Moye, Jersey.

1996. Allen, Sherilyn K. *The Official Book of the Neapolitan Mastiff.* TFH, New Jersey.

AFGHANISTAN

AFGHAN MASTIFF   AFGHANISTAN

Also known as the Aryan Molossus, the main function of this breed is to take part in pit contests to settle tribal disputes. In a secondary role the dogs also act as property and livestock guardians.

This massive dog, weighing even more than an English Mastiff, is geographically intermediate between the impressive Kangal Dog of Turkey and the great Tibetan Mastiff of the Himalayas, and may well be the result of a combination of these two ancient breeds. Its principal home is in Afghanistan, but it is also known to have spread its range over the border into Pakistan and into nearby regions of northern India.

These dangerous and powerful animals are kept by special 'dog men', who breed them and train them for the fighting arena. Whenever there is a dispute between two of the local Afghan tribes, two of these dogs are acquired and then set against one another. The tribe supporting the winning dog is considered victorious in the dispute and the argument is settled without tribal warfare or loss of human blood. For the dogs, the event is less symbolic, the loser being killed by its rival, or destroyed after the fight.

The fights always take place on neutral ground and the tribal affiliations of the contestants are identified by the bright colours painted on their high, curled-over tails. This is necessary because most of these dogs have similar brindled coats.

Afghanistan's miserable history in recent times, first with the brutal involvement of the Russian army and then with the domination of the unspeakable Taliban regime, has meant that the only survivors of this rare breed of huge fighting dog are those that inhabit the most remote corners and the farthest mountain ranges of this unhappy country. Because of the unsettled conditions there at the present time it is impossible to say how many of these imposing dogs still exist, but their numbers must necessarily be very small.

CHINA

SHAR PEI   CHINA

Also known as the Chinese Shar Pei or the Chinese Fighting Dog, this strange, wrinkled breed was developed especially for use in organized dog fights. Its name is said to mean 'draping sandpaper-like skin' or 'harsh sandy coat'.

There are no precise records to tell us about the origins of this bizarre dog from southern China, but it seems likely that both it and its close relative, the Chow Chow, are descended from the Han Dog, the ancient guard dog that existed in the Han Dynasty in China about 2,000 years ago. Effigies of that dog show an unwrinkled version of the Shar Pei and it would seem that, from its guard-dog beginnings, it developed in two diverging directions, leading by increased bulk and heavier coat to the food dog we call the Chow, and by increased skin-wrinkling to the fighting dog we call the Shar Pei. The reason we know that these two breeds are related is that they both possess a blue-black tongue, but they were specialized for different purposes and their anatomy reflects this fact.

When the Shar Pei puppy is born it is soon clear that it has a coat several sizes too large for it. Its skin lies over its body in loose folds that soon settle into characteristic, deep folds. These decrease as the dog grows into adulthood, but never vanish completely. This odd appearance could be obtained by a simple genetic change – a gene reducing the dog's body-size, but without reducing its skin-size. The reason that early Chinese breeders retained these oddities is that the looseness of the coarse, bristly coat made it extremely difficult for an opponent in a dog fight to gain a tight grip and then hold it. The Shar Pei that found itself clamped in enemy jaws could twist and turn with ease and quickly slither out of its rival's grasp. In addition, the harsh, bristly surface of the Shar Pei's thick coat would be unpleasant inside the other dog's mouth. So this 'genetic oddity' was, in reality, a godsend to a fighting dog and was carefully selected for and increased over the years. But then two misfortunes befell the breed and it nearly became extinct. First, the Chinese dog-fight organizers began importing much bigger, fiercer fighting dogs from Europe and, for these monsters, the Shar Pei was no match, even with its sliding skin. Second, in the 20th century, the Communist rulers in China became massively opposed to the existence of domestic dogs, seeing them as signs of Western triviality and decadence, and set about slaughtering every dog they could lay their hands on. Countless thousands of much loved pets were wantonly destroyed on the instruction of these barbaric politicians, and the Shar Pei was nearly wiped out.

In 1978 *The Guinness Book of Records* stated that this was the rarest breed in the world with only 60 dogs still alive. However, thanks to some canine enthusiasts in the havens of Hong Kong, Macao and Taiwan, a few were saved and used as the basis for a new breeding population. Their unique appearance appealed to certain breeders in the United States and within a few years their numbers were climbing again. Today they exist in their thousands and this unique animal is now safe for the future.

It is not without its problems, however, some physical, some mental. The deep folds in its skin cause health problems that are still being solved at the present time. In particular the heavy skin around the eyes has created difficulties that have often required corrective surgery. In personality, the Shar Pei has inherited a strongly aggressive personality, and reducing this by selective breeding is taking time. But rapid progress is being made in all these matters.

The standard of this extraordinary dog sums up its eccentric appearance. It must have a head like a Wu-Lo melon, ears like clamshells, a nose like a Guangzhou cookie, legs like Pae Pah musical instruments, a back like a shrimp, a tail like iron wire, a face like a grandmother, a neck like a water buffalo, a body like a wun fish, an anus that faces the sky, a rump like a horse, feet like garlic, toenails like iron and a mouth like a mother frog or a roof tile.

References

1980. Strang, Paul D. and Olsen, Eve C. *The Chinese Shar-Pei.* Denlinger's, USA.

1984. Redditt, Jo Ann Thrower. *The Chinese Shar-Pei Puppy Book.* Medea, Washington.

1985. Straus, Mary and Wood, Robin. *The Guide to the Chinese Shar-Pei.* Stockton, California.

1986. Debo, Ellen Weathers. *The Chinese Shar-Pei.* TFH, New Jersey.

1988. Davison, Betsy. *More about the Chinese Shar-Pei Puppy.* Medea, Washington.

1988. Gannon, Dee. *The Complete Chinese Shar-Pei.* Howell, New York.

1988. Nicholas, Anna Katherine. *Chinese Shar-Pei.* TFH, New Jersey.

1988. Redditt, Jo Ann. *Understanding the Chinese Shar-Pei.* Orient, Arlington, Virginia.

1991. Brearley, Joan. *Book of the Shar-Pei.* TFH, New Jersey.

1992. Nicholas, Anna Katherine. *The World of the Chinese Shar-Pei.*

1992. Ditto, Tanya B. *Shar-Pei: Everything About Purchase, Care, Nutrition, Breeding, Behavior, and Training.* Barron, New York.

1995. Cunliffe, Juliette. *The Chinese Shar Pei Today.* Howell, New York.

1996. Ackerman, Lowell. *Dr Ackerman's Book of the Shar-Pei.* TFH, New Jersey.

1995. Hunter, Devin. *Guide to Owning a Shar-Pei: Puppy Care, Grooming, Training, History, Health, Breed Standard.* TFH, New Jersey.

1996. Kleinhans, Karen. *A New Owner's Guide to Shar Pei.*

1996. Redditt, Jo Ann Thrower. *The Chinese Shar-Pei: An Owner's Guide to a Happy Healthy Pet.* Howell, New York.

1996. Zervas, Michael R. *Basic Guide to the Chinese Shar-Pei.* Dace Publishing.

1997. Gannon, Dee. *New Complete Chinese Shar Pei.*

Tate, Kelly Anne. *The Chinese Shar-Pei Veterinary Manual.*

JAPAN

AKITA   JAPAN

Also known as the Shishi Inu, the Nippon Inu, the Japanese Akita, or the Akita Inu, this dog takes its name from its home locality, Akita, in the northern part of the main island of Honshu. It was developed as a powerful fighting dog for specially staged contests.

The Akita is a magnificently formed, sturdy, muscular dog that oozes confidence, power and fitness. Descended from Northern Spitz dogs, with the typical spitz tail curled up over its back, it was refined into a fighting special-ist in the 17th century and was the foremost contest dog in Japan until the middle of the 19th century, when imported breeds began to alter the Japanese dog-fight scene.

In modern times, dog-fighting contests have fallen out of favour and the Akita has been forced to find other employment to survive. It has proved successful in five areas – as a guardian of property, a hunting dog, a police dog, a competitive show dog and a companion dog. In its role as a hunting dog it was used for the pursuit of both wild boar and deer, and was sometimes given the name of Japanese Deerhound.

In some countries, where the Akita is now a popular pedigree breed for the show-ring, there has been an attempt to conceal its brutal, pit-fighting origins. Its history has been conveniently rewritten to suit modern tastes. But the really remarkable feature of this dog is surely that it has overcome its fighting origins so well, to become a much loved and trusted modern pet. It owes its revival in a domestic role largely to Hiroshi Saito who pioneered the rebirth of the breed in the 1920s. It was first imported into England in 1937.

The most famous of all Akitas was, strangely enough, not a fighting champion, but a loyal companion of a Tokyo professor, Eizaburo Ueno. This learned man commuted to his office every day by rail and his loyal dog, called Hachi, would accompany him to the railway station each day, see him off on his train, and then return home on his own. When it was time to greet his master back from work, he would set off by himself for the station and wait on the platform for him to arrive. On 25th May 1925 his master suffered a stroke in his office and died. Hachi waited at the station for him and was distressed when he did not appear. The following evening the dog went again to the station, but again his master was not there. Hachi continued to make his lonely journey back and forth to the station every day for the next nine years until eventually he himself died. A bronze statue was raised to his memory and can be seen to this day at the Shibuya Station where this amazing dog continued his long vigil. The statue is called 'Chuken Hachi-ko', meaning 'Loyal Dog Hachi'.

References

1964. Van Der Lyn, Edita. *How To Raise and Train an Akita.* TFH, New Jersey.

1981. Van Der Lyn, Edita. *Akitas.* TFH, New Jersey.

1984. Linderman, Joan M. and Funk, Virginia B. *The Complete Akita, Natural Monument of Japan.* Howell, New York.

1985. Brearley, Joan McDonald. *The Book of the Akita.* TFH, New Jersey.

1990. Mitchell, Gerald and Mitchell, Kath. *The Akita.* Ringpress Books, Letchworth, Hertfordshire.

1994. Linderman, Joan M. and Funk, Virginia B. *The New Complete Akita.* Howell, New York.

1996. Andrews, Barbara J. *A New Owner's Guide to Akitas.*

1996. Bouyet, Barbara. *The Akita: An Owner's Guide to a Healthy Pet.* Howell, New York.

1997. Andrews, Barbara J. *The World of the Akita.*

1997. Rice, Dan. *Akitas: Everything About Purchase, Care, Nutrition, Breeding, Behavior, and Training.* Complete Pet Owner's Manual.

1997. Taylor, Jason. *Guide to Owning an Akita: Puppy Care, Grooming, Training, History, Health, Breed Standard.*

1999. Killilea, Dave and Killilea, Jenny. *The Akita Today.*

TOSA   JAPAN

Also known as the Tosa Inu, the Tosa Token, the Tosa Ken, the Tosa Fighting Dog, the Japanese Tosa, the Japanese Fighting Dog or the Japanese Mastiff, this breed takes its name from the Tosa region on the island of Shikoku, in the Kochi Prefecture. It is one of the greatest of all fighting dogs, bred to defeat every kind of canine opponent.

In their efforts to create the ultimate fighting machine, Japanese breeders crossed their local fighting dog, the Nihon Inu, with imported Bull Terriers, bulldogs (in 1872), mastiffs (in 1874), pointers (in 1876) and Great Danes (in 1924). The result was an imposing giant of a dog that was prepared to fight to the death in complete silence, fearlessly attacking its opponent without hesitation. National Champions were formally dressed in ceremonial aprons, these traditional costumes sometimes being valued at over $30,000.

This formidable breed was developed because the breeders of local fighting dogs were consistently losing out to the various imported breeds. By combining the indigenous dogs with the foreign ones, they were able to call the new, improved dog their own, while at the same time gaining the advantages of the introduced blood.

When it has not been engaged in brutal pit contests, the massive Tosa – weighing up to 200 lb (90 kg) – has proved to be a highly effective house guard. This is not surprising. Looking like a cross between a mastiff and a Great Dane, with a short, hard coat and a muscle-bound body, a single glance from this stately animal would be enough to send most burglars scuttling for cover.

In colour it is red, brindle, fawn or dull black. It is rare in Japan and outside that country is little-known, there being no more than a handful of breeders in Germany and the United States. In some countries it is a banned breed.

UNITED STATES

ALAPAHA BLUE BLOOD BULLDOG   UNITED STATES

Also known as the Plantation Dog, or to its friends simply as Otto, this breed was developed from its fighting-dog origins to become a valuable property guard, despite the fact that it still retains its old title of bulldog. It takes its name from the Alapaha River region of south Georgia.

This is an extremely rare breed, with no more than 120–150 dogs in existence today.

It was saved from extinction and fostered over a long period of time by the Lane family of Rebecca, Georgia. The dog's first great supporter was PaPa Buck Lane, and, continuing the family tradition, his grand-daughter Lana Lou Lane eventually started a registry for the breed. Its future is in good hands but, with such a small population, its long-term survival must still be in doubt.

This is a direct descendant of the original English Bulldogs that arrived in North America in the 18th century, and were used there for the traditional sports of bull-baiting and bear-baiting. It is an immensely powerful dog with a massive head and a heavy, muscular body. Its tail remains undocked. The short coat is white, patched with black, blue, buff or brown.

The founding father of the breed was called Otto, and all members of this breed are called 'Ottos' in his memory. When Otto's master was killed by a train in 1943, the dog insisted on visiting his grave, time after time. Nobody knew how the dog could iden-tify his master's grave, but he was somehow able to distinguish it from all the others. He continued to pay his visits, to sit with his dead master, until he himself pined away and died. Another famous member of this breed, called Henry, was faced with two intruders carrying a sawn-off shotgun. He jumped at them and knocked them down, forcing them to flee empty-handed. On another occasion the same dog jumped through a plate-glass window to attack a burglar. This is clearly a guard dog that demands respect.

In 1996 the Alapaha Blue Blood Bulldog Club was formed to promote and protect the breed. The club makes the point that this may be a massively powerful breed, but it is also agile, intelligent and very affectionate with its own human family. Because of careful selective breeding, it no longer goes looking for a fight, but it still responds vigorously when provoked.

ALTMAN WHITE ENGLISH BULLDOG   UNITED STATES

The ancestors of this breed were known as 'White English' and belonged to the larger, working type that existed before the English Bulldog was reduced for the modern show-ring.

The forerunners of this breed came to the United States in the 19th century. The pre-sent dog is a reconstruction of those dogs and was developed by Ray Altman of Waycross, Georgia. This impressive dog is now said to be gaining recognition in the United States as a separate breed, although it clearly has a similar background to the American Bulldog (see separate entry).

From its photographs this dog looks very similar to the modern English Bulldog of the show-ring, but its pictures conceal the fact that it is on a much larger scale. The standard of the Altman White gives a height of 15–21 in (38–54 cm), compared with only 12–14 in (31–36 cm) for the modern English Bulldog. The weight of the Altman White is 50–80 lb (23–36 kg), compared with only 40–50 lb (18–23 kg) for the modern English Bulldog. Another difference is that the tail of the Altman White is usually docked.

As regards their duties, it is said that they are good at guard work, farm work and field competition. It is also mentioned that 'they have fought wild dogs, bulls and fires to protect their masters'. How a dog fights a fire is not clear, nor is it immediately obvious why bulls and wild dogs would wish to attack the dogs' owners.

AMERICAN BULLDOG   UNITED STATES

This breed used to be known as the American Pit Bull Dog, but in order to avoid confusion with the quite distinct American Pit Bull Terrier, it has recently been given its new, official title. In its early days it was also called by a variety of other names, including the Old Country Bulldog, the Old Country White, the Old Time Bulldog, the Old English White, the English White, the White English, the Alabama and the Southern Bulldog. Its main patron, John D. Johnson, proposed calling it the Johnson American Bulldog, or the JDJ Bulldog. Its original role was to engage in pit contests and in fights against larger animals.

This massively powerful dog, probably one of the most ferocious ever created, is rare even in its homeland. It was developed in the south-eastern region of the United States and is best known in Alabama and Georgia.

According to some authorities, this breed was manufactured from crosses between the modern, short-legged English Bulldog, the American Pit Bull Terrier and the Bullmastiff, and is a reconstruction of the early English Bulldog. It should be mentioned, however, that despite this view, one particular expert still insists that the breed was brought to America by his ancestors, long ago in colonial times, and that its ancestry can be traced back to the working bulldogs of 18th-century England.

To him, and to the official supporters of the American Bulldog, modern examples of this breed are the direct descendants of the early English Bulldogs that arrived in North America in the 17th and 18th centuries. In England the shape of bulldogs has changed dramatically during recent times, but its American equivalent has remained faithful to the original, with much longer legs and a more athletic body. The main reason for this is that the American Bulldog did not become a show dog.

Its first duties were its traditional ones of bull-baiting and bear-baiting, with the exotic addition of American buffalo-baiting. When these so-called entertainments lost favour, Bulldogs in the United States nearly became extinct. The only ones to survive were the few that were employed on farms in isolated pockets of the south-east. There they were used as 'cattle-catchers' or 'catch-dogs', to attack and subdue wayward bulls, and as livestock guards, protecting valuable farm animals from attacks by packs of roaming, feral dogs. Their strength was such that they were said to be capable of confronting and single-handedly slaughtering an entire pack of stray dogs.

It is also, needless to say, an effective house guard against human intruders. The breed's main patron and breeder, John D. Johnson, commented in an interview:

> As time has gone on, our cities have enlarged and there are fewer and fewer small farms. In essence, the dog has lost his job. The Bulldog is the original working dog and his purpose is to do a job. When the job disappears, he no longer has a reason for existing. Now, with crime on the increase, the Bulldog is once again finding a new job and so we are seeing a complete resurgence in his popularity.

According to one report, Johnson was worried that cross-bred dogs were being labelled as 'American Bulldogs', and he proposed that his pure line should be given a more specific name, modestly suggesting that it be called the Johnson American Bulldog, or the JDJ Bulldog. It was reported that 'the JDJ Bulldog has been renamed by Mr Johnson himself to separate the true Johnson American Bulldog from the different crosses claiming to be Johnson American Bulldogs'.

Because this is a dog that will readily give its life to protect its owners or their property, it has become increasingly sought after in recent years. In 1989 the American Bulldog Association was formed to oversee the breeding of this powerful dog and to ensure its proper use. Sadly, illegal dog-fighting still occurs using this courageous breed, but this is officially opposed by all those involved in the promotion of the dog as a modern house guard.

Dogs belonging to this breed are registered with an organization called the Animal Research Foundation (ARF) or with the Game American Bulldog Club (GABC). Detailed records have been kept, pure breeding has been achieved, and an official breed standard has been issued.

Some specimens are huge, weighing up to 125 lb (57 kg), and in the standard there is no upper limit to the body weight. They have been variously described as 'big rough-and-tumble bulldogs', 'iron-jawed gangbusters', and 'fighting machines with alligator heads and python bodies' that are (rather disturbingly) 'still capable of wrestling down a cantankerous bull'.

References

1998. Blackwell, John. *American Bulldogs*. TFH, New Jersey.
1999. Putnam, Dave. *The Working American Bulldog*.

AMERICAN PIT BULL TERRIER UNITED STATES

This breed was formerly known by many names including the Pit Bull, the Pit Bull Terrier, the American Bull, the American Pit Bull, the American Pit Bull Dog, the Pit Dog, the Half-and-Half, the American Bull Terrier, the Yankee Terrier, the Yankee Bull Terrier, and the Staffordshire Terrier. It was developed as a fighting dog for pit contests in the United States.

In the 1870s Staffordshire Bull Terriers began to arrive in North America from England, for use in organized dog-fighting. Soon, it was felt that the dogs of the foundation stock were too small, so selective breeding was undertaken to make the body taller and heavier. The head and chest were also increased in size and the result was a massively powerful fighting machine.

Because of the dog's unsavoury associations, the AKC refused to recognize it, but those involved in breeding the animals wished to establish pedigrees and record blood-lines. In 1898 they therefore set up their own club, the United Kennel Club (UKC), with which they could register their dogs.

When pit-fighting was outlawed in America in 1900 it did not cease, but merely went underground. It is claimed that even as late as the 1990s it was still widespread and that 1,500 dogs died annually as a result of these savage contests. It is largely the high-stakes gambling involved that helps to keep the sport alive. In one police raid, for example, more than $500,000 in stake money was found on the 20 people arrested.

As with most fighting dogs, their animosity towards their own kind does not normally extend to people. Pit Bull Terriers are said by their owners to be 'loyal companion dogs... obedient, loving and protective'. Unfortunately their protective behaviour can easily become excessive and, with their bone-crushing jaws and complete lack of fear, they are capable of inflicting terrible damage on an imagined intruder in a few seconds.

When some of these dogs were imported into England in the 1980s there were several such incidents, and in 1991 the British government passed the Dangerous Dogs Act, banning the breed from the country. Those dogs that had already been imported had to be registered, neutered, tattooed and fitted with an identification microchip. In public they had to be muzzled and on a leash at all times. If any of these orders were ignored, the dogs were to be destroyed.

The British police had little idea how to identify an American Pit Bull Terrier and many innocent dogs were impounded. Their owners then set about suing for their release, and interminable court cases followed. One pet mongrel, for example, was held for 17 months before it was finally released back to its owner. At one point over 1,000 canine suspects were in police custody, awaiting death or release following the trials of their owners. Within two years there had been over 2,000 court cases with a total cost running into many millions of pounds. The reason for this extreme action was not just that there had been a few savage attacks on people, but also that the government wanted to prevent the growth of organized dog-fighting in Britain. They felt that unless they acted firmly, it would soon begin to spread and become as endemic as it was in the United States. In this, they appeared to be largely successful.

References

1976. Stratton, Richard F. *This is the American Pit Bull Terrier*. TFH, New Jersey.

1981. Stratton, Richard F. *The Truth about the American Pit Bull Terrier*. TFH, New Jersey.

1982. Stratton, Richard F. *The World of the American Pit Bull Terrier*. TFH, New Jersey.

1985. Stratton, Richard F. *The Book of the American Pit Bull Terrier*. TFH, New Jersey.

1988. Ely, Scott. *Pit Bull*. Weidenfeld & Nicolson, New York.

1989. Pierce, J. D. *Guide to Owning a Pit Bull Terrier: Puppy Care, Grooming, Training, History, Health, Breed Standard*.

1989. Sanford, William Reynolds. *The American Pit Bull Terrier*. Crestwood House.

1991. Semencic, Carl. *American Pit Bulls and Tenacious Guard Dogs*. TFH, New Jersey.

1995. Fraser, Jacqueline and O'Neil, Jacqueline. *The American Pit Bull Terrier: An Owner's Guide to a Happy Healthy Pet*. Howell, New York.

1995. Jessup. *Working Pit Bull*. TFH, New Jersey.

1995. O'Neil, Jacqueline and Fraser, Jacqueline. *The Ultimate American Pit Bull Terrier*. Howell, New York.

1995. Stahlkuppe, Joe. *American Pit Bull Terriers, American Staffordshire Terriers: Everything about Purchase, Care, Nutrition, Breeding, Behavior, and Training*. Barrows, New York.

1996. Fenstermacher, Todd. *A New Owner's Guide to the American Pit Bull Terriers*.

1997. Colby, Louis B. *Colby's Book of the American Pit Bull Terrier*. TFH, New Jersey.

1997. Pierce, J. D. *Guide to Owning a Pit Bull Terrier*. TFH, New Jersey.

1997. Rebenack, Butch. *Guide to Owning a Pit Bull Terrier*.

1997. Rocca, Frank C. *Fighting for Life: The American Bull Terrier, an Endangered Species*.

1999. Dunbar, Ian (Editor). *The Essential Pit Bull Terrier*. Howell, New York.

Rocca, Frank C. *American Bull Terriers: A Legacy in Gameness*.

AMERICAN STAFFORDSHIRE TERRIER   UNITED STATES

This breed was originally called simply the Staffordshire Terrier. Its modern name of American Staffordshire Terrier was introduced to avoid confusion. The breed's popular nickname today is AmStaff. It was originally developed as a fighting dog for pit contests in the United States.

The American Staffordshire Terrier is the show-dog version of the fighting dog called the American Pit Bull Terrier. Because the owners of the Pit Bull Terriers had been

keeping accurate records of the pedigrees and bloodlines of their dogs for over 30 years, it was clear, by the 1930s, that their animals should be considered as members of a proper breed and officially recognized. However, since it was suspected that the same animals were unofficially still being used in many cases for organized dog fights, the American Kennel Club faced a dilemma. It wanted to recognize a genuine American breed, but could not condone dog-fighting. The solution was to give the breed a new name and insist that any animal registered with the AKC could never be used in organized fighting.

With this in mind, the breed was officially registered with the AKC in 1935 as the Staffordshire Terrier. Later, when it was agreed also to recognize the smaller, English version of the Staffordshire in the United States, it was decided to emphasize the difference between the two breeds by calling the larger breed the American Staffordshire Terrier. This new name was registered with the AKC in 1972.

Although the two breeds – the American Pit Bull Terrier and the American Staffordshire Terrier – are virtually the same animal, small differences have started to appear since the show dogs have been separated from the 'working' dogs. The show dogs are judged on their appearance, the working dogs on their temperament. As time goes by, this will undoubtedly lead to the kind of divergence that has occurred in so many other breeds.

As with all bull terriers, this one is generally friendly with people and tolerant of children, despite the fact that it has such a potential for ferocity in its genetic background. It has been described by its supporters as 'a pleaser not a mauler'.

References

1948. Denlinger, Milo G. *The Complete Pitbull or Staffordshire Terrier*. Denlinger's, USA.
1989. Fraser. *American Staffordshire Terrier.*
1991. Nicholas, Anna Katherine. *Staffordshire Terriers: American Staffordshire Bull Terrier and Staffordshire Bull Terrier*. TFH, New Jersey.
1995. Stahlkuppe, Joe. *American Pit Bull Terriers, American Staffordshire Terriers: Everything about Purchase, Care, Nutrition, Breeding, Behavior, and Training*. Barron, New York.

ARKANSAS GIANT BULLDOG   UNITED STATES

This breed is sometimes called the Olde Bulldogge, but should not be confused with the Olde English Bulldogge (see separate entry) which, although its name is sometimes also shortened to Olde Bulldogge, has a different origin.

This breed was created in the late 20th century by arranging crosses with the English Bulldog and the American Staffordshire Terrier, or the Pit Bull Terrier. It is one of several recent attempts to recreate the old-style English Bulldog and to get away from the extreme show type of modern bulldog. As a breed it is still in the formative stages and shows too much variability to be considered as a pure-bred dog. Further breeding programmes may eliminate this variability, or the incipient breed may fail to develop.

At the present time, all colours are accepted. The height of the dog is 18–22 in (45–55 cm), and the weight is 55–66 lb (25–30 kg).

BOSTON TERRIER   UNITED STATES

In its early days this breed was called the Round-headed Bull-and-Terrier, the Round-headed Bull, the Round-headed Terrier, the Boston Bull Terrier, the Bullet Head or the Boston Bull. Its first official title was the American Bull Terrier, but this was rejected for competition use and was then replaced with the present title. This New England breed was originally developed as a fighting dog for pit contests.

The first Boston Terrier, the founding father of the breed, was in reality born in Liverpool in the 1870s and was shipped across the Atlantic to the city that would eventually give the breed its name. It had been created by crossing an English Bulldog with an English White Terrier. Its name was Judge and it became known as Hooper's Judge, because in 1875 it had been purchased by a Mr Robert Hooper of Boston.

This dog inherited brindle markings from its Bulldog parent and white markings from its Terrier parent, and a combination of brindle and white has remained the typical colouring of all Boston Terriers. It was mated with a bitch called Burnett's Gyp and their offspring provided the foundation stock.

At a later date some French Bulldog blood was thought to have been added, possibly to reduce the size to below its present 25 lb (11 kg) limit. Some authors think that the Bull Terrier was also involved in breeding plans, and even the Boxer has been mentioned.

In the early 1890s the Boston Terrier Club was formed and the breed was officially recognized for show-ring competition in the United States. Its fame soon spread beyond the Boston region and by the 1920s the breed had reached Europe. By the

1950s it was the most popular pedigree dog in North America. Its one drawback, as its size has gradually been reduced, appears to be the difficulty that some bitches have in delivering their big-headed puppies. For many the only solution is an expensive Caesarean operation.

References

1910. Axtell, Edward. *The Boston Terrier and All About It.*

1926. Rousuck. *The Boston Terrier.* G. Howard Watt, New York.

1928. Perry, Vincent G. *The Boston Terrier.* Judy Publishing, Chicago.

1932. Rine, Josephine Z. *The Ideal Boston Terrier.* Orange Judd, New York.

1937. Craven, Arthur. *The Boston Terrier as I Know It.* Privately published, Manchester.

1938. Penn, Penelope. *The Boston Terrier in England.* Tonbridge, Kent.

1954. Cline, Mrs Charles D. *Pet Boston Terrier.* All-Pets, Fond du Lac, Wisconsin.

1955. Denlinger, William W. *Complete Boston.* Denlinger's, USA.

1956. Miller, Madeline. *Boston Terriers: a Guide to the Training, Care and Breeding of Boston Terriers.* TFH, New Jersey.

1959. Miller. *How to Raise and Train a Boston Terrier.* TFH, New Jersey.

1967. Schneider, Earl. *Know Your Boston Terrier.* Pet Library, New York.

1968. Cline, Mrs Charles D. *Boston Terriers.* TFH, New Jersey.

1985. Huddleston, Arthur R. *The Boston Terrier.*

1994. Bulanda, Susan. *Boston Terriers: Everything About Purchase, Care, Nutrition, Breeding, Behavior, and Training.* Barron, New York.

1995. Staley, Beverly and Staley, Michael. *The Boston Terrier: An American Original.* Howell, New York.

1997. Flamholtz, Cathy J. (Editor). *Boston Terriers: The Early Years.*

1998. Lee, Muriel P. *The Official Book of the Boston Terrier.*

1998. O'Neil, Jacqueline F. *Guide to Owning a Boston Terrier.*

2000. Meade, Scottee. *The Boston Terrier: An Owner's Guide to a Happy Healthy Pet.* Howell, New York.

Braunstein, E. *Complete Boston Terrier.*

Nicholas, Anna Katherine. *Boston Terrier.*

OLDE ENGLISH BULLDOGGE   UNITED STATES

Sometimes called simply the Olde Bulldogge, this modern breed has been classified as a fighting dog, although its creator claims that it was developed specifically as an aggressive house guard.

In the early 1970s an American breeder, David Leavitt of Spring Grove, Pennsylvania, began a carefully planned programme to reconstruct the early type of the English Bulldog. Convinced that the modern Bulldog, with its short legs and flattened face, was a travesty of its former self, he started to make a series of crosses between it and the Bullmastiff, the American Bulldog and the American Pit Bull Terrier. He recorded the precise mixture of the foundation stock as: one-half English Bulldog; one-sixth

Bullmastiff; one-sixth American Bulldog; and one-sixth American Pit Bull Terrier.

The goal of his project was to produce an athletic Bulldog similar in appearance to the ones shown in the illustrations in early dog books. The result, which has already reached the stage where it is breeding true, is an awesome creation.

The officially stated function of this newly developed breed was not to bait bulls but to act as a powerful, fearless defender of the home, ready to take on any human intruders foolish enough to attempt to enter the premises. It is claimed that the Olde Bulldogge is so efficient that it can even tackle two opponents at once, making a rapid lunge at the first to incapacitate him and then quickly turning his attention to the second before he has time to escape.

On the basis of its proclaimed role to act solely as a guard dog, this dog should be classified in this book among the other property guards, but there are two good reasons for including it here, among the fighting dogs. First, its ancestry marks it out as a fighter, through and through. Second, it is included by Dr Carl Semencic in his book *The World of Fighting Dogs*.

PIT BULLMASTIFF   UNITED STATES

This breed was developed primarily as a fighting dog for pit contests in the western regions of the United States.

This recent breed is an attempt to create a larger and more powerful form of the Pit Bull Terrier. By mating Pit Bull Terriers with Bullmastiffs, breeders were able to produce a line of gigantic fighting dogs, apparently popular on the west coast of America for illegally staged dog-fights. According to witnesses of these savage contests, the greater strength of the Pit Bullmastiff gives it an advantage at the start of a bout, but the resilience and tenacity of the ordinary Pit Bull Terrier gives it greater staying power, providing that it has managed to withstand the initial onslaught.

SWINFORD BANDOG   UNITED STATES

This breed was named after its American creator, veterinarian John Swinford. It has sometimes been called the American Mastiff, the American Bandogge or simply the Bandog, but the last name is confusing as this dog is not related to the original, ancient Bandog breed. It was developed primarily as a fighting dog for pit contests in the United States.

The Swinford Bandog is the result of an attempt to create a giant version of the American Pit Bull Terrier, a dog that would prove invincible in the fighting pit. There is a curious irony in the fact that a veterinarian, dedicated to healing animals, should have been so keen to produce a breed that could inflict terrible damage upon them. It was in 1969 that Swinford first crossed American Pit Bull Terriers with mastiffs and called the result a Bandog, after the extinct house-guard dogs of earlier centuries. There are no records of precisely which kind of mastiff he employed, but after his death, when other breeders continued with his work, two alternative breeds were tried. The first was the Neapolitan Mastiff and the second the English Mastiff. The Neapolitan provided the necessary gameness for a fighting breed, but introduced hip dysplasia problems into the breeding programme. Use of the English Mastiff avoided this drawback, but this breed was felt by some to be too docile. The solution was to use a combination of both types of mastiff – first crossing the Neapolitan with the English Mastiff and then mating the offspring with Pit Bull Terriers. This method seemed to produce the best results and create a gigantic fighting machine of terrifying ferocity. Genetically this breed is still not stabilized.

It is said that these dogs are most often encountered in the north-eastern region of the United States, but that even there they are rather rare. Frankly, it is surprising to learn of the development of such a dog, a full century after the banning of dog-fighting in the United States. It poses an intriguing riddle: how do you ban a Bandog?

CUBA

CUBAN MASTIFF   CUBA

Also known as the Cuban Dog, the Cuban Bull-Mastiff or the Dogo Cubano, this breed was developed as a bull-fighting dog, although it had other duties, too.

The first examples of this rare breed to be seen in the Western world were a pair that arrived at the London Zoo, as a canine curiosity, early in the 19th century. According

to the zoo record books, the precise date is not known. It is given simply as '1830, or earlier'. According to Charles Hamilton Smith, writing a few years later, this pair allowed the public to become well acquainted with this impressive breed, and it is strange that so little has been written about it since.

Smith himself did discuss these dogs briefly and commented that he was informed by Spanish cattle-dealers on the south side of the island that great attention was given to preserving them. Bearing in mind that the Cuban Mastiffs were employed in the brutal sport of bull-fighting, which gave them some value locally, this is to be expected, but what is surprising is the observation that 'they were first kept at a Monastery in the ancient capital, St Jago'.

The ancestors of these dogs were apparently Spanish-owned mastiffs brought across the Atlantic to the West Indies in the 16th century for the purpose of what we would today call ethnic cleansing. Before they fought the bulls, they were used to fight the native Indians. According to William Youatt, writing in 1864, Spanish soldiers 'procured some of these Mastiffs, by whose assistance they penetrated into every part of the country, and destroyed the greater portion of the former inhabitants'. A Catholic priest who was present was horrified by the fact that the dogs 'had been trained to a thirst for human blood, so that before I left the island it has become almost entirely a desert'.

On the island, as time passed, these European mastiffs began to change, and the local island breed started to develop, in isolation, into a breed of its own. An eyewitness, a Mr Bennett, described these Cuban dogs as follows:

> ...larger than our common bull-dogs, and smaller than the mastiff, well made, and rather stout in their proportions; moderately high on the legs; muscular and powerful; their muzzle is short, broad, and abruptly truncate, with somewhat of an upward curve; the head broad and flat, and the lips elongated, and so deeply pendulous as to overlap the margins of the lower jaw; the ears which are of a middling size, are also partly pendulous, but not to such an extent as to be flat upon the sides of the head; the tail is rather cylindrical, and turned upwards and forwards towards the top.

In colour these dogs were said to be a 'rusty wolf-colour, with face, lips and legs black'.

This breed slowly faded from sight. It was still well known enough in 1912 to be included as one of a set of 50 cigarette cards, and it rated a brief mention in the great *Hutchinson Dog Encyclopedia* of 1935. After that it vanishes and appears to have become extinct. One recent student of mastiff breeds remarks that he does not know 'if the breed still exists, although I have heard rumours about breeders of Dogo Cubano in Holland'. Perhaps, like many rare breeds from earlier days, it has somehow managed to hang on in a few remote corners.

Livestock Dogs

A second major category of dogs comprises those breeds that are concerned with the protection or control of domestic livestock. Sporting dogs are all involved in helping with attacks on other animals – either by hunting for prey or by fighting rival dogs – but livestock dogs, in complete contrast, are dedicated to the welfare of their animal companions. They must aid their human owners by defending farm animals from thieves or predators, or by influencing the movements of groups of domestic stock. These are the fearless guardians and the nimble herders.

LIVESTOCK GUARDS

From the earliest days of mankind's partnership with the domestic dog, the duty of acting as a guardian has been of great importance. One of the earliest canine tasks was to protect the tribal settlements from intruders, but then, when farming began, there was an additional role – that of defending the livestock from thieves and predators.

Some breeds did not undertake this important new task. They remained in the settlements and acted exclusively as property guardians. Others took on the new duties during the day but then returned with the livestock at night and, in the dark hours, reverted to their original role of property guards. Still others became exclusive livestock protectors, day and night, and had no time for other duties. These powerful dogs had to act as sentinels, ever on the lookout for trouble and then, if danger was detected, had to be brave enough to attack the human thieves or animal predators approaching their flocks or herds.

Those dogs that protect only property are dealt with as a separate category. Those that protect livestock, with or without additional guard duties, are assembled here.

By the nature of their work, livestock guardians have to be large, heavily built dogs, with broad heads and powerful jaws. In personality, they are required to be sociable in a special way – they must be able to form a strong bond of attachment to their flocks or herds and never show any aggression towards them, even when they are left alone together. This requires a special character that has been developed and refined by selective breeding over hundreds of years. It also requires special individual training, and the puppies are introduced to their livestock companions when they are very young. They are also kept out of their owners' homes, so that their flocks or herds, rather than their owners' families, become their 'packs'. This means that, if they are working animals, they are essentially 'outside' dogs. Of course, if they are solely kept as show dogs, these rules do not apply.

This important group has not fared well in the classifications of show dogs. There is no special category for them. Some are included with the herding dogs, whose primary task is to control the movement of livestock, rather than defend them. Others are grouped with miscellaneous working dogs. This fails to do them justice as a specialized group, and it also conceals an interesting geographical difference. Because of the varying nature of the rural environments, there are far more livestock-guarding dogs in Eastern Europe, the Middle East and Asia than there are in Western Europe. And there are far more livestock-herding breeds in Western Europe than further east.

There are 39 breeds in this livestock-guarding category.

FRANCE

PYRENEAN MOUNTAIN DOG FRANCE

Also known as the Great Pyrenees, the Pyrenean Hound or the Chien de Montaigne des Pyrénées, this breed was given the title of Royal Dog of France by Louis XIV in the 17th century. It has been employed as a flock guard in the Pyrenees mountain range that separates France from Spain for several thousand years. Because of its work against marauding wolves and bears, it was sometimes called the Pyrenean Wolfdog or the Pyrenean Bearhound.

This huge, heavy-bodied dog with its thick white coat is perhaps the best-known of the large flock guards that have been employed to protect sheep from predators and thieves in the highlands of Europe. It is closely related to the Maremma Sheepdog of Italy and the Kuvasz of Hungary. Its great white bulk is so impressive that it has been referred to as the 'animated snowdrift'.

During its dangerous working days, this great dog was given the special advantage of a spiked iron collar, bristling with long nails, that helped to protect it if it was being savaged by wolves during the defence of its flocks.

In the 17th century, early French settlers took some of these dogs with them to Newfoundland, where they mated with black English Retrievers to produce the breed we now know as the Newfoundland.

With the disappearance of most of the Pyrenean predators during the 19th century, the breed gradually found itself out of work and out of favour. At the start of the 20th century it was verging on extinction, but was saved by its beauty. It became the darling of the show-ring and by 1935 had already been registered with both the AKC in the United States and the CKC in Canada. England was slower to follow suit and it was not until 1988 that the breed was accepted by the Kennel Club in London. Today it is to be found competing in dog shows all over the world and, whatever may happen to its working role in the Pyrenean Mountains, it is safe for the future in its new capacity as a much loved companion dog. In this respect it differs from some of its closest relatives, which have proved too aggressive to make the transition.

An anatomical oddity of this breed is that it has double-dewclaws on its hind legs. An occupational oddity is that these dogs were often used as smugglers. Equipped with bulging back-packs, they were despatched from one side of the Pyrenees to the other to deliver forbidden goods. Because they could take paths impassable to humans they were easily able to avoid customs officials and checkpoints.

References

1937. Trois-Fontaines, J. Harper. *Pyrenean Mountain Dogs*. Pyrenean Mountain Dogs Club of Great Britain.

1949. Crane, Mary W. *Handbook of Breed History, Being a Complete Chronicle of Breed Events from the Earliest History*. Privately published, Great Pyrenees Club of America.

1949. Trois-Fontaines, J. Harper. *My Travelling and My Dogs*. Privately published, Hyde Heath, Buckinghamshire.

1964. Smith, Edith K. *How to Raise and Train a Great Pyrenees*. TFH, New Jersey.

1975. Strang, Paul D. and Giffin, James M. *The Complete Great Pyrenees*. Howell, New York.

1978. Gordon. *The Pyrenean Mountain Dog (The Great Pyrenees)*.

1982. Duconte, Ch. and Sabouraud, J-A. *Pyrenean Dogs*. Kaye & Ward, Kingswood, Surrey.

1990. Johnson, Andrew M. *Great Pyrenees*. TFH, New Jersey.

1991. Strang, Paul D. *The New Complete Great Pyrenees*. Howell, New York.

SPAIN

MALLORQUIN SHEPHERD BALEARIC ISLANDS

Also known as the Majorca Shepherd Dog, the Majorca Sheepdog, the Perro de Pastor Mallorquin or the Ca de Bestiar, this breed has existed for centuries on the farms of the Spanish Balearic Islands in the western Mediterranean, working primarily as a livestock guard, but also as a herder and a general farm dog.

The origin of this breed is unknown, but in appearance it is very similar to the slightly larger Portuguese Cattle Dog. It is possible that one gave rise to the other, but it is not certain which was the earlier form.

Looking like a less stocky version of the Labrador, with a longer body and a more tapering muzzle, this big black dog exists in two versions — the short-haired and the long-haired. It has a lengthy, tapering, pointed tail.

Its special feature is that it can work in the intense heat of the Mallorcan summer and, for this reason, some of these dogs have been exported to Brazil, where they thrive as guard dogs on large estates.

This is strictly a working animal and has never been adapted for use as a pet or a household companion. A strictly rural, rather aggressive dog, with a powerful sense of territorial ownership, this is a pure breed not because of careful selective breeding programmes, but simply because of its long isolation in the hands of small island communities.

PYRENEAN MASTIFF SPAIN

Known in its home country as the Perro Mastin del Pireneo, the Mastin de los Pireneos or the Mastin d'Aragon, this massive dog has for centuries played an important role as the protector of the huge flocks of Spanish sheep during their annual migrations. It has also been recorded as the Navarro Mastiff.

During the first millennium BC, Phoenecian traders brought large dogs from the Middle East to the Iberian peninsula, where they became important working animals assisting in the movement and control of the enormous flocks of sheep that existed there. The biggest of these ancient dogs was a mastiff breed that was given the task of defending the flocks against attacks from wolves and bears. To assist the dogs in this task they were equipped with heavy, spiked collars.

The flocks had to be moved north every summer and south every winter, to find pasture and avoid the extremes of temperature, and the mastiffs went with them. There were only five mastiffs and one shepherd to a flock of 1,000 sheep, so their task was not easy.

As the years passed, each district developed its own local variant of mastiff and there were many regional 'breeds' that differed in little more than name. Then, in 1946, an attempt was made to bring some order to this situation and all these flock guards were reduced to two distinct types. The longer-coated, bicoloured dogs that came from the northern districts were given the name of Pyrenean Mastiff, while the smooth-coated, solid-coloured dogs from other regions were given the general name of Spanish Mastiff (see separate entry). The basic colour for the Pyrenean Mastiff is white, on which there are patches of black, brindle, grey, red or fawn. Its head is characteristically deep.

As often happens with very big dogs, this breed is gentle and calm when not threatened, and only shows its strength and aggressive power when an emergency occurs. Although it is rare today, this imposing dog is well protected by a group of devoted enthusiasts who are determined to see their ancient, native breeds flourish.

SPANISH MASTIFF SPAIN

The Spanish Mastiff has many names in its homeland, including Mastin Español, Mastin de Español, Mastin de la Mancha, Mastin de Leon and Mastin de Extremadura. Its traditional role is guarding livestock, but it has also been co-opted for boar hunting and, in recent times, has occasionally been employed to protect the home.

This impressive breed, with powerful jaws, broad head, large dewlaps, a strong neck and a massive body, has been in service in Spain for many centuries. It was first brought there by the Phoenicians back in the 1st millennium BC. From early records we know that in the 15th century AD its main function was to protect the flocks of sheep from marauding wolves, which were apparently no match for it. Because of its ingrained animosity towards its wild relatives, it had the reputation of being a danger in the presence of unfamiliar dogs. Despite this, the mighty Spanish Mastiff was said to be gentle with its human family and particularly 'gracious' with children.

In Spain today this great dog is still used as a guardian of flocks of sheep and herds of cattle in the more remote, hilly districts. It is claimed that these modern examples of the breed are no longer aggressive and satisfy themselves with barking an alarm and

leaving the rest to their human owners. They are even said to have become friendly towards other animals, and small numbers have been exported to enthusiasts in Switzerland, Germany and the United States. Whether the breed had been 'mellowed' genetically, or whether its change of character has been exaggerated, is not clear.

PORTUGAL

ALENTEJO HERDER   PORTUGAL

Also known as the Portuguese Watchdog or the Rafeiro do Alentejo, this breed has acted as a flock guard in southern Portugal for many years.

There are three Portuguese breeds employed as livestock guards: the Estrela Mountain Dog from the central region, the Portuguese Cattle Dog from the north, and this one, from the south.

The Alentejo Herder is thought to be descended from the Estrela and the Spanish Mastiff. The theory is that at one time flocks of sheep from central Portugal were brought further south to find winter pastures and that the Estrelas that came with them provided the ancestral stock. Locally, on the flat lowlands of the south near the border with Spain, these Estrelas were crossed with Spanish Mastiffs to produce a new breed, a large, fearsome, smooth-coated guardian, with a bear-like head, named after the province of Alentejo.

Aggressive, self-confident, independent, rowdy and dauntless are words that have been used to describe this breed. It has never been adapted for use in the home as a companion, is rarely seen as a show dog, and remains a practical working breed to this day. Its coat is white with either black, brindle, wolf-grey, fawn or yellow patches.

ESTRELA MOUNTAIN DOG   PORTUGAL

Also called the Portuguese Sheepdog or, in its homeland, the Cão da Serra da Estrela or the Berger da Serra da Estrela, this ancient breed has been protecting the flocks of sheep in central Portugal for many centuries.

Each spring this impressive flock guard accompanied the Portuguese sheep on their annual trek to the high ground for summer grazing, and then saw them safely back again in the autumn to the more sheltered, low-land pastures where they would pass the winter. A brave, powerful dog, it was quite capable of seeing off any hungry wolves that approached the flocks.

Because of the impressive appearance and aggressive behaviour of these dogs, local aristocrats decided to acquire some of them to use in a new role, guarding their large country estates against intruders. During the 19th century the numbers of Estrelas employed by the local shepherds began to fall, but these estate dogs retained their popularity. Because they were better fed, the estate dogs were bigger than the original sheep-guarding dogs, and this new, enlarged size was eventually to become the norm for the modern breed.

The dog first entered the show-ring in 1908 in Lisbon. In the 1930s there was a renewed interest in native Portuguese breeds and the Estrela began to flourish again. A breed standard was recorded in 1933 and a number of fine examples were exported to England and elsewhere.

Like most flock guards, this breed is renowned as much for its gentleness and friend-liness towards its owners as it is for its aggression towards intruders and its deep sus-picion of strangers. Over the centuries it has also developed a fearsome bark for rais-ing the alarm, a quality that can cause problems outside the original working context. In addition, at the slightest provocation, it is happy to display its ability to leap over very high fences. Despite these problems, those who keep Estrelas as companion dogs today report that, in the home, they are rewardingly benign and affable and especially good with children.

There are two versions of this dog, a short-haired type and a long-haired. The colours vary from fawn and wolf-grey to brindle, usually with a very dark face mask. The ears droop and the tail is long and bushy. At one point in the 20th century some crossings were made with German Shepherd Dogs, but this genetic interference was soon stopped.

References

1980. Pye, Roger F. *The Estrela Mountain Dog and its Background.* Privately published, Oporto.

PORTUGUESE CATTLE DOG PORTUGAL

Also known as the Castro Laboreiro Watch Dog, the Castro Laboreiro Dog, the Cão de Castro Laboreiro, or the Berger da Castro Laboreiro, this breed was originally developed to protect herds of cattle from the attacks of wolves and other serious predators. Its Portuguese title translates literally as 'the dog from the village of the labourers'.

This is a tough, dedicated and courageous dog that will protect its herds in all conditions, regardless of extremes of climate or terrain. Its original home was in the far north of Portugal, centred on the small village of Castro Laboreiro. Today it has been so successful as a working cattle guard that it is found throughout Portugal and has even spread abroad, as far afield as North America. Its supporters insist that it is the ideal breed for its particular task and is without equal.

It is such a reliable, efficient worker that it has acquired several secondary roles – as a property guard, a police dog and a protector of other kinds of livestock. In addition to being rugged and strong, it also happens to be extremely intelligent and capable of independent action whenever this is called for.

In origin, this breed is thought to have been the result of crossings, long ago, between the Estrela Mountain Dog of central Portugal and various local mastiffs. The tail is long and bushy and the dark coat is short, harsh and waterproof. In colour this intimidating breed varies from a dull grey to a dark brown or a grim black, either solid or brindled. It has an unusual voice which includes a threatening cry that has been formally described as 'an octave-climbing, chromatic vocalization'. To an intruder, this 'thundering bark', rising from a deep rumbling sound to a high-pitched climax, instils instant fear, usually followed by a rapid retreat. On the downside, it also makes the breed highly unsuitable for neighbourly urban living.

ITALY

MAREMMA SHEEPDOG ITALY

Also known as the Maremmes Sheepdog, the Abruzzi Sheepdog, the Pastore Abruzzese, the Mastino Abruzzese, the Maremmano, the Pastore Maremmano, the Cane da Pastore Maremmano, the Pastore Maremmano-Abruzzese, the Cane da Pastore Maremmano-Abruzzese or the Cane da Pastore dell' Italia Centrale, this breed has acted as a flock guard for many centuries.

The original function of this majestic dog was to protect the flocks of sheep from attacks by wolves and bears. Later, when these predators ceased to be a threat, the breed continued its vigil, but now against human thieves and packs of hungry stray dogs.

Sheepdogs of this type have been carrying out their duties for over 2,000 years. The ancient breed is described in detail by Varro, writing in the 1st century BC. He mentions that these dogs are 'preferably white in colour, so that they may be more readily distinguished in the dark' and that they should be 'of a leonine appearance'. When attacking marauding wolves, which at the time were a major problem, the flock guards were at serious risk and so, Varro explains: 'To protect them from being wounded by wild beasts, collars are placed on them, the so-called *melium*, that is a belt around the neck of stout leather with nails.'

The home range of this breed is from the Abruzzi to the Maremma plains of southern Tuscany. Its welfare has been jealously protected by Tuscan farmers who have resisted all attempts to see their dogs 'improved'. At one time there was a slight difference between the Abruzzi dogs and those from the Maremma plains, and they were then called by different names (the Abruzzese and the Maremmano), but in the 1950s Italian canine experts agreed that the thicker coats and sturdier bodies of the Abruzzese were insufficient to warrant a separate breed status. To keep both regions happy, the official Italian title of the breed became the cumbersome Cane da Pastore Maremmano-Abruzzese. Despite this diplomatic move, elsewhere the dog has remained universally known as the Maremma Sheepdog.

The first examples of this dog to arrive in England appeared at the London Zoo in 1827/1828, listed under the name of 'Italian Wolf Dog'. Occasional imports continued to appear during the Victorian period and Queen Victoria herself owned a pair, called Ruffo and Boldia. But it was not until the 1930s that serious attempts were made to breed Maremmas in England. Official recognition by the Kennel Club came in 1936 and the Maremma Sheepdog Club of Great Britain was formed in 1950. More recently the breed has found its way to Scandinavia, the United States and Australia. The Northern Maremma Association was founded in 1985, to further promote the breed.

A hardy breed, it is protected from the elements by its soft, dense, medium-length coat of pure white. As an extra defence against the weather, it is noted for its habit of digging sheltering burrows for itself when living outside at night alongside its flocks.

In personality this is a calm, courageous, docile, slow-to-anger dog, but one which, once it is stirred into action, is seriously aggressive. According to wartime legend a captured Maremma was placed in a holding pen overnight with seven military-trained German Shepherd Dogs. In the morning the Maremma was sitting quietly in the pen, surrounded by the corpses of seven GSDs.

GERMANY

HOVAWART   GERMANY

This breed takes its name from the early German words for farm or estate (hof) and watch or guard (wart), indicating that it was a 'guardian of the estate'. It was employed for centuries to protect the livestock and courtyards of German farms.

The earliest reference to this breed dates from 1220. In the Middle Ages it was recorded as an important courtyard guard. In more recent years the breed fell into decline. Then in the 1920s it was redeveloped by German breeders, especially Kurt König, using a mixture of farm dogs from the region of the Harz Mountains and the Black Forest. This reconstructed breed was recognized by the German Kennel Club in 1936. It did not reach the United States until the 1980s.

There are those who are sceptical about the 'rebuilding' of this breed. They believe that the modern Hovawart is merely a 'copy' of the old one, created by a careful mixing of Leonbergers, German Shepherd Dogs, Newfoundlands, Kuvasz and other breeds, to produce a 'fake' Hovawart that matched the original one in appearance but was not genetically related. Those who deny this are convinced that König and other breeders scoured German farms in the early years of the 20th century, seeking out remnants of the original breed, bringing them together and starting a new breeding programme. Nobody can be certain whether today's dogs are 'reinvented' copies, or resurrected originals, but either way, we do at least now have an animal that closely resembles the ancient, long-established livestock guardian, and we must be grateful for that.

A large, long-coated, drop-eared, bushy-tailed dog, this breed remains rare outside its homeland. It is said to be unusually intelligent, responsive, patient and reliable, with a playful streak even as an adult. The coat colour can be black, pale tan or black-and-tan.

SWEDEN

DALBO DOG   SWEDEN

An ancient Scandinavian livestock guardian, named after the Dalbo people of Sweden, this dog is also recorded as the Dahlbo Hound and the Dalbohunden. Its main centres of activity were in the Dalsland and Västergötland regions. It had a secondary role as a property guardian.

This impressive dog, described by an early traveller as 'a very lion', was employed for centuries in the northern forests to protect the local livestock from attacks by wolves, bears, wolverines and lynx. By the middle of the 19th century, however, these predators had been so widely destroyed that the value of the dogs was severely reduced. Their numbers began to decline and by the beginning of the 20th century the breed had almost vanished. A careful survey made in 1913 could not find a single living example, and it must be assumed that, by that date, the breed was extinct. Fortunately a few early photographs do survive to give us an accurate idea of its appearance.

The earliest written record of this breed dates from 1632, when the powerful livestock guards of the Dalbo people were praised for their efficiency in protecting their animals, even in the absence of human shepherds. But much earlier, even before AD 1000, there is evidence that a large livestock guardian was working in the region, because ancient examples of the typical, heavy, spiked collars worn by these dogs to protect them from the attacks of wolves have been found from that date.

This was a large, powerfully built, thick-coated dog with dropped ears, a long, muscular body and a long, fringed tail. The wolf-like colour of its coat was black with lighter patches, brown or yellow-grey. It stood 29–32 in (75–81 cm) in height.

POLAND

TATRA MOUNTAIN SHEEPDOG   POLAND

Also known as the Tatra Shepherd Dog, the Polish Tatra Sheepdog, the Polish Mountain Sheepdog, the Polish Mountain Dog, the Polish Mountain Herder, the Owczarek Podhalanski, the Owczarek Tatranski, the Iwczarej Tatrzabsju, or simply the Tatra, this breed has acted as a livestock guardian for several centuries. The Polish word for sheep is 'owca', and owczarek (pronounced 'of-shar-ek') means 'sheepdog'.

This breed hails from a region in southern Poland close by the Tatra Mountains. It is a courageous, tough, weather-resistant, independent, calm giant of a dog, standing up to 34 in (87 cm) at the shoulder. Its rich coat is so thick that combings from it are used for making woollen garments.

The Tatra is a heavily built mountain dog which is an out-and-out flock protector, with little interest in other ways of life. Attempts have been made to employ it for police, military or traction work, and as an urban guard dog, but although it is reasonably adaptable, it is only truly at home in the high pastures in the company of its sheep.

This imposing Polish flock guard is closely related to the Hungarian Kuvasz and the Slovakian Shepherd Dog. All three breeds have heavy bodies, long bushy tails and solid, creamy-white coats. It would take an expert to distinguish between them at a glance.

In the 1980s an American serviceman in Poland fell in love with this dog and imported three of them to the United States, where they formed the basis of a North American population and led to the formation of the Polish Tatra Sheepdog Club of America.

SLOVAKIA

SLOVAKIAN SHEPHERD DOG   SLOVAKIA

This is also known as the Slovak Cuvac, the Slovesnsky Tchouvatch, the Liptok, the Slovensky Kuvac, the Slovensky Cuvac, the Slovakian Cuvac, the Slovakian Chuvach or the Tatransky Cuvac. Until the recent political changes in the region, this dog would have been called a Czechoslovakian livestock guard, but today is it listed as a Slovakian breed.

This large, white, heavy-bodied, thick-coated, bushy-tailed flock guard is a close relative of the Hungarian Kuvasz, the Italian Maremma, the Greek Sheepdog and the Pyrenean Mountain Dog, and from a distance looks remarkably like them. It has been present in the rural highlands of what is now Slovakia since at least the 17th century, and probably much longer. Its traditional role was as a wolf-killer, ready at the slightest sign of danger to rush to the defence of its flocks.

It is a large, powerful dog with a personality that has been described as stubborn, fearless and independent, but which, with its human family, is also said to be calm, friendly and unusually demonstrative for such a big dog.

This has always been a rare breed and by the early part of the 20th century, with the near disappearance of European wolves, it was on the verge of extinction. Then, in the late 1940s, a rescue plan was started by an enthusiastic veterinary official at the Brno School of Veterinary Medicine, Dr Antonin Hruza. His carefully planned breeding programme saved the breed from disappearing altogether. The dog even started to become popular as a household companion, and its numbers began to rise until, in the 1960s, it was at last officially recognized as a pure breed.

There is a local legend, without any factual basis, claiming that this handsome dog is the result of a cross between a wolf and a greyhound. This story appears to have arisen because it combines the two qualities associated with these respective 'parents', being both very fierce and very fast.

HUNGARY

KUVASZ   HUNGARY

Sometimes called the Hungarian Kuvasz, this breed takes its name either from the Turkish word 'Kawasz', meaning an 'armed guard', or from the ancient Sumerian 'Ku-assa', meaning a 'horse-dog'. The plural of Kuvasz is Kuvaszok. It was developed as a guard for the flocks of sheep belonging to nomadic Hungarian shepherds.

This large dog, with its luxuriant, thick white coat, is a fearless flock guard that protects its livestock from the attacks of both wolves and human intruders. It is usually active at night, and its white colour makes it distinctive in the dim light. In the days of nomad shepherds this was an important breed, but it lost ground when more settled farming came to dominate the Hungarian countryside. As this progressed, the Kuvasz was reduced more and more to the role of a simple guard dog, wherever one was needed, in villages and eventually in towns.

This is an ancient breed, dating back thousands of years. Its ancestors are thought to have arrived in Hungary with migrant Turkish shepherds in the 12th or 13th century. In its modern form, the earliest written records date from the 17th century and the oldest illustration of one appears in 1815. A breed registry was started in 1905 and the first breed standard appeared in the same year. The breed was nearly wiped out by the chaos of World War II, but just managed to survive in a few isolated areas. A new breeding impetus followed, saving the Kuvasz from extinction. A modern standard was prepared in 1960 and the FCI accepted the breed in 1963. In 1966 revisions to the standard were added, and in 1974 the breed was accepted by the AKC in the United States.

In temperament this is an intelligent, loyal dog whose only fault is that it is sometimes too loyal and overeager to protect its human family from what it perceives as possible dangers. With its centuries-old flock-guarding background this is hardly surprising.

This breed is closely related to the Slovakian Shepherd Dog, and to the Tatra Mountain Sheepdog from Poland. All three have thick white coats and similar body shapes, and perform similar duties. It takes an expert eye to tell them apart. For the Kuvasz, the clue is in the shape of the head, this breed having a more distinctive, elegantly tapering muzzle.

References

1969. Alvi, Dana I. *How to Raise and Train a Kuvasz.* TFH, New Jersey.

1997. Alvi, Dana I. *Kuvasz: A Complete and Reliable Handbook.* TFH, New Jersey.

KOMONDOR   HUNGARY

The Komondor is known everywhere by its Hungarian name, the plural of which is Komondorok. In origin, the name is thought to come from the French word 'commandeur', meaning commander. This is the largest of the Hungarian native breeds and is used to protect the flocks of sheep, or herds of cattle, from attacks by thieves or predators, while the task of herding the livestock is left to smaller dogs.

The special feature of the Komondor is its white, massively thick, heavy, corded top-coat, with a dense, woolly undercoat. Described as 'the most profuse coat in the canine world', it serves to protect the animal in three ways: it keeps it warm in the cold winters, shields its skin from the burning sun in the hot summers, and makes it difficult for predators such as wolves to bite through to the dog's flesh. In addition, it acts as a disguise when the dog is mingling with a group of sheep, making it look like just another member of the flock and giving it the advantage of an element of surprise when responding to a predator attack. The predators include bears as well as wolves, and the Komondor must also be prepared to defend its flock against assaults from human thieves and brigands. In the United States this breed is now being employed in some regions to protect flocks from coyotes.

This is an ancient breed, thought to have arrived in Hungary with Mongolian hordes back in the 13th century. According to one authority, it is a descendant of the Aftscharka, which was found by the nomadic hordes on the southern steppes as they swept through Russia. However, the earliest definite record of the breed's name does not appear until 1544. A little later, in 1673, there is a comment that 'the Komondor guards the herd', confirming that this breed has been employed in its special role for at least 300 years. The first known illustration of the dog dates from 1815. Its appearance has changed little over the centuries, except that it has become slightly larger in size in modern times.

Komondor puppies are reared with their flocks, so that the dogs have a special attachment to them and will give their lives for them if necessary. They are exceptionally courageous, always vigilant and totally loyal. Inevitably, they are wary of strangers, but are extremely gentle with their close human companions. It is said that it is difficult to tell the changing mood of a Komondor, partly because its hair completely covers its face, concealing any expressions, and strangers are warned to approach one with caution. Despite its shaggy, cuddly appearance, this is not a breed that 'tries to please' or that enjoys being petted. It is a highly intelligent dog, which is prepared to learn (but is also capable of being remarkably stubborn) and is always ready to fight in defence of its livestock.

References

1966. Beregi, Oscar and Benis, Leslie. *How to Raise and Train a Komondor.* TFH, New Jersey.

1990. Evers, Irene. *Our National Treasure, the Hungarian Komondor.* Middle Atlantic States Komondor Club, Princeton, New Jersey.

1992. Kenez and Mut. *The Komondor Defined & a Description of the Shepherd Dog.*

1993. Beregi, Oscar. *Komondors.* TFH, New Jersey.

Levy, Joy C. *The Komondor in the United States, 1937–1976.*

SLOVENIA

KARST SHEPHERD
SLOVENIA

Also known as the Krasky Ovcar, the Karski Ovcar, the Krasski Ovccar, the Karst Schäferbund, the Karst Sheepdog, the Istrian Sheepdog or the Istrian Shepherd, this breed has been guarding the flocks in the Balkans since the Middle Ages. It takes the name of Karst from the region in which it is most commonly found.

This is an ancient breed, which was described in detail as long ago as 1687. In more recent times, until towards the end of the 20th century, it was regarded as a Yugoslavian breed, but since Slovenia declared its independence in 1990, it has been undergoing a revival there and is now classified as Slovenian.

The fighting in the Balkan states during the latter part of the 20th century decimated the dog population, but with the return of peace Slovenia has been quick to rebuild its population of indigenous animals. As a result the numbers of this breed are on the increase and its future appears to be assured. It is now listed as a 'Slovene Natural Treasure', and by the start of the 21st century there were reported to be no fewer than 1,000 of these dogs in the country. There are also active breeders in Germany and Italy.

This is a pastoral guard with a very heavy, dense coat, 4 in (10 cm) thick, and a primitive, wolf-like colouring. It has powerful jaws, drooped ears and a long, bushy tail. In personality it has been described at various times as cheerful, reliable, stable, loyal, serious, kind-hearted and calmly fearless. It sees itself as a partner rather than a subordinate.

It has a close relative in the Illyrian Sheepdog, further south in Macedonia (see separate entry).

BOSNIA-HERZEGOVINA

TORNJAK   BOSNIA- HERZEGOVINA

Also known as the Bonanski Ovcar Tornjak, this ancient breed has been protecting the flocks of sheep and cattle in Bosnia and Croatia for at least 1,000 years. The Croatian word 'tor' means a sheep-pen.

The earliest written description of this large dog is to be found in the archives of a bishop in the year 1062. It is mentioned again, in later archives, in 1374 and 1752. It has always been a dog of the hilly country, and in more modern times its largest numbers have been concentrated in the mountains of central Bosnia and western Herzegovina. There has been some argument as to whether this is truly a Bosnian or a Croatian breed and recently several books have appeared that list it as a 'Croatian indigenous and autochthonous breed'.

In origin this heavily built dog has been viewed as a descendant of the Tibetan Mastiff, with the later addition of spitz dogs and possibly some back-crossing to the wolf.

According to the shepherds who work with these dogs, keeping them close to their flocks day and night, they are capable of chasing away marauding bears and any one of them is more than a match for two hungry wolves. In addition to their bravery, they are also extremely loyal, often stubborn, wary of strangers and rather dignified. Their owners describe them as noble dogs, never looking for a fight, but ready to defend their flocks to the death if necessary.

The ears are folded. The tail is bushy and is held high 'like a banner' when the dog is active. The protective coat is long and thick. It is accepted in any colour or colour-pattern. The height is 24–27 in (60–70 cm) and the weight 77–99 lb (35–45 kg).

This rare breed is not yet recognized internationally and its numbers are low. In 1997 there were only about 200 of these dogs with registered pedigrees. They are, however, becoming more popular at local dog shows, and as many as 30 entries have appeared in recent times in a single show. This newly aroused interest in the breed bodes well for its future. In1996 it was given an extra boost when it was chosen to appear on a Bosnian postage stamp.

RUMANIA

CARPATHIAN SHEPHERD DOG   RUMANIA

This breed is sometimes referred to as the Carpathian Sheepdog. It also used to be called the Rumanian Sheepdog or the Rumanian Herder, but in recent years the Rumanian Kennel Club has recognized two native sheepdog breeds, separated largely on the basis of coat type. The old Rumanian Sheepdog is now called either a Carpathian or a Mioritic. Both are employed as flock guards.

This large, sturdy, long-coated breed is closely related to the flock guardians of Greece, Hungary, Slovakia and Poland. It is slightly smaller than its close relative, the Mioritic Shepherd Dog (see separate entry), with a narrower muzzle and a darker coat. The coat colour is variable, and may be black, black-and-tan, black-and-white, brindle, grey, or tan, in either solid, bicolour or tricolour patterns.

A curious custom of the Rumanian shepherds has been to dock the last third of the long bushy tails of their dogs. This is done, it seems, in order to encourage the surviving tail section to stand up more readily as a kind of identity flag when the dog is working among the sheep.

As with the Greek Sheepdog (see separate entry), a suspended log is sometimes attached to the collar in order to curb the attacking power of these aggressive dogs. This log also identifies them as 'owned' dogs as opposed to feral dogs which may be shot on sight.

The homeland of this breed is the region of the Carpathian Mountains in eastern Rumania. It has rarely if ever been seen outside that area and is becoming rare even within it. There has been a certain amount of genetic dilution caused by the infiltration of foreign breeds, but recently a special effort has been made by Rumanian canine enthusiasts to foster pure-breeding and keep the original type in an unaltered condition.

MIORITIC SHEPHERD DOG   RUMANIA

This breed is sometimes given the slightly different name of Mioritic Sheepdog. Like the Carpathian Shepherd Dog, it was once also known by the general title of Rumanian Sheepdog, but is now considered to be a separate breed. It is also employed as a guardian of the flocks.

This breed has a heavier head than its Carpathian relative. It also has a thicker, shaggier coat and a more stolid, stocky body. Its dense, sheep-like coat is usually solid white, but there may be some brownish markings in the head region.

This is an ancient breed. Medieval records reveal that, in 1359, a Mioritic Shepherd Dog called Molda died while trying to protect her master, King Bogdan, when he was being gored by an enraged bull.

Described as a natural, intelligent, charismatic dog, this breed has been largely ignored outside its homeland but that is now changing. It is a huge dog standing nearly 3 ft (90 cm) tall at the shoulder. It weighs almost 200 lb (90 kg), but despite its great size has a remarkably gentle disposition. Only when its flock is threatened does it become aggressive. Then it is transformed from a docile, calmly disciplined dog into a raging fury which knows no fear.

In Rumania the Mioritic has become a high-status breed. Both the son of the president and the minister of agriculture are owners of this impressive dog.

BULGARIA

KARAKACHAN DOG   BULGARIA

This large dog has been employed for centuries to protect the domestic livestock in Bulgaria from attacks by wolves. It is named after the Karakachan people, who are semi-nomadic livestock-breeders and shepherds.

This heavily built, thick-coated, white dog, with dark markings on the head and body, is an ancient flock guardian whose traditional role has been to defend its livestock against marauding wolf packs. It is a hard-working animal. Two dogs can successfully protect a flock of 300 sheep. Five dogs can protect flocks of 1,000 sheep.

In recent years, the breed has become increasingly rare. This has been due to the widespread hunting and poisoning of the wolves during the 20th century, which reduced their total population in Bulgaria to about 100 by the 1960s.

With this reduction in the threat from wolves, the role of the flock guardians became almost obsolete, and inevitably their numbers fell, too. But then, with attitudes towards wildlife changing, the population of wolves in Bulgaria began to rise once more and by the end of the 20th century it had grown to 800. The result has been an increasing number of attacks on livestock, and the Bulgarian forestry committee now feels that the wolf population should be reduced to between 150 and 200, to ease matters. More poisoning has been proposed. Conservationists and an organization called Semperviva, a biodiversity preservation society, are strongly opposed to this and believe that, if the domestic flocks can be adequately protected, the wolf population can be left in peace. There are, after all, wild ungulates, such as roe deer, red deer and wild boar, to provide natural food for the wolves if they can be kept away from the easy pickings of the domestic livestock. About 30 per cent of the country is still covered in forests, and it should be able to sustain a natural prey–predator balance of wildlife, if only the vulnerable flocks can be adequately guarded. To this end, Semperviva is now actively rearing the rare Karakachan Dogs at special breeding stations and is supplying free pairs of puppies to the shepherds. In this way, the organization hopes to see a return to the situation where the numbers of both the endangered wolves and the endangered flock guards can remain high enough to ensure the future survival of both.

In recent years a few Karakachan Dogs have been exported to the United States, where they are now being bred on the Circle Z Farm in Oklahoma. This will undoubtedly improve the breed's chances of thriving in the 21st century.

MACEDONIA

ILLYRIAN SHEEPDOG   MACEDONIA

Also known as the Ilirski Ovcar, the Jugoslovenski Ovcarski Pas-Sarplaninac, the Sarplaninac (pronounced 'shar-pla-nee-natz'), the Sar Planina, the Sar Planine, the Sharplaninec, the Charplanina or the Charplaninatz, this is a working dog that has been protecting the flocks of sheep in the Illyrian mountain pastures for centuries. Its local name is derived from the Sarplanina Mountains. Its international title of Illyrian Sheepdog refers to the ancient name of the region. It was once known as the Yugoslav Shepherd Dog or the Yugoslavian Herder, but since the break-up of Yugoslavia into several smaller nations at the end of the 20th century, it has been reclassified as a Macedonian breed. To its friends it is known simply as the 'Sar'.

This long-established, heavily built flock guard, with its thick, wolf-like coat and its long, bushy tail, is fearless in its defence of its livestock, taking on all-comers, whether human or animal, without hesitation. It is a rugged breed, sleeping outdoors in all weathers and quite capable of surviving even the most icy of winter conditions. Described by one author as 'the pearl in the snow', its main area of activity is the mountainous Massif of Sarplanina, Korab, Stogovo, Bistra and Mavrovo.

It is believed to have descended from the early molossian dogs of Greece and the livestock-guarding breeds of Turkey. In addition to protecting the flocks of sheep, it is also capable of guarding cattle and goats when the occasion arises.

It was first officially recognized as a distinct breed in 1930 and was accepted by the FCI in 1939, but it was not until the 1970s that it reached the New World. The first examples to arrive in America appeared in 1975 and 1977. Since then, in both the United States and Canada, it has found favour on ranches where it acts as a livestock guard against attacks by coyotes. An immensely powerful dog with large teeth, it is a match for any wild predator. Like many flock guards, it is calm when there are no threats to its territory, its family or its livestock, but once challenged it leaps into action and in an instant becomes a ball of fury.

SAR TIP

MACEDONIA

A close relative of the Illyrian Sheepdog, this little-known breed is a giant version of its better-known cousin.

Whereas the height of the Illyrian Sheepdog is 22–23 in (56–58 cm), that of the Sar Tip is over 25½ in (65 cm). It is an even more powerful dog, developed for 'heavy duty' work in certain areas. In other respects it is similar, both in appearance and character, to the smaller breed, being 'grave and undemonstrative in demeanour', but courageous when defending its herd. A faithful and obedient dog, the Sar Tip always remains suspicious of strangers.

ALBANIA

ALBANIAN WOLFDOG

ALBANIA

Sometimes described as the Albanian Wolfhound or simply the Albanian Dog, this ancient, extinct breed was employed to protect the flocks of sheep from attacks by marauding wolves. In a secondary role it was also occasionally used to hunt both wolves and wild boar.

In earlier days this flock guard was regarded as so ferocious that special warnings had to be given to strangers visiting the Albanian countryside. They were told that, under no circumstances, were they to shoot at the dogs to protect themselves. But the sight of one of these animals approaching aggressively was apparently so terrifying that, despite this warning, panic-stricken strangers did, indeed, occasionally draw their guns in self-defence. If this action was observed by the owners of these huge dogs, they had no hesitation in shooting the strangers dead on the spot, so valuable were their working animals.

Some authorities consider this breed to be one of the ancestral forms of the German Shepherd Dog. It was similar in many ways but, being a specialist 'guardian dog', lacked the modern German breed's herding ability.

Because of its reputation for ferocity, it aroused public curiosity and was a popular exhibit on the rare occasions when one was put on show. With this in mind, examples were exhibited at the London Zoo in the 19th century.

In retrospect it has to be said that the reportedly savage nature of this breed was probably an exaggeration. It seems to have been based on a wildly inaccurate, ancient tale told by Pliny the Elder in his great *Natural History* of AD 77. According to him, the king of Albania gave one of these dogs to Alexander the Great. It was an animal of 'huge and extraordinary bigness' and Alexander was so delighted by it that he decided to test it out by loosing it against bear, then against wild boar and finally against fallow deer. The enormous dog failed to respond, sitting quietly on the ground and making no attempt to attack the prey. Alexander misinterpreted the dog's behaviour, assuming that it was cowardly, and promptly had the unfortunate animal put to death.

When the king of Albania heard of this, he sent a second dog to Alexander, saying that the prey offered to the dog had been 'such little beasts' that it had ignored them, not because it was afraid, but because it considered the task beneath it. The king suggested that Alexander should offer the second dog some sport that was worthy of its brutal power, proposing lions and elephants as more suitable opponents. Alexander agreed and set the new dog against a lion. The Albanian Wolfdog fearlessly broke the lion's back and tore its body to pieces. He then set it against an elephant and the dog flew at the great animal, darting this way and that, until 'the Elephant grew giddy in the head, insomuch as he came tumbling down'.

It was this wildly inaccurate story, told and retold, that was probably the main source of the Albanian Wolfdog's fearsome reputation. In reality, the incident with the elephant took place in northern India and the dog in question was a gift from a defeated Asian king, who ruled the region now known as the Punjab (see entry for Neapolitan Mastiff). It happened in 326 BC, but two centuries later the Romans did import fierce dogs from Albania, and Pliny can be forgiven for confusing the two.

Canine authors writing in the middle of the 19th century have left us more factual details concerning the appearance of this breed. It was about the same size as a mastiff, with a height of 27–28 in (69–71 cm). It had close, silky hair, a pointed muzzle, powerful body and legs, and a long, bushy tail. The coat colour was fawn 'variously clouded with brown'.

GREECE/ALBANIA

GREEK SHEEPDOG   GREECE/ALBANIA

The Greek Sheepdog has been pure-bred by local shepherds for centuries as a flock guard.

This pure white dog has changed little over the years. In the 17th and 18th centuries it was slightly bigger than it usually is today, although even now in the more remote mountain districts it may retain its original, impressive size. Any non-white puppies appearing in litters have always been destroyed because they are thought to be unlucky.

A pastoral breed found in Epirus, Macedonia, southern Greece and the Parnassus ranges, it also occurs in the Balkan mountains and in Albania. It is closely related to the

other large, white-coated flock guards of Europe, especially the Hungarian Kuvasz, the Italian Maremma Sheepdog and the Polish Tatra Mountain Sheepdog.

There are two curious traditions involved in the way that this breed is treated by its sheep-herding owners. The first concerns its ears. The right ear only is cropped, while the left ear is left in its natural, drooping condition, giving the dog's head an asymmetrical appearance. This is done because it is believed that this strange procedure will improve the animal's hearing abilities. The second custom is to hang a small log from the collar around the dog's neck, supposedly to curb its energy and its aggression.

In personality, this is undeniably a ferocious breed, so well tuned to defending its flocks that it sometimes oversteps the mark. Any strangers approaching its territory, whether human or animal, are liable to be attacked. It has never been kept as a pet or exhibited in a dog show. It is purely a rural, working dog.

TURKEY

AKBASH DOG

TURKEY

Also known as the Turkish Guard Dog or the Akbas, this breed has been protecting the flocks of sheep and goats in western Turkey for many years. The word 'akbash' means 'white head'. It has also sometimes been called the Akkush Dog. 'Akkush' means 'white bird'.

This is one of the three flock-guarding dogs indigenous to Turkey recognized by Turkish canine experts. (For the other two – the Kangal from central Turkey and the Kars from eastern Turkey – see separate entries.)

The Akbash is a pure white guard dog, similar to those found protecting the flocks in the countries to the west of Turkey, such as Greece, Hungary, Poland and Italy. It appears in both short- and long-coated forms. Its white coat was developed to help the shepherds distinguish it from wolves in dim light.

Some American and European breeders have lumped this dog together with the two other regional breeds under the general heading of 'Anatolian Shepherd Dog'. They see the three merely as colour variants of one another, rather than as distinct breeds. However, in 1996, an International Symposium on the subject of Turkish Shepherd Dogs took place in Turkey, at the faculty of Veterinary Science in Konya, and it was categorically decided to reject this concept of a single breed of Turkish flock guard. It was agreed that in each of the three major geographical zones of the country — west, central and east — there exists a distinctive, true-breeding dog. The fact that, in the areas between the centres of these zones, there are intermediate types of dog does not invalidate this three-breed concept.

There is now an Akbash Dog Association International, based in the United States, which is actively promoting and supporting this breed as a flock guard in North America and elsewhere. In the United States it is sometimes used to protect livestock from attacks by coyotes.

When its flock is not under threat from predators, the Akbash is a stately, calm, steady dog that bonds tightly with its sheep from an early age. Little puppies are introduced to their livestock and become so attached to them that it is almost impossible to keep them apart in later life. This attachment is so extreme that it can even cause problems when shepherds are attempting to mate a pair of dogs, neither partner being prepared to abandon its flock, even for the excitement of a sexual encounter.

ANATOLIAN SHEPHERD DOG   TURKEY

This is the name given to the Turkish flock-guarding dogs by those authorities who believe there is only one breed of these dogs in the entire country. They accept that there are local variations, but do not consider these of importance. It has also been recorded as the Anatolian Shepherd or the Anatolische Herdershond. The Turkish name for these dogs is Coban Kopegi (also given as Koban Copegi or Choban Kopeyi), which translates simply as 'Shepherd's Dog'. These dogs have been used for thousands of years to protect the flocks of sheep and herds of goats from the attacks of predators.

In 1967, when stationed in Turkey, Lt Robert Ballard of the US Navy acquired a pair of working shepherd-dog puppies called Zorba and Peki. Zorba, the male, was a long-coated brown-and-white pinto, and Peki, the female, was buff-coloured. They came from a rural district near the capital, Ankara. He took them back to America where, in 1970, they produced their first litter and provided the foundation stock for the breed in the United States. A breed club was formed which, today, has over a thousand dogs on its register.

What Lt Ballard had ignored, in establishing this new breed, was the existence of three distinct regional types of flock-guard dogs in Turkey, one in the west (the Akbash), one in the central region (the Kangal) and one in the east (the Kars). In the zones between these three true-breeding centres, there are intermediate flock-guard dogs of varying type. The developing American breed, which had now been given the formal name of Anatolian Shepherd Dog, was from an intermediate zone and was based on stock that had not been breeding true in the past. The result was that puppies with a variety of colours, patterns and coat types were appearing. To the American breeders, these were no more than minor colour variations. They viewed their dogs as representing all Turkish flock guards and envisaged them as a single, if slightly variable breed.

Inside Turkey itself the title of 'Anatolian Shepherd Dog' was unknown. They named their working dogs by the localities in which they lived. In later years this would lead to heated controversy, with American breeders insisting that their dog, which, decade by decade, was steadily being improved by further careful selection, was the only true Turkish flock guardian, and that other so-called Turkish breeds were mere colour variants. Turkish experts, on the other hand, dismissed the American breed as the creation of 'amateur dog enthusiasts who had little idea of how to formulate hypotheses about Turkish dogs'. They went on to say that, when later Turkish stock was sought, to add to the American gene pool (in the 1980s), 'Anatolian Shepherd Dog fanciers took short trips to Turkey to rush about the countryside, buy a dog or two, and bring them back home'. American breeders retorted that these remarks suggested that someone was trying to 'start a fad' for dubious Turkish breeds. Robert Ballard himself entered the fray, stating: 'To regard the different colour patterns as separate breeds is, if not dishonest, at least misleading.'

Insults and counter-insults have been hurled back and forth in this way for some time. The irony is that everyone involved loves Turkish flock guards and looks upon them as magnificent, noble canines. For an objective outsider the simplest solution is to recognize four breeds. First, there is this one, the Anatolian Shepherd Dog, with its own breed standard that by now, after decades of planned breeding, differs from that of the three regional breeds (the Akbash Dog, the Kangal Dog and the Kars Dog) so strongly favoured by the canine experts inside Turkey. The Anatolian Shepherd Dog may have been started from a mixed gene base, but it has been steadily improved and is now much more inclined to breed true. This is partly because of a later, major injection of pure-breeding Kangal Dogs. Even this, however, does not appease the Turkish experts, who comment: 'So many Kangal Dogs have been imported or acquired for the Anatolian gene pool that increasing numbers of Anatolians do indeed look like Kangal Dogs. However, they are not purebred Kangal Dogs and the litters they produce continue to be highly variable in type.'

Be that as it may, to most dog enthusiasts in the West, the modern Anatolian Shepherd Dog remains an imposing, almost leonine presence in the show-ring, in the home or out working with livestock on the ranch. The breed has spread out from the United States to Canada, Mexico, Europe and Japan.

Inevitably these dogs still appear in a variety of colours, including both 'karabash' (black-headed) and 'akbash' (white-headed) forms. The muscular body is well balanced, carrying a massive head and a long tail that hangs low when the dog is quiet and curls up over its back, spitz-like, when it becomes active.

With careful training, Anatolians can be made into impressive house pets, but there are problems. After thousands of years of development as flock guards, they tend to view every visitor as a potential threat and act accordingly. As one owner put it: 'When arriving at our home, neither long-term friends nor strangers would be foolish enough to get out of their cars.' They must sit there patiently and await the arrival of the dogs' owners.

An anecdote gives some idea of the ferocious strength of these dogs. On an American ranch, a pack of hounds was pursuing a raccoon in the direction of a flock of sheep. The flock-guarding dog saw the pack approaching and stood its ground. As the pack came close, the huge dog methodically killed the hounds one by one, until the entire pack lay dead at its feet. No challenge is too great, when this mighty flock guard's sheep appear to be under threat.

KANGAL DOG TURKEY

In England this dog was given the name of Anatolian Karabash. The word 'karabash' means 'black head'. In earlier centuries it was sometimes known as the Samsun Dog. It was developed over thousands of years by the Kangal shepherds to protect their flocks.

This is one of the three Turkish flock guards recognized as true-breeding dogs by Turkish canine experts. It is found in central Turkey in the Kangal district of Sivas province, in the harsh, isolated plateau region where its geographical segregation has kept it free of cross-breeding for centuries.

The precise origin of this highly prized, localized dog from Turkey is unknown, but it is believed that its ancestors were a type of mastiff, bred to hunt lions in ancient times. This is a powerfully muscled, sturdy breed with a short but dense coat, and an up-curled, spitz-type tail. In colour it is usually cream, tan or pale greyish-brown, except for a dark face-mask and dark ears.

Some of these Kangal Dogs were exported to England in the mid-1960s, where an Anatolian Karabash Dog Club was formed to promote and support them. This club insisted on the correct Kangal colouring, of pale body with black head. They later came into conflict with the Anatolian Shepherd Dog Club of Great Britain, whose dogs were obtained, not just from the Kangal district of central Turkey, but from several other regions as well and who, as a result of this, agreed with their American counterpart in allowing a wide variety of colours. The Kennel Club in London did their best to resolve this conflict diplomatically by stating: 'All colours acceptable but it is desirable that they should be whole colours, cream to fawn, with black mask and ears.' This compromise has never satisfied the purists, who support a campaign 'to return to the original Turkish Kangal Dog standard for those dogs which can demonstrate pure Kangal lineage'.

In Turkey itself, the importance of the native Kangal Dog has at last been recognized and it is now being treated as a 'national treasure', appearing on postage stamps and being pure-bred in special kennels operated by the Turkish government and various academic institutions, where pedigrees are carefully maintained.

In personality, this is a loyal, obedient, dedicated dog with great physical stamina. Its movement is described as elegant. In its homeland it is strictly a working breed and is never used as a pet dog.

This is a ferocious, courageous breed. In the old days, when one of these great dogs had killed a wolf, it was rewarded with a special iron collar as a badge of honour; these collars also protected the dogs against throat-bites from wolves. During times of war, the dogs were trained to leap up and drag a mounted warrior from his saddle and hurl him to the ground.

KARS DOG   TURKEY

This little-known breed is the Turkish equivalent of the Caucasian Mountain Dog from Georgia. It is a flock guard from the far north-east of Turkey and is named after the town at the heart of the region where it is found. The town of Kars is located to the north of Lake Van near the border with Georgia.

The Kars Dog is one of three native flock guards found in Turkey. Coming from the most remote region, in the extreme east of the country, it is the least well documented. It has been described as a 'rough-looking, primarily dark-coloured dog' from the Pontic or 'Little Caucasus' Mountains. Another author calls it a 'multicoloured, heavy-coated dog'.

The first formal report on this breed was given by David Nelson at the 1996 International Symposium on the subject of Turkish Shepherd Dogs that took place in Turkey, at the faculty of Veterinary Science in Konya. It remains to be seen whether it attracts further attention in the future.

NORTH AFRICA

ATLAS SHEEPDOG   MOROCCO/ALGERIA/TUNISIA

This North African breed is known by many names, including the Atlas Dog, the Chien de l'Atlas, the Berber Dog, the Kabyle Dog, the North African Kabyle, the Kabil, the Ouled Naïl Dog, the Shawia Dog, the Douar Dog and the Aidi. It is employed by various Berber tribes to protect their goats and sheep, and has secondary roles as a watchdog and an occasional game-tracker.

This breed is essentially a refined, enlarged version of the common Pariah Dog of Africa, specially adapted for protecting domestic herds of goats and flocks of sheep in the Atlas Mountains of north-west Africa. It is 21–24 in (53–61 cm) in height and weighs about 50 lb (23 kg). It is typically off-white in colour, but may occasionally be cream, fawn, fawn-and-white, or black-and-white. Its coat is thick and soft and it has a powerful, muscular body, with pricked ears and a bushy tail.

It has been suggested that the Atlas Sheepdog may be the original ancestor of the Pyrenean Mountain Dog. The Moroccan Kennel Association has taken an interest in this dog in recent times and is making efforts to foster it as a pure breed.

The reason that this breed has so many names is that the Berber peoples are made up of a number of tribal subdivisions. When the dogs of one of these tribes are studied, they are usually named after that group. But if an overall view is taken, it soon becomes clear that, although there are some slight local variations, the Berber dogs of the Atlas region are all basically the same type and can best be described simply as Atlas Sheepdogs. Some of the local names are restricted to a region within a particular country. The Aidi, for example, is from Morocco and the Shawia, the Ouled Naïl, and the Kabyle from different parts of Algeria.

EGYPT

EGYPTIAN SHEEPDOG   EGYPT

This breed is also called the Armant, the Armenti, the Ermenti, the Sabe, the Hawara Dog or the Chien de Berger Égyptien. Armant is the name of a town on the left bank of the Nile, near Luxor. 'Sabe' is an Arabic word meaning 'lion' and referring to the breed's ferocity and its legendary roots. Hawara is the name of the local Berber tribe, who have for many years used these dogs as livestock guards.

This is a large, shaggy dog with a controversial origin. According to a much repeated tale, it is descended from European dogs brought to Egypt by Napoleon's army during his Egyptian campaign and left there in the vicinity of the village of Armant when they departed. (Armant has since grown into an industrial town.)

A rival view is that it is descended from a

guard dog left there by a Russian visitor some time before the middle of the 19th century. Both these views are clearly attempts to explain why a hot-country dog should be burdened with such a thick, cold-country coat.

Unfortunately, there is no evidence to support either of these views and it is now believed that this breed is, in fact, a modified, enlarged, true-breeding, shaggy version of the North African Pariah Dog, with a rough coat that may be black, black-and-white, tan-and-white, or grizzle-and-white.

In its earlier days this breed was valued for its power, its intelligence and its courage, but in recent times it has not been sufficiently protected from random cross-breeding, and its status is now in doubt. As a result it has become increasingly variable in type and has been dropped as a recognized breed by the FCI. Its best hope for the future is that there are isolated pockets of undiluted examples that could eventually be collected together to create the foundation stock needed to rebuild the breed.

A few of these dogs have been brought to Europe, many years ago, but there are no records of them having bred there. At present this appears to be an interesting breed badly in need of someone to champion its cause.

RUSSIA

CAUCASIAN MOUNTAIN DOG RUSSIA

Also called the Caucasian Sheepdog or the Caucasian Ovtcharka, this breed has many local names. Among its other titles are the Kawkasky Ovtcharka, the Kavkazskaya Ovcharka (in Russia), the Nagazi (in Georgia), the Gampr (in Armenia), the Kaukasische Herdershond (in Holland) and the Kaukasische Schäferhund (in Germany). The term 'ovtcharka' (sometimes spelled 'owtscharka' or 'ovcharka') indicates a shepherd's guard dog, rather than a herding sheepdog.

For more than six centuries these large dogs have protected the huge flocks of sheep that enjoy the pastures of the Caucasian mountain range in south-western Russia and neighbouring countries. The primary function of this breed has always been to defend the vulnerable sheep against attacks from predators such as wolves and from human thieves. Powerful dogs, usually with rather wolf-like markings, they have heavy, muscular bodies, and thick coats that protect them from the harshness of their environment. Their life is a hard one and it has created an aggressive, tough, fearless breed.

Because the mountain shepherds bred them for personality, strength and stamina, rather than for precise anatomy, there has been some variability in the appearance of these dogs, a variability that has kept them out of the show-ring. And their ruggedness has also kept them from becoming cosy house pets. Despite this, they are imposing, impressive dogs and deserve more attention than they have received in the past.

In temperament they are described as steady and even-tempered, willing and trainable, loyal and faithful, gentle and patient, intelligent and demonstrative. However, when they feel threatened, they are also bold and ferocious, and prone to bark noisily at the slightest nocturnal disturbance. In other words, like so many livestock guards, they have been bred for many generations to be affectionate with their owners, but as aggressive as possible with intruders and strangers.

Their origin is disputed. Some authorities believe they are the result of crossings between mastiffs and sheepdogs; others see them as descending from Tibetan Mastiffs about 2,000 years ago; others prefer a Mesopotamian origin; still others prefer to record them simply as indigenous dogs, and leave it at that. Whichever view is correct, it is certain that this is an ancient breed, created as a distinct type by its isolation from others. At least, that was the case until recently. Now, however, with increased movement in the region, it is claimed that between 70 and 80 per cent of today's Caucasian dogs have been genetically diluted by crosses with other breeds such as the St Bernard. Careful work is now being done to rectify this and to obtain full-blood Caucasian Mountain Dogs for future breeding programmes. The Caucasian Ovcharka Club of America, founded in 1991, is especially active in this area.

CENTRAL ASIAN SHEPHERD DOG RUSSIA

Also known as the Alabai, the Mid-Asian Shepherd, the Central Asian Sheepdog, the Central Asian Owcharka (also written as Ovcharka or Ovtcharka), the Middle Asian Owcharka, the Sredneaziatskaya Owcharka, or simply the Asian Shepherd, this ancient breed has been guarding livestock in remote areas of Russia for centuries.

With many breeds of big, heavily built dogs, it is popular to claim that they are 'probably descended from the Tibetan Mastiff'. This has also been said of the Central Asian, but one authority reverses this, listing it instead as 'believed to be an ancestor of the Tibetan Mastiff'. If this is true, it places this dog at the very root of the large-dog tree. One Russian author recently described it as 'the oldest Livestock Guardian breed in the world'.

This dog has existed over a huge range, from central Russia to Siberia and Mongolia, and there has undoubtedly been a certain amount of random crossing with other dogs in some areas. In other regions, however, it is so isolated that it has remained untainted for countless years. Today the purest form of the Central Asian is said to be found in the remote regions of Tadzhikistan, Uzbekistan and Kazakhstan. In Kirgyzstan, where it was once common, it is sadly now extinct, and as a working dog its numbers are in decline almost everywhere. In a few regions, however, it has recently been recognized as a 'national treasure' and support groups have been formed. This is true, for example, in Turkmenistan.

This strange dog, which traditionally has had its tail and its ears lopped off at birth, and which appears in many colour varieties and coat patterns, acts as a protector of livestock and also of the (often nomadic) people who own it. It is strictly a guarding dog and, as such, is capable of working in extremes of temperature and landscape. In temperament it is unusually lethargic, conserving its energy until the moment when it perceives that there has been an intrusion into its territory. Then it is instantly transformed into a fast, fearless and powerful defender.

The Central Asian Shepherd Dog was rarely been seen outside its vast homeland until recently, but towards the end of the 20th century a few of them were co-opted for other duties, such as competing in the show-ring and acting as urban house pets. Their popularity increased rapidly. At a major dog show held in Moscow in April 2000, there were no fewer than 270 examples of this breed on display. In the same year at an international dog show in Milan there were 42 Central Asians competing, including examples from Russia, Poland, Hungary, Italy and the Czech Republic.

Examples of this dog that have a contrasting dark-and-white coat pattern often display a balanced pair of 'eye markings' just above the real eyes. These small spots of pale colour sometimes stand out more conspicuously than the real eyes, and it seems probable that this breed is the one which, when it reached east to Mongolia, was referred to as the 'Four-eyed Mongolian Dog'.

SOUTH RUSSIAN SHEPHERD DOG   RUSSIA

Also known as the South Russian Sheepdog, the South Russian Ovtcharka, the Ovtcharka de Russie Meridionale, the Ioujnorousskaia Ovtcharka or simply the Owtchah, this breed has been employed for over 200 years to protect the flocks of sheep in the steppes of the Ukraine in southern Russia.

At the end of the 18th century, Spanish flock-guard dogs were taken to Russia where they were crossed with the local Russian flock guards to create this new breed, which came to be known as the South Russian Shepherd Dog. The reason for the importation of Spanish dogs was that Spanish sheep were being imported and their canine guardians came with them. These dogs were not, however, suited to the new environment, where wolves were a constant threat to the livestock. A bigger, tougher breed was required and the crossings with the local dogs created this ideal canine.

Nearly 3 ft (90 cm) tall at the shoulder, this gigantic animal was a match for any predator. The size of a Great Dane, but with a heavier body and a long, shaggy, white coat, this is a dog that commands instant respect. A Great Dane or an Irish Wolfhound weighs up to 120 lb (54 kg), while the South Russian weighs up to 165 lb (75 kg). Despite his huge size, however, he is amazingly alert at all times and incredibly fast to react, and to move, when there is a hint of danger.

Although friendly enough with its owners, this is a domineering and possessive animal that hates strangers, and it is not surprising to learn that it was co-opted for military guard duty by the Russian army. The military now value the breed so highly that they have actively discouraged its export to foreign countries. As a result, few have left Russia in recent times.

The small number of South Russians that have somehow managed to find their way to the West have proved something of a handful. It is said that, if they sense what they consider to be a threat to their owner, they will attack without hesitation and without warning. Unless strictly trained and controlled, they are liable to dramatically reduce the frequency of visitors to one's home. There is a saying that 'a pampered South Russian is a killer'. But it has to be admitted that this is a truly awe-inspiring canine specimen that lives up to its nickname of 'the White Giant'.

TRANSCAUCASIAN MOUNTAIN DOG   RUSSIA

Also known as the Transcaucasian Ovtcharka, this breed is employed as a livestock guardian in the Caucasus Mountains.

Closely related to the Caucasian Mountain Dog, this is the older of the two breeds. The finest examples come from Georgia, but it is also found in Armenia, Astrakhan, Azerbaijan, Dagestan, Grozny, Kraznodar, Rostov and Stavropol.

Like its close relative, this is a powerful, aggressive defender of its flocks, showing no fear in the face of attack from any source.

PAKISTAN

VIKHAN   PAKISTAN

The Sanskrit name of this dog has three distinct meanings — broken, noseless or hermit — but it is not clear which of these three unusual qualities typifies this little-known breed. Its main role is to guard the farmers' flocks against attacks by wild animals.

These large, ferocious dogs are employed to protect the sheep in the Chitral region in the extreme north-west of modern Pakistan. To give the dogs a fighting chance when pitted against marauding leopards, they are usually fitted with massive iron collars that prevent the big cats from sinking their fangs into the dogs' necks.

Looking like a collie, and with a body 'more calculated for swiftness than strength', the Vikhan appears in a variety of colours, including black, red or mottled. Its thick hair is sometimes used to make dark wool.

INDIA

BANGARA MASTIFF   INDIA

A local breed named after the Bangar district of Tehri Garhwal, which is employed to protect the herds of yak and the flocks of sheep from the attacks of wild animals.

This is a close relative of the Tibetan Mastiff, specially developed by the people of Tehri Garhwal (a mountainous region of the former Punjab hill states in north-west India) to control their livestock in the daytime pastures and, by night, to protect the animals from the attacks of large predators. For this role a powerful, courageous breed was needed and the Bangara Mastiff is such a dog, always ready to risk its life in defence of its livestock.

The usual colouring is black-and-tan, but paler coats also occur. The males are up to 25 in (64 cm) in height and have a strong, mastiff muzzle, a compact body and a heavily plumed tail that is curled to one side.

The local people do not appear to have called this dog by a particular breed name. It was given its official title of Bangara Mastiff by the Indian dog expert Major W. V. Soman in 1963. When he retired from the army he was asked to act as a judge at a dog show in Bombay and was dismayed to find that all the animals on display were imported pedigree breeds and that there was not a single native Indian dog to be seen. He set about correcting this by publishing a detailed list of Indian breeds, stating: 'My work will only be fulfilled if we see the pedigreed dogs of Indian origin in dog shows in India.' Where a local breed lacked a specific title, he created one, as with this distinctive mastiff from Bangar.

PATTI

INDIA

The nomadic Tamil tribes of India have used this dog for many years as a flock guard to protect their sheep from the attacks of foxes and other wild animals.

The Patti has the black-and-tan markings of the German Shepherd, but in shape looks more like a robust version of the Doberman Pinscher. The Tamil shepherds find this breed to be especially intelligent and hardy, but in recent times it has become increasingly rare, due to uncontrolled crosses with other dogs. However, there are still said to be some pure-bred specimens in existence from which a modern pedigree dog could be established with a carefully planned breeding programme.

INDIA/NEPAL

HIMALAYAN SHEEP DOG

INDIA/NEPAL

Also known as the Bhotia, this breed is sometimes used for herding sheep or protecting property, in addition to its main role as a flock guard. It has occasionally been recorded as the Bhotia Himalayan Mastiff.

The Himalayan Sheep Dog is found in the foothills of the Himalayas over a wide range, from eastern Nepal to Kashmir in north-west India. The typical form looks rather like a large, long-haired Labrador, but there is some variation in coat colour. It has small, drooped ears and its tail is described as 'heavily plumed and turned over the back'. Its height is 20–25 in (51–64 cm) and its weight is 50–60 lb (23–27 kg). It is a close relative of the more northerly and slightly larger Tibetan Mastiff.

This breed has a reputation for wandering and scavenging when it is not properly controlled, although this may simply reflect a response to an inadequate diet. As a working dog it is said to be 'ferocious and savage by nature' but again this may be due to the way it is treated. Those who have tried to keep it as a show dog instead of a working dog have remarked that it can (like almost any breed of dog) be transformed into a 'civilized companion'.

BHUTAN

BHUTIA SHEEPDOG BHUTAN

This is a larger form of the Himalayan Sheep Dog, found in the remote country of Bhutan, to the east of Nepal. In height it is 26–28 in (66–71 cm), compared with the 20–25 in (51–64 cm) of its relative to the west.

In Bhutan, the shepherds usually keep two or three of the dogs with every large flock, to defend them from the attacks of predators. The dogs are equipped with heavy leather collars that are covered in protective spikes. These devices help to prevent the choking throat-bite employed by some of the predators. Foreign visitors to Bhutan at the start of the 20th century were warned to avoid these dogs, because they 'will often attack Europeans without provocation'.

In general appearance these dogs are very similar to both the Himalayan Sheep Dogs and the Tibetan Mastiffs, although their tails appear to be less tightly up-curled. They are capable of twisting them up over their backs, but are also frequently seen with them hanging low. In colour the dogs are black-and-tan, solid red or grizzled.

SHEEP-HERDERS

From ancient times the shepherd has enjoyed the company and assistance of two types of dog – the flock guard and the herder. In earlier centuries flock guards were essential because of the lurking presence of wolves and other predators. In more modern times that need has lessened. In some countries, predators have been completely exterminated and flock guards have become obsolete. But the control of flock movement has remained a problem wherever grazing on open land occurs. For this, a smaller, faster, more nimble dog was still needed. The task also called for a quick-witted, sensitive animal that would respond to its master's signals with great precision.

The sheepdog, starting out centuries ago as a general farmer's dog, had to become refined as a specialist herder – a master tactician always on the alert to outwit the most wayward sheep. In this role it was of immense value to the shepherds, and many local breeds of sheepdog were developed in different parts of the world. Then another change occurred. In the more developed countries, the wild places started to vanish, to be replaced by orderly, enclosed fields, where the need for sheep control was drastically reduced. Just as wolf extermination had devalued the big flock guards, so land enclosure devalued the sheep-herder. Only in those countries with extensive, untamed, hilly regions did the working sheepdog manage to thrive in its natural state. Happily, in other countries the breeds often did manage to survive, not as working dogs, but as stars of the show-ring.

A few sheepdogs are also kept purely as pets, but because their temperament demands a very high work rate, they put great pressure on their owners to supply endless opportunities for physical activity and exercise. This makes them unsuitable for life in an urban environment.

There are 53 breeds in this category, some extinct, some on show and some still hard at work on the pasture lands.

ENGLAND

CUMBERLAND SHEEPDOG   ENGLAND

This breed is named after the county (now part of Cumbria) in the north-west of England that was its stronghold, and where for centuries it was busy controlling the flocks of sheep.

This working sheepdog was bred by the shepherds of Cumberland, Westmorland and the Peak District purely for their own use and has always been unknown outside this region. No attempt was ever made to formalize the status of the dog or to draw up a breed standard. Despite this it was a pure-breeding dog of long standing and was specially tailored to suit the rugged climate of the area. It was protected from the cold and the rain by an unusually heavy, dense, weatherproof black-and-white coat and a bushy tail.

Described by its chief patron, Lord Lonsdale, as 'agile, sagacious and reliable', it was a dog that worked 'quickly, quietly and low-to-ground'. It appeared each year at local sheepdog trials throughout the late 19th and early 20th centuries and always excelled. However, by the middle of the 20th century, its numbers were dwindling rapidly and some authorities now consider it to be completely extinct.

In appearance it was similar to the Border Collie that inhabited the region just to the north of its range, but was a more heavily built dog with a broader head and thicker coat.

SCOTLAND

BORDER COLLIE   SCOTLAND

Although this is an old breed it did not acquire its present title until 1915. Previously, it was known simply as one of the old Scottish Collies, or as the Working Collie. There are several theories concerning the origin of the name 'Collie'. The favourite is the suggestion that it relates to the Scottish Highland sheep called colley sheep. 'Colley' was an old Anglo-Saxon word for 'black' and these sheep had black markings. So the dog that attended the colley sheep was called the Colley Dog. An alternative theory attributes the origin of the name to the fact that 'Collie' is Gaelic for 'useful', as these were certainly useful dogs.

This remarkable dog, arguably the finest herder of sheep in the world, has been hard at work on the Scottish Borders for centuries. However, it was not until competitive sheepdog trials started in 1873 that its fame began to spread. It did so well in those early trials that it outshone the opposition and reserved a special place for itself in canine history. Many years later, when its feats were repeated on television, its remarkable skills became known to millions.

The Border Collie works silently, crouching, creeping and then springing into action, single-handedly marshalling its sheep and moving them from spot to spot with the control of a chess-master. It does this in cooperation with its shepherd, who communicates with it using a set of learned signals. When the dog is near at hand, spoken signals can be used, but when it is further away, the shepherd switches to whistled commands. The exact code varies slightly from shepherd to shepherd, but a typical, basic set would be as follows:

COMMAND	MEANING	SIGNAL
lie down	stop where you are	one long whistle
walk on	get up and start moving again	two sharp whistles
come by	circle round to the left of the sheep	short note repeated
away to me	circle round to the right of the sheep	longer note repeated
that'll do	stop working and come back to me	slap leg

Each shepherd has his own variations of these commands and adds further ones for special instructions. To watch man and dog cooperate using this unique language is to witness one of the most intimate and subtle of all human–canine interactions.

In personality, the Border Collie is a responsive, alert, eager workaholic. A graceful, lithe, beautifully balanced dog, it possesses amazing stamina. Its height is 18–21 in (46–53 cm) and its weight 30–49 lb (14–22 kg). It is nearly always a vividly marked black-and-white dog, although other colour patterns do occur. There are two types of coat: it is usually long, but may also be short.

Because this has always been first and foremost a working dog, it is no surprise to learn that it did not acquire a Kennel Club breed standard until 1976.

References

1937. Pasco, Luke J. *Heather Jean the Working Sheep Dog*. The Sheep Breeder, Chicago.

1938. Ritson, Kitty. *Lad: the Story of a Border Collie*. A. & C. Black, London.

1952. McCulloch. *Border Collie Studies*.

1958. Arnsonian (J. Boothman). *Training The Working Collie*. Duncan, Kilsyth.

1963. Holmes, John. *Farmer's Dog, the Border Collie, Training, Theory & Practice*. Popular Dogs, London.

1965. Ashcroft, Patricia Norah. *The Border Collie: Sheep Dog Extraordinary*. Times Press, Douglas, Isle of Man.

1979. Allen, Arthur N. *A Lifetime with the Working Collie. Their Training and History*. Privately published, Mcleansboro, Illinois.

1979. Combe, Iris. *Border Collies*.

1983. Vidler, Peidje: *The Border Collie in Australasia*. Gotrah.

1984. Billingham, Viv. *One Woman and Her Dog*. Patrick Stephens, Cambridge.

1984. McCaig, Donald. *Nop's Trials*. Crown, New York.

1987. Larson, Janet Elizabeth. *The Versatile Border Collie*. Alpine Publications.

1988. Collis, Joyce. *The Show Border Collie*. Letchworth, Hertfordshire.

1991. Collier. *Border Collies.* TFH, New Jersey.

1993. Bray. *Border Collies.*

1993. Combe, Iris. *An Owner's Companion to the Border Collie.*

1993. Grew. *Key Dogs of the Border Collie Family.*

1993. Quarton. *One Dog, his Man and his Trials.*

1995. Swann, Barbara Beaumont. *The Complete Border Collie.* Howell, New York.

1996. Burch, Mary. *The Border Collie: An Owner's Guide to a Happy Healthy Pet.* Howell, New York.

1996. McLeavy, Adrienne. *Pet Owner's Guide to the Border Collie.*

1997. Devine, Michael. *Border Collies: Everything About Purchase, Care, Nutrition, Breeding, Behavior, and Training.* Barron, New York.

1998. Hornsby, Alison. *The Ultimate Border Collie.* Howell, New York.

1998. Larson, Janet Elisabeth. *The Versatile Border Collie.*

1998. Powley, Robyn L. *A New Owner's Guide to Border Collies.*

1998. Quarton, Marjorie. *The Working Border Collie.* Irish Pets & Animals.

1999. Dunbar, Ian. *The Essential Border Collie.* Howell, New York.

1999. McGinty, Alice B. *Sheepherding Dogs: Rounding Up the Herd.*

1999. Price, Carol. *Understanding the Border Collie.*

2000. Dearth, Kim D. R. *Your Border Collie's Life: Your Complete Guide to Raising Your Pet.*

2000. Sheninger, Gene. *The Border Collie Headline Herder.*

(Note: For general books on collies see entry for Rough Collie.)

MARLED COLLIE   SCOTLAND

Also known as the Marbled Collie or the Harlequin Collie, this breed is no longer recognized, but was championed for a while in the 19th century.

Originally this distinctively marked, blue-marle Collie was viewed as no more than a colour variation of the Smooth Collie, but then a serious attempt was made to develop it into a separate breed. This was done by a collie expert by the name of W. P. Arkwright, who set up a careful breeding programme and eventually had the 'marbled'-coated line breeding true to type.

Arkwright had problems, however, finding that, if blue-marle was bred to blue-marle too often, there was a risk of deaf, blue-eyed, all-white puppies appearing in the litters. For this reason, he had to be especially careful in his breeding plans, which may account for the fact that, as a breed in its own right, the Marled Collie did not enjoy long-term success.

ROUGH COLLIE   SCOTLAND

In the days before there was also a Smooth Collie, this breed was known simply as the Scotch Collie. It is sometimes given the full name of Rough-coated Collie.

The early ancestors of this breed are believed to have arrived in the British Isles with the Romans about 2,000 years ago. The original version of this dog had shorter legs and a shorter nose. Its present elegant silhouette is thought to have been developed by the brief introduction of a Borzoi to the Collie bloodline. This would certainly explain the longer legs and the unusually long and slender muzzle.

When Queen Victoria took an interest in Collies in the 1860s, her royal patronage gave them a significant boost. (Even though she kept Smooth Collies, the Rough Collie also benefited, as the two breeds were often lumped together as one.)

A little later, at the start of the 20th century, Queen Alexandra preferred Rough Collies, and not only kept them but also exhibited them. Under her influence, selective breeding made them more glamorous. In all probability, it was when the czar of Russia brought Borzoi dogs as royal gifts that the Borzoi/Collie cross was made. (Some authors believe, however, that the Borzoi cross was made at a much earlier date.)

The fame of the Rough Collie reached even greater heights in the 20th century, when it was chosen by Hollywood as the star of the sentimental *Lassie* films. There were seven of these films, appearing from 1943 to 1951, not to mention a long-running TV series. Since then interest has waned slightly (to the relief of serious breeders and exhibitors), but it remains a very popular dog. Today it is essentially a companion and a show dog, its sheep-herding days far behind it.

In personality this is an alert, sensitive, obedient, cooperative dog, always eager to please its owner. Its long, flowing coat, with its impressively thick mane and frill, can be black and white; black, white and tan; or merle, white and tan. The ears are erect, but with their tips hanging forward. The Collie's height is 22–24 in (56–61 cm) and its weight is 50–75 lb (23–34 kg).

References

1890. Lee, Rawdon B. *A History and Description of the Collie or Sheepdog in his British Varieties.* Horace Cox, London.

1904. Dalziel, Hugh. *The Collie, as a Show Dog, Worker and Companion.* Upcott Gill, London.

1906. Packwood, H. E. *Show Collies, Rough and Smooth-Coated: a Complete History.* Our Dogs, Manchester.

1923. Baskerville, W. *Show Collies (Rough and Smooth) and Shetland Sheep Dogs.* Our Dogs, Manchester.

1927. Whyte, William. *The Sheep-Dog.* Auckland.

1934. Johns, Rowland (Editor). *Our Friend the Collie.* Methuen, London.

1947. Denlinger, Milo G. *The Complete Collie.* Denlinger's, USA.

1948. Puxley, W. Lavallin. *Collies and Sheep-Dogs.* Williams & Norgate, London.

1949. Kelly, R. B. *Sheep Dogs; their Breeding, Maintenance and Training.* Angus & Robertson, London.

1955. Miller, Madeline. *Collies as Pets.* TFH, New Jersey.

1957. Barbaresi, Sara M. *How to Raise and Train a Collie.* TFH, New Jersey.

1957. Kattell, Ted. *Pet Collie.* All-Pets, Fond du Lac, Wisconsin.

1958. Arnsonian (J. Boothman). *Training the Working Collie.* Duncan, Kilsyth.

1961. Osborne, Margaret. *Collies.* Foyles, London.

1962. Anon. (The Collie Club of America). *The Complete Collie.* Howell, New York.

1963. McCloskey, Esther. *This is the Collie.* TFH, New Jersey.

1965. Osborne, Margaret. *The Collie.* Popular Dogs.

1973. Cartledge, Joe and Cartledge, Liz (Editors). *The Complete Illustrated Collie.* Ebury Press, London.

1989. Bishop, Ada L. *All About The Collie (Rough and Smooth).* Pelham Books, London.

1993. Clark. *Rough and Smooth Collies.*

1994. Sunstrom. *Collies.*

1995. Lewis. *Guide to Owning a Collie.* TFH, New Jersey.

1996. Ackerman, Lowell. *Dr Ackerman's Book of Collies.* TFH, New Jersey.

1997. Starkweather. *Magnificent Collie.*

1999. Combe, Iris. *Rough Collie Records.*

Hunt, Hazel. *Rough Collies: An Owner's Companion.*

(Note: Some of the above books refer to collies in general rather than specifically to the Rough Collie.)

SHETLAND SHEEPDOG   SHETLAND ISLES

This breed is commonly referred to by its nick-name of Sheltie. In earlier days it was called the Dwarf Scotch Shepherd or the Shetland Collie. Its local Shetland names are the Toonie Dog (meaning Crofter's Dog) or the Peerie (Fairy Dog). In addition to its main duty of controlling the sheep, it also helped to bring the cattle home at milking time.

This is a miniature version of the Rough Collie, but despite its small size, it is a serious working dog. Its body may only weigh a third to a quarter of that of its larger relative, but in its rugged homeland it is a hardy, industrious companion that has always been highly valued by the crofters there.

As it comes from the Shetland Isles, which lie 50 miles (80 km) north of the mainland of Scotland, its reduced body-size is to be expected. Dwarfism in livestock has always been the norm there, from the tiny Shetland ponies to the small Shetland sheep. The Sheltie is not out of proportion to the animals it must control.

Despite its reduced size, the docile, friendly Sheltie is agile, fast and a good jumper. It is an intelligent dog, capable of controlling the sheep even in the absence of human supervision. In earlier days (if we are to believe old reports) when the sparse grazing was too poor, dogs and sheep were put in boats and taken to smaller, uninhabited islands in the Shetland group, where the grass was better. The flocks were left there to feed by themselves with only the dogs in charge. (How the dogs were fed and watered during these episodes is unclear, unless a small boat made a daily journey with supplies for them.)

Traditionally, one of the special tasks of this breed was to protect the crofter's growing crops. These were usually unfenced, and the more intelligent sheep would, from time to time, abandon their modest moorland grazing and try to sneak in for the richer pickings of the cultivated patches near the small crofts. The little Shelties were constantly on guard, ready to drive off the encroaching sheep with loud barking.

Because of its smaller, more manageable size, this is today the most popular of all the officially registered collie breeds. Interest in it as a companion dog had begun as long ago as the 19th century, when the British Navy visited the Shetlands and sailors starting buying the little dogs to take home as gifts. In 1908, at Lerwick, the capital of the Shetland Isles, the Shetland Sheepdog Club was formed to protect the breed and to ensure that the wider demand for it did not lead to a decline in its qualities. In 1909 the Scottish Shetland Sheepdog Club followed and then, in 1914, the English Shetland Sheepdog Club. At this point the dog was known as the Shetland Collie, but when the breed was registered at the Kennel Club, this had to be changed to Shetland Sheepdog, because the breeders of the bigger collies did not wish to be associated with a dwarf relative.

From this point onwards the Sheltie became increasingly favoured as a companion dog and a show dog, but was less and less in demand on the islands in its working capacity. This is because the small crofts were growing larger and therefore a bigger, imported sheepdog was more in demand. But although the Sheltie largely lost its original role, its fame in the show-ring spread far and wide, until, with its luxuriant coat and its obedient nature, it became known as a star attraction at competitions all over the world.

In colour it is usually black, white and tan; golden brown; or blue merle. Occasionally it is black-and-white or black-and-tan. Its height is 14–15 in (35–37 cm) and its weight 14–16 lb (6–7 kg).

References

1916. Thynne, Beryl. *The Shetland Sheepdog.* Illustrated Kennel News, London.

1943. Coleman, Catherine E. *Shetland Sheepdog.* Mail & Express, New York.

1948. Johnson, Margaret S. *Gay, a Shetland Sheepdog.* William Morrow, New York.

1954. Taynton, Mark and Goudy, Jean. *Pet Shetland Sheepdog.* All-Pets, Fond du Lac, Wisconsin.

1958. Gwynne-Jones, Olwen. *The Shetland Sheepdog Handbook.* Nicholson & Watson, London.

1959. Osborne, Margaret. *The Popular Shetland Sheepdog.* Popular Dogs, London.

1960. Miller, Evelyn. *How to Raise and Train a Shetland Sheepdog.* TFH, New Jersey.

1960. Moore, Catherine Coleman. *The Complete Shetland Sheepdog.* Denlinger's, USA.

1961. Herbert, Beryl M. and Herbert, J. M. *The Shetland Sheepdog.* Foyles, London.

1961. Johns, Rowland (Editor). *Our Friend the Shetland Sheepdog.* Methuen, London.

1966. Moore (Editor). *The English Shetland Sheepdog Club Handbook.*

1969. Weiss, Seymour N. *How to Raise and Train a Shetland Sheepdog.* TFH, New Jersey.

1970s. Schneider, Earl (Editor). *Know your Shetland Sheepdog.* Pet Library, New York.

1970. Simmonds, Jean Daniels. *The Illustrated Shetland Sheepdog Standard.* Privately published, Oneonta, New York.

1973. Taynton, Mark. *Shetland Sheepdogs.* TFH, New Jersey.

1974. Jeu, Jean C. and Saltzman, Lynette J. *The Shetland Sheepdog*. American Shetland Sheepdog Association.

1974. Riddle, Maxwell. *The New Shetland Sheepdog*. Howell, New York.

1974. Rogers, Felicity M. *All About the Shetland Sheepdog*. Pelham Books, London.

1975. Marriage, J. E. and Marriage, M. A. *The English Shetland Sheepdog Handbook*. Shetland Sheepdog Club.

1976. McKinney, Betty Jo and Rieseberg, Barbara Hagen. *Sheltie Talk*. Alpine Publications.

1977. Fletcher, Ron (Editor). *Shetland Sheepdog*. Menlo Park, California.

1977. Shiel. *The Shetland Sheepdog*. Bartholomew, London.

1979. Pisano, Beverly. *Shetland Sheepdogs*. TFH, New Jersey.

1980. Schneider, Earl (Editor). *Know Your Shetland Sheepdog*. Pet Library.

1984. Nicholas, Anna Katherine. *The Book of the Shetland Sheepdog*.

1985. McKinney, Betty J. *Sheltie Talk*.

1988. Baker, Maurice. *Shetland Sheepdogs Today*. Ringpress Books, Letchworth, Hertfordshire.

1990. Sucher, Jaime J. *Shetland Sheepdogs: Everything About Purchase, Care, Nutrition, Breeding, and Health Care*. Barron, New York.

1991. Riddle, Maxwell. *The New Complete Shetland Sheepdog*. Howell, New York.

1993. Davis, Mary. *The Shetland Sheepdog*. Howell, New York.

1995. Merrithew, Cathy. *The Shetland Sheepdog: An Owner's Guide to a Happy Healthy Pet*. Howell, New York.

1996. Credidio, Scott. *Guide to Owning a Shetland Sheepdog*. TFH, New Jersey.

1998. Churchill, Linda. *A New Owner's Guide to Shetland Sheepdogs*.

1999. Carriera, Joanne. *Shetland Sheepdogs at Work*.

1999. Dunbar, Ian (Editor). *The Essential Shetland Sheepdog*.

1999. McGowan, Clem Charlotte. *The Shetland Sheepdog in America*.

1999. Norman, Margaret. *The Complete Shetland Sheepdog*.

1999. Wilcox, Charlotte. *The Shetland Sheepdog*.

2000. Palika, Liz. *How to Train Your Shetland Sheepdog*.

SMOOTH COLLIE   SCOTLAND

This breed is also known sometimes as the Scotch Collie, when it is being treated as the same breed as the Rough Collie. It is sometimes given the full name of Smooth-coated Collie.

This breed is almost identical to the Rough Collie, except for its shorter coat. The two separate types of collie, rough and smooth, were known and illustrated as early as the 18th century. At the beginning of the 19th century, the smooth type was said to be 'more cloddy' than its modern equivalent, with a heavier head and shorter legs. At some point it was crossed with a greyhound, which made it taller and more slender. Later still, after it had become a show dog, it was crossed with the Rough Collie, with the result that the two breeds looked even closer than they had in the past.

It was on one of her visits to Balmoral in the early 1860s that Queen Victoria caught sight of these elegant working dogs. She was so impressed by them that she took some back with her to Windsor Castle. Her favourite was a dog called Sharp, whose grave

at Windsor is marked by a bronze statue.

This royal interest immediately elevated what had been a humble working dog to the level of a noble companion, and the breed's popularity soared. In the canine literature, Queen Victoria's dogs are sometimes referred to as Rough Collies, but this is an error. There is a photograph of her with Sharp, showing clearly that he is of the short-coated type. However, because the two breeds are so similar, and were often referred to collectively simply as 'collies', both breeds benefited from the royal patronage.

In the 20th century, with dog shows growing ever more important, the Rough Collie, with its impressively luxuriant coat, gradually overshadowed its short-haired relative. Indeed, on several occasions the Smooth Collie was on the verge of disappearing altogether, especially after World Wars I and II, but somehow it managed to survive, thanks to the work of a group of devoted enthusiasts. Despite their efforts, however, it never managed to catch up with its glamorous cousin. By the end of the century, for every Smooth-coated registration at the Kennel Club, there were 50 Rough-coated.

References

1906. Packwood, H. E. *Show Collies, Rough and Smooth-Coated: a Complete History.* Our Dogs, Manchester.

1923. Baskerville, W. *Show Collies (Rough and Smooth) and Shetland Sheep Dogs.* Our Dogs, Manchester.

1989. Bishop, Ada L. *All About The Collie (Rough and Smooth).* Pelham Books, London.

1993. Clark. *Rough and Smooth Collies.*

(Note: For general books on collies see entry for Rough Collie.)

WALES

OLD WELSH GREY

WALES

Sometimes known simply as the Welsh Grey, this is an ancient breed of sheepdog that has become increasingly rare and may now be extinct.

The Old Welsh Grey was most commonly found in Snowdonia, in north-west Wales. It was a rather untidy, shaggy dog that some believe may have been the ancestor of the Bearded Collie. As the Bearded Collie developed and became more and more popular, it seems likely that it overshadowed, absorbed and finally replaced its predecessor.

Some authorities are now convinced that the Old Welsh is extinct, but others feel that there may still be a few isolated specimens in remote corners of the Welsh mountains, last survivors that may not even be recognized as such.

Viewed objectively, this was not an imposing breed. Clifford Hubbard described it as 'an unbeautiful dog much like a small old-fashioned Bearded Collie'. In colour the harsh, shaggy coat was usually light tan or fawn. It was an alert, medium-sized dog with a long, bushy tail. Its height was 17–18 in (43–46 cm) and its weight 35–40 lb (16–18 kg).

When, in the early 20th century, Welsh emigrants settled in South America as sheep farmers, they took Old Welsh Greys with them. Once there, these dogs were kept busy controlling the huge flocks of sheep and protecting them from predators and thieves. They gradually began to change, as they adapted to this new way of life and the unfamiliar environment. Eventually they developed into a different breed, which was given the name of Patagonian Sheepdog (see separate entry).

WELSH BLACK-AND-TAN SHEEPDOG   WALES

This is one of the four indigenous sheep-herders of Wales, the other three being the Old Welsh Grey, the Welsh Blue-Grey and the Welsh Hillman. It is now believed to be extinct.

This breed and its predecessors have been hard at work in the Welsh mountains for over a thousand years. Evidence to support this view can be found in the ancient laws of Wales, dating from AD 920; these mention a dog called the Covert Hound or Gellgy, which was the Black-and-Tan's forerunner.

In appearance this breed has a striking resemblance to the Manchester Terrier, and it has been suggested that it was the ancestor, not only of that breed, but also of the Lancashire Heeler.

Like the other native sheepdogs of Wales, the Black-and-Tan was adept at working in both the Welsh valleys and the mountains, and had a special talent for dealing with the nimble and devious Welsh mountain sheep.

WELSH BLUE-GREY   WALES

A minor, local breed of sheepdog, this is still found in a few remote areas today.

This breed is distinguished by its unusual coat pattern which has been described as 'a beautiful slate blue haze all over the body'. In appearance it resembles a Border Collie.

It is said to be a remarkably efficient worker, and is highly regarded on the few farms where it can still be found. Because it is so rare and so localized, its survival in the long-term is under threat unless it manages to attract a few devoted enthusiasts to protect and promote it.

WELSH COLLIE WALES

This breed is also known as the Welsh Sheepdog. Unlike the other Welsh herders, this one is not an ancient inhabitant, but a comparatively new arrival.

It was in the 1820s that some Border Collies from Scotland first appeared in Wales. They were adopted by Welsh sheep farmers and modified slightly to suit their new environment. Because of their Scottish origin they were sometimes referred to as Highland Heelers.

Then, in 1873, the Welsh farmers organized the first-ever sheepdog trial competition (England and Scotland followed suit a few years later) and they called the participating dogs Welsh Sheepdogs, even though they were still very much like their recent Border Collie ancestors. The four ancient breeds of Welsh herders did not, apparently, compete and were increasingly overlooked as the trials, dominated by the collies, became more and more popular. Eventually, it was this new arrival, the Welsh Collie, that became generally identified as *the* Welsh Sheepdog.

As time went on, there were attempts to stabilize the Welsh Collie and to breed for greater uniformity. Because of its acute intelligence, its devotion to its human companions and its gentleness, it became a favoured companion animal as well as a trial dog and a working sheepdog.

Then, gradually, interest in the breed dwindled and its numbers started to fall. It was slowly absorbed into other breeds and was heading towards extinction as a pure breed. Happily, before it vanished completely, there was renewed interest in it on the part of Welsh farmers. In the 1990s sheep farmer John Davies called a meeting to promote the breed and with the help of over 60 other farmers was able to establish a breed register. They also formed a Welsh Sheepdog Society, called Cymdeithas Cwn Cymreig, and 44 dogs were considered to be suffcently pure to be placed on the initial list. The future for the breed now looks much brighter.

The colour of the medium-length coat is black, black-and-white, black-and-tan, tri-colour or merle. The ears are usually erect but often have fold-over tips. Odd-coloured eyes are admired by some Welsh farmers. The tail is long and bushy. The height is 17–20 in (43–51 cm) and weight 40–45 lb (18–20 kg).

WELSH HILLMAN WALES

One of the four native sheepdogs of Wales, the Welsh Hillman is on the verge of extinction. In addition to herding sheep, it was also co-opted to control Welsh cattle.

Like the Black-and-Tan Sheepdog, this breed is probably descended from the Covert Hound of the tenth century. It is taller than the Black-and-Tan, however, and its smooth coat is different, sometimes being a rich golden colour with white markings, and sometimes being brindle.

It has been suggested that this particular breed may have originally been brought to Welsh shores by ancient Phoenician traders in the first millennium BC, when they were shipping in livestock from North Africa. The dogs would have accompanied the livestock to help the traders control them. Alternatively, the dogs may have arrived a little later, with the Romans.

Writing in the 1980s, sheepdog breeder Iris Combe stated her belief that, despite pessimistic reports to the contrary, this breed was not, at that date, completely extinct. In her opinion a few of them could still be found on remote farms in certain outposts of rural Wales. One or two enthusiasts had been trying to assemble a breeding nucleus of these survivors, but without much luck. The problem was that the farming people who owned them were not aware of how important they were and had often spayed the bitches, dramatically reducing the chances of setting up serious breeding programmes.

However, as long as a few breeding pairs of Hillmans still exist, all is not lost. It remains to be seen whether this interesting and ancient breed manages to survive in the 21st century.

IRELAND

IRISH COLLIE   IRELAND

The Irish Collie barely exists in a pure form today, having been swamped out by introduced breeds. For many centuries, however, it was an important working dog right across rural Ireland.

It is believed that the Irish Collie was the original form of sheepdog in the British Isles, having been brought to Ireland by the early Celts. When these Celts spread to western Scotland they took their livestock and sheepdogs with them. So the Irish Collies were the ancestors of the Scottish breeds.

In the Wicklow region of the Republic of Ireland there was a local type of sheepdog, called the Wicklow Collie, that looked like a larger version of the Border Collie, except that it was born with a bobtail or stumpy tail. Today it has been absorbed into mixed stock by interbreeding with imported Scottish dogs, and the bobtail feature has been lost.

According to sheepdog breeder Iris Combe, although most working collies in Ireland today look like Border Collies, 'on a few isolated farms in west Galway and County Clare one or two Irish Collies can still be found'. With luck, local enthusiasts will isolate and pure-breed these last survivors of the important ancestral Celtic sheepdog, to prevent it vanishing altogether. (Note: at one time the collies found in Galway were named as a distinct breed called the Galway Collie.)

FRANCE

BEAUCERON   FRANCE

Also known as the French Shorthaired Shepherd, the Beauce Shepherd, the Berger de Beauce or the Bas Rouge, this breed has been controlling flocks of sheep in France since at least the 16th century. The name Beauceron refers to the plains around Paris, and the alternative name of Bas Rouge refers to the tan markings on the dog's legs.

The Beauceron is a muscular, deep-chested, long-tailed, short-coated herding dog that has been busy working in the French countryside for centuries. It is a fierce-looking dog, especially in the cases where its ears have been brutally cropped to form sharp, vertical points. It was well described by one author as having a superficial resemblance to a cross between a Dobermann and a German Shepherd. In modern times, with an increasing distaste for cosmetic mutilations, its ears are left intact and hang down to give the dog a softer, less intimidating appearance.

The first mention of the breed dates from a manuscript of 1587, but it did not acquire its breed title of Berger de Beauce until 1809, when attempts were being made to separate the then rather variable French herders into distinct types. The short-haired ones were named after the Beauce region, and the long-haired ones after the Brie district.

In 1900 the Beauceron made its first appearance at a dog show and in 1911 its first specialist breed club was formed. During the two World Wars it fared better than many other breeds because it proved of great value to the military. It was employed by them in the dangerous task of carrying messages to the front lines and even ran the gauntlet of enemy fire with replacement ammunition belts strapped to its athletic body. In more recent years, towards the end of the 20th century, the popularity of this dog spread to Belgium, Holland, Germany and, in a small way, the United States, but its major stronghold remains its French homeland, where it is increasingly used as a guard dog or for police work.

The typical colour-pattern of this breed is black-and-tan, but there is also a rare harlequin form. One oddity of this breed is the required presence of rear double-dewclaws. According to ancient superstition, these useless appendages are of great value to the dog, and this fanciful belief has survived even into modern times. As a result a Beauceron lacking this trivial feature is disqualified from any competition.

This is a potentially aggressive breed, ready to attack when the occasion demands the defence of its territory, its family or its livestock. If badly handled by its owner it can sometimes become a problem dog, but if well trained it remains a loyal and fearless companion. A sensitive owner can control his Beauceron with no more than a disapproving word and, by gentle training, can create a faithful, intelligent dog that is always eager to please. Harsh training simply does not work with this breed and can easily produce a neurotic misfit.

French author Colette was a great admirer of this breed, calling it 'un gentilhomme campagnard' – a country gentleman – but another enthusiast went even further, giving it the title of 'king of sheepdogs'. With accolades such as these, it is surprising that it has not become more popular worldwide.

BRIARD

FRANCE

Known in its homeland as the Berger de Brie, this spectacular sheep-herder has been active in the French countryside for centuries. It is named after the district of Brie, famous for its cheese-making. In addition to herding sheep, the Briard is quite capable of defending its flock from attacks by predators. In modern times it has acted as a war dog (sentry, messenger and rescue dog), a guide dog for the blind, and a police dog.

Described as a giant teddy-bear of a dog, or a 'heart wrapped in fur', it has a long, wavy coat, its most spectacular feature. Solid fawn, black or grey are the possible colours. Bicolours are not permitted. The face is adorned by a long beard and moustache. The ears used to be cropped to stand upright, but today they are preferred in their natural condition and hanging down. The spurious argument that cropping the ears improves the health of the dogs has long since been discredited.

An ancient breed, it is thought to have arrived in France with invaders from the East at some point during the Middle Ages. There is a 14th-century legend about the Briard which depicts it in a movingly heroic role. A man known as Aubry of Mondidier was murdered, but his dog witnessed the killing and followed the assailant relentlessly until the king, hearing of the matter, ordered a trial by combat in which the faithful dog was pitted against his master's murderer. Needless to say, the dog won the duel and avenged his master's death. It is argued that, because that particular sheepdog was known as 'Aubry's Dog', its modern title 'de Brie' is a play on 'd'Aubry'.

Napoleon loved this breed, as did Thomas Jefferson, who imported some into the United States at an early date. The dog appeared in the show-ring at the very first French dog show, held in Paris in 1863. Its first breed standard appeared in 1897 and a French breed club was formed in 1909. In 1928 the Briard Club of America was founded, to promote and protect the breed in the New World. The dog did not arrive in Britain until the 1960s but then quickly gained an enthusiastic following.

Only two or three of these vigorous, active dogs are needed to deal with a flock of up to 700 sheep. An amazingly energetic dog, it is capable of covering up to 50 miles (80 km) a day. It is a close relative of the Beauceron and, like that breed, possesses the unusual feature of rear double-dewclaws.

References

1965. Tingley, Mary Lou. *How to Raise and Train a Briard*. TFH, New Jersey.
1982. McLeroth, Diane. *The Briard*.
1983. Luquet. *Le Berger de Brie ou Briard*.
1993. Bixler-Clark. *Briards*. TFH, New Jersey.
Bumstead, Ruth. *Briards in England*.

CÉVENNES SHEPHERD   FRANCE

This breed is named after a hilly district to the south of the Massif Central and to the west of Marseilles. The dog is also known in France as Le Chien de Berger du Languedoc, or more simply the Berger du Languedoc, a title which is less specific, since the Languedoc region covers most of southern France.

Little information is available about this breed because it is now virtually non-existent. In the 19th century it was a common sheep-herder working in the hills and mountains of southern France, but although it was popular then, the modernization of herding techniques and the devastations of two World Wars brought it close to extinction. Its numbers became so small that eventually its name was dropped from the register of the FCI.

When herding, members of this breed operated alone, working with a single shepherd, and each dog was in control of a flock of 450 sheep – the officially allocated

number. Although influencing the movements of the flock was its main duty, this dog was also sufficiently strong to defend them, should they be attacked by wolves. According to one report it was the 'biggest, strongest, most vigorous of all the French herders'. This conflicts with another account that described it as 'small to medium size and only 16–22 in (40–56 cm) in height'.

The apparent contradiction concerning the size of the breed is probably due to its great variability in earlier days. It was bred for function, not for precise measurements or anatomy, and there were no fewer than five different types in existence at one time. Some early authors classified these as five different breeds: the Camargue, the Larzac, the Carrigues, the Grau and the Farou. Each was named after its special locality within the Languedoc region, but there is no information as to how these 'breeds' differed, one from another. The general opinion is that they were no more than local varieties of the same type of dog. Some may have been big wolf-slayers and others smaller, more modest versions of essentially the same animal.

In colour, this breed was said to be fawn, or fawn-and-black. Its protective, double coat was usually short, but was sometimes of medium length. Its tail was traditionally docked and its ears cropped.

PICARDY SHEPHERD

FRANCE

Known in France as the Berger Picard, the Berger de Picardie, or the Chien de Berger de Picardie, this large sheepdog will also herd cattle or act as a livestock guardian.

The early ancestors of this imposing breed, traditionally regarded as the oldest of all the French sheepdogs, are reputed to have appeared in north-eastern France in the ninth century with the arrival of the Celts. However, some authorities doubt the validity of this claim, arguing that hard evidence is lacking.

The most surprising aspect of this impressive breed is that it is so rare. Its dramatic appearance, with its long, shaggy coat, its tall, pointed, erect ears and its dignified, bearded face, mark it out as a potential star for major dog shows. Yet despite this its numbers remain small even in its native country.

A close relative of the Briard and the Beauceron, it appeared at the very first French dog show, back in 1863. A few decades later, in 1898, a programme of careful selective breeding was initiated to fix its type. But during the 20th century it suffered greatly when the battles of both World Wars were raging in the countryside where it normally worked – in the valley of the river Somme. When hostilities were finally over, its numbers had dropped to a dangerously low level, from which they have never truly recovered.

The rough, tousled coat of this dog, with its dense undercoat, is wonderfully weather-resistant. In colour it is any shade of red, often with black tipping; the most common form is grizzled fawn.

In personality, this lanky, versatile sheepdog has been described as spirited, lively, spontaneous, energetic, agile, rugged and loyal. It is also said to be mischievous, rowdy, assertive and sometimes stubborn.

PYRENEAN SHEEPDOG   FRANCE

Also known as the Pyrenees Sheepdog, the Pyrenean Shepherd Dog, the Labrit, the Labri, the Chien de Berger des Pyrénées or the Berger des Pyrénées, this breed is used for controlling the flocks of sheep in the Pyrenean Mountains during the five warmer months, when the livestock is grazing on higher ground. Its friends often refer to it as the Petit Berger (Little Shepherd).

This is a smaller version of the Catalan Sheepdog. It usually works in tandem with the larger Pyrenean Mountain Dog (see separate entry). The smaller dog controls the movements of the flocks and the bigger one acts as a guard against predators and thieves.

In origin, it has been argued in the past that this breed, the smallest of the French sheepdogs, is a descendant of the Briard, but recent opinion is against this and suggests instead that this is an indigenous breed of great antiquity.

The range of its operations stretches right along the Pyrenees, and it is also known in the Basque country to the west. Working with the mountain shepherds it is capable of covering over 20 miles (32 miles) a day. It is renowned for its speed and its quick reactions. One observer described it as a 'ball of fire'.

It is a hardy dog with a great deal of nervous energy – vivacious, quick-witted, mischievous, intelligent, brave and sure-footed. It shows impressive stamina even at high altitudes. Like many herding dogs, it is rather wary of strangers. In colour, it may be fawn, grey, blue, brindle or black. Its height is 15–22 in (38–56 cm). Working dogs traditionally had both the tail and the ears cropped, but this custom is now in decline.

It was first formally recognized as a breed in 1926. The Kennel Club in London registered it in 1988. Two forms exist – the goat-haired and the long-haired. The goat-haired has a medium-length coat and is viewed as no more than a minor variation of the long-haired form. These two are lumped together under the title of the Pyrenean Sheepdog. A third, smooth-faced type is considered sufficiently different to be classed as a separate breed (see separate entry for Savoy Sheepdog).

Savoy Sheepdog   France

Also known as the Savoie Sheepdog, the Berger de Savoie or the Berger de Savoy, this is a localized, regional French sheep-herder which is also used in a secondary role to herd cattle.

Found only in the Alpine frontier region of Savoy in south-east France, this little-known breed is a tough, hard-working, thick-coated dog employed in difficult terrain. It has a strong head, a long, well-muscled body, ears with tips that drop forward, a medium-length tail with a curled tip, and a coat sufficiently luxuriant to protect against the rigours of the Alpine climate. There is a conspicuous neck ruff.

In colour, this is basically a grey dog, but with patches of blue or brown. Its height is 18–22 in (46–56 cm) and its weight is 45–55 lb (21–25 kg).

Smooth-faced Pyrenean Sheepdog   France

Known in France as the Berger des Pyrénées à Face Racée, this breed is closely related to the more common, long-haired Pyrenean Sheepdog. Like its better-known relative, it is employed to control the movement of flocks of sheep in the mountains. It has also been recorded as the Smooth-faced Berger des Pyrénées, the Smooth-muzzled Berger des Pyrénées or the Smooth-muzzled Pyrenean Shepherd Dog.

Apart from its different coat type, this breed is very similar to the ordinary Pyrenean Sheepdog, but it is said to be less highly strung and less suspicious of strangers. It is a generally livelier dog and easier to handle.

Its body is slightly shorter and its feet more compact, but in other ways it is anatomically the same. Its height is 16–22 in (41–56 cm).

BELGIUM

BELGIAN GROENENDAEL SHEEPDOG BELGIUM

This breed is also known as the Belgische Herdershond Groenendaeler. In the United States it is known simply as the Belgian Shepherd, and is considered as a separate breed in its own right. In some other countries it is viewed as no more than a variety and is lumped with the Malinois, the Tervuren and the Laekenois as a single breed, called collectively the Belgian Sheepdog, the Chien de Berger Belge, the Belgische Herdershond or the Belgischer Schäferhund. It has been employed for centuries as a Belgian sheep-herder, but is today more likely to be encountered in the show-ring.

At the end of the 19th century, after centuries of flock-herding, the Belgian Sheepdogs were rapidly becoming obsolete and in danger of disappearing. In 1891 the Club de Chien de Berger Belge was formed to save them from extinction and to ensure their future. The problem was that they had always been bred for performance rather than precise looks, and in appearance were rather variable. A collection of 117 of them was assembled by Professor Adolphe Reul, a Belgian veterinary official, who then attempted to classify them and divide them into distinct types. He decided that, although they were anatomically very similar, they could be split up into six varieties, based on coat type and colour. Later, the six types were reduced to four, as follows:

1   The Groenendael, long-haired and solid black
2   The Malinois, short-haired and fawn-and-black
3   The Tervuren, long-haired and black-tipped fawn
4   The Laekenois, rough-coated and fawn

Once these firm distinctions had been made, it was possible to start standardized breeding programmes and to fix the different types more firmly, eliminating any inter-mediates in the process. In 1897, after hesitating and delaying for several years, the Belgian Kennel Club finally decided to recognize only three distinct breeds, the Groenendael, the Malinois and the Tervuren. In the United States, the AKC followed suit much later, in 1959.

The Groenendael, with its tall, pricked ears, its long, bushy tail, its narrow, pointed muzzle, its lanky, athletic legs and its luxurious, black coat, is the most striking of the group. It is also the best-known and the most widespread. It was created in 1885 by Nicholas Rose, owner of the Château de Groenendael situated just south of Brussels. He possessed a long-haired black bitch called Petite and, liking the look of her, spent a year searching for a similar male. He found one in the shape of a dog called Piccard D'Uccle and together these two black dogs became the foundation pair for what was later to become known as the Groenendael breed.

The first examples of this attractive black dog to reach the United States arrived there in 1907. England had to wait until 1931 to welcome the breed.

It is an intelligent, sensitive dog which, in recent years, has been co-opted for work as a police dog, army dog and property guard. Lively, intelligent and affectionate, it also makes a good companion.

References

1964. Dykema, Frank E. *How to Raise and Train a Belgian Sheepdog.* TFH, New Jersey.
1989. Bossi, Erna. *The Belgian Shepherd Dog and Its History.*
1990. Dykema, Frank E. *Belgian Sheepdogs.* TFH, New Jersey.
Turnquist, Marge. *The Belgian Sheepdog.*

BELGIAN LAEKENOIS SHEEPDOG   BELGIUM

This breed is also known as the Belgische Herdershond Laekense, or simply as the Laekense or Laeken. In the United States this dog is not recognized as a separate breed. In some other coun-

tries it is viewed as no more than a variety and is lumped together with the Groenendael, the Malinois and the Tervuren as a single breed, called collectively the Belgian Sheepdog, the Belgische Herdershond or the Belgischer Schäferhund. It takes its name from the Belgian Château de Laeken. Like the other types, it has been employed for centuries as a Belgian sheep-herder, but is today more likely to be encountered in the show-ring. Laekenois is pronounced Lake-n-wah.

A rare breed, the Laekenois owes its survival, not so much to the Belgians themselves, as to enthusiasts in Holland and France. Even today, 90 per cent of the existing Laekenois are to be found, not in Belgium, but in the Netherlands.

This shaggy, wiry-haired dog is the only rough-coated Belgian Sheepdog. With its tawny-gold colouring and its long, rough coat, it was the favourite breed of the Belgian queen, a fact which greatly enhanced its social status.

BELGIAN MALINOIS SHEEPDOG   BELGIUM

This is also called the Belgische Herdershond Malinois, the Chien de Berger Malinois, the Mechelen or the Mechelaar. In the United States this dog is known simply as the Malinois, and is considered as a separate breed in its own right. In some other countries it is viewed as no more than a variety and is lumped together with the Groenendael, the Tervuren and the Laekenois as a single breed, called collectively the Belgian Sheepdog, the Belgische Herdershond, or the Belgischer Schäferhund. It takes its name from the north-western Belgian location of Malines, or Mechelaar, where this type was originally most commonly found. Like the other types, it has been employed for centuries as a Belgian sheep-herder, but is today more likely to be encountered in the show-ring.

As a working flock-herder, the short-haired, black-masked Malinois used to be the most popular of the Belgian Sheepdogs, but in its modern role as a show dog it has been less favoured. It has undoubtedly suffered because of its superficial resemblance to the much better-known German Shepherd Dog. However, closer inspection reveals that its head has a different structure, its body is more fine-boned, and it is longer in the leg.

This breed is more of an outdoor dog, and is less suitable as a household pet than its close relative, the Tervuren. It was the first Belgian breed to be employed as a police dog or a border-patrol dog. In the early part of the 20th century some of these dogs were exported to New York and New Jersey to work as police dogs there. They were also popular for police and customs work in their home country, especially for night patrol work.

References

1989. Bossi, Erna. *The Belgian Shepherd Dog and Its History.*

BELGIAN TERVUREN SHEEPDOG   BELGIUM

This is also known as the Belgische Herdershond Tervuerense. In the United States this dog is known simply as the Belgian Tervuren and is considered as a separate breed in its own right. In some other countries it is viewed as no more than a variety and is lumped together with the Groenendael, the Malinois and the Laekenois as a single breed, called collectively the Belgian Sheepdog, the Belgische Herdershond or the Belgischer Schäferhund. This breed was named after the Belgian town of Tervuren, at the centre of the region where it originated. It has been employed for centuries as a Belgian sheep-herder, but is today more likely to be encountered in the show-ring.

This is a long-haired version of the Belgian Sheepdog with black-tipped, fawn hair and a black face-mask. The man who originally fostered this breed was a Monsieur M. F. Corbeel from the town of Tervuren. He owned the foundation pair, who were called Tom and Poes.

The first examples of this breed to appear in the United States arrived there in the 1940s, and the first litter to be born on American soil made their debut in 1954.

Like the other three breeds of Belgian Sheepdog, this one is vigilant, brave, agile, alert, trainable and hard-working. In recent years it has been employed as a police dog, a drug-sniffing customs dog, a security dog, and a guide dog for the blind.

References

1965. Laurin, Mrs Edeltraud. *How to Raise and Train a Belgian Tervuren.* TFH, New Jersey.

1989. Bossi, Erna. *The Belgian Shepherd Dog and Its History.*

1990. Anon (American Belgian Tervuren Club). *The Complete Belgian Tervuren.* Howell, New York.

1992. Anderson-Allen, Moira. *Belgian Tervuren.* TFH, New Jersey.

HOLLAND

DUTCH SHEPHERD   HOLLAND

Also known as the Dutch Herder, this Dutch working dog exists in three forms – the Coarse-haired, the Long-haired and the Short-haired. There is little difference between them apart from their coat types. Some authorities say that Dutch Shepherds did not exist before the early part of the 19th century, but it is known that they must have been around since before the early 18th century because it was then that some were exported to Australia.

The formal division of the Dutch Shepherd into three types occurred at the end of the 19th century. Prior to that date there was widespread variability in coat type because the dogs' owners bred for working ability rather than for specific appearance. But then, when dog shows started, it was decided to separate them into the three distinctive forms. Great interest in the three types arose in the 1890s, and a club for all three was formed in 1898.

COARSE-HAIRED DUTCH SHEPHERD

This version of the Dutch Shepherd is also known as the Rough-haired Dutch Shepherd, the

Rough-coated Dutch Shepherd or the Wire-haired Dutch Shepherd. In its homeland, it is the Ruwhaar Hollandse Herdershond, or the Hollandse Herdershond Ruwhaarige. It has been herding sheep in Holland since the 18th century.

The Coarse-haired is the oldest of the three types of Dutch Shepherd. In the 1940s the Coarse-haired was the most popular, but it has since lost ground and is now very scarce.

This dog has a wiry, hard coat. The ears are pricked and the face displays a moustache, a beard and tufts of hair over the eyes. Its muzzle is slightly more square than that of its two close relatives. In colour it may be yellow, red-brown, ash blue, streaked, grey-blue or salt-and-pepper. Its body height is 23–25 in (58–63 cm). In personality, this is a reliable, adaptable, obedient dog that has been described as a workaholic.

LONG-HAIRED DUTCH SHEPHERD

This form of the Dutch Shepherd is known in its homeland as the Langhaar Hollandse Herdershond, or the Hollandse Herdershond Langhaarige. Sometimes the two languages are mixed together and it is given the name of Long-haired Hollandse Herdershond. Like its two close relatives, it has been used for herding sheep and for other duties for many years.

This attractive version of the Dutch Shepherd has a flat, harsh coat with a pronounced woolly undercoat. It displays a prominent mane and trousers. The ears are pricked and the tail is long and feathered. In colour it is chestnut, with gold or silver brindling.

This type of the Dutch Shepherd is allowed to be slightly smaller than the other two – down to 21 in (53 cm) in height.

Like the other two versions, the Long-haired is descended from a mixture of German Shepherd Dogs and Belgian Sheepdogs. Some authorities believe that the Giant Schnauzer may also have been involved in its ancestry at some point.

The Long-haired Dutch Shepherd has become increasingly rare as a working dog, supposedly because its coat needs more grooming than that of its Short-haired relative. In the 1980s it was calculated that there were only about 200 of them left alive, and since then some authorities have expressed the fear that the dog may soon become extinct.

SHORT-HAIRED DUTCH SHEPHERD

In its homeland the short-haired version of the Dutch Shepherd is known as the Korthaar Hollandse Herdershond, or the Hollandse Herdershond Korthaarige. It is sometimes also referred to as the Nederlandsche Herdershond. Like its close relatives, the Coarse-haired and the Long-haired Dutch Shepherds, it has been herding sheep in Holland for many years.

This version of the Dutch Shepherd has a short, dense, flat coat with a protective undercoat. In colour it may be chestnut, yellow, or brown, brindled or streaked with silver or gold. There is a black face mask. The body height is 23–25 in (58–63 cm).

Today this is by far the most popular version of the three types of Dutch Shepherd, but although it is a popular dog in Holland, internationally it is overshadowed by the global success of its neighbour, the German Shepherd.

In addition to its primary role as a sheep-herder, this amazingly versatile animal has been co-opted for the following secondary duties: police dog, military dog, guide dog for the blind, household companion, show dog, security dog, vermin-controller, property watchdog, cart-puller, drover, livestock-protector, farm guard and even retriever.

In recent years a few of these hard-working dogs, with their alert, tractable, tireless, undemanding, rugged, affectionate personalities, have been exported to the United States, where, thanks to their remarkable stamina and speed, their owners are convinced that they will become increasingly popular.

SCHAPENDOES   HOLLAND

This breed is also known as the Dutch Sheepdog, but employing that English title risks confusion with the better-known Dutch Shepherd. The Schapendoes has been used to herd sheep since the 19th century.

This delightful, rough-and-tumble, Dutch sheep-herder can easily be distinguished from the Dutch Shepherd by its long, shaggy coat and its drooped ears. When the dog is active, its long, heavily haired tail is often carried erect like a flag, but is never curled over the back. Its profuse, dense coat protects it from the harshest weather. The preferred colours range from black to grey, but others are allowed.

In origin, it is thought to have descended from crosses between the Bearded Collie, the Bergamasco, the Briard, the Puli, the Polish Lowland Sheepdog and the German Schafpudel (Sheeppoodle), but the truth is that nobody is certain. It first appeared as a recognized breed early in the 19th century, but later almost vanished. One of the reasons for its disappearance was that any sheep-herding that had to be done in Holland was increasingly carried out by super-efficient, imported Border Collies.

The Schapendoes only began to re-emerge in the 1940s when several Dutch breeders, under the leadership of a well-known Dutch canine expert called Toepoel, decided to salvage their little-known native sheepdog. As a result of their hard work, the breed was formally accepted in 1952 and has now once again become popular with the Dutch people, although it remains virtually unknown outside its home country. It was recognized by the FCI in 1970. Even today, however, only an estimated 250 puppies are born each year.

It is said of this dog that, if sheep are not present, it will herd almost anything, and can sometimes be observed trying to round up children. Its method of controlling sheep involves nudging them with either its nose or its shoulder. In personality it has been described as cheerful, willing, playful, tireless, alert, lively, brave, intelligent and non-aggressive. Its only weakness appears to be that it can sometimes be rather highly strung.

SPAIN

CATALAN SHEEPDOG   CATALONIA

Also known as the Catalan Shepherd, the Catalonian Shepherd, the Catalonian Sheepdog, the Catalan Herder, the Catalaanse Herdershond, the Gos d'Atura, the Gos d'Atura Catala, the Perro de Pastor Catalan, or, more fully, the Perro de Pastor Catalan de Pelo Largo.

This friendly-looking, shaggy-coated dog from the extreme north-east of Spain is related to the Pyrenean Sheepdog, which it closely resembles. Its history goes back to at least the 18th century, and probably much earlier, but its breed standard was not compiled until 1929.

In addition to its main duty of herding sheep, the Catalan is also occasionally employed to round up horses or cattle. A determined dog in the field, it is said that it 'can inspire obedience in the meanest bull or the wildest colt'. During the Spanish Civil War, it

was used as a despatch dog to carry important messages. It also excelled at the task of locating wounded soldiers and bringing assistance to them.

The coat colour is variable and includes fawn, tawny, tan, brindle, black-and-tan, grizzle, and black. The dog's head displays an attractive beard and moustache. In the past its drooping ears were sometimes cropped to make them stand erect. Traditionally, the tail has been either left in its natural state or docked to 4 in (10 cm). In personality it is said to be an intelligent dog, energetic and eager to learn.

SHORT-COATED CATALAN SHEEPDOG   CATALONIA

Also called the Short-haired Catalan Herder and known locally as the Gos d'Atura Cerda or the Perro de Pastor Catalan de Pelo Corto, this breed has been employed to herd sheep in north-eastern Spain for several centuries.

This breed is very similar in everything but its hair type to the better-known, shaggy-coated Catalan Sheepdog. It appears to have been developed in order to create a working breed for the hotter, lowland districts and it has the added advantage that it needs little grooming attention. It is a powerful dog and in the past has been co-opted for work with the police and the military.

In colour it is black with tan extremities. Its height is 18–20 in (46–51 cm). This is an extremely rare breed and little is known about it. It has been suggested that it may be on the verge of extinction.

PORTUGAL

PORTUGUESE SHEEPDOG   PORTUGAL

Also known as the Cão da Serra de Aires, or the Monkey Dog, this breed should not be confused with the Estrela Mountain Dog (see separate entry) which is also sometimes given the name of Portuguese Sheepdog. The main difference is that the Estrela is a flock guard, while this one is a shaggy-coated sheep-herder.

The origin of this breed, which is found mainly on the southern plains, is unknown. The dog has some similarity to the Catalan Sheepdog, but there is no evidence that they are closely related. In 1900 a local nobleman imported two Briards and there are stories that these dogs contributed to the ancestry of the Portuguese Sheepdog, but again there are no details available.

In addition to its main duty of controlling the movements of flocks of sheep, it can also be used to work with cattle, horses, pigs and goats. When it is not busy herding, it also makes a good guard dog.

In personality, this is a high-spirited, loyal, intelligent dog that is quick to learn. It possesses great stamina and its only weakness is a stubborn streak if it is not properly trained. In colour, it is known in a variety of shades, from black and brown through to grey and yellow, but white and particolours are not acceptable.

Kept solely as a a working dog by shepherds in the south of Portugal, this breed was nearly extinct by the 1970s, but was then saved by a group of enthusiasts who were reluctant to see an old, indigenous breed disappear. They began a salvage operation and the future of the breed now seems assured.

ITALY

BERGAMASCO ITALY

Also known as the Bergamese Shepherd, the Italian Bergama Sheepdog, the Bergamaschi Herder, or, in its homeland, the Cane de Pastore Bergamasco, this ancient breed has been controlling flocks in northern Italy for centuries.

This large, excessively hairy dog has been working in the mountains around Bergamo, near Milan, ever since its Asian sheepdog ancestors were brought here from the Middle East by Phoenician traders in pre-Roman times. French canine experts have insisted that it is a descendant of their Briard dog, but Italian authorities counter-claim that, on the contrary, the Briard must be a descendant of the Bergamasco. They point out that, because it originated in the Middle East, it must have arrived in Italy before it appeared in France. Geographically this makes sense and it does seem as though the Italian claim is sound, making this dog a true ancestor not only of the Briard but probably of several other European sheep-herders as well.

It would not be exaggerating to describe this breed as the shaggiest dog in the world. Its most prominent feature is its extraordinary coat. Authors attempting to describe the curious matting that develops on adult Bergamascos are at a loss to find the correct word for it. One of them depicts the hair as 'naturally matted not in corded curls but in flat stripes'. Another says the hair 'hangs in matted shanks'. Yet another speaks of the coat 'falling in wavy locks'. And finally, one says that the 'long hair cords into strong, wavy flocks'. Whether the flattened cords are stripes, shanks, locks or flocks, the fact is that, along with a thick undercoat, they do provide these dramatic-looking dogs with an ideal protection from the high-altitude cold which they must face during their busy, working lives in the mountains. In colour, all shades of grey are accepted, from light to almost black; also pied coats in white, black, red or fawn.

This is a strong, intelligent, loyal dog, docile with its master, but fearless if its flock is threatened. Sadly, after World War II it became increasingly rare in its homeland, and its future was by no means secure. In recent years, however, a number of enthusiasts in the United Kingdom, Sweden, Finland, Switzerland, the Czech Republic, the United States and Canada have begun serious breeding programmes, and although it remains rare, its numbers are steadily increasing. There is now an International Bergamasco Sheepdog Association to protect its interests.

GERMANY

GERMAN SHEEPPOODLE   GERMANY

This breed is also referred to as the Schafpudel, the Sheeppudel or the Poodle Sheepdog.

This is a rare dog which is little known today. Some authors have even questioned whether it may have become extinct in recent years. It appears to be completely unknown outside its homeland.

In appearance this is a shaggy sheepdog, with a wavy, poodle coat and a tendency to become corded. One rather harsh critic commented that it is a dog of 'heavy and uncouth' appearance. It has drooped ears, a long tail and a coat that is either white or pied, with various forms of shading. In height it is 24 in (61 cm). It has been described by various authors as clever, attentive, vigilant, good-natured, devoted, sociable, gentle, tolerant and affectionate.

It is thought that its ancestors included the Barbet and the Poodle. The Puli has also been mentioned as a close relative and it is believed that the movements of flocks of sheep between Germany and Hungary in earlier times may have played a significant role in the development of this breed.

German Shepherd Dog

Known in its native home as the Deutsche Schäferhund, or simply the Schäferhund, this breed has two different names in Britain: inside the world of show dogs it is called simply the GSD; outside, the general public usually refer to it as the Alsatian. Its original function was to influence the movements of large flocks of sheep. Its name has occasionally been recorded as the Alsatian Hound, the Alsatian Shepherd or the Alsatian Wolfdog.

For countless years, large dogs had been needed to control the flocks of sheep in Germany and prevent them from straying from their pastures onto the unfenced arable land. Each district had its own type of herding dog until, late in the 19th century, a concerted effort was made to breed the perfect German sheep-herding dog. Crosses were made between the existing dogs in the north of the country and those from the central districts, and the result was the forerunner of the GSD.

The primary role of this breed was to keep moving around on the edges of the flock, watching out for any individual sheep that might start to wander away. The dog would then silently usher the stray sheep, gently but firmly, back into the fold. It could not do this by barking, because that might alarm the whole flock, and it could not (like a cattle dog) nip its legs, as this too might cause panic or perhaps injury. The sheepdog therefore had to possess a special kind of canine personality: swift and intelligent, silent and stealthy, and calm and steady. It also needed power, stamina and the ability to concentrate for long periods of time. The GSD scored highly on all these points.

In 1901 a specialist breed club was established in Stuttgart. (Its headquarters were later moved to Munich and then to Berlin.) It was called Der Verein für Deutsche Schäferhunde. Known as the SV for short, it kept detailed breeding records and had very strict rules that ensured the purity of this new race of sheepdog. The next decade was a time of great development for the GSD. This was interrupted by World War I, after which it once again became a favoured breed. In England and France its name was now changed to the Alsatian, to sidestep any anti-German feelings in the wake of the conflict.

The early members of this breed were straight-backed, longer-legged and shorter-bodied and had a generally squarer, more upright build than modern GSDs. Their popularity was such that they spread all over the world and soon became one of the most common of all breeds. The only shadow cast over them was the rumour that the wolf had been used in early crosses to give the dog its handsome, powerful, vulpine appearance. This was quite untrue, but the mud stuck and whenever a maltreated GSD lashed out and bit someone, it was reported that the 'wolf in it' was reasserting itself. Despite this, the hard-working GSD won many friends and, during World War II, proved to be of great use both to the Army and the Royal Air Force. It also revealed its capacity for patient restraint when it was co-opted for use by the Guide Dogs for the Blind Association, and assisted in a wide variety of other helpful duties.

In the show-ring, the GSD has been made increasingly 'streamlined' with a thinner, shorter body and finer bones. It is displayed in contests with its back sloping downwards towards the tail, and with its rear legs bent. To the supporter of the new style this gives the animal an attractive posture, as if crouched ready to spring into action. But it has to be admitted that the changes that have occurred during the course of the 20th century have not met with universal approval. Some critics have insulted the modern display posture by calling it the 'urinating bitch' posture or the 'cringing with fear' posture. They also accuse it of causing damage to the dog's hips and have insisted on a return to the original, more upright type of dog, with its back parallel to the ground. Their ideas have been roundly rejected and controversy has raged. The result has been the recent creation of a 'reconstructed' version of the early GSD, a dog called the Shiloh Shepherd (see separate entry). But whichever view you take, the GSD remains a magnificent breed, well deserving of its global popularity.

References

1921. Stephanitz, Max von. *Der Deutsche Schaferhund in Wort und Bild.*
1922. Schwabacher, Joseph. *The Popular Alsatian and All About It.* Popular Dogs, London.
1923. Horowitz, G. *The Alsatian Wolf Dog – Its History and Show Points, Working Capabilities, Etc.* Our Dogs, Manchester.
1925. Brockwell, David. *The Alsatian.* Hutchinson, London.
1925. Stephanitz, Max von. *The German Shepherd Dog in Word and Picture.*
1932. Johns, Rowland (Editor). *Our Friend the Alsatian.* Methuen, London.
1936. Ash, Edward C. *The Alsatian as a Companion, Show and Working Trial Dog.* Cassell, London.
1947. Denlinger, Milo. *The Complete German Shepherd.* Howell, New York.
1950. Pickett, F. *The Book Of The Alsatian Dog.* The Weald Press, London.
1950. Ross, John (Editor). *Alsatians.* Beveney Publishing.
1954. Schalk, E. C. Mansfield. *Pet German Shepherd.* All-Pets, Fond du Lac, Wisconsin.
1955. Dodge, Geraldine R. and Rine, Josephine Z. *The German Shepherd Dog in America.* Orange-Judd, New York.
1955. Goldbecker, William and Hart, Ernest H. *This is the German Shepherd.* The Practical Science, Orange, Connecticut.
1955. Leonard, Lillian. *Alsatians: A Guide for the Novice.* Our Dogs, Manchester.
1955. Miller, Madeline. *German Shepherds as Pets.* TFH, New Jersey.
1956. Leonard, Lillian. *Alsatians.* Foyles, London.
1957. Barbaresi, Sarah M. *How to Raise and Train a German Shepherd.* TFH, New Jersey.
1961. Elliot, Nem. *The Complete Alsatian.* Nicholas Vane, London.
1964. Pickup, Madeleine. *The Alsatian Owner's Encyclopedia.* Pelham, London.
1966. Cleveland, Reginald M. *Your German Shepherd.* Hawthorn Books, New York.

1967. Hart, Ernest H. *Your German Shepherd Puppy.* TFH, Jersey City.

1967. Schwabacher, J. and Gray, T. *The Alsatian (The German Shepherd Dog).* Popular Dogs, London.

1968. Elliott, Nem. *Modern Bloodlines in the Alsatian.* Kaye & Ward, London.

1969. Pickup, Madeleine. *German Shepherd Guide.* Pet Library.

1970. Bennett, Jane, et al. *The Complete German Shepherd Dog.* Howell, New York.

1973. Pickup, Madeleine. *All About the German Shepherd Dog.* Pelham, London.

1974. Strickland, Winifred Gibson and Moses, James Anthony. *The German Shepherd Today.* Macmillan, New York.

1975. Migliorini, Mario. *German Shepherds.* Arco, New York.

1976. Leonard, Lillian. *German Shepherd. Alsatians.* Arco, New York.

1976. Willis, Malcolm B. *The German Shepherd Dog.*

1977. Cree, John. *Training the Alsatian (German Shepherd Dog): the Obedient Companion or Working Partner.* Pelham, London.

1977. Ixer, Joyce. *The Alsatian (The German Shepherd Dog).* Bartholomew, London.

1978. Denlinger, Milo, et al. *The Complete German Shepherd Dog.* Howell, New York.

1978. Gordon, John Frazer. *The German Shepherd Dog (the Alsatian).* John Bartholomew, Edinburgh.

1978. Tidbold, May E. *The German Shepherd Dog, Its Care and Training.* K. & R. Books.

1979. Kern, Francis G. *German Shepherd Dogs.* TFH, New Jersey.

1981. Pickup, Madeleine. *The German Shepherd Dog Owner's Encyclopaedia.* Pelham, London.

1982. Bennett, Jane. *The New Complete German Shepherd Dog.* Howell, New York.

1983. Nicholas, Anna Katherine. *The Book of the German Shepherd Dog.* TFH, New Jersey.

1985. Antesberger, Helmut. *The German Shepherd Dog: Everything About Purchase, Care, Nutrition, Diseases, and Training.* Barron, New York.

1985. Hart, Ernest H. *The German Shepherd Dog.* TFH, New Jersey.

1986. Abbott, Brenda E. (Editor). *The German Shepherd Dog.* Hoflin Publishing.

1986. Schwabacher, Joseph, Gray, Thelma and Pickup, Madeleine. *The German Shepherd Dog.* Popular Dogs, London.

1987. Nicholas, Anna Katherine. *A Complete Guide To German Shepherds.*

1988. Wootton, Brian H. *The German Shepherd Dog.* Howell, New York.

1990. Lanting, Fred. *The Total German Shepherd Dog.* Loveland, Colorado.

1991. Walkowicz, Chris. *The German Shepherd Dog.* Denlinger's, USA.

1993. Willis, Malcolm B. *Pet Owner's Guide to the German Shepherd Dog.* Ringpress Books, Lydney, Gloucestershire.

1995. Palika, Liz (Editor). *The German Shepherd Dog: An Owner's Guide to a Happy Healthy Pet.* Howell, New York.

1996. Ackerman, Lowell. *Dr Ackerman's Book of the German Shepherd.* TFH, New Jersey.

1996. Allan, Roy, et al. *A Dog Owner's Guide to German Shepherd Dogs.* Tetra Press.

1996. Fogle, Bruce. *Dog Breed Handbooks: German Shepherd.* Dorling Kindersley, London.

1996. Hegewald-Kawich, Horst. *The German Shepherd Dog: Expert Advice on Training, Care, and Nutrition.* Barron, New York.

1996. Kallen, Stuart A. *German Shepherds.*

1996. Mars, Julie. *German Shepherds.*

1996. Orban, Timothy. *Guide to Owning a German Shepherd: Puppy Care, Grooming, Training, History, Health, Breed Standard.*

1996. Schwartz, Charlotte. *A New Owner's Guide to German Shepherds.*

1996. Siegal, Mordecai and Margolis, Matthew. *The Good Shepherd: A Pet Owner's Guide to the German Shepherd Dog.* Little, Brown, Boston.

1996. Wilcox, Charlotte. *The German Shepherd Dog.*

1998. Dunbar, Ian, et al. *The Essential German Shepherd Dog*. The Essential Guides.

1998. Palika, Liz. *How to Train Your German Shepherd*.

1998. Rankin, Sheila (Editor). *The Ultimate German Shepherd Dog*. Howell, New York.

1999. Berger, Todd R. *Love of German Shepherds*.

1999. Coile, D. Caroline. *The Complete Idiot's Guide to German Shepherd Dogs*.

1999. Orban, Timothy. *German Shepherd*.

1999. Pavia, Audrey. *Your German Shepherd's Life: Your Complete Guide to Raising Your Pet from Puppy to Companion*.

1999. Rice, Dan. *Training Your German Shepherd Dog*.

2000. Brazil-Adelman, Mary Belle. *The German Shepherd Handbook*. Barron, New York.

Alderton, David. *Beginner's Guide to German Shepherds*. Howell, New York.

Allan, Roy. *The Essential German Shepherd Dog*.

Ashabranner, Brent. *Crazy About German Shepherds*.

Novesky, Thomas. *Marta the Best in the West: The Life Story of a German Shepherd Dog*.

Sanford, William R. *The German Shepherd*.

GERMAN WOLFSPITZ   GERMANY

Known in France as the Chien Loup, this dog was originally a sheep-herder, but in later years it was increasingly employed as a guard dog or companion. In its role as the guardian of the vehicles of German carriers, it was called the Fuhrmannsspitz.

The German term 'spitz', meaning 'sharp point', was first introduced in the 15th century to denote northern dogs with pointed muzzles, erect, pointed ears, up-curled tails, stocky bodies and thick, double coats. It is thought that the Wolfspitz arrived in Germany from the north even before that date and may have been working as a herder for centuries before it acquired its modern title.

The German spitz dogs are currently recognized in five different sizes (from large to small, they are: wolf, giant, standard, miniature and toy). Despite its name, the 'Giant' is much smaller than the Wolfspitz. The Giant weighs only 38–40 lb (17–18 kg), while the Wolfspitz registers 60–70 lb (27–32 kg). The colours accepted vary from size to size. The Wolfspitz is recognized only in wolf grey.

Some authorities consider that this herding dog and the Dutch barge dog, the Keeshond, are one and the same, but it is now generally agreed that they must be regarded as two separate breeds. Even though they may be similar in appearance, it would be surprising if, after generations of specialization as barge dogs, the Dutch type had not developed a distinctive and very different temperament and personality. It is also, incidentally, slightly smaller than its German relative.

ICELAND

ICELAND DOG

This breed has also been called the Icelandic Sheepdog, the Iceland Spitz, the Islandske Spidshunde, the Islandsk Farehond, the Friaar Dog, or the Fiaarhundur. In addition to its main task of controlling the flocks of sheep, it has also been used for rounding up ponies.

The ancestors of the Iceland Dog arrived on the island in AD 874, along with the first Norwegian settlers and their flocks of sheep. It is therefore assumed that the Iceland Dog is a relative of the slightly larger Norwegian Buhund, which it closely resembles.

This ancient, northern dog was referred to in the Icelandic Sagas a thousand years ago, and has been mentioned in the canine literature since the 16th century. Writing in 1570, Caius describes the breed as 'Iceland dogs, curled and rough all over'. Even Shakespeare makes a specific reference to the breed in *Henry V*: 'Pish for thee, Iceland Dog! Thou prick-ear'd cur of Iceland.' In 1744 visitors to the island remarked of these dogs that 'they carry the tail upright and they have a small pointed muzzle'. Ten years later, Buffon provides the first illustration of the breed, his engraving showing a typical spitz dog with a pointed muzzle, up-curled tail, pricked ears and a thick black-and-white coat. So the type of this dog has clearly been fixed for centuries.

In the 19th century two disasters befell this breed. One was a heavy infestation of tapeworm, acquired from the sheep, that was passed on to the human population. The situation was so bad that at one time it was estimated that over two per cent of Icelanders were infected. The other was a major epidemic of distemper that wiped out three-quarters of the dog population. They became so rare that desperate farmers were offering a horse and two sheep in exchange for a single Iceland Dog.

The working life of these dogs involved some heavy labour. In the autumn of each year they were especially active, because it was then that the sheep, which had scattered during the summer grazing months, had to be brought down from the hills to the lower ground for the winter. Each dog knew every sheep in its flock individually and would travel for miles over difficult terrain to locate each one and bring it back to the shepherd.

The first written breed standard for the Iceland Dog appeared in Danish in 1887, but it was not until 1969 that a specialist breed club was formed to protect and promote the dog.

References

1956. Watson, Mark. *A Research on the Iceland Dog.* Wensum Kennels, Nicasio, California.

NORWAY

NORWEGIAN BUHUND NORWAY

Also known as the Norwegian Sheepdog, the Norsk Buhund or the Nordiske Sitz-hunde, this ancient breed has been used primarily as a sheep-herder, but has also been co-opted for general farm work. The Norwegian word 'bu' means a shed, booth, stall or homestead, and refers to the crude dwellings constructed by shepherds when they were out with their flocks during the summer grazing months.

The Icelandic Sagas tell of the ancestor of the Iceland Dog arriving from Norway in the ninth century AD. That ancestor was the Norwegian Buhund and those early writings give us a record of just how ancient this breed must be.

Despite this long history, the Buhund remained solely a shepherd's working dog, unknown in the show-ring or to the outside world, until the 1920s. It was then that its impressive spitz body, with its tightly curled tail and pricked ears, attracted the attention of dog-breeders. The patron of the breed, who first set up a serious breeding programme, was John Saeland. In 1936 he had stabilized the type sufficiently to be able to form the first Buhund breed club.

The breed was brought to England just after the ending of World War II, in 1946 or 1947. More examples arrived there in the 1950s and 1960s and it was first given official recognition in 1968. In the show-ring it really took off in the 1970s, having the right kind of 'lively presence' that suited the competitive world of the dog show. It has also been exported to France, Australia, the United States and elsewhere around the world.

In colour it varies from solid cream to light brown, to red and to black, but it is the wheaten shades that are most strongly favoured. In personality it is fearless, loyal, intelligent, energetic and full of life. Its urge to herd is deeply ingrained and, if starved of sheep, it will round up anything that may be available, including goats, turkeys, geese, ducks and even chickens in a farmyard. It is well described as 'a dog that is never off-duty'.

References

1972. Heffer. *The Norwegian Buhund.* Privately published.

POLAND

POLISH LOWLAND SHEEPDOG POLAND

Also known as the Polish Sheepdog, the Valée Sheepdog, the Lowlands Herder, the Berger Polonais de Vallée or, in its homeland, the Polski Owczarek, the Polski Owczarek Nizinny, the Owczarek Nizinny, or the Owczarek Polski Nizinny, this breed has been herding sheep in the lowlands of Poland since at least the 16th century. In Poland it is known to its friends as the Pons, in England as the Nizzy. It is named after the Nizinny district which was once its stronghold.

This shaggy-coated, medium-sized sheepdog is an ancient breed thought to have descended from the Hungarian Puli and various Eastern European, long-coated mountain herders. For centuries it has been working on the Polish lowland plains, where its method of flock control is unusually gentle. More restrained than many other sheepdogs, it uses its eyes and a few gentle shoulder nudges to influence the movements of the flock. It possesses a highly effective 'sheepdog eye' – an intense stare

accompanied by a rigid body posture – that the sheep instantly respect and respond to. As a result of this technique, it makes a much better household companion dog than many other working sheepdogs.

Polish sailors were in the habit of taking some of these dogs with them on their travels and this helped to spread the breed abroad in earlier times. At the beginning of the 16th century, a male and two females were taken to Scotland, where they were exchanged for a ram and a ewe. From that foundation trio, a new type of shaggy sheepdog appeared in the British Isles. Over the years it would change and develop and give rise to several new breeds, including the Bearded Collie, the Bobtail or Old English Sheepdog, the Welsh Collie and the now possibly extinct Old Welsh Grey.

After World War II the breed was nearly extinct, but a few breeders in remote rural districts managed to keep it alive. A Polish breeder by the name of Danuta Hrzniewicz scoured the country and found six bitches and two males of sufficient quality to act as the foundation stock for rebuilding the breed.

Although it arrived in the United States, in very small numbers, in the 1970s, it did not reappear in Britain until 1985, when dog-breeder Megan Butler visited Poland, selected some high-quality stock and imported them to her English kennels, to start a serious breeding programme. Her success in this venture has already led to the dog being officially recognized by the Kennel Club in London.

This is an alert, affectionate, bouncy, playful dog which is both intelligent and easily trainable. In Poland it is known in three sizes, of which the medium one, called the Sredni, is of principal importance. It has a short tail, which traditionally may be docked. Some are said to be born naturally tailless. Its coat appears in all colours, but is usually white, white-and-black, white-and-grey, or grey.

References

1995. Brown, Jane E., et al. *The Official Book of The Polish Lowland Sheepdog.* TFH, New Jersey.

HUNGARY

MUDI   HUNGARY

Sometimes referred to as the Hungarian Mudi, or the Hungarian Sheepdog, this breed's primary function is to herd sheep. It also has several secondary roles — controlling the herds of cattle, destroying vermin on farms, acting as a watchdog and, on special occasions, hunting wild boar.

A rare breed, with probably no more than a few hundred in existence, the Mudi is hardly ever encountered outside its homeland. Its rough, curly coat is usually solid black, but may also be white or pied.

Although a valuable defence against the elements, its coarse hair gives this dog a strangely unkempt, untidy appearance. Traditionally its tail is docked to protect it when working, and this again does not help the animal's appearance because it has the kind of body that cries out for a long, swishing tail to balance its shape. Interestingly, recent photographs of the breed in Hungary show specimens without docked tails. These immediately look better-constructed dogs, worthy of a place in a dog show.

This is the least-known of the indigenous Hungarian dogs and was not considered as a separate breed until the 1930s, when a careful study was made of the different types of sheepdog working in country districts. It was then given its modern name of Mudi by Dezsö Fényesi, the director of a local museum in the town of Balassagyarmat. He was the first person to take a special interest in the dog and to organize selective breeding in an attempt to stabilize it. Previously its breeding had been left entirely to shepherds and herdsmen, and even today there are still some local variations in the appearance of the breed.

PULI HUNGARY

Sometimes given its full name of Hungarian Puli, this strange-looking dog has been used for herding sheep in its native land for many centuries. Its name first appears in Hungarian writings in 1751 and is said to be derived from 'Puli Hou', meaning 'Hun destroyer' — a reference to its links with the Magyars.

The heavily corded 'Rastafarian' Puli is one of the most distinctive of all dogs to be seen in the modern show-ring. Only its giant cousin, the Komondor, has a similar appearance today. The details of the dog's head and its body shape are completely obscured beneath its thick covering of hair.

In origin it is thought that, in ancient times, the ancestors of these dogs arrived from the east, possibly from Tibet, and that the Puli and today's Tibetan Terrier may come from common stock.

This ancient dog has been herding sheep on the Puszta — the Hungarian plains — since at least the ninth century, when it arrived with the Magyar invaders who were spreading west from Siberia. The nomadic shepherds who inhabited the plains knew the dog's value to them and treasured it, so that it remained almost unchanged over the centuries. These shepherds worked with two different breeds — a large white dog (either a Kuvasz or a Komondor) to guard the flocks at night from attacks by thieves or wolves, and the faster, smaller Puli to control the movements of the flocks by day. They took special care not to interbreed these two types.

The breed was first studied carefully in the 1920s, when the professor at Hungary's veterinary college, Dr Emil Raitsitz, began to take an interest in the classification of all the indigenous Hungarian breeds. Up to this point the dog had been bred exclusively for its working potential, but now, with new interest from the show-ring, the Puli began for the first time in its long history to undergo minor changes.

Its thick, corded coat became even thicker and longer, to a point where, had the dog been required to work with flocks of sheep, it would have been severely handicapped. The old, working Puli was a much more agile, unencumbered dog (and each year was shorn with the sheep, to keep it cool in the heat of the summer), but the new show-breeders preferred a dramatically exaggerated coat and that is the one we marvel at today.

In modern times, solid colours, usually but not always black, are the fashion for the show-dog Puli, but in its working past, mixed colours were also common.

References

1976. Owen, Sylvia C. *The Complete Puli*. Howell, New York.
Anderson, E. *How to Raise and Train a Puli*.
Benis, Leslie. *This Is the Puli*.
Weil, Martin. *Puli*.

PUMI   HUNGARY

The name of this dog is probably a local variant of Puli, a better-known breed with which it used to be confused. It is sometimes given the longer title of Hungarian Pumi, but this is super-fluous as there are no Pumis in other countries. Its original task was to herd sheep. It is not over-specialized and will also undertake the control of cattle or pigs with equal zest, and in recent times has, in fact, been used more for cattle than for sheep. It has also been employed to act as a property guard and to control vermin.

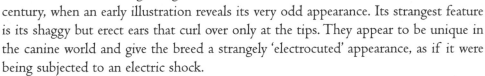

This breed emerged in the 17th or 18th century, when its ancestors were the Hungarian Puli, the German Spitz, the French Briard and some kind of terrier. The terrier blood was important because it gave this breed its distinctive personality. In fact, it was at one time called 'the Sheep Dog Terrier'.

The first accurate description of this breed dates from the beginning of the 19th century, when an early illustration reveals its very odd appearance. Its strangest feature is its shaggy but erect ears that curl over only at the tips. They appear to be unique in the canine world and give the breed a strangely 'electrocuted' appearance, as if it were being subjected to an electric shock.

For many years the Pumi was not regarded as distinct from the Puli, but this was due to ignorance and a muddled use of their two names. It was the Hungarian dog expert Emil Raitsitz who, back in the early decades of the 20th century, first decided to make a marked distinction between the two breeds. In 1921 he compiled a separate breed standard for the Pumi, and from then on it was no longer classed as 'a regional varia-tion of the Puli'.

As soon as Raitsitz started to organize separate breeding programmes, the differences between the Puli and the Pumi became even more obvious. The coat of the Puli was com-pletely different from that of the Pumi. In place of the heavily corded Puli hair, the Pumi had a shorter, wirier coat. The dramatic appearance of the Puli meant that it became the darling of the show-ring, while the shaggier-looking Pumi strengthened its position as the working dog of the countryside. The modern standard for the Pumi was drawn up in 1960, by which time the breeding programmes had fully stabilized the breed. Included in the standard was the requirement that only solid coat colours should be allowed.

The primary function of this breed requires a comment. Some recent English and American authors have labelled it as a cattle drover, one going so far as to say that 'the Pumi was created for the defined purpose of droving cattle... and remains a favourite cattle dog of the Hungarian people'. However, Hungarian canine authorities firmly classify its primary role as that of a sheepdog, placing it with the Puli and the Mudi, and stating: 'The name Pumi is first mentioned in 1815, describing a kind of sheep dog.' As this is one of the nine indigenous Hungarian breeds, all of which the Hungarian experts have studied in great detail, they must be respected in this decision. The reason for the disagreement is probably due to the fact that the Pumi began as a sheepdog but was later increasingly co-opted for cattle work. Even the Hungarian authors comment that 'now Pumis are mainly bred by herdsmen', but this does not alter the original function for which the breed was developed.

CROATIA

CROATIAN SHEEPDOG   CROATIA

Known in its homeland as the Hrvaski Ovcar, this breed is primarily a sheep-herder, although it has sometimes wrongly been labelled as a flock guard.

This little-known breed, which has been controlling the movements of flocks in Croatia for at least a thousand years, bears a striking resemblance to the Mudi that is found further north in Hungary. It is a black or blackish-grey dog with a dense, curly coat. The tail is sometimes docked and sometimes left in the long, natural state. The hair on the face and the fronts of the legs is shorter than elsewhere on the body.

This is a typically rugged, working sheepdog, with a ready aggression should its flock be threatened. However, protecting its livestock is not its primary role. It normally leaves that task to a companion specialized in defence, such as the Karst Shepherd or the Illyrian Sheepdog. Usually the sheep are under the care of a trio made up of the shepherd, the herder and the flock guard. The herder, as is so in this case, is nearly always a lighter, more athletic build than the guarder, so that it is ready to run and run in its attempts to control the activities of the flock.

The Croatian has a height of 16–20 in (40–51 cm) and weighs 30–35 lb (13–16 kg). It is still busily working in the pasture lands today

but is also increasingly observed living a less demanding life as a companion animal. It is rarely, if ever, encountered outside its native Croatia.

According to Croatian Sheepdog expert Barry Marjanovich: 'Today's breed can be considered a direct descendant of the Tresetni and Sojenicki (Soyenichki) dog, originating from Asia, and which the Hungarians unsuccessfully attempted to adopt.'

SAHARA/MIDDLE EAST

BEDOUIN SHEPHERD DOG   SAHARA/MIDDLE EAST

Also known as the Ishtarenhund, this is a tough, hard-living, resilient dog that herds sheep (and sometimes goats or camels) for the nomadic tribes of North Africa and the Middle East.

This hardy breed of dog has to survive the sweeping sandstorms, the intense desert heat, a meagre diet, and the harsh lifestyle of the Bedouin tribes. In origin, it is a wandering Pariah Dog that has been brought under control by the Bedouin and domesticated by them, converting an unspecialized feral dog into a more specialized herder.

Its coat is variable in colour and is left matted and unkempt by its owners. It has a long head with a tapering muzzle, drooped ears, a robust body and a bushy tail. It is a fast-moving dog, fearless and eager to please its masters. In height it is 20–24 in (51–61 cm) and its weight is 40–55 lb (18–25 kg).

RUSSIA

EAST EUROPEAN SHEPHERD   RUSSIA

Known in its homeland as the Byelorussian Owtcharka, this breed was developed early in the 20th century as an important working dog. In addition to herding sheep it was also co-opted as a war dog and a property guard.

This impressive dog is an enlarged version of its direct ancestor, the German Shepherd. In the 1920s the German dogs were imported into Byelorussia and after several decades of selective breeding had been adapted to the harsh environment in which they had to work.

Compared with the German breed, the East European is not only bigger, but also has a longer muzzle, a squarer, more muscular body, and a thicker, denser coat. It soon became immensely popular and began to spread right across Russia. Then, with the chaos of World War II, it inevitably suffered a major setback. It survived, however, and enjoyed a widespread revival.

In colour it usually shows primeval wolf-like shading in black-and-tan, but may also be seen in solid black and occasionally brindle. In height it is up to 29 in (74 cm) and tips the scales at just over 100 lb (48 kg), compared with 25 in (64 cm) and 70 lb (32 kg) for the German Shepherd.

A particularly intelligent dog, with a courageous, tough, determined personality, it has acquired a secondary role as a favourite of the KGB. By tradition, those dogs that are used to patrol the Kremlin are always solid black.

INDIA

DHANGARI DOG   INDIA

The name of this dog is sometimes spelled Dhanagari. Some writers refer to it as the Maharashtrian Dhangari Kutra. The name comes from 'dhangar', the local word for a shepherd. It is used to herd large flocks of sheep and goats in hilly country.

This is a rare dog from the region of Maharashtra, to the east of Bombay in central India. Some authorities believe that it is nearing extinction. Its rarity is due to the fact that it is now interbreeding rather too freely with local mongrels. As a result, pure-bred specimens are increasingly hard to find. A recent report from India suggests that the best places to seek out pure-bred specimens today are near Chikaldara in Vidharbha, where they are kept by the local Korku people, and at Dhavalpuri in Ahamadnagar.

Like all good herding dogs, it is nimble, alert and endlessly energetic, ever watchful for the slightest unusual movement of the grazing animals, or for a small signal from its master. It has remarkable stamina and is capable of working non-stop for a full day, even in a difficult environment. If owned by nomads it always moves with their caravan and at night acts as a useful watchdog around the camp. It may occasionally be taken on hunts for small prey.

The typical colouring of the Dhangari Dog is black above and white below, but this can vary. It weighs about 30 lb (14 kg) and stands about 20 in (51 cm) high. Its long, bushy tail is usually carried over its back, and it has eyes 'sparkling like fire'. In general appearance it is said to be reminiscent of the slightly larger Tibetan Mastiff.

TIBET

TIBETAN TERRIER

TIBET

In the past this breed has also been known as the Dhokhi (or Dhoki) Apso, the Bhutan Terrier, the Bhutanese Dog, the Bhuteer Terrier, the Bhuteer Dog and the Lhasa Terrier. In addition, it has been recorded as the Tibetaanse Terrier or the Darjeeling Terrier. It was used in its homeland both to herd sheep and as a companion dog.

This profusely haired Tibetan sheepdog has been described as resembling a 'miniature Old English Sheepdog'. It also looks like a larger, longer-legged version of its close relative, the Lhasa Apso. Indeed, at the start of the 20th century, there was some confusion between the two Tibetan breeds, and many reports on the talismanic role of the Lhasa Terrier were, in reality, accounts of the smaller Lhasa Apso.

In 1895 the first written mention of the Tibetan Terrier as a distinct breed appeared, when it was stated that, at first glance, it could be taken to be 'neither more nor less than a rough terrier'. Unfortunately, this vague description was taken too literally, with the result that the breed was given the unsuitable title of 'Terrier'. Because it is rather small for a sheep-controlling dog, it did have a superficial resemblance to a shaggy-coated terrier, but it has neither the temperament nor the occupation of an earth dog. Despite this, the name has stuck and is now in general use.

One of the advantages of the comparatively small size of this sheepdog was that it was capable of deftly running over the backs of the sheep when they were in narrow ravines. In the summer, the coats of the working dogs are clipped at the same time as those of the sheep, and the long hair is mixed with yak strands to create a woven cloth.

The first person to bring this breed out of Tibet and to the West was a surgeon called A. R. H. Greig. In the early 1920s, when she was the doctor-in-charge of a hospital on the border between Tibet and India, she was given a female Tibetan Terrier called Beauty, as a reward for saving the life of a Tibetan patient. Two years later she acquired a male for Beauty and started breeding from her. She found these dogs not only endearing, but also courageous. On one occasion, when she was about to be attacked by a rabid dog, one of her Tibetan Terriers leapt to her defence, was badly bitten and subsequently died.

Dr Greig was soon able to persuade the Indian Kennel Club to recognize the breed, and when she returned to England in the 1930s, she achieved the same goal with the Kennel Club in London in 1937. In the United States, dog breeder Alice Murphy imported one of Dr Greig's puppies in 1956. She was quickly converted, acquiring ten more and establishing the breed in North America. In 1957 she founded the Tibetan Terrier Club of America and was eventually successful enough to see the breed officially recognized by the AKC in 1973.

Unlike the smaller Lhasa Apso, the Tibetan Terrier has never become widely popular on either side of the Atlantic, although those who do know the breed are completely won over by it. They find its 'bouncy gait and gentle disposition' especially attractive. Strangely, among certain owners there is a reluctance to admit to the herding origins of this breed. They see the dog exclusively as a companion animal. It is certainly true that in the West this is its role, but in its homeland it is still employed in its primary activity, controlling the movements of sheep. Because of the Chinese Communist slaughter of Tibetan dogs, there are few left now, but on a visit in 2000, Tibetan breed expert Juliette Cunliffe was able to report that it is still possible to see an occasional Tibetan Terrier tending its sheep in the countryside. Seeing this with her own eyes, she was able to report that 'now I have proof that they do indeed still work in this way, and understand that those that do are much valued and cherished'.

References

1964. Murphy, Alice. *How to Raise and Train a Tibetan Terrier.* TFH, New Jersey.

1964. Reif, Jane. *The Tibetan Terrier Book.* Southfarm, Middletown.

1977. Mulliner, Angela. *Tibetan Terrier.* Privately published.

1997. Keleman, Anne. *Tibetan Terrier: a Complete and Reliable Handbook.* TFH, New Jersey.

Reif, Jane. *Reflections on the Tibetan Terrier: a Collection of Writings about the Tibetan Terrier.*

AUSTRALIA

AUSTRALIAN KELPIE   AUSTRALIA

This breed has also been called the Australian Sheep Dog, but is best known simply as the Kelpie. The origin of the name is disputed. One theory is that it is Scottish for 'water sprite' — a spirit that assumes various shapes. Another states that it is Gaelic for 'spirited colt'. A third suggests that it is simply the pet name that was given to the bitch which founded the breed. The primary function of the Kelpie is to control the movements of the huge flocks of sheep that exist in the farmlands of Australia.

As a sheep-herder, this dog is the ultimate workaholic. It is capable of covering more than 30 miles (50 km) in a single day, as it darts here and there, marshalling flocks of sheep that sometimes run to literally thousands of animals. In its sure-footed determination to exert its influence, it may even run over the backs of the sheep as they huddle together. As a working dog it is doubtful if there is a tougher canine in existence.

Its story begins in Scotland in the middle of the 19th century. Farmers travelling to the southern hemisphere to try their luck in the Australian outback often took their Scottish sheepdogs with them. From these, it is the Rutherford strain of the Smooth Collie that is thought to have provided the ancestral basis for the development of the Kelpie. Once in Australia, however, with its heat, its vast open spaces and its enormous flocks of sheep, a new, more sturdy kind of dog was called for. According to some authorities this was achieved simply by selective breeding from a mixture of various kinds of imported sheepdog, but others reject this idea. They insist that the Kelpie stemmed from a cross between a Collie and a Dingo bitch. A black-and-tan female offspring from this union, called Kelpie, was in turn mated with another Collie called Caesar. One of their female offspring resembled its mother so closely that it was called Young Kelpie or Kelpie II. Her descendants were claimed to be the foundation stock for the breed. In appearance, the modern examples of this breed certainly look as though they may have descended from a mixed ancestry that combined the collie herding personality with the stockier, heavier-headed, broader-chested Dingo body-shape. But without DNA tests we cannot be sure.

In the 1870s these early Kelpies made a name for themselves by winning top honours in sheepdog trials. The breed went from strength to strength until it was commonplace all over the continent. Recent assessments of the numbers of Kelpies still working at the end of the 20th century vary wildly from as low as 70,000 to as high as 450,000. A rare breed it is not. Nor is it likely to become one. Ranchers say that one Kelpie can do the work of ten men, and if any working dog's future is assured, this is the one. No mechanical invention will ever be able to replace it.

The words used to characterize this breed all stress its legendary endurance. It is described as energetic, tireless, fast, agile, light-footed, intelligent and conscientious. Its only drawback as a companion dog is that it is liable to become neurotic if it is not allowed to spend its days working incessantly at full throttle. If it has no access to sheep, it will, in desperation, herd anything in sight, from cattle or goats to chickens or geese.

References

1997. Sloane, Steve. *Australian Kelpie.* TFH, New Jersey.

BARB

AUSTRALIA

The Barb, also known as the Black Kelpie or the Australian Barb, was named after a black racehorse that won the Melbourne Cup in 1869. It was developed as a sheep-herding dog on Australian ranches.

This black, sheep-herding dog is very closely related to the Australian Kelpie, and many authors state that the two should be considered as a single breed. Others have gone to lengths to separate them. One of the world's greatest canine historians, Clifford Hubbard, commented in the 1940s that, in addition to being jet black, the Barb 'constitutes a very real breed on its own'. It is, he says, at least 2 in (5 cm) taller in the leg than the Kelpie and has a heavier body. He concludes that, although it is undoubtedly a relative of the Kelpie, its ancestry is slightly different and probably includes some Kangaroo Dog crosses that have given it its extra size. He gives the maximum height and weight for the Kelpie as 20 in (51 cm) and 30 lb (14 kg) and for the Barb as 24 in (61 cm) and 45 lb (20 kg). Another author puts the Barb's maximum weight as high as 55 lb (25 kg).

Angela Sanderson, in her 1980s book *Australian Dogs*, suggests that the situation has changed. She says that 'any black Kelpies were called Barb, and for some time it was believed that these dogs were a different strain to the Kelpie'. The truth, ultimately, will lie with the breeders of Barbs and Kelpies. If the two kinds of dog are kept separate, they will remain two distinct breeds, but if they are freely crossed with one another they will eventually merge into one.

NEW ZEALAND

NEW ZEALAND HUNTAWAY

NEW ZEALAND

This breed is also known as the New Zealand Sheepdog, or simply as the Huntaway. It is purely a working dog, used for controlling large flocks of sheep.

This is a barking sheepdog – one that controls the flock by using its voice. Most sheepdogs carry out their duties silently, running this way and that, but in this instance the dog clusters the sheep together and then moves to the back of the flock. From there it drives the sheep forward and influences the direction they take by barking loudly at them.

This unusual form of sheep control became a popular spectacle at sheepdog field trials. In New Zealand these barking competitions were called 'huntaways', and gave this breed its unusual title. The earliest definition of 'huntaway', in 1933, was as follows: 'Huntaway: a dog whose work is to drive sheep forward when mustering. As a verb the word is used in two senses… "That dog hunts away well" and "I hunt away with that dog".'

Although it is a specialized dog and has been breeding true for at least a century, it has never been formally recognized by any canine authority. This is not because its authenticity as a fully established breed is in any doubt, but simply because its owners have never been interested in such matters. For them, it is a field dog, through and through, and official Kennel Club documentation is of no importance to them.

This is a short-coated, long-tailed dog with a black body and tan extremities. It is a muscular, sturdily built and well-balanced dog lacking in any extreme features. As a breed, it is little-known outside its homeland, but a few of them have been brought back to Britain as working animals and for field trials.

UNITED STATES

AUSTRALIAN SHEPHERD   UNITED STATES

Despite its name, this is an American breed, developed in California for controlling large flocks of sheep. There are slight variations in its name, some authors referring to it as the Australian Shepherd Dog or the Australian Sheepdog. Its nickname is the Aussie.

This bobtailed, wavy-coated sheepdog with its complex coat patterns has an unusual, globe-spanning origin. Its forerunner was the Pyrenean Sheep Dog which was taken to Australia by Basque farmers to control the large flocks of Australian sheep. There it was crossed with various types of Collie. When the dogs resulting from these crosses were brought with their sheep to California in the mid to late 19th century, they were assumed to be pure Australian, although their true origins had been European. As a result, the Californian farmers called them Aussie Sheepdogs, or simply 'Aussies', and that is how their present, official title was born. But the main development and fixing of the breed took place in the years that followed, on American ranches.

This breed has been a popular herding dog in the United States for over a century, much admired for its 'workaholic' personality and its ability to deal with cattle and other livestock in addition to its main duties with sheep. Purely a working dog, it has not been seen in the show-ring until very recently, but there is now an organization – The Australian Shepherd Club of America – to support the breed, and it is recognized by the AKC. A miniature version of the dog also exists, bred down from the full-sized working animal to create a household companion (see separate entry).

The Australian Shepherd is known for its unique pattern of coat markings. They are so variable and complicated that no two dogs look alike. The harsh, wavy coat has a dense undercoat and there is a thick neck ruff. The tail is either naturally bobbed or is docked. The dog's height is 18–23 in (46–58 cm) and its weight is 27–40 lb (12–18 kg).

In personality it is described as loyal, protective, affectionate, active, brave, playful and adaptable. It is sturdy, tireless and prepared to work in any weather, and its main appeal to ranchers is its almost desperate need to please its owner. It is said to 'have a sixth sense about what the owner wants'. A rather silent dog, it occasionally emits a strange call that is somewhere between a bark and a howl.

In recent years this versatile dog has branched out into a whole range of new activities including field trial competitions, narcotics detection work, hearing service for the deaf, search and rescue work, and even Frisbee displays, at which it is said to be a champion competitor.

References

1990. Hartnagle, Joseph. *Australian Shepherds.* TFH, New Jersey.
1995. Palika, Liz. *The Australian Shepherd. Champion of Versatility.* Howell, New York.
1996. Hartnagle-Taylor. *All About Aussies.*
1997. Palika, Liz. *An Owner's Guide to the Pet The Australian Shepherd.* Howell, New York.

BASQUE SHEPHERD   UNITED STATES

This recent breed of American sheep-herder is named after the region in northern Spain which was the homeland of its ancestors. It has also been called the Basque Herder.

The Basque Shepherd is a variant of the better-known Australian Shepherd. Some Australian Shepherd enthusiasts were alarmed by the spinal problems created by selective breeding for natural bobtails. They also felt that the docking of individuals that lacked the natural bobtail had the effect of unbalancing the dog. They therefore started to breed away from the short-tailed lines and also ceased docking the fully tailed lines.

The result of this new trend is an attractive working animal with a long, flowing tail that seems much more appropriate for a sheep-herding dog – an animal that must twist and turn as it works to control its flocks. Its supporters are convinced that the Basque Shepherd will one day come to overshadow its awkwardly de-tailed relative.

ENGLISH SHEPHERD UNITED STATES

Despite its name, this is an American breed. It is called the English Sheepdog because it was imported into North America from England by early settlers arriving in the New World. In recent times there has been much debate about the correct name for this breed, and many rival proposals have been put forward, including Farm Shepherd, Old Time Farm Shepherd, Farm Collie, Old Farm Collie, North American Old Farm Collie, Old Working Collie, Scotch Collie, Old Scotch Collie, Holmesian Collie (after John Holmes), and Victorian Collie (suggested by the Classic Victorian Collie Club). In addition to herding sheep, this versatile breed can also be worked with any form of livestock, from cattle to poultry. In the southern states it is sometimes given an extra role as a hunting dog and is used for treeing squirrels. In some rural districts, where this activity is popular, the breed has been referred to as the Treeing Farm Shepherd or the Treeing Shepherd.

This is a descendant of the old type of sheepdog that was active in England centuries ago, but is no longer to be seen there. According to American enthusiasts, it alone has remained honest to its original, working form, unlike other modern sheepdog breeds, which have been refined for the show-ring. Compared with the elegantly elongated Rough Collie, for example, it has a much broader skull and shorter muzzle.

It may seem strange that the English Shepherd is to be found today in America and not in its homeland, but there is a simple explanation for this. Back in the 16th century this breed is mentioned in the earliest of all dog books, *Of Englishe Dogges* by John Keys (also known as Johannes Caius), where it is described as follows:

> Our Shepherd's Dog is not huge, vast, and big; but of an indifferent stature and growth, because it hath not to deal with the bloodthirsty wolf, since there are none in England... This dog, either at the hearing of his master's voice, or at the wagging and whistling in his fist, or at his shrill and hoarse hissing, bringeth the... straying sheep into the selfsame place where his master's will and wish is... either to have them go forward, or stand still, or to draw backward, or to turn this way, or to take that way...

It is clear from this description that, back in 1536, when the book was written, England could boast a classic, sheep-herding dog. However, in the 18th century, new land enclosure laws restricted the movements of flocks and largely removed the need for working sheepdogs. In Scotland and Wales, however, there were plenty of wild, hilly places that escaped this restriction. That is why Scottish and Welsh sheepdogs were able to outlive the English kind. And, of course, in the wider, open spaces of North America, those farm dogs that accompanied the early settlers in the 17th century were also able to continue to fulfil their original role and could therefore survive as a breed.

Having said this, it must be pointed out that, as with many working dogs, performance has always been more important than appearance, and America's English Shepherd is to this day sufficiently variable to have been ignored by the strict pedigree world of the AKC. Only the more liberal-minded United Kennel Club has accepted it for registration as a true breed.

The extent of the variability of these dogs is clear from their breed standard. Their ears may be pricked, folded, low-set or 'on the side'; their body-type may be heavy or lean; their height may vary from 18 to 24 in (46 to 61 cm) and their weight from 35 to 90 lb (16 to 41 kg); their eyes may be brown, blue or one of each; their glossy coat may be straight or wavy; their tail may be long, sabre, up-curled or bobtailed; and their coat colours are many. Yet despite all these variations, the English Shepherd is very much its own dog, with its own special character. It is easy to see why it is hard to judge it in the show-ring, but that does not mean that it should be ignored as a genuine, working breed.

In personality, this is said to be an ideal companion dog and is especially good with children. It is responsive, cheerful, dependable, calm, loyal, brave, gentle, intelligent and athletic. If it is not required as a hard-working farm labourer, it will make a most rewarding pet, providing it is allowed to enjoy plenty of daily exercise.

McNab Dog UNITED STATES

This working sheepdog was named after its creator, Alexander McNab, who left Scotland to settle on a ranch in California. It is also referred to as the McNab Shepherd.

The origins of this breed stretch back to Scotland in the early 19th century. It was then that Bruce McKinsey and his family left the Highlands of the north and settled in the Grampian Hills of central Scotland. They brought with them their sheepdogs, an early kind of collie called the Fox Shepherd. Their new neighbour, Alexander McNab, started breeding these dogs and established them in the region. In 1868 he emigrated to California and established himself there as a sheep farmer on a large ranch near the town of Ukiah in Mendocino County. In 1885 he returned briefly to Scotland to obtain some of the sheepdogs he had developed there. He took one, called Peter, back with him to California, and others would follow later, to work on his ranch.

Once in California, the Scottish dogs were mated with female Spanish sheepdogs that had been imported by Basque farmers who were also settling in the region. The crosses resulting from these matings provided the foundation stock for the McNab breed which was to be developed over the years ahead.

In perfecting the new breed, it was important to adapt it to the hotter, American climate, and there was strong selection for short-coated dogs. Other changes took place until the McNab was truly its own, distinctive breed. Today it is still popular in the great central valley of California, but is seldom heard about elsewhere, or seen at dog shows, because it is first and foremost a working stockdog, whose character is considered more important than its precise appearance.

The McNab typically has a predominantly black coat, with white markings. These markings usually consist of a white muzzle, a white flash on the head, white on the neck, chest and tail-tip, and on one or more feet. Its tail is not bushy. Its height is 18–22 in (46–56 cm) and its weight is 40–50 lb (18–23 kg), although some strains are reported to be smaller than this.

This is a fast, alert, agile dog, and a quick learner. It is direct and forceful in its working style, employing barking, growling and nipping in a manner that sets it apart from the typically silent, stealthy Border Collie.

ARGENTINA

PATAGONIAN SHEEPDOG ARGENTINA

In its homeland this breed is also known as the Barbucho, which translates as 'little beard' and refers to the dog's hairy face. In addition to controlling the movement of huge flocks of sheep, this herder has the added task of defending them from attacks by predators.

At the start of the 20th century a number of Welsh sheep farmers emigrated to Argentina, taking their sheepdogs with them. Prominent among these dogs was the shaggy-coated Old Welsh Grey and it is this breed that the Patagonian Sheepdog most closely resembles, strongly suggesting that it was the main ancestor of the new breed.

In the South American landscape, with its vast, open grasslands, the sheepdogs from Wales faced incredibly hard work. With thousands of sheep to be rounded up from enormous grazing areas, there must have been intense selection for stronger, more muscular dogs, and with this pressure, the old Welsh hill dogs would have rapidly developed into the new Patagonian breed.

CATTLE-HERDERS

Herding cattle is a more dangerous task than the more common canine duty of herding sheep. Irritated cattle can lash out with a hoof and injure a dog that is too slow to react, so cattle-herding dogs have to be agile, cunning and quick-thinking. To deal with the much larger livestock, they also have to be powerful and aggressive. Their duties range from guiding herds of cattle on the wide open spaces of big ranches, to driving cattle through busy streets on the way to market. In addition to barking and generally worrying the cattle to go in the desired direction, many of these breeds also control them by nipping their feet. Such dogs have to be carefully controlled to ensure that they do not bite the cattle too seriously and cause damage.

When they are not actively herding cattle, these dogs are often employed as useful livestock guards or property guards. Geographically, they have their origins in Europe, North America and Australia. There are 22 breeds in this category.

ENGLAND

BOBTAIL   ENGLAND

This breed has also been called the Bobtailed Sheep Dog, but it is best-known by the highly mis-leading name of Old English Sheepdog, or OES. The truth is that it is not very old, is only partly English and is not a sheepdog, which is why that name is not used as the main title here. The breed was developed as a drover's dog and employed to control the movements of cattle. Any work carried out with flocks of sheep was secondary.

The earliest known date we have for this breed (and even that is uncertain) is the late 18th century. It may have been created by crossing English drover's dogs, and possibly Bearded Collies, with European breeds such as the Italian Bergamasco or the Russian Ovtcharkas, but there is no hard evidence for this. Once it was established, we do know that its main centre of development was in the West Country of England.

The reason usually given for the bobbing of the tail of this breed is that it was a tax-avoidance scheme. At one time, drovers' dogs were exempt from certain taxes and this breed was supposed to have been docked in order to display clearly its working status. The true sheep-herding dog could not be modified in this way because it needed its long tail to assist with its complex, rapid sideways movements as it rounded up the flock. Driving slower-moving cattle did not involve that type of fast, athletic twisting and turning, so a 'rudder' tail was less important.

These cattle dogs were often given subsidiary duties. In addition to occasionally looking after sheep and other farm livestock, they were also sometimes trained to act as retrievers in the hunting field. And once a year they were shorn like sheep and their woolly coats used to make yarn for weaving warm garments. Each dog produced 3–5 lb (1–2 kg) of wool. Today they are almost exclusively companion or show dogs.

This breed was first exhibited at a dog show in 1865 and was recognized in America by the AKC as early as 1888.

In recent times it has become widely known as a profusely hairy champion dog and has impressed audiences the world over with its dramatic coat texture, its appealing personality and its rolling, ambling gait that makes it look like a big, friendly, shaggy bear. Its typical colour-pattern is blue-grey with a predominantly white head, neck, front and feet.

In the home it is a faithful dog, protective, intelligent, loving, watchful and fearless, but its need for exercise and grooming requires regular attention. It is also undeniably photogenic, which has led to its use in commercial product endorsement. This in turn has given rise to the mixed blessing of even greater popularity among those who know little about its special requirements.

References

1905. Hopwood, Aubrey. *The Old English Sheep Dog*. Bickers & Son, London.

1914. Megnin. *Les Chiens De Berger Anglais (Old English, Collie & Shetland)*.

1933. Tilley, Henry Arthur. *The Old English Sheepdog*. Watmoughs, London.

1935. Johns, Rowland. *Our Friends the Old English and Shetland Sheepdogs*. Methuen, London.

1936. Smyth. *Inordinate Affection – Old English Sheepdog*.

1961. Keeling, Jill Annette. *The Old English Sheepdog*. Foyles, London.

1967. Berkowitz, Mona. *How to Raise and Train an Old English Sheepdog*. TFH, New Jersey.

1973. Davis, Ann. *The Old English Sheepdog*. Popular Dogs, London.

1973. Gould, Jean. *All About The Old English Sheepdog*. Pelham Books, London.

1974. Brearley, Joan Macdonald. *This is the Old English Sheepdog*. TFH, New Jersey.

1976. Mandeville, John. *The Complete Old English Sheepdog*. Howell, New York.

1977. Edwards, George Hampden. *Old English Sheepdogs in Australia*. Wentworth Books, Sydney.

1978. Boyer, Alice. *Your Old English Sheepdog*. Denlinger's, Fairfax, Virginia.

1980. Pisano, Beverly. *Old English Sheepdogs*. TFH, New Jersey.

1989. Brearley, Joan MacDonald. *The Old English Sheepdog*.

1993. Smith, Christina. *The Complete Old English Sheepdog*. Howell, New York.

1999. Walker, Joan Hustace. *Old English Sheepdogs: Everything About Purchase, Care, Nutrition, Behavior, and Training*. Barron, New York.

Sanford, William Reynolds. *The Old English Sheepdog*.

Woods, Sylvia. *Old English Sheepdogs*.

CUR DOG
ENGLAND

One theory suggests that the name of this dog is taken from 'cur-tail' – to shorten – and relates to the fact that the animal's tail was docked or naturally short. The other sees 'cur' as being the noise ('grrrr') that a dog makes when giving a low growl. This was originally a powerful, cattle-controlling dog, sometimes called the Drover's Dog.

Today the word 'cur' is used as an insult, or to indicate a lowly mongrel, but in earlier centuries it was employed to describe a specific breed of early English herding dog. Writing in 1790, Thomas Bewick comments that the Cur Dog is 'a trusty and useful servant to the farmer and grazier... especially in the north of England, and such great attention is paid in breeding it, that we cannot help considering it as a permanent kind'.

Some authors refer to them as sheepdogs, but Bewick makes it clear that 'they are chiefly employed in driving cattle; in which way they are extremely useful. They are larger, stronger, and fiercer than the Shepherd's Dog; and their hair is smoother and shorter'.

Sydenhan Edwards, writing a little later, in 1801, makes a similar point, adding that the Cur Dog has longer legs than the Sheepdog. He believes that it is the result of crosses between the Sheepdog and the Lurcher, or possibly the Mastiff.

In dealing with the cattle, the Cur Dogs were typical heelers, with a keen bite, and were even capable of driving large bulls. Ever watchful, they immediately detected strange cattle intruding on their herd and quickly drove them away. If one of their own herd began to stray, they swiftly rounded it up.

In personality they were said to be cunning and clever, active and busy, restless and noisy. The coat colour was usually black-and-white. The ears were half-pricked. Some puppies were born with short tails and so avoided docking; these were called 'self-tailed dogs'. It is not certain when or why this breed vanished, or why the name 'cur' should have ended up as a widely used insult. It seems likely that the dog disappeared at some point in the 19th century, when it was replaced by that hairier cattle dog, the Bobtail (see separate entry).

LANCASHIRE HEELER ENGLAND

Also known as the Ormskirk Heeler or the Ormskirk Terrier, this breed was developed primarily as a cattle-driving dog.

In the days when cattle were walked to market, small dogs were employed to drive them along by nipping at their heels. This was a delicate task because if the bite was too weak it had no impact and if it was too strong it panicked the cows and there was a risk of a sudden stampede. So breeding the perfect heeler was a refined art. One such animal was the Lancashire Heeler.

This breed originated from crosses between Welsh Corgis and Manchester Terriers. Originally, this is supposed to have happened almost by accident when Welsh cattle were being driven to market at the Lancashire town of Ormskirk. There, the Corgis met and mated with the local terriers, creating a slightly taller, leaner, black-and-tan version of the Corgi, or, if you prefer, a stumpier, more stolid version of the Manchester Terrier. In the Victorian era, local gypsies employed these dogs to drive their goats along when caravans were on the move, and farmers discovered that this breed was a useful, dual-purpose worker. Not only could it drive cattle, thanks to its Corgi ancestry, but in a secondary role it was also a useful ratter, courtesy of its Manchester Terrier ancestry.

This dual personality meant that, when mechanization arrived and the drover's dog suddenly became obsolete, there was still a useful vermin-control task for the Lancashire Heeler to perform, so it managed to cling on at a time when some other cattle-driving breeds were becoming extinct. Surviving the transport revolution, it was later taken up as a pedigree show dog. It then increased in numbers in this new role and was eventually recognized by the Kennel Club, who finally awarded it Championship Certificate status in 1999.

Recently, dissenting voices have been raised concerning the history of this breed. They claim that, when cattle were no longer walked to market, but were instead carried in lorries, the Lancashire Heeler did become extinct. This is said to have taken place early in the interwar period, as heavy motorized transport started to become a serious commercial proposition. They insist that the breed was then artificially recreated as a show dog in the 1960s, by making new, deliberate crosses between its two ancestral breeds. The Lancashire Heeler Club refutes this, stating that although a few modern breeders may have produced 'reconstituted' Heelers in this way, the old breed certainly did not become extinct and, indeed, some families have breeding records going back over a period of 70 years.

Happily, regardless of this dispute, the dog is now finding favour on an international scale. Many breeders and owners are attracted by its lively and appealing personality, and although it is by no means a common breed, its future seems assured.

SMITHFIELD COLLIE   ENGLAND

Also known as the Smithfield Drover, this extinct cattle dog was important in its role as ancestor to several other breeds.

Little is known about this dog, which appears to have become extinct in the 19th century. It was presumably employed to drive herds of cattle to Smithfield Market in London, which had been established there since the 12th century.

The name of this breed is repeatedly mentioned in connection with its ancestral role in the creation of other breeds. For example, during the 1830s it was crossed with Dingoes in Australia, in attempts to create a tougher form of working cattle dog for the rugged conditions of the outback. The offspring from this cross were called Timmon's Biters, and in the 1840s these dogs were used in further crosses that led, in the end, to the creation of the Australian Cattle Dog, or Blue Heeler (see separate entry).

In the United States, the creation of a sheepdog breed there called the Australian Shepherd (see separate entry) also involved the Smithfield Collie, in crosses with the Border Collie, the Rough Collie and the Pyrenean Sheepdog.

SCOTLAND

BEARDED COLLIE   SCOTLAND

This breed has also been called the Highland Collie, the Hairy Mountain Dog, the Mountain Collie, the Beardie or simply the Beard. In the early days it was known as the Scot's Colley Dog. This is primarily a drover's cattle dog, although it has also been used to control sheep.

There are several theories concerning the origin of this breed:

1 It began as a cross between the Scotch Collie and the Bobtail, or Old English Sheepdog. This is unlikely because the Bobtail was not an early breed.

2 It is a descendant of the shaggy-coated Polish Lowland Sheepdog (see separate entry), three of which were brought to Scotland in the 16th century. From that trio, via crosses with indigenous Highland Collies, there came a variety of early, long-haired herding dogs, including the Bearded Collie.

3 It was developed from another shaggy British sheepdog – the Old Welsh Grey, now possibly extinct.

4 It was descended from the Icelandic Dog.

5 It was an ancient and indigenous Scottish sheepdog which gained added protection from its longer coat in the freezing winter Highlands.

For several centuries the working ancestors of the modern Beardie were engaged in hard labour as drover's dogs, controlling the herds of cattle on the hills of Scotland. It also played an important role in driving the livestock (including both cattle and sheep) when they were being taken to market. It is said that in the 17th and 18th centuries there were two slightly different types – the Border strain and the Highland strain, differing in colour. As the years passed, these two became so intermixed that, in the end, there was only a single version. This type became more or less fixed in the 19th century and at the same time switched its main duties from its original cattle work to controlling sheep.

In 1912 a breed club (now defunct) was established and the first breed standard was drawn up. But the Beardie was falling slowly out of favour and, towards the end of World War II, was almost gone. Then a lucky accident occurred, which would eventually lead to a revival of the breed. A Mrs Olive Willison asked a Scottish farmer to supply her with a working Shetland Sheepdog. The puppy she received, called Jeannie, was not what she expected. It grew up to be a delightful Bearded Collie bitch. Mrs Willison became so attached to Jeannie that she decided to breed from her. The problem was to find a suitable mate. In January 1944 she located a Beardie called Bailey in the south of England. He was the ideal partner for Jeannie and Mrs Willison managed to acquire him.

From that pair she established a new line that was to prove immensely successful. In fact, virtually all the modern Beardie show dogs can trace their ancestry back to her kennels. She not only improved the stock (it is thought that a small amount of Bobtail was added along the way) but campaigned vigorously to promote the breed. By 1955 a new Bearded Collie Club had been formed, and by 1959 the breed had been accepted by the Kennel Club in London. Its fame soon spread around the world and by 1969 the Bearded Collie Club of America had been formed. The AKC accepted the breed in 1976.

The crowning moment for the revived breed came in 1989, when a Bearded Collie won Best in Show at Crufts. What had started out as a rough-and-ready, tousled-looking drover's dog had become groomed and refined into a glamour star of the show-ring. Since then, its flowing grey-and-white coat, combined with its lively personality, has made it increasingly popular, but this is an exuberant, high-spirited, energetic dog which can easily become bored if it does not have enough work to do. Its personality should be borne in mind if it is to be taken on as a modern pet. If it is to flourish, it must be given adequate exercise and activity.

References

1978. Rieseberg, Barbara and McKinney, B. J. *Beardie Basics: The Complete Guide to Bearded Collies.* Alpine Publications.

1979. Collis, Joyce. *All About the Bearded Collie.* Pelham Books, London.

1985. Walkowicz, Chris. *Bearded Collie.* Denlinger's, USA.

1990. Gold, Carol. *Bearded Collies.* TFH, New Jersey.

1990. Moorehouse. *Talking about Beardies.*

1992. Collis, Joyce and Jones, Pat. *The Complete Bearded Collie.* Howell, New York.

1999. White, Brenda. *The Bearded Collie.* Pet Owner's Guide Series. Ringpress Books, Lydney, Gloucestershire.

WALES

CARDIGAN WELSH CORGI   WALES

Known to its friends as the Cardi, this dog has acted as a heeler, driving cattle to pasture or to market, for many centuries. An earlier spelling for its name was Kergie. In the Welsh language it has been called Ci Llathaid, indicating that it is a yard long, from the tip of its nose to the tip of its tail. (The old Welsh yard was 40 in [102 cm].) The word 'Corgi' is Celtic for 'Dog' and was at one stage corrupted to 'Curgi' and then to 'Cur'. In this last form it was no longer related to the Corgi breed.

Welsh Corgis (of two types, the Cardigan and the Pembroke) have been working as cattle heelers in Wales for at least a thousand years. It was their task to drive the herds of cattle along by nipping at their legs. On long journeys, they drove the cattle by day and guarded them by night. In earlier centuries they were slightly taller, more robust dogs than those of the modern show-ring.

The Cardigan breed is distinguished from the closely related Pembroke Corgi by its long, bushy tail and its larger, rounder ears. It is slightly bigger, heavier-boned and with a longer body. The Cardigan, with its favoured blue-merle (blue-grey flecked with black) coloration, is usually darker than the Pembroke. The Cardigan typically shows white patches on its feet, chest, neck and face. These patches may also occur in the Pembroke but are less common there. Both Corgi breeds come from south-west Wales, but the homeland of the Cardigan is further north than that of the Pembroke.

At one time the Cardigan and the Pembroke were allowed to interbreed freely, but then, in 1927, Crufts listed them as two types and in 1934 they were fully recognized as two separate breeds. In 1935 the Cardigan was accepted by the AKC in the United States.

This breed has been described as 'hard as nails', energetic, muscular, strong and sturdy. Both breeds of Corgi carry the personality of a large dog in their small bodies.

References

1952. Hubbard, Clifford L. B. *The Cardiganshire Corgi Handbook.* Nicholson & Watson, London.

1954, Johns, Rowland (Editor). *Our Friend The Welsh Corgi, Pembroke and Cardigan.* Methuen, London.

1990. Nelms, Hemming. *Cardigan Welsh Corgis.* TFH, New Jersey.

1999. May, Richard G. *Welsh Corgis: Pembroke and Cardigan: Everything About Purchase, Care, Nutrition, Grooming, Behavior, and Training.* Barron, New York.

(Note: General books on Corgis are listed under the entry for the Pembroke Welsh Corgi.)

PEMBROKE WELSH CORGI   WALES

Known to its friends as the Pembi and in the Welsh language as Ci Sawdl, or Ci Sodli, meaning 'to heel', this breed, like its close relative the Cardigan, has been employed as a cattle dog for more than a thousand years. In earlier days it was sometimes called the Welsh Heeler.

The easiest way to distinguish the Pembroke from the Cardigan is by the absence of its tail. Puppies either are born tailless or are docked to appear tailless. Curiously, an early ban on tail-docking in this breed was imposed by the Kennel Club in London in 1931. The ban lasted for three years but was then lifted.

Queen Elizabeth II has championed this breed since 1933, when she acquired her first Pembroke, called Dookie. The choice of a small cattle dog as a royal companion is unusual and has not been without its problems. Frustrated in their deeply ingrained urge to herd cattle by biting their legs, the royal Corgis have occasionally snatched an opportunity to revert to type by nipping the legs of palace staff. They are on record as biting two Grenadier Guardsmen, one Irish Guardsman, one policeman and one royal clock-winder. Off the record they are said to have given the term 'footman' a new meaning. In 1991, one Corgi even committed treason

by biting the Queen herself when she tried to break up a dog fight. Despite these unfortunate incidents the Monarch's 'breed loyalty' has proved unswerving, and several generations of Pembrokes have remained much loved pets at Buckingham Palace over a period of nearly 70 years.

Within two decades of the start of royal patronage of the breed, the Pembroke's popularity had risen by 20 times, easily outstripping the Cardigan. Today it is nearly eight times as popular as the Cardigan. It was recognized by the Kennel Club in London in 1934 and by the AKC in the United States in 1936.

References

1948. Johns, Rowland (Editor). *Our Friend the Welsh Corgi; Pembroke and Cardigan*. Methuen, London.

1952. Hubbard, Clifford L. B. *The Pembrokeshire Corgi Handbook*. Nicholson & Watson, London.

1954. Lister-Kaye, Charles. *The Popular Welsh Corgi*. Popular Dogs, London.

1955. Forsyth-Forrest. *Welsh Corgis*.

1958. Perrins, Leslie. *Keeping a Corgi*. Rockliff, London.

1964. Niccoli, Ria. *How to Raise and Train a Pembroke Welsh Corgi*. TFH, New Jersey.

1970. Albin. *The Family Welsh Corgi*.

1970. Osborne, Margaret. *Know Your Welsh Corgi*. The Pet Library, New York.

1975. Anon. *An Illustrated Study of the Pembroke Welsh Corgi Standard*. Pembroke Welsh Corgi Club of America.

1976. Elias, Esther. *Profile of Glindy: A Welsh Corgi*. Christopher Publishing, North Quincy, Massachusetts.

1978. Berndt, R. J. *Your Welsh Corgi: Cardigan-Pembroke*. Denlinger's, Fairfax, Virginia.

1979. Sargent, Mary Gay and Harper, Deborah S. *The Complete Pembroke Welsh Corgi*. Howell, New York.

1989. Nicole. *Pembroke Welsh Corgis*. TFH, New Jersey.

1994. Harper, Deborah S. *The New Complete Pembroke Welsh Corgi*. Howell, New York.

1999. May, Richard G. *Welsh Corgis: Pembroke and Cardigan: Everything About Purchase, Care, Nutrition, Grooming, Behavior, and Training*. Barron, New York.

2000. Ewing, Su, et al. *The Pembroke Welsh Corgi: Family Friend and Farmhand*.

Dunbar, Ian (Editor). *The Essential Pembroke Welsh Corgi*.

BELGIUM

BOUVIER DES ARDENNES   BELGIUM

This is also known as the Ardennes Cattle Dog. In addition to its main role as a cattle-herder, the breed has been employed as a farm watchdog.

Today this is an extremely rare breed, and may soon vanish altogether. It was created from crosses between the more popular Bouvier des Flandres (see separate entry) and the Belgian Malinois Sheepdog, with possible additions of Briard, in an attempt to produce the perfect cattle dog. In the 1940s its future looked bright and a group of these dogs was even exported to the United States, but as a breed it did not thrive and is now nearly extinct.

The tail is traditionally docked, but the ears have never been cropped, unlike those of the Bouvier des Flandres.

BOUVIER DES FLANDRES   BELGIUM

Also sometimes called the Flanders Cattle Dog or the Belgian Cattle Dog, but known internationally by its local title, this breed has been used as a cattle-herder for centuries and has also been employed in the subsidiary roles of cart-puller and property guard. The word 'bouvier' translates literally as 'bovine-herder'. Earlier names for this breed include Vuilbaard ('Dirty Beard'), Koehund ('Cowdog'), Toucheur de Boeuf ('Cattle Drover') and Pic ('Cattle-drover').

The origin of this large, powerful, shaggy-coated dog is obscure, but it is thought to have descended from a mixture of Tibetan Mastiffs, Brabanters, Schnauzers, Griffons and Beaucerons.

This is the last of the Belgian bouviers to exist in any numbers. Several, including the Bouvier de Roulers, the Bouvier de Moerman and the Bouvier de Paret, have already become extinct, and the only other survivor, the Bouvier des Ardennes, is almost gone. But over the years the Bouvier des Flandres has acquired a wide following in many countries and is an imposing presence in the show-ring. It first appeared as a show dog in 1910, in Brussels.

It was the terrible battles of World War I that decimated the Bouviers and their herds, but this particular breed managed to find new, temporary employment as a messenger dog and an ambulance dog. A Belgian army vet by the name of Captain Barbry did his best to protect the breed during its darkest hours and after the war was able to start a breeding programme and prevent it from disappearing altogether. His dogs became the foundation stock for the modern breed and since his day the breed has increased steadily in numbers. It soon crossed the Atlantic and was recognized by the AKC in 1929. Later, the fact that President Kennedy's beautiful wife's maiden name was Jacqueline Bouvier gave the breed an unexpected social boost in the United States.

Traditionally this breed has had both its ears cropped and its tail docked, but this custom is rapidly losing ground. When the ears were cut they stood up as small, erect points, looking outlandishly small for such a big animal. Today, left in a natural state, they fold over. The coat colours include solid black, brindle, grey, fawn or white.

In personality, this breed is said to be extremely friendly with its family, but aggressive with strangers, as befits a powerful guard dog. With its exaggerated eyebrows, moustache and beard it has a distinctive appearance and a rugged, commanding presence.

References

1965. Leggett, Gerene Coates. *How to Raise and Train a Bouvier des Flandres.* TFH, New Jersey.
1981. McLean, Claire D. *Bouvier des Flandres.* Denlinger's, USA.
1990. Lucas, Miranda. *Book of the Breed: Bouvier des Flandres.*
1991. Engel, J. *Bouvier des Flandres: The Dogs of Flandres.*
1991. McLean, Claire D. *Bouviers in America: Record Book.* Denlinger's, USA.

PORTUGAL

SÃO MIGUEL CATTLE DOG   AZORES

Also known as the Azores Cattle Dog, the Cow Dog, the Açores, the Fila de São Miguel or the Cão de Fila de São Miguel, this breed's title refers to the fact that its home is on the remote Island of São Miguel, which is situated in the south-eastern part of the Azores archipelago in the middle of the North Atlantic. The dog's alternative title of Açores is taken from the first name given to this group of islands by the Portuguese when they were colonizing them in the 15th century.

This is a rare breed, little-known outside its island home. Described as 'rustic and aggressive', it spends almost its entire life out of doors, protecting its herds from danger when it is not performing its main duty of actively controlling their movements.

Its origin is not certain, but it seems to be closely related to another Azorean dog called the Fila da Terceira. Terceira is a smaller island in a more central position in the Azores group, and this Fila da Terceira is a watchdog that was itself descended from

467

the Rafeiro da Alentejo, which is a flock guardian from southern Portugal. Bearing in mind the history of the islands, this ancestry makes good sense.

As an efficient cattle drover, the breed encourages movement by nipping very low and avoiding all contact with the udders of the cows. It is an intelligent dog, quick to learn and highly responsive to commands. It is completely trustworthy and is said to demonstrate 'blind obedience'.

Its muscular body can reach a height of up to 24 in (60 cm). The head is heavy, with powerful jaws. The thick coat is fawn, grey or yellow brindle, with a marked fringe in the rump region. When it walks, it has a characteristic waddling gait. Although recognized by the Portuguese canine authorities, this breed has yet to be officially accepted elsewhere, although it is being seriously considered by the FCI.

ITALY

CANE CORSO

SICILY

Also known as the Sicilian Branchiero, the Branchiero Siciliano, or simply the Branchiero, this breed is a recreation of an extinct cattle drover, a molossian dog called the Cane di Macellaio ('Butcher's Dog'), or Macellaio Herding Dog.

A fearsome-looking animal with the appearance of a thickset mastiff, the ancestral form was descended from bull-baiting dogs. This savage origin has left a mark on its cattle-herding style. Most breeds that control the movements of cattle do so by nipping at their heels. The heelers dart this way and that, rather like sheepdogs, approaching each cow from behind and encouraging it to hurry up or move in the desired direction by gently biting at its legs. It is an exhausting process, like sheep-herding on a grand scale.

The Cane Corso employs a completely different technique. It concentrates solely on the leader of the herd, approaching this influential animal and directing its attack at the cow's head. This is a bull-baiter's strategy. Of course, the dog has to inhibit its assault. If it carried the attack through and clamped its powerful jaws on the nose of the leading cow, it would damage the animal. So it must only make threatening lunges. These are enough, however, to influence the leader, who changes direction in order to avoid the dog. By making the leader alter course in this way, the dog can control the movements of the entire herd, since all the cows that are following behind will automatically imitate the change of direction of the leader. This clever, cattle-herding adaptation of the ancient sport of bull-baiting appears to be unique to the Cane Corso.

This breed possesses a heavy, broad head equipped with massive jaws that are capable of doing serious damage if the dog is not properly trained and controlled. Traditionally, the ears have been cropped and the tail docked. Black or brindle are the favoured colours.

The breed became extremely rare after two World Wars, but has since been salvaged by some carefully planned breeding programmes. It is little-known outside Sicily and is not seen on nearby mainland Italy, but a few puppies were exported to the United States in the 1980s, to form a breeding nucleus for North America.

Note: According to the Italian canine expert Flavio Bruno, it is wrong to consider the Cane Corso and the Branchiero Siciliano as the same breed. He points out that the Corso has 'pelo de vacca' (short hair with 'underwool') while the Branchiero has 'pelo raso' (short hair without 'underwool'). He believes that the two types have been sufficiently isolated from one another to justify their separation.

SWITZERLAND

APPENZELL CATTLE DOG

SWITZERLAND

Also known as the Appenzeller Sennenhund, the Bouvier d'Appenzell, the Appenzell Mountain Dog or simply the Appenzeller, this breed was used as a general-purpose farm dog in addition to its main function of herding cattle.

This is one of the four Swiss Mountain Dogs, distinguished from the other three by its tightly curled, spitz tail. Although, as its name suggests, its principal duty was herding and driving cattle, it has, over the years, proved to be a valuable all-purpose farm dog. After helping with the movement of the cattle, it was employed to keep guard over the herds. It was also enlisted to herd both sheep and goats when the need arose. At home, it acted as a property watchdog, and, on market days, as a draught dog, pulling carts piled high with produce from farm to market-stall. When avalanches occurred it was co-opted as a rescue dog. On special occasions, Appenzellers can still be seen wearing their broad, decorated collars, adorned with brass images of cattle, a reminder of their primary function.

The earliest description of this breed dates from 1853, when a book on animal life in the Alps was published. In it, there is reference to 'a clearly barking, short haired, medium size, multicolour cattle dog of a quite even "Spitz type", which can be found in certain regions and is used partly to guard the homestead and partly to herd cattle'. The region in question is Appenzell in the east of Switzerland, near the border with Austria.

The Appenzeller Sennenhund Club was founded in 1906, thanks to the interest of Professor Albert Heim, with the intention of protecting and preserving this rare breed.

A stud book was started and all puppies were registered from that date onwards. The breed gradually spread from its restricted home locality, and in 1936 the first examples arrived in Britain. By 1989 it had became an internationally recognized breed. A breed standard was established, thanks to the work of Head Forester Max Siber, who had become its main champion, and it started to appear at Swiss dog shows.

This is a tricoloured dog with symmetrical markings in black, tan and white. In personality, this dog is described as self-assured, fearless, cheerful, high-spirited, reliable, but suspicious of strangers.

ENTLEBUCH MOUNTAIN DOG SWITZERLAND

Also known as the Entlebucher Cattle Dog, the Entlebucher Sennenhund or simply the Entlebucher, this breed was primarily employed as a cattle drover, but was also used to guard the herds and as a general watchdog and farm dog. It is named after the river that runs through the valley where it is found, in central Switzerland.

This is the smallest of the four Swiss Mountain Dogs (the other three being the Greater Swiss, the Bernese and the Appenzell). In the 19th century these dogs were rather variable and were not recognized as distinct breeds. Then, in 1908, Professor Albert Heim, a Swiss canine expert, with the cooperation of the Swiss Kennel Club, set about standardizing and classifying them. He separated out the different types that were centred in distinct districts and gave them names according to their localities. In the valleys to the west of Lucerne, he recognized the Entlebuch breed. It had shorter legs and a smaller body than the others. Its short coat was tricoloured in black, tan and white, and its tail was severely docked.

This breed had originated as a servant of the Lucernese herdsmen. Its main function was to assist in driving their cattle up into the high pastures for the summer, where it stayed with them to guard them. Then, at the end of the summer, it would help to bring them back down again to the shelter of the valleys for the harsh winter period. It was also employed to drive cattle to market and to move them though mountain passes when they were being used in local trading.

In personality this dog has been described as quiet, trustworthy and trainable, docile with people, eager to work and intelligent and agile with cattle. As a pet animal, it remains active and playful even as an adult, often jumping up and hitting its human companions with its body, as if trying to herd them.

A highly localized breed, it has always been small in number and in the early part of the 20th century was nearly extinct. Although more common now, it has remained comparatively rare and is hardly ever seen outside its native country.

GERMANY

GIANT SCHNAUZER   GERMANY

Called the Riesenschnauzer in its homeland, or simply the Schnauzer, this breed was once known as the Munich Schnauzer, the Münchener or the München Dog. It was first exhibited at a dog show in Munich in 1909 under the title of Russian Bear Schnauzer. The breed has been employed as a cattle drover in southern Germany for many years.

The original ancestor of this powerful, vigorous dog was the Standard Schnauzer which had been employed in Germany for centuries as a rodent-controller. Cattlemen from Bavaria acquired some of these dogs and used them as the basis for creating a much larger, stronger cattle drover. They crossed them with a variety of bigger breeds, including, it is said, the Great Dane, the Rottweiler, possibly the Bouvier des Flandres, and local sheepdogs. The result was a Schnauzer that was about 8 in (20 cm) taller than the Standard form, capable of dealing with even the most wayward of cattle.

The Giant Schnauzer was developed in the region around Munich, and for many years was employed to drive the herds of cattle to market, until this activity was overtaken by the introduction of rail transport in the 19th century. Rendered obsolete as cattle-herders, these dogs then found a new role as urban property guards and later as pets, police dogs and show dogs.

With its special trim, complete with bushy eyebrows, moustache and chin whiskers, this impressive, usually black or 'salt-and-pepper', wire-coated dog looks like a gigantic terrier, but it is a true drover. It used to be the custom to mutilate the ears of this breed by cropping them into an erect, pointed shape, but they are now usually left in their natural, drooped condition. The tail has been traditionally docked to a short stump.

Combining strength and agility, this tough, muscular breed is intelligent, bold, fast-acting and weather-resistant.

References

1964. Lockley, Arthur S. *How to Raise and Train a Giant Schnauzer.* TFH, New Jersey.

1981. Fiorone, F. *Le Schnauzer — Schnauzer Moyen, Schnauzer Géant, Schnauzer Nain.* Éditions de Vecchi, Paris.

1985. Galuszka, Martha (Editor), et al. *What You Should Know about the Giant Schnauzer.* Giant Schnauzer Club of America.

1985. Hammarstrom, Sylvia. *The Giant Schnauzer in America.* Privately published.

1993. Lockley, Arthur S. *Giant Schnauzers.* TFH, New Jersey.

1996. Gallant. *World of Schnauzers: Standard, Giant, Miniature.*

ROTTWEILER

Today this breed is known universally as the Rottweiler, but in earlier times it was sometimes called the Rottweil Dog. To its friends it is known as the Rottie. In Germany it was first called the Rottweiler Metzerhund, which translates literally as the 'Butcher's Dog from Rottweil'. Rottweil is a market town in the Würtemberg district of south-west Germany. Although this dog's original function was to control the movements of cattle on their way to slaughter, it also acquired other duties, acting as a livestock guardian and eventually as a protector of property. Today it is primarily known as a guard dog, a police dog or a show dog.

This is an impressive breed which, like the Bulldog, has seen its name borrowed to describe a particular type of human being — one who is a fiercely tenacious defender of a cause or person. Because there have been several cases of Rottweilers causing severe injuries to strangers or children, it has acquired a bad reputation which it does not deserve. Careful investigations of the incidents involving Rottweiler attacks reveal that, in all cases, the animals either were being tormented or had not been properly cared for or trained by their owners. A well-loved and properly trained Rottweiler is no more dangerous that any other powerful breed of dog. As a result of its long history as a working dog, it has a natural tendency to defend itself or its territory from individuals that it sees as a potential threat, and it does have powerful jaws capable of inflicting serious injury, but, like all dogs, it is susceptible to conditioning and discipline. Recent calls for the banning of the Rottweiler breed, following isolated, tragic incidents, are unjustified.

The early ancestors of this dog were the cattle-driving dogs of the ancient Romans. As the Roman army spread across Europe, they took large dogs with them to control their cattle. When they left, some of these dogs stayed behind and were later crossed with local German sheepdogs. The result was the Rottweiler. This was then developed and improved by the butchers and cattle-dealers of Rottweil, to create the perfect drover's dog.

The cattle-dealers spent a great deal of time on the rough roads around Rottweil, buying cattle and driving them to market. To help them in this task they needed a dog that was a good drover and also an intimidating companion to protect them from the thieves and bandits that infested the region. Fearful of losing their moneybags to these marauders, they attached them to the collars of their loyal dogs. Any strangers attempting to steal the purses from these canine guardians would find themselves in serious trouble, and it was said that the neck of a Rottweiler was safer than any bank vault.

With the arrival of the industrial revolution in the 19th century, these brave dogs faced a crisis. Cattle were now being moved by rail rather than along country roads, and the Rottweiler gradually became obsolete. Its numbers fell lower and lower until, by the start of the 20th century, it was almost extinct. Then, with the outbreak of war in 1914, it found an important new role in the service of the German army. After the war a new career as a guard dog blossomed, and its numbers began to rise again. In the 1930s Rottweilers were exported to both Britain and the United States. The breed was officially recognized by the AKC in 1935 and by the Kennel Club in London in 1966.

The Rottweiler is a short-coated, black-and-tan dog. The black colour predominates, with the tan markings confined to the legs, chest, throat and face. The head is broad, the ears drooping, the body compact and powerful, and the tail heavily docked.

In personality, this dog has been described as bold, devoted, intelligent, courageous, calm, enthusiastic, responsive and self-assured. It is strongly territorial, but is only aggressive when roused.

References

1962. Hall, Patricia. *The Rottweiler in Australia: The First 20 Years.* Privately published.

1964. Klem, Joan R. and Rademacher, P. G. *How to Raise and Train a Rottweiler.* TFH, New Jersey.

1968. Korn, Hans. *Der Rottweiler.*

1969. Macphail, Mary. *Studies in the Breed History of the Rottweiler.*

1970. Zopp. *The Rottweiler in Word and Picture.*

1976. Bresson, H. *Rottweiler.*

1976. Hurley, Clara (Editor). *Regulations/Breeding Matters for Rottweiler.* Allgemeiner Deutscher Rottweiler Club.

1981. Nicholas, Anna Katherine. *The Book of the Rottweiler.* TFH, New Jersey.

1981. Schanzle. *Studies in the Breed History of the Rottweiler.* Powderhorn Press, Hollywood, California.

1982. Kerfmann, Woodrow. *How to Raise and Train a Rottweiler.* TFH, New Jersey.

1982. Anon. *Rottweiler in Word and Picture.* Rottweiler Club of Germany.

1983. Chardet, D. *Know Your Rottweiler.* Powderhorn Press, Hollywood, California.

1984. Freeman, Muriel. *The Complete Rottweiler.* Howell, New York.

1984. Smith, Beverlee. *Rottweiler Critiques.*

1985. Hodinar, Dogmar. *Rottweiler: An International Study of the Breed.*

1985. Stratton, Richard F. *The Rottweiler.* TFH, New Jersey.

1985. Yrjola, J. A. U. and Tikka, Elvi. *Our Friend the Rottweiler.* Powderhorn Press, Hollywood, California.

1986. Stiefel, Emil. *Fifty Years with Rottweilers.*

1987. Macphail, Mary. *All about the Rottweiler.* Pelham Books, London.

1987. Elsden, Judy and Elsden, Larry. *The Rottweiler.* Popular Dogs, London.

1987. Blackmore, Joan. *Dog Owner's Guide to the Rottweiler.* Tetra Press, Morris Plains, New Jersey.

1988. Pettengell, Jim. *The Rottweiler.* David & Charles, Newton Abbot, Devon.

1989. Stratton, Richard F. *The Rottweiler.*

1990. Biene, Heinrich V., et al. *Step by Step Book about Rottweilers.*

1991. Elsden, Judy and Elsden, Larry. *The Rottweiler Today.* Ringpress Books, Letchworth, Hertfordshire.

1991. Kern, Kerry V. *Rottweilers: Everything About Purchase, Care, Nutrition.*

1991. Nicholas, Anna Katherine. *The Professional's Book of Rottweilers.*

1993. MacPhail, Mary. *Pet Owner's Guide to the Rottweiler.* Howell, New York.

1994. Price. *Rottweilers.*

1995. Forster, Jean. *An Owner's Guide to the Rottweiler.* Howell, New York.

1995. Brace, Andrew H. *The Ultimate Rottweiler.* Howell, New York.

1995. Braun, George W. *Guide to Owning a Rottweiler.* TFH, New Jersey.

1995. Klem, Joan R. and Rademacher, Susan C. *Proper Care of Rottweilers.* TFH, New Jersey.

1996. Ackerman, Lowell. *Dr Ackerman's Book of Rottweilers.* TFH, New Jersey.

1996. Arnn, Barbara. *Rottweilers.*

1996. Klem, Joan R. and Rademacher, Susan C. *The Rottweiler Experience: From the Golden Age to Predictions for the 21st Century.* Howell, New York.

1996. Wilcox, Charlotte. *The Rottweiler.*

1996. Zervas (Editor). *Basic Guide to the Rottweiler.*

1997. Jones, Stephen W. (Editor), et al. *Basic Guide to the Rottweiler.*

1998. Stockdale, Renee (Editor), et al. *The Essential Rottweiler.*

1998. Hutchinson, Robert, et al. *For the Love of Rottweilers.*

1998. Palika, Liz. *How to Train Your Rottweiler.*

1996. Ochsenbein, Urs. *A New Owner's Guide to Rottweilers.*

1998. Michels, Linda and Thompson, Catherine M. *The Rottweiler: Centuries of Service.*

1999. Dearth, Kim D. R. *Your Rottweiler's Life: Your Complete Guide to Raising Your Pet from Puppy to Companion.*

1999. McNinch, Barbara L. *Training Your Rottweiler.*

DENMARK

DANISH BROHOLMER DENMARK

Sometimes referred to simply as the Broholmer, this rare breed was named after the location of its greatest supporter, Count Niels Frederik Sehested of Broholm-Funen. This large dog was primarily employed to drive the cattle to market, and in this role was sometimes referred to as a slagterhund, or butcher's dog. An early name for it was Slagterhund. It was also used as a watchdog.

In appearance this impressive dog resembles an elegant, more athletic version of the English Mastiff. This is not surprising because its ancestry consisted of English Mastiffs sent as gifts by the English court to the Danish courts of Frederik II and his son Christian IV, in the 16th century. Once there, they were crossed with local dogs to create a more streamlined version of the great English guard dog. Some remained in

the royal courts while others started work as cattle-herders, the first of these presumably tending the royal herds.

Although, over the centuries, they were developed as working dogs, the royal courts retained an interest in them. Indeed, as late as the middle of the 19th century, some Broholmers were still noble dogs, favoured by royalty. In 1859 one was portrayed lying at the feet of the then king, Frederik VII, and his consort, the countess Danner.

It was at this point that Count Sehested took the breed in hand and started to develop it and standardize it. Its popularity spread and all Sweden began to enjoy this majestic dog. An official breed standard was recorded in 1886. The typical coloration of its short, coarse coat was established as fawn, but black was also permissible.

But then, in the 20th century, the ravages of World War I and World War II between them managed to bring this attractive breed to the verge of extinction. It was such a large dog and so expensive to keep and feed that its numbers plummeted. In 1974, the Committee for National and Forgotten Breeds, appointed by the Danish Kennel Club, started a rescue mission. At first, they could find only two surviving dogs of the original type in the entire country. But then, with the help of a nationwide campaign, they managed to locate a few more in remote corners. Brought together, these were used to rebuild the breed. Eventually, in 1982, it was formally recognized by the FCI.

There are some sceptics, however, who argue that the original Broholmer did become extinct and that the modern versions of the breed are no more than recreations of what the dog should look like, based on a clever mixture of other breeds. Given the fact that an officially appointed committee of canine experts was involved, this seems unlikely.

SWEDEN

SWEDISH VALLHUND   SWEDEN

Also known as the Swedish Cattle Dog, the Swedish Herder Spitz or, in its homeland, the Väsgötaspets or Väsgöta-Spitz, this breed was once called the Vikingarnas Dog because of its supposed Viking origins. Its Swedish name of Väsgötaspets translates as 'Spitz Dog of the West Goths'. The name Vallhund means simply 'Farm Dog'. Its original function was as a heeler, controlling the herds of cattle in Sweden, especially in the Vastergotland region in the south-west of the country.

This sturdy little dog, with its wolf-like coat colouring and its alert, pricked ears, is superficially reminiscent of the Welsh Corgi, and some believe that the resemblance goes deeper. There are two rival theories. Corgi owners insist that ancestors of their working dogs were pillaged from Wales by Viking raiders, taken back to Scandinavia, and there developed into the Vallhund. Owners of Vallhunds, inevitably, claim that the ancestors of their dogs were taken to Wales by Vikings and left there, where, over the centuries, they developed into Corgis. Although, with the scanty evidence available, it is hard to choose between these two theories, the Viking connection itself does seem to be firmly established, because images of these dogs have been found as ornamentations on the remains of old Viking ships discovered in Ireland.

This is a watchful, alert, energetic little dog which, despite its short legs, is capable of covering a great deal of ground. It is slightly taller than the Corgis – they are only 12 in (31 cm) high, while the Vallhund is 13–14 in (33–36 cm). In most cases, the bobtail is naturally short. Docking is forbidden in Sweden, although permitted in some other countries.

In addition to driving the herds of cattle, this breed was also employed to catch vermin on the farms and act as a watchdog. Despite its usefulness, it nearly became extinct in the 1930s, but was saved for future generations by the efforts of Count Bjorn von Rosen and a group of dedicated breeders. Its numbers gradually rose again as it found favour both as a show dog and as a household companion. It was recognized by the Swedish Kennel Club in the 1940s and by the Kennel Club in London in the 1980s.

Note: This breed has sometimes misleadingly been called the Swedish Shepherd or Swedish Sheepdog. Although it has occasionally been employed to herd sheep, this is not its main function.

References

1989. Gascoigne, Nicky. *The Swedish Vallhund.* Wakefield.

AUSTRALIA

AUSTRALIAN CATTLE DOG   AUSTRALIA

Also known as the Queensland Heeler, the Australian Queensland Heeler, Hall's Heeler, the Blue Heeler or the Australian Heeler, this breed was developed specifically as a cattle drover, although when asked to do so it will skilfully control horses, goats and even ducks.

The early cattle ranchers of Australia required a tough, no-nonsense dog that would be capable of controlling cattle by nipping at their hind legs without damaging them. Imported breeds were not adequate for the job so, as early as the 1830s, a serious effort was made, through deliberate crosses, to produce the ideal Australian cattle drover. The first cross was between Smithfield Collies and Dingoes. The cross was given the name of Timmon's Biters, an appropriate title, because it was found that they nipped the legs too hard.

Ten years later, a second cross was made, this time between blue-merle Smooth Collies and Dingoes, and it proved to be more successful. The offspring of this cross were mated with the Timmon's Biters and other experimental half-breeds and then a little Kelpie, Bull Terrier and Dalmatian blood was added. By 1893, a true-breeding, hard-working, perfected cattle dog had been created and this has remained a busy working breed in Australia ever since.

These fearless dogs work silently, a trait inherited from their Dingo ancestry. In this way they can control the movements of the cattle without causing a general panic in the herd. In appearance they have been rather unflatteringly described as looking like 'stunted Alsatians', although in personality they are more like giant Corgis.

References

1954. Atwater, Montgomery M. *Cattle Dog*.

1967. Hamilton-Wilkes, Monty and Cumming, David. *Kelpie and Cattle Dog. The Australian Dogs at Work*. Angus & Robertson, Sydney.

1987. Freud, Jan L. and Johnson, Dorothy L. *Australian Cattle Dog Champions, 1980–1986*. Camino Book Company.

1988. Redhead, Connie. *The Good Looking Australian – Australian Cattle Dog*.

1990. Robertson, Narelle. *Australian Cattle Dogs*. USA.

1993. Holmes, John and Holmes, Mary. *The Complete Australian Cattle Dog*. Howell, New York.

1997. Beauchamp, Richard G. *Australian Cattle Dogs: Everything About Purchase, Care, Nutrition, Breeding, Behavior, and Training*. Barron, New York.

1998. Buetow, Katherine. *The Australian Cattle Dog: An Owner's Guide to a Happy Healthy Pet*. Howell, New York.

1999. Robertson, Narelle. *A New Owner's Guide to Australian Cattle Dogs*.

Harling, Donn. *Australian Cattle Dogs: the First Five Years, 1980–1985*.

Shaffer, Mari. *Heeler Power: A Guide to Training the Working Australian Cattle Dog*.

STUMPY-TAIL CATTLE DOG   AUSTRALIA

Also known as the Smithfield Heeler, the Stump-tail Cattle Dog was developed to control cattle on Australian ranches.

This breed is very close to the Australian Cattle Dog, but differs in several small details. The most obvious distinction is that, whereas its relative has a long, bushy tail, the Stumpy-tailed breed is born with only an abbreviated tail, less than 4 in (10 cm) long, or without any tail at all. It also has a shorter back and a stockier body. In other respects its form and character are the same as its more commonly encountered relation.

UNITED STATES

BLUE LACY   UNITED STATES

Also known as the Blue Lacy Game Dog, this breed is named after its founding fathers, the Lacy brothers, who developed it in the 19th century, to act as cattle drovers in the American West.

In 1858 the brothers Frank, George, Erwin and Harry Lacy, and their farm dogs, left Kentucky in covered wagons and set off for Texas. They settled there in the granite hill country near Marble Falls. To help them in the arduous task of controlling their cattle, they developed their dogs into a droving breed of exceptional quality. The Blue Lacy was such a hard worker that each one of these canine helpers was said to be worth five cowhands. It was a dog that needed little training, taking naturally to its task of driving the herds.

This breed, centred in the south-western states, is related to the Catahoula Leopard Dog, which carries out similar duties in the south-east. In origin, the Blue Lacy is traditionally described as descending from crosses between greyhound, scenthound, droving dog and coyote. Despite this claim, it is highly improbable that the coyote was actually involved. Instead, it is much more likely that that particular element in its ancestry was 'feral dog'.

The Blue Lacy is a fearless breed, capable of dealing with the most bad-tempered and uncooperative of cattle. However, although it is a tough, energetic and dedicated dog, it is also highly sensitive to harsh treatment by its owners, and responds much better to a soft command than a shouted one. With children it is remarkably gentle and friendly.

In addition to its main duty of cattle-herding, the dog has also been employed in a number of secondary roles, including hunting wild hogs, tracking wounded animals, treeing game and even herding poultry.

Despite its name, this short-coated breed is found in a variety of colours, including black, tan, black-and-tan, grey, yellow or cream, and in solids, bicolours or tricolours. Solid colours are the most common, but such dogs often carry a small patch of a second colour.

For about a century these dog proved immensely valuable on the cattle ranches, but then, with the arrival of motorized herding, modernization overtook them. Their numbers fell dramatically and they were rapidly becoming a rare breed, with a real risk of vanishing altogether. In the 1970s H. C. Wilkes set out to save the breed and his efforts have proved successful. There is now a Lacy Game Dog Registry which is keeping accurate records of the breed, and its future is in good hands.

CATAHOULA LEOPARD DOG   UNITED STATES

Also known as the Blue Leopard Dog, the Blue Spotted War Dog, the Catahoula Cur, the Catahoula Hog Dog, the Catahoula Leopard Cowdog, The Catahoula Leopard Stockdog, the Louisiana Catahoula, the Louisiana Catahoula Leopard Dog, the Texas Leopard Cowdog or simply the Leopard Dog, this breed has been developed as a cattle driving dog in the deep south of the United States. Among its owners it has acquired the nickname of 'the Cat'. The word 'leopard' in its title refers to its typically spotted coat.

This is a breed with a most unusual history. Its ancestors were employed by the early Spanish explorers in the New World to brutally drive the native Indians from their lands. Pursuing them into Louisiana, the Spaniards arrived at the marshy land around the Catahoula Lakes in the north-east of the region, where they and their horses sank into the swamps. The Indians climbed into trees to escape and later were able to adopt the abandoned Spanish war dogs. Over the years, they interbred them with their own native dogs. Then, in the middle of the 16th century, shipbuilders moved into this region and obtained some of the Indian dogs as working animals. These were later given the task of controlling the movements of cattle and were eventually developed as specialized cattle drivers. It is thought that some hound blood was introduced at one stage to improve the breed.

Some owners also use these dogs to control the movements of pigs. The dogs are renowned for their fearless behaviour when dealing with escaped or difficult pigs and cattle and are described as hard heelers best suited to rough stock. Tough, sturdy and strong-jawed, they are said to be extremely hard-working and dedicated to their dangerous tasks. One owner referred to them as 'walking sledgehammers'. In personality they are dominating dogs with a strong character, and they require a firm hand. This is not surprising bearing in mind the way they deal with the livestock. Their technique is not to gently drive the animals along, but to attack them boldly, bite them and then run for it. The enraged cattle or hogs chase them to retaliate and find themselves led precisely where the dogs want them to go. The dogs eventually run into a penned area with the livestock following close behind. The gates are slammed shut, the dogs quickly leap over the back fence and their bewildered victims are secured.

Concerned about the random crossing that was threatening to destroy the purity of this early American breed, local enthusiasts have recently studied its history and have set up a registry to record pedigrees. In 1977 the National Association of Louisiana Catahoulas was founded, and in 1979 the breed was accorded the honour of being named the State Dog of Louisiana. In 1984, a special gathering of these dogs was able to display as many as 168 examples, and its future now appears to be assured.

One strange feature of the dog is that an individual sometimes displays odd eye colours, the right eye being dark and the left one pale. When this occurs, the pale eye looks strangely artificial, leading to an early reference to the animal as 'the dog with a glass eye'. Some dogs have two pale eyes, giving them a striking expression which is favoured in the show-ring.

References

1979. Eaves, B. A. *The Catahoula Collection.* Privately published, Denham Springs, Louisiana.

1983. Stodghill, T. D. *History of the Catahoula Leopard Cowdogs.* Animal Research Foundation, Quinlan, Texas.

1996. Abney, Don. *The Louisiana Catahoula Leopard Dog.* Doral Publishing, Oregon.

CUBA

CUBAN CATTLE DOG   CUBA

This is a little-known dog which is probably extinct. Early in the 19th century it was recorded as having a body like a Great Dane, but with the colouring of a wolf. There was a black spot over each eye, and the small pendulous ears were also black. It had a long 'truncated' tail and the coat was described as being 'rugged'. It is thought to have been created from crosses between some kind of Spanish cattle dog, taken to the West Indies by the early Spanish settlers, and local Cuban Mastiffs.

This breed was specialized in at least one important and specific task, namely bringing newly arrived cattle ashore safely. The design of early seagoing vessels did not make it an easy matter to transfer large animals from the deck to the seashore. The somewhat rough and ready method employed in Cuba was described in 1839 by Charles Hamilton Smith in the following words:

> We have often witnessed, when vessels with livestock arrive in our West Indian colonies, and the oxen are hoisted out by a sling passed round the base of their horns, the great assistance they [the Cuban Cattle Dogs] afford to bring them to land. For, when the ox first suspended by the head is lowered, and allowed to fall into the water, men generally swim and guide it by the horns; but, at other times, this service is performed by one or two dogs, who, catching the bewildered animal by the ears, one on each side, force it to swim in the direction of the landing-place, and instantly release their hold when they feel it touch the ground, for then the beast naturally walks up to the shore.

DEER-HERDERS

In the countries of the far north, where large herds of domesticated reindeer are kept, several breeds of dog have become specialized for controlling the movements of these docile, if somewhat stubborn animals. At present there are five distinct breeds in this functional category, and also one little-known, extinct breed.

SWEDEN
Swedish Lapphund   482

FINLAND
Cockhill's Finnish Lapphound   482
Finnish Lapphund   483
Lapland Herder   483

RUSSIA
Nenets Herding Laika   484
Samoyed   485

SWEDEN

SWEDISH LAPPHUND   SWEDEN

*Also known as the Ruotsinlapinkoira, the
Lapplandska Spets, the Swedish Lapp Spitz, the
Lapland Spitz and sometimes simply the
Lapphund, this breed is occasionally employed
today for herding animals other than reindeer,
such as sheep and cattle. Unlike the more specialized herders, this breed not only helps to control
the movements of the deer, but also guards them
from attacks by predators.*

This is an old-established breed, developed by the Sami people of Lapland in the far
north of Scandinavia to help them control the movements of their large herds of reindeer. It is generally accepted today that this is an early descendant of the ancient
Siberian Samoyed. It differs very little, except in preferred colour, from the Finnish
Lapphund (see separate entry).

The Swedish Lapphund is a typical 'spitz' breed, with a heavy coat, stocky body,
pricked ears and a curled-up tail. A popular colour form is solid black, which helps to
make the dogs more conspicuous in the snowy wastelands. There are slight colour variations, however, with some dogs being dark brown ('bear-brown') instead of jet black,
and occasionally showing a few small patches of white.

This dog was recognized as an official breed in Sweden in 1944 and by the FCI in
1946. It is an energetic, active, intelligent animal that responds well to training, providing this is persuasive rather than harshly disciplinarian.

FINLAND

COCKHILL'S FINNISH LAPPHOUND   FINLAND

*This is an extinct breed that enjoyed a brief existence for a few decades, starting in the inter-
war period of the 20th century.*

When the long-established, working Lapland Dogs were brought south in Finland in
the 1930s they were cross-bred with the long-haired Karelian Bear Dog to create this
rare breed. It flourished for a while, but was eventually abandoned when the Finnish
Kennel Club officially recognized the Lapland Herder and the Finnish Lapphund as
two distinct types.

FINNISH LAPPHUND   FINLAND

Also known as the Suomenlapinkoira, the Lapinkoira, the Finnish Lapland Dog or the Lapland Dog, this breed is known to its friends simply as the Lappy. In modern times the task of herding sheep and cattle has been added to its traditional role of reindeer-herding.

The Finnish Lapphund is closely related to its Swedish counterpart. A typical spitz breed with a stocky body, pricked ears, a thick coat and a twisted-up tail, it appears in a variety of coat colours and patterns. Typically, on each dog, one colour dominates and the others are confined largely to the extremities. A common pattern is a black body with tan-to-white feet, tail and face.

This working dog from the far north was first brought to southern Finland in the 1930s and soon became a popular pet. Its attractive markings, its courage in the face of danger, its lively, active personality and its noisy barking made it a favourite sentinel dog for security-conscious property owners.

Before the Finnish Lapphund was brought south it was essentially the same breed as the Swedish Lapphund. They were simply Lapland reindeer-herders, and their working qualities were more important than any consideration of fine coat detail or anatomy. But once some of them had come south to Finland and others to Sweden, the two types began to diverge very slightly. The Swedes preferred solid, dark colours, while the Finns favoured patterned coats. Other very minor differences developed, and each country claimed their dog as the true representative of the northern working breed. To keep the peace, the FCI recognized both dogs, but it has to be admitted that their separation into two distinct breeds is more a matter of politics than of canine biology.

LAPLAND HERDER   FINLAND

Also called the Lapinporokoira, the Lapland Reindeer Dog, the Lapland Sheepdog, the Lapponian Herder, the Lapponian Shepherd, the Lapponian Vallhund or the Lapsk Vallhund, this breed is known colloquially as the Lappy.

This is an 'improved' reindeer-herder, created in southern Finland by deliberate crossings to combine the hardiness of the northern, cold-country spitz breeds with the highly developed herding abilities of European sheepdog breeds. This was achieved by arranging matings between the Finnish Lapphund, the German Shepherd Dog and working Collies, creating a 'Nordic herder' capable of working in freezing conditions, but with the advanced manoeuvring skills of the typical sheepdog. It is said to be capable of covering 60 miles (97 km) in a day, and it is often claimed that 'one of these dogs is worth five men'.

This carefully planned breed has the erect, pricked ears of its spitz ancestor, but the less stocky body, the longer legs and head, and the uncurled tail of its sheepdog ancestor. Its low-hanging tail, in particular, sets it apart from the other northern dogs.

The introduction of the motorized snowmobile in the 20th century resulted in a sudden modernization of reindeer-herding techniques and rendered the Lapland Herder almost obsolete. Its numbers fell rapidly and there was a serious risk of it becoming extinct, but in the 1960s the chairman of the Finnish Kennel Club began a salvage operation and in 1966 it was given an official breed standard. By the end of the 1960s the population of these dogs had risen to five times the figure for the start of that decade.

An interesting breeding system was devised for the working dogs. In the north the stockworkers kept only males. In the south, the breeders kept females. Each year the best males would be brought south to mate and the best male puppies would then be taken north again for future reindeer duties. Surplus puppies would be sold off as pets.

Colour forms include white with dark shading; black body with tan extremities; and black.

RUSSIA

NENETS HERDING LAIKA   RUSSIA

Also known as the Reindeer Herding Laika or the Nenets Laika, this breed was developed by the Nentsy, a tribe of northern nomads, to assist them with reindeer-herding and also, when at base camp, to act as a watchdog and a guard dog. It has at times, rather confusingly, also been called the Samoyed Laika, the Russian Samoyed Laika, the North Russian Samoyed Laika or the Reindeer Samoyed, but these names fail to distinguish it from its close relative, developed by the Samoyede tribe. Its name has also been given as the Stenezkajapastuschja-Laika.

The Nentsy are an ethnic group living in an Arctic region that spreads from north-eastern Europe to western Siberia. Their main activity is reindeer-herding and they are assisted in this by their Laika dogs.

Despite the fact that their dogs are indispensable to their survival, the tribes look down on them and consider them dirty. This is because the dogs will eat excrement, intestines, rotten meat — anything they can find. It is a sad comment on these people that they do not understand that it is they themselves who force the dogs to be dirty by the way they treat them. And it is a remarkable testament to the resilience of the dogs that they continue to work so hard for their masters.

It is true that the dogs are allowed to come into the shelters for warmth at night, but this is only because they are seen as useful working aids and not out of any sense of sympathy for the animals' need for comfort.

The Samoyede tribe and the Nentsy tribe each developed their own breed of dog, selecting those animals that were most useful for the particular tribal needs. Because the needs of the two groups were so similar, it was inevitable that their two dog breeds would also resemble one another closely. As a result, the Nenets dog looks very much like the more familiar and better-known Samoyed. The main difference between them is in their coat colour. The Nenets dog can be tan, grey, black or white, either solid or bicoloured, whereas the modern Samoyed is traditionally pure white.

The ears are erect, the chest is deep, the coat very thick and dense, the neck ruff heavy (especially in the males) and the tail twisted up over the back in the typical spitz position.

SAMOYED   RUSSIA

Known in its homeland as the Samoyedskaja and to its friends simply as the Sammy or Sam, it takes its name from the tribe that fostered it, the Samoyede people of northern Siberia. (The original spelling for this dog was, in fact, Samoyede.) A variant spelling of its name is Samojed. It has also been recorded as the Reindeer Dog, the Smiling Dog or the West Siberian Dog. This ancient breed was sometimes used for sledge-pulling work in addition to its main activity of reindeer-herding, but the Arctic Husky was the preferred dog for sledge work.

The brilliant white Samoyed, with its thick, luxuriant coat, is a glamorous and highly distinctive breed. When an early explorer first encountered it in the Arctic steppes in the 18th century, he recorded that its owners were wearing heavy garments made from dog fur. So it would seem that, in addition to controlling its owners' livestock, and occasionally helping them to drag their belongings from place to place in their relentlessly hostile world, the dog was also killed from time to time to provide its owners with pelts to keep their bodies warm in the desolate, frozen wastelands. Despite this, the Samoyed dog was treated extremely well while it was alive, often being taken into the shelter of its owners' sleeping quarters at night and treated as a family pet.

At the end of the 19th century, fur traders and explorers returning from expeditions to the frozen north brought a small number of Samoyeds back to England with them. There, with their dramatic appearance, these showy animals soon became popular with pedigree-dog breeders. It has been estimated

that the whole of the modern breed has descended from about 12 of those imported dogs. Queen Alexandra became devoted to the Samoyed, and her patronage quickly helped to raise its social status.

A typical spitz dog, with pricked ears, a tightly up-curled tail and a stocky body, it displays an almost leonine mane around the neck. In its earlier days this breed appeared in several coat colours, including black-and-white and also sable, but in its modern form, solid white is the colour for which it is famous.

This is a friendly, active, alert and intelligent breed, but it is also a dog of independent nature that needs careful discipline to keep it under control. It has been described as 'casually obedient', stubborn and easily bored, requiring a great deal of social contact with its human family. But it is also much loved by its devoted owners. The Samoyed, says one, is not part of the audience, it is the star.

In the field, as one might expect, it shows great stamina and powers of endurance. Because Samoyeds were easier to obtain that other Arctic breeds at the end of the 19th century, early polar explorers such as Nantsen, Shackleton and Scott employed this dog for the sledge work on their historic expeditions.

An oddity in the history of this breed is that one of its founding fathers in England came, not from the frozen north, but from the unlikely source of Sydney Zoo in Australia. This dog, called Antarctic Buck, was a survivor of the second Scott expedition to the South Pole, and was shipped back to English kennels to join the foundation stock being assembled there.

References

1934. Puxley, W. Lavallin. *Samoyeds.* Williams & Norgate, London.

1936. Johns, Rowland (Editor). *Our Friends the Samoyed and Keeshond.* Methuen, London.

1950. Keyte-Perry, Marion. *The Truth about the Samoyed.* Privately published.

1951. Croft, Donna Maria. *The Samoyed in Brief.* Northern California Group of the Pacific Coast Division of the Samoyed Club of America.

1961. Baillie, Pearl M. and Auckram, Valerie E. P. *The Samoyed.* Cliff Press, Hastings, New Zealand.

1963. Keyte-Perry, Marion. *The Samoyed: Survey from Ancient History to the Present Day.* Privately published.

1964. Kroman, Vera. *How to Raise and Train a Samoyed.* TFH, New Jersey.

1971. Ward, Robert H. and Ward, Dolly *The Complete Samoyed.* Howell, New York.

1975. Brealey, Joan Macdonald. *This is the Samoyed.* TFH, New Jersey.

1983. Reynaud, Joyce. *Samoyeds.* TFH, New Jersey.

1985. Ward, Robert H. and Ward, Dolly. *The New Complete Samoyed.* Howell, New York.

1989. Sanford, William R. and Green, Carl R. *The Samoyed.* Crestwood House, New York.

1990. Nicholas, Anna Katherine. *The Samoyed.* TFH, New Jersey.

1998. Grounds, Beryl and Grounds, Geoff. *All About the Samoyed.*

1998. Siino, Betsy Sikora. *Samoyeds: Everything About Purchase, Care, Nutrition, Grooming, Behavior, and Training.* Barron, New York.

1999. Wilcox, Charlotte. *The Samoyed.*

2000. Taylor, Pamela. *The Samoyed Today.*

Kauzlarich, Jan. *Your Samoyed.*

LLAMA-HERDERS

This is a minor functional category, with only one breed represented. This dog was employed by the Incas along the western coast of South America during the seasonal drives when the llama herds were corralled to be used as a source of wood and food.

PERU
Inca Dog   488

PERU

INCA DOG PERU

In addition to the hairless Peruvian breeds, there were two ancient haired breeds – this one and the Long-haired Inca Dog that was used as a source of hair for weaving. The ordinary, short-haired Inca Dog was mainly used as an aid to controlling the domesticated llamas, and we have 17th-century drawings to confirm this.

Described as a heavily built collie in appearance, the Inca Dog was the largest of the Peruvian breeds. In addition to its herding duties it was also expected to help in tracking and hunting, and to stand guard duty. It was of great value to the native tribes and they frequently honoured it by mummifying it and placing its corpse in a special burial site.

The coat was a pale yellow with darker patches. It was the only breed of American Indian tribal dog to have its ears cropped, but nobody knows why this was done. The Inca Dog had a sharp pointed face, shortish legs, and a tail that curled up, over its back.

Most of the ancient tribal dogs of the Americas have long since vanished, but in the case of the Inca Dog it seems that there may still be a few left. In the late 19th century every Peruvian shepherd had one, but then they started to decrease dramatically in numbers. Today it is thought that, in the most remote regions, they can still be found scratching a living as backstreet strays, or as family pets in obscure native villages. It is a pity that this ancient breed does not have a modern champion to organize a serious rescue programme.

FISH-HERDERS

This is a rare, but fascinating, functional category. Dog breeds that have developed a powerful urge to control the movements of herds of animals can be persuaded to direct their attention to almost any group of living things, even to shoals of fish. Of the two breeds that have become specialists at fish-herding, one is now extinct but the other still survives, if only as a show dog.

PORTUGAL		CHILE	
Portuguese Water Dog	490	Fuegian Dog	491

PORTUGAL

PORTUGUESE WATER DOG

PORTUGAL

Also known as the Portuguese Diving Dog, the Portuguese Fishing Dog, the Portuguese Curly Water Dog, the Pelo Encaracolado, the Cão de Agua, or simply the Portie, this ancient breed of fishermen's dog was originally used to herd fish into nets and carry out other marine tasks.

Although this tough, curly-coated dog is closely related to the water dogs of Europe that specialize in retrieving waterfowl, it cannot be classified as a retriever because its main duties were so different. It acted as a marine aid to the fishermen of the Algarve on Portugal's southern coast, taking to the water to herd the fish, move the nets and even catch the odd fish that managed to escape from the nets.

Apart from fish-herding, this breed also carried out various other, subsidiary duties. When a fleet of small fishing boats was out together, the dogs could be used to carry messages from one vessel to another. With their keen eyesight they also acted as look-outs, barking an alarm when they spotted a shoal of fish. If fog descended, they adopted yet another role, acting as barking 'fog-horns' to warn other vessels and avoid collisions. Assisting them in this role was their unusual, 'rising-and-falling' bark.

They carried out these duties for centuries and were so highly valued that anyone harming one of these dogs was in serious trouble. But then modern technology caught up with the breed and advanced fishing techniques rendered them more or less obsolete. By 1960 a survey revealed that they were on the verge of extinction, with only about 50 left alive. Fortunately, it was such an attractive dog that it was saved from disappearing by enthusiasts who valued it, not for its fish-herding abilities, but for its personality and its striking appearance. Finding yet more roles to add to its repertoire, it became a show dog and a companion dog. Examples were exported to the United States where it soon acquired enough admirers for the breed to gain recognition by the AKC in 1984.

After centuries of sitting patiently in small boats, this friendly, relaxed dog has developed a remarkable degree of self-control and is eminently trainable and adaptable. Its charming personality will no doubt keep it safe for the future.

There are five colour forms: solid white, solid black, solid brown, black with white markings, or brown with white markings. There are also two coat textures: long and wavy, or compact and curly. And there are two coat trims: overall the same length; and the lion-trim, in which only the rear-end of the body is clipped very short. This second trim was originally supposed to reduce drag when the dog was swimming in the water, but today, as with the poodle-cut, it is adopted purely for show.

One unusual anatomical feature of this breed is the way it carries its tail. When the dog is alert, its tail rises up and curls over into what could be described as a 'semi-spitz' position. It is not a tight curl, like that of the typical northern dogs, but it is certainly very different from the tail posture of other European water dogs, and sets this breed slightly apart from them.

References

1986. Braund, Kathryn. *The Complete Portuguese Water Dog.* Howell, New York.
1997. Braund, Kathryn. *The New Complete Portuguese Water Dog.* Howell, New York.
1999. Foster, Verne. *Portuguese Water Dog: A Guide for the New Owner.*

CHILE

FUEGIAN DOG   CHILE

This unique breed, also called the Tierro Del Fuego Dog, was developed as a specialized fish-herding dog.

The southern-most tip of the South American continent, with its notoriously hostile environment, is the ancestral home of the Indian tribes that Darwin called 'the most miserable humans' he had ever encountered. Their very survival depended on the cooperation of their amazing dogs. To avoid starvation, the tribes were forced to hunt for fish, seals and sea-otters in the freezing waters. When hunting fish, the men waded waist-deep into the icy water, holding their nets, and waited while their dogs swam further out. The dogs then turned and drove the shoals inshore and into the nets. To do this, these astonishing dogs dived below the surface and controlled the fish like submarine sheepdogs, surfacing every so often for air and barking excitedly each time they did so. Seals and sea-otters were caught in a similar way, the little dogs chasing them underwater towards the Indians' boats, where the fleeing animals could be speared.

In any other tribe, when the group was facing starvation, they would not hesitate to kill and eat their dogs, but the reverse was the case with the precious Fuegian Dogs. When there was no food for a prolonged period, the old women of the tribe were killed and their flesh was fed to the dogs to ensure the animals' survival.

The physical appearance of this remarkable breed is known to us from only two sketches. The first, from the Darwin visit in 1832, shows a dog with a fox-like head and body, but with longer legs. The second, from 1883, provides more detail, showing a handsome little dog with a black-and-white coat, a strong neck, a small head with a tapering muzzle and a bushy tail.

Curiously, there is an entry in the archives of London Zoo that states that examples of these dogs were placed on exhibition there in '1830 (probably earlier)', under the name of 'Terra de Fuego Dog'. How these animals were acquired, and whether they were successfully bred, is not recorded.

Service Dogs

Sporting dogs and livestock dogs are all concerned with duties involving other animals – hunting them, fighting them, guarding them or herding them. But there is another major canine category comprising breeds that aid their human owners without interacting with other animals. These are the service dogs, breeds which carry out a wide variety of canine duties, from offering companionship, carrying out work in the house, providing their own meat as food, providing their own hair for clothing, guarding human property, rescuing human victims, assisting in transportation or searching for truffles.

HOUSEHOLD COMPANION DOGS

These are breeds specifically created as companion animals. Of course, many working breeds, originally created to carry out a specific task, have been adopted as popular pets in modern times, but those dogs are correctly classified under their primary functions. This is necessary because their canine duties influenced their appearance, their anatomy and their temperament. We can only understand them fully if we see them in their original colours, before they became much loved family pets or modern show-ring competitors. But, from the earliest days, certain – usually very small – breeds have been created and refined *solely* as companions.

In previous centuries these dogs were sometimes given the title of 'comforters'. More recently they have been called 'toys' or 'pets', but these terms tend to denigrate breeds whose existence has provided so much more than mere amusement. For countless thousands of human beings, these little animals have given endless hours of companionship and emotional support, and deserve better than to be given a title that labels them as being little more than animated soft toys or wind-up playthings. Unfortunately, the word 'toy' has been enshrined in many of their breed names and cannot be ignored, but it can, at least, be removed from their group title.

There is one special category of companion dog that requires a preliminary word. This is a very recent American innovation and has caused considerable controversy. Critics have referred to the members of this group as 'Poo Dogs' or 'Designer Dogs' and have made loud protests over their very existence. The trend began in the 1960s with the creation of a breed called the Cockapoo. This was a deliberate cross between Cocker Spaniels and small Poodles. The idea was not to create a mongrel but to invent an entirely new breed that would combine the best qualities of its two parent breeds. There was nothing new about this. For centuries, similar experimental matings had been carried out and some of today's most revered pedigree breeds started out their existence in this way, before breeding true and becoming fully established. The novelty lay more in the humorous, catchy name the new breed was given. The Cockapoo was so successful that it soon spawned imitations – the Lhasapoo, the Maltipoo, the Pompoo and so on.

Before long a whole trend was started and many American breeders began to invent their own, personal version of the double-pedigree dog. The two parent breeds were always dogs with impeccable ancestries, brought together with the specific intention of creating an exciting new, luxury pet. Some people love these new breeds, while others loathe them, and it is important to recognize both sides of the controversy that now surrounds them.

The following claims are made in their defence:

1   Some of the long-established pedigree breeds have developed health problems. By deliberately crossing these ancient breeds with one another, it is possible to reduce these problems and to create more healthy stock that enjoys the 'hybrid vigour' seen in typical 'accidental mongrels'.

2   By carefully selecting the two parent breeds, it is possible to combine the best qualities of each of them. For example, it should be possible to take the attractive appearance of one parent breed and combine it with the non-shedding coat of the other, or perhaps to take the intelligence of one breed and combine it with the athletic qualities of another.

3   By experimenting with different parent breeds, it should be possible to create exciting new canine forms of a type never seen before. So many companion dogs started out as working breeds and had to be adapted to the role of pets. By contrast, these new dogs are, from the start, 'designed' as ideal pets. (Hence the tag of 'designer dogs'.)

Their critics respond with the following comments:

1   There is no guarantee that the crosses will automatically be healthier. They could, indeed, combine the worst health problems of both parents, making the new breeds doubly weakened.

2   When two breeds are combined there is no guarantee that they will produce a single, new type. A wide variety of types may appear, with many different shapes, colours and temperaments. Rather than a specific new form, there could be unpredictable, anatomical chaos.

3   Just by giving these new dogs a catchy name and advertising them as rare 'exotics', the breeders concerned are exploiting gullible buyers, who imagine they are part of a trendy new revolution in canine development, when in reality they are paying a fortune for mixed-breed mongrels of a kind that could be obtained for a fraction of the price at any dog pound, animal sanctuary or rescue centre.

There are some valid points in both views. Traditionalists involved with well-known breeds possessing long-established pedigrees have a stubborn resistance to any interference with their dogs, no matter what form it takes. They cannot envisage any possible gain in mixing their breed with any other, and dismiss the inventors of new 'designer' breeds as running 'puppy mills' or 'puppy farms'.

The supporters of the 'designer' breeds reply that they are merely trying to create interesting new forms and that, over a long period of time, they may yet be able to produce exciting companion breeds for the future. They accept that there will be a phase of variability, but insist that, by careful selective breeding, they will eventually be able to stabilize a new type of dog that will be pure-breeding, healthy and well suited in its role as family pet.

In a few instances this does, indeed, seem to be the case, and those new breeds are included here and given full entries in this section on companion dogs. In a number of other cases, however, it does seem possible that the criticisms of the traditionalists are entirely justified and that unscrupulous commercial breeders are entering this arena with spurious claims and exploiting dog-lovers. All they have to do is to put two well-known breeds together, invent a funny name and offer a 'rare exotic' for sale.

There are over 20 of these new 'designer' breeds at present and, with many of them, so little is known about their history that it is impossible to tell whether they are part of a serious, carefully planned breeding programme or not. These examples are not described here, but are listed in the 'Obscure Breeds' section towards the end of the dictionary. Their inclusion there is not an endorsement, merely a record of the fact that they exist, and in some cases may eventually develop into fully recognized breeds.

In the general category of household companions, both ancient and modern, there are 81 breeds.

ENGLAND

BICHON YORKIE   ENGLAND

*This new breed of companion dog is still in the early
stages of development.*

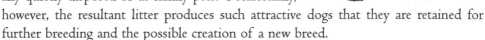

When an unintended mating takes place between two
well-known pedigree dog breeds, the puppies are usually quietly disposed of as family pets. Occasionally,
however, the resultant litter produces such attractive dogs that they are retained for
further breeding and the possible creation of a new breed.

This is what occurred in the 1980s when a Yorkshire Terrier mated with a Bichon Frisé.
London veterinary expert Dr Bruce Fogle who first reported the 'Bichon Yorkie', sang its
praises because of its hybrid vigour. As a practising vet, he all too often has to deal with
the medical problems that arise with prolonged 'pure' breeding, and he welcomed the
cross, pointing out that it 'is less likely to have slipping kneecaps or retained baby teeth'
than either of the two parent breeds. A further advantage is that it 'has both the tenacity
and resilience of the Yorkshire Terrier, as well as the insulating coat of the Bichon'.

In appearance, the Bichon Yorkie is a mixture of the two parents, perhaps slightly
favouring the Yorkie. The height is 9–12 in (23–31 cm) and the weight 7–13 lb (3–6 kg).
Further breeding of this dog was planned, but it remains to be seen whether it eventually graduates to become a true breed in its own right.

BULL BOXER   ENGLAND

This is another new breed of companion dog that is still in the early stages of development.

In the 1990s an accidental mating occurred between a Boxer and a Staffordshire Bull
Terrier. The offspring proved to be unexpectedly attractive and, in addition, lacked
some of the problems facing both the parent breeds. Because of this, it was decided to
develop the cross as a new breed in its own right, with a properly planned breeding programme, to fix the type. Whether this succeeds and it becomes fully established as a
new pure-breeding dog at some time in the future remains to be seen.

Enthusiasts claim that this new breed-in-the-making is superior
to both its parents. Inevitably, breeders of Boxers and Staffordshire
Bull Terriers dislike it and see it as a 'bad mix'. They also criti-
cize the claim that the Bull Boxer is healthier than
either of their breeds. For the present, therefore,
it remains controversial.

In appearance, as might be expected, it is intermediate between the two parent breeds. It has longer legs than the Staffie and a more pointed muzzle than the Boxer. In height it is 16–21 in (41–53 cm) and its weight is 37–53 lb (17–24 kg).

DORGIE

ENGLAND

Only one breeder has championed this breed, but as that breeder also happens to be the Queen of England, it is worthy of note. Elizabeth II has displayed a lifelong passion for Welsh Pembroke Corgis. She even took one with her on her honeymoon. She has bred them repeatedly, but the puppies that she keeps for herself are always female. This fact did not escape Pipkin, the male Miniature Long-haired Dachshund belonging to her sister, Princess Margaret. On one of his friendly visits to the Queen's home, he achieved the impossible – performing an illicit sexual act inside the precincts of Buckingham Palace. The result of his wanton disregard for royal protocol was a litter of seven delightful little puppies. The Queen found them so appealing that, instead of having them secretly whisked out of a side entrance by palace staff, she christened them Dorgis and became their determined champion. She even arranged repeat matings with some of her other Corgi bitches, to carry on the tradition. One of Pipkin's problems was that his legs were too short, but royal help was now at hand. When Norman Parkinson, the royal photographer, asked how such a tiny Dachshund could achieve such glory, the Queen explained: 'Oh, it's quite simple. We have a little brick.'

The Dorgie is one of the few cross-breeds ever to have found favour in royal palaces. Traditionally, all the kings and queens of Europe have kept dogs with pedigrees as long as their own. Furthermore, Queen Elizabeth is also the Patron of the Kennel Club in London, the very heartland of pure canine breeding. This gave rise to an embarrassing situation when the royal portrait was being painted, to hang in the club's entrance hall. As she was to be depicted surrounded by her beloved dogs, it was politely pointed out to her that among all the famous dog paintings hanging in the club's fine rooms, there was not a single cross-breed on view. As the Kennel Club was totally committed to pure breeding, it would not be possible for the Queen's Dorgi to be included in the portrait. They were sure she would understand and were startled by her blunt reply: 'No Dorgi, no portrait!' They had little choice but to concede to their Patron's wishes and so it is that a royal Dorgi, of undeniably mixed parentage, takes pride of place in the august club's entrance.

The then secretary of the Kennel Club was overheard to comment dryly: 'The Dachshund was evolved to chase badgers down holes, and Corgis to round up cattle. If anyone loses a herd of cattle down a badger hole, these are just the dogs to get them out.'

BLENHEIM SPANIEL   ENGLAND

This early breed of Toy Spaniel is named after Blenheim Palace, the seat of the Dukes of Marlborough at Woodstock in central England. It is no longer recognized as a distinct breed.

This is a 17th-century breed, easily identified by its bold red-and-white markings. The First Duke of Marlborough, John Churchill, was so attached to these dogs that it is said he insisted on having one with him as a mascot when he fought the Battle of Blenheim. Others were with his wife at the time and legend has it that she was so nervous that she pressed her thumb onto the forehead of a pregnant bitch sitting on her lap, and that when this bitch produced its puppies, each of them had a red thumb-mark on its head. Although the story is nonsensical, this red 'beauty-spot' became an ideal feature of the very best examples of the Blenheim after that date. In later years, however, the 'Blenheim Spot', as it came to be called, was not easy to obtain, and was recorded as 'often missing'.

The ancestors of these Blenheim Spaniels were said to have come originally from Spain, and to be dwarf versions of sporting dogs similar to Cocker Spaniels, created by progressive inbreeding. (A rival theory suggests that they came from China.) The 17th-century version was a bigger dog than its later 'improved' descendants, with longer legs and a longer, more pointed muzzle. They still had their longer faces when painted by Landseer in 1838, but during the Victorian period it became the fashion to select for smaller bodies and for flatter and flatter faces, and the Blenheim gradually lost its original shape.

At the start of the 20th century, the tradition of breeding Blenheim Spaniels at Blenheim Palace itself was still active, and there the modernization of their breed was not met with approval. Working against the fashion of the day, the Palace insisted on keeping to the original type, and even went so far as to declare them a separate breed, calling their long-faced dogs Marlborough Blenheim Spaniels, or simply Marlborough Spaniels, to distinguish them from the flat-faced Blenheims of the show-ring.

In 1910, the Chairman of the Kennel Club in London took up the cause, publishing an attack on the flat-face extremes, stating: 'The tendency of exhibitors is, unfortunately, often to encourage exaggerations of special points until the stage of monstrosity is reached... It is a great pity that this beautiful breed of Spaniel should be spoiled by the fancier's mania for something *outré.*'

Help was on the way, but it would take another 18 years before steps were taken to support the Chairman's remarks (see entry for Cavalier King Charles Spaniel). Before then, in 1923, any red-and-white individuals that still existed were officially reduced to a mere colour form of the King Charles Spaniel.

CAVALIER KING CHARLES SPANIEL

ENGLAND

This is the latest of the English Toy Spaniel breeds, developed in the 1920s to recreate the original type of the King Charles. The word 'Cavalier' was added to its name to distinguish it from the modern King Charles, which it seeks to replace. Its nickname is the Cav.

From the 17th century to the early 19th, the King Charles Spaniel had a pointed muzzle. Then, in the Victorian era, it became fashionable to breed for shorter and shorter faces, until a flat-faced dog was created. At the same time, the dog's body grew slightly smaller. Many were unhappy with this change and wished to see a return to the earlier type.

Nothing was actively done about this until 1926, when an American by the name of Roswell Eldridge visited England and was upset to discover that the traditional form of King Charles Spaniel, which he had always admired, had effectively become extinct and had been replaced by a smaller, pug-faced dog. He took the extraordinary step of offering money prizes for the best 'long-faced' King Charles Spaniels at the next five Crufts shows.

Eldridge's challenge started a movement which, in 1928, led to the formation of the Cavalier King Charles Club. Bigger, longer-faced dogs were bred and put into competition against the smaller, short-faced ones. The two types were in direct competition until 1945, when it was accepted that they were now effectively two different breeds and should be treated as such. From that date onwards they were given separate classes. The Cavalier was by now 2 in (5 cm) taller and 3 lb (1.3 kg) heavier that its rival.

As the years passed, the Cavalier began to get the upper hand. Its flat-faced rival gradually lost ground until, by the late 20th century, it had been completely overshadowed. At the very end of the century, the annual Kennel Club registrations for the two breeds were: Cavalier King Charles – 12,702; King Charles – 221. Even more impressive was the fact that the Cavalier was by then the most favoured of all the 23 recognized toy breeds, outstripping even the popular little Yorkshire Terrier. It had also appeared for some years among the 'top ten' of *all* registered dog breeds.

Traditionally this breed should be seen only in black-and-tan, but because the early Prince Charles (tricolour), Blenheim (red-and-white) and Ruby (solid red) breeds had disappeared, their colours were also accepted for the Cavalier.

References

1951. Stopford, Richard R. *The Cavalier Spaniel and its Derivations.* Stockwell, Ilfracombe.
1964. Stenning, Eilidh M. *Cavalier King Charles Spaniels.* Foyles, London.
1965. Spalding, Elizabeth C. *How to Raise and Train a Cavalier King Charles Spaniel.* TFH, New Jersey.
1967. Forwood, Mary. *The Cavalier King Charles Spaniel.* Popular Dogs, London.

1975. Burgess, Susan. *The Cavalier King Charles Spaniel.* K & R Books, Edlington, Lincolnshire.

1983. Booth, Evelyn. *All About the Cavalier King Charles Spaniel.* Pelham Books, London.

1985. McKenzie, Barbara. *Your First Cavalier.* Maypole, Essex.

1989. Pennington, Alicia. *Royal Toy Spaniels.* Ringpress Books, Letchworth, Hertfordshire.

1990. Evans, John. *Cavalier King Charles Spaniels.* Crowood Press, Wiltshire.

1991. Anon. *The English Toy Spaniel Handbook.* English Toy Spaniel Club, USA.

1991. Cuddy, Beverly. *Cavalier King Charles Spaniels.* TFH, New Jersey.

1995. Field. *Cavalier King Charles Spaniels.*

1995. Smith. *Cavalier King Charles Spaniels Today.* Howell, New York.

1998. Coile, Caroline. *Cavalier King Charles Spaniels: Everything About Purchasing, Care, Nutrition, Behavior, and Training.* Barron, New York.

1998. Garnett-Smith, Barbara. *The Cavalier King Charles Spaniel in North America.*

2000. Moffat, Norma. *The Cavalier King Charles Spaniel: An Owner's Guide to a Happy Healthy Pet.* Howell, New York.

COMFORTER   ENGLAND

This old breed of lapdog was described in the 16th century, when it was given the alternative name of Spaniel Gentle. It is the earliest form of the group of closely related breeds that are collectively known as the English Toy Spaniels.

The physician of Queen Elizabeth I, John Keys (also known as Dr Johannes Caius), whose book *De Canibus Britannicis*, published in 1570, was the first dog book ever written, includes a section on this breed, as the tiny dog that ladies keep close to their bodies for comfort. In the 1576 translation of this work, called *Of Englishe Dogges*, his description of the 'delicate, neat, and pretty kind of dogs, called the Spaniel Gentle, or the Comforter' reads as follows:

> These dogs are little, pretty proper, and fine... the smaller they be, the more pleasure they provoke, as more meet playfellows for mincing mistresses to bear in their bosoms, to keep company withal in their chambers, to succour with sleep in bed... to lay in their laps, and lick their lips as they ride in their wagons...

Later, he adds that 'these little dogs are good to assuage the sickness of the stomach, being often times thereunto applied as a plaster preservative, or borne in the bosom of the diseased and weak person, which effect is performed by their moderate heat'. In other words they were used as living hot-water bottles, to comfort the poorly.

Two centuries later, Thomas Bewick, writing in 1790, gives us an illustration that makes it clear that the Comforter is, indeed, a dwarf spaniel, the forerunner of all the later forms of English Toy Spaniel. He has mixed feelings about it, describing it as 'a most elegant little animal... generally kept by ladies as an attendant of the toilette or the drawing-room. It is very snappish, ill-natured, and noisy; and does not readily admit the familiarity of strangers.'

As the years passed, the name of the Comforter was heard less and less. In its place came the Toy Spaniels, divided into separate types, colours and breeding lines. Some of these were mentioned as new imports from Spain and elsewhere, but such comments must be taken with a pinch of salt, because, since the 16th century at the very least, the dwarf spaniel called the Comforter had been happily embedded in English society, ready and available to act as the ancestral form of any little toy dog that would become the height of fashion in later days.

GREDIN ENGLAND

This extinct breed is mentioned in Buffon's 'Natural History', but little is known about it. The literal translation of the name of this breed is 'rogue' or 'scoundrel', and it may be significant that one of the royal dogs in 17th-century London had the pet name of Rogue.

Writing in 1750, Buffon says: 'There are Black Spaniels, also called Gredins, and which are known as English Spaniels because they originate in that country.' He goes on to say that there is also a variant, which he calls a Pyrame, that, although mostly black, also has 'fire-marks' in the form of small tan markings over the eyes, on the muzzle, the throat and the legs. The Pyrame is clearly the Black and Tan Spaniel, or King Charles Spaniel.

From this report it would seem that there was a largely forgotten black Toy Spaniel in the very early stages of the development of the English Toy Spaniel. A clue comes from the fact that, when Charles I was walking to his execution in 1649, he was accompanied by a small spaniel with the pet name of Rogue. Charles II, his son, who was to become obsessed with small spaniels and was to give his name to the black-and-tan breed, was 19 when his father was beheaded. It seems likely that he inherited some of his father's dogs. This might have included Rogue, but one of the Roundheads kidnapped the dog after the axe fell and, that same night, exhibited it in a sideshow to earn a few pennies. It was never seen again, and the black spaniel tradition seems to have faltered after this. There were a few, scattered later reports of black spaniels being called King Charles Spaniels, but as time passed, nothing more was heard of them, and the black-and-tan came to dominate the scene.

Curiously, a special type of black spaniel did reappear many years later, in the form of the Toy Trawler Spaniel (see separate entry), which was said to be a 'throwback' to the early, black King Charles Spaniel, but the relationship between that and the Gredin is not known.

KING CHARLES SPANIEL   ENGLAND

In earlier centuries this breed was sometimes called King Charles's Dog, or the Black and Tan Spaniel. Its nickname was the King Charlie, or simply the Charlie. Outside England it has often been referred to as the English Toy Spaniel, but when this is done it is lumped together with all the other forms of dwarf spaniel, including the Prince Charles, the Ruby, the Blenheim, the Toy Trawler and the Cavalier King Charles.

This tiny spaniel was the favourite dog of the English king, Charles II, and later took his name. He is reputed to have imported it from Spain in the 17th century, but the fact is that dwarf spaniels had been present in England for many years. Whether he added new blood from abroad is a matter of debate, but it is unlikely that he started an entirely new breed.

Whatever its true origins, the king became an avid breeder, and his palace at Hampton Court was overrun with the little dogs. Samuel Pepys, in his famous *Diary*, comments that the king's dogs went everywhere with him and accompanied him 'even upon State occasions'.

In colour this breed was traditionally always black-and-tan. Essentially it was a black dog with limited tan markings, and some early Toy Spaniel enthusiasts found it too sombre in appearance, preferring instead the showy, white-and-red Blenheim. (King Charles also had black-and-white Toy Spaniels, and pure black ones, as we know from portraits, but these seem to have been conveniently forgotten.)

During the Victorian period this breed, along with its close relatives, underwent two anatomical changes, imposed upon them by the fashions and whims of the day: they became smaller and flatter-faced. This trend persisted until the 1920s, when a group of breeders rebelled against it and set about returning to the original, large, long-muzzled type. They called their 'recreated' breed the Cavalier King Charles (see separate entry) to set it apart, but the flat-faced King Charles did not die out. Instead, it continued in favour, alongside the Cavalier, and today these two breeds are both still recognized by the Kennel Club.

One other change has also occurred and that concerns the coat colour of the breed. Today, both the King Charles and the Cavalier King Charles are available in four coat patterns: black-and-tan; tricolour; red-and-white; and solid red. Traditionally they should both be seen only in black-and-tan, but it was decided to add the other three coat types when the old breeds associated with them (the Prince Charles, the Blenheim and the Ruby, respectively) disappeared.

In personality, this is a cheerful, devoted and extremely affectionate dog. In many ways it is the ideal pet, especially for urban families. It is only 10–11 in (25–27 cm) tall and weighs no more than 14 lb (6 kg).

References

1953. Hauer, Odd. *My Friend King Charles*. Oslo.

1960. Birchall, M. Joyce. *King Charles Spaniels*. Foyles, London.

1964. Paine, Mrs Milton J. *How to Raise and Train an English Toy Spaniel*. TFH, New Jersey.

1974. Forward, Mary. *The King Charles Spaniel*. Popular Dogs, London.

1989. Pennington, Alicia. *Royal Toy Spaniels*. Ringpress Books, Letchworth, Hertfordshire.

1997. Paine, Mrs Milton J. *English Toy Spaniel: a Complete and Reliable Handbook*. TFH, New Jersey.

PRINCE CHARLES SPANIEL   ENGLAND

This breed, which is no longer recognized, was also known as the Tricolour Spaniel, because its coat pattern was black, white and tan.

The Prince Charles was one of the later forms of English Toy Spaniel, created in the Victorian period. One of them can be seen in a painting by Landseer (called *The Cavalier's Pets*) in 1845. It first appeared in the Kennel Club's stud book in 1892.

This was the most attractive form of the various Toy Spaniels, with a white coat carrying large patches of black on both head and body, and with tan markings on the cheeks, over the eyes, on the insides of the ears, on the insides of the legs and on the underside of the tail. It was obtained by carefully planned crossings between the other Toy Spaniels, probably taking the black-and-tan from the King Charles and the White from the Blenheim.

In 1923 any tricolour individuals that still existed were officially reduced to a mere colour form of the King Charles Spaniel.

RUBY SPANIEL   ENGLAND

The Ruby Spaniel is no longer recognized as a breed, but has been treated as one in the past.

This is the solid red form of the English Toy Spaniel, created in the 1880s by crossing the Blenheim with the King Charles. Prior to the 1880s, all-red puppies were destroyed as unwanted, but then it was decided to make a special breed of them.

The coat of the Ruby, ideally in a rich, deep red with no lighter patches, was not as long as that of its close relatives. The ears were often too short and the body too long, and few of the Rubies were said to be free of these faults, which is probably why it failed to develop as a separate breed and was eventually abandoned. It is given a separate section in dog books published as late as 1910, but then appears to have been swept away by the chaos of World War I.

In 1923 any solid red individuals that existed were officially reduced to a mere colour form of the King Charles Spaniel.

TOY TRAWLER SPANIEL   ENGLAND

A now vanished breed of English lapdog, also known as the Trawler Spaniel, the Miniature Toy Trawler or the Miniature Trawler Spaniel.

At the beginning of the 20th century, this little dog was described as the 'modern representative' of the old type of curly King Charles Spaniel. One author called it a 'throwback' to the original, curly, all-black King Charles.

Although so little is known or written about this dog today, in its heyday it does appear to have reached the show-ring. For example, Robert Leighton records that there were 27 entries in a dog show at Horsham at the beginning of the 20th century. Writing in 1907, he comments that 'at present it is regarded as a toy, and kept as such in growing numbers'. He goes on to say that the breed was also becoming popular on the continent, especially in Holland and Italy. Despite these encouraging words, it does not appear to have survived long after World War I and must now be considered as an extinct breed.

A preserved specimen of this breed is on display at the Tring Zoological Museum in Hertfordshire. It is a dog called Robin, bred by Lady Wentworth, and was born in 1911. It died in 1920, when the breed was said to be 'nearly extinct'.

The dominant feature of this breed was its very curly, glossy, silky coat. It was the curly quality of the coat that set it apart from the other Toy Spaniels, and which suggests a link to some kind of ancestral water spaniel. The favoured colour was 'brilliant black

with white waistcoat', but it also sometimes appeared in black-and-white or red-and-white. In height it was 11–13 in (28–33 cm) and its weight was 12–15 lb (5–7 kg). The well-feathered tail, which did not curl up over the back in the spitz style, was docked to a length of 4–5 in (10–12 cm). In temperament the dog was said to be bold and courageous and never timid.

MINIATURE BULLDOG   ENGLAND

A now extinct, dwarf version of the Bulldog, this breed was originally called the Toy Bulldog. This was sometimes abbreviated to Toy Bull. It was developed as a ladies' companion in 19th-century England.

When bull-baiting was banned in England in 1835, the Bulldog was suddenly out of work. Some, who liked the breed for itself rather than for its violent lifestyle, started to breed smaller and smaller specimens until a miniature form was developed. This became a popular companion animal in certain districts and was given the name of Toy Bulldog to emphasize its new, non-violent status. Its appearance was intended to be as close to that of the large Bulldog as possible in every respect except size.

In the 1850s, some of these Toy Bulldogs were taken to northern France, where they were crossed with other breeds to create the French Bulldog (see separate entry). In England they lost favour for a while and nearly became extinct, but they enjoyed renewed interest towards the end of the Victorian era. At the turn of the century, one titled English lady burbled effusively: 'There is nobody who is anybody who does not nowadays both know and highly appreciate coffee, caviar and Toy Bulldogs. Not to do so would be, indeed, to argue oneself unknown!'

However, all was not well with the breed. Writing at about the same time, Mrs Leslie Williams, an expert on toy dogs, reported:

> Toy bulldogs are yearly becoming more popular. They are absolutely ideal dogs as to temper and all the other qualities necessary for a pet and companion, and almost uncannily intelligent, but alas! they are delicate beyond denying. They are hard to breed, and hard to rear; few of the bitches are good mothers, while their babies have little stamina; they are shy breeders moreover, and altogether need incessant care and watchfulness.

The upper weight limit for Toy Bulldogs was 20 lb (9 kg), and breeders found this increasingly hard to maintain. Already struggling with the dogs' severe breeding problems, the leading supporters of this little dog were about to face a new threat. In the 1890s the greatly improved French Bulldog arrived in London from the boulevards of Paris. This impressive descendant of the Toy Bulldog had been modified by various crosses which, among other small changes, gave it a dramatic new feature – a pair of erect, bat-like ears. It attracted immediate attention and a host of new admirers. Those loyal to the original Toy Bulldog, with its curled-over ears, were outraged

by this continental invasion and hurled insults at the French pretender. Arguments raged, but there was no stopping the bat-eared competitor. Eventually the matter was settled in 1902 by establishing two rival clubs, one for the English Toy Bulldog, with curled-over ears, and one for the French Bulldog, with erect bat-ears.

Objections were raised by the Kennel Club to the use of the word 'toy' for the English breed, with the result that in 1906 the English Toy Bulldog was renamed the Miniature Bulldog. In the years that followed, the French Bulldog went from strength to strength, while the Miniature Bulldog sank into obscurity and eventually disappeared. The last record of it is from 1914, after which it did not appear to recover from the ravages of World War I. In 1920 the Kennel Club formally recorded that registration of Miniatures had ceased.

TOY BULL TERRIER ENGLAND

Sometimes known simply as the Toy Bull, this little pet dog was popular at one time in the 19th century, but has since vanished.

The Toy Bull Terrier was a tiny dog, bred down from the Miniature Bull Terrier until, in exceptional cases, it was one of the smallest dogs in existence, weighing less than 3 lb (1.4 kg). Such extreme reduction was not favoured, however, the preferred weight being 8–10 lb (4–5 kg). The favourite colour was white, but brindle and black were also acceptable.

This now extinct breed was a prick-eared, rat-tailed, short-coated midget of a dog, with the defensive spirit of an animal ten times its size. It is said that the only way to prevent it from attacking a giant dog was for the toy dog's owner to run away as fast as possible. This would encourage the little assailant to follow suit, and avoid an embarrassing incident.

The Toy Bull was moderately well supported during the Victorian period but then, at the start of the 20th century, it began to fall out of favour. During the Edwardian period it lost its social status and ended up confined largely to the East End of London and the mining districts of the Midlands. One noble lady, writing in 1907, commented: 'Their plucky qualities appear to appeal to a certain rough kind of man... This is a pity because their Lilliputian self-assertion is most amusing.' She goes on to describe how one of her own Toy Bull Terriers was even prepared to fly at a herd of cattle and attack them, until it was kicked into the air by an angry hoof. It would seem that, despite its dwarf body, inside its brain it still considered itself to be a full-blown Bull Terrier.

With its owner it was lively, affectionate and always cheerful. It made a good watchdog and was always ready to destroy any rodents it encountered. But its main role was as a lapdog, or to be more precise, a pocket dog, since it was usually small enough to be carried on its owner's body.

One reason given for the breed's disappearance was that, the more its size was reduced, the more apple-headed it became, with a narrower muzzle, which resulted in it losing the typical Bull Terrier head-shape. Another problem it faced was that its owners found it difficult to ensure that it bred true to type, so not many dog shows would include classes for them.

WHITE COLLIE   ENGLAND

Although this breed is closely related to Scotland's Rough Collie (see separate entry) and was developed in the United States, its true origin was in Victorian England, where it briefly became the height of fashion. It is technically a sheepdog, but it is doubtful if it ever saw a sheep; its function was solely that of a high-status pet and a show dog.

Nobody can say how many pure white collies appeared as colour variants in the early days of working sheepdogs. When white puppies were born they were probably destroyed, because shepherds preferred dogs that offered a contrast with their white sheep. But at a later date, when the Rough Collie had become a fashionable pet and a glamorous show dog, this prejudice against white dogs was removed.

Two collie breeders by the names of J. and W. H. Charles, who had kennels at Wellesbourne in Warwickshire, in central England, presented a White Collie of their breeding to Queen Victoria and a second one to the Prince of Wales. The acceptance of these animals by royalty created an immediate craze for this type of dog, and a new strain of White Collies was soon on offer. It is believed that a little Samoyed had been used at some point to boost the whiteness of the coat, and judging by the appearance of Queen Victoria's dog, this does seem very likely.

Traditionalists disliked the new colour form, but admitted that, since the dog was now being bred 'purely for the fancy', there was no good reason why it should not prosper. For a while it did indeed do so and, towards the end of the 19th century, various princesses were pictured with their exotic white dogs. This news filtered across the Atlantic and, before long, fashion-conscious American owners were delighting in their imported White Collies. From this point, the breed lost favour in England and soon disappeared, but in the United States it flourished. It quickly had its own breed club there, was treated as a distinct breed and was given separate classification at dog shows.

There is even a portrait of a White Collie hanging in the White House in Washington.

The modern White Collie looks very much like a Rough Collie, having a longer, more pointed muzzle than Queen Victoria's original dog. It is seldom totally white, usually having darker marks in the head region and sometimes on the tail.

FRANCE

FRENCH BULLDOG   FRANCE

Known affectionately as the Frenchie, Frogdog or Bat Ears, and in France as the Bouledogue Français, this little dog was developed primarily as a companion animal. In England at one stage it was known as the French Toy Bulldog.

This is a miniaturized, bat-eared bulldog, with a body height of only 12 in (31 cm) and a weight of 22–28 lb (10–13 kg). Some authors describe its original function as 'bull-baiting', but the truth is that, from the moment the French Bulldog existed as a distinct, separate breed, it was essentially a pet animal.

Its early history has been hotly debated, but the most likely version is as follows. In the early 1850s a dwarf bulldog breed, called the Toy Bulldog, was common in London, Nottingham, Birmingham and Sheffield. In Nottingham it was especially popular with the local lace-makers. The Industrial Revolution in Britain at that time meant that 'cottage industries' such as lace-making were under threat. The lace-makers tried their luck elsewhere and many settled in northern France, taking their small bulldogs with them. Once there, these little companion animals became popular in rural districts. In addition to their value as family pets, they showed a fondness for ratting; some say that, as a way of improving this feature, a little terrier blood was added. Others believe that some Pug crosses also occurred.

After several decades, a new breed that could justifiably be called the French Bulldog had developed. Unlike all other bulldogs or their relatives, it had now sprouted large, erect, bat-like ears. Parisians heard about this unusual little dog and it was soon taken up as an urban pet, at first by the Belles de Nuit (Ladies of the Night) and then, a little later, by those wishing to appear socially daring. It was paraded proudly up and down the Champs-Élysées, and French artists Degas and Toulouse-Lautrec immortalized the breed in their paintings of Paris social life.

Eventually, because of its delightful personality, the demand for this little dog spread wider and wider, and it rose to become one of the most favoured of all French breeds. It found its way to other European countries such as Holland, Austria and Russia, and even crossed the Atlantic to be taken up in the United States, where its bat-ears were especially admired.

In the 1890s this now essentially Gallic breed also made what was intended to be a triumphant return to Britain in its new form. Instead it was met with out-and-out hostility. The very name 'bulldog' was thought to be uniquely British. National pride was at stake, and the French Bulldog was written off by certain breeders as an inferior variant of the English Toy Bulldog 'hampered by many undesirable features'. There were furious arguments, a major split occurred, and in 1902 a splinter group of British enthusiasts banded together to form the French Bulldog Club of England. They held their first show in 1903, when no fewer than 51 examples of this breed were displayed.

On 1st January 1906, the Kennel Club in London gave the breed its official approval under the title of Bouledogue Français. In 1912 they changed its name to French Bulldog. It later went on to triumph over the English breed and, unlike its rival, is still with us today.

In temperament, this breed is brave, loyal, affectionate, vivacious and intelligent. With children it is endlessly playful. Furthermore, unlike so many breeds of dog, this one is ideally suited to life in towns and cities. In colour it can be brindle, pied or fawn. Its naturally short tail is left undocked.

The breed has one sad distinction: a French Bulldog is said to have been the only pet animal to have perished when the *Titanic* sank in 1912.

References

1926. Anon. *The French Bulldog. History of the Origin of the Breed, its Cultivation and Development.* The French Bulldog Club of America & The French Bulldog Club of New England.

1965. Pronek, Neal. *How to Raise and Train a French Bull Dog.* TFH, New Jersey.

1988. Eltinge, Steve. *The French Bulldog.*

1989. Nicholas, Anna Katherine. *French Bulldogs.* TFH, New Jersey.

2000. Dannel, Kathy. *The French Bulldog: An Owner's Guide to a Happy Healthy Pet.* Howell, New York.

LÖWCHEN

FRANCE

The name of the little dog translates from the German as 'Little Lion' and, in the past, it has also been called the Little Lion Dog or the Petit Chien Lion. One author insisted on calling this breed the Leoninus (or 'lion-like'). The correct pronunciation of the word Löwchen is 'lerv-chun'.

This small, shaggy dog is usually seen wearing its own version of the poodle-cut — shaved legs and a shaved rear end, except for the feet and tail-tip. Two reasons have been given for this 'lion-cut', as it is called. The first is that, back in the Middle Ages, when nights were often chilly, the exposed skin of these little dogs was comfortingly hot to the touch. Keeping them in their beds, ladies were able to use them as 'hot-water bottles'. The second explanation is that the dogs were half-shaved to give them the look of a male lion with a thick mane of hair. The lion was a symbol of strength and power, and the little dogs were supposed to have acquired that power symbolically by virtue of their leonine appearance.

It is fairly obvious that the Löwchen is a member of the Bichon family and that it is related to such breeds as the Maltese, the Bolognese and the Bichon Frisé. However, as with several European lapdog breeds, there is a dispute over its true country of origin. The fact that its name is German implies a German origin. But it was also known, as early as the 16th century, not only in Germany but also in Russia, Holland, Italy, Spain and France. The current feeling is that, despite its name, it was primarily developed in France, and it is usually listed as a French dog, although, to be truthful, we do not have a definitive answer.

Back in the 1960s and 1970s this breed had fallen so dramatically from favour that for several years its name appeared in *The Guinness Book of Records*. In the 1973 edition it is stated: 'The rarest breed of dog is the Löwchen, of which only 65–70 were reported in March, 1973.'

Since that time there has been a revival of interest, and several serious breeders have taken it up and have initiated carefully planned breeding programmes. Even so, it remains essentially a rare dog. More recently still, it has been made famous by the popular American television series *Hart to Hart*, in which an unclipped example starred as the family pet, called Freeway. It remains to be seen whether this will have influenced its future popularity.

In personality, this is a rather strong-willed dog that refuses to acknowledge its small size. It has been described as outgoing, lively, robust, even-tempered, affectionate, intelligent, energetic and sensible. It appears in several solid colours, including white, cream, blue and black. Its weight is rather variable, ranging from 9 to 18 lb (4 to 8 kg). Its height is 10–13 in (25–33 cm).

BELGIUM

PAPILLON   BELGIUM

The name Papillon means 'butterfly' in French and refers to this breed's appealing butterfly-shaped ears. In France it was also called the Épagneul Nain, or Dwarf Spaniel. This was sometimes given in a longer version as Épagneul Nain Continental, Papillon. Another title was the Chien Écureuil, or Squirrel Dog, because of its bushy, squirrel-like tail. It has also been known as the Butterfly Spaniel, the Squirrel Spaniel or the Continental Toy Spaniel. Its modern nickname is the Pap.

This graceful, seemingly delicate little dog is in fact quite hardy and can stand both hot and cold extremes. It has been one of the top lapdogs of continental Europe for over 200 years. Its direct ancestor, the Phalène, which differs only in the shape of its ears, had been a favourite long before that, since at least the 13th century.

The Papillon developed as an erect-eared version of the Phalène in the 18th century. According to one report, somewhere in Belgium a mutation in the Phalène gave rise to the butterfly ears. A rival theory suggests that the Phalène was crossed with some kind of prick-eared miniature spitz dog to produce the erect ear shape.

Whichever story is true, once this feature had appeared, the new type soon overtook the Phalène in popularity and effectively replaced it, so that in later years people imagined that the Phalène was merely a minor variant of the Papillon, instead of its ancestor. Because of this, the Phalène was sometimes called the Drop-eared Papillon, when it would have been more correct to call the Papillon the Prick-eared Phalène. Edward Ash, for example, writing in the 1920s, remarked: 'There are two varieties of Papillons, the prick-eared and the drop-eared.' In some countries, even today, these two dogs are exhibited as variants of one breed.

The Phalène and the Papillon were always high-status dogs, immensely popular at royal courts throughout Europe. They were the boudoir companions of many noble ladies including both Madame Pompadour and Marie Antoinette. When, in her last days, the latter was awaiting the guillotine, her little pet, called Thisbe, is said to have waited patiently for her outside her prison. Many great artists, including Titian, Goya, Rubens, Rembrandt, Fragonard, Watteau and Boucher, added these little dogs to their portraits of the famous.

Despite its widespread popularity in continental Europe, the Papillon did not appear in England until 1901. It was not accepted by the Kennel Club in London until the mid-1920s, or by the AKC in the United States until the mid-1930s. This late arrival in the English-speaking world was probably due to the entrenched position of the King Charles Spaniel, which occupied a similar social niche.

In personality, the Papillon has been described as a quick and impulsive breed. Known fondly as 'beauty-and-brains', it is an alert, affectionate, adaptable, lively little dog that lacks aggression, but can, if necessary, attack and kill any rodents it encounters. It is only 8–11 in (20–28 cm) in height and weighs only 9–10 lb (4 kg). Its long, silky coat is basically white, but has darker markings.

References

1959. Roberts, Peggy and Roberts, Bob Russell. *The Papillon Handbook.* Nicholson & Watson, London.

1964. Gauss, Mrs D. C. *How to Raise and Train a Papillon.* TFH, New Jersey.

1976. Christensen, Runa. *Papillon.* Clausen Boger, Copenhagen.

1976. Waud, Clarice and Dowle, Pat. *The Butterfly Dog: Papillon and Phalene.* The Canine Library.

1978. Tamm, Suzanne. *Papillon och Phalène.* ICA Vasteras, Sweden.

1985. Waud, Clarice and Hutchings, Mark. *The Papillon 'Butterfly' Dog.*

1987. Bolt, Erika. *Schmetterlingshundchen: Papillon and Phalène.* Kynos-Verlag, Mürlenbach Eifel.

1987. Sharwarny, Lis. *Papillon.* Clausen Bøger, Copenhagen.

1989. Newton, Virginia. *Papillon Primer – The Basic Book.* The Papillon Club of America.

1990. Gauss. *Papillons.* TFH, New Jersey.

1992. Roe, Caroyn and Roe, David. *The Complete Papillon.* Ringpress Books, Letchworth, Herts.

1992. Swann, Gwen. *Papillons and Other Friends.*

2000. Wood, Deborah and Thomas, Susanna. *The Papillon. An Owner's Guide to a Happy Healthy Pet.* Howell, New York.

SPAIN

BICHON FRISÉ   TENERIFE

This small lapdog used to be known as the Bichon Tenerife, the Tenerife Dog or the Canary Islands Lap-dog. At one time it was also known simply as the Bichon, or as the Tenerife. Its modern name (which is an abbreviation of Bichon à Poil Frisé) is often mispronounced as Bee-shon Freese, instead of the correct Bee-shon Free-zay. The name Bichon is a contraction of Barbichon, which means 'little Barbet', the Barbet itself being an ancient form of water spaniel.

It may seem strange that such a sophisticated little dog should have originated in the Canary Islands off the north-west coast of Africa, but the history of those islands explains its presence there. When Spanish explorers first arrived on the islands in the 15th century, they saw many large dogs but no small ones. And yet, by the 16th century, the Bichon Tenerife was already a popular lapdog among the ladies of the Spanish court. The only explanation is that it was the Spanish who took their own lapdogs with them to the Canary Islands, left them there and then later took some of the dogs' descendants back to mainland Spain. Doing this implies that, during their stay on the island between the 15th and 16th centuries, these little dogs underwent some kind of change that made them especially attractive, otherwise there would have been no point in returning them to the courts from which their ancestors originated.

Back in Spain, they remained popular among the nobility from the 16th to the early 19th century and appeared in some of the great paintings of the period, including several by Goya. They also found favour at the French court. Towards the end of the 19th century, however, this particular breed went out of fashion, and descended to the level of a circus and fairground performer. It was not until 1933 that it was taken seriously again, when French and Belgian enthusiasts came to its rescue, established a breed standard and changed its name from Bichon Tenerife to Bichon à Poil Frisé, meaning 'the bichon with a curly coat'. Since it was they who rescued it, they can be forgiven for registering the breed as 'French/Belgian', rather than Spanish.

After World War II, the breed slowly increased in popularity, but it was not until it was taken up by American breeders in the late 1950s that its appeal became more widely appreciated. By the 1970s, it was recognized both by the AKC and by the Kennel Club in London and was destined to become a spectacular star of the show-ring.

This is a confident, lively, playful, outgoing, intelligent little dog that makes the ideal pet for anyone who is prepared to devote a great deal of time and effort to grooming the profuse, fluffy white coat, which is officially described as 'fine, silky, with soft corkscrew curls'.

The Bichon Frisé has three close relatives: The Maltese, the Bolognese and the Havanese (see separate entries). It differs from the other three in having a double coat.

References

1972. Beauchamp, Richard G. *The Bichon Frisé Handbook.* Rohman, California.
1972. Crepin-Labond. *Le Bichon (Frisé et Maltais).* Paris.
1973. Brearley, Joan McDonald and Nicholas, Anna Katherine. *This is the Bichon Frisé.* TFH, New Jersey.
1975. Beauchamp, Richard G. *The Bichon Frisé Workbook.* Rohman, California.
1978. Ransom, Jackie. *The Dog Directory Guide to the Bichon Frisé.* Dog Directory, Berkshire, Bracknell.
1978. Walin, Dorothy. *The Bichon – Grooming and General Care.* Milwaukee, Wisconsin.
1981. Weil, Martin. *Bichon Frisé.* TFH, New Jersey.
1982. Beauchamp, Richard G. *The Bichon Frisé Today.* Rohman, California.
1984. Ransom, Jackie. *Bichon Frisé Great Britain Pedigree Book.*
1985. Anon. *The Bichon Frisé: Twenty Five Years.* The Bichon Frisé Club of San Diego, La Jolla, California.
1986. Hutchison, John E. *The Bichon Frisé – a Practical Approach.* Australia.
1990. Ransom, E. Jackie. *The Bichon Frisé.* Witherby, London.
1990. Stubbs, Barbara B. *The Complete Bichon Frisé.* Howell, New York.
1995. Beauchamp, Richard G. *The Truth About Bichons.*
1995. Dylan, Jamie. *Guide to Owning a Bichon Frisé.* TFH, New Jersey.
1995. Hearn, Ann. *Proper Care of Bichon Frisé.* TFH, New Jersey.
1995. Nicholas, Anna Katherine. *This is the Bichon Frisé.*
1996. Beauchamp, Richard G. *Bichon Frisés: Everything About Purchase, Care, Nutrition, Breeding, Behavior, and Training.* Barron, New York.
1996. Nicholas, Anna Katherine. *The World of the Bichon Frisé.*
1996. Vogel, Mary, et al. *The Bichon Frisé: An Owner's Guide to a Happy Healthy Pet.* Howell, New York.
1999. Dunbar, Ian. *The Essential Bichon Frisé.* Howell, New York.
1999. Ransom, Jackie. *The Bichon Frisé Today.*
1999. Wyatt, Chris, et al. *The Bichon Frisé, an Owner's Companion.*
2000. Palika, Liz. *How to Train Your Bichon Frisé.*

ITALY

BOLOGNESE
ITALY

Also known as the Bichon Bolognese, the Bolognese Toy Dog, the Bologneser, the Gutschen Hundle or the Schoshundle, this dog has been popular as a household companion in northern Italy for centuries. It has been known by several nicknames, including the Bolo, the Botoli and the Bottolo.

This small, white-coated member of the bichon family (which includes the Bichon Frisé, the Maltese and the Havanese) is distinguished from its close relatives by its unusually fluffy hair, sometimes described as 'flocked'. There is no undercoat – the dog being well adapted to a hot climate – and the main hairs are 'raised from the body'.

This little lapdog has a history stretching back to at least the 11th century, and has been the pampered favourite of many European aristocrats and members of royal houses, including Madame Pompadour, Louis XIV of France, Philip II of Spain, and Catherine the Great of Russia (who shared her bed with one). The ruler of the Austrian Empire, Queen Maria Theresa, loved her Bolognese dog so much that when it died she had it taxidermized, so that it could remain near her for ever. Her pet can still be seen today, on display in a Vienna museum. During the Renaissance, the Medicis not only kept these dogs but actively bred them and sometimes sent groups abroad as special gifts to other leading families in Europe.

According to early records, this cherished breed was so revered that it was sometimes fed from solid-gold bowls and, in 18th-century Italy, servant women were occasionally known to suckle Bolognese dogs as a special service for their titled superiors.

There are two theories concerning its ancestry. The most popular one sees it as a descendant of the Maltese dog that originated further south, on the Mediterranean island of Malta, and then spread north through Italy until it arrived in the region of Bologna. The other views it as a descendant of the now extinct Shock Dog, a petite water dog.

One curious report suggests that, when Pope Julius II drove the wanton Giovanni II out of Bologna in 1506, the disgraced ruler took his Bolognese dogs with him and retreated into exile on Malta. Once there, his pets are said to have crossed with very small local dogs to create the Bichon breed we know today as the Maltese. Clearly, there is a major contradiction here. One theory depicts the Bolognese as a descendant of the Maltese and the other depicts the Maltese as the descendant of the Bolognese. At present, the evidence is too scanty to decide between these two diametrically opposed opinions.

In personality, this attractive animal, with its up-curled tail and soft, fluffy coat, has been called serious, reserved, devoted, loyal, alert, intelligent and quick to learn. It becomes so strongly attached to its owners that it is like a shadow, never leaving their side. It is healthy, long-lived and, after centuries of noble living, markedly non-aggressive. In size it is 10–12 in (25–31 cm) tall and weighs only 5–9 lb (3–4 kg). Today, all dogs of this breed are pure white, but in earlier centuries they were sometimes black, or black-and-white.

Despite its ancient pedigree and obvious appeal, it remains today a rare breed. It did not appear in the United States until the 1980s, when the Bolognese Club of America was founded, following the arrival of the first imports from Italy.

ITALIAN GREYHOUND ITALY

Known in its homeland as the Piccolo Levriero Italiano, this tiny dog has been kept as a companion animal for thousands of years.

We know from paintings, reliefs and sculptures dating from early civilizations that this little dog was popular, not only in ancient Egypt (where it was sometimes mummified by the pharaohs), but also in both Greece and Rome. It was probably one of the very first dog breeds created exclusively as a companion. By breeding down from full-sized greyhounds to this diminutive creature, early pet-keepers were able to develop a dog which, although it could no longer take part in serious hunting, was of great value as a high-status adornment about the house.

This situation continued for many years. In the 15th century, for example, great artists such as Jan van Eyck and Hans Memling both included this dog in their paintings. In Britain it became a highly fashionable breed in the Tudor and Stuart periods and, by the start of the 19th century, its popularity had become so great that it was vying with the little Maltese and the King Charles Spaniel for the role of top dog in high society.

Royalty has frequently fallen under its spell and monarchs who have owned dainty, high-stepping, Italian Greyhounds include Charles I, Queen Anne and Queen Victoria, not to mention the African King Lobengula, who fell in love with one to such an extent that he exchanged 200 head of Matabele cattle in order to possess it.

Sadly, this craze for high-status pet Italian Greyhounds resulted in progressive miniaturization until the breed was in serious danger. As it became smaller and smaller, many unsound specimens began appearing. The breed was on its way to extinction, but towards the end of the Victorian period, in the 1890s, a group of serious breeders came to its rescue and began to return it to its former, stronger self.

Today the breed is fully recovered and a hardy little dog once more, despite its frail appearance. One owner recently observed his tiny Italian Greyhound leaping 15 ft (4.5 m) down from an open window and then, after a brief shake, running off across a lawn, all four of its matchstick legs perfectly intact.

In personality, it is fastidious, rather shy, gentle, retiring, good-natured, undemanding and comfort-loving. A discerning dog, it takes time to make friends, but for those who know it well, it is the ideal urban pet, and it is surprising that it is not more popular in this role today.

References

1956. Incontri, Marie Luisa. *Il Piccolo Levriero Italiano.* Sansoni, Florence.

1964. Russo, Louis F. *How to Raise and Train an Italian Greyhound.* TFH, New Jersey.

1964. Worthing, Eileen M. *Life and Legends of the Italian Greyhound.* The Italian Greyhound Club of America.

1968. Thring, E. D. *The Italian Greyhound.* The Italian Greyhound Club, UK.

1972. Haegel, E. P. *Le Petit Lévrier Italien.* Le Club Français du Petit Lévrier Italien.

1983. Barber, Lilian. *The Italian Greyhound Guide.* Italian Greyhound Productions, Washington.

1983. Oliver, Annette. *Living with Italian Greyhounds.* Italian Greyhound Club, London.

1987. Barber, Lilian. *The Complete Italian Greyhound.* Italian Greyhound Productions, Washington.

1989. Russo, Louis F. *Italian Greyhounds.* TFH, New Jersey.

1992. Oliver, Annette. *Italian Greyhounds Today.* Ringpress Books, Letchworth, Hertfordshire.

1994. Barber, Lilian. *The New Complete Italian Greyhound.* Italian Greyhound Productions, Washington.

1999. Keppler, Dean. *Italian Greyhound: A Complete and Reliable Handbook.* TFH, New Jersey.

PHALÈNE   ITALY

Also known misleadingly as the Drop-eared Papillon (when, historically speaking, the Papillon should have been called the Prick-eared Phalène) this breed of lapdog was also known as the Épagneul Nain, the Dwarf Spaniel or the Continental Toy Spaniel, or sometimes as the Épagneul Nain Continental, Phalène. The French word 'phalène' means 'moth', likening the folded ears of the dog to folded moth-wings.

This graceful little animal was one of the top lapdogs of continental Europe between the 13th and the 18th centuries. Then, during the reign of Louis XVI of France, an erect-eared version was developed in Belgium and given the name of Papillon (see separate entry). The appeal of this new breed, with its stylish 'butterfly ears', was so great that it quickly eclipsed its direct ancestor. For the next 200 years the Papillon was the favoured breed, but the Phalène did not disappear completely and can still be seen today, although in greatly reduced numbers.

In some countries the Phalène and the Papillon are exhibited as two varieties of one breed, but elsewhere they are considered separately. (For the sake of consistency, it would seem that if the Norwich and Norfolk Terriers are to be classed as two different breeds on their ear-shape, the Papillon and Phalène should be treated in the same way.)

There has been great speculation concerning the country of origin of this breed. The situation is so confusing that some authors capitulate and say simply that it comes from 'continental Europe'. Others insist that it is a French breed because of its name; a Belgian breed, because it was so popular in that country; a Spanish breed, because of the 'spaniel' element; and even a Mexican breed, because it looks rather like the Long-haired Chihuahua. The best guess, however, is that it originated in central Italy, where its ancestors may well have been ensconced since the days of ancient Rome. We know, for example, that Louis XIV of France employed the services of an Italian dog-dealer called Giovani Filliponi to provide his court with the pick of the best examples of these little dogs, carefully transported from Italy to France in small cages on the backs of mules.

This is a delightfully sprightly little dog which is proud, extroverted and appealingly possessive of its owner.

References

Waud, Clarice. *The Butterfly Dog: Papillon and Phalène.* The Canine Library.

POTSDAM GREYHOUND   ITALY

Despite its name, this breed originated in Italy. It gained its title because it was championed by Frederick the Great, who kept these dogs at his Potsdam Palace. It was developed purely as a companion.

This dog was a larger cousin of the tiny Italian Greyhound. It was intermediate in size between a typical hunting greyhound and the tiny toy version. Its height was 20 in (51 cm), compared with the Italian Greyhound's 13–15 in (33–38 cm), or the English Greyhound's 27–30 in (69–76 cm).

It was an elegant, decorative breed, with a fine-textured coat in fawn, blue, black, bronze or silver-grey. It was described as the ideal indoor dog, 'born to lie in graceful attitudes on drawing-room sofas'.

Frederick the Great was passionately fond of his Potsdam Greyhounds and was distraught when he accidentally poisoned two of them. He was about to drink a cup of chocolate, when he decided to offer it to his two favourite greyhounds. They lapped it up, promptly went into convulsions and died in front of him. The drink had been poisoned by his enemies and Frederick angrily sent for his French cook. On hearing the news, the cook put a gun to his head and blew out his brains. He had been in the pay of the Austrians and could not face the consequences.

Frederick's Potsdam Greyhounds, pampered dogs served by their own valets, were so important to him that the breed was kept as exclusive to his palace. After his death a day arrived when there was only one pair left alive, and these were acquired by the Countess Marie Munster. She bred from them and eventually there were examples in both England and Ireland. The breed was still in existence as recently as the early part of the 20th century. After that, it seems to have faded away and does not appear to have survived the ravages of World War I.

VOLPINO ITALY

Also known today as the Volpino Italiano, the Italian Spitz or the Florentine Spitz; this dog was called the Volpino di Firenze (the Florentine Volpino) in the 18th century. The word 'volpino' translates as 'little fox'. In the 19th century the breed was known as the Cane de Quirinale (the Quirinal Dog).

This is the Italian equivalent of the German Pomeranian, with a stronger head and a muzzle which, although short, is slightly longer and more pointed than that of its more northerly relative. The favoured colour of its long, dense coat is pure white. In the past, this breed has also appeared in fawn, black or sable colours, but these varieties appear to have vanished in recent times. Although it does have a ruff, it is less dense than that of the Pomeranian.

The Volpino is an early breed and there has been some debate about whether it is the ancestor of the Pomeranian. Records suggest that it existed before its German relative, but detailed evidence is lacking.

This tiny spitz dog, with its foxy face, pricked ears and up-curled tail was a favourite among the Italian ladies of the Renaissance, when its body was often adorned with expensive ivory collars and bracelets. It remained in favour with the nobility for centuries and its 19th century name of Quirinal Dog reflects its high-status role. (The Quirinale was the Royal Palace in Rome and is now the Presidential Palace.)

In personality, this healthy, long-lived dog is lively, noisy, exuberant and affectionate. It height range is 11–12 in (27–30 cm) and its weight 9–11 lb (4–5 kg). Despite its obvious appeal, it remains rare in its homeland and virtually unseen elsewhere.

GERMANY

GERMAN GIANT SPITZ

GERMANY

Also known as the Great Spitz, the Large Spitz, the Grand Loulou and, in its homeland, the Deutscher Grösser Spitz or the Deutscher Grosspitz, this breed, despite its size, was developed exclusively as a pet dog.

This is not really a giant breed, being only of medium size and not even as large as its relative, the sheep-herding Wolfspitz. But it gained its name because it is bigger than the Standard, Miniature or Toy Spitz breeds. It is a rare breed today, because breeders have tended to favour the smaller sizes of German Spitz dogs, especially the tiniest of them all – the Pomeranian.

In origin, it is said that the ancestors of this breed, and its relatives, were brought to Germany from the north by the Vikings. The German Spitz dogs are certainly early breeds, there being a mention of them (before they split into different sizes) in the literature of the mid-15th century.

The Giant form is accepted only in solid colours: white, black or brown. Since at least the 17th century, each of these colours has been associated with a particular region of Germany. The white were favoured in Elberfeld, the black and the brown in Würtemberg.

In height, this breed is 16 in (40–41 cm); in weight it is 38–40 lb (17–18 kg).

GERMAN STANDARD SPITZ

GERMANY

This middle-sized German Spitz is known in England as the German Spitz (Mittel), and in its homeland as the Deutscher Mittelspitz.

During the course of the last few centuries, the German Spitz dogs have been progressively reduced in size from the big, northern dogs that were their early ancestors. The situation has become progressively complicated, with different authorities recognizing different phases in this reduction process. At the present time, there are five different sizes recognized, and this one falls in the middle of the range, with the Wolfspitz and the Giant Spitz above it and the Miniature Spitz and the Toy Spitz below it.

Its height is given as 11–14 in (29–36 cm) by one authority, and 12–15 in (30–38 cm) by another. The outer coat is harsh and long, while the undercoat is soft and woolly, providing good protection from even the coldest weather. Colours are varied. Solid colours are most commonly seen, but others are permitted.

Although this breed had been recognized by the FCI for some time, it was not until 1985 that it was accepted by the Kennel Club in London. Previously the British preference had been for the ever-shrinking Pomeranian, which had first arrived in England in the 18th century as a medium-sized dog and had then been selectively bred for smaller and smaller sizes until the tiny, modern Pom had been reached. In the 1970s several English breeders decided that they wanted to reverse this process and imported larger German Spitz dogs which they then crossed with the minute Pomeranians. The idea was to reverse, to a small degree, the extreme dwarfism which had developed. The idea of calling the larger dogs resulting from these crosses 'Pomeranians' was offensive to the devotees of the very small Poms, and the Kennel Club decided to classify the new, enlarged Poms as a separate breed. Even this did not settle matters entirely, because there were now two 'levels' of enlarged Pom. These were given the new names of German Spitz (Mittel) and German Spitz (Klein), which linked them to their continental size-equivalents, the Standard German Spitz and the Miniature German Spitz.

GERMAN MINIATURE SPITZ GERMANY

Also known as the Miniature German Spitz, the Small German Spitz, the German Spitz (Klein) or the Deutscher Klein Spitz, this little companion dog has been separated from its close relatives purely by size. It is smaller than the Wolfspitz, the Giant Spitz and the Standard Spitz, but larger than the Toy Spitz and the Pomeranian. It has sometimes been called the Victorian Pom, because it is closest to the type of dog that was first imported into England by Queen Victoria in the 19th century.

There has been considerable confusion over the different German Spitz breeds. Some canine authorities recognize only three forms of German Spitz – the large German Wolfspitz, the German Spitz and the tiny Pomeranian. In those cases, the Giant, the Standard and the Miniature are lumped together as one breed, called simply the German Spitz. The FCI, on the other hand, recognizes five breeds: the Wolfspitz, the Giant, the Standard, the Miniature and the Toy.

The situation was further complicated in the 1970s, when British breeders, alarmed by the problems arising with the smallest Pomeranians, imported both Standard and Miniature Spitz dogs to boost their size. These larger specimens were originally called Pomeranians, but this was unsatisfactory and eventually the Kennel Club allowed them to be separated and called the German Spitz (Mittel) and the German Spitz (Klein).

The height of the Klein, or Miniature, breed is given as 9–11 in (23–28 cm), which fills the size-gap between the Mittel, or Standard, and the Toy.

These quibbles over classification do not, happily, affect the personality of these dogs. From the rare Giant down to the tiniest Pom, they are all essentially the same kind of dog, even if they come in different-sized packages. They are all buoyant, lively, adaptable pets with almost identical spitz proportions, and provide ideal urban companionship.

This particular breed, the Miniature, may appear in both solid and bicolour forms. Although it had become quite rare, since 1985 there has been a revival of this version of the Spitz family in Germany, perhaps following in the wake of its official recognition by the Kennel Club in London.

GERMAN TOY SPITZ   GERMANY

Also known as the Toy German Spitz, the Dwarf Spitz or the Loulou (abbreviation of Loup Loup), or in its homeland as the Zwerg Spitz, this breed was developed exclusively as a companion dog.

This is the smallest of the German Spitz breeds, a dwarf form developed as a toy dog ideally suited to life in a restricted, urban environment. In personality it still considers itself to be a large dog and announces this fact without hesitation. For those with limited space, or the inability to undertake long walks, this is a tailor-made breed.

There has been confusion between this and the Pomeranian breed. Both have been created by selective breeding that has favoured smaller and smaller individuals, but the development of the Toy Spitz has taken place in Germany and other parts of continental Europe, while the Pomeranian has been refined in England and elsewhere outside continental Europe. Some authorities treat them as one and the same, but others separate them as two distinct breeds (as is done here). The reason for separating them is that they have been bred as distinct lines for well over 100 years and the size of the Pomeranian has been reduced even below that of the German Toy Spitz. They may have paralleled one another's progress, but they are not the same breeding stock.

The German Toy Spitz is a favourite lapdog on continental Europe, but is little-known elsewhere because its niche is already occupied by its 'parallel breed', the English-developed Pomeranian.

In height, this breed is under 9 in (23 cm); in weight it is under 7 lb (3 kg). It is accepted in solid colours with black, orange, brown, grey and white being the favourites, and also in particolours.

HARLEQUIN PINSCHER

Also known as the Harlekinpinscher, this rare breed is now thought to be nearly extinct. It was developed primarily as a companion dog.

This is essentially an odd-coloured Pinscher with a blotched coat. Traditional Pinscher supporters scorned it and refused to recognize it, but some fanciers liked its unusual 'merle' (blue-grey flecked with black) markings and tried to develop it as a separate breed. They succeeded for a while, but by the 1930s new registrations had largely dried up and few examples of the breed managed to survive World War II.

It is not known precisely which breeds were crossed with the typical Pinschers to obtain the Harlequin's 'merle' colouring, but the chances are that they were not terriers because the Harlequin has a gentler personality. This is why it is more suitable as a companion dog than as a working terrier, and also why working-terrier men look upon it as a useless reject.

KROMFOHRLÄNDER

A recent German terrier breed which was named after the Krumme Furche district in which it was created. It is known to its devotees as either the Kromi or the Länder. Despite its ancestry, it has never been a working terrier and has been developed exclusively as a companion dog.

This breed owes its origins to the chaos of World War II. Fighting their way through France, American troops adopted a little brown-and-white, harsh-coated French terrier as their mascot. It was probably a Breton Griffon, or something very similar, and it accompanied them as they pushed on into Germany in 1945.

At the Westphalian town of Siegen, in the Krumme Furche region about 100 miles (160 km) north-west of Frankfurt, the dog, now known by the name of Peter, jumped off its American Army truck and ran up to a German woman called Ilse Schleifenbaum. She took pity on Peter, who by this time was dirty, unkempt and underfed, and kept him as a pet. He became attached to her neighbour's terrier bitch, Fiffi, and the pair produced a litter of puppies. Because Fiffi was a mongrel (whose ancestors had at some stage been on friendly terms with a Fox Terrier), it was expected that the offspring would prove to be a mixed bag. Surprisingly this was not the case. They were of uniform type and so appealing that it was decided to use them as the foundation stock for a new breed, to be called the Kromfohrländer.

Ten years later, in 1955, the breed was sufficiently established to gain recognition from the German Kennel Club and eventually from the FCI. By the end of the 20th century, the population of Kromfohrländers stood at just over 1,000, of which 750 were in Germany and the rest in Finland, Switzerland and Holland. It has never become a working terrier and throughout its entire existence has been kept solely as a pet. Its main appeal is its lively intelligence and its ever-alert interest in its owners and their world. It also manages to avoid trouble with farmers because, it is said, this breed 'is totally disinterested in the hunt, even if hares, rabbits or other wild animals cross its way directly in front'.

POMERANIAN GERMANY

A small pet dog developed from the larger spitz types by reduction through selective breeding, this dog originated in Germany, but was fostered and developed in England. It has sometimes been called the Dwarf Spitz or the Loulou by those who do not distinguish between it and its continental equivalent, the German Toy Spitz. It takes its name from the extreme northern German district of Pomerania. To its friends it is known simply as the Pom.

The ancestors of the Pomeranian arrived in England from Germany in the 18th century, when the German-born Queen Charlotte came to the British throne and brought with her the favourite court dogs of her country. She called them Pomeranians, but these were white spitz dogs weighing 20–30 lb (9–14 kg), which places them in the size-range of what we today call the Standard or Mittel Spitz. Devoted, vivacious and affectionate companions, these white spitz dogs soon became popular in Britain and were painted several times by Gainsborough. By the 19th century the Pom was a favoured Victorian breed.

In 1888 Queen Victoria was on a visit to Florence when she saw some small examples of the breed (equivalent in size to today's Miniature Spitz) and brought them home with her. They were added to her kennels and this royal accolade resulted in a further rise in the Pomeranian's popularity. The Queen not only went on to breed them but also exhibited them and won great acclaim for her dogs. She exhibited six of them at the 1891 Cruft's show in London and one of them, called Windsor Marco, won the breed class. (It would have been a brave judge to have placed her second.) When Queen Victoria died in 1901, her favourite black Pom, Turi, was with her to the end, lying at the foot of her bed. In the years that followed, the size of these little dogs continued to shrink, heading down towards the dwarf dog we know today. Its modern height is only 7–8 in (18–22 cm); its weight only 4–5 lb (1.8–2.2 kg). These tiny examples became so favoured that the earlier, larger types vanished in Britain (although they did, of course, survive in continental Europe).

The first Pomeranian Club was formed in 1891, and the following year the first examples arrived in the United States. In 1911 the American Pomeranian Club held its first show.

Fondly described as 'animated puff-balls', Poms appear in 12 different colour forms: black, brown, chocolate, beaver, red, orange, cream, orange sable, wolf sable, blue, white and particoloured. The coat is amazingly thick and upstanding, with an exaggerated ruff that completely surrounds the small, foxy face, and a fluffy tail which is held up over the back.

References

1906. Hicks, G. M. *The Pomeranian.* Our Dogs, Manchester.
1911. Ives, Lilla. *Show Pomeranians.* Our Dogs, Manchester.
1928. Parker, Mrs E. *The Popular Pomeranian.* Popular Dogs, London.
1934. Johns, Rowland (Editor). *Our Friend the Pomeranian.* Methuen, London.
1950. Denlinger, Milo G. *The Complete Pomeranian.* Denlinger's, USA.
1958. Miller, Evelyn. *Pomeranians as Pets.* TFH, New Jersey.
1959. Liebers, Arthur and Sheppard, Mrs George. *How to Raise and Train a Pomeranian.* TFH, New Jersey.
1962. Ricketts, Viva Leona. *The New Complete Pomeranian.* Howell, New York.
1965. Spirer, Lousie Ziegler and Spirer, Herbert F. *This is the Pomeranian.* TFH, New Jersey.
1967. Harmer, Hilary. *The Pomeranian.* Foyles, London.
1968. Ricketts, Viva Leona. *Pet Pomeranian.* All-Pets, Fond du Lac, Wisconsin.
1980. Pisano, Beverly. *Pomeranians.* TFH, New Jersey.
1987. Tietjen, Sari Brewster. *The New Complete Pomeranian.* Howell, New York.
1990. Hughes, Pauline B. *The Pomeranian.*
1991. Stahlkuppe, Joe. *Pomeranians: Everything About Purchase, Care, Nutrition, Breeding, Behavior, and Training.* Barron, New York.
1996. Ellmann, Vikki. *Guide to Owning a Pomeranian: Puppy Care, Grooming, Training, History, Health, Breed Standard.*
1996. Jones, Happeth A. *The Pomeranian: An Owner's Guide to a Happy Healthy Pet.* Howell, New York.
1999. Dunbar, Ian (Editor), et al. *The Essential Pomeranian.*

MEDIUM POODLE   GERMANY

This is a recently designated breed, based on a subtle size distinction.

The Kennel Club in London, like many other canine organizations, recognizes only three sizes of Poodle: Standard, Miniature and Toy. In recent times, however, a fourth size has been accepted as a separate breed by some authorities, although many Poodle experts view this as a case of unwarranted hair-splitting. This fourth breed is called the Medium Poodle and is intermediate in size between the Standard and the Miniature. The FCI lists the four breed sizes as follows:

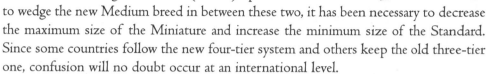

BREED	SIZE
Large (Standard)	45 cm up to 60 cm
Medium	More than 35 cm up to 45 cm
Miniature	More than 28 cm up to 35 cm
Toy	Below 28 cm

Other organizations, adhering to the three-size system, see Miniatures measuring up to 15 in (38 cm) in height and Standards measuring from 15 in (38 cm) upwards. In order to wedge the new Medium breed in between these two, it has been necessary to decrease the maximum size of the Miniature and increase the minimum size of the Standard. Since some countries follow the new four-tier system and others keep the old three-tier one, confusion will no doubt occur at an international level.

If the Medium Poodle differed in some way other than mere size, it would be easier to accept the breed, but since this does not yet appear to be the case, its status must remain doubtful. In its defence, it can be said that its justification lies in the need to reduce the overcrowded Poodle classes at many major shows.

It should be noted that the Miniature Poodle is unfortunately also known as the Caniche Moyen, or Medium Poodle, in some countries, adding further confusion.

MINIATURE POODLE   GERMANY

This breed was developed as a companion animal by breeding down in size from the Standard Poodle. In France it is known as the Caniche Nain.

This is a simple case of dwarfism, the large, original Poodle having been selectively bred down until a dog with a height of no more than 15 in (38 cm) was created. It retained all the good qualities of its big cousin, especially its lively intelligence, but was now small enough to fit into more restricted living environments.

Up until 1907 the Miniature Poodle was called the Toy Poodle, but then, when an even smaller breed was produced by further selective breeding, it had to be given a new name. The tiniest version became the Toy and the name of the existing Toy was changed to Miniature.

The history of the Miniature Poodle is unusual because, uniquely, the circus appears to have been a major influence. When the high intelligence of large Poodles was first exploited to transform them into acrobatic performers, it was clear that smaller dogs would be even easier to handle and to transport in the restricted conditions of a travelling circus. This was to be an important factor in motivating breeders to bring down the size of these dogs and create the miniaturized version. The responsive, quick-witted and fun-loving nature of these high-spirited animals was immediately obvious and they were soon on the way to becoming one of the most popular companion dogs of all time. By the middle of the 20th century they were at their peak, but there followed a period of over-production of puppies, to meet the huge demand, and in the process the quality of the breed suffered. This was later corrected.

References

1960. Brauer, Dorothy. *Poodles without Tears: My Way of Rearing and Training a Miniature or Toy Poodle Puppy.* Privately published, London.
1960. Price, P. Howard. *The Miniature Poodle Handbook.* Nicholson & Watson, London.
1969. Sabella, Frank T. *Your Poodle: Standard, Miniature, and Toy.* Denlinger's, USA.
1997. Fogle, Bruce. *Dog Breed Handbooks – Poodle – Standard, Miniature, & Toy.* Dorling Kindersley, London.
(Note: For general books about Poodles, see entry for Standard Poodle.)

TOY POODLE   GERMANY

Although, in origin, all poodles must be classified as German dogs, this dwarf version was largely developed in the United States as an urban companion dog. It has sometimes been called the Caniche Toy.

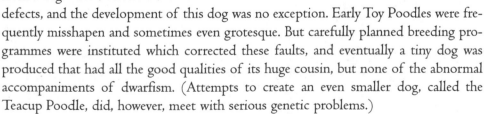

The Toy Poodle was created in the first half of the 20th century as a luxury town dog, being bred down from what are now called Miniature Poodles. It was first recognized as a separate breed in America in 1943. England did not follow suit until 1957.

Creating a dwarf dog by scaling down from a large breed often leads to unfortunate defects, and the development of this dog was no exception. Early Toy Poodles were frequently misshapen and sometimes even grotesque. But carefully planned breeding programmes were instituted which corrected these faults, and eventually a tiny dog was produced that had all the good qualities of its huge cousin, but none of the abnormal accompaniments of dwarfism. (Attempts to create an even smaller dog, called the Teacup Poodle, did, however, meet with serious genetic problems.)

The perfected Toy Poodle blossomed into a perfect small-scale replica of the large breed and by the 1960s had reached its peak. The breed's progress was crowned by the award of Best in Show at Crufts in 1966.

These jaunty little dogs are the epitome of canine playfulness and self-confidence.

Despite their small size, they fear no man and will courageously defend their mistresses' honour whenever it appears threatened, even on special occasions when those particular services are not required.

References

1960. Brauer, Dorothy. *Poodles without Tears: My Way of Rearing and Training a Miniature or Toy Poodle Puppy.* Privately published, London.

1969. Sabella, Frank T. *Your Poodle: Standard, Miniature, and Toy.* Denlinger's, USA.

1997. Fogle, Bruce. *Dog Breed Handbooks – Poodle – Standard, Miniature, & Toy.* Dorling Kindersley, London.

(Note: For general books about Poodles, see entry for Standard Poodle.)

CZECH REPUBLIC

Prazsky Krysavik   CZECH REPUBLIC

This is the most recent of all European companion dogs. Its name translates as 'Prague Beauty', and it has been bred exclusively as a pet dog for urban living.

This tiny, short-coated, black-and-tan dog, with bat-like ears, a pointed muzzle and spindly legs, was created in the 1980s in Prague. By the end of the 20th century there were approximately 600 of them in existence, nearly all to be found in Prague itself. Although it is such a new dog, it is already breeding pure and has been included in some European dog shows. It was developed by local canine enthusiasts who wanted to own a tiny lapdog that was unique to their country.

In height it is only 7–8 in (18–20 cm) and it weighs only 2–6 lb (1–3 kg), making it smaller than a Yorkshire Terrier and roughly the same size as the Chihuahua.

MALTA

Maltese   MALTA

Also known in the past as the Maltese Terrier, the Maltese Spaniel, the Maltese Dog, the Maltese Lion Dog, the Maltese Poodle, the Bichon Maltais, the Melita Dog, the Melitaie Dog, the Melitae Dog, the Ancient Dogge of Malta, the Roman Ladies' Dog, or the Shock Dog, this small breed is one of the earliest of all lapdogs.

This is the ultimate luxury dog, with a long, soft, pure white coat, dark, black-rimmed eyes, drooped ears and an up-curled tail. In earlier centuries these dogs were often carried on the bodies of their owners and were described as 'the jewels of women'.

The history of the Maltese is difficult to trace because of the breed's variability in previous centuries. From at least the time of ancient Greece, ladies of high social status frequently owned tiny pet dogs, which they loved, groomed, fed on delicacies and allowed to sleep on their beds. These little companion animals were so highly valued that an international trade in them had begun even before the time of Christ. In the first millennium BC, the Phoenicians, in particular, were active in the Mediterranean region, and the island of Malta was one of the focal points of their commercial enterprises. Nobody knows where they might have discovered tiny lapdogs, but it seems likely that it was they who first took them to Malta, and then distributed them from there to the various centres of ancient civilization.

Judging by the images that we see on ancient artefacts, many of these early dogs looked remarkably like modern Maltese dogs, but others looked more like tiny Pomeranians, or other toy breeds. There seems to have been little serious line breeding until more recent times, and many historical reports on the Maltese are in reality only very loosely related to this specific breed. One can speak of the Maltese as a true breed only from about the middle of the 19th century.

There are many ancient references to the Maltese dog, but not using its modern name. To the Greeks and Romans, Malta was known as Melita or Melite (taken from the Greek word for honey, 'meli') and the small dogs that came from there were called the Melitae or Melitaie. (It has been suggested that the island of Melita where the dogs lived is not the one we know today as Malta, but another one with the same ancient name situated in the Adriatic, off the coast of Yugoslavia. However, the ancient history of that island, now called Mljet, rules it out.)

The name Melitae for these dogs lasted for over a thousand years and in AD 1600 one author still spoke of 'the melitane dog bred only for delight, whose force is small, though voice be loud and shrill'.

Early in the 17th century it was reported that the island of Malta was 'no longer famous for its dainty little dogs, as only poor shepherds live there'. From this date onwards, the breed seems to have become rare on the island, but in 1805 we do, for the first time, have a local record of it. In that year a Knight of Malta commented: 'There was formerly a breed of dogs in Malta with long silky hair, which were in great demand at the times of the Romans, but have for some years past greatly dwindled, and indeed are become almost extinct.' They did not die out altogether, however, because in 1833 an accurate portrayal of the breed in Maltese settings appears in paintings now housed in the Royal Library of Malta.

Throughout the 19th and 20th centuries the Maltese became increasingly popular. No longer restricted to the nobility, it developed a wide following both as a pet dog and as a show dog, and is now known around the globe. It appeared early in the show-ring – in 1859 in England, and in 1877 in the United States.

Despite its small size and its glamorous appearance, this is a tough little dog, sprightly, vigorous, friendly, trusting and alert. In earlier times it appeared in a variety of coat patterns, but pure, solid white was always a favourite and today is the only colour form accepted. Early pictures often show a wavy-haired, shaggy dog, but in the modern show-ring, the silky coat is long, flat and flowing. There is no undercoat. The weight of the Maltese is only 4–6 lb (2–3 kg) and its height is at most 10 in (25 cm).

References

1953. Leitch, Virginia T. *The Maltese Dog.* John Vir Kennels, Maryland.

1959. Iveria, Miki. *Maltese Dogs, the Jewels of Women.* The Maltese Club of Great Britain.

1961. Miller, Evelyn. *Maltese as Pets.* TFH, New Jersey.

1962. Liebers, Arthur. *How to Raise and Train Maltese.* TFH, New Jersey.

1967. Howell, Patricia M. *The Modern Maltese.* Pollyanna Press, Minnesota.

1970. Leitch, Virginia T. and Carno, Dennis. *The Maltese Dog.* International Institute of Veterinary Science, New York.

1971. Stuber, Marge. *I Love Maltese.* Ohio.

1975. Berndt, Robert. *Your Maltese.* (Your Dog Books). Denlinger's, Fairfax, Virginia.

1976. Stuber, Marge. *Breeding Toy Dogs – Especially Maltese.* Ohio.

1983. Di Giacomo, Kathy and Bergquist, Barbara J. *Maltese.* TFH, New Jersey.

1984. Brearley, Joan McDonald. *The Book of the Maltese.* TFH, New Jersey.

1984. Nicholas, Anna Katherine. *The Maltese.* TFH, New Jersey.

1986. Cutillo, Nicholas. *The Complete Maltese.* Howell, New York.

1989. Beuttler, S. *Dein Malteser.*

1995. James. *Guide to Owning a Maltese.* TFH, New Jersey.

1996. Fulda, Joe. *Maltese: Everything About Purchase, Care, Nutrition, Breeding, Behavior, and Training (Complete Pet Owner's Manual).* Barron, New York.

1996. Henrieff, Vicki, et al. *The Maltese Today.* Howell, New York.

1998. Linden, Bobbie. *The Maltese: An Owner's Guide to a Happy Healthy Pet.* IDG Books Worldwide.

1999. Dunbar, Ian (Editor), et al. *The Essential Maltese.* IDG Books Worldwide.

Schneider, Earl. *Know Your Maltese.* Pet Library, New York.

MADAGASCAR

COTON DE TULEAR   MADAGASCAR

Also known as the Royal Dog of Madagascar, this breed, the cotton-haired dog of Tulear, has always existed solely as a household companion animal.

The ancestors of this small, fluffy white dog arrived at the southern Malagasy port of Tulear in the 17th century on trading ships from the small Indian Ocean island of Réunion. Once there, it is recorded that they are supposed to have interbred with local dogs (although it is hard to imagine that there was anything suitable for them to mix with in such a place at that time) and developed into the attractive breed we know today. The noble families of Tulear adopted them as pets and enjoyed their company so much that they guarded them jealously, even passing a law prohibiting the common people from owning them. They were also extremely reluctant to allow any of their pets to leave the island, with the result that these dogs remained isolated from the rest of the world and were breeding true for centuries.

The Cotons were rediscovered by visiting Europeans in the middle of the 20th century, and a few were allowed to be taken away. These were soon being carefully bred to type and by 1970 the FCI had formally recognized them. A club for their protection was established in Tulear in the same year. Even so, they remain rare on the island.

In 1974 an American biologist, Robert Russell, visiting Tulear, was greatly impressed by these dogs, which he had not encountered before, and took several home with him to New Jersey, where his parents established a breeding kennels for them. By 1976 they had formed the Coton de Tulear Club of America. Within a few years this exciting breed, so old and yet so new to the West, was gaining rapidly in popularity.

Its appeal lies not only in its appearance, but also in its personality. After centuries of living as a highly valued possession, this breed has developed a character that makes it the perfect companion animal. It is intelligent, calm, remarkably unaggressive, playful, and with a fondness for walking on its hind legs. It enjoys a good run, but is less demanding for exercise than most dog breeds. It will sit quietly indoors for long periods, providing it can remain close to its owners.

The Coton's soft, light, fluffy, odour-free, non-shedding coat has a dry, cottony texture. It is never silky. The typical colour is white, but there are also white dogs with cream patches, white dogs with black patches, and tricolours which are white with cream patches and beige patches.

In 1999, after months of negotiation, a young male Coton de Tulear was brought from Madagascar to New York to improve the breeding stock. This was the first member of the breed to arrive in America from the island for over a decade.

RÉUNION

COTON DE RÉUNION RÉUNION

This extinct breed, with a long, cotton-like coat, was the ancestor of the well-known Coton de Tulear of Madagascar. The small island of Réunion lies 500 miles (800 km) to the east of Madagascar, in the Indian Ocean. It was settled by the French in the 17th century and has been under French control for most of its history since then. It is therefore believed that the little Coton de Réunion dog was first taken to the island from France, as a companion for the elite among the French settlers in the coastal capital of St-Denis. From there it was taken to the trading port of Tulear in the south-west of Madagascar, where it reputedly interbred with small local dogs to create a new companion breed – now know as the Coton de Tulear. With the opening of the Suez Canal in the late 19th century and a shorter trade route between Europe and the Orient, Réunion lost much of its commercial importance and before long its little luxury dog had also faded away (although whether any canine expert has searched the more remote settlements on the island for surviving examples is not clear).

RUSSIA

MOSCOW TOY TERRIER RUSSIA

Also known as the Moscovian Miniature Terrier, this breed was developed specifically as a small companion dog in the Russian capital.

This is a newish breed that was first recognized by the former Soviet Kennel Club in the 1960s. Its precise origin is not known, but it was probably created from crosses between

English Toy Terriers (known to have been favourites at the Russian court in earlier days), Long-haired Chihuahuas, Papillons and perhaps some small, local mongrels. The result is the ideal urban Russian apartment dog. Russian dog-lovers living in cities often have severe problems with space for their pets, and this breed has been tailor-made to be tolerant of restricted living conditions. It has also been bred to be friendly with other city dogs, to bark less than usual, and to be less aggressive than the more typical, outdoor Russian dogs. Weighing 5–6 lb (2–3 kg), with a height of only 8–11 in (20–28 cm), this is a true 'toy' breed. It is described as an inquisitive, lively, playful dog that is obedient and quick to learn. There are two varieties, short-haired and long-haired, and three main colour forms – black, red or tan. Traditionally the tail has been docked.

The recent history of the breed begins in 1950 when a group of Moscow canine enthusiasts led by E. Zrovoin decided to stabilize it as a pure-bred animal. They developed a breeding programme, gave it its modern name of Moscow Toy Terrier, and introduced it at a dog show in 1964, when 24 examples were on display. Their breed standard was formally recognized in 1966.

In recent years the breed has been in great demand and has been exported to Russia's neighbouring countries, including Finland, Poland, the Czech Republic, Hungary, Germany and Estonia.

BHUTAN

DAMCHI   BHUTAN

This little-known breed is named after the Himalayan village of Damchi and is a popular pet in Bhutan.

The Damchi is a close relative of the Tibetan Spaniel, but is larger and more strongly built, and has a longer muzzle. Colours are variable, although a black body with tan-and-white extremities appears to be the favoured pattern. The plumed, spitz-like tail curls up over the back.

In its homeland this is a celebrated dog – one was owned by the King of Bhutan – and the breed was commemorated in a 1972 set of postage stamps featuring Bhutanese dogs. It has hardly ever been seen elsewhere in the world, although a few were taken to Europe by a German breeder who came across them on a visit to Asia.

TIBET

LHASA APSO   TIBET

Sometimes more accurately called the Tibetan Apso, this breed is known formally in its homeland as the Apso Seng Kye (which translates literally as 'Hairy Lion Dog' and not as 'Bark Sentinel Lion Dog' as so many authors insist). Conversationally, the Tibetans refer to this dog simply as the Apso, pronounced 'Apsok'. Earlier names included the Talisman Dog, the Shantung Terrier and the Sheng Trou. Prior to the 1930s, before a formal distinction was made between the larger Tibetan Terrier (a working sheepdog) and the smaller Lhasa Apso (a monastery dog), they were both frequently called Tibetan Terriers, which causes confusion when consulting early writings. Although its primary role was that of a companion dog, it also acted as a watchdog.

This is one of the most ancient of companion breeds, having been kept by Tibetan monks for many centuries in the isolation of their great monasteries. These dogs were pure-bred and jealously guarded from outside influences. It was believed that when monks died they might be reincarnated as one of the monastery dogs. When one of the Apsos died, a small child was sometimes identified as having become its human reincarnation.

It was impossible for foreigners to buy these sacred Apsos, and they were only rarely made available to the outside world as special, diplomatic gifts. From time to time, between the 16th and 20th centuries, the Dalai Lama sent a pair as a presentation to the Imperial families of China. The last two were sent in 1908. The dogs were believed to have talismanic powers and to bring good luck and prosperity to their owners. (In earlier works, it is stated that Tibetan Terriers were presented as talismans, but the dogs involved were the smaller Apsos and not the larger sheepdogs that we today call by the name of Tibetan Terrier.)

There is a special mythology attached to this breed. It is believed that there was once a flying, gliding, white-headed, bone-eating animal goddess called Sako. She made her nest high up in the mountains and each year gave birth to two offspring, one with wings and one without. The wingless one was a little Apso, but because it could not fly, it fell to its death. This happened for several years until Sako decided to place her latest baby Apso safely on her back and fly down with it to the ground. In this way, the first Apso arrived in Tibet.

The factual origin of the Apso is unclear. It has been suggested that, many centuries ago, the smallest puppies of the sheep-herding Tibetan Terriers were given to the monks as monastery dogs. These little animals, whose legs were too short for herding sheep, became the foundation stock for the Apso breed. This is pure conjecture and the truth is that we have no convincing explanation of how the breed originated. Only one small clue exists: the word Apso is not Tibetan but Mongolian, suggesting a northern source for the breed.

Because they were so closely guarded in Tibet, Lhasa Apsos were late arriving in the West. One or two may have managed to filter through in the late 19th century, and there are some Victorian oil paintings of small, Apso-like dogs to support this view. However, even if isolated examples did manage to make the long journey, they soon disappeared without leading to the establishment of breeding stock.

Then, at the start of the 20th century, the first recorded importations occurred and serious breeding began. This succeeded to the point where, in 1908, the breed was recognized by the Kennel Club in London. However, it was then known as the 'Lhasa Terrier, 10-inch [25-cm] type' (to distinguish it from the 'Lhasa Terrier, 14-inch

[36-cm] type', which in the 1930s would be separated under the name of Tibetan Terrier). Between 1914 and 1918, World War I nearly exterminated the breed, but it reappeared in the 1920s.

In 1922 Colonel and Mrs Eric Bailey acquired a pair of Apsos when living in Sikkim, on the Tibetan border. They bred from them and eventually, in 1928, returned to England with six of their dogs. These were shown (still as Lhasa Terriers) in 1929. In 1934 it was finally decided to separate the smaller Lhasa Apso from the bigger Tibetan Terrier and all was set for their future development. Sadly, World War II intervened and the population of Apsos in England was again decimated, to be slowly rebuilt when peace returned. The Kennel Club in London agreed to Championship status in 1965.

In the United States the breed had fared better. Between 1930 and 1940, Mr and Mrs Suydam Cutting of New Jersey were given three Apsos by the 13th Dalai Lama. Three more followed later and together these formed the foundation stock for the breed in North America.

During the second half of the 20th century, the Lhasa Apso progressed in leaps and bounds on both sides of the Atlantic, until it had become one of the most popular of all the smaller breeds. In 1984, an Apso won Best in Show at Crufts. In stark contrast, in its Tibetan homeland it was virtually exterminated by the Chinese Communists who invaded that country.

Occasionally a pedigree bitch Apso produces smooth-coated puppies. These have been called Prapsos and in the past have appeared spasmodically in a number of separate breeding strains of Apsos. A careful study in 1960 revealed that, at that time, six per cent of all Apso puppies were short-haired. It was found that bitches which produced Prapsos when mated with one particular male, did not do so with other males. In recent years there has been less talk of Prapsos, and selective breeding appears to have gone a long way to eliminating them.

With its long, flowing coat and its proudly up-curled tail, this is a dignified, self-confident breed which, after centuries of monastery life, is more content than most dogs with the confined spaces of urban living. For those who are prepared to keep it well groomed, it has proved to be one of the most rewarding of all modern companion dogs.

References

1950. Duncan, Ronald Cardew. *Tomu from Tibet*. Methuen, London.
1965. Chenoweth, Patricia and Chenoweth, Thomas. *How to Raise and Train a Lhasa Apso*. TFH, New Jersey.
1970. Schneider, Earl. *Know Your Lhasa Apso*. The Pet Library, Harrison, New Jersey.
1970. Sefton, Frances. *The Lhasa Apso*. Pet 'n' Pedigree Books, New South Wales.
1974. Berndt, Robert J. *Your Lhasa Apso*. Denlinger's, Virginia.
1977. Brearley, Joan McDonald. *This is the Lhasa Apso*. TFH, New Jersey.
1979. Herbel, Norman and Herbel, Carolyn. *The Complete Lhasa Apso*. Howell, New York.
1979. McCarty, Diana. *Lhasa Apsos*. TFH, New Jersey.
1983. Vervaske-Helf, Sally Ann. *Lhasa Lore*. Alpine Publications, Colorado.
1985. Bracksieck, G. 'On the Trail of the Original Apsos'. *KTR Reporter No. 2*. (In German)

1989. Nicholas, Anna Katherine. *The Lhasa Apso.* TFH, New Jersey.

1990. Cunliffe, Juliette. *All about the Lhasa Apso.* Pelham Books, London.

1990. Wehrmann, Stephen. *Lhasa Apsos.* Barron, New York.

1992. Herbel, Norman and Herbel, Carolyn. *The New Complete Lhasa Apso.* Howell, New York.

1996. Zeppi, Jennifer. *Guide to Owning a Lhasa Apso.* TFH, New Jersey.

1998. Herbel, Carolyn. *The Lhasa Apso: an Owner's Guide.* IDG Books Worldwide.

1998. Valencia, Patricia Duque. *El Nuevo Libro del Lhasa Apso.* Susaeta Ediciones, SA.

1999. Cunliffe, Juliette. *Lhasa Apso.* Interpet Publishing.

2000. Cunliffe, Juliette. *Pet Owner's Guide to the Lhasa Apso.* Ringpress Books, Lydney, Gloucestershire.

TIBETAN SPANIEL   TIBET

Inside Tibet, these dogs were given the name of Jemtse Apso, translating literally as 'scissored Apso'. Some of them were called simply 'Palace Dogs'. In Kathmandu they were known as Nepalese Palace Dogs. They have also been recorded as Tibetaanse Spaniels. The name Tibetan Spaniel was given to them when the first examples arrived in the West in the late 19th century. To its friends today, it is known as the Tibbie. In its homeland, its primary role was as a companion dog, but it also acted as a watch-dog. According to some authors, one of its special duties was to turn the large prayer-wheels in the monasteries and it has, in the past, been given the name of Tibetan Prayer Dog.

Looking at a modern example of this breed, with its blunt-muzzled face, silky mane, up-curled, richly plumed tail, small body and tiny feet, it is clear that it is not a spaniel of the hunting field. When it was first encountered in Tibet by European visitors, it reminded them of another kind of spaniel – the toy spaniel, or 'spaniel gentle', as it used to be called. This is confirmed by its first European nickname, which was 'the King Charles of the East'.

It was quite distinct from that other small favourite of the Tibetan monks, the dog we now call the Lhasa Apso, which had a different origin. The need for these two small dogs in the great monasteries appears to be connected with their different duties. The Tibetan Spaniel had a special role as a 'labour-saving device', helping the monks to say their prayers without any physical effort on their part. A monastery tradition of these holy men was that, by spinning a wheel carrying a written prayer on a rolled-up scroll, the prayer was 'said' over and over again. Small, personal wheels were held in the hand and spun round with little trouble by the monks themselves, but the monasteries also had huge, circular 'prayer-drums' that had to be rotated, and it was to these that the little dogs were harnessed, to pull them round and round. Some have queried this story, but if the Tibetan Spaniel had a specialized duty of this kind it would explain why both this dog and the Lhasa Apso existed side by side in the monasteries.

The origin of the Tibetan Spaniel has been the subject of much debate. According to one view, it is an ancient Tibetan breed which, when it was sent to China as a royal gift, was developed into the Pekingese. If this seems unlikely, it is worth recalling that the early form of the Pekingese was far less 'extreme' than its present show-dog form. In fact, a glance at early photographs of Pekinese Spaniels (as they used to be called) reveals dogs that were remarkably similar in appearance to the Tibetan Spaniel.

A modified version of this view suggests that it was the early Ha-pa Dog (see separate entry) that gave rise to the Tibetan Spaniel, the Pug and the Pekingese, each of which gradually diverged from the other two, as time passed.

Another opinion sees the early form of the Pekingese, presented as a royal gift to the Tibetans by the Chinese rulers, as the ancestor of the Tibetan Spaniel. Still others believe that when the early Pekingese arrived in the Tibetan monasteries they were crossed with the Lhasa Apsos that were already there, to create the Tibetan Spaniel. When such varied and contradictory ideas are put forward, there is only one safe conclusion: that they are all clever guesses and hard facts are missing.

Once European visitors arrived in Tibet in late Victorian times, more solid information was available. It was clear that the Tibetan Spaniel showed some variability. In size, it ranged from as little as 4 lb (2 kg) to 16 lb (7 kg). Some had longer muzzles, others had shorter muzzles. Significantly, the ones found near the Chinese border had the shortest muzzles of all.

The Tibetan Spaniel first arrived in England in the late 19th century, and Maud Earle painted a skilful portrait of three colour variants in 1898. Its numbers were never great, however, and during World War II the English examples died out altogether. More were imported from Asia after the war, starting in 1946, and in 1957 the Tibetan Spaniel Association was founded. In the late 1960s the breed reached the United States, and the Tibetan Spaniel Club of America was formed in 1971. The breed was recognized by the AKC in 1984.

In personality, this is an intelligent, alert, assertive, active, loyal, and self-confident dog. Its height today is 10 in (25 cm) and its weight is 9–15 lb (4–7 kg). It makes an ideal urban pet and it is perhaps surprising that it has not become more popular in recent years. In the West it seems to suffer from competition with the Pekingese and the Cavalier King Charles Spaniel.

References

1972. Mayhew, Phyllis M. *The Tibetan Spaniel*. Colwell, Malvern & Worcester Publishing.

1974. Wynyard, Ann. *The Dog Directory Guide to the Tibetan Spaniel*. The Dog Directory.

1980. Wynyard, Ann. *Guide to Owning a Tibetan Spaniel*. Privately published.

1982. Wynyard, Ann. *Dogs of Tibet and the History of the Tibetan Spaniel*. Book World, Rugby.

1986. Wynyard, Ann and Holsapple, Jeanne. *The Tibetan Spaniel Handbook*. Prinit Press, Indiana.

1996. Miccio, Susan W. *The Tibetan Spaniel: a Gift from the Roof of the World*. OTR Publishers.

1998. Miccio, Susan. *Tibetan Spaniel: a Complete and Reliable Handbook*. TFH, New Jersey.

CHINA

CHINESE CRESTED

CHINA

Sometimes given the slightly longer name of Chinese Crested Dog, in China this toy breed was originally known as the Treasure House Guardian. In addition to the hairless type there is also a fully haired version called the Powderpuff.

This dog has caused a greater division of opinion than any other breed. Few are indifferent to it; it is either loved or hated. Almost entirely naked, with only a few tufts of hair on its head, tail and feet, this breed has in the past been described as a freak, and naked puppies have often been culled by breeders. Despite this unpromising beginning, it has survived and grown steadily in popularity until today it can boast a strong and devoted following. This is largely due to its happy-go-lucky personality, for this is a dog that exudes an infectious playfulness and joy of living.

Its origins have long been debated. An early opinion was that its ancestors came from Africa and then moved east to Asia and Orient. After this it is supposed to have continued its expansion until it arrived in the Americas, to give rise to the Mexican Hairless and various New World Indian breeds of naked dog. This theory sees the gene for nakedness appearing only once and then spreading outwards from its source. An alternative view would suggest that, instead, the gene for hair reduction appeared independently on a number of occasions, in a variety of locations worldwide.

When naked dogs were encountered by early European travellers and explorers, they made an immediate impact as 'living curiosities' and were sometimes acquired and brought back to Europe for their novelty value. One of the earliest accurate portrayals of a Chinese Crested dog appears in Robert Plot's *Natural History of Staffordshire*, published in 1686. He described the dog in question as 'being curiously spotted, and for the most part naked, his head only adorned with an English Peruque, and his tail with a single tuft at the end'. His illustration shows a dog that is almost identical to the modern Chinese Crested.

The tufts of hair on the feet are called 'socks', on the tail the 'plume' and on the head the 'crest'. The ears are held erect. The reduced dentition that accompanies the nakedness of this breed involves the absence of premolars. The body skin is hot to the touch, a fact which has given rise to various medical myths. For instance, it is claimed that arthritis can be cured by using one of these little dogs as a 'heating pad'. And in 1928 the breed was briefly given the title of 'Fever Dog', because it was believed that simply to touch its skin would cure a patient of a feverish condition.

The advantage of owning a naked dog is that it has no body odour, no heavy shedding and no fleas. And people who are allergic to other, hairier breeds, may find that this one causes them no problems. The disadvantage is that a naked dog must wear protective clothing of some kind during cold winter months, and be kept out of the hot sun in the summer.

In England a Chinese Crested Dog Club was established in the 1960s. In the United States a similar club was formed in the 1970s, and the breed was accepted for registration with the AKC in the 1990s. Because of the draconian attitude of the Chinese Communist government, which sees the ownership of a pet dog as a decadent bourgeois act, the breed has become an extreme rarity in the land of its birth. Fortunately there are already enough of these intriguing little dogs in other, more enlightened countries, to ensure the breed's future survival.

In the United States the famous striptease artiste Gypsy Rose Lee owned several Chinese Crested dogs (presumably because her dogs, like herself, were notorious for being semi-naked) and helped to make them famous there.

References

1964. Van der Lyn, Edita. *How to Raise and Train a Chinese Crested.* TFH, New Jersey.
1986. Cardew, Mirrie. *A Chinese Crested Dog for Me.* Midland Counties, Leicester.
1988. Jones, Brenda (Editor). *The Chinese Crested Dog: a Practical Handbook.* The Chinese Crested Club of Great Britain.
1990. Jones, Brenda. *The Complete Chinese Crested.* Ringpress Books, Letchworth, Hertfordshire.
1998. Rachunas, Joseph. *A New Owner's Guide to Chinese Crested.*

HA-PA DOG

CHINA

Several spellings exist for the name of this breed, including Hapa Dog, Happa Dog, and Hah-pah Dog. In Chinese 'hah-bah' means 'small pet dog'.

This ancient oriental breed is essentially a short-haired Pekingese. Some authors refer to it as the ancestor of the Tibetan Spaniel, the Pug and the Pekingese, and one student of Chinese dogs comments that 'the Chinese pug was evolved from a short-haired type of toy dog [the Ha-pa?], bred along with a long-haired type that subsequently developed into the Pekingese'. Whatever their precise relationship, it is clear that the four breeds – the Ha-pa (short-haired, short-legged), the Pug (short-haired, longer-legged), the Pekingese (long-haired, short-legged) and the Tibetan Spaniel (long-haired, longer-legged) – were closely related to one another. One author dismisses the Ha-pa as having the bad qualities of both the Pug and the Pekingese, but none of their good qualities. It appears to have vanished at some point during the 20th century, although nobody has specifically declared it extinct.

Assembling any detailed information on this elusive dog is difficult. A report from Shantung in 1867 described a toy breed existing there which originated to the west ('Western Foreign') and which was 'low, small, clean and cunning, with which you can play; it is called "ha-pa dog"'. It is not clear how far west was being indicated and it is pointed out that Tibet would be too cold for a small, short-haired dog. A later statement suggests, rather surprisingly, that Turkey may have been the original source of the Ha-pa: 'A small and alert class are the Turkish dogs which nowadays are called "ha pa" dogs.'

The first Ha-pa Dogs to be seen in the West were two that were imported from Peking by Mrs Lancelot Carnegie in 1906. It was stated rather vaguely that they had been 'purloined from the Imperial Palace'. One was black-and-tan and the other fawn-and-white. The following year, one of them was displayed at the first show organized by the Pekingese Club, when the little dog was led around the ring by a Chinese nurse in native costume. Amazingly, it is still on display in England a century later, now in the form of a preserved specimen at the Tring Zoological Museum in Hertfordshire. It was estimated that, in life, the animal weighed no more than 5–6 lb (2–3 kg) and was about 9 in (23 cm) in height.

In 1991 Juliette Cunliffe, a Tibetan dog expert on a visit to neighbouring Nepal, encountered a small, short-haired dog living in a monastery near Pokhara, which the monks there insisted was a Ha-pa Dog. Although its legs were too long and its face too pointed for a typical Ha-pa, its existence suggests that the genetic influence of the original breed is still present in the region.

PEKINGESE   CHINA

Also recorded as the Pekinese, the Peiching Kou, the Pekin Spaniel, the Pekinese Spaniel, the Chinese Lion Dog, the Dragon Dog, the Sun Dog, the Mandarin Pug, the Peking Palace Dog or the Peking Palasthund, this is an ancient companion dog created exclusively for the Chinese nobility. In earlier times it varied in size and the Miniature Pekingese was often called the Sleeve Dog, or Sleeve Pekinese. To its friends today it is known simply as the Peke.

The origin of the Pekingese is unknown. It has existed in China for many centuries, although in earlier times it did not look like the extreme form seen in the show-ring today. Up until the 19th century, it was closer in appearance to the Tibetan Spaniel than to the modern show Peke. Its ears were shorter, and its legs long enough to see daylight beneath its body. During the 20th century the demands of show-ring competition saw its body get lower, its neck shorter, its ears longer, its face flatter and its coat even more luxuriant.

In their heyday, the royal Pekingese were treated with enormous respect, and amazing tales are told of the pampered lives they led. Only the Chinese nobility were allowed to own them, and anybody found guilty of stealing one faced death. Eunuchs were employed to care for their every need.

When the British stormed Peking in 1860, the royal court fled, taking most of their dogs with them. According to romantic legend, three young British officers – an army captain, John Hart Dunne, and two naval officers, Lord John Hay and Sir George Fitzroy – entered a shuttered room in a deserted pavilion in the Summer Palace, where they found five royal Pekingese noisily protecting the corpse of the Emperor's aunt, who had committed suicide rather than be taken prisoner by Western vandals. Dunne took one of the dogs, and Hay and Fitzroy a pair each. Dunne's dog, insensitively named Lootie, was taken back to London by him and presented to Queen Victoria. The others followed a few years later.

That is the endlessly repeated tale, but unfortunately the captain's diary tells a different ent story. In reality, he went to a French army camp to buy 'trifles' (that is, looted goods) and while he was there also purchased 'a pretty little dog, smaller than any King Charles, a real Chinese sleeve dog. It has silver bells around its neck.' When he later offered it to Queen Victoria, he improved on this story, saying that the dog 'was found by me in the Palace of Yuan-Ming-Yuan near Pekin'. In this way are canine fables born.

As for the other four dogs, they were probably acquired in a similar manner at a later date because, at the time the palace was being sacked, the two naval officers, Hay and Fitzroy, were in reality on duty on board their vessels, guarding the Peking River.

Because of its rarity, its exotic origins and its royal patronage, the breed aroused great interest in the British press, and efforts were made to find additional examples. A few more did manage to filter through, nearly always with great difficulty, to England, Ireland and France in the late 19th century and at the beginning of the 20th century. (One of them cost a eunuch his life – he was stoned to death for selling it.) Together these dogs formed the foundation stock for what was destined to become one of the most popular of all small breeds. It prospered both as a lapdog in the home and as a star of the show-ring, and was soon spreading around the world.

In China itself, following the sacking of Peking, the royal court returned and re-established itself. The Palace Pekingese now entered an important new phase, under the patronage of the extraordinary Dowager Empress Tzu Hsi. She introduced new rules for the care of the dogs and made a serious attempt to fix the breed. She even wrote a breed standard for it, a poetic document which included phrases such as: 'Let its eyes be large and luminous; let its ears be set like the sails of a war-junk; let its nose be that of the monkey-god of the Hindus.' When she died in 1908 her royal kennels were destroyed and the history of the Pekingese dog in China came to an abrupt halt.

In personality, the Pekingese belies its soft appearance. It may luxuriate on silk cushions, but it is a remarkably confident, fiery little dog, with a stubborn streak and a fearless dignity more appropriate to a mastiff. It has also been variously described as wilful, aloof, independent, fastidious, sensitive, courageous and bold. To paraphrase an owner of these remarkable little animals, 'a Pekingese is to other dogs what a goldfish is to other fish'.

References

1909. Smythe, Lillian C. *The Pekingese*. The Kennel, London.

1912. Allen, Minna Loftus and Astley, L. P. C. *The Perfect Pekingese*. Illustrated Kennel News, London.

1914. Verity-Steel, Queenie. *The Book on Pekingese*.

1917. Anon. *The Pekingese Spaniel*. CSR, New York.

1923. Allen, Minna Loftus. *Show Pekingese*. Our Dogs, Manchester.

1924. Breese, Vinton P. *The Pekingese, a Symposium*. Field & Fancy, New York.

1924. Hopkins, Lydia. *The Pekingese*. Field & Fancy, New York.

1924. Vlasto, John A. *The Popular Pekingese*. Popular Dogs, London.

1929, Vlasto, John A. *The New Popular Pekingese*. Popular Dogs, London.

1931. Dixey, Annie Coath. *The Lion Dog of Peking*. Peter Davies, London.

1931. Soutar, Andrew. *A Chinaman in Sussex. Reflections of a Worldly Peke*. Hutchinson, London.

1932. Cross, Mrs C. Ashton. *The Pekingese Dog*. Privately published.

1932. Johns, Rowland. *Our Friend the Pekingese*. Methuen, London.

1934. Lansdowne, Charmain. *The Imperial Dog of China. The Pekingese*.

1935. Dilssner, Hede. *Die drei Pekingesen*. Berlin.

1936. Ash, Edward, C. *The Pekingese as a Companion and Show Dog*. Cassell, London.

1939. Nicholas, Anna K. *The Pekingese*. TFH, New Jersey.

1949. Denlinger, Milo. G. *The Complete Pekingese*. Denlinger's, USA.

1949. Harman, Ian. *Pekingese*. Williams & Norgate.

1950. Daly, Macdonald. *The Pekingese*. Findon, London.

1951. Hubbard, Clifford. *The Pekingese Handbook*. Nicholson & Watson, New York.

1954. Howe, Elsa and Howe, Ellic. *Pekingese Scrapbook*. Chapman & Hall, London.

1954. Krieger, Grace A. *Pet Pekingese*. All Pets, Fond du Lac, Wisconsin.

1957. Davidson, George B. *The Pekingese Manual*. Lexicon, California.

1957. Hill, Herminie Warner. *Pekingese*. Foyle, London.

1959. Scott, Alice. *How to Raise and Train a Pekingese*. Sterling, New York.

1962. Godbold, Bridget. *Pekingese in Australia*. Jacaranda, Brisbane.

1962. Katz, Louise. *This is the Pekingese*. TFH, New Jersey.

1964. Quigley, Dorothy. *The Quigley Book of the Pekingese*. Howell, New York.

1966. Schneider, Earl. *Know Your Pekingese*. Pet Library, New York.

1967. Schneider, Earl. *Enjoy Your Pekingese*. Pet Library, New York.

1969. Sefton, Frances. *The Pekingese Guide*. Pet Library, London.

1975. Nicholas, Anna K. and Brearley, Joan M. *The Book of the Pekingese*. TFH, New Jersey.

1976. Hamilton-Wilkes, M. *All about the Pekingese*. Rigby, Adelaide.

1977. Godden, Romer. *The Butterfly Lions. The Pekingese in History, Legend and Art*. Macmillan, London.

1977. Tocagni, Hector. *El Perro Pekines*. Esitorial Albatross, Buenos Aires.

1978. Berndt, Robert J. *Your Pekingese*. Denlinger's, USA.

1982. Wittenburg, H. and Wittenburg, G. *Der Pekingese*.

1989. Dearn, Dorothy. *The Modern Pekingese*.

1990. Aubrey-Jones, Nigel. *The New Pekingese*. Howell, New York.

1990. Pisano, Beverly. *Pekingese*. TFH, New Jersey.

1990. Williams, Vandella and Summers, Adele. *Pekingese*. Crowood Press, Wiltshire.

1996. Coile, Caroline. *Pekingese*. Barron, New York.

1999. Stannard, Liz. *The Complete Pekingese*. IDG Books Worldwide.

1999. Ulmer, Deann. *A New Owner's Guide to the Pekingese*. TFH, New Jersey.

PUG

CHINA

Known in France as the Carlin, in Italy as the Carlino, in Germany as the Mops Hund, in Holland as the Mopshond, in Sweden as the Mops, in Finland as the Mopsi, in Spanish as the Doguillo, and in China as the Lo-sze, this ancient form of companion dog was originally described in England as the Dutch Pug or the Pug-Dog. In Old Chinese it was called the Ha Ba Gou, and in Gaelic the Smutmhadra.

This thick-skinned, short-coated, curly-tailed, flat-faced little dog presents three mysteries: how did it get its name, where did it originate, and who are its ancestors? There are no definitive answers to these questions, although many suggestions have been offered in the past.

First, as regards the name, there have been five proposals:

1   Pug is taken from 'pugnus', the Latin for 'fist', because its frontally squashed head has the shape of a clenched fist.

2   Pug is taken from 'Pugnaces' – the ancient fighting dogs, because it is a dwarf version of such dogs.

3   One 18th-century definition of the word 'pug' was 'anything tenderly loved'. It is assumed that this is its true root because the owners of these dogs always doted on them.

4   The word 'pug' also meant 'monkey'. So a Pug-dog (the breed's original name) was a monkey-faced dog. (The Affenpinscher obtained its name in this way.)

5   The word 'pug' was also used to mean a hobgoblin, puck or imp. Applied to a dog it indicated a goblin-like creature, or dwarf animal.

Second, in respect of the breed's origins, there have been eight theories:

1   The breed originated in China and was brought from there to England, where it became immensely popular and spread throughout the world of dogs.

2   It originated in Holland and was brought to England in the late 17th century by the Protestant couple, William and Mary of Orange, when they took over the English throne in 1688. Their much loved pugs accompanied them and started a craze for the dogs in 17th-century England. This is why one of the first names for the breed was the Dutch Pug.

3   It originated in Russia, where it acquired its spitz tail from Arctic ancestors. From there it travelled to Holland and then England.

4   It originated in western China in 700 BC, when it was called the Lo-chiang-sze, which was shortened to Lo-sze. It was carried west, via Tibet, where it was known as the Lags-kyi, to Russia, then to Holland, and then to England.

5   It originated in China and was brought from there to Holland by the Dutch East India Company. There it found royal favour with William I and became the symbol of the House of Orange. It then moved from Holland to England with William III in the late 17th century.

6   It originated in China, then spread to Europe via the first European traders — the Portuguese — who arrived in AD 1516. The Portuguese brought it back to their country and from there it travelled to Holland and then, finally, to England.

7   It originated in ancient Rome and was brought to Britain during the Roman occupation.

8   It originated in ancient Egypt and was brought from there to ancient Rome by Phoenician traders and from Rome to England.

Third, with regard to the breed's ancestry, there have been four suggestions:

1   It is a 'bulldog in miniature'. (Comparison of the skulls rules this out. And the Pug is, in any case, the older breed of the two.)

2   It is a dwarf mastiff. (It was once called the Dutch Mastiff.)

3   It is a 'smooth-coated, long-legged variety of the Pekingese'.

4   It is the ancestor of the Pekingese.

All these ideas have been put forward in the past by serious scholars of canine history. However, when there as many theories as these concerning the name, the origin and the ancestry of a breed, only one thing is sure: that they are all guesses, some educated, some outlandish, and that nobody is certain of anything. For the time being, the little dog retains the mystery of its beginnings.

The Pug's original colour was fawn, with a black mask and saddle mark. In the mid-19th century the breed split into two types, the Willoughby and the Morrison, named after two rival sponsors of the breed. Willoughbys were silver-fawn, or 'stone-fawn', and Morrisons were golden-fawn, or apricot-fawn, and the two camps competed for top honours. Later, the two types became mixed and the distinction was eventually lost. Solid black was a new colour, not formally introduced until 1877. In 1896 the Kennel Club in London granted separate classes for the Black Pug.

In personality this dog is the perfect household companion — patient, non-aggressive, good-natured and wonderfully tolerant with children. Furthermore, it is odour-free, requires little grooming and is not yappy like some other small dogs. Its only weakness is a tendency to enjoy its food too much and become overweight.

The Pug's popularity has always been high, and twice in English history (the middle of the 18th century and again in the mid-Victorian period of the 19th century) it was the most popular dog in England. It first entered the show-ring in 1861 and the Pug Dog Club was formed in 1883. The breed standard drawn up in the 1880s remains essentially unaltered to this day.

References

1891. Cryer, M. H. *The Prize Pugs of America and England.* Fancier's Publishing, Philadelphia.

1930. Swainston-Goodger, Wilhelmina. *The Pug-Dog: its History and Origin.* Watmoughs, London.

1947. Denlinger, Milo G. *The Complete Pug.* Denlinger's, USA.

1947. Trullinger, V. W. *The Complete Pug.* Howell, New York.

1952. Featherstone, G. *The Pug Dog.*

1956. Doherty, Filomena. *Pet Pug.* All-Pets, Fond du Lac, Wisconsin.

1959. Hubbard, Clifford. *The Pug Handbook.*

1959. Miller, Evelyn. *Pugs as Pets.* TFH, New Jersey.

1959. Swainston-Goodger, Wilhelmina. *The Pug Handbook.* Nicholson & Watson, London.

1960. Miller, Evelyn. *How to Raise and Train a Pug.* Sterling, New York.

1962. Daglish, E. Fitch. *Pugs.* Foyles, London.

1965. Weall, Susan Graham. *The Pug.* Popular Dogs, London.

1968. Spier, Louise Ziegler and Spier, Herbert F. *This is the Pug.* TFH, New Jersey.

1972. Wolf, Esther E. *Your Pug.* Denlinger's, USA.

1973. Gordon, J. F. *The Pug.* John Gifford, London.

1980. Brearley, Joan McDonald. *The Book of the Pug.* TFH, New Jersey.

1981. Pisano, Beverly. *Pugs.* TFH, New Jersey.

1990. Thomas, Shirley. *New Pug.* Howell, New York.

1994. Maggitti, Phil. *Pugs: Everything About Purchase, Care, Nutrition, Behavior, & Training.* Barron, New York.

1995. Swainston-Goodger, Wilhelmina. *The Goodger Guide to the Pug.*

1996. Patterson, Edward. *The Pug: An Owner's Guide to a Happy Healthy Pet.* Howell, New York.

1997. Cannon, Ariel. *Guide to Owning a Pug.*

1998. Hutchinson, Robert, et al. *For the Love of Pugs.*

1999. Dunbar, Ian (Editor). *The Essential Pug,* Howell, New York.

2000. Thornton, Kim Campbell. *Your Pug's Life.*

Brown, Ellen S. *The Complete Pug.*

Trullinger, James W. *The Complete Pug.*

SHIH TZU   CHINA

The name of this breed, which translates as 'Lion Dog', is usually mispronounced in the West. The Chinese rendering of it is 'sher-zer'. In earlier days it was known as the Chrysanthemum Dog, or the Lhasa Lion Dog.

The Shih Tzu originated as an ancient cross between what we now call the Lhasa Apso and the Pekingese. Several centuries ago there were Lhasa Apsos in the great monasteries of Tibet and an early form of the Pekingese in the great courts of China. From time to time the Dalai Lama would make a special gift of some of Tibet's most precious dogs to the rulers of China. These Lhasa Apsos would make the long and difficult journey to the Chinese capital, where they would disappear into the Forbidden City. Living there in splendid isolation from the outside world, they would inevitably come into contact with the royal Pekingese. Matings occurred and the result was what could loosely be described as a 'Shaggy Peke' or, if you prefer, a 'Flat-faced Apso'. Either way, the cross-breed was an immensely attractive little dog

and was soon on its way to becoming a pure breed in its own right. It was known in the Imperial Palace as the Lhasa Lion Dog, presumably to distinguish it from the Chinese Lion Dog (the Pekingese).

This happened during the 17th century, or perhaps even earlier. The dog then remained hidden to the West until the 20th century, when it finally emerged from the shadows and entered the glare of the show-ring. In 1934 the Peking Kennel Club was formed and held its first international dog show. Lhasa Apsos and Lhasa Lion Dogs were both entered and were judged together. There was clearly confusion between them at this time.

The breed description of the Lhasa Lion Dog given by the Peking Kennel Club must be one of the most poetic ever written for a dog. It includes the following features: the head of a lion; the round face of an owl; the lustrous eyes of a dragon; the oval tongue of a peony petal; the mouth of a frog; teeth like grains of rice; ears like palm-leaves; the torso of a bear; the broad back of a tiger; the tail of a phoenix; the legs of an elephant; toes like a mountain range; a yellow coat like a camel; and the movement of a goldfish.

Although golden-yellow was the favourite coat colour, others were permitted and each colour had its own special Chinese name. Solid yellow dogs were called Chin Chia Huang Pao; yellow dogs with a white mane were called Chin Pan To Yueh, meaning 'golden basin upholding the moon'; black-and-white dogs were Wu Yun Kai Hsueh, meaning 'black clouds over snow'; solid black dogs were Yi Ting Mo, meaning 'lump of ink'; multicoloured dogs were called Hua Tse, meaning 'flowery child', and so on.

During the 1930s a few of these cherished dogs managed to find their way to the West. A black-and-white one called Lung Fu Ssu arrived in Ireland in 1930 and in the same year a black-and-white pair called Hibo and Shu Ssa reached England. In 1932 a trio – a dog and two bitches – also reached Norway and established the breed there.

The owners of the English pair, Sir Douglas and Lady Brownrigg, showed them alongside Lhasa Apsos in 1933, and it was then realized that the two forms were, beyond any doubt, different breeds and should not be lumped together. It was at this point that it was decided to give them separate, distinctive names; the type with a narrower skull and longer muzzle was called the Lhasa Apso, and the type with a rounder skull and shorter muzzle was called the Shih Tzu.

In the following year the Shih Tzu Club of England was formed, and during the

1930s and 1940s a few more specimens were imported from the East to add to the gene pool. The breed was officially recognized in England in the 1940s and before long was gaining rapidly in popularity. In 1952 a controversial back-cross was made to a black-and-white Pekingese in an attempt to overcome some faults due to inbreeding. Some felt that this improved the breed, but purists were unhappy and there were heated arguments. One of the debates concerned the size of the breed in the West, many feeling that it was being allowed to become too big, when compared with the Imperial Palace dogs of Peking.

The breed's popularity continued to rise in the second half of the 20th century. It arrived in the United States in the 1960s and was soon competing in dog shows all over the world.

Words used to describe the personality of the Shih Tzu include extrovert, vivacious, confident and dignified. It is one of the few breeds that is ideally suited for modern urban living, having for centuries been forced to adapt to a life in the confines of the Imperial Palace in Peking.

References

1939. Moulton, H. L. *Shi Tzu Shavings*. H. L. Hawkins.

1960. Easton, Allan. *This is the Shih Tzu*. TFH, New Jersey.

1964. Smythe, R. H. *How to Raise and Train a Shih Tzu*. TFH, New Jersey.

1973. Mooney, Will C. *Your Shih Tzu*. Denlinger's, USA.

1974. Dadds, Audrey. *The Shih Tzu*. Howell, New York.

1980. Brearley, Joan and Easton, Allan. *The Book of the Shih Tzu*. TFH, New Jersey.

1981. Parker, Robert P. and Collins, Gerard M. *The Shih Tzu*. TFH, New Jersey

1982. Seranne, Ann and Miller, Lise M. *The Joy of Owning a Shih Tzu* Howell, New York.

1988. Ferrante, Jon C. *The Heritage of the Shih Tzu*.. Denlinger's, USA.

1991. Sucher, Jaime J. *Shih Tzus*. Barron, New York.

1992. Cunliffe, Juliette. *The Complete Shih Tzu*. Ringpress Books, Letchworth, Hertfordshire.

1994. Gurney, Dorothy. *Pet Owner's Guide to the Shih Tzu*. Howell, New York.

1994. Joris, Victor. *The Complete Shih Tzu*. IDG Books Worldwide.

1995. Dadds, Audrey. *The Shih Tzu, World of Dogs*. TFH, New Jersey.

1996. Ackerman, Lowell. *Dr Ackerman's Book of Shih Tzu*. TFH, New Jersey.

1996. Regelman, Joanne. *A New Owner's Guide to Shih Tzu*. TFH, New Jersey.

1996. Soy, Teri. *Guide to Owning a Shih Tzu*. TFH, New Jersey.

1998. White, Jo Ann. *The Official Book of the Shih Tzu*. TFH, New Jersey.

1999. Dunbar, Ian, et al. *Essential Shih Tzu*. IDG Books Worldwide.

1999. Soy, Teri. *Shih Tzu*. Popular Dog Library, Chelsea House.

Beute-Faber, R. M. A. *Pekingese, Shih Tzu, Lhasa Apso*.

Dallison. *The Shih Tzu*.

Farr. *Owner's Guide to the Shih Tzu*.

Mann, Clarence E. and Mann, Jayne D. *Bring on the Clowns: An Assessment of the Origin of the Shih Tzu*.

Sanford, William Reynolds and Green, Carl R. *The Shih Tzu*. Top Dog Series.

Schneider, Earl. *Know Your Shih Tzu*. Pet Library. TFH, New Jersey.

Widdrington, G. *Shih Tzu Handbook*.

JAPAN

JAPANESE CHIN   JAPAN

This breed used to be called the Japanese Spaniel, the Japanese Pug or simply the Japanese, but today, in English, it is always referred to as the Japanese Chin, or the Chin. Its early nickname was the Jap. It began life as a revered lapdog of the nobility. One school of thought claims that the name 'Chin' means 'of China', and indicates that it came to Japan from that country; another suggests that it means 'cat-like'.

This is a graceful, high-stepping, ancient breed whose image can be seen on early Japanese pottery, tapestries, silks and temple walls. There are four theories concerning the dog's origin:

1   It was brought to Japan from China by Buddhist monks in the 6th century AD. These monks are supposed to have been accompanied by their little Lion Dogs, which symbolized the Lion of Buddha, and some of these dogs remained to develop into the Chin.

2   It originated in Korea as a breed called the Ssuchan Pai and, in the year AD 732, was brought to the Japanese court as a gift from a Korean prince.

3   It arrived as a royal gift from the Chinese rulers for the Japanese Emperor, brought back by his envoys, returning from China some time between the seventh and tenth centuries.

4   It was taken to Japan on trading ships that came from the West.

Once in Japan, by one or more of these routes, it was developed and modified until it had become the dog we know today, making it a truly Japanese breed. At first it was exclusively owned by the Japanese nobility and was not available to the general public. It lived a pampered existence and it is rumoured that, in an effort to keep the breed's size small, the dogs were given a diet of rice and saki. The penalty for stealing one of these noble animals was death.

The first examples of this breed to reach Europe were brought back by Portuguese sailors, probably in the 17th century. In England it was first exhibited in 1873 at the Birmingham show. It appeared in America in 1882 and was registered with the AKC as early as 1888. The Japanese Spaniel Club of America was founded in 1912. (The named was changed to the Japanese Chin Club in 1977.) After World War II, the population of this breed inside Japan was so depleted that new bloodstock had to be imported from England and elsewhere.

This breed has a luxuriant, silky coat, an up-curled tail, a flattish face and drooping ears. In colour it is either black-and-white or brown-and-white (in various shades of

'brown', from lemon to red). It is a very small dog, having a height of only 9 in (23 cm) and a weight of only 4–7 lb (2–3 kg). It is the Japanese counterpart of the King Charles Spaniel, the Tibetan Spaniel or the (old-style) Pekingese.

According to one Asian authority, the five rules of Japanese Chin beauty used to be: (1) the butterfly head; (2) the sacred V (a white V-shape marking on the head); (3) the bump of knowledge (a round black spot between the ears); (4) the vulture feet; and (5) the chrysanthemum tail.

In personality it has been described as the perfect companion, elegant but comical, dignified but prepared to be playful. It is alert, quick to learn and sensitive. Unlike many breeds, it is prepared to live in quite a small space, making it the ideal apartment dog, but even so, it enjoys a daily walk. It used to be said that, in developing the breed, the Japanese tried to create a blend of cat and dog – in other words, a feline dog. It is certainly true that in several ways the little Chin is rather catlike: it jumps well, climbs deftly, is fastidious and is feline in the way it uses its front feet. A special point in its favour is that, unlike some other lapdogs, it is not 'yappy' and rarely barks.

References

1929. Muller-Probster, Paule. *Der Vornehme Zimmerhund.* Chr. Moser, Nürnberg.

1960. Schenck, Vera E. *Japanese Spaniels as Pets.* TFH, New Jersey.

1968. Alexander, Mrs Claude V. *How to Raise and Train a Japanese Spaniel.* TFH, New Jersey.

1982. Legl-Jacobsson, Elisabeth. *Japanese Chin.* GPR Förlag, Göteborg, Sweden.

1990. Alexander, Mrs. Claude V. *Japanese Chins.* TFH, New Jersey.

1997. Stern and Mather. *The Complete Japanese Chin.* Howell, New York.

JAPANESE SPITZ   JAPAN

This is the Japanese version of the popular small spitz dogs that are found in many parts of the world, acting as lively household companions and show dogs.

This is a typical spitz dog with an up-curled tail, a foxy face, a pointed muzzle, pricked ears and a dense, pure white coat with an impressive ruff. In appearance it looks remarkably like a dwarf Samoyed, its height being only 12–14 in (30–35 cm) and its weight only 11–13 lb (5–6 kg).

Although some authors refer to this as an ancient breed it is, in reality, quite recent, and appears to have several sources. If we are to believe all the different reports on its history, its ancestors arrived in Japan in several stages. First, in about 1900, came some

small Samoyeds, via Mongolia. Then, in about 1920, white-coated German Spitz dogs were brought to Japan (some say from Poland, others via Siberia and China). They were exhibited in Tokyo in 1921. Then, in 1923, more white spitz dogs arrived, this time from Canada. It is believed that these may have been American Eskimo dogs. In the 1930s still more came, this time from Canada, the United States, Australia and China. They were joined by Russian Spitz dogs from Manchuria. The gradual mixing together of all these spitz dogs continued through the 1930s and 1940s, and the type was eventually stabilized. In 1948 the Japan Kennel Club unified the breed standard and made it permanent.

Needless to say, since detailed facts are scarce, this 'blending of breeds' scenario has given rise to much argument. Some feel that the Samoyed was vitally important, others that it was not involved at all. Some are convinced that the white German Spitz played the key role in the foundation of the breed. Some are doubtful as to whether the American Eskimo played a serious part. Until DNA testing on the various breeds has been carried out, we cannot be sure.

One thing is certain, however – this is a glamorous little dog, and one that has made many friends in recent years. In personality, it is bold, lively and intelligent. The offspring of some that had been exported to Sweden were an immediate success when they arrived in England in the 1970s, and from there they spread in many directions. The Kennel Club in London recognized the breed in 1977.

JAPANESE TERRIER   JAPAN

Also know as the Nippon Terrier, the Nihon Terrier, the Mikado Terrier or the Oyuki (Snowy) Terrier, this breed was created as a companion animal rather than as a working terrier.

When Europeans first started serious trading with Japan in the 18th century, they sometimes took their small dogs with them. Some of these remained in the Far East and were interbred with other local dogs to create new breeds. Among those early canine imports were Smooth Fox Terriers, brought to the port of Nagasaki by Dutch sailors during the Edo period. These were used to develop a Japanese Terrier that was essentially a pet animal, rather than a working dog. Its main centres were Yokohama and Kobe. In Kobe it was sometimes referred to as the Kobe Terrier.

For many years this little terrier progressed from generation to generation without any serious attempt to control its type. Then, in 1916, in the Nada district near Kobe, the founding father of the modern breed, a male called Kuro, was born. He was the result of crosses between the ancestral terriers, an English Toy Terrier and a Toy Bull Terrier. From his offspring a new, improved terrier breed was developed and, in the 1930s, Japanese enthusiasts in the region of Osaka began a breeding programme with the aim of producing a fixed, pure-breeding line. The result was an athletic, elegantly slim little dog with a short white coat bearing dark markings, and with a black head and neck. The slightly arched shape of its slender body suggests that among its ancestors were whippet-like animals of some kind, most probably Italian Greyhounds.

The Japanese Terrier is still a rare breed and, sadly, its numbers are on the decline, but local canine conservationists are said to be coming to its rescue. It is still almost unknown outside its native country, although in the 1990s a few examples did arrive in Europe, thanks to the efforts of French and Italian breeders.

References

1992. Takahara, Jun and da Castejon, Luisa Gonzalez. *The Japanese Terrier.*

PHILIPPINES

MANILLA SPANIEL   PHILIPPINES

This toy spaniel is named after the capital (now spelled Manila) of the Philippines, the city which was the breed's stronghold.

A small companion breed, rarely mentioned today, this was popular at the end of the 19th century and the start of the 20th, when there was an attempt by a British breeder, called Miss Pidgely, to established it in England. She was impressed by its physical appeal, by its intelligence and quickness to learn, and by its longevity, one of her dogs living to the age of 18.

The Manilla was a member of the bichon group, very similar to the Maltese but much larger. It weighed 16 lb (7 kg), compared with the 6 lb (3 kg) of the tiny Maltese. Breeders in the Philippines claimed that it was a native breed, but the chances are that it was one of the highly valued little lapdogs that were carried around the world by early trading ships, for use in exchanges of luxury goods. This would put it in the same category as the Bichon Frisé from Tenerife, the Havanese from Cuba and the Coton de Tulear from Madagascar.

The Manilla Spaniel had a long, white, wavy coat, a jet black nose and large, lustrous black eyes. In Europe, it seems to have disappeared at some time during the early part of the 20th century, but it is not clear whether some survivors still exist in the Philippines.

AUSTRALIA

AUSSIE BULLDOG   AUSTRALIA

Despite its ferocious ancestors, this breed has been developed exclusively as a pet animal. Although it looks intimidating, it is never used as a guard dog. It is sometimes called the Australian Bulldog.

This is a new breed, developed in Queensland, Australia, towards the end of the 20th century. It is the creation of dog-breeder Pip Nobes of Toowoomba, who loved the British Bulldog but was upset by the health problems it was encountering in its exaggerated, modern form. The stated intention was 'to eliminate defects seen in many Bulldogs, such as breathing difficulties due to an elongated soft palate, skin fold eczema, and caesarean births'.

Of course, bulldog experts are themselves undertaking selective breeding to eliminate these hazards, but Nobes took a more drastic step, using a mixture of breeds to create the 'perfect' Australian Bulldog.

By making a series of controlled crosses with Boxer, Bullmastiff and Bull Terrier, a new bulldog breed was created. It was one that retained the temperament of the traditional bulldog, but gave it a healthier body. It has longer legs, a smaller head and chest, a less flattened muzzle and broader hips. Its height is 16–20 in (40–50 cm), compared with 12–14 in (31–36 cm) for the British Bulldog. Its weight is 55–77 lb (25–35 kg), compared with 50–55 lb (23–25 kg). In colour it is usually red or fawn or brindle, with white.

The Aussie Bulldog has a temperament that has been colourfully described as 'affectionate, elephantine and lazy'. When it does become excited, it reveals a 'bulldozing nature... that can bowl over unsuspecting adults'. It is praised, however, for its friendly and outgoing personality, completely lacking in shyness, which makes it an ideal pet dog. Because it has been created purely as a household companion, no attempt has been made to draw up a breed standard, and there is no intention to enter it in competitive dog shows.

AUSTRALIAN SILKY TERRIER   AUSTRALIA

Also known as the Silky, the Australian Silkie, the Sydney Silky Terrier, the Sydney Silky, the Silky Terrier, the Silkie Terrier or the Silky Toy Terrier, this diminutive terrier was developed purely as a companion breed — a household pet — from its larger, working cousin, the Australian Terrier.

In a country where most dogs must work hard to earn their living, this is Australia's only 'toy' breed, developed purely as a pet. During the 19th century, the larger

Australian Terrier had established itself as the country's champion vermin-killer and had become a national favourite. By crossing it with tiny Yorkshire Terriers it was possible to reduce its size while retaining its personality. It is thought that the Skye Terrier may also have been involved in a minor way, which would explain the Silky's prominent, pricked ears.

The result of this mixing was an intelligent, lively, fun-loving, high-spirited companion with fine, silky hair, weighing no more than 10 lb (5 kg) and ideal for urban living. As a bonus, it is an excellent watchdog, noisily announcing the arrival of any stranger. Its coat does not shed and it lacks the dog odour common in many breeds.

In the Australian show-ring, this breed made its debut in the early years of the 20th century. There was great rivalry between Silky breed clubs in Victoria and New South Wales, each putting out its own version of the breed standard. The Sydney faction tried to claim the breed as its own by calling it the Sydney Silkie, and it was not until 1959 that a national standard was finally established.
In this same year the breed was recognized by the American Kennel Club, under the name Silky Terrier. The Silky has been slower to catch on in Britain, probably because of the enormous popularity of the Yorkshire Terrier, and a British breed club was not formed until 1979.

References

1963. Young, Betty. *How to Raise and Train a Silky Terrier.* TFH, New Jersey.
1964. Wheatland, W. A. *The Australian Terrier and the Australian Silky Terrier.* Hawthorne Press, Melbourne.
1965. Hamilton-Wilkes, Monty. *The Australian Silky Terrier.* Angus & Robertson, London.
1972. Lehnig, Beverly. *Your Silky Terrier.* Denlinger's, USA.
1972. Young, Betty. *This is the Silky Terrier.* TFH, New Jersey.
1981. Weil, Martin. *Australian Silky Terriers.* TFH, New Jersey.
1990. Seabrook, Dot. *Getting to Know Your Silky Terrier.* Loveland.
1990. Smith, Peggy. *The Complete Silky Terrier.* Howell, New York.
1997. Boyce, Jan. *Australian Born, Australian Bred: The Australian Silky Terrier.*
1997. Hingeley, Marshall and Hingeley, Wren. *Silky Terriers Today.* Howell, New York.

MINIATURE LABRADOODLE   AUSTRALIA

This is a reduced version of the Labradoodle, produced as a companion animal for people with smaller homes.

Influenced by the appeal of the larger Labradoodle (see separate entry), this small version was recently created by crossing a male Toy Poodle, or a Toy Poodle x Miniature Poodle cross, with a Golden Labrador bitch. At least 150 puppies have been bred in this programme so far and they have apparently grown into ideal, shaggy-coated family dogs. They are said to be intelligent, tolerant, patient, easy to train and without any signs of aggression. They are especially suitable for older owners.

UNITED STATES

ALASKAN KLEE KAI   ALASKA

This breed was originally given the name of Klee Kai of Alaska, but it was changed to Alaskan Klee Kai in 1995. It is a new breed, developed exclusively as a companion animal. In the Inuit language, 'klee kai' means 'little dog'.

This is a small, 'apartment-sized' version of the big, northern sled dogs, bred down from Siberian Husky and Alaskan Malamute ancestors, with Schipperke and American Eskimo crosses introduced to help reduce its size. It was the creation of one breeder, Linda Spurlin of Wasilla, Alaska. She started developing it in the early 1970s, but it was not until 1988 that she was sufficiently satisfied with her stock to allow examples to go to other breeders.

The Klee Kai was an immediate success and, by the end of the 20th century, there were estimated to be about 500 in existence, with owners scattered all over the United States. There are three sizes: the toy, at 13 in (33 cm) in height; the miniature, at 13–15 in (33–38 cm); and the standard at 15-17 in (38–43 cm). For comparison, its large ancestor, the Alaskan Malamute, is 23–25 in (58–63 cm) tall. Like its big relatives, it displays a striking face mask and an attractive coat pattern.

This is a lively little dog, described by its owners as curious, quick, energetic, proud, tenacious, intuitive and observant. It is very friendly with its own human family, but rather reserved with strangers. A cunning escape artist, it is a remarkably agile climber, an ability which can sometimes cause problems. It is also an active hunter, killing and eating rabbits, squirrels, mice, snakes and bugs, whenever the opportunity arises. If Klee Kai dogs are kept together in breeding kennels, they often enjoy group howling sessions, singing together early in the morning and late at night.

The Klee Kai National Kennel Club was formed in 1995, when a breed standard was established for the first time.

AMERICAN ESKIMO (STANDARD)   UNITED STATES

Originally known as the American Spitz, this dog acquired its new name in 1917. Its nick-name is the Eskie. It was bred exclusively as a household companion dog.

This breed has been popular in America since the beginning of the 20th century, but it is little-known elsewhere. Its main ancestors first arrived in the United States during the 19th century with German immigrants who could not bear to be parted from their white spitz dogs. At about the same time, Volpinos from Italy, Keeshonds from Holland and Pomeranians from Germany were also appearing in American cities, and some of these other European spitz breeds may have contributed in a minor way to the ancestry of the new, American breed.

(Note: Several recent authors have suggested that the German white spitz dogs arrived in the United States in the 17th century, but this is incorrect since major German immigrations did not occur until the 18th century and it was not until the middle of the 19th century that Germans of the social class most likely to have kept these little companion dogs arrived in the New World.)

Looking rather like a miniature Samoyed, with its thick white coat, dense ruff, pricked ears, and heavily plumed, up-curled tail, this hardy breed was gradually reduced in bulk by careful, selective breeding, until it was the ideal size for a household companion. Its owners claim that it has the perfect canine personality, being unusually intelligent, sensitive, alert, playful, energetic, cooperative, trainable, devoted and ideal with children. Although a good watchdog, it only barks and never bites. Some owners admit that it can occasionally be stubborn and headstrong, but point out that with proper training, this is not a problem.

Although this is a snow-loving breed, the American Eskimo is badly named, because its modern title misleadingly suggests that it is a miniature version of the big, sled-pulling Canadian Eskimo Dog, rather than a descendant of German spitz breeds. The explanation for the change in name from Spitz to Eskimo is simple. The political climate in America during World War I was such that nobody wished to have a dog with obvious German connections. The German term 'Spitz', meaning 'sharp point', which was first introduced by them in the 15th century to denote northern dogs with pointed muzzles, erect, pointed ears, up-curled tails, stocky bodies and thick, double coats, had to be replaced. Just as the German Shepherd Dog became the Alsatian, so the American Spitz became the American Eskimo, and thus distanced itself from its true, Germanic origins.

In 1985 the American Eskimo Dog Association was formed and the breed was officially recognized by the AKC in 1995.

References

1990. Beynon, Barbara. *The Complete American Eskimo: a Special Kind of Companion Dog.* Howell, New York.

1995. Coile, Caroline D. *American Eskimo Dogs: Everything about Purchase, Care, Nutrition, Breeding, Behavior, and Training.* Barron, New York.

1996. Hofman, Nancy J. and Flamholtz, Cathy J. *The New American Eskimo.* OTR Publications.

1998. Siino, Betsy Sikora. *Guide to Owning an American Eskimo.*

1999. Beauchamp, Richard. *A New Owner's Guide to American Eskimo Dogs.*

AMERICAN ESKIMO (MINIATURE)   UNITED STATES

Almost as soon as the American Eskimo dog had been developed as a pure breed, early in the 20th century, the process of miniaturization began. Before long there was a distinct, smaller version that soon because separately recognized as the Miniature American Eskimo.

The Standard American Eskimo is 15–19 in (38–48 cm) in height whereas the Miniature is only 12–15 in (31–38 cm). The Standard weighs 20–35 lb (9–16 kg), while the Miniature tips the scales at only 11–20 lb (5–9 kg). Apart from this size difference, the two breeds are virtually identical.

AMERICAN ESKIMO (TOY)   UNITED STATES

For many years, the smallest American Eskimo was the Miniature, but then, after years of selective breeding, an even more reduced breed was created, to be called the Toy American Eskimo.

This breed is 9–12 in (23–31 cm) in height and 6–10 lb (3–5 kg) in weight. There is still argument as to whether it should be classified as a separate breed, but if its popularity increases, this distinction will eventually gain general recognition, as it has with other types of diminutive companion dog.

AMERICAN HAIRLESS TERRIER   UNITED STATES

The only hairless breed originating in the United States, this has been developed purely as a companion dog.

In 1972 a naked puppy appeared in a litter of otherwise normal Rat Terriers. Her name was Josephine and she was to become the first of an entirely new breed of small, hairless companion dogs. Her owners, Edwin and Willie Scott of Trout, Louisiana, bred from her and were successful in obtaining another naked female puppy, which they named Gypsy. Eight years later, after giving birth to many litters of fully haired puppies, Josephine once again produced a naked female puppy, this time called Jemima, and, more importantly, a naked male, which was named Snoopy. In 1983 Snoopy was mated with all his sisters and many more naked puppies were born.

The Scotts now established Trout Creek Kennels to further develop the breed and year by year have increased their population of American Hairless Terriers. They kept careful records and eventually set up the American Hairless Terrier Association. Because they have found that individuals vary in size from 7 to 14 lb (3 to 6 kg), they have decided to treat the smaller ones as a separate form and classify them as 'Toys'.

At birth the naked puppies do possess a little sparse, fuzzy hair, but it soon starts to fall out and by the age of six weeks it has all gone, except for a few stray eyebrow hairs and whiskers. The skin of these lively, friendly, intelligent little dogs is usually a mottled white, showing small dark spots and some larger blotches. For anyone allergic to animal fur they make the ideal house pet and have the added advantage that they can never leave hairs on furniture. Their only shortcomings are that they would soon become chilled in a cold climate – not a problem in their native Louisiana – and that, like their human owners, they can easily suffer from sunburn.

BULLNESE   UNITED STATES

A recent American pet breed that takes its name from its two ancestors, the French Bulldog and the Pekingese.

Developed from French Bulldog/Pekingese crosses, this breed was created by Bobby Rice of Florida at the end of the 20th century. It has bandy legs, bat ears and a snub nose. The head is large and square and the tail is slightly curled. The short, thick coat is soft and dense. Fawn is popular, but any coat colour is acceptable.

Its movements are described as graceful, with a smooth, flowing gait. In temperament it is said to be alert and friendly, making an ideal family pet. Its height is rather variable, from 6 to 12 in (15 to 30 cm). Its weight also varies considerably, from 12 to 25 lb (5 to 11 kg), suggesting that, as a breed, it is not yet fully stabilized.

CHINESE TEMPLE CH'IN   UNITED STATES

Also known as the Chinese Imperial Ch'in or the Chinese Temple Dog, this breed is a modern American recreation of one of the ancient temple dogs of China.

Despite its name, this is an American dog. A United States breeder crossed a 'believed Temple Dog male' with a large female Japanese Chin. Starting from this basis, the new breed was developed. It remains very similar to the Japanese Chin, but has a longer muzzle, and its body is slightly longer and lower. Its ears hang close to the head, and a plumed tail is curled up over the back. Its long cottony coat is nearly always black-and-white. Other colours do appear, but only rarely.

There are four size classes: the Giant, the Classic, the Miniature and the Sleeve. The biggest examples are about 14 in (36 cm) in height and weigh 20 lb (9 kg). The smallest are tiny, no more than 3 in (8 cm) tall and weighing as little as 1.5 lb (700 g). This newly revived breed is said to be growing rapidly in popularity.

COCKAPOO
UNITED STATES

The name of this new breed is sometimes given as Cockerpoo. It was developed in America exclusively as a companion dog.

This new breed is a straightforward mixture of Cocker Spaniel and Poodle. It came into being to provide a companion dog that had the good qualities of both its parent breeds. The idea was to retain the 'sweet nature, patient disposition and sturdy build' of the Cocker Spaniel and to combine it with the 'extraordinary intelligence and non-shedding coat' of the Poodle. The result, its supporters claim, is the 'perfect family pet', with a wonderful disposition and a 'hybrid vigour' that avoids many of the health defects of its pedigree parents.

This modern breed did not exist before the 1960s, but is steadily increasing in popularity in the United States and now has its own Cockapoo Club of America to 'protect and promote' it. They have made the following formal statement: 'We do not plan to be associated with the AKC as our focus and purposes are different. We... focus on the unique personality, health, temperament and longevity with a much less important focus on beauty.' In other words, they accept some variability of form (which would rule them out as dog-show competitors) in order to concentrate on perfecting the personality of the Cockapoo. If, with the passage of time, its form stabilizes nonetheless, there will undoubtedly be a moment when a set of breed standards is drawn up. This has happened with other popular breeds, like the Jack Russell, and it will probably happen here too.

KING SHEPHERD
UNITED STATES

This rare breed was recently created to provide an unusually impressive companion dog and show dog, but also one with good working potential as a guard or herder.

This massive new breed dates only from the latter part of the 20th century. A powerful, rugged, vigorous, agile and intelligent dog, it is a giant version of the German Shepherd, created by American enthusiasts by careful selective breeding for increased size.

The minimum height for males is 27 in (68.5 cm) and for females 25 in (63.5 cm). For comparison, the German Shepherd itself has a height range of only 22–26 in (55–66 cm). The ideal weight of this dog is 130–150 lb (59–73 kg) for males and 90–110 lb (41–50 kg) for females, which compares with only 75–95 lb (34–43 kg) for the German Shepherd. There are two coat varieties, the coarse-haired and the long-haired.

Kennels in at least five different states (New York, New Jersey, Connecticut, Delaware and Pennsylvania, all in the north-east of the United States) are now focusing on this breed, which promises to be popular in the future. For the present, however, it remains a rare animal.

KYI LEO   UNITED STATES

This recent Californian breed acquired its title from the Tibetan name for dog (Kyi) and the Latin name for Lion (Leo). At an earlier stage of its development it had been referred to as the Lhasa-Maltese Shaggie. Some authorities prefer to call it the American Lamalese. It was developed solely as a companion dog.

In the 1940s a family in San Francisco bred a cross between a Lhasa Apso and a Maltese. They continued with these attractive crosses for several generations, at which stage they were approached by a San Jose dog-breeder who obtained a pair from them, a black-and-white male and a gold-and-white female. This breeder was so fascinated by them that she started a line of what she called Lhasa-Maltese Shaggies, using the original pair, another Lhasa Apso/Maltese cross – a gold and white male – and a small black and white male Apso. These four dogs were her foundation stock which was eventually to lead to the Kyi Leo breed.

Harriet Linn, of Concord, California, acquired one of the San Jose puppies, a black-and-white female called Mitzi, and later obtained a mate for her, a black-and-white male called Impy from the same source. Their first litter arrived in 1967 and the puppies were so appealing that Harriet Linn began a serious breeding programme to initiate a new breed. By 1972 there were 60 of these dogs in existence and the demand for them was growing. In was in this year that a breed club was formed and they were given their new name of Kyi Leo. By 1986 their numbers had swollen to 190, the dogs were breeding true, and this attractive new addition to the family of domestic dogs was safely on its way. Instead of the usual breed shows, Harriet Linn held 'non-competitive reunions' for the descendants of her foundation stock, events she much preferred because they had all the fun of serious dog shows, but without the stresses of judging, winning and losing.

The majority of Kyi Leos are black-and-white particoloured, but some are gold-and-white and a few are solid colours. As might be expected, they are smaller than Apsos and bigger than Maltese. Superficially they look like their Lhasa Apso ancestors, but on closer inspection it is clear that they have slightly longer noses, slightly shorter coats, and slightly less prominent eyes. Their exuberant, playful personalities are winning them more and more devotees and it seems certain that they will increase in popularity as the years pass.

It should be mentioned that there is an identical breed listed by some American canine organizations as the American Lamalese. This appears to be simply an alternative name for the Kyi Leo, presumably coined by a rival breeder. It remains to be seen which of the competing names is finally adopted. Kyi Leo is used here because, at present, it is more widely employed, but with such a recently developed breed this could easily change.

LONG-HAIRED CHIHUAHUA   UNITED STATES

Also known as the Longcoat Chihuahua, or the Chihuahua Langhaar, this is to many people merely a variant of the typical, short-haired Chihuahua, differing only in coat length. To others it is a separate breed.

Those who support the idea that this is a distinct type do so because they believe that it is the result of one or more matings with other breeds. In other words, it was not merely a Chihuahua with a long-hair gene, but a new type of lapdog created by crossing the Chihuahua with other small companion breeds. These crossings are said to have occurred in the United States in the early part of the 20th century, only a few decades after the first Smooth-coated Chihuahuas had been brought back from Mexico as exotic pets.

The Pomeranian is the favourite candidate as the most important of the other foundation breeds, but the Papillon and the (early type of) Pekingese were also said to have been used on a number of occasions. A careful comparison of the smooth-haired and the long-haired versions of the Chihuahua does show slight differences that go beyond hair length.

In 1952 the Longcoat Chihuahua Club of America was founded and treated this dog as a separate entity. Interbreeding between the short- and the long-haired forms was no longer permitted.

The earliest record of a Long-haired Chihuahua in Mexico dates from as recently as 1959, and that dog was owned by a German and had been imported from the United States. As late as 1965 there were only 12 registered in Mexico, compared with huge numbers in the United States, supporting the view that this type of Chihuahua is not an early local variant of the smooth-coated dog, as some have claimed.

MI-KI

The name of this new breed is pronounced Mee-Kee. It is being developed in the United States exclusively as a lapdog and a show dog.

This is one of several new American toy dog breeds being created to satisfy the needs of urban apartment dwellers. In this role, one of the Mi-Ki's advantages is that it seldom barks, a major consideration in areas of high-density housing.

In personality, this little dog is said to be sociable, alert, friendly, good-natured, non-aggressive and intelligent. Unlike many small dogs, it is not wary of strangers. Its breeders recommend it as a companion for the elderly or the disabled and state that, for apartment owners, it can be trained to use a litter box like a cat. In height, it is 11 in (28 cm) or less. Its weight is 5–8 lb (2–4 kg).

The Mi-Ki is a dog of rather vague origins. It probably began as an accidental cross between two well-established toy dog breeds, such as the Maltese and the Japanese Chin. In appearance it looks remarkably like an intermediate between these two. There is no official word on its precise background, other than that the dog 'is thought to be Asian', can perhaps be traced back to Penang and shares 'common ancestry with the Papillon, the Maltese, and the Japanese Chin'. Confirmation of the fact that its beginnings are obscure comes from the report that Donna Hall, the vice-president of the Mi-Ki Club of America, has submitted DNA samples from three of the foundation dogs for laboratory analysis at Universities in Switzerland and New Zealand.

This breed has an apple-domed head and a spitz-like tail curled up over its back. At present, its anatomy appears to be somewhat variable. The muzzle varies from ½ in (1 cm) to 1½ in (4 cm). The ears may be erect or drooped. The coat may be either long, fine, silky and straight, or smooth and lying close to the body. A beard and moustache may be present (with the long coat) or absent (with the smooth coat). For show purposes, dewclaws must be removed, the feet must be shaved and, in the case of the long-coated variety, the head must also be shaved. All colours are accepted.

This developing breed first appeared in the United States in the 1980s and the Mi-Ki Club of America was founded in Wisconsin in 1996. It has to be said that some dog authorities are highly critical of this breed; one has gone so far as to say: 'I am convinced that the Mi-Ki is not a breed.' And it has been pointed out that 'in all of the AKC publications… there has never been any mention of a breed called Mi-Ki'. It remains to be seen whether it will manage to establish itself in the future.

MINIATURE AUSTRALIAN SHEPHERD UNITED STATES

Also known as the North American Shepherd and, to its friends, as the Mini Aussie, this recent breed was created as a companion dog by producing a smaller version of a working sheepdog.

This recent addition to the companion dogs of America was created by breeding down in size from the Australian Shepherd Dog, an active working breed employed to control large flocks of sheep. Despite its name, the Australian Shepherd Dog (see separate entry) is a Californian herder extremely popular on local ranches.

In the 1960s a Californian woman obtained a few rather small examples of this breed, dogs that she found working on the rodeo circuit, and began selective breeding to reduce their size even further. The body height was taken down from 18–23 in (46–58 cm) to 13–18 in (33–46 cm), and the weight from 35–70 lb (16–32 kg) down to 15–30 lb (7–14 kg). She called them Miniature Australian Shepherds, and the new breed type was fixed by 1980. Then, in 1993, this name was changed to North American Shepherd to give the new dog the illusion of being more distinct from its immediate ancestor.

It was then pointed out that, since back-crosses were still being made to the ancestral breed to improve the gene pool, this new name was unsuitable, so there was a move to revert to the original title. A specialist breed club was formed, called the Miniature Australian Shepherd Club of America (MASCA). This upset the members of the North American Shepherd Club, who solved the problem by creating a compromise name that will almost certainly be ignored, a name that only a committee could invent: the North American Miniature Australian Shepherd. Fortunately everyone concerned with the breed calls it the Mini Aussie, so no harm is done.

Blissfully ignorant of all this name-calling, the dog itself continues to delight its owners as an ideal household companion and show dog. Because of its recent ancestry, it retains a very high level of intelligence, loyalty and confidence. Traditionally it has either a naturally bobbed or an artificially docked tail. Its coat colour is always mixed, never solid, and there are many accepted colour combinations.

MINIATURE SHAR PEI UNITED STATES

Sometimes called the Min Pei or Mini Pei, this dog was bred down from the typical Shar Pei solely as a companion dog.

The full-sized Shar Pei was a Chinese fighting dog, but when it was first brought to North America in the 1970s it created a sensation as an exotic pet dog, in particular because its puppies were covered in thick, wrinkled flesh. This gave them the unique look of a small dog wearing the skin of a big dog. As each puppy grew up, it lost a great deal of this wrinkling and, in the process, some of its special charm. Some American breeders decided to breed down in size to a dwarf form that would have the double advantage of being much smaller – for urban living – and retaining the heavily wrinkled condition all its life.

The breeders who have created these miniatures in recent years have met with hostility from some of those dedicated to the full-sized version, but this has not stopped them. They have been busy fixing the dwarf form so that it will breed true. For them, the maximum height is 16 in (40 cm), compared with 20 in (50 cm) for the larger version.

OCHERESE UNITED STATES

This new breed was created at the end of the 20th century specifically as an ideal companion animal. The name is a combination of 'ocher' and 'ese'. 'Ocher' is the American spelling for the earth colour 'ochre' and was used because it reminded the breed's creator of 'a beautiful sunset with a little red, a little orange, and a dash of golden tones'. The ending 'ese' is borrowed from Pekingese and Maltese, two of the three breeds involved in the creation of this dog.

Canine traditionalists are aghast at the number of newly invented companion breeds that have been appearing in the United States in recent years. Some of these dogs may well be no more than passing fads, but others have a more serious purpose. Faced with the health problems caused by the excessive inbreeding of some of the best-known pedigree dogs, some American breeders have responded by undertaking dramatic cross-breeding programmes with the ultimate goal of developing new companion breeds that will benefit genetically from 'hybrid vigour'. The Ocherese is a recent example of this trend.

Pekingese breeder Janet Dilger, from the small town of Mariah Hill in southern Indiana, had become increasingly concerned by the birth defects she was discovering in her newborn puppies and decided to take action. Her goal was to produce a small, calm, healthy animal, with long hair that did not shed. To achieve this end she crossed her show Pekingese with a small Toy Poodle. The results, known as Pek-a-Poos, aimed her in the direction she wanted to go, but she was not satisfied with the coat texture. The final step was taken when she then mated one of her female Peke/Poodle crosses with a male Maltese. The puppies from this mating were, it was said, 'nothing short of marvellous', and she decided to continue with these as the foundation stock of a new breed, which she christened the Ocherese. (This word is apparently pronounced O-shur-ese, and not O-ker-ese, as one might have expected.)

The Ocherese Club of America was soon formed, but it remains to be seen whether the dog will fulfil its early promise and eventually become recognized as a fully fledged breed.

The Ocherese has soft, silky, non-shedding, non-matting hair, in a wide variety of colours. The body is compact, with short, feathered legs, and a long, plumed tail that is carried over the back. The height is only 9–12 in (23–30 cm) and the weight 5–12 lb (2–5 kg).

In personality, this is an eager, intelligent, sprightly, trusting and vigorous little dog, seen by its creator as the ideal household companion. When its existence became known, it attracted immediate attention, and proved so popular that demand soon out-stripped supply, facing the breeder with a long waiting list for puppies.

ORI PEI   UNITED STATES

A new, exotic companion dog developed by an American breeder. The name is short for Oriental Shar Pei.

This breed was created in the United States in the 1970s by Aaron Silver. As a breeder of Chinese Shar Pei for some years, he had become increasingly concerned about the medical difficulties, especially the skin problems, encountered with that fascinating dog. Wishing to keep the good qualities of the breed but lose the bad ones, he started a care-fully designed breeding program in which, by crossing Miniature Shar Peis with Pugs, he was able to create a smaller animal that was much healthier.

The Ori Pei eventually had a pedigree history of more than six generations and could be considered as a new breed. Several other breeders joined in to help establish it.

Described as a lively, intelligent little dog with a regal appearance, it has a height of only 12–15 in (31–38 cm), compared with 18–20 in (46–51 cm) for the full-sized Shar Pei. The 12 in (31 cm) Ori Peis are much preferred. It is said that, to have one of these dogs, is to own a Shar Pei that never grows up. The adult Ori Pei looks remark-ably like a six-month-old Shar Pei.

The typical colour is fawn, but others are allowed, even particolours, which are referred to as 'flowered'. There are two types of coat – the ancestral, thin, 'prickly' type, called the Horse Coat, and a slightly longer one which is softer to the touch, called the Brush Coat. The latter is more popular. As with its Chinese ancestor, both the body and head are liberally supplied with skin-wrinkles.

PEKEPOO   UNITED STATES

A recent experimental breed created by crossing Pekingese with Miniature Poodles. The result is an appealing little dog but is as yet without any official recognition. It is being developed purely as a companion dog and is restricted to the United States at the present time.

It is described as a friendly, protective, active, affectionate dog that is patient with children. It is suited to apartment life, although it is said to be a somewhat noisy barker. Its height is approximately 11 in (28 cm) and its weight 9–20 lb (4–9 kg).

A slighty smaller version, created by crossing Pekingese with Toy Poodle, was involved in the development of the Ocherese (see separate entry) and was given the similar name of Pek-a-Poo.

SCHNOODLE UNITED STATES

One of several new American breeds developed from deliberate crosses between two well-known pedigree dogs, it was created purely as a household companion. The name is formed from the first part of Schnauzer and the last part of Poodle.

This recent breed is based on crosses between Miniature Schnauzers and Miniature Poodles. According to Shelly Hanson, a Schnoodle breeder from Isanti, Minnesota: 'These dogs do not shed and are great for people with allergies… They are not yappy dogs, but they are good watchdogs.'

In temperament they are said to be the perfect family dog – intelligent, loyal, adaptable, and good with children. Their height is 13 in (33 cm) and their weight is 10–15 lb (5–7 kg). The tail is docked.

SHILOH SHEPHERD UNITED STATES

Named after the Shiloh Kennels in New York, where it was created, this variant on the German Shepherd Dog has been created specifically as a companion dog.

The recently developed Shiloh Shepherd is a large, good-natured, straight-backed version of the German Shepherd Dog – an attempt to return to the early form of that breed. It has been developed at the Shiloh Kennels in New York in a carefully monitored breeding programme that began in 1962.

American dog-breeder Tina Barber was born and raised in Germany and vividly recalled from her childhood the 'big, strong, easy to train… mountain herding dogs that stole everyone's heart'. These were the old-fashioned German Shepherd Dogs, and when she looked at their modern equivalents she was horrified to

see what had happened to them. Their bodies were longer and thinner, their bones were finer, their overall size was reduced and, in temperament, they had become what she called 'spooky-shy', or 'fear-biters'. Calm, stable intelligence had been sacrificed to create a flashy show dog. She resolved to do something about this and set about reinventing the original dog, as she had known it when she was young.

When the breeding programme started in 1962, Tina Barber's kennel name was Konigin. After 12 years of struggling to breed the perfect dog, with 'super intelligence, huge size and great hips', she despaired of ever being able to combine all three qualities. Then in 1974 she changed her kennel name to Shiloh and continued with renewed energy. By the 1990s, over 30 years after she first began, she had succeeded in achieving her goal and the Shiloh Shepherd was, at last, the animal she had dreamed of. Many other German Shepherd devotees, also longing to return to the original type, acquired puppies from her kennels, spreading the success of the Shiloh across North America.

Most of her breeding work was done with carefully selected German Shepherd Dogs, always aiming to intensify the breed's original features, but in 1989, she did introduce one additional element – a cross with an unusually large Malamute, to give the new breed better hips and increased size.

Although Tina Barber's programme has been laudable in every way and has created a magnificent dog, her choice of name for the reconstituted breed is unfortunate. The Biblical town of Shiloh was an ancient settlement located 17 miles (27 km) north of Jerusalem, and implies a Middle Eastern connection for this dog which is misleading. Back in the 1920s and 1930s, when German Shepherd Dogs conformed to the original type that Barber is honouring, they were referred to in Britain as Alsatians (because of anti-German feelings stemming from World War I). So perhaps the name Alsatian Shepherd Dog would have been more appropriate for the new breed.

TOY FOX TERRIER UNITED STATES

This small breed is also referred to as the American Toy Terrier, the Amertoy or simply the TFT. It was developed from larger working terriers primarily for use as a companion dog, although it is still capable of ridding a house of rodent pests.

This breed is a miniature version of the Smooth Fox Terrier, created largely by breeding from successive generations of litter runts, until dogs weighing less than 7 lb (3 kg) started to arrive and eventually began to breed true. They are small enough to be carried in one hand. It has been suggested that both Chihuahua and Toy Manchester Terrier may have been introduced during breeding programmes to assist in size reduction.

The TFT was first registered as a separate breed with the United Kennel Club in

America in 1936. In 1949 the National Toy Fox Terrier Association was formed in Ohio.

In character, the breed has been described as self-possessed, energetic, spirited and determined. In other words, despite its small size it retains a true terrier personality. Although all dogs prefer a rural setting, with plenty of opportunity for exercise, this tiny breed can adapt more easily than most to the restrictions of urban living. Its height is only 10 in (25 cm), its weight 4–7 lb (2–3 kg).

References

1967. Hart, Ernest H. *Toy Fox Terrier.* TFH, New Jersey.
1988. Hopkins Eliza L. and Flamholtz, Cathy J. *Toy Fox Terrier.*
1993. Krueger. *Toy Fox Terriers.* TFH, New Jersey.
1994. Baker-Kreuger, Sherry. *Toy Fox Terrier.*

TOY MUNCHKIN UNITED STATES

This lapdog is claimed by its promoters to have an ancient heritage, but there is no evidence that it is anything other than a recent cross-breed, or dwarfed breed, created specifically for the toy dog market. Whether it becomes established in the future, or remains a brief 'flash-in-the-pan' gimmick, remains to be seen.

This controversial breed has appeared recently in the United States and has caused a great deal of public interest. The facts surrounding it, however, remain obscure. It is thought to be either a cross between Pomeranians and Chihuahuas, or an example of unusually small Pomeranians. As yet, it is not recognized by any major canine authority, and has attracted criticism from some quarters. One author referred to the breed as the 'Half Chihuahua/Half Pom: Out-to-Lunchkin!'.

The acceptance of the breed will undoubtedly depend on its creators providing more information on its ancestry and the history of their breeding programme. At present they have said only that it 'has a history that goes back several hundred years' and that 'the ancestors of these affectionate little dogs were the favourite companions of the Royal families'. The ancestral form was a larger and usually white dog that has 'been bred down to its present size over a period of time'.

With a minimum height of 4 in (10 cm) and a minimum weight of only 2 lb (900 g), this must be the smallest dog on earth. The average weight is about 3–5 lb (1.5–2.3 kg). There are no colour restrictions. It is usually seen in what is called a 'lion-cut' – that is to say, with its rear end shaved, except for the last inch (the last couple of centimetres) of its tail. Some owners prefer to leave the thick, dense coat in its natural state.

This is said to be an alert, eager-to-please, intelligent little dog which is not 'yappy' or hyperactive like some other toy breeds. Because of its size it is being recommended as the ideal apartment dog, and has the special advantage that it can be trained to use a litter box like a cat. When Munchkin-owners venture into the outside world, they can carry their minute pets in 'designer purses'.

This dog appears to have been established by two breeders who sell only male puppies or sterilized females, making it impossible for anyone else to set up a breeding pro-gramme. At the end of the 20th century there were fewer than 100 examples of this breed in existence. Prices asked were up to $4,000 for each puppy, with the demand for them fuelled by appearances on American television talk shows, where they created a sensation.

TOY RAT TERRIER   UNITED STATES

This breed was specifically created as a companion dog and was too small to undertake serious farm or hunting work.

The ancestor of this breed was the American Rat Terrier, an efficient, small vermin-destroyer, imported from England in the 19th century, which was an active working dog on many North American farms. At some point it was crossed with the even smaller Toy Manchester and the minute Chihuahua, to create a miniature version known as the Toy Rat Terrier.

The average weight of the standard Rat Terrier is 35 lb (16 kg), while that of the Toy version is only 4–7 lb (2–3 kg). Despite its small size, the little Toy is tough and sturdy and is capable of fearlessly nipping an intruder, if it feels threatened.

WHITE GERMAN SHEPHERD   UNITED STATES

This pure white form of the German Shepherd Dog has been developed primarily as a companion and show dog. It has been known by the longer name of American-Canadian White Shepherd Dog and the shorter name of White Shepherd.

This has been a controversial breed. For GSD traditionalists the white coat is looked upon as a flaw. For the supporters of the breed it is the dog's crowning glory.

The earliest mention of a White German Shepherd has been traced back to 1882, in Europe. The first Whites to be registered with the AKC in the United States date from 1917. More arrived in America in the 1920s, but then, in the 1930s, the breed lost favour. In 1933 the breed standard of the German Shepherd Dog recorded a white coat as a 'disqualifying fault'.

In the 1960s canine authorities in Germany began a campaign against the White dog, insisting that it should be outlawed. As a result, White Shepherds virtually disappeared from Europe. America followed suit and in 1968 the breed was disqualified from competing in the show-rings there, too.

There was a backlash against this ban and in 1969 the White German Shepherd Club of America was formed to support the breed. Since that time, groups in both the United States and Canada have developed the breed and have treated it as a separate entity. The White German Shepherd Dog Club International was founded in America in 1977.

In the 1970s White Shepherds were reintroduced into Europe and found favour there with a small number of enthusiasts in Switzerland. The dog's reacceptance grew steadily and, by the end of the 20th century, there were several thousand White Shepherds living in Europe. Switzerland, Holland, Denmark and the Czech Republic all came to recognize this dog as a new breed in its own right. Resistance to it still exists in many quarters, however.

The White Shepherd is not an albino. It has dark brown eyes, nose, eyelids and pads. Apart from its white hair it is virtually the same as a normally coloured GSD, except that it is usually slightly larger. White dogs of over 28 in (71 cm) in height and weighing 130 lb (59 kg) are common, compared with 26 in (66 cm) and 95 lb (43 kg) maximums for the standard GSD.

References

1988. Hearne, Vicki. *The White German Shepherd.* Atlantic Monthly Press Book, New York.
1999. Plummer, D. Brian. *Polly: a White German Shepherd Dog.* Perry Green Press, Sudbury.
Neufeld, Peter Lorenz. *The Invincible White Shepherd.*

MEXICO

CHIHUAHUA   MEXICO

Also known as the Smooth-coat Chihuahua, or the Chihuahua Korthaar, this minute dog, with its apple-domed head, is named after the Mexican state in which it was first encountered by visiting Americans in the late 19th century. Earlier names include the Mexican Dwarf Dog, the Ornament Dog, the Raza Fina and the Pillow Dog.

The Chihuahua is famous for being the smallest breed of dog in the world. This is a slight exaggeration, as the record is held by a freakishly tiny Yorkshire Terrier, but it is true that the average Chihuahua is smaller than the average Yorkie, so in general the claim can stand. The Chihuahua's weight is only 2–6 lb (1–3 kg) and its height 6–9 in (15–23 cm). This remarkable breed has several key features: a molera (a soft spot on the top of the skull), a flattened, furry tail and a strange, talon-like foot with long curved nails.

There are several conflicting theories concerning the origin of this breed. The first sees it as a dwarf form of one of the ancient American Indian dogs. It is claimed that, during the Aztec period, tiny dogs were sometimes cremated with their owners, the idea being that these little animals would then act as guides to show their owners the way to the afterlife. Some of the more common Indian dog breeds were fattened for the pot, but it is conjectured that the tiniest ones would have had special ritual value or been kept as pets. From these, the Chihuahua is thought to have descended.

Supporting this view is the presence in Mexico of a number of small, short-haired breeds of Indian dogs, from any one of which the little Chihuahua could have been developed. In addition, there is an Aztec depiction of a cremation ritual which includes what appears to be the body of a small, reddish-coloured dog.

The second view sees the Chihuahua as a European breed developed from the small Comforter dogs of the Middle Ages. It is supposed that, after the conquest of the New World, the wives of high-ranking Spanish settlers, or colonial officials, would have taken their beloved pets dogs with them for comfort. Some of these dogs would have spread from the great estates and become pet dogs on a wider scale, eventually ending up as companions of the local Indians.

Supporting the second view is a Chihuahua-like dog depicted in a painting by Botticelli which he completed ten years before the conquest of the New World had occurred. Also, it is pointed out that the little red 'dog' shown in the cremation picture of the Aztecs was more likely to have been some kind of fattened rodent, taken along by the deceased as food for the journey to the other world.

Some other authors have pinpointed the original homeland of this breed as being Malta, because there was supposed to be a tiny, short-haired lapdog there centuries ago, called the Maltese Pocket Dog. Still others have suggested China as the primary source, claiming that Chinese visitors brought their little flat-faced companion dogs to Mexico in the 18th century. This view is based on the fact that China has always favoured small, flat-faced dogs. There is little hard evidence to support any of these views and for the present it is best to favour the least complicated explanation, which is that the Chihuahua was a dwarf pet dog developed from some larger breed in ancient Mexico.

By the 19th century, the history of the breed is less confusing. In the 1880s American visitors to Mexico came across these tiny dogs and started buying them from local Indians for a few dollars, to take them back home as exotic pets. Many were delicate and badly nourished and soon died but enough survived to establish a breeding base in the United States. The first Chihuahua was registered there in 1903 and by 1923 the Chihuahua Club of America had been formed. The little dog gradually rose to become one of the most popular breeds in North America, ideal for urban living — easy to house and easy to feed – and with a lively and endearing personality. In 1958 over 48,000 Chihuahuas were registered in the United States alone.

The Chihuahua has changed in appearance since its early days. Photographs of the first ones to be taken to the United States clearly depict dogs with longer, more tapering snouts, smaller eyes, and bigger, bat-like ears. (These were called 'bambi' dogs because they were more fawn-like.) Progressive selective breeding through the decades of the 20th century has gradually created a more 'juvenile-looking' animal, with big baby eyes and a much more domed, rounded head. This anatomical shift increases the dog's 'infantile' appeal and makes it even more attractive as a small companion dog to be carried in the arms.

References

1933. Garrett, Ida H. *The Chihuahua.* Minsky, New York.

1936. Hasse, G. *Le Chihuahua.* Brussels.

1950. Denlinger, Milo G. *The Complete Chihuahua.* Denlinger's, USA.

1952. Kauffman, Russell E. *The Chihuahua.* Judy, Chicago.

1954. Thurmer, Tressa E. and Gentile, F. L. *Pet Chihuahua.* All-Pets, Fond du Lac, Wisconsin.

1955. Miller, Madeline. *Chihuahuas as Pets.* TFH, New Jersey.

1956. Wall, Charles H. *This and That about Chihuahuas.* Buddy Press, Toronto.

1958. Ferguson, Estelle and Barbaresi, Sara M. *How to Raise and Train a Chihuahua.* TFH, New Jersey.

1959. Riddle, Maxwell. *This is the Chihuahua.* TFH, New Jersey.

1961. Gray, Thelma. *The Popular Chihuahua.* Popular Dogs, London.

1963. Casselli, Rosina. *The Complete Chihuahua.* Howell, New York.

1966. Harmar, Hilary. *Chihuahua.* Foyles, London.

1966. Murray, Ruth L. *Your Chihuahua.* Hawthorn, New York.

1968. Harmar, Hilary. *Chihuahua Guide.* Pet Library, New York.

1970. Schneider, Earl (Editor). *Enjoy your Chiuhuahua.* Pet Library, New York.

1972. Harmar, Hilary. *The Complete Chihuahua Encyclopedia.* Arco, New York.

1976. Huxham, Mona. *All About the Chihuahua.* Pelham, London.

1979. Dickerson, S. M. *Who's Who in Chihuahuas.*

1980. Johnson, Walter. *Chihuahuas.* Almeda Kennels, Las Cruces, New Mexico.

1983. Pisano, Beverly (Editor). *Chihuahuas.* TFH, New Jersey.

1985. Biala, Karin. *Der Chihuahua.* Cosmos Verlag, Germany.

1986. Gehring, Hugo. *Der Chihuahua.* Müller, Köln.

1988. Nicholas, Anna Katherine. *The Chihuahua.* TFH, New York.

1990. Terry, E. Ruth. *New Chihuahua.* Howell, New York.

1995. Coile, D. Caroline. *Chihuahuas: A Complete Pet Owner's Manual.* Barron, New York.

1996. Sisco, Roberta. *Guide to Owning a Chihuahua: Puppy Care, Grooming, Training, History, Health, Breed Standard.* TFH, New Jersey.

1996. Terry, E. Ruth. *The Chihuahua: An Owner's Guide to a Happy Healthy Pet.*

1999. Mondshine, Marion. *A New Owner's Guide to Chihuahuas.*

1999. Thornton, Kim Campbell. *Your Chihuahua's Life: Your Complete Guide to Raising Your Pet from Puppy to Companion.*

1999. Wilcox, Charlotte. *The Chihuahua.*

2000. Coile, D. Caroline. *The Chihuahua Handbook.* Barron, New York.

Schneider, Earl (Editor). *Know your Chiuhuahua.* Pet Library, New York.

Watson, James, et al. *The Complete Chihuahua.* Howell, New York.

TOY XOLOITZCUINTLI MEXICO

Also known as the Toy Mexican Hairless Dog, this tiny, naked breed was developed in modern times specifically as a companion dog.

This is the smallest of the three types of Xoloitzcuintli. The slightly bigger Miniature and the full-sized Standard versions are both of ancient origin, but this Toy-sized one, measuring less than 12 in (31 cm) at the shoulder and weighing as little as 9 lb (4 kg), was created by the Mexican Kennel Club in the 1950s to provide the perfect hot-country lapdog.

CUBA

HAVANESE CUBA

Also known as the Cuban Shock Dog, the Bichon Havanais, the Havana Silk Dog, the Havana Spaniel, the Havana Bichon or simply the Havana, this breed has been a high-status family pet on the island of Cuba for several centuries.

This long-coated, spitz-tailed, high-spirited little dog was once the pampered favourite of rich Cuban families, especially those living in the capital, Havana, but with the arrival of Castro's Communist regime in 1959, it fell out of favour and became rare on the island.

The breed has been saved for the future by the efforts of the Cuban refugees living in the United States and, through them, by American breeders themselves. The Havanese Club of America was founded to support and protect it, and a survey in the 1980s calculated that there were then about 500 of these dogs registered in the country.

The precise origin of this member of the bichon family is disputed. One view sees it as a descendant of the Bichon Frisé, brought to the West Indies from the Canary Isles by Spanish colonizers. Another view portrays it as arriving from Italy with Italian sea captains and derives it from either the Bolognese or Maltese dogs. A third envisages a more complex beginning, with northern Italian émigrés from Emilia taking Bolognese dogs to Argentina, where they were crossed with some kind of small Poodle. Some of these new companion dogs later found their way to the West Indies and, when they reached Cuba, were developed into what we know today as the Havanese. As yet, there is no hard evidence to decide between these three opinions.

In temperament this is an alert, intelligent, responsive dog which is reported to be unusually non-aggressive when kept in groups of its own kind. It is, however, wary of strangers, and makes a good watchdog.

It is a healthy, long-lived, sturdy breed that is comfortable in a wide range of temperatures. The preferred colour is white, but it also appears in cream, gold, silver, blue, brown and black, and various combinations of these. It has a slightly longer, more tapering muzzle than the other bichon breeds. In height it is only 8–11 in (20–28 cm), and it weighs no more than 7–13 lb (3–6 kg).

BARBADOS

BAJAN TOY TERRIER   BARBADOS

A rare toy breed developed on the Caribbean island of Barbados in the 1960s and 1970s. Weighing in at 8 lb (4 kg), with a smooth, shiny coat, pointed muzzle, pricked ears and a long, plume-tipped tail, this attractive, intelligent little dog was soon breeding true to type. Its coat colour is restricted to a rich honey shade.

In addition to its primary role as a household companion, this active, alert breed is capable of hunting down mice, lizards and frogs and, despite its small size, is prepared to challenge any strangers intruding on its home territory.

Canadian-born residents in Barbados, Mr and Mrs Dusty Miller, are the main champions of this recent breed and were largely instrumental in its creation and development.

PERU

ALCO   PERU

The name of this breed is said to be an ancient Inca word, but there has been some confusion concerning its precise identity.

Writing in the 18th century, Buffon mentioned the existence of a small Peruvian breed of dog called the Alco and later, in 1840, Charles Hamilton Smith gave the breed a whole section to itself, describing it as a little companion dog: 'All writers agree that it is a small animal, kept as a kind of lapdog by the women, and yet occasionally returning to the state of independence.'

By that date of 1840, one example had already been brought to Europe. where its stuffed body had been put on exhibition as a curiosity. That particular individual was illustrated by Smith and was described as having rather a large head, pendulous ears, and long, soft hair on its body. In colour it was 'white, excepting a large black spot covering each ear, and part of the forehead and cheek, with a fulvous mark above each eye, and another black spot on the rump; the tail was rather long, well fringed and white'.

The difficulty with this breed stems from the fact that several authors have identified it as hailing from Mexico. The example sent to Europe was itself 'brought from Mexico' by an enterprising traveller called Mr W. Bullock. It is possible that he acquired it in Peru and then took it to Mexico before shipping it home to England. Unfortunately this led to its being labelled as a Mexican Dog, regardless of the fact that it has an Inca name.

HOUSEHOLD WORKING DOGS

In earlier centuries some breeds of dog were developed specifically to assist with household chores. They have long since vanished, and we know of them now only from old records, drawings and etchings. These breeds have been made redundant by advances in domestic technology, and are usually ignored by modern canine authors, but they were once part of canine history and deserve to be mentioned in any survey that aims to include all breeds of dogs.

In addition to those obsolete breeds, there are some very recent ones which have been developed to fulfil a new type of household duty, such as assisting the deaf or guiding the blind. Most of these duties are carried out by old established breeds, but in a few cases attempts have been made to develop specialized dogs that are uniquely suited to these tasks.

There are ten breeds in this category of household working dog.

ENGLAND
Labrahuahua 577
Turnspit 578
Water Drawer 579

EGYPT
Egyptian Hairless Dog 579

SRI LANKA
Ceylon Hairless Dog 580

CHINA
Manchurian Hairless Dog 580

AUSTRALIA
Labradoodle 581

MEXICO
Izcuintli 581

CENTRAL AMERICA
Mayan Hairless Dog 582

ECUADOR
Ecuadorian Hairless Dog 582

ENGLAND

LABRAHUAHUA ENGLAND

This new breed was created by the charitable organization called 'Hearing Dogs for Deaf People' specifically to act as a canine hearing-aid.

At the end of the 20th century, attempts were made to create the perfect dog to carry out the household duty of assisting people with acute hearing problems. Seeking to combine the placid helpfulness of the typical Labrador with the much smaller body size of the Chihuahua, 'Hearing Dog' staff decided to try crossing these two breeds. This was achieved by providing a male Chihuahua with a platform, from which it could mount a female Labrador. The platform consisted of two large bags of dog biscuits.

The six puppies resulting from this cross are being used as the foundation stock of a new breed which the organization hopes to establish. They report that: 'The Labrahuahuas are very sociable, alert, willing to please, affectionate pups... they are looking very promising at this stage.'

It remains to be seen whether this cross can be refined to create a genuinely useful, new type of dog. If these miniature Labradors (or Giant Chihuahuas, depending on your point of view) breed true and do not experience throw-back problems, with tiny bitches struggling to give birth to huge puppies, the experiment may work, producing small companions with ideal temperaments for the household duties demanded of Hearing Dogs.

Inevitably, the traditionalists were outraged at this 'corruption' of their favoured breeds. Chihuahua specialists have been quoted as saying: 'The experiments have to be stopped immediately. We are horrified that our breed is involved.'

The charity's response to these comments was to point out that there is an increasing requirement for 'small dogs to meet the demand from elderly and disabled people with special needs'. And they emphasized that, in order to obtain the ideal dog for this work, they were careful to take veterinary advice when deciding which parent breeds to employ, to give them the best chance of creating 'a small dog that is willing to please, sociable and tolerant to sound'.

TURNSPIT ENGLAND

The now extinct Turnspit is recorded in the very first English dog book, in 1576, where it is called the Turnespete. This ancient breed also has the distinction of having been included in Linnaeus's 18th-century classification of dogs, where it is listed as the Canis vertigus. Buffon refers to it as the Basset à Jambes Torses. Other names include the Kitchen Dog and the Vernepator. It was a small working dog that was employed to run in a wheel, for the purpose of turning meat that was roasting before a fire.

The Turnspit was a household breed that was in great demand prior to the 19th century. Writing in 1809, the Revd Bingley remarks: 'It is now on the decline and, in the course of another century, will probably be extinct in Great Britain.' With the advent of the Industrial Revolution, and the arrival of efficient mechanical devices, its demise was more rapid than he anticipated.

In pre-industrial days, large kitchens usually kept several Turnspits, so that they could act as a team, replacing one another in the wheel as each tired. According to one early observer, 'they take their hours for labour in regular rotation'. And it appears that they came to recognize certain days as 'roasting days' and were reluctant to work at other times. Some individual dogs were so keen to do their work that they would jump into the wheel of their own accord, while others would hide themselves away on roast days, and had to be encouraged to take to the drudgery of their task. Bearing in mind that, in those days, a large family roast, turning constantly on the spit, took three hours to cook, it is clear that the labours of the kitchen Turnspits were arduous. Some observers reported that these little dogs were often ill-treated by the cooks and that 'the poor turnspit performs his task by compulsion, like a culprit on a tread-wheel, subject to scolding or beating if he stops for a moment to rest his weary limbs'.

From the early depictions of the Turnspit that are left to us, it is clear that this was a dark, short-legged, long-bodied little dog with drooping ears and an erect, curled tail. Its front legs were often said to be crooked, but this may have been purely occupational. According to Bewick, it often had odd-coloured eyes, 'the iris of one eye black, and the other white'. As they were regarded as a lowly breed, little or nothing has been recorded about their ancestry or their relation to other dogs. One author, writing in 1874, describes them as 'nearer to the terriers than any thing else' and that is probably as close as we will ever get to understanding their lineage.

WATER DRAWER   ENGLAND

We know nothing about this extinct breed other than its role in life, which was to assist with the drawing of water from the well. For this duty a large, powerful dog was developed.

In his classic work *Of Englishe Dogges*, published in 1576, Johannes Caius has this to say of them: 'This kind of dog is also called, in Latin, Aquarius; in English, a Water Drawer. And these be of the greater and weightier sort, drawing water out of wells and deep pits, by a wheel which they turn round about, by moving of their burthenous bodies.'

EGYPT

EGYPTIAN HAIRLESS DOG   EGYPT

This extinct breed was reputedly employed for healing purposes in the households of ancient Egypt.

This was a close relative of the African Sand Dog (see separate entry) and may, indeed, have been its ancestor. Like several other hairless dogs, it was used as a cure for aches and pains, probably by a direct application of its hot-skinned body to the troubled part. It also played a secondary role as a household companion dog, and, as a talismanic animal, it was thought to bring good luck to its owner.

The Egyptian Hairless was a small dog, standing only about 16 in (41 cm) in height. It had drooped ears, long feet, and a smooth, naked skin which was spotted or blotched with dark markings, contrasting with its white, cream or light grey background colour.

Little is known about the personality or behaviour of this dog, except that it disliked getting wet and spent a great deal of its time resting in small hollows which it dug out of the sandy soil.

In 1833 the London Zoo received some small naked dogs that were labelled as Egyptian Hairless Dogs, but these clearly belonged to a separate breed, having unblotched skin and tall, pricked ears. They are discussed in the entry for the African Sand Dog.

SRI LANKA

CEYLON HAIRLESS DOG   SRI LANKA

This breed was employed for medicinal purposes. Superstitious rural communities believed that the dog had the power to relieve pain if it was held against the aching part of the sufferer's body.

A now extinct breed, the Ceylon Hairless Dog was employed as a 'heat pad' to relieve localized aches and pains. The naked skin of all hairless dogs is remarkably hot to the touch and some of the edible breeds (see entry for Xoloitzcuintli) also had a secondary use as 'healers', or simply as 'hot-water bottles' on cold nights. In the case of the Ceylon Hairless Dog, however, this appears to have been its only function, there being no evidence that it was ever employed as a food source.

This slender breed is said to have resembled a Whippet in shape. Its height was 19 in (48 cm). Like the Chinese Crested, it was not entirely naked, having tufts of hair on the feet and the tip of the tail, in addition to a crest. The ears were semi-erect.

Local superstitions made a distinction between light-coloured dogs and dark ones. A light individual was thought to bring bad luck to any household it entered, other than that of its owner. A dark individual was believed to be the most effective at healing.

CHINA

MANCHURIAN HAIRLESS DOG   MANCHURIA

This little-known breed is employed in the cold north-eastern region of China as a household bed-warmer.

The naked, hot-skinned Manchurian Hairless Dog is favoured in the more remote districts of northern China as a means of keeping warm at night. Held against the body as a living hot-water-bottle, it provides comfort to its owners in their bitterly cold environment.

This is a short-nosed dog with a domed head. Its smooth skin is flesh- or copper-coloured and it has a short crest of white hair on its head and neck. In addition, there is thick hair on much of its tail and on its unusually long feet. Its height is 18–20 in (46–51 cm). It appears to be a close relative of the Chinese Crested dog (see separate entry).

AUSTRALIA

LABRADOODLE AUSTRALIA

Known affectionately as the Doodle, this new breed was first developed specifically as a companion for the blind.

Some of the new experimental breeds are no more than a breeder's whim and have little serious thought behind them, but this is certainly not the case with the Labradoodle. Despite its comical name, it came into being for a serious purpose. It was first developed in Australia in the 1980s, by Wally Conron of the Australian Guide Dog Association, who was trying to create a guide dog that could be used by blind people who suffered from allergies to canine hair. By crossing a Standard

Poodle with a Labrador trained as a guide dog, it was hoped to produce a dog that would have the non-shedding curly coat of the Poodle combined with the obedience and steady temperament of the Labrador. It is early days yet to be certain, but the indications are that the combination works well, although more breeding is necessary to fix the new type.

MEXICO

IZCUINTLI MEXICO

The ancient name of this breed translates simply as 'dog'. It has sometimes been spelt Izucuintli, or Izucuiltly. Its household duties are mystical rather than physical. A rare breed, it is kept in village houses in a talismanic role, to bring the owners of the properties good fortune.

Although this little-known breed is nearly extinct, it is claimed that examples can still be found in the region around the town of Rio Balsas, located in the mountainous state of Guerrero, roughly halfway between Acapulco and Mexico City.

This is one of the naked dogs, a close relative of the Xoloitzcuintli, or Mexican Hairless Dog, but with a longer crest of coarse hair on top of the head. Its height is about 18 in (46 cm) and it has semi-pricked ears. The slightly wrinkled skin is typically slate grey in colour, with a few pale blotches.

CENTRAL AMERICA

MAYAN HAIRLESS DOG   CENTRAL AMERICA

It has been claimed that this ancient, hot-skinned breed, sometimes called the Mayas Hairless Dog, was used as a 'heat pad' to relieve the aches and pains of its owners.

This extinct dog was said to be popular at the end of the first millennium AD, when it was employed by the Mayans as a living hot-water bottle. A smallish dog, with a height of only about 15–16 in (38–41 cm), it is known largely from clay effigies which show an animal that is not as fat as the local edible dogs, nor as large as the local hunting dogs. The skin is depicted as being of a light colour, with some wrinkling, and with tufts of hair on the head, feet and tail-tip.

ECUADOR

ECUADORIAN HAIRLESS DOG   ECUADOR

This hairless breed is employed as a household healer, to reduce discomfort when its owners are suffering from aches and pains, by applying its hot-skinned body to the trouble spot.

This is one of the rarest of the hairless dogs and also the most naked-skinned of them all, retaining only a few short hairs on its flat-topped head. Its golden-coloured skin is exceptionally soft and smooth. This is an elegant, long-legged animal with elongated, slender feet. It lacks premolar teeth. In height, it ranges from 15 to 18 in (38 to 46 cm).

In Ecuador, this dog is found in its pure form only in remote villages, and even there it is far from common. According to one authority it was originally developed from crosses between the Inca Orchid Dog from Peru, to the south, and the smaller form of the Xoloitzcuintli, from Mexico, to the north.

EDIBLE DOGS

As with horses, man's first interest in dogs was as a source of food. Of course, in those prehistoric days, there were no domestic dog breeds, only wild wolves and their cubs. But some of the cubs that were brought back to primitive settlements to be fattened for the pot probably endeared themselves to their owners sufficiently to be allowed to stay on as camp guardians. From this point onwards, the story of the multi-talented, domesticated wolf we now call 'the dog' unfolded. In a dozen different ways these early canine companions became specialized for specific roles and duties, and for many people their original function as part of the food supply was forgotten. They were too useful now in other capacities. They had become friends and partners and the idea of eating them was repugnant.

There were, however, exceptions to this rule. Wherever animal protein was in short supply, the ancient custom of eating dog flesh persisted and several breeds were created and improved specifically with this in mind. Today these are mostly rare or extinct, but a few still survive, even though they have long ago been removed from the human menu.

There are 16 breeds in this category.

CHINA

CHOW CHOW

CHINA

The Chow Chow was supposedly named after the pidgin-English expression used to cover all the small items being added to a sailing ship's cargo (in the 18th century). It other words, it means 'etcetera'. A rival theory suggests that the word 'chow' is derived from the Cantonese for 'edible' and it has also been called the Food Dog, the Edible Dog, the Chinese Edible Dog, the Chow Kow, the Chinese Spitz, the Cantonese Butcher-dog and simply the Chow. Its Chinese names included Lang Kou (Wolf Dog), Hsiung Kou (Bear Dog), Hei She-T'ou (Black-tongued), Kwantung Kou (Dog of Canton) and simply Wonk, meaning 'dog'. A short-haired version was known as the Smooth-coated Chow Chow, or the Shan Dog. A colloquial name for the breed, in the past, has been the Teddy Bear Dog. In early China, the Chow was an important source of food, but it also acted as a guard dog, a hunting dog and a traction dog.

The extraordinary Chow has the mane of a lion, the tongue of a bear, the fur coat of a dowager, and the stiff gait of a ceremonial guardsman. It is one of the most unusual of all breeds but unfortunately little is known about its origins. One theory sees it as arising from crosses between Tibetan Mastiffs and Samoyeds, but this would not explain its unique black tongue. Another view sees it as representing an extremely ancient, ancestral breed from which all other spitz dogs have descended.

The first Chows to arrive in Britain appeared in 1780. In his famous work *The Natural History of Selborne*, Gilbert White records the fact that a pair of Chinese dogs with an awkward gait, bristling coat and black eyes, lips and tongues, were brought home by a member of the East India Company as curiosities. They did not catch on, however, and were still viewed as oddities in 1828, when the London Zoo recorded the arrival of some 'Wild dogs of China' called the Black-mouthed Chinese. Their status only rose when Queen Victoria acquired one, after which their popularity was assured. They were first shown in the United States in 1890 and were recognized as a true breed by the Kennel Club in London in 1894.

In its homeland, in earlier days, the Chow Chow was used as an important source of food in a protein-starved culture. Those destined for the table were kept in special enclosures, fed on an all-grain diet and butchered when young and tender. Their pelts provided fur-coat trimmings. The first reports received in the West about this unusual dog indicated that supplying meat for human consumption was its main role, and the breed was first shown in Britain (in 1870) as 'The Edible Dog'. We now know, however, that it had several other important duties as well. These included, not only guarding the home, the caravans, the junks and the sanpans, but also accompanying hunters, pulling sleds and guarding the flocks. And it was frequently given an important part to play in the cultural life of China. One Tang Emperor, for example, who lived in the 8th century AD, is reputed to have maintained a kennel complex that housed no fewer than 5,000 Chows, attended by 10,000 huntsmen.

The Chow's personality has been described as aloof, independent, detached and strong-willed. It is sensitive to rebuke, restrained with its affections and disapproving of strangers. Like most dogs, however, it is fiercely loyal to its owners. It is perhaps the least playful, most serious-minded of all dog breeds, another reason for seeing it as being close to an ancestral form.

References

1906. Lindley, Samuel. *Chow Chows.* Woffenden's, Huddersfield.

1914. Dunbar of Mochrum, Lady N. *The Chow Chow.* Pitman, London.

1926. Dietrich, Edith L. and Davies, L. Mae. *The Chow Chow. A Complete Book of Guidance and Information Regarding the Chow Dog.* Judy, Chicago.

1928. Leighton, Robert and Baer, Mrs W. S. *The Popular Chow Chow.* Popular Dogs, London.

1932. Johns, Rowland (Editor). *Our Friend the Chow Chow.* Methuen, London.

1933. Judy, Will. *The Chow Chow.* Judy, Chicago.

1954. Ingeton, Lydia and Rybot, Doris. *The Popular Chow Chow.* Popular Dogs, London.

1959. Collett, C. E. *The Chow Chow for the Novice Breeder and Exhibitor.* Nicholas Vane, London.

1965. Burrows, E. A. *The Early History of the English Chow.* Privately published, Bournemouth.

1965. Shryock, Clifford. *How to Raise and Train a Chow Chow.* TFH, New Jersey.

1975. Green. *The Chow Chow.*

1977. Draper, Samuel and Brearley, Joan McDonald. *The Book of the Chow Chow.* TFH, New Jersey.

1980. Pisano, Beverly. *Chow Chows.* TFH, New Jersey.

1985. Nicholas, Anna Katherine. *Guide to Owning a Chow Chow.* TFH, New Jersey.

1988. Atkinson, James. *Chow-Chows.* Barron, New York.

1988. Kopatch, L. J. Kip. *The Complete Chow Chow.* Howell, New York.

1989. Phillips, Diana. *A Dog Owner's Guide to the Chow Chow.* Tetra Press, Blacksburg, Virginia.

1992. Draper, Samuel and Brearley, Joan M. *The World of the Chow Chow.*

1995. Banghart, Love. *Proper Care of Chow Chows.* TFH, New Jersey.

1996. Braun, Paulett. *An Owner's Guide to the Pet Chow Chow.* Howell, New York.

1999. Wilcox, Charlotte. *The Chow Chow.*

KOREA

NOO-RUNG-YEE   KOREA

The Korean name of this breed means literally 'yellow dog'. The breed is also known as the Korean Edible Dog.

Every year, millions of dogs are tortured to death by Korean butchers. The method of killing is made as painful as possible for the animals because it is believed that this will improve the taste of their flesh when it is served in Korean restaurants. It is estimated that about a quarter of the Korean population consumes dog meat, despite the fact that this practice has resulted in most people in the Western world looking upon Korea as a barbaric, uncivilized country.

Compared with Korea's National Treasure, the carefully protected Jindo, the Edible Dog has a larger frame with more flesh on its bones. Its ears are drooping rather than pricked like the Jindo's.

These dogs are specifically raised for meat, but before they are killed, they may be expected to act as general-purpose house guards. Despite the recent introduction of foreign breeds, the Edible Dog has kept true to its type. This is said to be because Korean dog-eaters do not like the taste of foreign dogs and wish to keep their food-breed pure for the table. Cross-breeding is therefore avoided.

It should be added that there are strong moves afoot within Korea to outlaw dog-eating and that many Koreans are outraged by what takes place.

PHILIPPINES

PHILIPPINES EDIBLE DOG   PHILIPPINES

Also known as the Philippines Islands Dog or the Philippines Native Dog, this breed was considered to be a special food delicacy, although it was employed for other duties as well.

Philippine farmers used this dog as a valuable aid in controlling their other livestock, but ultimately their only way of showing their gratitude for this work was to fatten the dogs up, kill them, stuff them with rice, seasoning and spices, and then roast them over wood embers. Their flesh was said to be delicate and delicious, yet it seems a strange way to repay a lifetime of canine friendship and hard labour. But as a nation the Filipinos have never been accused of excessive sentimentality.

The Philippine centre for dog-eating was Northern Luzon, where the Igorot tribe were the breed specialists, developing a short-coated dog that bred to type and looked like a primitive form of smooth-coated terrier.

In recent years, there has been great controversy in the Philippines concerning the continued widespread practice of dog-eating, including the barbaric custom of beating the animals slowly to death (because this was believed to improve the taste of the meat). Despite vigorous attempts to stamp out these activities, they have continued almost unabated. At one stage, Madame Imelda Marcos insisted on outlawing the custom, but when her husband, the president, was overthrown, her influence was lost and the problem remained. In 1998 an Animal Welfare Act to ban dog-eating was passed by the Philippines government, but it is widely ignored and thousands of diners devour dog dishes at restaurants every night.

SUMATRA

BATAK DOG SUMATRA

Also known as the Battak Dog, the Batak Spitz, the Sumatran Battak, or the Sumatraanse Batakhond, this breed has three roles to play in the lives of the tribal Batak people of northern Sumatra — as a source of food, as a guard and as a pack-hunter.

Roast Batak Dog is a highly prized dish and its sweet-tasting flesh is said to be considered a great delicacy. Rather unusually, the animals are cooked in their own blood. In addition to their culinary use, these dogs are employed as sentinels and as hunting companions. Living in small, tribal communities, they are unused to newcomers and are unduly shy and retiring with visitors. They spend a great deal of time inside the tribal huts, which often have to be reached by climbing ladders that may be up to 15 ft (4.5 m) in height — a difficult task for any dog.

The modern Batak people are the descendants of the notorious Sumatran headhunters — the cannibals who used to curse their enemies with the phrase 'I pick the flesh of your relatives from between my teeth'. The punishment for adultery, theft, incest or murder was to be eaten by the other members of your village. For serious crimes you were eaten alive. With the coming of Christianity and Islam, these human items were struck off the Batak menu, but they continued to devour their dogs, despite the fact that this practice was considered repulsive by non-Batak Sumatrans.

This is a small, spitzy, short-necked, curly-tailed dog, with a tough, compact body. Its short coat appears in a variety of colours including red-and-black, grey-and-black, all black, brown, brindle, or yellow-and-white. In personality it is active and intelligent. As a watchdog it is timid but watchful. When used for hunting it often has its tail docked and one of its ears cropped.

There is a curious anomaly in some recent reference works, where, in addition to the Sumatran Batak Dog, there are entries for a breed called the Batak Spitz. This is described as a 'medium-sized hunting and watchdog of Africa', but few details are given. Since there are no Bataks in Africa and the Batak tribes are restricted solely to northern Sumatra, it would appear that an error has occurred here and that the Batak Spitz is simply another name for the Sumatran breed. How it acquired an African label is unclear.

NEW ZEALAND

KURI NEW ZEALAND

Also known as the Guri, the Maori Dog or the New Zealand Native Dog, the most important use of this breed was as a sacrificial offering, although it was also eaten at other times.

This now extinct breed was taken to New Zealand in AD 900 by colonizing Maori people, and its remains have been found in archaeological sites from that period onwards. The dogs were allowed to eat the left-overs of fish at Maori settlements, but their hunger also took them into the wilds where they found indigenous species unused to advanced predators. Local lizards, frogs and ground birds, including the unusual New Zealand parrot, the Kakapo, were easy prey for them. The Kuri thrived in New Zealand until the arrival of the later, European settlers, who brought with them a variety of European dogs. Then, uncontrolled interbreeding took place and by the end of the 19th century it was impossible to find a pure-bred native dog anywhere in the country.

Descriptions of the Kuri by visiting Europeans were remarkably consistent over a period of 80 years, confirming that it constituted a genuine breed. It was a moderate-sized animal, weighing about 35 lb (16 kg), with shortish legs, prick ears, a sharp, pointed snout, a bushy spitz tail and a short, white coat with black markings. Like other Pacific dogs it did not bark, but was known to howl.

Its image appears in early rock paintings and in wood carvings, indicating that it was of some significance to the first settlers. This is confirmed by reports that the Maoris ritually killed these dogs for their flesh when preparing sacred dishes on special occasions. According to Captain Cook, their flesh tasted like freshly killed lamb. A study of bones in ancient settlements has revealed that 40 per cent of the native dogs were killed when immature – in other words, when their flesh was tender. So it would seem that, in addition to sacrificial dishes, they were also probably on the menu for everyday meals as well.

The Maori were not wasteful, making good use of almost every bit of their dogs. In addition to eating their meat, they wore their skins as cloak decorations, used the long hairs from their bushy tails to ornament their spearheads, and fashioned their bones into spear-points, awls and fish-hooks. And the living Kuri were also co-opted for the secondary function of guarding property.

HAWAII

POI DOG   HAWAII

This breed is also known as the Hawaiian Poi Dog or the Ilio. It was originally a dog used exclusively for food, but is now extinct.

Many food dogs were allowed to exist as lively, active companions before they were eventually culled and cooked. With Poi Dogs there was a different tradition. They were kept by the Hawaiian islanders, not as alert, athletic animals, but as fat, short-legged,

waddling, pig-like livestock. It is true that infants were allowed to keep the puppies as pets and the children's mothers were even known to suckle the little animals, but when the dogs grew larger they were treated more as commodities. They achieved their bloated shape by being overfed on a meat-free diet of breadfruit and a granular paste called 'poi', which consisted of ground, baked and fermented taro root. Their flesh was considered to be a special delicacy and they were usually offered as a gourmet dish to important visitors when there were celebratory feasts.

The Poi Dog is thought to have arrived on the islands with the Polynesians about 1,000 years ago. Captain Cook reported seeing the breed when he visited Hawaii in 1779. According to official sources, it has been extinct for 200 years. When it was on the verge of disappearing, at the beginning of the 19th century, the Honolulu Zoo made a valiant attempt to save it from extinction, continuing their efforts for over a decade, but eventually gave up the struggle. It has been claimed that today there are fresh attempts to 'reconstruct' it, but anyone hearing of a Poi Dog for sale should be warned that in the relaxed atmosphere of the modern Hawaiian Islands, any mongrel may be referred to fondly as a 'Poi Dog'. This is not to mislead, but is simply a nod in the direction of early island traditions.

NORTH AMERICA/CARIBBEAN

LARGE INDIAN DOG   NORTH AMERICA/CARIBBEAN

This has also been called the Common Indian Dog because it was found over such vast areas of North America during the heyday of the native tribes, before the coming of the Europeans. It was used as an important source of food, but it did also have several other functions.

This dog was first observed in 1492 by Columbus and was written about in some detail by the Spanish explorer Oviedo in 1535. He described it as the 'regular fare' of the Caribbean Indians and he himself dined on it, saying that it tasted like lamb. He even described the method of preparing it, reporting that the dogs were 'split along the spine and roasted on one side.' In times of plenty, dog flesh was considered a great luxury, usually reserved for great feasts, presumably because the animals were valued for their other uses. But in times of deprivation, they were widely eaten without such reservations.

Studies by Indian dog experts such as William Pferd have revealed that the Large Indian Dog was eaten by most of the native tribes of the sub-Arctic, the eastern woodland, the south-east and the Caribbean, but this breed was also employed by some tribes as hunting companions and as beasts of burden. In appearance it looked rather like a slender wolf, with a coat that was either black, white, black-and-white or reddish brown.

MEXICO

COLIMA DOG
MEXICO

The Colima Dog is known only from finely polished ceramic works that were made between AD 300 and AD 600 in north-west Mexico. All these carefully fashioned, hollow pottery figures show the same type of dog, a short-legged, pot-bellied, prick-eared breed, with no sign of any coat, suggesting that it was almost certainly a hairless dog. It is known that these animals were deliberately fattened as a delicacy and that their main, if not sole, function was as a food source. It is reported that the Aztecs, Tarascans and Mayas, as well as the Colima people, all enjoyed eating dog meat. According to one archaeologist, 'puppy-dog roast was regarded as a delicacy fit for kings'. Another comments that they were 'specially fattened for consumption by forced feeding like Strasbourg geese', although it is not clear how this was discovered. The many ceramic dogs found in the tombs were probably placed there to provide a succulent meal on the long journey to the afterlife.

The anatomy of these beautifully crafted dog figurines is remarkably consistent, and it is clear that the legs of these early dogs were much shorter than those of today's living Mexican Hairless Dogs. Either they belong to a distinctly different breed, or they are all meant to represent young puppies. Although puppies would be more succulent as food, some of the figurines show more 'juvenile' individuals than others. This suggests that the Colima Dog was, indeed, a different breed with shorter legs, and this view is strengthened by the fact that even very young puppies of the Mexican Hairless Dog have longer legs than those of the little Colima animals.

IZCUINTLIPOTZOTLI
MEXICO

In Spanish this breed is known as the Perro Jorobado, or Hunchbacked Dog. Its ancient name has the same meaning (izcuintli means dog and potzotli means hunchback). Alternative spellings are Izcuintepozotli or Ytzcuinte Porzotli. It is thought to have been bred purely as a source of food.

This extinct breed would easily have won any contest to find the ugliest dogs in the world. Grossly misshapen animals, they were ritualistically buried with their owners, presumably to supply convenient food for them on the long journey to the afterlife.

This unusual dog was first described by the Spanish author Francisco Javier Clavijero. Writing in 1780 he recorded that it was 'the size of a Maltese Terrier' and that its skin was covered in white, black and brown spots. This suggests a naked dog or one with a very short coat. It had a small head with a prominent nose-ridge, drooped ears, a short thick neck, a heavy, lumpy body and a short tail. It was found in the Tarascan region of Michoacán, on the west coast of what is now Mexico. The last sighting of it was in 1843, when Madame Calderón de la Barca saw a dead one hanging from a hook at an inn about 30 miles (48 km) north of Mexico City. She described it as 'a species of dog, with a hunchback, a head like a wolf and no neck, a perfect monster'.

It is the only known example of a dog breed with a humped back, and it may be significant that, among the ancient pottery remains of the region, there are also clay effigies of human hunchbacks. If these individuals had some special, magical significance, it is possible that the dogs were bred in imitation of their condition.

TECHICHI   MEXICO AND THE AMERICAS

Also known as the Small Indian Dog, this breed was primarily used as a source of food by Indian tribes in the Pre-Columbian Americas. Its Indian name is sometimes given as Techici. It has also been called the Carrier Dog, although acting as a beast of burden does not appear to have been one of its regular duties.

A slender, small-headed, sharp-nosed, fox-like little dog, the Techichi extended its range into both North and South America, although Mexico seems to have been its stronghold. It was common among the native tribes of the east coast of North America, right across the southernmost parts, down into Central America and even into north-western South America.

The first European to encounter the Techichi was the Spanish explorer Francisco Hernandez, who reported its existence in 1578. He commented that the native Americans ate them as commonly as his own people ate rabbits. In other words, they were not specially reserved for sacrificial ritual or celebratory feasting, but were everyday food items. The Spaniards themselves, as they investigated the New World, were frequently short of meat and ate dog flesh whenever they had the chance. It has been estimated that at least 100,000 Techichis must have been consumed by them during their expeditions. Not surprisingly, later travellers found few of these dogs, and by the 19th century they appear to have vanished altogether.

The breeding of these dogs for food seems to have been well organized by the indigenous tribes. Certain stud males and brood females were kept to produce as many litters as possible and young males that were destined to be eaten were castrated to make them grow fat, to provide as much flesh as possible. The puppies were used as playthings for the tribal children.

In colour, the dogs' coats varied from brown, brown-and-white and black-and-white, to black. Their pricked ears were sometimes cropped close to the head, but their tails were left in the natural state.

XOLOITZCUINTLI   MEXICO

This breed, also known as the Standard Mexican Hairless Dog, is more usually called by its ancient name of Xoloitzcuintli. In the Nahuatl tongue, this complex word (pronounced sholo-its-quintli) meant 'dog of the god Xolotl'. Xolotl was the Aztec god of twins, of things which are deformed, and of the Aztec ball-court game. It has also been called the Pelon, or Bald Dog. Breeders usually refer to it simply as the Xolo (pronounced sholo). Its primary function in ancient times was as a source of food.

This ugly but strangely appealing breed, with the dark, mottled, wrinkled skin of a shrunken elephant, has a confusing history. Many authors, including even the Mexicans themselves, have tried to relate it to the other naked dog breeds in Asia, Africa and else-where. They postulate arrivals from the Far East or the European West but without the slightest shred of hard evidence to support their views. In reality, it is much more likely that the hairless gene has cropped up as a mutation independently in different parts of the world at different times. We know from ancient artefacts that the Colima Dog from western Mexico was available locally as a precursor for the modern Xoloitzcuintli, long before any Europeans arrived on the scene. And it is highly unlikely that naked dogs would have survived the long trek down from the freezing north in the company of the earliest Asiatic settlers of the Americas. So it is best at present to call this breed a local Mexican mutation – an indigenous dog with very early origins.

As an important source of protein, this 'oven-ready' dog was of great value to the early tribal peoples. But it had other functions in addition to providing food. Its naked skin is hot to the touch and this feature also gave it a secondary role as a healer. Pressing the warm animal next to a part of the body that was hurting was believed to 'draw out' the pain. It was said to be especially useful for curing headaches, asthma, rheumatism, aching muscles, insomnia and even malaria. In addition, for healthy people, it made a useful hot-water bottle on cold nights and a protective, ever-alert watchdog.

Its body is not entirely bereft of hair. There are sparse tufts on the top of the head and the lower part of the tail. And in every litter of naked pups there is usually one with a full coat – a so-called 'powder-puff' dog. A weakness of the breed, apart from the fact that it cannot stand extreme heat or cold, or bright sunlight, is the reduced dentition. It seems as if the gene that removed most of the hair also removes many of the teeth, especially in the molar region of the jaws.

Surprisingly the breed was first exhibited at a dog show as early as 1883 – in the United States. But it remained extremely rare and by 1959 the AKC had removed it from its list of recognized breeds. It was not until the 1980s that it at last began to grow in popularity. There are now serious attempts being made to ensure its survival, not only in the United States and Mexico but also in Europe.

In personality it is a calm, dignified, obedient, sensitive animal. It is intelligent, but may not demonstrate this too freely because it is also rather wary of strangers. If one can accept its wrinkled, naked appearance, it has several special advantages as a companion, namely that it is flealess and odourless, and does not cause the allergic responses found with most hairy dogs.

References

1920. Allen, Glover W. 'Dogs of the American Aborígenes.' *Bulletin of the Museum of Comparative Zoology.* Harvard University, Cambridge, Massachusetts.

1945. Fernández de Córdoba, Joaquin. *Los Perros pre-Colombinos de América.* Revista 'El Hijo Prodigo', Mexico.

1960. Wright, Norman Pelham. *El Enigma del Xoloitzcuintli.* Instituto Nacional del Antropología e Historia, Córdoba, Mexico.

1997. Anon. *El Xoloitzcuintle en la Historia de Mexico.* Museo Dolores Olmedo Patiño.

MINIATURE XOLOITZCUINTLI   MEXICO

Also known as the Miniature Mexican Hairless Dog, or the Tepeizcuintli, this dog differs only in size from its larger relative.

The Xoloitzcuintli is now recognized in three sizes: the Standard, which is above 18 in (46 cm) at the shoulder; the Miniature, which is 13–18 in (33–46 cm); and the Toy, which is below 13 in (33 cm). The Toy is a recent breed created in the 1950s specifically as a modern lapdog; the Standard is the full-sized animal, descended from ancient stock, and the Miniature is simply a reduced version of this, being about the size of a small terrier. It weighs 13–22 lb (6–10 kg), and has come into existence as a breed simply because, originally, size was not a controlled feature. There was a whole range of different-sized hairless dogs, with no pressure to breed for a specific weight. Then, when interest in pure-breeding these dogs grew, it was a natural development to categorize them into different types and, from then on, to keep them separate. The Mexican

Kennel Club recognized the Standard and the Miniature as distinct breeds in 1956.

All three sizes of Xoloitzcuintli remain rare and it has been estimated that, even taking the three sizes together, there are fewer than 500 of them in existence in the world today.

PERU

PERUVIAN HAIRLESS DOG   PERU

Also known as the Perro sin Pelo del Peru, or the Inca Hairless Dog, this was originally the same breed as the Peruvian Inca Orchid. Its original function was as a source of meat.

This breed differs from the Peruvian Inca Orchid largely in its colour, which is uniformly dark instead of mottled. Because of the dense pigment in its skin, this naked animal was better protected from the sun than the pale Peruvian Inca Orchid, and was allowed outside during daylight hours. The two kinds were known as the daytime dog and the night-time dog.

In its earliest days, when its flesh was eaten, the colour of its skin was obviously of little importance, and this dog and the Peruvian Inca Orchid would then have been a single breed. When they were taken over by the Inca nobility and became high-status pets, their appearance did begin to matter and it was probably then that the two types – light and dark – were developed and eventually kept separate as distinct breeds.

The Peruvian Hairless is similar to the Mexican Hairless, but it is not known whether they are closely related or whether their naked genes arose independently. Every author who has considered this problem has automatically assumed that there must have been one primary source for all hairless dogs and that they were then taken from this location, across the globe, to widely different sites. But it is just as likely – probably more likely – that the hairless mutation arose separately on a number of occasions, and that the Peruvian Hairless Dogs were indigenous to Peru.

PERUVIAN INCA ORCHID   PERU

This hairless breed is also known as the Moonflower Dog, the Inca Moonflower Dog, the Perro Flora, the Inca Orchid Dog, the Peruvian Inca Orchid, or the Perro sin Pelo del Peru. It is often referred to simply as the PIO. Its ancient name in the Quecha language was 'Caa-alleppo' or 'Caa-allego' ('dog without clothes'). Additional names include Chien Nu du Pérou, Peruanischer Nackthund, Perunkarvatonkoira and Peruaanse Haarloze Hond. It began life as a food dog, but was later adopted as a high-status companion dog of the Inca nobility.

Although this breed is called an 'Inca Dog', it was known long before it became a favourite of the Inca nobles. Like most hairless dogs, its original function was to provide dog meat. In ancient Peru the inhabitants of the regional kingdom of Huanca were so greedy for dog flesh that they were known as the 'dog-eaters' and their most important feasts were dog banquets. When they went to war they blew on horns made of dogs' heads. After these brutal Huancas (who skinned their prisoners alive and used their pelts to make drum-skins) were subjugated by the Incas in 1460, they were forbidden to exploit dogs and were told to make their horns out of the heads of deer instead.

The powerful Incas almost certainly acquired their hairless dogs from these defeated dog-eaters and carried the little animals home as treasured, protected pets. Unlike the Huancas, the Inca nobility were disgusted by the idea of eating dog flesh and looked upon the hairless dogs as their friends, admiring them for their pale, mottled skin. The paler the skin, the more they valued the dog. The delicate animals were kept in darkened, orchid-filled rooms and only exercised at night, hence the alternative name of Moonflower Dog.

When the Inca empire collapsed, these dogs became extremely rare, but the breed never vanished completely and is still kept in small numbers in Peru even today. In the 20th century, examples have been exported to both North America and Europe, although it has never become a common breed anywhere.

A calm and intelligent little dog, it is lacking in any aggression and is highly sensitive. Its delicate, light-boned body exhibits several defects. Not only is its skin prone to various ailments, but its teeth also suffer from weaknesses that often need attention. From time to time, there are hair-covered individuals in the litters and these are retained for breeding purposes, as they do not suffer from dental deficiencies and help to keep the breed stable.

PERUVIAN PUG-NOSED DOG PERU

The Pug-nosed Dog is a third breed from ancient Peru, but unlike the other two this one has long been extinct. Judging by the plump, rounded shape of its effigies, it was probably used as food, but we cannot be certain of that.

We can tell from the analysis of tomb contents that this was a small dog with a yellowish-white coat bearing dark patches, a fat body and a flattened 'bulldog' face. It has been recorded from burial sites in the Peruvian highlands and from the central coastal region of Chancay. Its remains were first encountered by archaeologists in 1885. Its short, pug-nosed skull astonished its finders, who could not understand how its ancestors — assumed to be European flat-faced dogs — could have been brought to South America several centuries before the Spanish discovery of the New World. The answer, almost certainly, is that the flat-face gene arose independently in Europe and in Peru.

What *is* surprising, however, is that the flattening was so extreme. Chancay pottery effigies of these dogs, dating from the 11th–13th century AD, reveal a skin-wrinkled face that is as squashed as that of a modern Pekingese. In fact, this extreme facial type is from such an early epoch that it may well have pre-dated the flat-faced dogs of other regions, rather than have been one of their descendants.

It is not known for certain when (or if) these little dogs became extinct. There is a faint possibility that a few of them may still exist in a remote corner of modern Peru. If so, it would be extremely interesting to study them and to compare them in detail with the flat-faced breeds from other continents.

BOLIVIA

KHALA   BOLIVIA

Khala (sometimes given as Kala or Ccala) is a Bolivian Quecha Indian name which means simply 'naked'.

This breed differs little from the Peruvian hairless breeds. Its ancestors were imported into Bolivia from Peru and became popular there, being adopted as a 'national breed'. However, the Peruvian canine expert Tullio Peschiera Magnani, of Lima, believes that 'all American hairless dogs should be called "PreColumbian Hairless Dogs", because they all have the same origin, and the different names are due to geographic and linguistic differences'.

At the end of the 20th century, following Magnani's suggestion, American breeders of hairless dogs that originated in Latin America decided to lump them together under a new name and chose Khala. They recently founded the American Khala Association.

This action ignores the possibility that the Bolivian dog has developed into a distinct breed, differing slightly from the hairless dogs of Peru. Time will tell whether their action is justified. They have already felt the need to recognize two forms of Khala, the Khala Medio, which is 14–17 in (36–43 cm), and the Khala Grande, which is 17–20 in (43–51 cm). The first is called the 'Pottery Type' and the second the 'Gazehound Type' or 'Sighthound Type'.

This breed is described as alert, active and agile. It is noisy in play, but good-tempered. One owner calls them 'mind-readers'.

HAIR DOGS

Long-coated dogs of several species – the Chow Chow, for example – have occasionally been exploited for their hair, but this is nearly always a minor, secondary use. There have been five breeds, however, whose main function was to supply hair to their owners. One is from Asia and four from the New World.

INDIA
Naga Dog   598

CANADA
Nootka Dog   599

UNITED STATES/CANADA
Clallam-Indian Dog   598

PERU/CHILE
Long-haired Inca Dog   600

UNITED STATES
Long-haired Pueblo Dog   599

INDIA

NAGA DOG

ASSAM

This rare breed is found only in the Naga Hills of Upper Assam. A certain Colonel Shakespear, of the Gurkhas, acquired some and kept them for a number of years in India. He reported that they were most commonly found among the Trans-Dikkoo tribes. In appearance they were similar to the Chinese Chow Chow, but lacked that dog's black tongue. They also differed in their coat, which was pure white, except for lemon-tipped ears. With their thick coats, pricked ears, throat ruffs and up-curled tails, they looked remarkably like the typical spitz dogs of the far north.

The colonel gave an account of the way in which the tribespeople utilized these dogs:

> The coat is very long and silky, and they are valued by the Nagas on this account; the tribes using the hair, which takes a good dye, for weaving the tribal designs into their cloth. The hair is plucked, not cut, and the method adopted is to peg down the dog, muzzled, and stupefy him with some drug, while the operator plucks out small bunches of hair, rubbing the bare patch of flesh with some dry powdered herb which soothes the irritated skin. The process is necessarily a long one, not completed in a single day. Although so frequently subjected to this treatment I have always found them most friendly and good-tempered creatures.

UNITED STATES/CANADA

CLALLAM-INDIAN DOG

UNITED STATES/CANADA

A native Indian dog found in the extreme north-western corner of the United States and the extreme south-western corner of Canada, from Tacoma in the south, to the lower parts of Vancouver Island in the north of its range.

This is the most unusual of all the dogs owned by the tribes of North America. It was first observed by George Vancouver, near the location that was later to bear his name, when he was surveying the region in 1792. He noted that these white, woolly-haired, poodle-like dogs were being shorn of their dense fleeces just as if they were domestic sheep. And he was surprised to see families of Indians walking along accompanied by a 'flock' of 40 of these shorn dogs.

This was, in fact, a highly specialized breed, developed specifically to provide thread for the looms of the tribal weavers. Paintings of these dogs were made in the middle of the 19th century by the artist Paul Kane. They show a white-coated, medium-sized dog, not unlike an unclipped poodle, with small, rounded ears and a thick, bushy tail, sitting serenely next to a woman working on a vertical loom.

The dog wool was employed in the making of native blankets, leggings and hats. For the blankets, mountain-goat's wool was used for the warp and dog wool for the weft. Unfortunately, when Europeans starting selling cheap blankets to the Indians, the tribes stopped making their own goods and the remarkable 'wool-dog' became obsolete. By the end of the 19th century it has vanished and was never seen again.

UNITED STATES

LONG-HAIRED PUEBLO DOG   UNITED STATES

A long-extinct dog that was originally used to provide wool for making coloured wigs, cloaks, shirts and other tribal garments.

This breed, developed by the Pueblo Indians of Arizona and New Mexico, reached its zenith in the 13th century AD, when their tribes were flourishing. It was still common several hundred years later, but then savage drought robbed the Pueblo of their affluence, and by 1540 the dog had become rare. Finally, when sheep and goats arrived with the Europeans in 1599, its time was up. This Pueblo Dog is thought to have been a long-haired version of the more common Plains-Indian Dog, with native Pueblo breeders progressively selecting for longer and longer coats. It was about the size of a modern collie, covered in what was described (from a mummified specimen) as: 'a dense coat of long woolly hair, of a pale yellowish colour, clouded on the head and back with brownish'. The longest individual hairs were about 4 in (10 cm) long.

CANADA

NOOTKA DOG   CANADA

Also known as the Asiatic Nootka Dog or the Nootka Sound Dog, this breed has sometimes been called the Nootka Sheepdog, not because it herds sheep, but because it has a sheep-like coat, so thick that it could be used as a source of wool.

This is an apparently extinct breed of native Indian dog that was found in the region of Nootka Sound, on what is now known as Vancouver Island, in the extreme south-west of Canada.

Some authors have confused this dog with the Clallam-Indian Dog, but it is clearly a different breed. It was accurately described by Charles Hamilton Smith in 1840 as being 'large, with pointed upright ears, docile, but chiefly valuable on account of the immense load of fur it bears on the back, of white, and brown, and black colours, but having the woolly proportion so great and fine, that it may well be called a fleece'. This description clearly distinguishes it from the Clallam-Indian Dog, whose ears were not pointed and whose coat was all-white.

The dog was regularly shorn like a sheep, and it was reported that its fur was so dense that 'it is sufficiently interwoven to lift the whole produce of one animal by grasping a single handful'. This abundant hair was then worked in with other types of wool and used in the spinning of Indian garments.

As a fleece-producing dog, it was so impressive that there was an early suggestion that it might be introduced, on a commercial basis, into Scotland. In this connection, the Zoological Society of London, whose original aim was the 'introduction and exhibition of such subjects of the animal kingdom as may be of utility'. acquired living examples of the 'Nootka Sound Dog' in 1842/43, no doubt with the thought in mind of developing them as a new kind of wool-producing animal. For whatever reason, nothing seems to have come of it, and the Nootka Dog was soon to vanish.

PERU/CHILE

LONG-HAIRED INCA DOG   PERU/CHILE

This shaggy dog from the coastal regions of Peru and Chile was a vital source of hair for native weavers. It was first identified as a distinct breed by 16th-century Spanish explorers, who noted that its luxuriant hair was employed by the Chonos Indians in the making of warm, short cloaks for the winter months. The reason that the dogs were exploited in this way was that there were no large game animals from which the Indians could make furs and skins to shield themselves from the cold. They subsisted on marine food and small game and, had it not been for their dogs, would have been unable to survive the cold seasons. Their dogs were so important to them that, on occasion, they honoured them by mummifying them and giving them special burials.

We know from their mummified remains that these were yellow-coated dogs with exceptionally long hair. They had slender bodies and were similar in general appearance to the modern collie.

PROPERTY GUARDS

One of the earliest duties of the domestic dog was guarding the property of its owners. Smaller, weaker breeds acted as watchdogs – their barking alerted their owners to possible danger, but they did not themselves attack intruders. Bigger, stronger breeds barked the alarm and then proceeded to attack the intruders. The attacks were sometimes so fearsome that these bigger dogs had to be chained up outside their homes. This gave their owners the option of releasing them to carry out an attack in emergencies, but avoided unwanted assaults.

Most modern breeds will act as property guards when at home, even if their main duties lie elsewhere. Some, however, have been developed as property-guard specialists and these are the breeds that make up the present category. There are 37 breeds in this group.

ENGLAND

BANDOG ENGLAND

This ancient breed has also been known as a Band-dogge (1425), a Bondogge (1440), a Bonde Dogge (1499), a Bandogge (1576), and a Tie Dog or Banddog (1577). The name is taken from the band or tie that held them chained to a fixed point. The function of this fearsome breed was to guard the house against intruders.

This was the name given to the early house-guarding dogs that were so fierce that they had to be chained up to prevent them from killing strangers approaching a dwelling. Their very presence was a deterrent in itself. Johannes Caius, in his 16th-century treatise *Of Englishe Dogges*, offers a colourful description of the Bandog — it is 'vaste, huge, stubborne, ougly, and eager, of a heuy and burthenous body, and therefore but of little swiftness, terrible, and frightfull to beholde, and more fierce then any Arcadian cur'. He goes on to explain that the dog's function is to deal with any 'theefes, robbers, spoylers, and night wanderers'. He was very impressed by the strength of their jaws, commenting that 'the faste hold which they take with their teeth exceedeth all credit'.

In 1790, Thomas Bewick provided an illustration of a typical Bandog and describes it as a breed similar to the Mastiff, but lighter, smaller, more active and more vigilant. He says that it attacks with eagerness and that its bite is 'keen and dangerous'. Just over a hundred years later, another author described the Bandog as a 'sort of light Mastiff' and suggests that it must have been created by crossing a Mastiff with a Foxhound. It appears that, at some point during the 19th century, this breed became extinct, but it is not clear why, since the need for an impressive guard dog certainly remained.

In appearance the Bandog was said to have a coat that was rough and of a yellowish or sandy-grey colour, streaked with black or brown.

BULLMASTIFF ENGLAND

This breed takes its name from its two ancestors, the Bulldog and the Mastiff. It is sometimes referred to as the English Bulmastiff. Its primary use, historically, was as a property guard, employed by gamekeepers to protect great estates from poachers. It was originally known as the Gamekeeper's Night Dog.

The Bullmastiff is 40 per cent Bulldog and 60 per cent Mastiff and, as might be expected, it is intermediate in size between its two parent breeds. It looks rather like a Mastiff with a Bulldog's head.

Despite its Bulldog ancestry, this was never intended to be a baiting or pit-fighting dog. It was created with one specific purpose in mind — to be strong enough and fearsome enough to terrorize and overpower human intruders. It was created at a time when large country estates were being subjected to a plague of thieving and poaching. The landowners needed a new weapon to help their gamekeepers and their other estate staff in the struggle to keep this problem under control.

The Bullmastiff was the perfect answer. It was capable of finding, pursuing, overtaking and subduing any stranger it encountered, by day or night. Thanks to its Bulldog blood it was faster and more aggressive than a Mastiff, and thanks to its Mastiff blood it was bigger and less wantonly savage than a Bulldog — the ideal mixture.

Although stubborn and difficult to train, this dog, once it was properly controlled, was a model exponent of the 'restrained attack'. When it captured its victim it did not proceed to rip the man to pieces. Instead, it simply knocked him down, applied its Bulldog grip with Mastiff power, and held the intruder until help arrived. In the 19th century, when the workload for the breed was at its height, this technique led to many desperate struggles between dog and man, because at that time poaching was a crime that carried the death penalty. A frantic intruder, pinned to the ground by a huge Bullmastiff, had nothing to lose if he fought the dog to the death, because he was going to die anyway. But he rarely succeeded because the implacable courage of the great dog was unshakeable. In making the Bullmastiff, the dog-breeders had succeeded in creating a canine mantrap.

Such was the reputation of this dog that the breed soon spread around the globe and is still popular on large estates to this day, not only in Europe and North America, but also as far afield as Asia and South America. Its modern role is more that of a watchdog and a deterrent, but it has lost none of its original power or determination, should an emergency arise. For its owners, however, it makes a delightful companion, surprisingly quiet and docile with its known companions. It is often said of small breeds that their bark is worse than their bite. With Bullmastiffs the opposite is true. Because it is capable of clamping iron jaws onto any criminal intruder it encounters, it has nothing to prove and is therefore remarkably calm and friendly when all is well.

In recent years the breed has also become a successful show dog. It was officially accepted by the Kennel Club in London in 1924 and by the AKC in the United States in 1933. In this new role, its coat colour has undergone a shift from the dark, cryptic brindles favoured during its early, silent night-work, to a more visually appealing fawn for the show-ring, although it still retains its dark face mask. From the time of the breed's first official recognition in 1924, no more Bulldog/Mastiff crosses were made. From that point onwards, Bullmastiffs were pure-bred among their own kind.

References

1932. Craven, Arthur. *The Bull-Mastiff as I Know it.* Privately published, Manchester.
1938. Makins, Eric. *The Bullmastiff.* Our Dogs, Manchester.
1957. Hubbard, Clifford L. B. *The Bullmastiff Handbook.* Nicholson & Watson, London.
1964. Prescott, Mary A. *How to Raise and Train a Bull Mastiff.* TFH, New Jersey.
1979. Pfenninger, Adele (Editor). *The Bullmastiff.* The American Bullmastiff Association.
1988. Oliff, Douglas B. *Mastiff and Bullmastiff Handbook.* Howell, New York.
1989. Prescott, Mary. *Bullmastiffs.* TFH, New Jersey.
1992. Walkey, Bill. *The Bullmastiff Fancier's Manual.* Coastal Arts, Sechelt, British Columbia, Canada.
1993. Hubbard, Clifford. *The Bull Mastiff.* Beech Publishing House.
1996. Hancock, David. *The Bullmastiff; A Breeder's Guide.* Chapwynne Dog Features.
1996. Pratt, Lyn. *Bullmastiffs Today.* Howell, New York.
1996. Prescott, Mary A. *Bullmastiffs Today.* TFH, New Jersey.
1999. Roach, Geraldine M. and Shastid, Jack. *The Bullmastiff: Peerless Protector.* Howell, New York.
1999. Rostron, Alan. *Bullmastiffs; An Owner's Companion.* Crowood Press, Wiltshire.
Beans, Carol and Pfenninger, Adele. *A Practical Guide to the Bullmastiff.* Hoflin Publishing, Colorado.

ENGLISH MASTIFF   ENGLAND

This breed is sometimes referred to as the Old English Mastiff, or simply as the Mastiff. Its primary function has always been that of a powerful guard dog, although its dramatic, secondary role as a fighting dog has overshadowed this fact. In earlier centuries its name appeared in many forms, including such variants as Mestyf and Mastie.

The popular image of the Mastiff is of a huge, aggressive, leonine dog, immensely strong and savagely violent. This is a gross distortion. Of course, the unfortunate animal has frequently been driven to behave in this extreme way, but by nature it is a kind and gentle, noble and protective breed. Its story begins in the first millennium BC when, it is claimed, Phoenician traders brought the ancestors of the English Mastiff as valuable cargo on their trading voyages to the British Isles. They had undoubtedly obtained them from the Middle East, where they had been popular as royal dogs for some time. It is true that the archaeological evidence for this origin is slim, but one important fact supports it. When the Romans first arrived in Britain in 55 BC, they found that the inhabitants possessed huge mastiff dogs. One Roman author commented: 'Soon after Britain was discovered, the *pugnaces* of Epirus… were pitted

against the *pugnaces* of Britain, and the latter completely beat them.' The visitors were so impressed by this that, following later Roman settlement, a special Roman official was appointed to oversee the export of the British 'pugnaces' for use in the Colosseum.

The use of mastiffs in the Colosseum arena explains their name. 'Mastiff' is a corruption of the Roman word 'mansuetus' meaning 'tame'. At first sight, this is odd, because the Romans only saw these dogs in brutal combat with lions and other wild beasts. But that was the point – the mastiffs were the only tame animals to be seen fighting in the Colosseum; all the other animals there were wild.

As the centuries passed, the great English Mastiff was enrolled for many secondary duties. In addition to its primary role of aggressively guarding property, it was set to work wolf-hunting, dog-fighting, bear-baiting and bull-baiting. These 'rude and nasty pleasures', to quote Samuel Pepys, were eventually banned in 1835 and the Mastiff's future suddenly looked grim. Its numbers started to dwindle and, by 1908, only 35 were registered with the Kennel Club in London.

By the end of World War II the breed was nearly extinct. There were then only 14 remaining in the British Isles, mostly well past their prime. Luckily they were slightly more common in the United States and some imported stock helped to rebuild the breed. Even so, it is still not a common dog, largely because of its huge size and gargantuan appetite. But for those who do undertake the weighty task of owning them, they represent one of the most lordly and ancient of all types of dog.

References

1873. Kingdon, H. D. *The Old English Mastiff.* Privately published, London.

1886. Wynn, M. B. *The History of the Mastiff.* William Loxley, Milton Mowbray.

1936. Bukllen, W. and Dickin, Norah. *The St Bernard and the English Mastiff and All About Them.* Watmoughs, London.

1964. Moore, Marie Antoinette. *How To Raise and Train a Mastiff.* TFH, New Jersey.

1978. Moore, Marie Antoinette. *The Mastiff.* Denlinger's, USA.

1982. Carp-Gordon, Norman Howard. *The Making of the Modern Mastiff.* North and East Mastiff Fanciers, Texas.

1988. Oliff, Douglas B. *Mastiff and Bullmastiff Handbook.* Howell, New York.

1990. Camino. *Mastiff Champions 1952–1988.* Camino Books.

1993. Baxter, Elizabeth J. and Baxter, David. *The Complete Mastiff.* Howell, New York.

1993. Hahn, Joan. *Grandeur and Good Nature, the Character of the Mastiff: An International Collection of Photos and Commentaries Portraying 'the Lion of Dogdom'.* Privately published.

1995. Camino. *Mastiff Champions, 1989–1993.* Camino Books.

1998. Becknell, John M. *The Mastiff: An Owner's Guide to a Happy Healthy Pet.* Howell, New York.

1999. Andersson, Dee Dee. *The Mastiff: Aristocratic Guardian.* Doral Publishing.

1999. Oliff, Douglas (Editor). *The Ultimate Book of Mastiff Breeds.* Howell, New York.

1999. Thornton, Kim. *Mastiffs: Everything About Purchase, Care, Nutrition, Grooming, Behavior, and Training.* Barron, New York.

Baxter, Elizabeth J. and Hoffman, Patricia B. *The History and Management of the Mastiff.* Scan Book.

Powers, Judy and Hahn, Joan. *Champions: A View of the Mastiff in America.*

LYME MASTIFF   ENGLAND

An extinct breed of mastiff, this was named after Lyme Hall in Cheshire, where it was bred and kept as an estate guard.

This was an exclusive breed of mastiff developed by the Leghs at Lyme Hall in Cheshire. The Legh family were resident at Lyme Hall, with its 1,320 acres of park-land, for 600 years and rarely allowed examples of their highly valued mastiffs to leave their estate. The dogs were well known to be pure-bred and of the highest quality, but they were seldom seen because the family guarded them jealously from external inter-ference and hardly ever permitted the puppies to be sold or given away to outsiders.

In the 19th century this mastiff was said to be the 'purest and most valuable strain of blood in the kingdom'. Because of its centuries-long isolation it would certainly have been the purest, but whether or not it was the most valuable, we have to take on trust. Even then, in the Victorian period, certain expert voices were already being raised in protest about the probable effects of the breed's prolonged inbreeding at Lyme Park.

SPAIN

ALANO   SPAIN

Regarded as an extinct form of Iberian mastiff, this breed has suffered from great variation in the spelling of its name. It would seem that the Alano is the same breed as the Alan, the Allan, the Aland, the Alain, the Alaunte, the Alauntz and the Alaunt. All appear to take their name from their original owners, the Alans or Alani, a Caucasian people who moved into western Europe in the 4th century AD. Although this dog's ancestors had primarily been used as guard dogs, this particular breed was perfected as a bear- and bull-baiting animal.

There is great confusion over the origin of the mastiff breeds. The general view is that the Tibetan Mastiff is the original version and that some of these dogs were brought, in the first millennium BC, to the Middle East, where, when they were not acting as palace guards, they were taken on lion hunts by the Assyrian kings. A little later, Alexander the Great acquired some of them and in ancient Greece these were developed into the Molossus. The Romans then obtained this breed from the Greeks and, as they spread across Europe, took their big dogs with them. Local versions of these dogs became modified, improved and specialized for slightly different tasks in different countries and gave rise to a whole range of large, fierce breeds. One of these would have been the Spanish Alano.

Set against this view is the theory that the dog arrived in Spain slightly later, in the fourth century AD, courtesy of the Alani tribe. Whichever is true, it is clear that once it had arrived in Spain the Alano was to become a major canine force. It was first used for guarding property and cattle and for hunting, but was later enlisted for bull-baiting, bear-baiting and perhaps dog-fighting.

In character, the Alano was described as a 'speedy attacker', pug-nosed, long-bodied and well boned, with a big head, hanging lips and drooping ears. It was called a 'clutching dog' because 'when it fights, it holds its adversary only by the head, in absolute silence and totally indifferent to any pain'.

Velázquez portrayed them in action in the hunting field and Goya showed them capturing a bull. They were also the dogs that accompanied the Spanish Conquistadors to the New World and helped the invaders to subdue the indigenous peoples there. It was said that ten soldiers with one Alano were worth a hundred without.

When competitive dog shows began in Spain, some of the indigenous Alanos were included for exhibition along with the other, more familiar breeds. The last ones to be exhibited appeared at the Retiro Park show in Madrid in 1963. In the early 1980s the Spanish Kennel Club reported that the Alano 'for all practical purposes, may now be considered to be an extinct breed'. Despite the opinions of several top dog experts, there are those who refuse to accept that the breed has vanished altogether. They have written that the breed's disappearance has been reported 'without any scientific basis to justify this audacity'. Time will tell.

PORTUGAL

FILA DA TERCEIRA   AZORES

Also known as the Terceira Island Watch-Dog, this rare, isolated breed is named after the small island in the Atlantic Azores group, which is its only home. There, it is employed as a house guard by the islanders.

The remote Island of Terceira, which is situated in the central region of the Azores archipelago in the middle of the North Atlantic, is the only location where this dog has ever existed. It is descended from the Rafeiro da Alentejo, which is a flock guardian from southern Portugal, and is a close relative of the São Miguel Cattle Dog, a livestock dog found on another of the Azores islands.

The Portuguese colonized these small islands in the 15th century and from time to time took their dogs with them from the mainland, establishing them there as local breeds. As the centuries passed, the dogs changed as they became adapted to their island habitats, and developed into new, highly localized breeds.

The Terceira dog is described as being 'rather like a Bull Mastiff, but shorter on the leg, although supposed to be heavier'. Its coat is short and smooth and in colour it is 'yellow, fawn, orange and white with yellow, red or tan markings'. It has a heavy, broad head, with cropped ears. Its height is 23 in (58 cm) and its weight is 120 lb (54 kg).

SWITZERLAND

ALPINE MASTIFF

SWITZERLAND

This ancient breed, the ancestor of the St Bernard, was employed as a watchdog in the Swiss Alps. It became extinct when it was transformed into the larger rescue dog in the 18th century. It has occasionally been recorded as the Alp Mastiff, or the Bernadine Dog.

In the 10th century a monk called Bernard de Menthon founded a hospice in a treacherous pass in the Swiss Alps, to provide emergency aid to travellers trying to cross from one side of the mountain range to the other. Centuries earlier, the Romans had left behind some of their Mollosian war dogs and those that had survived had managed to find a role as watchdogs guarding the properties scattered in the Alpine valleys. The monks adopted some of these mastiffs and used them as watchdogs. It was these Alpine Mastiffs that would eventually be developed into the famous rescue breed we know today as the St Bernard (see separate entry).

The Alpine Mastiff was a smaller dog than the St Bernard and had a smoother, shorter coat. We cannot be certain about the exact date when it was stabilized at the monastery, as a breed in its own right, but it was certainly fully established by the early 17th century. Two paintings of these dogs dating from 1695 give us an idea of its appearance.

The earliest record we have of the monastery watchdogs being adapted for use as live-saving rescue dogs dates from 1774, so it would appear that it was during the 18th century that the ancient Alpine Mastiff watchdog faded into history, to be replaced by the huge, modern St Bernard (although a dog presented to the London Zoo in 1835/36 was entered under the name of Alpine Mastiff).

GERMANY

BOXER

GERMANY

There are four theories concerning the origin of the name of this breed: (1) that it is a corruption of 'Beisser', meaning 'biter'; (2) that it is a corruption of 'Boxl' or 'Boxeln', which was the nickname of one of the ancestors of the Boxer, a now extinct breed called the Brabanter; (3) that it was applied simply because the dogs were 'prize fighters'; (4) that it was a name given to the breed by an Englishman who was impressed by the way these dogs sparred with one another using their front legs. This fourth explanation is highly unlikely, but it is hard to choose between the others. In earlier days the breed was sometimes known as the German Bulldog.

The ancestors of this well-known breed were the German Bullenbeisser and the English Bulldog. The Bullenbeisser had been working as a German hunting dog for centuries, employed in the pursuit of bear, boar and deer. Its task was to seize hold of the nose of the prey and hold it fast until the hunters arrived to kill it. In later years faster dogs were favoured and the Bullenbeisser grew smaller and was then called the Brabanter.

In the late 19th century it was this smaller type of Bullenbeisser that was to be crossed with an English Bulldog to start the line that would lead to the modern Boxer. In 1894 three Germans by the name of Roberth, Konig and Hopner decided to stabilize the breed and put it on exhibition at a dog show. This was done in Munich in 1895 and the next year they founded the first Boxer Club. During the years that followed there was a great deal of heated argument about the precise standard for the dog. Rival Boxer clubs were formed and fought with one another. At last, in 1910, they were amalgamated and peace reigned. In a few years, however, a new kind of war broke out – World War I erupted and the Boxer was co-opted for military work, acting as a valuable messenger dog and pack-carrier.

It was not until after World War II that the fame of the breed spread around the world. Boxer 'mascots', taken home by returning soldiers, introduced the dog to a much wider audience and it was soon becoming a favourite, both as a companion animal and as a show dog.

In personality this breed has been characterized as a boisterous, self-confident, playful dog. Faced with danger it becomes determined, athletic, and brave, but with its human family it is docile, affectionate and gentle with children. Unlike some other breeds, it is not good in extremes of heat or cold.

Its lean, muscular body with its dramatic, flat-faced head used to be displayed with savagely cropped ears and severely docked tail. Today, ear-cropping is increasingly outlawed, but the Boxer still manages to present an impressive appearance. In colour it is either brindle or fawn, with or without white markings.

References

1939. Wagner, John P. *The Boxer*. Orange Judd, New York.

1940. Gordon, Dan M. *The Boxer*. Judy, Chicago.

1945. Meyer, Enno. *Judging the Boxer*. Orange Judd, New York.

1951. Dunkels, Joan. *The Boxer Handbook*. Nicholson & Watson, London.

1951. Johns, Rowland (Editor). *Our Friend the Boxer*. Methuen, London.

1952. Denlinger. *The Complete Boxer*. Denlinger's, USA.

1954. Davis, Mrs Paul Newhall. *Pet Boxer*. All-Pets, Fond du Lac, Wisconsin.

1955. Daly, MacDonald. *The British Boxer*. Chambers, London.

1955. Miller, Madeline. *Boxers as Pets*. TFH, New Jersey.

1955. Somerfield, Elisabeth. *The Boxer*. Arco.

1955. Somerfield, Elisabeth. *The Popular Boxer.* Popular Dogs, London.

1957. Barbaresi, Sara M. *How to Raise and Train a Boxer.* TFH, New Jersey.

1957. Hemery, M. E. *Boxers.* Ernest Benn, London.

1960. Wiley, Constance and Wiley, Wilson. *Boxers.* Foyles, London.

1964. Volpe, Stanley U. *This is the Boxer.* TFH, New Jersey.

1970. Gordon, Dan M. *All About The Boxer.*

1973. Meyer, Lorraine C. *Your Boxer.* Denlinger's, USA.

1976. Royle. *The Boxer.* KR Books.

1979. Pisano, Beverly. *Boxers.* TFH, New Jersey.

1984. Nicholas, Anna Katherine. *The Boxer.* TFH, New Jersey.

1989. McFadden, Billie. *The New Boxer.* Howell, New York.

1993. Russell. *Boxer.*

1996. Abraham, Stephanie. *The Boxer: An Owner's Guide to a Happy Healthy Pet.* Howell, New York.

1996. Ackerman, Lowell. *Dr Ackerman's Book of the Boxer.* TFH, New Jersey.

1996. Rutledge, Patti. *The Guide to Owning a Boxer.* TFH, New Jersey.

1996. Thiel, Johanna, et al. *Boxers: Everything About Purchase, Care, Nutrition, Breeding, Behavior, and Training.* Barron, New York.

1998. Hutchings, Tim. *The Complete Boxer.* Howell, New York.

1998. Tomita, Richard. *The World of the Boxer.* TFH, New Jersey.

1999. Dunbar, Ian (Editor). *The Essential Boxer: Total Care, Training, Companionship.*

2000. Abraham, Stephanie. *The Boxer: Family Favorite.*

2000. Mulvany, Martha. *The Story of the Boxer.*

2000. Palika, Liz. *Your Boxer's Life: Your Complete Guide to Raising Your Pet from Puppy to Companion.*

2000. Wilcox, Charlotte. *The Boxer.*

DOBERMANN

GERMANY

Originally known as the Thuringer Pinscher or the Plizeilich Soldatenhund, this breed was renamed the Dobermannpinscher (a single word) in 1899 to honour its creator, Louis Dobermann, who died in 1894. In 1949 'pinscher' was dropped from its title and it became simply the Dobermann. In the Americas, however, it is still known as the Doberman Pinscher, with its creator's name misspelt. This breed was developed as a guard dog of a special kind, its working role being to defend its creator (a tax collector) from attack.

The dramatic-looking Dobermann was developed in the late 19th century by Louis Dobermann, a German tax collector from Apolda in Thuringia. In the 1870s he arranged complicated crosses to create a dog that would be aggressive enough to protect him as he made his rounds collecting taxes. He wanted a dog that would not only be fearless when the occasion demanded, but would also look fierce, to act as a deterrent. Fortunately, in addition to being a dog-breeder, he was also in charge of the local animal shelter, where he had access to a wide variety of breeds. Sadly, he did not keep records of the crosses he made, and there have been endless debates about precisely what he did use.

Attempting to unravel the confused arguments of rival experts, it would appear that Louis Dobermann started by crossing local mongrels with German Pinschers. The mongrels in question were the offspring of a cross between a 'blue-grey bitch, a sort of Pinscher' and a black-and-tan dog that was itself a cross between a Butcher's Dog and a sheepdog. There were later crosses involving a black-and-tan Manchester Terrier and a black greyhound bitch. Other breeds that may possibly have been added to the genetic history of the breed at some point include the Beauceron, the Rottweiler, and German pointers.

By 1899 the new breed had been stabilized and the following year it was officially recognized by the German Kennel Club. It was such an impressive dog that it was quick to spread to other countries. By the 1920s it was to be found all through Europe, including Russia, and as far away as South Africa and the United States, and it was soon on its way to becoming one of the worldwide breeds.

In personality, the Dobermann is quick, alert, intelligent, strong, lively, courageous and, above all, aggressive. It proved to be the ideal dog for security work and property guarding. It also became a favourite for police work and, during wartime, for army patrol duties. More recently it has been recruited for search-and-rescue work and has even been employed as a guide dog for the blind.

With its slender, athletic body, its dark, black-and-tan coat, its severely cropped ears and its docked tail, it has become a symbol of canine defiance. In countless film thrillers, when the intruders scale the wall of a large property, it is the snarling faces of Dobermann guard dogs that greet them. With its owner, however, the dog is incredibly loyal and obedient, always eager to please. Furthermore, since its early days, its temperament has been mellowed considerably, to enable it to become a more easily handled show dog and companion animal. Many years ago, when the breed first entered the ring, judges were said to be reluctant to open the dog's mouth to inspect the teeth and, as a result, one animal managed to achieve Championship status with several teeth missing. Today's Dobermann is a much more friendly dog, although still perfectly capable of fearlessly undertaking any protection duties to which it may be assigned.

References

1940. Schmidt. *The Doberman Pinscher in America.*

1953. Denlinger, Milo G. *The Complete Dobermann Pinscher.* Denlinger's, USA.

1958. Curnow, Fred. *The Doberman Pinscher.* Privately published, Warmingford, Sussex.

1958. Stebbins. Natalie and Barbaresi, Sara. *How to Raise and Train a Doberman Pinscher.* TFH, New Jersey.

1959. Gruenig, Philipp. *The Doberman Pinscher.* Orange Judd, New York.

1961. Carey, Len. *Pet Doberman Pinscher.* All-Pets, Fond du Lac, Wisconsin.

1963. Spirer, Louise Ziegler and Miller, Evelyn. *This is the Doberman Pinscher.* TFH, New Jersey.

1970. Harman, Hilary. *The Dobermann.* Foyles, London.

1972. Curnow, Fred and Faulks, Julia. *The Dobermann.* Popular Dogs, London.

1976. Brearley, Joan Mcdonald. *The Book of the Doberman Pinscher.* TFH. New Jersey.

1978. Walker, Joanna. *The New Doberman Pinscher.* Howell, New York.

1979. Donnelly, Kerry. *Doberman Pinschers.* TFH, New Jersey.

1982. Rietveld, Simon. *History of the Dobermann.* Foundation Dobermann Magazine.

1985. Kerfman. *The Doberman Pinscher.* TFH, New Jersey.

1986. Irven, Jan. *All About the Dobermann.* Pelham, London.

1986. Nicholas, Anna Katherine. *The World of Doberman Pinschers.* TFH, New Jersey.

1986. Tocagni, Hector. *El Perro Doberman / the Doberman Pinscher.*

1988. Irven, Jan. *A Dobermann's Day.*

1989. Ladd, Mark. *Dobermanns – An Owner's Companion.* Howell, New York.

1989. Richardson, Jimmy. *A Dog Owner's Guide to the Doberman.* Salamander.

1990. Hogg, Alf. *Dobe is a Four Letter Word.* Valmara.

1990. Schuler, Gerhard. *Der Dobermann (Portrat einer Hunderasse).* Urania Verlagh, Leipzig.

1994. Bakondi, C. and Ferencz, C. *The Dobermann World in Pictures.* Gyongyos Association of the Hungarian Kennel Club.

1995. Gudas, Raymond, et al. *Doberman Pinschers: Everything About Purchase, Care, Nutrition, Diseases, Breeding, Behavior, and Training.* Barron, New York.

1995. Richardson, Jimmy. *Doberman Pinschers Today.*

1996. Ackerman, Lowell. *Dr Ackerman's Book of the Doberman Pinscher.* TFH, New Jersey.

1996. Beauchamp, Richard G. *The Doberman Pinscher: An Owner's Guide to a Happy Healthy Pet.* Howell, New York.

1996. Schau, Joseph P. *Guide to Owning a Doberman Pinscher.*

1997. Jones, Stephen W. and Zervas, Michael R. (Editors). *The Basic Guide to the Doberman Pinscher.*

1997. Zervas, Michael R. (Editor). *Basic Guide to the Doberman Pinscher.*

1998. Palika, Liz. *How to Train Your Doberman Pinscher.*

1998. Strauss, Faye. *A New Owner's Guide to Doberman Pinschers.* Akc Rank.

1998. Wilcox, Charlotte. *The Doberman Pinscher.*

1999. Humphries, Rod and Walker, Joanna. *The Doberman Pinscher.*

Brown, Robert M. *Doberman Owner's Medical Manual.*

Maanen, Willem G. van. *Vrouw met Dobermann: verhalen.*

Migliorini, Mario. *The Doberman Book.*

Nicholas, Anna Katherine. *A Complete Introduction to Doberman Pinschers.*

Schneider, Earl (Editor). *Know Your Doberman Pinscher.* Pet Library, New York.

Wilhelm, Andre. *Doberman.*

Winkler, Bernadette E. *Beginner's Guide to Doberman Pinschers.*

Sanford, William Reynolds and Green, Carl R. *The Doberman Pinscher.*

GREAT DANE   GERMANY

Despite its name, this is a German breed and is also known as the German Mastiff or Deutsche Dogge. It is a dog of many names and at one time or another has been called the Ulm Dog, the Ulmer Dogge, the Ulmer Mastiff, the Ulmer Hund, the Boarhound, the German Boarhound, the Danish Dog, the Great Danish Dog, the English Dogge, the Tiger Dog, the Tiger Mastiff, the Grand Danois, the Grosse Dogge, the Hetzreude, the Saufanger, the Saupacker, the

Fanghund or the Dogo Aleman. In the 17th century, the best type was called Kammerhunde ('Chamber Dog'), the second best Liebhunde ('Life Dog'). In its present form the only working role for this dog has been that of a guard dog, although its earlier ancestors were variously employed as war dogs, fighting dogs, bull-baiters and boar-hunters.

Described as the Apollo of Dogs, this majestic breed, with its statuesque, athletic build, holds the record for the tallest canine in the world. *The Guinness Book of Records* lists a huge male called Shamgret Danzas (1975–1984) as standing 41.5 in (105.4 cm) high. He weighed 238 lb (108 kg).

The forerunners of this breed have been known from ancient times, although not in the refined form we see in today's show-rings. The early ancestral types were heavier, less elegant dogs, built for ferocity rather than appearance. In the Middle Ages they were the high-status dogs of the hunting field. On one memorable occasion, a German Duke arrived for a boar hunt accompanied by a pack of 600 of them.

It was not until the 19th century, in Germany, that the breed was developed into something approaching today's impressive giant. In 1876, it was declared the National Dog of Germany. In the 1880s breed clubs were formed in both England and the United States. It caused a sensation when it first appeared at a dog show and was soon a favoured breed for competition.

A gentle giant, the modern Great Dane has been selectively bred for docility – a wise move for a breed of such power. Its deep bark is worse than its bite, and it is kind and patient with children, even allowing them to ride on its back. It has been said that the greatest threat it now offers is the size of its food bills.

Despite its huge size, it is a graceful dog with a noble bearing. In personality it is even-tempered, affectionate and dignified. Traditionally it had its ears severely cropped to make them pointed and erect, but this custom is now increasingly outlawed and the ears are seen hanging down in their natural shape, giving the dog a more friendly appearance. Its short coat appears in five colours: fawn, blue, black, brindle and harlequin.

Although the breed holds the record for the world's tallest dog, the individual that held that record was an exceptional animal. On average, the Great Dane's size is in fact slightly less than that of the Irish Wolfhound: 32–34 in (80–86 cm).

References

1905. Becker, Frederic. *The Great Dane (Deutsche Dogge)*. Our Dogs, Manchester.
1912. MacKenzie, Morell. *Great Danes, Past and Present*. Our Dogs, Manchester.
1933. Hale, D. E. *The Great Dane*. Judy, Chicago.

1934. Johns, Rowland (Editor). *Our Friend the Great Dane.* Metheun, London.

1938. Booker, Beryl Lee. *Great Danes of To-Day.* Watmoughs, London.

1949. Keckler, Virginia. *Great Dane.* Judy, Chicago.

1950. Denlinger, Milo G. *The Complete Great Dane.* Denlinger's, USA.

1960. Miller, Evelyn. *Great Danes as Pets.* TFH, New Jersey.

1961. Lanning, Jean. *Great Danes.* Foyles, London.

1963. Denlinger, Milo G., et al. *The New Complete Great Dane.* Howell, New York.

1967. Hart, Ernest H. *This Is the Great Dane.* TFH, New Jersey.

1975. Osbourne, H. M. *Your Great Dane.*

1980. McCarty, D. *Great Danes.* TFH, New Jersey.

1981. Carroll, Nancy. *The Great Dane: Dogdom's Apollo.*

1982. Ostovar, Pat. *Great Danes in Canada.* Denlinger's, USA.

1988. MacDonald, Bruce. *All About the Great Dane.* Pelham, London.

1988. Nicholas, Anna Katherine. *The Great Dane.* TFH, New Jersey.

1972. Basquette, Lina. *Your Great Dane.* Denlinger's, USA.

1994. Johnson. *Great Danes Today.* Howell, New York.

1994. Stahlkuppe, Joe, et al. *Great Danes: Everything About Purchase, Care, Nutrition, Breeding, Behavior, and Training.* Barron, New York.

1995. McCracken, Mary J. *The Great Dane Handbook.*

1996. Ackerman, Lowell. *Dr Ackerman's Book of the Great Dane.* TFH, New Jersey.

1996. Lorg, Garth, et al. *Guide to Owning a Great Dane: Puppy Care, Health, Feeding, Training, Showing, Breed Standard.*

1997. Jones, Stephen W. and Zervas, Michael R. (Editors). *Basic Guide to the Great Dane.*

1997. Wilcox, Charlotte. *The Great Dane.*

1997. Zervas, Michael R. (Editor). *Basic Guide to the Great Dane.*

1998. Swedlow, Jill. *The Great Dane: An Owner's Guide to a Happy, Healthy Pet.* Howell, New York.

1999. Swedlow, Jill. *The Great Dane: Model of Nobility.*

LEONBERGER GERMANY

Also known in the past as the Leonberg Dog, this breed is named after the south-western German town of Leonberg, where it was employed as a guard dog. In a secondary role, it has also been employed as a draught dog in Holland and Belgium and occasionally as a livestock guard.

Surprisingly, this fine breed began life as a discarded dog. When, in the 1830s and 1840s, the monks of St Bernard were trying to improve the breed of dog that takes their name, they experimented by importing some Newfoundlands to inject new blood. From these St Bernard/Newfoundland crosses they selected and retained the examples that looked most like their own breed. The others were discarded and it was from these rejects that the Leonberger was created. Some of them were acquired by Heinrich Essig, the mayor of Leonberg, and he felt they were so imposing that he used them as the foundation stock for a new breed that would later take the name of his town.

Essig's goal was to create a massive dog that would look like the heraldic lions in his town's coat of arms. He added other breeds to the bloodline, in particular the Pyrenean Mountain Dog. The result is a huge animal with a height of 32 in (80 cm) and the colouring of a lion. The thick, long coat is usually fawn but can also be grey-fawn or orange. There are often darker markings in the head region. It has drooped ears and a bushy tail.

By the end of the 19th century this imposing dog was fully established as a new breed — a powerful and impressive property guard. It found favour, not just with local property owners, but also with a number of famous European figures, including the Prince of Wales, the Russian Czar, the King of the Belgians, Bismarck, Garibaldi and Wagner.

Then, during World War I, the breed all but vanished. By the end of hostilities in 1918 there were only five of them left alive. Carefully organized breeding led to a revival of the breed until, once again, it fell victim to the ravages of war: World War II proved to be no kinder to it than World War I. This time, when peace returned, there were only eight examples surviving. Once again great care was taken to protect the breed and its numbers rose. Twenty-five years later, the hard work of the breeders had been rewarded and the Leonberger was at last re-established and has remained so ever since. It is now recognized by the Kennel Club in London and has been exported to a number of other countries across the globe.

This is a self-confident breed ('Where does it sleep?' — 'Wherever it chooses.'). When there is no challenge, it is relaxed and genial, but it is also majestically strong when it is roused. With small dogs and children it is endlessly patient and surprisingly affectionate, and has been given the title of 'Gentle Lion'. Thanks to its Newfoundland ancestry, it loves water and, given the slightest excuse, will plunge in for a swim.

References

2000. White, Angela. *The Leonberger.* TFH, New Jersey.

GREECE

MOLOSSUS   GREECE

This ancient, extinct breed is named after the Molossi, tribespeople who inhabited the mountainous region in what is now north-west Greece, between the 5th and the 2nd centuries BC. It was primarily a guard dog, but also had other duties. In the past it has also been called the Molossan, the Molossian Hound or the Molosscicus, and today it is sometimes referred to as the Molosser.

There are two conflicting opinions concerning this famous, ancient breed. The popular view is that it was the early forerunner of the mastiffs, and that it was the epitome of canine ferocity and aggression.

Writing in the first century BC, the Roman poet and philosopher Lucretius vividly describes how 'the angered Molossians' slack, wrinkled snouts lay bare in yawning jaws the threatening fence of fangs, in repressed snarl now raging their visceral fury'. This fearsome image is the one that has been handed down over the centuries.

The general feeling is that some kind of gigantic guard dog was brought to Greece from a location lying to the east. There it became associated with the Molossi tribes and acquired their name. Later, this impressive breed moved on towards Rome, where it was employed as the guard dog of the Roman army, accompanying the troops as they spread out across Europe. Wherever the armies went they left behind a few of their dogs and it was from these that most heavyweight breeds of Europe were descended.

That view has been challenged by some authorities, who claim that it is based on guesswork and lacks detailed historical support. They point out that the pastoral Molossi tribes were regarded by the Greeks as backward barbarians living outside the enlightened Hellenic world, and were hardly likely to have developed a special breed of giant guard dogs. What they did have, apparently, was a more lightly built hunting dog that was swift, nimble, tall, with straight legs, a firm belly and soft ears that flowed back as it ran. This description of the Molossus dog, from the writings of Nemesianus in the 3rd century AD, sounds more like the big Greek Saluki than any kind of mastiff.

M. B. Wynn, in his classic 1886 work *The History of the Mastiff,* states categorically that 'the Molossus was not in reality a Mastiff... the true Mollosian was an erect-eared, slate coloured or fawn, swift-footed wolfish-looking dog'.

The best explanation of these contradictions seems to be that the Molossi had more than one type of dog. It is worth remembering that Alexander the Great's mother was a Molossi princess and that Alexander, in the spectacular military wanderings that took him far to the east, is said to have encountered giant dogs which impressed him so much that he sent some home. It would seem that, although the typical Molossus dogs may have been lighter, faster animals, some exceptional giant ones were also present in the 4th century BC, thanks to Alexander. It was these, presumably, that became the foundation stock for the mastiffs that were to follow. Whether we call Alexander's exotic, imported dogs by the name Molossus or not is largely a matter of taste. This is what has been done by most modern writers, who have chosen to ignore the native Molossian dog. It might be historically more accurate to call them something else, but that would only confuse matters.

SULIOT DOG   GREECE

Also known as the Suliot Boarhound, this extinct breed was employed as a property guard and, during wartime, as a protector of military outposts.

During the 17th and 18th centuries, the Suliots were a tribe inhabiting the mountains near Parga in what is now the extreme north-western corner of modern Greece, and this dog was their impressive guardian. It was a local form of the ancestors of the breed which today we call the Great Dane.

Described as 'full in mouth, fierce, coarse in aspect and rugged in coat', this huge guard dog is reputed to have been the largest canine that ever existed, standing 4 ft (121 cm) tall. As a guard dog, its ears were traditionally cropped. Writing on the history of the mastiff in 1886, M. B. Wynn comments: '...the true Molossian... identical or almost so, with the modern Suliot Boarhound.'

SOUTH AFRICA

BOERBOEL   SOUTH AFRICA

According to an exaggerated claim by the supporters of this dog, it 'is the only breed in the world specifically bred to guard and protect'. It is known to its friends as the Bole.

This large, powerful South African breed is descended from the old Boer Dog which was itself created from crosses between mastiffs and bulldogs. In early colonial days, that ancestral dog was used by the Boers for hunting big game as well as for protecting white farmers on remote ranches, but the Boerboel that was later developed from it was employed exclusively as a family guardian.

The Boerboel was prominent in this protective role for many years, but during the course of the 20th century the breed was increasingly diluted by careless crossing with others dogs. Then, in the 1980s, five founder members of a newly formed Boerboel Association agreed to restore the breed to its former, pure-bred glory. They started a search in the more remote areas, travelling for thousands of miles to locate examples of genuine, full-blood Boerboels. Their aim was to locate dogs that were so isolated geographically that they had not been subjected to random matings. These enthusiasts were eventually successful in rebuilding the breed as it was originally intended to be and, in 1990, made a television documentary about it.

One of the special features of this dog is that it 'should know when you approve or disapprove of a stranger and share your feelings'. In other words, this is not a crudely aggressive protector, confronting all-comers, as happens with some other breeds of guard dog; it is sensitive enough to distinguish between friendly or neutral strangers and those with hostile intentions.

The parent association, formed to support this breed, called the Suid Afrikaanse Boerboeltelers Vereniging, has recently been joined by foreign organizations such as the All-Russian Boerboel Association and the United States Boerboel Association, and interest in the breed as a highly efficient guard dog is spreading around the globe.

RUSSIA

BLACK RUSSIAN TERRIER   RUSSIA

Sometimes called the Russian Black Terrier, the Tchiorny Terrier, the Chornyi or the Blackie, this 20th-century breed was specifically created as a military guard dog for the Red Army. In France it is known as the Terrier Noir Russe, and in Germany as the Schwarze Russische Terrier.

A powerful, black, thick-coated guard dog, the Black Russian has perhaps the most complex origins of any dog breed, involving no fewer than 17 different parent-breeds. So often, the origins of a breed are said to be 'lost in the mists of time' but uniquely this breed's history has been meticulously recorded since its very beginning. The breeding programme was initiated after World War II, when the Russian army decided it needed to develop its own specialized guard dog, an animal that would be able to stand up to the rigours of an often hostile climate. The dog population of Russia had suffered terribly during the war and there was no pure-bred strain readily available, so it was decided to gather together various breeds from both home and abroad and start from scratch with the creation of an entirely new type of dog.

The first dog to be assigned to this military breeding programme was a Giant Schnauzer called Roi (born in 1947). He was mated with several Airedale Terrier bitches, then with several Rottweiler bitches and then with several Moscow Retriever bitches. The Moscow Retrievers themselves were descended from a mixture of Newfoundlands, Caucasian Sheepdogs and Eastern European sheepdogs. Among other breeds known to have been involved at some stage were the Great Dane, the Borzoi and the Laika. First they aimed for a dog that was stable in temperament, then they went on to standardize its appearance. By the 1980s they had achieved their goal and in 1984 the new breed was recognized by the FCI. By the 1990s there was already an enthusiastic Black Russian Terrier Club in the United States, eager to see this impressive new breed in the show-ring.

The result of this elaborate, long-term project was a perfected military canine servant, a formidable guard dog that would effectively protect any army installation against intruders. It has been described as a solid, robust, rugged, fearless, aggressive but trainable, high-spirited, imposing dog, able to withstand huge climatic variations. Its luxurious, 4-in (10-cm) long, slightly wavy, black coat not only keeps it warm in the Russian winters, but also camouflages it from prying eyes during night-time duties.

MOSCOW WATCHDOG   RUSSIA

In the 1950s, Russian dog-breeders carried out a series of planned matings to create a new type of large property guard. In its homeland this breed has been referred to as the Moskovskaya Storozhevaya Sobaka.

After World War II, an attempt was made to find an improved form of watchdog for Moscow. Crosses were made between the Caucasian Mountain Dog, or Ovtcharka, and the St Bernard, and the offspring from these matings were stabilized by further selective breeding to create the impressive Moscow Watchdog.

The object of this exercise was to produce a breed that combined the

aggressive alertness of the Mountain Dog with the size and power of the great St Bernard. The Caucasian Mountain Dog, by itself, was renowned for its assertiveness, but was not considered to be heavy enough to act as an urban guard. The St Bernard had the huge bulk and great strength, but on its own was too slow and ponderous. Bringing the two together kept the personality of the flock guard and the body of the St Bernard, and the result was a formidable defender of the home.

This big-boned breed, with its thick coat, massive head and long bushy tail, has a height of 25–27 in (64–69 cm). Its weight is 100–160 lb (45–74 kg). Its colour is always red-and-white. Despite its obvious appeal as a house guard, this even-tempered, intelligent breed is, for some reason, unknown outside Russia.

AFGHANISTAN

POWINDER DOG   AFGHANISTAN

This rare breed is also known as the Kooichi Dog or the Koochi. It has also been recorded as the Koochi Greyhound, the Afghan Koochi Dog, or the Sage Koochi. Its name is sometimes confused with those of the Kooiker Dog of Holland and the Kuchi Dog of India. Its role is to guard the property of the nomadic Powinder tribe.

The Powinders are Afghan nomads who used to migrate south each autumn to the warmer regions of India. In recent times, however, their southward trek has reached no further than the Indian border, where they have been forbidden entry. Each spring they travel north again, and their tribal dogs accompany them at all times. Each Powinder caravan consists of about 1,000 tribespeople, along with their livestock, consisting of several hundred camels, sheep, goats and donkeys – and a pack of about 20 guard dogs. These dogs have the special duty of protecting the caravan each night, wherever it comes to rest. Although by day they are friendly enough, after dark their personality changes dramatically and they become ferociously aggressive. As one author put it, to go into the Powinder campsite after nightfall 'is like entering death valley'.

The Powinder Dog looks like a smaller version of the Great Dane – an alert, heavy-boned, solidly built, strong-jawed animal with a thick, harsh coat. It is particularly savage towards strange dogs that may approach the caravan, and this has been given as the reason why it has remained a pure, undiluted breed for such a long period of time.

Because of the important role they play in defending the caravans, these dogs are well treated and well fed. Great care is taken of the puppies that are born during the nomadic journeys. They are given pride of place in special carrying bags on the camels, while their mothers trot alongside, ready to feed them whenever a halt is called. The adults are strong dogs, able to travel up to 20 miles (32 km) a day. It is doubtful if this breed will ever be taken up as a house pet or show dog because they cannot stand confinement and will always be a risk when encountering other kinds of dogs.

INDIA

ALUNK   INDIA

This little-known southern Indian breed, also called Sonangi, is employed as a watchdog.

Found in the Tanjore region south of Madras, in the extreme south-east of India, this is a miniature breed with very little hair. Despite its small size it is said to be a ferocious, intelligent defender of the property which it is given the task of protecting. In appearance it is similar to the African Sand Dog and the Mexican Hairless.

BISBEN INDIA

A Himalayan breed similar in size and shape to a mastiff, the Bisben is used to protect the flocks of sheep and may sometimes accompany the hunt for local game. It has the reputation of being exceptionally fierce as a guard dog. In colour it is usually black-and-white, but may also show small patches of red. It has a long shaggy coat as a protection from its cold environment, a long, bushy tail that curls up, and a long, pointed head.

KANAWAR DOG INDIA

This little-known guard dog from Himachal Pradesh state in north-western India is described as a large, ferocious dog that is kept chained up during the day (because it is so aggressive towards strangers) and allowed to wander at night. A hardy breed, it is noted for its thick, black, woolly coat. The largest specimens come from the district of Disehur.

SHIKARI DOG INDIA

This little-known breed from the Kumaon region of the Himalayas, south of Tibet, is said to be used primarily as a watchdog but also for hunting.

Described by Indian dog expert Major W. V. Soman as being very strong and standing well over 36 in (91 cm) in height, the Shikari Dog of the Kumaon people is apparently very similar in appearance to the feral Pariah Dogs of the Indian plains.

Soman makes the remarkable claim that this breed of Indian dog is a descendant of the Dhole – the Indian wild dog – and this statement has unfortunately been uncritically accepted by recent authors of dog books. It must be stressed that there is no firm evidence that the Dhole (*Cuon alpinus*) has ever been domesticated. It is not even a member of the Caninae – the subfamily that contains all the wild relatives of domestic dogs – and it has a very different personality. Dholes are ferocious pack-hunters that prey on large animals such as deer and have even

been known to kill bears and tigers. Strangely they do not attack domestic livestock and have always given human settlements a wide berth. One zoologist who spent 5,000 hours watching out for them in the wild only managed to clock up 100 hours of direct observation. So, although it is not impossible, it does seem highly unlikely that any of these animals have ever been domesticated and employed as guard dogs. It should be added that Dholes are only 16–21 in (41–53 cm) in height, compared with the 36 in (91 cm) claimed for the Shikari Dog. On the scanty evidence we have available, it is much more likely that the Shikari Dog is a tamed relative of the feral Pariah Dog of India.

SINDH HOUND INDIA

This is an ancient breed, sometimes called the Sindh Mastiff, that has existed for as long as people can remember in the desert regions of north-western India. It is a large dog, 30 in (76 cm) tall, and similar in appearance to a Great Dane. Its main employment is as a watchdog, but in the past it has also been used for hunting boar. It displays a powerful, broad head with a strong neck, heavy shoulders and deep chest. The tail is carried low, like that of the Great Dane. It has a smooth, dense coat that is usually pale in colour, matching its desert surroundings.

VAGHARI DOG INDIA

This rare breed takes its name from the jungle-dwelling, nomadic Vaghari tribe of Saurashtra. The dogs are used to guard the tribal camps from intruders.

The Vaghari Dog is such an aggressive protector of its tribal campsites that attempting to visit one is considered dangerous. A large dog of roughly greyhound shape, with a thin, shining coat, a long face and drooping ears, it is either black, brown or tan in colour, or a mixture of these three. The dogs accompany the tribesmen when there is a hunt and are prepared to attack wild boar, deer and even wolves. Occasionally they set off on a hunt on their own, in a pack, and are then capable of killing an animal as powerful as a leopard. Little appears to be known about their current status.

NEPAL

BLACK HILL DOG NEPAL

This large, jet black dog from the northern hills of Nepal is employed primarily as a property guard, but also has several subsidiary roles.

In addition to guarding the home, this breed is sometimes trained to herd sheep or goats, and sometimes to act as a flock guard, protecting the domestic animals against attacks from leopards, tigers, wolves and jackals. Occasionally it is also used as a hunting dog in the pursuit of wild boar and deer, but protecting the homesteads is the main task for which it has been developed as a distinct breed.

Isolated from other kinds of dogs for many years, the Black Hill Dog now breeds true and has become remarkably uniform right across its range, from the north-west to the north-east of Nepal. In the settlements, each dog is attached to a particular household and is never allowed to roam free or to mate with the local feral dogs.

This breed is closely related to the Tibetan Shakhi, from which it is believed to have descended. Unlike the Tibetan breed, however, it lacks the curled-up, spitz tail. Its long, bushy tail is carried low when it is stationary and is held in a slight curve when the dog is moving.

As a property guard it is said to be very sensitive to the arrival of strangers, and can detect their approach even when they are a long distance away, responding with a loud, continuous barking.

Its thick, protective coat is slightly wavy and is usually solid black. Rarely, some individuals do, however, show a dark brown colouring, and there may be a few specimens that show small white patches, usually on the feet or the front of the body. This is a strong, muscular dog which is described as brave, intelligent, alert and active. It is important to its owners and is usually well cared for by them. A medium-sized dog, it stands about 18–20 in (45–50 cm) in height and weighs 44–55 lb (20–25 kg).

An unfortunate aspect of one of the minor roles of this dog is that it is sometimes used by poachers in the illegal pursuit of the rare and heavily protected musk deer. The musk gland of the male deer produces a strong-smelling secretion that is immensely valuable to the perfumery trade, and Black Hill Dogs can be trained to follow this scent. When the deer have been killed, the poachers remove the glands and smuggle the contents to India, where they fetch huge prices.

TIBET

SHAKHI TIBET

Also known as the Tibetan Guard Dog, the Congkhi or the Kongpo, this breed was developed as a sentinel and a guardian of Tibetan camps and rural settlements.

Not to be confused with the heavier and better-known Tibetan Mastiff, or with the smaller Black Hill Dog of Nepal, this medium-sized property guard is found in country districts of both Tibet and neighbouring Nepal. The height of this dog is about 22 in (55 cm), while that of the Tibetan Mastiff is a massive 28–35 in (70–90 cm), and the Black Hill Dog only 18–20 in (45–50 cm).

The Shakhi is first and foremost a property guard, but is also occasionally employed as a herding dog or for hunting. Compared with the Black Hill Dog, it is longer in the leg and less heavily built, but with a similar, broad, flat-topped head. The ears are folded forward and the bushy tail is carried high and curled over the back in a position which is halfway to a full, spitz curl. The long, thick coat is variable in colour but is typically rather light. Some animals are white with a few minor black markings on the head. Others are red-and-sandy, sometimes with additional white patches.

Examples of this breed that are found in Nepal today nearly always belong to Tibetan immigrants or Nepalese people with Tibetan ancestry.

Note: This breed should not be confused with the Tibetan hunting dog called the Kongbo or Kongkyi (see separate entry). The names Kongbo/Kongpo and Kongkyi/Congkhi may well be translations of the same Tibetan word, but it is clear from the descriptions of the dogs that two distinct breeds are involved.

TIBETAN KYI-APSO TIBET

This is a rare property guard from a remote region of Tibet. Pronounced 'kee-OP-so', its name means, literally, 'hairy dog'. The main role of this little-known breed is to protect homes and settlements, but it may also defend livestock when the need arises.

Looking like a shaggy-headed, longer-eared, more slender-bodied, longer-legged version of the Tibetan Mastiff, this ancient breed is found in the high plateau district of the sacred mountain called Mount Kailash. With its up-curled tail and its bearded face, it has sometimes been called the Bearded Tibetan Mastiff, or the Bearded Kyi-Apso. Its height

is 26 in (65 cm) and its weight about 80 lb (36 kg). It is basically a black dog with pale extremities, although other colours do occur.

This breed is agile and athletic, moving with a characteristic 'rolling, bouncy trot'. It is also energetic, independent, stubborn and highly intelligent. Aggressive towards strangers, it requires special training to control its deeply ingrained territorial defensiveness. It possesses an impressively deep, resonant bark, which it uses whenever it senses a stranger approaching its home base.

This intriguing dog was not known to the outside world before 1937, when it was encountered by Mrs Eric Bailey, whose husband was attached to the British Diplomatic Mission in Lhasa. She photographed one that was being kept by the 13th Dalai Lama.

Little more was heard of the breed until the 1970s, when American field-workers operating in north-western Nepal observed some that were brought over the border by traders. In the years that followed, other American field-workers managed to penetrate as far as Mount Kailash and there acquired a trio of Kyi-Apso puppies, a male and two females.

Eventually, by the 1990s, a total of six of these rare dogs had been imported into the United States, and enthusiasts there were making a desperate bid to salvage the breed, which was threatened with extinction in its native Tibet. Their foundation stock was soon breeding successfully and the numbers were steadily increasing. A Tibetan Kyi-Apso club was formed to support the breed.

TIBETAN MASTIFF   TIBET

Also recorded as the Tibetan Dog, the Thibet Dog, the Thibet Mastiff, or the Tibetaanse Mastiff, this is one of the world's most ancient breeds. It has been used by Tibetans for centuries as a guard dog. Its primary role is to guard the home, but some are also used as village guardians and occasionally as protectors of livestock. They are often chained up outside and act as barking sentinels rather than attack dogs. These tethered mastiffs are called Do-Kyi, meaning 'gate dog' or 'tied dog'.

It is believed by many authorities that this ancient and noble dog is the ancestral form from which all modern mastiffs are descended. Tibet offered the ideal situation for the development of such a breed. The Himalayan region, because of its altitude and climate, would tend to favour larger individuals. They would be more resistant to the freezing, mountainous conditions. Also, the Tibetan people were vulnerable to intruders and needed the protection of the biggest dog possible. So it is not surprising to find that it is here that one of the first truly massive breeds was to develop.

There is historical evidence to show that early travellers visiting the Himalayan region were impressed by the giant dogs they saw there. Some of these impressive animals were taken away as special gifts and were later used to establish the mastiff strain in the Middle East and Europe. In Tibet itself, the Tibetan Mastiff remained an important presence, protecting the people, their homes, settlements, monasteries, palaces and livestock. The Dalai Lama employed eight of them to guard the gates to his summer residence at Norbulinka — a pair of dogs for each of the four entrances.

One of the earliest records of these huge dogs appearing in England dates from 1828, when an example was presented to the London Zoo by the king, George IV. It was listed as 'Thibet Mastiff or Watch Dog'. In 1847 the viceroy of India sent one as a gift to Queen Victoria. Later, in 1874, the Prince of Wales brought two back from Asia.

After World War II, the Dalai Lama gave a pair to the American president, Dwight Eisenhower. In the 1970s Nepalese drug smugglers employed the Tibetan Mastiff in a new and unusual guarding role. They shipped their illegal drugs into the United States in the false bottoms of dog crates carrying these mastiffs and in this way ensured that no customs official would risk close examination.

During the brutal period when China annexed Tibet, orders were given by the Communist authorities that all dogs must be beaten to death by their owners, or the owners themselves would be beaten to death. As a result, the Tibetan Mastiff nearly became extinct in its homeland. Only a handful of dogs living in the most remote rural districts managed to survive this canine holocaust. Fortunately, by this time, enough Tibetan Mastiffs had been exported to Europe and America for the breed to be saved.

This is a powerful, heavy-boned dog with a massive head, folded ears, and an up-curled, spitz-tail. The thick, insulating coat is unusually dense. Its favoured coat colour is black-and-tan, but other colours from black to golden also appear. A white 'heart-spot' on the chest is traditionally said to signify bravery. In earlier centuries it was the custom to adorn these big dogs with a special woollen collar, made from yak hair and dyed red.

In ancient times this dog was described as being 'as large as a donkey' and there is a record of one, presented to a Chinese emperor in the 12th century, that was claimed to be four feet (124 cm) tall at the shoulder. In the unlikely event that the tale is true, this would indeed make the emperor's dog as big as a large donkey — the most enormous dog that has ever lived.

It is certainly true that the Tibetan Mastiff was once bigger than it is today. Body weights of over 220 lb (100 kg) have been reported, but the modern show-dog version is much smaller, with average weights of no more than 120 lb (55 kg). It seems as if, once it is away from its Tibetan highlands, this breed starts to lose its great bulk and revert to a more moderate size.

In personality, the breed has been described as calm, patient, aloof and independent, but with its human family it is also affectionate, playful and gentle. With intruders, it is aggressive and fearless. It has one primitive, wolf-like feature, namely a single annual breeding season.

References

1981. Rohrer, Ann and Flamholtz, Cathy J. *The Tibetan Mastiff: Legendary Guardian of the Himalayas.* OTR Publications, Fort Payne, Alabama.
1981. Rohrer and Larsen. *The Tibetan Mastiff Book.*
1995. Siber, Max and Flamholtz, Cathy. *The Venerable Tibetan Mastiff.* OTR Publications, Centreville, Alabama. (Originally published as *Der Tibethund* in 1897.)

CHINA

CHINESE FOO DOG CHINA

Also known as the Sacred Dog of Sinkiang, the Chinese Choo Hunting Dog, the Chinese Temple Forest Dog, the Happiness Dog, the Chinese Celestial Dog (Chinese T'ien Kou) or the Chinese Dragon Dog (Chinese Lung-Kou), this was a versatile guard dog that was also used for several other duties.

According to the Chinese Foo Dog Club of America, this 3,000-year-old breed was thought to have become extinct, but was recently rediscovered. It is said to have taken its name from the city of Foochow, now called Minhow, located in south-east China. In origin it is believed to have been derived from crosses between the Chow Chow and hunting dogs from northern Europe, although how this occurred is not clear. A more fanciful suggestion is that it resulted from crosses between the Chow Chow and the Chinese wolf.

In its homeland, the Foo Dog is reputed to have been a general-purpose dog, employed in hunting, herding and sled-pulling in addition to its duties as a guard and watchdog. In appearance it resembles a less extreme form of Chow Chow. According to its breed standard its tongue may be either black or pink, reflecting its part-Chow ancestry. Its size is variable and it is at present offered in Standard, Miniature and Toy versions. In personality it is said to be agile, alert, bold and energetic, and from its Chow ancestry it has inherited a dignified independence of spirit.

This breed is being actively promoted in the United Sates by Mr Brad Trom, the director of the Chinese Foo Dog Club of America and the International Chinese Foo Dog Association. It should be added that no information has been forthcoming about the foundation stock of this breed or how or when it travelled from China to the United

States. It is certainly an attractive breed, but critics have queried its oriental origins and believe it may have been created by crosses between Chow Chows and other, smaller breeds in the United States, currently the only country where it is being developed.

HAN DOG
CHINA

An ancient breed, the Han Dog was developed as a house guardian and, in effigy, was also employed as a tomb guardian.

This extinct breed was popular during the Han Dynasty in China about 2,000 years ago. Although many of the dogs that we know only from ancient art are too variable in form to be labelled as specific breeds, in this particular case there is a remarkable consistency in the way that the animal is depicted. It is consistent, not only in its anatomy, but also in the details of the restraining harness that it wears. This was clearly a stocky, ferocious house guard that was kept tied up outside a property to deter intruders and to sound the alarm at their approach. It had a curled tail, shortish legs widely set, forward-folded or cropped ears, a thick neck, a broad head and strong jaws. Its mouth corners were wide and often open in a snarl. Its heavy, double harness consisted of a thick collar connected to a chest strap, with a strong ring at the nape of the neck.

In shape, the Han Dog was reminiscent of the short-coated Chow Chow and its relative, the Shar Pei. It may well be that it represents the ancestral form from which, many centuries later, both the popular Chow and the wrinkly Shar Pei were to descend.

Effigies of this formidable dog were placed in the tombs of the Eastern Han culture that flourished in China between AD 25 and 220. It has been suggested that, inside the tombs, their symbolic role was to protect their dead masters, as live dogs had done during life. These ceramic dogs may be glazed or unglazed and it is clear that the artists who modelled them knew the breed extremely well and were always able to remain faithful, not only to its anatomy, but also to its fiercely protective personality.

JAPAN

SANSHU DOG
JAPAN

Also known as the Sanshu Inu, this breed was specially developed as a medium-sized guard dog.

A little-known breed from the central, Aichi region of Japan, the Sanshu Dog is a typical spitz-type breed, with a thick coat, curled tail, pricked ears, muscular neck and

powerful body. It was deliberately created, start-ing in 1912, at the end of the Meiji period. Local breeders decided that they wanted to pro-duce an ideal, medium-sized guard dog, so they crossed their local Shika Inu hunting dog with imported Smooth-coated Chow Chow. The result was a robust, sturdy, intelligent dog, 20–22 in (51–56 cm) in height, with various colour combinations of black, red, tan and white.

It looks rather like a small Akita, with a com-pact, stocky body and an intent gaze. Its tail, although curved up over its back, is not as tightly curled as that of other spitz dogs. In recent years this breed has become increasingly popular as a companion dog but, despite this, it has not, as yet, been offi-cially recognized as a pedigree breed.

KOREA

CHEJU DOG CHEJU ISLAND

A rare breed of guard dog, the Cheju Dog is found on the island of Cheju about 50 miles (80 km) south of the Korean mainland.

This ancient breed was introduced to Cheju Island about 5,000 years ago. According to official reports, it is 'currently under protective supervision, with a careful breeding programme taking place… on Cheju Island'. This is good news for the Cheju Dog, because in 1996 it was announced that two slaughterhouses were about to be opened on the island, for the preparation of dog meat for local restaurants. Presumably a dis-tinction is made between nondescript dogs for the pot and specially revered native breeds for preservation. The island of Cheju, which is in an isolated position, equi-distant between Korea and Japan, has become a popular tourist holiday resort in recent years, and many new hotels and restaurants have been opened there.

This local native dog, which was once plentiful, was reduced to near-extinction during the Japanese occupation that occurred between 1910 and 1931. The Japanese authori-ties ordered the slaughter of almost all the indigenous domestic dogs in Korea, and very few escaped. The Haenam Dog of the Haenam region in the south-west of the main-land, and the Gujae Dog on Gujae island were both completely exterminated during this period, but a handful of the Cheju Dogs somehow managed to survive. From these, the population was very slowly rebuilt so that, by the end of the 20th century, there were about 100 of these rare dogs in existence, all living on the island. Now that they are pro-tected, it is hoped that this figure will continue to rise in the 21st century.

SAPSAREE

SOUTH KOREA

The name of this breed appears in several alternative spellings: Sap-Sar-Gae, Sapsari, Sapsalyee and Sapsal-Gae. It has been used to guard property in Korea for 2,000 years. For the first 1,000 years of its history it was considered a noble dog and was employed only to protect royal properties, but after that it was also used by the general population.

This appealing, shaggy dog acts as a property guard in an unusual way. In addition to the down-to-earth business of barking at intruders, it is also reputed to possess a supernatural power to repel evil spirits. Its name means, literally, 'drives out devils', and for centuries the breed has been kept in houses in the belief that its presence will protect both the building and its occupants from the Evil Eye and other malevolent forces. So powerful was the spell it cast that, in the seventh century, General Kin Yoo-Shin took his Sapsaree dog into battle with him as an additional form of protection, and scored a great victory over a rival kingdom. Today a Sapsaree symbolically stands guard at the Tokdo island lighthouse, watching over the nation's territorial waters. It is said that 'even a ghost dare not appear before a Sapsaree'.

At one stage in its recent history this intriguing dog nearly became extinct. A survey in 1969 revealed that its numbers had dwindled to no more than 50. By the end of the 20th century, largely thanks to the devoted efforts of Professor Ha Chi-Hong of Kyungbuk University, these numbers rose to 350, but it remains a rare dog. In 1992 it was declared Natural Monument No. 368, and the Korean government is now sponsoring a conservation project to ensure the breed's safety. Internationally, Korea has an appalling reputation regarding its treatment of edible dogs, and the government obviously hopes that by fostering this exceptional Korean breed, it will be possible to improve the country's cultural image abroad.

This is a hardy breed, well protected from the elements by its long, thick, shaggy coat, which covers its entire body, including its eyes, and gives it a 'lion-maned' head. Its drooped ears are also almost hidden by its long coat. During the harsh winter months, rain, cold and snow hold no fear for it. Its body height is only about 20 in (50 cm) but it is said to be powerful enough and brave enough to tackle any opponent, from a large dog to a bull. At home it is obedient and docile with its master, despite its hostility to other dogs outside. Although its jaws are shorter than average, it has large, sharp teeth and is reputed to fight to the death once threatened by another dog.

There are two colour forms of Sapsaree. The Blue Sapsaree, or Chung Sapsaree, has long, black hair streaked with light grey that gives it a bluish tinge in certain lights. The Yellow Sapsaree, or Hwang Sapsaree (sometimes misleadingly referred to as the Yellow Poodle), has a yellow coat mixed with black and white hairs. The Yellow form is slightly larger and more gentle; the Blue form is slightly smaller but more aggressive, suggesting that they are beginning to separate into two distinct types. The puppies of both colour forms are born with black coats, but after four to six months they moult into the adult colours.

Despite its interesting history and attractive appearance, this breed has been conspicuously absent from the canine literature in the past. Perhaps the fact that it has been chosen as the official mascot for the 2002 World Cup in Korea will bring it wider recognition in the future.

THAILAND

THAI RIDGEBACK

THAILAND

The primary function of this multi-purpose dog is to protect the homes of its peasant owners while they are at work. Known in its homeland by the name Mah Thai Lang Aan, it is now recognized as the National Dog of its country and has been given the official title of Royal Dog of Thailand.

It has been claimed that the Thai Ridgeback is depicted in Cambodian and Thai cave paintings that are at least 3,000 years old, but this handsome dog was virtually unknown to the outside world until as recently as 1975. For centuries it had stood guard over the peasant homes in the remote, isolated villages of eastern Thailand. The villagers hardly ever visited the urban centres of the country. Had they wished to do so, the journey would have taken them many days. As a result, the Thai Ridgeback has remained largely undiluted by other dogs, making it one of the purest breeds in the world. Then, in 1975, the Dog Association of Thailand was formed and the Ridgeback suddenly gained the international recognition it deserved. Even now, however, it remains an extremely rare breed that is seldom seen in the West.

In addition to its primary role as a guard dog, it accompanies local hunters and helps to track down quarry such as rabbits and deer. Packs of Ridgebacks are also used to corner wild boar. They are not trained to hunt – the young dogs simply learn from the old ones. When the peasants set off on a special journey, the Ridgebacks accompany their carts as escort dogs.

This is a fierce, proud, powerful animal, weighing about 50 lb (23 kg). A remarkably athletic dog, it is capable of jumping 6 ft (1.8 m) into the air. It has a short, smooth coat bearing its extraordinary, trademark ridge of hair down the middle of the back – hair that grows in the 'wrong' direction – which gives the dog its distinctive appearance. This curious marking stops short of both the tail and the nape of the neck, and experts have identified several different shapes of ridge. They have given these various names, such as Needle Pattern, Hands-in-prayer Pattern, Lute Pattern, Violin Pattern, Horse-saddle Pattern, Arrow Pattern and Bowling-pin Pattern. The most favoured one is the Arrow Pattern. The Thai Ridgeback is claimed to be the ancestor of the African breed known as the Rhodesian Ridgeback as a result of examples having been taken from Thailand by trading ship in ancient times. This is entirely possible, but it is also feasible that the gene for the ridge pattern occurred spontaneously in two widely separated locations. Future DNA tests may settle this matter.

VIETNAM

PHU QUOC DOG   VIETNAM

Like its very close relative, the Thai Ridgeback, this breed acts primarily as a property guard.

Some authors believe that this dog is identical with the Thai Ridgeback, but others claim that, because of its even greater isolation on the island of Phu Quoc, it is closer to its ancient ancestors than the mainland breed is. Local experts insist that the perfect Phu Quoc Dog should possess seven key features: (1) a black tail-tip; (2) dark nails; (3) a dark nose; (4) dark speckles on its tongue; (5) a back-ridge showing an arrow-pattern; (6) a reddish-coloured coat; and (7) a triangular root to the tail. When examined recently, the island dogs were found to carry more of these special characteristics than the typical mainland dogs. A local expert concluded that 'the Thai dogs are now inferior to the dogs on Phu Quoc in terms of purity and quality'. So, although the two breeds undoubtedly share a common ancestor, they have diverged slightly with the passage of time and for the time being can be treated as separate breeds. The differences between them have been summed up as follows: the Phu Quoc Dogs have larger bodies, more sword-like tails, deeper chests, slightly longer coats and darker snouts.

During the Vietnam War, the island of Phu Quoc was turned into a prisoner-of-war camp and many of the dogs were eaten, but enough survived to keep the breed alive. Although Phu Quoc island – which is in the Gulf of Siam, 124 miles (200 km) south of Bangkok – used to belong to Thailand, it has now become part of modern Vietnam, which means that this breed must now be officially listed as a Vietnamese dog.

Many of these island dogs roam unattended and find food for themselves. They are particularly adept at catching crabs on the beaches, and are also expert diggers in their never-ending search for small prey. It is said that they will eat almost anything that moves. Their future as a separate breed is uncertain. If the island and mainland forms are considered by Thai authorities to be one and the same, the chances are that they will be freely crossed with one another in the search for an improved show dog. If this happens on a large scale, the two types, the Phu Quoc Dog and the Thai Ridgeback, will indeed soon become a single breed.

References

Mersman, R. Ch. E. *In search of the Phu Quoc Dog.*

INDONESIA

KINTAMANI DOG   BALI

A rare, local breed of house guard, named after the Balinese town of Kintamani, this is a family pet as well as an alert protector of its owners' property.

This sturdy, spitz-like dog, with its thick, double coat, its erect ears and its up-curled tail, is bred in the remote mountain districts around the famous Gunung Batur volcano in the north-east of the island of Bali. The puppies are brought down to the local towns to be sold. Kintamani, on the great crater rim, is the main centre for the breed. According to one guidebook for the region, 'Kintamani has more angry dogs per square mile than any other place on Bali'.

This little-known breed appears in a variety of colours, but the most favoured one is a tricolour of white, yellow and black.

CANADA

VALLEY BULLDOG   CANADA

This localized breed, developed in Annapolis Valley, Nova Scotia, the district from which it takes its name, is employed as a powerful and intimidating watchdog.

The Valley Bulldog has been described as either a 'tall Bulldog' or a 'short Boxer', and is the result of crosses between these two parent breeds. It has a muscular body, a massive head and a very short tail – either a stump or a screw-tail. In colour its short coat is brindle, brindle and white, or any mixture of brindle, white, black, tan, fawn or red.

It is said to have a calm and gentle personality and, despite its fearsome appearance, is unusually playful. If kept indoors more than usual, it occasionally goes on a brief rampage, lasting several minutes, during which time it rushes crazily around the house before settling down again.

URUGUAY

PERRO CIMARRON URUGUAY

Also known as the Perro Criollo or the Perro Gaucho, this breed is so little-known outside its homeland that it does not yet have an English name. The word 'cimarron' means, literally, 'untamed' or 'wild'. It is also used as an alternative name for the Rocky Mountain Sheep. Neither usage translates well in the title of this dog. The word 'criollo' means, literally, 'native to the locality'. This breed is employed as a watchdog and guardian for property.

The Perro Cimarron is a descendant of the Spanish Mastiffs brought to South America in the 17th century. These mastiffs are thought to have been crossed with imported sighthounds to create a tough but athletic guard dog, especially for use on the often remote ranches in the Uruguayan countryside.

Its body is of medium height, about 22–24 in (56–62 cm). The preferred colours of the short coat are fawn and brindle. Black and white are forbidden in the breed standard, as is a long coat. It is an agile dog, compact, muscular and fast. Although aggressive to intruders, with its owners it is said to display a 'tranquil' temperament.

In recent years this property guard has acquired an important secondary role as a hunter of wild boar. These pigs were introduced early in the 20th century, and, having few natural enemies, have become something of a plague, causing farmers many headaches. They damage the crops and create problems for the flocks of sheep. Something has to be done to reduce their numbers, and groups of Cimarron dogs are sent into action to tackle them. This has recently become a favourite local sport, born of necessity.

The Perro Cimarron is the National Dog of Uruguay, and has become extremely popular there but, despite this, it is seldom mentioned outside that country. The Kennel Club Uruguayo (founded in 1938) and the Sociedad de Criadores de Cimarron (the Cimarron Breeders Society) are doing their best to persuade the FCI to grant official recognition to this well-established breed.

BARGE DOGS

Over the centuries two breeds have become specialized as barge dogs, combining a vessel-guarding role with that of vermin-controller and boatman-companion. They are found in the Low Countries – Belgium and Holland – where the network of waterways and canals has been a main source of commercial transportation for centuries.

A dog that is prepared to live on a small boat for long periods of time has to have a special temperament, and it has taken many years of selective breeding for the Belgian Schipperke and the Dutch Keeshond to achieve this, resulting in two unique canine personalities.

BELGIUM		**HOLLAND**	
Schipperke	637	Keeshond	638

BELGIUM

SCHIPPERKE

The Belgian name of this breed is pronounced 'skeep-er-ker'. It first acquired this title in 1888, before which it had been known simply as the Spitske. In English, it was at first called the Belgian Barge Dog, the Canal-boat Dog or simply the Barge Dog, before its Flemish name was adopted. There are two interpretations of the meaning of this name. According to one, Schipperke is the diminutive of 'schipper', meaning 'skipper', which makes it 'the little skipper'. According to the other, it is the diminutive of 'schip' meaning 'boat', which makes it 'the little boatman'. In England it is known to its friends as the Skip, in America as the Schip. It is a compact little dog that has been employed on the Flemish canal systems since at least the 15th century.

This breed has the unique claim to have been the world's very first show dog. As early as the 17th century, Flemish craftsmen were holding what they called 'Sunday Beauty Contests' with their dogs. One of these competitions was held in the Grand Palace of Brussels in 1690, when the competing dogs were displayed wearing intricate, hammered-brass chokers.

Despite their early popularity with craftsmen, the main duty of these little black dogs was to act as sentries and ratters on board the many barges that transported goods through the local canals. It was essentially a working-man's dog until, in 1885, the Belgian queen, Marie Henriette, acquired one as a pet and immediately raised its social status. By the end of the 19th century it had already become the most popular house-hold dog in Belgium. The first Schipperke to be seen in England appeared in 1887 and the Schipperke Club of England was formed in 1890. It arrived in America in 1888 and the Schipperke Club of America was founded in 1929.

According to local legend, the breed lost its tail in a strange way. In 1609 a shoemaker became so angered over the thieving behaviour of a neighbour's dog that he cut off its tail. The result of his assault looked so attractive that it was decided to perform this operation on all members of the breed. Today it is said that a small proportion of Schipperke puppies are born naturally tailless. Others have their tails amputated close to their bodies, leaving less than 1 in (2.5 cm), to give the dog its characteristic silhouette.

There are three theories concerning the origin of this breed:

1   The first sees it as a small edition of a spitz dog. Supporting this view is the breed's alert expression, its pricked ears, pointed muzzle and stocky body with a distinctive ruff.

2   The second insists that it is a reduced sheepdog. A now extinct, black Belgian sheepdog called the Leauvenaar is believed to have split into two modern

breeds, growing bigger to become the modern Groenendael Sheepdog and shrinking down to become the little Schipperke.

3   The third claims that it is a cross between the Pomeranian and some kind of terrier. This last idea seems unlikely, but it is difficult to choose between the other two theories. Eventually DNA studies will be able to settle the matter.

In colour, the classic Schipperke is jet black, although in some countries other solid colours are also permitted, even though these offend the purists. It is smaller than its Dutch barge counterpart, the Keeshond, being only 9–13 in (22–33 cm).

In personality, this small dog has at various times been described as mischievous, frisky, agile, energetic, resilient, lively, curious, bustling and vigilant. Because of its watchdog role, it is always suspicious of strangers. Critics have called it petulant, stubborn and a little street-fighter. Back in the 15th century it was even dubbed 'the incarnation of the Devil'.

References

1907. Freeman, C. D. *The Schipperke.* Our Dogs, Manchester.

1934. Holmes, E. B. *The Schipperke.* Hotspur Press, Manchester.

1940. Ormiston. *The Schipperke: The Best All Around Small Dog.*

1950. Ormiston. *The Schipperke Comes of Age.*

1964. Martin, Janice F. *How to Raise and Train a Schipperke.* TFH, New Jersey.

1978. Root, Vella M., et al. *The Official Book of the Schipperke.* Sponsored by the Schipperke Club of America. Howell, New York.

1981. Smith. *The Schipperke.*

1993. Anon (The Schipperke Club of America). *The Complete Schipperke.* Howell, New York.

1998. Coronetz, Melanie. *Schipperkes: Everything About Purchase, Care, Nutrition, Breeding, Behavior, and Training.* Barron, New York.

HOLLAND

KEESHOND   HOLLAND

The word Keeshond is pronounced 'kays-hawnd'. This breed is also known as the Dutch Keeshond, the Dutch Barge Dog or the Smiling Dutchman. At one stage in its history it was referred to as the Foxdog. It is sometimes also called the Wolfspitz or the Chien Loup, by those who believe that it should be lumped with the closely related German Wolfspitz as a single breed.

This is a typical spitz dog, with pointed muzzle, pricked ears, up-curled tail, thick coat, stocky body and wolf-like colouring. The impressively dense coat stands away from the body and includes a huge, spectacular ruff. It is a medium-sized dog, a reduced version of its more northerly, Arctic ancestors, with a height of only 17–19 in (43–48 cm). It is slightly smaller than the very similar German Wolfspitz from which it is descended.

As a barge dog it was a jack-of-all-trades, catching and killing vermin, watching over cargo, guiding barges through the fog, and acting as a guard dog.

There are two theories concerning the origin of the breed's name. The first states that it is derived from Cornelis de Witt, whose nickname was Kees, and who was murdered by a mob of Orangemen in 1672. He owned one of these dogs and after his death the breed became known as Kees's Dog, or Keeshond. It was popular among the peasantry, in opposition to the Pug, which was the favoured breed of the Dutch nobility.

The second theory suggests that the name is derived from an 18th-century Dutch revolutionary called Cornelis (Kees) de Gyselaer (or Gyzelaar), who came from Dordrecht. Politically, Holland was deeply divided at the time, with the Prinsgezinden (supporters of the Prince of Orange) lining up against the Patriotten (supporters of the middle classes). Kees de Gyselaer was one of the leaders of the Patriots, and his pet dog became the group's official symbol. When the Patriots were defeated in 1787, the dog associated with them also lost favour and its numbers declined dramatically. In the 19th century the breed suffered a further blow when modernization of commercial transportation began to erode the dog's function as a barge worker. Bigger and bigger barges appeared and larger breeds were employed to protect them.

Happily, just as its role as a barge dog was becoming obsolete, the Keeshond was discovered by foreign breeders. The first imports into England arrived in 1905 and serious breeding soon began. They were first shown in 1923 at the Birmingham National Show, under the title of Dutch Barge Dog, and in 1925 the Dutch Barge Dog Club was formed to support and promote the breed. In 1926 the club's title was changed to the Keeshond Club and before long the dog had established itself as a dog-show favourite. Inspired by the English interest in the breed, serious dog-breeders in Holland also 'rediscovered' the dog in the 1920s, and by 1933 had issued an official breed standard.

The American Kennel Club accepted the breed in 1930, and the Keeshond Club of America was founded in 1935. In its home country the Keeshond has now become recognized as the National Dog of Holland. In some countries, however, the breed has never been recognized because distinguishing it from the German Wolfspitz is thought to be impossible.

Because of its history as a barge dog, the Keeshond is prepared to accept more confined spaces than many breeds although, like any dog, it enjoys an outing. In modern times its main role has become that of an urban companion dog and watchdog. In personality it is vivacious, alert, 'impertinent', intelligent and outgoing. Its only weakness is that it barks a great deal, a legacy of the days when it was left to guard its barge against intruders.

References

1936. Johns, Rowland (Editor). *Our Friends the Samoyed and Keeshond.* Methuen, London.

1938. Gatacre, Alice. *The Keeshond.* Country Life, London.

1960s. Glover, B. *Belonging to a Keeshond.* Privately published, Houghton, Hampshire.

1964. Wescott, William Dennison. *How to Raise and Train a Keeshond.* TFH, New Jersey.

1972. Digby. *My Life With Kesshonden.*

1983. Weil, Martin. *Keeshonds.* TFH, New Jersey.

1984. Nicholas, Anna Katherine. *The Keeshond.* TFH, New Jersey.

1987. Cash, Carol, et al. *The New Complete Keeshond.* Howell, New York.

1993. Stahlkuppe. *Keeshonden.*

1998. Pavia, Audrey. *Guide to Owning a Keeshond.* TFH, New Jersey.

Peterson, Clementine. *The Complete Keeshond.*

RESCUE DOGS

In modern times, many breeds have been co-opted for search-and-rescue work. Some have specialized in mountain rescue, sniffing for skiers buried under snowdrifts and avalanches. Others have been employed to search for lost travellers in remote, uninhabited regions, such as the Australian outback, and have even adapted to the daunting challenge of being parachuted into the rescue zone with their trainers. Others have become expert at sniffing out living survivors in buildings destroyed by major earthquakes. But the breeds used for these tasks have already been well known in other capacities. They are not dogs that have been especially developed for such a role. Even that well-known water-rescue breed, the Newfoundland, does not owe its development as a breed to its ability to save fishermen from drowning. Its brave rescue acts were rare events in its busy working life.

There appears to be only one type of dog that was specifically developed as a rescue animal and was moulded into a new breed in the process, and that is the famous dog of the Swiss Alps, the St Bernard. It is true that the ancestors of this dog were originally employed as guards, rather than as rescue dogs, but that was before they had been refined into the breed they are today.

SWITZERLAND
St Bernard   642

SWITZERLAND

ST BERNARD   SWITZERLAND

This is a dog of many names, including Alpendog, Alpine Dog, Alpine Spaniel, Barry Dog, Good Samaritan Dog, Holy Dog, Hospice Dog, Monastery Dog, Mountain Dog, Mount St Bernard Dog and St Bernardshund. The name Alpendog was suggested in 1828. The name Alpine Dog was proposed by the Germans in 1878. The name Barry Dog was favoured by the Swiss in the mid-19th century, to commemorate the most famous example of the breed. The final name of St Bernard Dog was not adopted until 1880, after which all the earlier names fell into disuse.

This breed, the National Dog of Switzerland, has the distinction of being one of the heaviest canines in the world. The record is held by an American dog weighing in at 295 lb (133 kg), but this huge size is a modern development and is not typical of the working dog of earlier centuries.

The story of the St Bernard begins in the tenth century when a monk by the name of Bernard de Menthon established a hospice to offer aid to travellers in the Swiss Alps. The first dogs employed by the monks were mastiffs obtained from the nearby valleys. These were the descendants of the Roman Mollosian war dogs, left behind in ancient times. They were, at this stage, not rescue dogs, but watchdogs, employed to guard the properties. The monks used them in this way for many years before their special rescue abilities were discovered. These Alpine Mastiffs (see separate entry) were the ancestors of the modern St Bernard. They were smaller dogs, with shorter hair, but otherwise similar in shape, with powerful bodies, heavy heads and long, bushy tails.

Then, in the 18th century, their role changed. It was recorded in 1774 that they were being used for rescue work, locating lost travellers in need of help. It is clear from this report that, by this date, their role as rescue dogs had been established for some years, so we can assume that the transformation had occurred at least by the mid-18th century. It is also known that the monks were undertaking breeding experiments to improve their remarkable dogs and that the animals were growing in body size. Some authors believe that crosses with Great Danes were made to achieve this. Others feel that Bloodhounds were also involved, creating heavier jaws and a deeper face.

By the end of the 18th century, the fame of these life-saving dogs was beginning to spread, and many names were suggested for them, such as Good Samaritan Dogs. Two of them arrived in London at the beginning of the 19th century and were painted by the famous Victorian animal artist, Edwin Landseer. His depiction of these dogs saving the life of a stranded traveller was highly romanticized and, in order to embellish the scene, he added a wooden cask of brandy to the neck of one of the dogs. This fanciful invention of his was soon universally accepted as fact, so that, in the years that followed, no drawing or cartoon of a St Bernard was complete without it.

Landseer, as late as 1825, was still using the name of Alpine Mastiff for what was now plainly a new, improved type of dog, and it was not until 1880 that the modern title of St Bernard was adopted as the official and lasting name for the breed. In the interim there was a strong bid to have the big rescue animal called the Barry Dog. This was because the most famous individual life-saver went by that name. Between the years of 1800 and 1812, Barry saved no fewer than 40 lives. When he died, in 1814, his body was preserved and can still be seen today in the Museum of Natural History in Bern.

In the early part of the 19th century the winter storms in the Alps were so severe that several of the rescue dogs perished, so it was decided to improve the thickness of their coats. This was done in 1830 by obtaining some Newfoundlands and crossing them with the short-coated rescue dogs. (Some authors think that the Pyrenean Mountain Dog was also added at about this time.) The result was a much heavier-coated dog, better protected from the icy winds. There appears to have been some disagreement about this step, however, certain people arguing that the heavier coats would 'ice-up' and weigh down the dogs, while others felt that the thinner, old-style coats did not offer sufficient blizzard protection. As a result, neither type managed to eliminate the other and, to this day, both the dogs with thick, rough coats and those with thinner, smooth coats can be seen. However, when the great St Bernard finally made the 20th century transition to show dog and companion, it was the more spectacular, rough-coated one that was to dominate the scene.

It has been calculated that over 2,000 lives were saved by the St Bernard dogs during the centuries when they were at their most active. Some authors are sceptical about this, but there seems no reason to doubt it. Whatever the truth, the fact remains that the St Bernard was one of the most majestic of all breeds, and remains so to this day.

References

1888. Dalziel, Hugh. *The St Bernard.* Upcott Gill, London.
1891. Dalziel, Hugh (Editor). *The St Bernard Stud Book and Show Record.* Upcott Gill, London.
1929. Zulliger, Gottleib. *The Saint Bernard.* Judy, Illinois.
1936. Bullen, W. and Dickin, Norah. *The St Bernard and the English Mastiff and all about them.* Watmoughs, London.
1936. Fleischli, Joseph H. *The St Bernard.* Judy, Illinois.
1951. Barazetti, W. F. *The Saint Bernard Book.* Privately published.
1952. Denlinger, Milo. *The Complete St Bernard.* Denlinger's, USA.
1963. Denlinger, Milo. *The New Complete St Bernard.* Howell, New York.
1963. Chanoine, Marquis. *Aumonier de l'Hospice les chiens du Grand St Bernard et leurs sauvetages.*
1967. Kay, Helen. *Man and Mastiff; The Story of the St Bernard Dog Through History.* Macmillan, New York.
1990. Weil. *Saint Bernards.* TFH, New Jersey.
1992. Muggleton, Pat. *The Complete Saint Bernard.* Howell, New York.
1998. Beaver, Richard. *All About the St Bernard.* Kingdom Books, Waterlooville, Hampshire.

SLED DOGS

The sled (or sledge) is a vehicle that moves on parallel runners. Once invented, it proved to be an invaluable mode of transport across the snowy wastelands that make up no less than one third of the land mass of this planet. Pulled by teams of dogs, it enabled northern peoples to trade, hunt and move their belongings at speeds previously unimaginable. Bearing in mind the difficult terrain and the huge distances often involved, the task of pulling these sleds called for an extremely powerful dog, with tremendous stamina, willing to work in a coordinated group, and able to survive in extreme cold.

The solution to this problem came in the form of amazingly resilient dogs given the general name of huskies. At first, the title of 'husky' (a variant of the word 'Eskimo') was applied to all these northern haulage dogs. They were bred for strength and endurance, rather than looks, and there was a great deal of variability in their appearance from region to region. Then, as the years passed, different types began to develop. The differences were not created deliberately, but they were to a large extent caused by the isolation of one group of northern people from another. This led to local inbreeding of the sled dogs and a gradual establishment of a number of regional forms. Each of these eventually bred true and could justifiably be described as a breed. The differences between them were not great because the demands put upon all of them were much the same, but inevitably small features arose that made each one distinctive.

After a time, each of these breeds was given its own, special name, usually derived from the region in which it was found: the Mackenzie River Dog, the Greenland Husky, and so on. When traders and visitors from the south began to penetrate these northern communities, however, they often brought their own southern dogs with them, or introduced northern dogs from other regions. The result was that new mixings began to occur and some of the pure, local breeds began to suffer from almost random crossings. Some of the differences between them were lost and, in the end, only a few distinctive northern breeds managed to survive undiluted.

In the early part of the 20th century, the first man to reach the North Pole, the American explorer Robert Peary, found it hard to tell one husky breed from another and commented that it would be better if we treated all the sled dogs as mere variants of one major breed. Anyone attempting to unravel all the local forms today has some sympathy with this view. The fact remains, however, that, at a time when they were valid, before they had been diluted by modern interference, a dozen or more breeds did exist and were faithfully recorded in the literature. For the purposes of this book they are listed here, although only a few of them are now officially recognized. The minor, local breeds may have disappeared in the 21st century, but they were part of the history of dogs and deserve a brief, passing mention, for the sake of completeness. As a result, there are altogether 19 breeds in this category.

Regarding the three main breeds that are recognized today by the leading canine authorities, their relationship can be clarified as follows: (1) Malamute – heavyweight, very powerful but slower; (2) Eskimo Dog – middleweight, powerful with moderate speed; and (3) Siberian Husky – lightweight, strong but smaller and faster.

Note: There has been much debate over the rival use of the names Eskimo and Inuit (or Innuit). Both have been in use for many years to denote the indigenous peoples of the Arctic north of the New World, from Greenland to eastern Siberia. Europeans have employed the name Eskimo since the 16th century. It is an Algonquian Indian word and is descriptive of the special diet of the northern people. In recent times, it has been considered 'politically correct' to replace the word Eskimo with Inuit, which is a title the northern people gave to themselves. Ironically, Inuit is not a tribal name, but a racist term, implying the inferiority of Europeans. It was first recorded in the 18th century when the inhabitants of Labrador 'looked upon Europeans as upon dogs... but called themselves Innuit, which signifies men'.

GERMANY

EURASIER

Also known as the Eurasier Dog or the Eurasian, this dog represents a modern attempt to recreate an old breed. Originally created as a sled dog, it has since become a popular companion animal and show dog in its native Germany.

In the 1940s a German professor from Bergstrass in Weinheim, Julius Wipfel, crossed some Chow Chow males with large German Wolfspitz bitches. Some of the offspring of these crosses were then selected for further breeding. He chose those that were intermediate in appearance between the two parent breeds and called them Wolf-chows. The next step was to mate some of the Wolf-chow bitches with a male Samoyed. After this phase, no further cross-breeding was allowed and he continued to develop his new type of spitz dog.

The professor had been inspired by the work of the Austrian naturalist Konrad Lorenz, and the object of his breeding experiment was to create the perfect spitz dog by combining the best examples of European and Asian stock. Twenty years of carefully planned breeding followed his initial crosses and, by the 1960s, his new breed was fixed. It was officially recognized by the FCI in 1973.

This is a typical spitz dog, with pointed muzzle, heavy head, erect ears, solid body, thick, luxuriant coat and up-curled tail. Colours include fawn, red, grey, black and wolf pattern. Its height is 19–24 in (48–61 cm) and its weight 40–70 lb (19–32 kg). One anatomical oddity of the breed is that it often shows the blue-black tongue so characteristic of its Chow parentage.

In personality, the Eurasier is eager to please and a quick learner. It is shy, but not aggressive, with strangers. One of the problems that arise with this dog is that it becomes so strongly attached to the owners who rear it that it takes badly to any change of ownership, or to kennel-boarding.

RUSSIA

NORTHEASTERLY HAULING LAIKA

Also called the North-eastern Sleigh Dog, this breed is known in its homeland as the Sewero-Wostotschnaja Jesdowaja Sobaka. This is the working sled dog of the extreme eastern region of Siberia, where, even with all the technological advances of modern times, there appears to be no more efficient way of transporting people and goods across the frozen tundra.

The Hauling Laika is the specialized sled dog of Siberia. Other Russian spitz breeds occasionally act as haulage dogs, but they also carry out other important duties such as hunting and herding. This one is exclusively a sled-puller.

Without these hard-working animals, life could not go on in this desolate part of the world. They transport all kinds of goods, including mail, and also deliver doctors or vets when emergencies arise. Their work rate is almost beyond belief. They can cover up to 50 miles (80 km) a day for a six-day journey of 300 miles (480 km), pulling a weight of 100 lb (45 kg) per dog, in temperatures that are as low as —50° F (—45° C).

As with all sled dogs, the double coat, which may appear in any colour, is typically thick and weather-resistant. The neck is especially strong and muscular. When the dogs are moving, the tail is curled up over the back, and slightly to one side. This is a large dog, with a height of 23–27 in (58–69 cm) and a weight of 75–110 lb (34–50 kg).

The cumbersome title of this breed was given to it by a committee of Soviet canine experts in the 1940s. They were surveying the many different types of spitz dogs that were working in the frozen north of what was then the Soviet Union. There had been confusion over how many true breeds there were and how many local variants or strains. Laying down the law, they decreed that there were six official breeds: four were hunting dogs that also occasionally pulled sleds; one was a herding breed that could also pull sleds; and one, the Hauling Laika, was a pure sledding breed. Their classification, although it overlooked some of the finer details, has been generally accepted and is followed here.

SIBERIAN HUSKY   RUSSIA

This important breed of sled dog is also known as the Siberian Dog, the Arctic Husky, the Siberian Chukchi, the Chukchi Sled Dog, the Chukchi or the Chuchi. The name Chukchi is taken from a local tribe that lives in the Yakutsk region of the extreme north-east of Siberia, in the basin of the Kolyma River, north of the Stanovoi Mountains. There are two theories concerning the origin of the word 'husky' — it is thought to have arisen either as a European mispronunciation of 'chukchi' or as a slang abbreviation of 'Eskimo'.

This is one of the most ancient and most undiluted of all the northern sled dogs. It is claimed that it was pure-bred for as long as 3,000 years in a remote, isolated region in the extreme north-east of Siberia, where its presence meant the difference between life

and death for the local nomads. When they were forced to expand their territory in order to survive, only their Huskies made this possible.

The Chukchi custom was to castrate all but the best lead dogs and, in this way, to ensure regular genetic improvement in the breed. The task of the women was to care for the dogs when they were not working. This meant that the animals had to be near the children and this, in turn, meant that only non-aggressive individuals were favoured. So, for century after century, both the working abilities and the temperament of these dogs were gradually improved, until the Chukchi people had developed a super-dog.

This is the smallest and the fastest of the sled dogs, built for carrying lighter loads (such as killed game) at high speeds over amazingly long distances. At the end of the 19th century, Americans began to hear tales about this exceptional working dog, and when a team of imported Huskies took part in a major Alaskan sled race in 1909, they created a sensation. Very soon they were winning nearly all the races, easily beating the larger, more powerful, but slower Malamutes and Eskimo Dogs. They were soon regarded as the supreme racing sled dog.

Greater fame came to the Siberian Husky in the winter of 1925, when there was a serious diphtheria epidemic in the city of Nome in Alaska. Live-saving serum was needed urgently and it was transported there by a relay of Husky dog teams. This heroic 'Serum Run', as it became known, led by the champion Norwegian dog-driver Leonhard Seppala, was so admired that a team of his Siberian Huskies went on an appearance tour of the United States afterwards. A statue commemorating one of those dogs can still be seen in Central Park in New York. This event made the breed widely known, and only a few years later, in 1930, it was officially recognized by the AKC.

During World War II, the breed was used as a highly valued 'search and rescue dog' in the Arctic Circle by the United States military. Since then it has become increasingly popular in the United States and its numbers have grown so greatly that, in the 1960s, it was exported in some numbers to Scandinavia and Europe. There, its elegant shape and impressive bearing quickly made it a favourite, not only as a working dog, but also at major dog shows.

Words of praise used to describe this imposing dog include tireless, dignified, athletic, agile, friendly, gentle, independent and alert. It reveals its wolf-like personality in the way that it rarely barks, but does enjoy bouts of communal howling. All colours are permitted, but there is usually some kind of facial mask of contrasting pale and dark patches. In height it is 20–23 in (51–60 cm) and it weighs 35–60 lb (16–27 kg).

References

1945. Montgomery. *Husky.*

1957. Overs, Robert. *Huskies.* Bell, London.

1960. Carrighar, Sally. *A Husky in the House.* Michael Joseph, London.

1964. Demidoff, Lorna B. *How to Raise and Train a Siberian Husky.* TFH, New Jersey.

1974. Brearley, Joan McDonald. *This is the Siberian Husky.* TFH, New Jersey.

1978. Demidoff, Lorna B. and Jennings, Michael. *The Complete Siberian Husky.* Howell, New York.

1978. Peat, Neville. *Snow Dogs: The Huskies of Antarctica.* Whitcoulls, Christchurch.

1979. Pisano, Beverly. *Siberian Huskies.* TFH, New Jersey.

1985. Eylat, Martin. *Vous et Votre Husky.* Les Éditions de l'Homme, Quebec.

1990. Kern Kerry V., et al. *Siberian Huskies: Everything About Purchase, Care, Nutrition, Breeding, Behavior, and Training.* Barron, New York.

1992. Jennings, Michael. *The New Complete Siberian Husky.* Howell, New York.

1995. Sikora-Siino, Betsy, et al. *The Siberian Husky: An Owner's Guide to a Happy Healthy Pet.* Howell, New York.

1996. Kanzler, Kathleen. *A New Owner's Guide to Siberian Huskies.*

1996. Montoff, Alexei. *Guide to Owning a Siberian Husky.* TFH. New Jersey.

1998. Palika, Liz. *How to Train Your Siberian Husky.*

1998. Schlegl-Kofler, Katharina. *Huskies: A Complete Pet Owner's Manual.* Barron, New York.

1998. Wilcox, Charlotte. *The Siberian Husky.*

1999. De Beer, Hans. *Piuma: E Il Cucciolo Di Husky.*

1999. Dunbar, Ian (Editor). *The Essential Siberian Husky.*

2000. Bonham, Margaret H. *Your Siberian Husky's Life: Your Complete Guide to Raising Your Pet.*

UNITED STATES

ALASKAN HUSKY   UNITED STATES

This is the name given by Alaskan sled-racers to their fast, local dogs, specially bred for competition.

This is not a breed in the strict, anatomical sense, but it is certainly a 'type' of dog that means a great deal to the sled-dog racers. Its breed standard is measured largely by its miles-per-hour.

When southern traders arrived in the frozen north, they sought entertainment and found it in competitive sled races. Some of the local working dogs had great stamina, but lacked speed. As a result, faster-running southern dogs were mixed with the traditional sled dogs in an attempt to create champions.

The casual races that had been going on for some years were formalized in 1906 with the foundation of the Nome Kennel Club. Later, in 1948, the Alaska Dog Musher's Association was formed in Fairbanks and weekly races began. Then, in 1950, the Alaskan Sled Dog and Racing Association was established in Anchorage and the regular racing events attracted more and more attention.

As the popularity of the sled-racing grew, so did the quality of the dogs. There were all kinds of complicated breeding programmes in progress and each region had its own 'line'. All these local lines, together, were given the general label of 'Alaskan Husky', regardless of their precise appearance.

It was a highly competitive field and some breeders even went so far as to import southern sighthounds to add to the genetic mix. Labradors, Setters, German Shepherds, Samoyeds and even Springer Spaniels were all added to the mating programmes by one breeder or another, in desperate attempts to improve racing speeds. Thoroughbred racing this was not. A few of the 'lines', such as the Aurora Husky and the Huslia Husky (see separate entries), became so well established and eventually were breeding true for so long that they graduated to become minor breeds in themselves.

So, to sum up, Alaskan Husky is the name given to the northern racing dogs. It should not be confused with any of the ancient and genuine breeds of northern working dog, such as Siberian Husky or Alaskan Malamute.

ALASKAN MALAMUTE UNITED STATES

This breed is one of the oldest and strongest of the northern sled dogs. It takes its name from that of an Eskimo group called the Mahlemut or Malemuit. Occasionally it is given the longer title of Alaskan Inuit Malamute, but it may also be abbreviated simply to the Malamute. It has occasionally been recorded as the Arctic Malamute. Its nickname is the Mal.

This noble breed was first discovered by Russian explorers when they visited the Kotzebue Sound district of the Pacific Coast region of Alaska. They were surprised by how well the dogs were cared for by their owners. Most northern sled dogs were harshly treated and kept in order with the whip. But the Malamute people showed nothing but kindness to their animals and even shared their simple dwellings with them.

The intimacy between these people and their dogs was remarkable. On one occasion, a bitch Malamute, lying down to suckle her puppies, allowed a tiny naked baby to crawl over and join in, enjoying her milk, with the full approval of the baby's mother.

This was a big dog, with a height of 23–28 in (58–71 cm) and a weight of 85–125 lb (38–56 kg). It was a 'heavy-hauler', with incredible stamina. A team of these dogs was able to drag half a ton of goods a distance of 1,100 miles (1,770 km) over difficult mountainous trails.

In addition to this main duty of sled-pulling, the Malamute also performed various secondary tasks. In the summer, when it was impossible to employ sleds, the dogs were used as pack animals, often carrying as much as half their body weight in goods. They were capable of transporting burdens of as much as 50 lb (23 kg) for 20 miles (32 km) a day. At other times, they might be required to guard the herds of caribou, or assist in hunts for bear, moose or even wolf.

From 1890 until 1918 many outsiders arrived in Alaska and the sport of sled-racing became immensely popular. Although the Malamute was extremely powerful and could travel long distances, it was not built for speed. Because of this, the outsiders crossed these northern dogs with southern breeds that were built specifically for fast running. Much money was wagered on these races and every effort was made to breed champions, without any consideration for the local canine traditions. The Malamute tribesmen had always guarded their sled dogs against this kind of interference and had purebred them consistently for centuries. Now all that was lost and the special quality of the dogs inevitably went into a steep decline.

Fortunately, in the most remote outposts, enough of the original, undiluted Malamutes had been kept away from this trend. In the 1920s, two canine enthusiasts, Eva and Milton Seeley, spent 18 months living in an Eskimo village and did their best to gather together a group of these pure, untouched Malamutes, to use as the foundation stock for rebuilding the breed. Their efforts were rewarded and before long the show-ring beckoned. Apart from its athletic power, this was a breed with boldly attractive markings, especially its black cap over its pale face. An Alaskan Malamute Club was soon formed and by 1936 the breed had been recognized by the AKC.

References

1945. Caldwell, Elsie. *Noble Alaska Trail Dogs.* Richard S. Smith, New York.
1963. Berger, Charles J. *How to Raise and Train an Alaskan Malamute.* TFH, New Jersey.
1975. Brearley, Joan McDonald. *This is the Alaskan Malamute.* TFH, New Jersey.
1977. Riddle, Maxwell and Seeley, Eva B. *The Complete Alaskan Malamute.* Howell, New York.
1979. Gordon. *The Alaskan Malamute.*
1983. McCarty, Diane. *Alaskan Malamutes.* TFH, New Jersey.
1990. Riddle and Harris. *The New Complete Alaskan Malamute.* Howell, New York.
1995. Le Kernec. *Alaskan Malamutes.* TFH, New Jersey.

AURORA HUSKY   UNITED STATES

One of the minor Alaskan sled-dog breeds, the Aurora Husky was created especially for competitive racing.

When dog-racing became popular in Alaska in the first part of the 20th century, the earliest champions were nearly always imported Siberian Huskies. Attempting to improve on the speed of those remarkable, pure-bred dogs, local breeders began to experiment with a wide variety of crosses. They cared little for pure breeding, instead defining their dogs purely by their speed. This hotchpotch of cross-bred racers were collectively called Alaskan Huskies (see separate entry), but there were some that became sufficiently distinctive to be considered as separate, minor breeds. We know little about these today, as few detailed breeding records were kept, but we do have some details about one of them, the Aurora Husky.

This breed was the creation of a racer called Gareth Wright. Between the late 1940s and the early 1950s he started acquiring Yukon-Tanana River dogs from a well-known local 'musher' called Johnny Allen. Wright began mating these dogs with Irish Setters, Siberian Huskies, Targhee Hounds and other breeds, with the intention of producing a super-racer. It is reported that he even added some wolf to the mixture.

When this new breed of his was 'perfected', he called it the Aurora Husky and entered it in the sprint races, with enormous success. The dog was described as 'a red-coated, floppy-eared, blue-eyed animal that looked a bit goofy, although there was nothing goofy about its performance'. Wright boasted: 'Because of their gait, running 20 mph [32 kph] is nearly effortless for Aurora Huskies.'

This was not a flash in the pan. Wright and his daughter, Roxy Champaine, continued racing the Aurora Huskies over a period of 40 years and during that time managed to win every major sprint race in Alaska. In later life, Wright scorned the endless cross-mating that he saw going on around him, commenting: 'Once I got my principal strain going, I didn't cross any other breed into it for over 20 years.' This statement alone justifies calling the Aurora Husky a true breed.

CHINOOK   UNITED STATES

This sled dog, created in America, takes its title from the pet name of an exceptional husky owned by the breed's creator, Arthur Walden. The word 'chinook' translates as 'warm winds'.

This is a breed created by one man — the American explorer Arthur Walden. Born in New Hampshire, he left to face the challenges of Alaska in 1869. Once there he became fascinated by the local working dogs and acquired great skill as a sled-driver. In 1898 he acquired a half-breed Mackenzie River Husky called Chinook, a brilliant lead dog that he admired above all others.

When Walden returned home from Alaska, he decided to create his own special breed of sled dog. It had to be a dog with four qualities: strength, stamina, speed and friendliness. To achieve this, he started by mating a 'Greenland Husky' bitch with a 'mastiff-type' dog. The Husky in question came from a good line, being a direct descendant of Polaris, the lead dog of Robert Peary, who had been the first man to reach the North

Pole in 1907. The 'mastiff-type' had a more obscure origin, being described by Walden as 'a mongrel with perhaps a trace of St Bernard'. In 1917 a litter was born and the best puppy was given the name of Chinook, in memory of Walden's earlier favourite. This second Chinook, a large golden-coloured animal with a dark muzzle and drop ears, proved to be a wonderful lead dog and Walden decided to make him the founding father of this new breed. He crossed him with both German Shepherd and Belgian Shepherd, and then crossed the offspring back to Chinook to strengthen his qualities in the new stock. These dogs were the basis of Walden's developing breed.

When Chinook was 12 years old, Walden joined the Admiral Byrd Expedition to Antarctica. He was appointed lead driver and his dogs proved themselves to be outstanding. But Chinook went missing one day and his body could not be found. When Walden returned to his home in New Hampshire he found himself deeply in debt and was forced to sell his kennels. Later, in the 1930s, the surviving examples of the sled dog he had created were given the breed name of Chinook in his honour.

After this, the stock of Chinooks was sold on several times. Walden died in 1947, saving his wife's life when their house burned down. New owners of the dogs did little to increase their numbers. By 1966 there were only 60 Chinooks alive in the world. By 1970 this figure has fallen to a mere 12 and the breed seemed destined to disappear. But they were remarkable dogs and aroused sufficient interest to avoid complete extinction. By 1985 the number had risen back to 60, and a special survey in 1986 revealed that there were now 82 of them, of which 45 were suitable for breeding. Enough dedicated enthusiasts were now involved to ensure the future of the breed, even though it still had to be classified as a rare dog. In 1993 a national breed club was founded, called Chinooks Worldwide, and a global registry was started.

Because of its mixed ancestry, the Chinook does not look much like the other, more familiar sled dogs. With its drooped ears, its uncurled tail and its solid tawny colouring, it looks superficially more like a golden Labrador than a typical, northern spitz dog. But somewhere inside its brain lurks the intense, ancient desire to run and run over frozen wastes. As a companion, it is boisterous when young, but calm and relaxed when older. It shows great patience with children and is non-aggressive. Like all sled dogs, the world over, it 'lives to please'.

HUSLIA HUSKY   UNITED STATES

One of the minor Alaskan sled-dog breeds, this was created especially for competitive racing.

The Alaskan village of Huslia was a centre for dog-breeding in the early part of the 20th century. The huskies bred there were of a particular type. Although we know few details of their anatomy, we do know that they were identifiable as Huslia Huskies and that they had considerable success in the competitive sled-racing that was so popular in Alaska at that time.

A dog-racer by the name of George Attla won the Anchorage World Championship with this breed in 1958. Using the same breed of dog, he was then successful in the Fur Rondy race, winning it ten times, which was more than any other competitor. He also won the Fairbanks North American race on eight occasions.

The Huslia Husky was one of the breeds that together made up the type of mixed-parentage racing dog generally referred to as the Alaskan Husky (see separate entry).

INDIAN HUSKY   UNITED STATES

Like the Kugsha Dog (see separate entry), this is a breed that was recently developed at a single location in the United States, being a refinement of various long-established breeds.

This little-known dog was developed in the 1970s at Taylor, South Carolina, by the breed's founder, Becky Galliher. It was the result of blending between three northern breeds, the Siberian Husky, the Alaskan Husky and the Eskimo Dog (see separate entries). In size, it has a height of 21–26 in (53–66 cm) and a weight of 40–90 lb (18–41 kg).

The anatomical stability of these dogs is questionable, since it is stated that they 'come in three sizes with both long and short double coats'. They also appear in a wide variety of coat colours. However, although they may be variable in these respects, it is claimed that years of selective breeding and research have been carried out in order to create a sled-dog breed that has an unusually friendly temperament, is highly intelligent, is visually attractive, and has no health problems.

This breed is registered with an organization called the Northern Country Kennels and Breeders Association, which was founded in 1999 and is located in the North Georgia Mountains. The Northern Country Kennels also lists four other 'breeds' – the Alaskan Indian Husky, the Inuit Husky, the Alaskan Indian Malamute and the McKenzie Indian Husky, but these appear to be little more than variants of the Alaskan Husky, the Eskimo Dog, the Alaskan Malamute and the Mackenzie River Dog respectively.

KLAMATH-INDIAN DOG   UNITED STATES

A rare and little-known breed from the north-western United States, this dog is employed for pulling sleds and for other duties.

The dog of the Klamath tribe, who lived in a region that is today on the border of Oregon and California, was a breed distinguished from the more common and widespread Plains-Indian Dog by its short tail. It was first described by railway surveyors who encountered it in 1860. They recorded it as a large dog with a tail that was no more than 6–7 in (15–18 cm) long, a tail which was 'bushy, or rather broad, it being as wide as a man's hand'. These were not docked tails. All the puppies were born with 'bobtails', and it was clear that this was a feature that had been carefully selected by the Klamath tribe, for some reason that was not clear. Perhaps it was simply a way of identifying the animals as Klamath dogs — a way of labelling them as different from the long-tailed dogs of other tribes. Another unusual feature was that these dogs were nearly all of a brindled grey colour. Little more is known about them, except that, in addition to their haulage work, they assisted in hunting trips and acted as household pets for the women and children of the tribe.

KUGSHA DOG UNITED STATES

This is a recent breed, developed for long-distance freight haulage.

The intention, when this modern breed was being created, was to produce the ideal dog for heavy weight-pulling. To achieve this, three separate bloodlines were mixed together. They were:

1   From Pennsylvania, a Wolfen Kennels line that was refined in the mid-1970s. This type of sled dog was added to the Kugsha mix to contribute superior temperament, grace and trainability.
2   From Virginia, a HabbenHaus Kennel line based on some large, primitive sled dogs that were located in a remote region of the north-east of Alaska in the mid-1970s. Fourth-generation progeny from this line were added to the Kugsha mix to contribute a good temperament, dense bone and large webbed feet.
3   From South Carolina, a Graystone Ranch line based on large working dogs obtained from an Eskimo group near Wasilla in Alaska. This line was added to the Kugsha mix to contribute more subdued temperament, good stamina, and fluid movement.

The result of the blending of these three lines was a large, handsome, gracefully moving sled dog. Work began on the creation of this new breed in 1980 and the Kugsha breed club was eventually formed in 1998. The bushy tail is carried low, not curled over the back. The coat usually has a grizzled, wolf-like pattern, but paler forms are also known. In personality this is an intelligent, alert, untiring dog. It is shy with strangers. With other dogs it is highly competitive and soon establishes a dominance order. It remains to be seen whether it will establish itself on a long-term basis, but it certainly appears to have an enthusiastic breed organization behind it.

TARGHEE HOUND   UNITED STATES

This little-known American breed was created purely as a fast racing dog to compete in sled races. It is named after a location in the Rockies.

This dog started as a cross-breed, specially developed for sled-racing speed, and was particularly popular in the American Dog Derby in the 1920s and the 1930s. According to one report it was based on a cross between setters and greyhounds. According to another, it was, more specifically, a cross between an Irish Setter and an American Staghound. This is less of a contradiction than it may appear because the Staghound in question not only looks like a huge, rough-coated greyhound, but was also once called the Cold-blooded Greyhound. It was a fast, powerful wolf-hunting dog with enough strength, stamina and energy to make an ideal ancestor for a racing sled-dog breed.

In Alaska, the Targhee Hound was used by champion racer Gareth Wright as one of the foundation breeds when creating his famous Aurora Husky in the 1940s. By mixing the Targhee Hound with the Siberian Husky, the Irish Setter, the wolf and Yukon-Tanana River dogs, he was able to develop a super-racer that would eventually win him a number of important sled-racing prizes.

TIMBER-WOLF DOG   UNITED STATES

This breed is the biggest and the most aggressive of all the northern sled dogs. Its name refers to the fact that it is an Eskimo Dog which has been strengthened by the occasional addition of timber-wolf blood.

This is the 'king-dog' of the sled team. Because of its immense power, it always becomes the leader of any group. So determined is it to become the dominant individual, that it is usually impossible to include more than one of these ferocious animals in any team. Together, two Timber-wolf Dogs would fight so badly that they would disrupt the group.

Its use spread from Alaska to as far away as Hudson Bay. It is normally confined to carrying heavy loads over short distances. Longer trips do not, apparently, suit its temperament.

Anatomically, its special features are an unusually long back; ears that are drooping instead of pricked; a long muzzle; and a long, bushy, low-hanging tail. Its grizzled coat carries wolf-like markings.

CANADA

BAFFINLAND HUSKY CANADA

This is a regional breed of sled dog named after Baffin Island in north-eastern Canada.

Geographically, Baffin Island lies between Canada's Northwest Territories and Greenland and, as might be expected, its local sled dog is also intermediate between those on either side of it.

This is a medium-sized dog, found not only in the coastal areas of Baffin Island – which is 900 miles (1,450 km) long – but also further south, in the northern regions of Quebec. Compared with its close relatives, it has a longer back, a shorter muzzle and an unusually bushy tail.

In colour, this breed is nearly always black-and-white. White eye-spots are common. In rare cases, a tan-and-white pattern may occur. Its height is 26 in (66 cm) and its weight 80–85 lb (36–39 kg). A muscular, sturdy, heavy-boned dog, it has great power and endurance. A neighbouring breed, the Labrador, is thought to have contributed to its bloodline.

In the early part of the 20th century this dog was recorded as a breed in its own right, but today it is generally considered to be no more than a minor variant. Nevertheless, in referring to this as merely a 'local' breed, it is worth remembering that the British Isles are less than two-thirds the size of Baffin Island.

ESKIMO DOG CANADA

Also known as the Esquimaux or the Canadian Eskimo Dog, this ancient sled-pulling breed is sometimes called the American Husky, apparently as a way of distinguishing it from the Siberian Husky. In modern times, those who wish to rewrite history refer to it as the Inuit Sled Dog or the Canadian Inuit Dog. The northern people themselves call it the Qimmiq, or Kingmik.

There has been some confusion over this breed. The term Eskimo Dog has been applied in both a general and a special sense. In the general sense it has been employed to refer to almost any sled dog ever used by the Eskimo people of the Arctic. In the special sense, it has come to mean one particular breed that is now recognized as a separate entity by major canine authorities. It is in the latter sense that it is discussed here. The Canadian Kennel Club have clarified this situation by stating: 'The existing strain of Canadian Eskimo Dog originated from stock primarily bred by the Eskimo Dog Research Foundation in the Northwest Territories.'

This is the ancient sled dog of the Canadian Arctic. It was once common and widespread, but its numbers have been drastically reduced in recent times. There have been two reasons for this. First, the introduction of the Siberian Husky to North America did it no favours. The Siberian animal was smaller and faster, and when sled-racing became a major sport in the north, the Eskimo Dog could not compete. Second, the introduction of the snowmobile in the late 1960s removed a great deal of the need for the Eskimo Dog as a working animal. The northern dream now was not for a magnificent team of hard-working dogs, but for a shiny new machine.

It is estimated that in the 1920s there were 20,000 Eskimo Dogs working in the north. By the 1970s this impressive figure had shrunk to a dangerously low level of a mere 200. But then the Canadian Kennel Club and other interested parties came to the rescue and initiated a project that ensured the survival of this historic breed. There are now organizations called the Canadian Eskimo Dog Association and the Inuit Sled Dog International to protect and promote it. It also has its supporters in the United States where one kennel alone, the Wintergreen, maintains a large group of 50 dogs. It is registered with the Canadian Kennel Club, the Kennel Club in London and the FCI.

This is a powerful dog with the typical spitz configuration of strong body, dense coat, pricked ears and up-curled tail. In colour it may be white, buff, red, grey, brown or black, with or without white markings. In height it is 20–27 in (51–69 cm) and its weight is 60–105 lb (27–48 kg). Described as the 'Sherman Tank of the mushing world', it has amazing stamina and strength, but is built for long-distance work rather than fast running. Although extremely friendly and non-aggressive with people, it is intensely hierarchical and each team of dogs has been carefully selected to allow for internal dominance relationships.

References

1923. Baynes, Ernest Harold. *Polaris, the Story of an Eskimo Dog.* Macmillan, New York.
1997. Montcombroux, Genevieve. *The Canadian Inuit Dog: Canada's Heritage.* Canada.

MACKENZIE RIVER DOG   CANADA

Also known as the Mackenzie River Husky, this breed is named after its main location in north-west Canada.

In the vast, frozen area just to the east of the northern Rockies, this sled dog is the local, regional breed. It has a wide distribution, from Athabaska Lake, north to the Great Slave Lake and the Great Bear Lake.

It is very similar to the other Arctic sled dogs, but has a longer coat which is finer in texture and which lies flatter on the body. In colour, it is usually grey with dark points, but may also be fawn with white markings, or white with grey or tan points. Its height is 25 in (64 cm) and its weight 75–80 lb (34–36 kg).

In the early part of the 20th century this dog was recorded as a distinct breed in its own right but today it is generally considered to be no more than a minor variant.

TOGANEE   CANADA

This little-known breed of sled dog from north-west Canada is found mostly on the eastern slopes of the Canadian Rockies and in the Klondike region, near the border with Alaska.

This is an all-purpose haulage dog that appears to be an intermediate between the Mackenzie River Dog and the Timber-wolf Dog. A large and exceptionally powerful breed, with great stamina, it is taller and heavier than the Mackenzie River Dog.

Its coat is profuse, long, and harsh on the back and neck. The coat pattern is always tricolour – black, tan and white. Tan eye-spots are common. Its height is 26 in (66 cm) and its weight 85–90 lb (39–41 kg).

In the early part of the 20th century this dog was recorded as a distinct breed in its own right but today it is generally considered to be no more than a minor variant.

GREENLAND

GREENLAND DOG   GREENLAND

The Greenland Dog has also been known as the Grünlandshund, the Grønlands Hund or (in earlier days) the East Greenland Husky or Østgronlands Hund. And it has sometimes been called the Angmagssalik Husky, after the south-east Greenland settlement where it was most commonly found.

This typical spitz breed was first recorded in 1784, but it had been in existence for centuries before that. It is one of the most ancient of northern dogs, superbly adapted for haulage work in the frozen wastelands of the Arctic. It has managed to escape the genetic dilution that has ruined several other northern breeds, as more and more introduced dogs have arrived with their owners and mated with the indigenous spitz dogs.

The importation of foreign dogs into Greenland is now forbidden, so it would seem that this breed is at last safe for the future.

This dog was originally called the East Greenland Husky, until its neighbour, the West Greenland Husky, was wiped out by random crossing with imported dogs and the arrival of a major epidemic. The East Greenland escaped both these disasters and went on to become the sole breed in Greenland.

Special features of this dog are the ears which, although pricked in the usual spitz manner, are smaller than those of its close relatives. Its thick coat is also much longer and softer, giving it added protection against the elements. There are no colour restrictions. Its height is 22–25 in (56–64 cm) and its weight 66–70 lb (30–32 kg).

In recent years this breed has become increasingly rare in its homeland, where snow-mobiles have taken over many of the transport duties. It is still popular for sled-racing, however, and is sometimes used for seal-hunting. Abroad, it has also found a new role to play as a leisure dog, acting as a hiking companion in several Scandinavian countries.

WEST GREENLAND DOG   GREENLAND

Also called the West Greenland Husky or the Vestgrønlands Hund, this breed has now been absorbed into the East Greenland Husky to create a single breed, the Greenland Dog.

In the middle of the 19th century, this was a pure breed in its own right, larger than the East Greenland Dog and quite distinct from it. Then, in 1864, Baffinland Dogs from the east coast of Baffin Island arrived in west Greenland and mixed with the dogs there, diluting the local breed and destroying its purity. In addition to this genetic dam-age, the introduced dogs brought with them a virulent disease, an Arctic form of canine distemper called piblockto. This nearly wiped out the west coast dogs and the West Greenland breed effectively became extinct. The East Greenland Dog was unaffected, absorbed any survivors, went on to thrive, and became the sole breed in Greenland.

What little we know about the West Greenland Dog is that it was a typical spitz breed, with great strength and stamina, powerful legs and a stocky body. The bushy tail was carried high, curled up over the back. The colour was black, sable or grey, always with a white face mask, white throat, underparts and tail plume. In height it was 26 in (66 cm) and its weight was 75–80 lb (34–36 kg).

TRAVOIS DOGS

The semi-nomadic, native tribes of North America employed transportation dogs in two capacities – as sled dogs and as travois dogs. The sled, with parallel runners, was used over snow. The travois, with pointed ends dragging on the ground, was used over earth.

The front of the travois was harnessed to the shoulders of the dog. From here the poles sloped downwards until their rear ends touched the substratum. It was a primitive haulage device but, in the absence of wheels, it provided a rough-and-ready way of removing personal belongings and tribal supplies from one settlement site to another.

Three dog breeds were developed as specialists in this demanding form of canine service.

CANADA

HARE-INDIAN DOG

CANADA

This sub-Arctic dog was employed by North American tribes principally as a beast of burden to haul their belongings from place to place. It has also been recorded as the Indian Haredog, or simply as the Indian Dog.

The Hare-Indian Dog was named (after one of the tribes that kept it) by the first Europeans to explore the north-west region of Canada. In 1829 John Richardson, on this first expedition, was attracted to this smaller breed of dog, which was quite distinct from the big sled-pulling dogs such as the Malamute. It was not much bigger than a fox and, with its tapering muzzle, its erect ears and its bushy tail, was often mistaken for one. Richardson tells the story of a puppy of this breed which he adopted and which ran on the snow alongside his sled for a distance of 900 miles (1,450 km) without tiring. Its reward for this astonishing feat was to be killed and eaten by a hungry Indian who claimed that he thought it was a wild fox.

The Hare-Indian Dog appears to have been developed as an animal that could run fast over soft snow without sinking into it. Its lighter body combined with its very broad paws enabled it to do this. The native tribes employed it for hunting small game and, when food ran out, ate the dog itself. If the dog was killed as food, its coat was used to make fur coverings. But its main role appears to have been as a somewhat diminutive beast of burden. Early paintings show these little dogs dragging along the household goods of travelling tribespeople as they moved from camp to camp. Some were laden as pack animals, others pulled toboggans and still others struggled along with their load resting on a travois (two sloping poles).

In personality, this little dog was said to be docile, affectionate, gentle, playful and sensitive. It hated confinement and reacted badly to punishment. Its voice was more like that of a coyote than a domestic dog, being strong on howling and weak on barking.

There is an early record at the London Zoo which indicates that examples of this type of dog were exhibited there early in the 19th century. The entry reads: 'Hare-Indian, or MacKenzie River, 1827, or 1828.'

NORTH AMERICA

PLAINS-INDIAN DOG

NORTH AMERICA

Sometimes called the Song Dog, or the American Indian Dog, this medium-sized breed was employed by the Plains Indians of North America for haulage work during their frequent moves to new campsites.

What the sled dogs were to the northern tribes, this breed was to the tribes of the Great Plains. A well-balanced, sturdy dog with a superficial resemblance to the coyote, it was used to drag their belongings to new locations, pulling them along on a travois. This consisted of a pair of long poles, harnessed to the dog, with the lower, rear ends of the poles dragging along the surface of the ground. The larger objects were dragged along in this way by ponies, the smaller objects by the hard-working dogs.

Although this was their main function, the Plains-Indian Dogs were also employed as sentinels, trackers, herders (of buffalo) and bed-warmers. On rare occasions — for special ceremonial feasts, or when the tribe was suffering serious starvation — they were eaten. In other words, they were general-purpose native dogs, but with a primary role as beasts of burden.

These dogs had an ancient ancestry, having been bred by the American native tribes for thousands of years. In earlier days, coyote crosses were introduced from time to time, to strengthen the domestic bloodlines. Bitches on heat were tied out to be mated by wild coyote males, but this practice ceased long ago.

At one time the Plains-Indian Dogs were extremely common. In the late 18th century, European explorers reported that the Commanche and the Blackfoot tribes alone possessed no fewer than 20,000 of them. However, with the arrival of European settlers, the cultural upheaval that followed meant that they were at a serious disadvantage. Not only did their resemblance to coyotes mean that they were frequently shot as pests, but they also suffered from the severe restrictions imposed on the movements of their tribal owners. As the Native Americans were increasingly confined to Indian reservations, the need for transportation dogs declined. Their numbers dwindled rapidly and they were soon facing extinction. Many of those which did manage to survive interbred with imported European dogs, and their breed purity was lost.

In some books it is claimed that, by the end of the 19th century, like most other breeds of Native American dogs, these attractive animals had vanished for ever. Happily this is not true. A few did manage to survive and, thanks to the efforts of one man, they are now on the road to recovery. Kim LaFlamme of Selma, Oregon, is the great-grandson of a Blackfoot Indian and he remembered playing with his grandfather's dogs as a child. When he was told that his ancestral dogs no longer existed, he found it hard to believe and so started to investigate. He managed to find a few surviving pure-bred animals, and gathered these together to start a serious breeding programme. After several decades he had increased their number to nearly 200 and had even allowed a few to go to other countries.

There are now 40 breeders of this dog in North America, and its future looks secure at last. By the year 2000 it was estimated that there was a world population of about 250. Outside the United States, in Wales, Sarah Harrison is also breeding them and finds them an 'exceptional breed... humble, quiet, observant and eager to please'. They are inquisitive, alert and attentive, but they are also sensitive dogs with a tendency to become shy if they are not allowed to mix with a variety of people from an early age. They rarely bark but communicate freely with one another in a characteristic, high-pitched voice. Their 'song' consists of a strange, musical howling – a characteristic that seems to relate them to the New Guinea Singing Dog. Their body language is unusually expressive, which may be the result of their ancient coyote genes. Unlike many breeds of dog, they are not aggressive towards strangers. Their height is 18–21 in (46–53 cm) and their weight about 35 lb (16 kg). They are exceptionally long-lived and suffer from none of the usual dog ailments or genetic weaknesses.

References

1996. Harrison, Sarah A. *Out of the Past Comes a New Dawn: The American Indian Dog.* Song Dog Kennel Europe.

UNITED STATES

SIOUX DOG UNITED STATES

This larger cousin of the Plains-Indian Dog was used primarily for traction.

It has been estimated that in the heyday of the Plains Indians there were 200,000 dogs accompanying the tribes. Of these, about 150,000 were the medium-sized Plains-Indian Dogs and 50,000 were the much bigger Sioux Dogs. These were used for pulling the travois loaded with goods and, when rivers were frozen, were attached to sleds to drag heavier loads. They were also used in a secondary way, as guard dogs and hunting dogs.

These Sioux Dogs were a genuine breed, a large wolf-like dog similar in appearance to the German Shepherd Dog. They were not allowed to breed freely, but were controlled and carefully selected to keep the qualities required. Puppies that were not considered to be suitable were killed and thrown in the river. One member of the Sioux, named Buffalo-Bird-Woman, recalls: 'We had but one breed of dog in the village in old times.' The coat colour varied (white, black-and-white, grey), but in other respects it was a uniform, true-breeding dog.

The Sioux Dogs were much loved and respected by the tribespeople, and the greatest compliment they could offer to visitors was to sacrifice one of their favourite dogs for a celebratory feast. On one occasion when this had been done, the chief rose and proclaimed: 'We give you our hearts in this feast – we have killed our faithful dogs to feed you – and the Great Spirit will seal our Friendship.'

CART DOGS

Dogs have been used to pull heavy weights for many centuries. The earliest record of this activity dates from 6,000 BC. Today, when we think of transport dogs, we visualize Arctic sled dogs speeding over the snow, but in earlier times many canines were also used in other ways. In ancient Rome, for example, when the charioteers and horse-breeders went on strike in the first century AD, during the reign of the Emperor Nero, dogs were brought in as strike-breakers and were trained to pull the chariots, so that the popular races could continue. It was easy to find suitable dogs for this task as they were already in daily use, pulling loads around the city streets. They were favoured in this role because they were less expensive to keep than horses and because the ancient streets were often very narrow.

In later centuries many dogs were still used as urban beasts of burden, like miniature cart horses, dragging cumbersome wheeled vehicles behind them. In 18th-century England there were estimated to be as many as 20,000 cart dogs in service. The road surfaces were often sharp and rough, the carts heavily loaded, and the dogs ill-fed and cruelly treated. The result was that, in the 19th century, following the banning of bull-baiting and bear-baiting, a vigorous campaign was mounted against this form of canine labour. By 1840 it had been outlawed in London, where 4,000 cart dogs had been at work, and by 1855 it had been banned throughout the entire country. This ruling remains in place today and anyone employing dogs to pull vehicles of any kind (including sleds) on public highways of Britain is breaking the law. The recent enthusiasm for using Arctic dogs in light-hearted sporting events, pulling wheeled sleds on dry roads, is therefore only legal if it occurs on private land.

Other countries did not all follow Britain's lead in this matter. In Switzerland, for example, cart dogs could be seen working in the streets in the 20th century.

There are five breeds in this specialized category.

BELGIUM

BELGIAN MASTIFF BELGIUM

Also referred to as the Mâtin Belge, or the Chien de Trait Belge, this breed was best known as a cart-pulling dog, although when not on the road it was also employed as a property guard. The title 'Chien de Trait' means literally 'pulling dog' or 'draught dog'. It has also been recorded as the Belgian Draught Dog, the Flemish Draught Dog or the Vlaamsche Trekhond.

This impressively powerful dog is now believed to be extinct. Its role as a cart-pulling dog became obsolete in the 20th century and, with the ravages of two World Wars, its numbers were so reduced that it never recovered and eventually vanished altogether. The Belgian Kennel Club says that 'it may be extinct', holding out the slender hope that, somewhere, in a remote corner, a few members of this imposing breed are still clinging on. In some parts of the world this might well be possible, but in a country as dog-conscious as Belgium, it seems highly unlikely that, if they did still exist, they would not be known and recorded.

As might be expected, the Belgian Mastiff was a huge, heavy-boned, muscular dog, with a thick neck and large head. Its tail was docked very short to protect it from damage during its cart-pulling labours. It had a height of up to 31 in (78 cm) and a weight of up to 110 lb (50 kg). The short, smooth coat appeared in fawn or brindle colours, sometimes with a dark mask or with white markings. In personality the dog was said to be intelligent, calm and obedient. Little is known about its background except that it is believed to have descended from large French dogs at some point in the distant past.

SWITZERLAND

BERNESE MOUNTAIN DOG SWITZERLAND

Known in its homeland as the Berner Sennenhund, this breed also had several older names, such as the Gelbbacker ('Yellow Cheeks'), the Vieraugen or Vieraugli ('Four-eyes'), the Dürbächler or the Durrbacher. This last title referred to the district of Durrbach from which the breed foundation examples were taken. In its earlier days it was often referred to locally as the Cheese Factory Dog, the Cheesery Dog, the Butcher's Dog or simply the Farmer's Dog. Its principal duty was to act as a draught animal. In France it is known as the Bouvier Bernois. It has

occasionally been recorded as the Bernese Cattle Dog, because controlling the cattle was one of its secondary duties.

This handsome dog, with its long, symmetrically marked, tricolour coat of black, tan and white, is increasingly popular in the show-ring, but also has a long working history. It is said to have descended from ancient crosses between mastiffs and local flock guards and to have laboured in the valleys of the Swiss Alps for centuries, before becoming the focus of interest for modern canine experts.

Its numbers had started to fall in the second half of the 19th century and it was being gently absorbed into other breeds, when a Burgdorf innkeeper by the name of Franz Schertenleib set out to rescue it. He began to scour the countryside for pure specimens and found one in 1892 in Durrbach. He and other enthusiasts then started to collect more examples and after a few years a professor of geology from Zurich, Albert Heim, added his weight to the project. By 1907 a breed club had been formed and the Bernese was starting to enjoy success as a show dog.

In 1936 the first Bernese Mountain Dog arrived in the United States and a breed club was formed there in 1968. The first one to appear in England arrived in 1936, but during World War II the breed died out completely there and was not seen again until 1969, with the first English breed club being established in 1971.

When it was a working dog, the major role of this breed was to act as a beast of burden on market days. It laboured as a draught dog for weavers, butchers, dairymen and toolmakers. These craftsmen and small farmers were too poor to own horses, and dogs had to take their place. One of the main tasks was to transport fresh milk. In the 1850s cheese-making became popular and many cheeseries were built. The dogs were then employed to deliver heavy containers of milk from the dairy farms. When they were not kept busy in this way, they acted as general farm dogs, helping to guard and control the livestock.

In personality, this breed is quiet, obedient, patient, non-aggressive, loyal and ever-willing. It is particularly gentle with children.

References

1981. Cochrane, Diana. *The Bernese Mountain Dog.* Westgrove House, Warwickshire.
1989. Simonds Jude. *The Complete Bernese Mountain Dog,* Letchworth, Hertfordshire.
1992. Petch, Paddy. *The Bernese Mountain Dog.* Dickson Price.
1993. Ostermiller. *Bernese Mountain Dog.* TFH, New Jersey.
1994. Russ, Diane. *The Beautiful Bernese Mountain Dogs: A Complete American Handbook.*
1994. Smith, Sharon Chesnutt. *The New Bernese Mountain Dog.* Howell, New York.

1995. Ludwig, Gerd, et al. *The Bernese and Other Mountain Dogs: Bernese, Greater Swiss, Appenzellers, and Entlebuchers: Everything About Purchase, Care, Nutrition, Breeding.* Barron, New York.

1995. Smith, Sharon Chesnutt. *The New Bernese Mountain Dog.* Howell, New York.

1998. Willis, Malcolm B. *The Bernese Mountain Dog Today.* Howell, New York.

2000. Hubbard, Coleen. *Mountain Dog Rescue: A Story of a Bernese Mountain Dog.*

Bèartschi, Margret. *Hunde Sehen, Zèuchten, Erleben: das Buch vom Berner Sennenhund.*

GREATER SWISS MOUNTAIN DOG   SWITZERLAND

Also known as the Large Swiss Mountain Dog, or the Grosser Schweizer Sennenhund, this breed is a short-haired relative of the Bernese Mountain Dog, and is employed as a draught dog for transporting goods in carts. Its nickname is the Swissy.

This breed is very similar to the Bernese Mountain Dog, with the same, symmetrical, tricolour pattern, but in weight it reaches 135 lb (61 kg) instead of only 97 lb (44 kg). And whereas the Bernese has a long, soft, silky coat, this dog has a short, dense coat.

Late in the 19th century, as modern methods of transport replaced the old dog carts, the breed had become increasingly rare, and most people imagined that it was already extinct. Swiss canine expert Professor Albert Heim of Zurich was certainly of this opinion, and was therefore delighted when Franz Schertenleib, who was also instrumental in saving the Bernese Mountain Dog, was able to show him a pure-bred specimen that he had discovered living on a remote farmstead. Early in the 20th century a few more examples were found and serious breeding began to save this important, native Swiss dog.

In 1910 the breed was recognized by the Swiss Kennel Club. The following year the first specialist breed club was formed – by a Swiss butcher. By 1923 there was also a club in Germany and the breed was well on the way to recovery, its future ensured by its success as a show dog, even though its cart-pulling duties were now greatly reduced. The first examples to reach the United States arrived there in 1968, and an American breed club was soon formed.

Like the Bernese, in its earlier days this breed was used to haul all kinds of local produce, especially fresh milk to the cheese factories and cheeses to the markets. The dogs usually worked in pairs, with specially designed harnesses made of wide leather straps that were carefully fitted to ensure the dogs' comfort. As with its close relative, this dog has a patient, kindly, affectionate personality and shows no aggression. It is calm and steady and always ready to work.

References

1994. Hennigan. *The Greater Swiss Mountain Dog.*

1995. Ludwig, Gerd, et al. *The Bernese and Other Mountain Dogs: Bernese, Greater Swiss, Appenzellers, and Entlebuchers: Everything About Purchase, Care, Nutrition, Breeding.* Barron, New York.

1997. Barton. *The Greater Swiss Mountain Dog; a Complete and Reliable Handbook.* TFH, New Jersey.

CANADA

LANDSEER   CANADA

This breed is named after the Victorian artist Sir Edwin Landseer, whose sentimental portraits of the dog first made it famous. It is sometimes referred to as the Landseer Newfoundland. Its original role was as a fisherman's draught dog.

The Landseer is so similar to the Newfoundland (see separate entry) that in both Britain and North America it is considered to be no more than a colour form of that well-known dog. In some other countries, however, it is regarded as a distinct breed in its own right.

There was a time during the Victorian period when this black-and-white version of the Newfoundland was more popular than the typical, all-black form. Landseer was not the only 19th-century artist to depict it. Sydenham Edwards, Philip Reingale and Samuel Jones all portrayed the Newfoundland as a black-and-white dog.

As time passed, however, the black dog became more popular and the breeding of the two forms – solid colour and bicolour – split apart. After a while, this meant that other minor differences began to creep in. For example, the Landseer gradually grew taller, with longer legs, less bulk, and a longer, more tapering head than the Newfoundland. Its coat was curlier, while that of the Newfoundland was wavier. It was because of this drifting apart that some countries insisted on calling them separate breeds. In 1976, the German Landseer Club was founded, and Belgium and Holland later followed their lead.

As regards its origins, its history, its early working roles, and its temperament, the Landseer remains basically the same as the Newfoundland.

NEWFOUNDLAND

CANADA

This breed is named after north-east Canada where it was developed. Its original duty was to act as a fisherman's draught dog, but it later became famous for its seagoing rescue feats. In its earlier days it was known as the Greater St John's Dog.

This large, heavily built breed has been described as a 'huge, cuddly bear of a dog' and is one of the gentlest of all breeds, renowned for its love of children and its endless patience when enduring their more annoying habits. It has a thick coat that is usually solid black in colour, but can also appear in a dark, rich brown. Black-and-white (Landseer pattern) examples are accepted in some countries.

There is a fanciful tale that, in origin, the early ancestors of this breed were Tibetan Mastiffs brought over the Polar region by migrating tribes. It seems more likely, however, that European fishermen settling in Newfoundland brought with them large canines of the Pyrenean Mountain Dog type. Once there, these hardy dogs mated with even tougher Eskimo Dogs, to create the perfect fisherman's working companion.

This does not appear to have happened in ancient times, however. A careful survey of Newfoundland carried out by a British naval officer in 1768 revealed that the indigenous Indian tribes possessed no native dogs of any kind. Yet, by the end of the 18th century, Newfoundlands were well established there. Presumably, as soon as a few large European dogs appeared at the northern fishing ports, perhaps at about the same time as sled dogs arriving from other parts of Canada, they were found to be so useful that they were quickly bred in large numbers.

We may not know for certain how Newfoundlands originated, but we do know that their formidable duties included the following:

1   Hauling fishermen's carts, piled high with cod, to markets and to packing sheds.
2   Hauling logs from the forest for the lumbermen.
3   In the winter, dragging carts laden with fuel from the forests to the settlements.
4   As pack animals, carrying burdens strapped to their bodies.
5   Powering blacksmiths' bellows.
6   Powering turners' lathes.
7   Jumping into the freezing water and pulling the fishermen's nets ashore.
8   Jumping from fishing boats to retrieve equipment lost overboard.
9   Acting as couriers from boat to boat.
10 Carrying lifelines to shipwrecked vessels.
11 Rescuing people from drowning.

Their earliest challenges were the heavy, cart-pulling duties. But then it was discovered that they were strong swimmers and could be trained as seagoing aids on board ship. Webbed feet developed and the oiliness of their double coats was increased by selective breeding as they became increasingly specialized as marine working dogs. They became a regular fixture on the fishing vessels and it was then discovered that, in emergencies, they would plunge into the freezing water to rescue a drowning man. This last feat is the one for which they became famous throughout the world. Even though, for them, it was only a rare activity and not part of their daily routine, it was so dramatic that it would eventually come to overshadow all their other working roles.

Much later, when they became popular companion and show dogs, it was their delightful temperament for which they became justly renowned. Glowing words used by owners to describe their Newfoundlands include: benign, friendly, gentle, even-tempered, devoted, easy-going, mild and robust. Long-suffering could also be added to this list, with regard to those dogs who worked for the fishermen in the early days of the breed's history. The tasks they were asked to perform then must have been the most demanding and arduous of anything ever required of a domestic dog. Despite this, the duties were always performed without hesitation and without complaint by this truly remarkable canine.

The only mildly discordant note ever uttered in connection with this much loved breed came from the American humorist Josh Billings in 1885, when he commented: 'Newfoundland dogs are good to save children from drowning, but you must have a pond of water handy and a child, or else there will be no profit in boarding a Newfoundland'. Although it is true that pet Newfoundlands, with so little work to do these days, tend to rescue people who do not actually wish to be rescued, it would be hard to find any owner who would agree with Mr Billings's remark.

References

1927. Heim. *Der Neufundlanderhund.*

1955. Chern, Margaret Booth. *The Complete Newfoundland.* Denlinger's, USA.

1956. Stetson, Joe. *This is the Newfoundland: Official Breed Book of the Newfoundland Club of America.* Practical Science, Orange, Connecticut.

1987. Chern, Margaret Booth. *The New Complete Newfoundland.* Howell, New York.

1964. Drury, Kitty and Linn, Bill. *How to Raise and Train a Newfoundland.* TFH, New Jersey.

1969. Drury, Mrs Maynard K. (Editor). *This is the Newfoundland: Official Breed Book of the Newfoundland Club of America.* TFH, New Jersey.

1985. McDonnell, Betty. *The Newfoundland Handbook.*

1990. Drury, Kitty and Linn, Bill. *Newfoundlands.* TFH, New Jersey.

1992. Jager. *Great Balls of Fur: Life With Newfoundlands.*

1994. Bendure, Joan C. *The Newfoundland: Companion Dog – Water Dog.* Howell, New York.

1996. Kosloff, Joanna. *Newfoundlands: Everything About Purchase, Care, Nutrition, Diseases, Breeding, Behavior, and Training.* Barron, New York.

1996. Lerman, Rhoda. *In the Company of Newfies: A Shared Life.*

1998. Richards, Hedd, et al. *Newfoundlands Today.*

2000. Wilcox, Charlotte. *The Newfoundland.*

Bruno, Emmy. *The Newfoundland.*

CARRIAGE DOGS

There is only one breed in this unusual category, namely the Dalmatian. Its primary role was to accompany carriages, either to defend the occupants against attack, or to display the high status of its owners.

ENGLAND
Dalmatian 673

ENGLAND

DALMATIAN

Also known as the Coach Dog, the Brighton Coach Dog, the Spotted Coach Dog, The Carriage Dog, the Spotted Dog, the Spotted Dick, the Plum Pudding Dog or simply the Dal, this breed's main role was to accompany carriages. When working with horse-drawn fire engines, it was called the Firehouse Dog, and when accompanying long-distance coaches, it was given the name of the Marathon Runner. It has also been recorded as the Dalmatinac.

This spectacular, spotted dog is one of the most famous breeds in the world, needing little description, and yet its ancestry is one of the most mysterious and little-understood of all. The title by which it is universally known today is the biggest mystery. It was first used by Thomas Bewick in 1791, but nobody can tell where he found the connection between the animal and the Dalmatian coastal region of the Balkans. One thing seems certain – there were no Dalmatian dogs living in Dalmatia when he gave it that name. The first ones ever seen there were imported in 1930 by a millionaire ship-owner who rejoiced in the name of Bozo Banac. He bought his dogs in England and took them to live and breed in the place after which they had been named. Even stranger is the title given to these dogs by the great French naturalist Buffon. Writing between 1749 and 1767, he called the breed 'le Braque de Bengale' ('the Hound of Bengal'), and in 1790 he called it the Harrier of Bengal. There was no known connection between the dogs and Bengal in India.

The earliest European depiction we have of a dog looking like a Dalmatian is Dutch, dating from 1647. But there is no clue as to its source.

An educated guess suggests that the Dalmatian was a mutant European scenthound of some kind, with a gene for a spotted coat. Because the pattern was conspicuous and unique, it would have had immediate appeal and would have led to this type of dog being bred for its looks rather than for its scenting ability. Where this breed first appeared we will never know, but its development into a modern 'transport worker' certainly took place in England and it can therefore best be described as an English dog. As one author put it, its birthplace may be unrecorded, but England was its cradle and its nursery.

Dalmatians were transport dogs with a special duty. They did not pull weights like the traction breeds. Instead they acted as transport guards, running or walking alongside travellers to protect them or their property as they ventured forth on the highways and byways. There were three stages in the history of this activity. (1) In the early days of the breed these dogs were used as property guards in a special way. When the farmer's wife rode on her pack-pony to the nearby town to sell her produce at market, the dogs accompanied her to ensure her safety and that of her goods. It was at this stage that these dogs were sometimes called Talbots (suggesting that perhaps the old, white Talbot

Hound was the ancestor of this breed), and some English inn signs carried (and still carry) the name of 'The Packhorse and Talbot'. (2) Later, the dogs ran alongside carriages as deterrents to highwaymen, who were a common hazard on journeys in earlier centuries. (3) The conspicuous spotted dogs were employed as high-status displays when the carriages of the rich set off to attend special events or great social occasions.

Inevitably, being such a showy dog, the Dalmatian became an early favourite at competitive dog shows. Its first breed club was formed in 1890 and it was soon on its way to becoming a major star in the show-ring. In the second half of the 20th century, it would also become a star in the cinema, in Disney's *101 Dalmatians*.

The puppies are born pure white – the dark spots do not appear until the third week of life. The spots may be either black or liver brown. For show purposes, the best dogs are those in which the individual spots are clearly separated from one another and do not run together in irregular blotches. In the old days the ears were nearly always cropped, but today this practice is outlawed and the ears fold down close to the head.

References

1927. Willock, Franklin J. *The Dalmatian*. Ernest Gee, New York.

1932. Saunders, James. *The Dalmatian and All About It*. Watmoughs, Bradford.

1947. Denlinger, Milo G. *The Complete Dalmatian*. Denlinger's, USA.

1954. Johns, Rowland (Editor). *Our Friend the Dalmatian*. Methuen, London.

1956. Nelson, Evelyn S. *Pet Dalmatian*. All-Pets, Fond du Lac, Wisconsin.

1957. Hubbard, Clifford L. B. *The Dalmatian Handbook*. Nicholson & Watson, London.

1958. Miller, Evelyn. *Dalmatians as Pets*. TFH, New Jersey.

1959. Liebers, Arthur. *How to Raise and Train a Dalmatian*. TFH, New Jersey.

1962. Gore, Catherine. *Dalmatians*. Foyles, London.

1964. Frankling, Eleanor. *The Popular Dalmatian*. Popular Dogs, London.

1975. Schneider. *Know Your Dalmatian*.

1980. Pisano, Beverly. *Dalmatians*. TFH, New Jersey.

1986. Nicholas, Anna Katherine. *The Dalmatian*.

1991. Ditto, Tanya B. *Dalmatians*. Barron, New York.

1992. Treen, Alfred, et al. *The New Dalmatian; Coach Dog, Firehouse Dog*. Howell, New York.

1995. Howison. *The New Dalmatian*. TFH, New Jersey.

1995. Kosloff. *Guide to Owning a Dalmatian*. TFH, New Jersey.

1995. Strand, Patti. *The Dalmatian: An Owner's Guide to a Happy Healthy Pet*. Howell, New York.

1996. Ackerman, Lowell. *Dr Ackerman's Book of the Dalmatian*. TFH, New Jersey.

1996. Kallen, Stuart A. *Dalmatians*.

1996. Mars, Julie. *Dalmatians*.

1996. Shue. Helen W. *A New Owner's Guide to Dalmatians*.

1998. Palika, Liz. *How to Train Your Dalmatian*.

1998. Wilcox, Charlotte. *The Dalmatian*.

1999. Dunbar, Ian (Editor). *The Essential Dalmatian*.

1999. Schlegl-Kofler, Katharina, et al. *Dalmatians*.

2000. Quasha, Jennifer. *The Story of the Dalmatian*. (Dogs Throughout History)

Gregory, Geraldine. *Pet Owner's Guide to the Dalmatian*.

Sanford, William Reynolds. *The Dalmatian*. (Top Dog Series)

Silverstone, Patches. *Dalmatians Today*.

TRUFFLE DOGS

The truffle is a subterranean fungus of immense value to the world of haute cuisine. In appearance it is quite unremarkable, being described by one irreverent Italian truffle-hunter as 'something a donkey might drop while the President is giving a speech'. Despite this, gourmets and chefs will pay large sums for this hidden culinary gem and for centuries it has been hunted using the scenting ability of either pigs or dogs. The dogs in question have varied considerably over the years, but there is one form that can justifiably be called a true breed.

ITALY
Truffle Dog   676

ITALY

TRUFFLE DOG   ITALY

Also known as the Romagna Water Dog and, in Italy, as the Lagota, or the Lagotto Romagnolo, in France as the Truffleur, and in Germany as the Wasserhund der Romagna, this breed is descended largely from water-retriever ancestry. Its Italian name Lagota or Lagotto is derived from the Italian word 'lago', meaning a lake; Romagnolo refers to the northern Italian district where it originated. To grateful truffle-hunters it is known as 'the King of the Woods'.

Despite the great value of a fully trained Truffle Dog, this breed has rarely been praised by canine experts for its appearance. In 1871 it was referred to as 'nothing more or less than a bad small-sized poodle'. In 1880 it was 'a poodle with a dash of terrier'. A century later it was called a 'special little yappy mongrel dog' with a 'rustic appearance'.

The truth is that the Truffle Dog does indeed look rather like a scruffy, off-white, curly-coated little poodle, but it has never been bred for its looks. All that matters with this dog is its ability to detect the hidden truffles and its willingness to forgo distractions in the form of any game animals that might cross its path or be disturbed by its busy woodland investigations.

It is believed that the ancestors of this little dog were water retrievers working in the region of the Ravenna lagoons in Italy back in the 16th century. From there it spread to the nearby plains and then into the Romagna hills, where its main role changed to truffle-hunting. In the 20th century, the truffle men began crossing their dogs with other breeds in attempts to improve its nose, and this explains the 'mongrel' insults that have been levelled at it in recent publications. However, enough of the original type have survived and the 'poodle factor' has somehow managed to remain dominant, so that it is still possible to recognize it as a distinct breed.

In the 1970s, canine experts began to take an interest in the Truffle Dog and set about fixing the type. In 1988 the Club Italiano Lagotto was formed and by 1993 the FCI was persuaded to give it full recognition as a true breed. In 1998 a further organization was formed, the Worldwide Association of the Clubs of the Romagna Water Dog, with a view to protecting the breed on an international scale. Truffle dogs are known to be active, not only in Italy, but also in Spain, France, Norway and Sweden.

In personality this dog has been praised for its noble character and its athletic strength and perseverance. Its task is not an easy one, for the truffles it seeks usually lie 12 in (30 cm) below the surface, where they are attached to the roots of trees growing in stony soil. The white truffles are the most sought-after and fetch several thousand pounds per kilo at market. They are eaten raw, shaved into thin slices to add their unique flavouring to a wide variety of dishes.

Other Dogs

Apart from the 30 groups of dog breeds already listed under sporting dogs, livestock dogs and service dogs, there are the following which cannot be placed in any one functional category. They are the hybrids, the feral dogs and the wild dogs.

In addition, there are the obscure breeds, dogs about which so little is known that they cannot be given a full entry in this book. In some cases, only a name is known; in others, there may be a few facts, but not enough to provide a proper breed description. These breeds are included in the compilation of obscure breeds.

WOLF/DOG 'HYBRIDS'

Crosses between wolves and dogs have been made for hundreds, probably thousands, of years. It has been a common practice among Eskimos and other peoples of the extreme north to stake out a bitch husky or other type of sled dog, when on heat, and allow her to be mated by male wolves. This was done only occasionally, however, just enough to add a small amount of wolf blood to improve the strength of the working dogs, and to avoid canine inbreeding in isolated communities. It was not viewed as strange or dangerous, because the northern peoples knew a great deal about wild wolves and were fully aware that the only serious risk in making these crosses was that it might make the hybrid offspring rather shy, like their wolf parent. By allowing the crosses only rarely and keeping the wolf element very low, they were able to avoid this problem.

Recently, in both Europe and the United States, there have been cases where wolf–dog hybrids have been created and attempts have been made to stabilize these crosses to develop a powerful new breed, having the friendliness of the domestic dog, but some of the natural wild features of the wolf. There are three examples in this category.

HOLLAND
Saarloos Wolfdog   679

CZECH REPUBLIC/
SLOVAKIA
Czechoslovakian Wolfdog   680

UNITED STATES
American Tundra Shepherd   681

HOLLAND

SAARLOOS WOLFDOG   HOLLAND

Sometimes called the Saarloos Wolfhound, the Dutch Wolfdog or the European Wolfdog, this breed takes its name from its creator, the Dutchman Leendert Saarloos (1884–1969).

This remarkable animal was the creation of a Dutch breeder who had become critical of the state of modern domestic dogs. He felt that, through centuries of selective breeding, they had lost their true canine nature and had become 'degenerate'. He decided to put back some of the wild, ancestral, lupine personality by arranging matings between the domestic dog and the wolf. Saarloos started his experiments in the interwar period – the 1920s and 1930s – and was soon completely obsessed with his unusual project.

The starting point of the Saarloos Wolfhound was a cross he made between a male German Shepherd Dog called Gerard and a female wolf called Fleur. Together these two produced a total of 20 half-wolves. Back-crossing with the sire created a group of quarter-wolves. He started to train these as working dogs, but met with little success. What he had overlooked was that the main difference between the wolf and the dog is that the wolf (against all popular beliefs) is an extremely shy animal. It is this acute shyness that 12,000 years of domestication has bred out of the modern dog.

In personality his animals proved to be attentive, careful dogs, timid with strangers and cautious of novelty. To his dismay, he found that they were useless as a working dog, because they were too cautious; useless as a guard dog because they refused to attack; useless as a watchdog because they were reluctant to bark; useless as a guide dog for the blind because they withdrew the moment there was any sign of trouble; and useless for dog trials, because they were strong-willed and resisted the usual training methods.

This was not the result he had hoped for, but they were majestic animals nonetheless and he persevered. In 1963 he introduced new wolf blood, crossing one of his wolf-dogs with a female wolf called Fleur II. In 1969 Saarloos died, and in the years that followed, the breed went into a rapid decline, with too little control over breeding programmes. In 1975, Dutch canine authorities stepped in and saved the breed. Up to this point it had been known as the European Wolfdog, but now they renamed it the Saarloos Wolfdog, in honour of its creator, and gave it official recognition.

It is a large dog, with a height of 28 in (70 cm). Its wolf-like colouring, its large, prick ears, its long muzzle and strong jaws, its bushy tail and its powerful, athletic body make it an impressive sight that draws respectful attention from those who encounter it for the first time.

The breeding cycle of this dog is intermediate between that of wolves and that of domestic dogs. The bitch comes into heat only once a year, like a wolf, but she does not have a specific breeding season, which is a dog-like quality.

CZECH REPUBLIC/SLOVAKIA

CZECHOSLOVAKIAN WOLFDOG   CZECH REPUBLIC/SLOVAKIA

This dog is sometimes known as the Czech Wolfdog, but because both Czech and Slovak breeders were involved in its creation, and because it was developed before Czechoslovakia split into two, it is more correct to give it its full historical name of Czechoslovakian Wolfdog. In its homeland it is called the Ceskoslovensky Vlcak.

In the 1950s a Czechoslovakian breeder by the name of Karel Hartl started a programme involving crosses between a German Shepherd Dog called Cesar and a Carpathian wolf called Brita. His first successful mating occurred in 1958. He then crossed the wolf with another German Shepherd Dog, called Kurt, and obtained a second litter of puppies. A third mating took place between a wolf called Argo and a German Shepherd called Astra. The puppies from these three matings formed the foundation stock for the new breed.

Much later, in 1974, a third wolf was introduced into the programme. This one, called Sarik, was mated with third-generation Wolfdog bitches. A final crossing took place in 1983, between a wolf called Lady and a German Shepherd Dog called Bojar. After this, no more crosses were permitted and the bloodline was closed. All future matings took place solely between Wolfdogs.

Official recognition of this unusual breed had been resisted for many years by the canine authorities in Czechoslovakia, but in 1982 they finally agreed to accept it. A registry of puppies was started and by 1991 no fewer than 1,552 had been officially enrolled.

This is described as a loyal, docile breed, but one with quick reactions. It is suspicious and never attacks without cause, but is fearless if threatened. It has great stamina and can thrive in almost any weather conditions. In appearance it is remarkably wolf-like, thick-coated in winter, less so in summer. In height it is about 28 in (70 cm).

UNITED STATES

AMERICAN TUNDRA SHEPHERD   UNITED STATES

Sometimes known as the American Wolfdog, this is a highly controversial breed recently developed in North America.

Crosses between German Shepherd Dogs and wolves have been made in the United States and have given rise to a great deal of public debate. Ten states have so far banned these hybrids outright, and there have been many calls for them to be totally outlawed. This is partly because of the false reputation of the wild wolf, and partly because of the supposed motives of people who have been keen to own such hybrids.

The wolf has always had an undeserved reputation as a fearless, bloodthirsty killer, ready to rip out the throat of any human it encounters. In reality, wolves are extremely shy and retiring animals that give human beings a wide berth if at all possible. So the wolf element of any hybrid, far from adding to its imagined ferocity, should actually be reducing it. However, those people who want to own a Wolfdog are often individuals who wish to cause a stir and impress others with their unusual companion. In other words, they prey upon the same misguided belief that wolves are highly dangerous.

Because of the wolf's natural timidity, this would not matter unless the genetic mixture worked in a different way. If the (bold) dog element in the cross overcame the (shy) wolf element, then the hybrid animal would become, effectively, an 'un-shy wolf'. This type of animal, owned by someone who wished his Wolfdog to be, say, an aggressive personal defender, and trained it accordingly, might be a canine time bomb waiting to explode.

The experience from the carefully studied Saarloos Wolfdogs in Holland suggests that this would be highly unlikely, but it cannot be ruled out. The United States American Wolfdog Association, which was founded in 1986, will meet great opposition unless it can effectively control and screen the ownership of these powerful dogs. The figures given recently for the numbers of Wolfdogs existing in North America are frankly hard to believe. The lowest quoted figure is 80,000 and some place it as high as 600,000.

There are several forms of American Wolfdog, varying according to whether the Malamute, the Husky or the German Shepherd Dog is the domestic partner. Apparently, the only version to have been stabilized to any degree is the American Tundra Shepherd, which is based on German Shepherd Dog–wolf crosses. This has been described as a dog of limitless energy, which is strong-willed, highly intelligent, inquisitive, but cautious with strangers. It is always ready for action and needs a great deal of exercise. A tall, well-built, gracefully athletic dog with immense power, it is by any standards an impressive presence.

References

1984. Prendergast. *Wolf Hybrids.*
1994. Prendergast. *Above Reproach; a Guide for Wolf Hybrid Owners.*

FERAL DOGS

There are literally millions of domestic dogs in the world today that are living rough. Some have reverted to the wild state and are thriving in remote regions. Others have remained semi-wild and have stayed near human settlements, scratching a living as best they can. Often half-starved and diseased, they disgrace the human species. We domesticated their ancestors and tamed them. We had a working contract with them, stating that we would look after them if they would carry out certain tasks for us. Once this arrangement had been established and developed over thousands of years, we had created a whole range of domesticated breeds that relied upon us for their welfare. These dogs depended upon us, but we repeatedly ignored our responsibilities to them and abandoned them to their own fate.

Faced with the unfair challenge of competing with wild species, these stray dogs were now at a grave disadvantage. They raided our refuse, ate any filth they could find, and did their best to survive. We owe them a living but we have done precious little to help them. Occasionally we try to exterminate them – to put them out of their misery. But they are still there, in their millions, reminding us of our failure to honour our contract with the domestic dog.

In a few cases they have developed into true, local breeds, and some of these have become the focus of special interest in recent years.

There are 15 'types' in this special category.

ISRAEL

CANAAN DOG

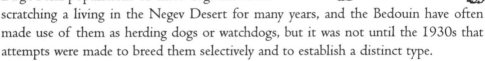

ISRAEL

Also known as the Israel Canaan Dog, the Kelef K'Naani or the Kelef Kanani, this is a feral dog of the Middle East that is becoming increasingly 'owned' and domesticated. It has also been recorded as the Kanaänhond or the Kanaan Hund.

The Canaan Dog has been described as 'the re-domestication of the Middle East Pariah Dog'. Feral populations of these dogs have been scratching a living in the Negev Desert for many years, and the Bedouin have often made use of them as herding dogs or watchdogs, but it was not until the 1930s that attempts were made to breed them selectively and to establish a distinct type.

Animal behaviour experts Dr Rudolph Menzel and his wife, Dr Rudolphina Menzel, became fascinated by this breed in 1934, when the couple arrived in Palestine from Europe. In 1935 Rudolphina Menzel was asked to recruit selected dogs for army service, and to train them in mine detection. She set about rounding up Pariah Dogs, as they were then generally known, from all over Palestine. Once they were captured they were put through a careful domestication process and those that adapted best were used for planned breeding programmes. In this way the type could be stabilized and the pedigree Canaan Dog could gradually be refined from the native Pariah. (It was Dr Menzel who gave the dog its modern name.) The breed was recognized by the Israel Kennel Club in 1953.

In addition to their military work, Canaan Dogs were soon being co-opted for use as guide dogs for the blind and for police work. The Red Cross used them for search-and-rescue duties, and they were widely employed as sentry dogs for private homes, factories and kibbutzim.

Dr Menzel recognized four variants of Pariah Dog: the heavier, flock-guard type; the curly-tailed Dingo type; the lighter collie type; and the lanky sighthound type. She chose the collie type as the basis for the Canaan Dog, and the breed standard that was drawn up by the Israel Kennel Club and the FCI in 1973 was based on this.

A medium-sized, spitzy dog, it has a basically white coat, with coloured patches that vary from cream to black. The muzzle is pointed, the ears are pricked and the bushy tail is curled over the back when the dog is active. In personality it is very alert, active and easy to train, devoted to its owners but wary with strangers. There are those who believe that it is related to the Basenji of Africa, but there is no hard evidence to support this.

This breed has a few special features that relate to its earlier life in the harshly arid conditions of the Middle Eastern deserts. It can survive on far less water or food than any other breed, and it can dissipate heat more efficiently. It also shows a powerful urge to dig holes — presumably harking back to its need to construct protective burrows when it was in a feral condition.

There are now Canaan breed clubs in both the United States and Canada, in addition to the one in Israel. Four dogs were imported to North America in 1965 by Ursula Berkowitz, and the numbers there now run into the hundreds. (It was reported that by 1986 there were 600 of them in North America.)

The Israel Kennel Club has adopted the Canaan Dog as its official symbol and it has also been named as the National Dog of Israel. In England the breed was recognized by the Kennel Club in London in 1971 and in America by the AKC in 1989.

References

1985. Shiboleth, Myrna. *The Israel Canaan Dog.* Alpine Publications, Colorado.

SOUTHERN AFRICA

AFRICANIS
SOUTHERN AFRICA

The feral dog of southern Africa has recently been adopted as a pure breed and treated with a new respect. Inevitably, it had already acquired many local, tribal names, but has now been given the official title of Africanis, which is an abbreviation of 'African Canis'. In Swahili it is called the Umbwa wa Ki-shenzi, meaning 'Traditional Dog'. In the past it has also been known as the Bantu Dog or the South African Pariah Dog. Old local names included Sica, Isiqha, Ixhalaga, Ixalagha, Isigola, I-Twina and Itiwina.

This elegant dog looks rather like a cross between a greyhound and a Dingo. Although there are some minor variations in appearance, it does breed true to a remarkable degree, considering that for thousands of years there has been no selective pressure on it from human owners. It has a well-balanced physique and appears to have built up a strong enough 'type' to resist most outside influences from random matings with other domestic dogs. The variations that do occur include a wide variety of markings and colour-patterns, ears that may be pricked, half-erect, or drooped, and the occasional presence of a ridge of hair down the back. This last feature is an obvious link to the Rhodesian Ridgeback.

This is a slender, short-coated, athletic dog, with an effortless gait, capable of running at very high speeds. It has a well muscled body of medium size, its height being 20–24 in (50–60 cm). It has an elongated head, long legs and a tail with a slightly up-curving tip. An interesting primitive feature is a dark patch high on the outside of the tail at the spot where the caudal gland is found on the wild wolf.

The Africanis claims descent from the dogs of ancient Egypt and can trace its ancestry back to the Nile Delta in 4700 BC. From there it spread, with human tribes, first to the Sahara and then, about AD 200, down towards the southernmost parts of the great continent, arriving in southern Africa at the latest by AD 570. Loosely attached to human settlements, when not running free it was often used for livestock control, as a hunting dog, a watchdog or simply a companion animal. One powerful tribal chieftain controlled his 7,000 cattle with 70 of these dogs.

This animal is renowned for its 'wisdom', a quality that cannot be doubted in a domestic breed that has managed to survive for thousands of years in a continent so full of wild predators. Although a friendly dog when being kept as a companion, it retains a natural caution when faced with novel situations. Unlike some modern show-dog breeds, it suffers from no health problems or inherited weaknesses, and has a built-in resistance to many kinds of parasitic infection.

There is now an Africanis Society of Southern Africa, based in Pretoria, which has been formed to protect and promote this breed. Their aim is to avoid the dog being split up into different types, and to retain its natural, feral character. Its long history of self-sufficiency has created one of the healthiest, most intelligent of all breeds, and that is what the Society wishes to conserve.

References

1971. Epstein, H. *The Origin of the Domestic Animals of Africa*. Africana Publishing, New York.

INDIA

PARIAH DOG   INDIA

This breed takes its name 'pariah' from the word that was used to describe the lowest caste in India. The literal translation of 'pariah' is 'drummer' and refers to drums beaten at certain Indian festivals. The term was extended to mean any human outcast and the Pariah Dog was therefore by definition an 'outcast dog'. It is also known as the Pi-Dog, Pye-Dog or Pie-Dog, taking this name from the Hindi word meaning 'outsider'.

Although they show some variability, the typical, short-coated Pariah Dogs of India usually look rather like Australian Dingoes. It would seem that, in most instances where domestic dogs have gone wild for any length of time, they all end up looking remarkably similar, as if they are reverting to an ancestral type. One might expect this type to look wolf-like, but that is rarely the case. Instead the Dingo type emerges time after time, suggesting that the ancestral wolf which gave rise to the domestic dog thousands of years ago was a small, short-coated, hot-country race and not the big, thick-coated form that we think of today as the typical wolf.

Dogs similar to the Indian Pariah are found all through southern Asia, the Middle East and North Africa. In each country they are given different, local names, but they are all much the same in appearance. They only show major variations of type in districts where recent European strays have mixed with the older feral population.

In Nepal, once a year, on the day of Swana boli, the Pariah Dogs enjoy a special event, when they are celebrated in an ancient festival. They are collected from the streets by the devout, and are bathed, groomed and garlanded. The red tika mark is placed on their foreheads and they are given a magnificent feast. Splendid as it may be, this act of benevolence is put into perspective by the fact that for the next 364 days these feral dogs must do their best to survive by scavenging on human refuse.

SRI LANKA

SINHALA HOUND
SRI LANKA

This native dog takes its name from the major ethnic group in Sri Lanka, the Sinhalese.

There is fossil evidence of the presence of domesticated dogs in Sri Lanka in prehistoric times, more than 11,000 years ago. When the legendary progenitor of the Sinhalese race first set foot in the country, back in the 5th century BC, he is said to have been greeted by the barking of dogs. And there is a Sri Lankan chronicle dating from 500 BC that refers to domestic dogs having been associated with the 'Stone Age ancestors of the Vaddhas, the Yakkas'.

Clearly, the domestic dog has a long connection with Sri Lanka, and the native dogs that still exist in a feral condition today doubtless have an ancient ancestry. Local canine experts see them as a primeval link between the Basenji of Africa, the Singing Dog of New Guinea and the Dingo of Australia, each type being a surviving legacy of prehistoric human migrations. Like all such dogs, however, familiarity has bred contempt and the local dog shows have ignored them in favour of imported 'exotics' from Europe and elsewhere. Only very recently has the Sri Lanka Kennel Club been encouraged to include the Sinhala Hound and to give it official recognition.

This dog is described as alert, watchful, amiable and obedient, with a sharp sense of scent, and is, when properly cared for, a 'doting pet'.

TIBET

CORPSE DOG

In earlier days, before the Chinese invasion of Tibet, it was the custom to lay the human dead on little mounds outside the villages so that they could be devoured by dogs. It was believed that if the dogs ate the body quickly, its soul would enjoy a swift flight to heaven. The dogs that performed this duty were of a particular type, called Corpse Dogs. They lived wild, without specific ownership, and roamed the countryside in search of food. For them, the occasion of a human death was a time for feasting and sustained them through the leaner periods.

In origin these dogs were degenerate, reduced forms of the great Tibetan Mastiff, and were described by a European visitor as 'only about the size of Irish Terriers'. They are often depicted on Tibetan 'thankas' (wall-hangings depicting religious subjects) where they are usually shown in the act of devouring human flesh or sitting next to skeletal remains. Interestingly, there are two types of Corpse Dog shown in these paintings: a pale one with pointed ears, and a black one with more rounded ears. The black one is more heavily built and is shown wearing a wide, decorative red collar. Both have a long tail that may be carried low or curled over the back. The implication of these images is that, in earlier centuries, corpses were eaten by both 'owned' (decorated) dogs and by scavenging, feral ones, as part of the ritual of death. Later, it would seem, this grue-some task was left solely to the feral Corpse Dogs.

In addition to scavenging near towns and villages, the Corpse Dogs sometimes grouped together into hunting packs and set off to attack the local fauna, reverting to an almost wolf-like existence.

MALAYSIA

TELOMIAN

This breed takes its name from the Telom river in the jungles of Malaysia, where it was first obtained. It has also been recorded as the Telemonian.

An early form of feral dog still existing today in the remote tribal territories of Malaysia, the Telomian is related to the Dingo and the New Guinea Singing Dog. It is remarkable for its climbing ability, developed because its tribal owners live in raised huts that can only be reached by ascending a primitive wooden ladder. Once inside the huts, the dogs make it their business to attack and kill any pests found there, including rats and snakes. For this service they are allowed to share their tribe's meals, but are also able to find food for themselves in the nearby bush and are even seen to catch fish from the local streams. They have managed to survive to the present day, but how long they will remain untainted by mixing with other recently imported breeds, it is hard to say.

This rare breed first appeared in the West as recently as 1963 when anthropologist Orville Elliot sent a pair back to the United States, where they were studied by canine expert J. P. Scott. They bred successfully and in 1970 the Telomian Dog Club was formed to encourage the breed. A second pair was obtained by Dr Elliot in 1973 and sent to join the others to improve the gene pool. All Telomians in the West are descended from just these four dogs.

This unusual breed produces a strange howling noise, described by one owner as a 'howl/growl/crowing' sound. Like the Basenji, the New Guinea Singing Dog and the wolf, the females only have one period of heat a year, instead of two like more typical domestic dogs. Because of its geographical position, the Telomian has been described as the 'missing link' between the (African) Basenji and the (Australian) Dingo.

INDONESIA

TENGGER DOG   JAVA

Also recorded as the East Java Dog or Javanese Dingo, this rare breed took its other name from the mountains that were its main stronghold.

This is an apparently extinct feral dog from the Tengger Mountains of eastern Java. When first discovered, it was thought to be a wild species and was named *Canis tenggeranus*. It was recorded as such in 1896 and the scientific description of the new species included the following details, paraphrased here:

The head has a well-defined stop. The ears are pricked. The fleecy coat is light brown in colour, with a reddish hue. There are some blackish-brown stripes, one of which extends from the head to the tip of the bushy tail. Another forms a dark collar. Other stripes lead from the back, down to the belly and thighs. The ears, nose and eyebrows are dark brown. The extremities of the dog are a lighter brown than the rest of the body. The underline is white. It skull is similar to that of the Dingo. Its body is 39 in (98 cm) long and the tail is 12 in (30 cm). The ears are 4 in (10.5 cm) long.

On the basis of this information it was argued that the Tengger Dog was the last remnant of a wild ancestor to the Dingo. Later studies of the skeleton of this dog confirmed that, in reality, this was a fully domesticated dog and not a wild species. It was concluded that this animal was an intermediate form between the common Pariah of India and the Dingo. As such it provides an interesting, geographical 'missing link' between the two well-known and common feral dogs of India and Australia.

One point of special interest is the striping of the coat colours. There are spotted domestic dog breeds, but apart from this Tengger Dog, there are no striped ones. A striped coat is a typically 'wild' feature among mammals. Therefore, if this dog truly was a feral, domestic breed, its striped coat was unique. For that feature alone, it would be well worth a search through the region of the Tengger Mountains today, to ascertain whether, perhaps, this fascinating breed is still surviving in some remote corners.

NEW GUINEA

GOODENOUGH ISLAND NATIVE DOG   GOODENOUGH ISLAND

This highly localized breed takes its name from the tropical island where it was discovered.

This is a true-breeding native dog that was first encountered on Goodenough Island in 1895–6 by one of Lord Rothschild's collectors who was working in the south-west Pacific. Goodenough measures only 20 x 15 miles (32 x 24 km), and lies 20 miles (32 km) off the eastern tip of New Guinea. On this small island the indigenous dog had developed in isolation from other breeds, and over the years had grown into a natural breed.

Looking like a cross between a spitz-type dog and a Papuan hill breed, its colouring is black with white markings. The coat is short and smooth, the ears small and erect, and the tail bushy. The head is described as 'flat and bullet-shaped'. The dog's height is about 14 in (36 cm) and its weight 25 lb (11 kg). Its present status is unknown.

NEW GUINEA SINGING DOG   NEW GUINEA

This dog is also sometimes referred to as the New Guinea Wild Dog, although that is a misleading title as the dog is, in origin, a domestic breed.

This fascinating feral dog is on the verge of extinction, which is a tragedy, since it is estimated to be the most primitive form of all the 500 breeds of domestic dogs. DNA studies have suggested that it is genetically more distant from all other dog breeds than any of them are from one another.

The weakness of this breed is that it is too domesticated to be protected by wildlife enthusiasts and too wild to become a favoured companion animal. It falls between these two stools and its future looks bleak. In origin, its story is similar to that of the slightly larger Dingo of Australia, which it closely resembles. When early humans began to colonize the southernmost regions of the world, thousands of years ago, they took with them their companion dogs. Some of these remained close to the tribal villages while others took off into the bush where they found plentiful animal food in the form of species not used to such efficient predators. All round South-east Asia and down into Australia, these early dogs spread out and flourished. Today they are less successful and, despite the increasing popularity of imported pedigree breeds, they themselves are on the decline everywhere. In New Guinea it is feared that the local Singing Dogs are almost extinct and those that have been exported to other parts of the world are also very low in numbers.

The breed first became famous back in 1957, when a pair from the Southern Highlands District of New Guinea was given to Taronga Zoo in Australia by the zoologist Ellis Troughton. He considered them to be a new species of wild dog – hence his gift to a zoo – and gave them the scientific name of *Canis hallstromi*. It was later realized that they were not wild, but feral dogs. They bred in the zoo without difficulty and their offspring were given to various other zoos in Europe and North America.

When the famous English orchestral conductor Sir Malcolm Sargent was performing in Sydney in the early 1960s, he was presented with a pair and had them sent back to London Zoo. On his return to England he visited them there but was not impressed by their singing abilities and quickly lost interest in them. Comedian Spike Milligan also inspected them and agreed with Sir Malcolm, commenting, memorably, that their Bach was worse than their Bitehoven. Their song is, in fact, a strangely patterned form of howling, with each dog joining in with a slightly different pitch, which gives the impression of the 'song' being composed into an eerie, counterpointed sequence. Someone remarked that, in full song, it sounds like a cross between a wolf and a whale.

Studies of these highly unusual dogs have revealed a number of special features, including dental features more wolf-like than dog-like; eyes that shine bright green in dim light; only one period of heat per year, like Basenjis and wolves; no 'play-invitation' bow, as seen in other domestic breeds; the use of an open-mouth play-bite, found in wolves but not other dogs; a shyness with strangers, similar to that seen in tame wolves; and their unique howl, unlike that of any other canines.

In 1997 a survey of the breed was carried out and it was established that only about 100 of these rare dogs were still alive in various zoos in Europe and North America. Many of these were old animals, beyond breeding age. All of them are descendants of no more that eight animals taken from New Guinea – the original pair and six more that were obtained later. Attempts to find additional examples have been made in the 1990s, but without success, suggesting that they have become extremely rare in their original home.

AUSTRALIA

DINGO

Also known as the Warrigal or Australian Native Dog, this feral breed has, in addition, a number of local names including Boolomo, Maliki, Mirigung and Noggum. The first one to be registered at the London Zoo, in 1828, was referred to simply as the Australian Dog. It is unfortunate that the name Dingo comes from the Australian Aboriginal term of contempt for imported European dogs. Their own name for their native dog was Warrigal, but in modern times the name Dingo has become too widely used to be abandoned, despite the fact that it is inappropriate. In Holland it is called the Australische Wilde Hond.

The Dingo is one of the few cases of feral dogs thriving in a wild environment. Most domesticated dogs that have to fend for themselves are forced to scratch a meagre living, usually scavenging near human settlements. The Dingo has been more fortunate, however. It was originally brought to the Australian continent by early human settlers several thousand years ago. The oldest known Dingo fossil dates from 1450 BC, but the dogs were probably there long before that date. Once they started to stray from human control on this vast new land mass, they found themselves in a carnivore's paradise, with no advanced mammalian rivals to bother them and a wide variety of marsupial species which provided easy pickings for a fast, canine predator. Wallabies and wombats became their main source of food.

Later, when Europeans arrived and introduced rabbits, the food supply grew even richer. Wild Dingoes gorged on the rabbits, but then, when the rabbits themselves became a pest, sheep farmers started poisoning them on a major scale. Their disappearance encouraged the Dingoes to turn their attention to the farmers' livestock, especially the lambs, and this in turn led to the persecution of the Dingoes. Despite this, the numbers of wild-living Dingo are still considerable. In Queensland alone it is estimated that there are between 200,000 and 350,000 of them. They are currently classified as vermin in Australia and it is illegal to keep one as a pet, although this rule is often broken. They can, however, be observed as exhibits in a number of zoos. The main threat to the breed is that it could eventually be swamped out by hybridization with feral dogs of recently imported European breeds. In recent years organizations such as the Australian Native Dog Foundation and the Dingo Study Foundation have been formed to ensure that this fascinating breed is better understood.

The importance of the Dingo is that it is, almost certainly, the oldest pure breed of dog in the world, having been left in isolation from other dogs for thousands of years. It differs in several respects from more modern breeds. Its teeth are more like those of the wolf, and the females only experience a single breeding season each year. Also, like wolves, it howls a great deal but barks very little.

One oddity of the Dingo is that, unlike wolves, and unlike many other types of feral dog, it rarely hunts in packs. It may sometimes hunt in pairs or in small family groups, but careful observations have revealed that in 73 per cent of cases the hunter is a solitary animal.

The Dingo is a short-haired dog with pricked ears and a long tail. (However, 1.5 per cent are born with short bobtails.) It is a medium-sized animal weighing 22–44 lb (10–20 kg) and with a maximum height of 21 in (53 cm). Any so-called 'Dingo' that is larger than this is the result of a cross between a pure-bred animal and a European breed.

The most commonly observed colour is a 'yellow-ginger' or tawny shade of brown, but there are several alternative colour forms, including one that is predominantly black and another that is almost white. Others show a black-and-tan or black-and-white bicolour pattern. One colour feature they all have in common, however, is pale feet and a white tip to the tail. A recent survey revealed that, of present-day wild feral Dingoes, 89 per cent are yellow-ginger, four per cent are black and tan, two per cent are white and the rest are white and a dark colour. The common yellow-ginger colour varies from light golden to deep red.

References

1968. Wright, S. *The Way of the Dingo*. Angus & Robertson, Sydney.

1980. Williams, Max. *Dingo: My Life on the Run*. Fontana/Collins, Melbourne.

1988. Breckwold, Roland. *A Very Elegant Animal: The Dingo*. Angus & Robertson, Sydney. (Contains detailed listings of scientific papers on the Dingo)

1994. Corbett, Laurie. *The Dingo in Australia and Asia*. Cornell University, Ithaca, New York.

POLYNESIA

TUAMOTUAN DOG   POLYNESIA

On the Tuamotu archipelago in the South Pacific (to the east of Tahiti) there was a native dog with long white hair which was skilled at catching fish for itself in the shallow lagoons. It was recorded as a distinct breed in the 18th century, but is now thought to be extinct. It was known to the native people as the Kurio and was probably related to the Kuri of the New Zealand Maori people.

UNITED STATES

CAROLINA DOG   UNITED STATES

Sometimes called the North American Native Dog, this ancient feral breed from the deep south of the United States is now extremely rare in the wild state. Ist local nickname is Old Yaller, referring to its pale coat colour.

Looking like a smaller version of the Australian Dingo, the Carolina Dog, with its short, dense, golden coat, its wedge-shaped head, its pointed ears and its long, curved tail, represents one of the last remnants of the native dogs that once roamed the whole of North and South America, as companions of the original Indian tribespeople.

The ancestors of these dogs must have arrived here thousands of years ago with the first human groups to colonize the vast spaces of the Americas. Attached to their human families, they first stayed close to settlements, but then many of them reverted to a wild state and fended for themselves in the rich environment that suddenly opened up for them.

As the centuries passed, most of these feral dogs eventually perished or cross-bred with more recently imported European dog breeds, until pure specimens were few and far between. Some of the specific types that are known to have vanished are the Basketmaker Dog of the Indian tribes of the south-eastern region, which also looked remarkably like the Dingo, and the Kentucky Shell Heap Dog, known from its fossils.

Only in a few remote, uninhabited corners did the ancient native dogs manage to survive. One such corner was part of the Savannah River region of South Carolina where the public are not permitted to enter. A biology professor called Lehr Brisbane discovered a population of primitive dogs there which had somehow avoided dilution from random matings with modern dogs and were still living naturally as pure-breeding stock. He called them Carolina Dogs and made a special study of them, discovering that their bones were almost identical to those of Neolithic dogs found in ancient burial grounds. He has since set up a group to monitor them.

Great care is being taken to protect these last remaining wild-living animals and, in addition, some of them are being bred and reared in a domesticated context. These home-bred ones are still rather shy, compared with modern breeds, but carefully reared from a very early age they do show the potential for becoming a fine companion dog, despite their many years of isolation from close human contact.

COYDOG   UNITED STATES

In the 1930s a previously unknown member of the dog family appeared in the extreme north-east region of the United States. The wolf had been exterminated there by the end of the 19th century, and these new animals had taken its place. They were too big to be coyotes and too small to be wolves. Zoologists did not know what to call them, but the public had no hesitation in giving them a name – they christened them Coydogs, believing that they were the result of crosses between wild coyotes and domestic dogs.

In the 1960s a litter of Coydog puppies was found and hand-reared. The dogs were bred and studied closely for a number of years by Walter and Henelette Silver of the New Hampshire Fish and Game Department, and eventually a judgement was made as to precisely what they were. They summed up their findings by stating: 'The unidentified canids are more nearly like coyotes but possess some wolf- and/or dog-like characteristics.'

As coyotes and wolves never mix when they meet in the wild, the obvious implication is that these animals are indeed the result of fertile crosses between coyotes and domestic dogs. However, they do not seem to be recent crosses and it is wrong to call these dogs 'hybrids', because the mixed genes have been present long enough for the population to have become stabilized and to be breeding true.

In other words, long ago, some coyotes met and mated with some kind of domestic dog. The offspring survived and continued to breed until a new feral animal, the Coydog, had developed of its own accord, without human assistance.

References

1942. Dice, L. R. 'A Family of Dog-Coyote Hybrids.' *Journal of Mammalogy*, Vol. 23. pp. 186–192.
1952. Cook, R. 'The Coy-Dog; Hybrid with a Future?' *Journal of Heredity*, Vol. 43. pp. 71–73.
1962. Carson, H. S. 'Coyote, Coy-Dog, or Dog.' *Maine Fish and Game, Spring*. pp. 4–7.
1969. Silver, Henriette and Silver, Walter T. 'Growth and Behaviour of the Coyote-like Canid of Northern New England with Observations on Canid Hybrids.' *Wildlife Monographs, No. 17*. The Wildlife Society, Washington.
1983. Gentry, Christine. *When Dogs Run Wild. The Sociology of Feral Dogs and Wildlife*. McFarland, Jefferson, North Carolina.

HAITI/DOMINICAN REPUBLIC

ST DOMINGO DOG   HAITI/DOMINICAN REPUBLIC

In the past, this breed has been called the St Domingo Greyhound, or simply the Feral Dog of St Domingo.

This breed developed naturally from descendants of the dogs taken to the New World by the early Spanish explorers. Some of those dogs ran wild and survived in the wooded areas of St Domingo – the Caribbean island that is now divided into Haiti and the Dominican Republic. They bred there as a feral population and gradually developed into a unique, local breed, adapting to their hot-country environment.

Buffon was one of the first to mention this St Domingo breed. Writing in the 18th century, he comments: 'Those domestic dogs which were abandoned… in America, and have lived wild for 150 or 200 years… changed from their original breed… Travellers say that they resemble our greyhounds… that they have long flat heads, thin muzzles, a ferocious air, and thin meagre bodies.' Later, in 1840, Charles Hamilton Smith published a colour plate of the breed and remarked that it had a striking appearance, being 28 in (71 cm) in height, with a short coat that was 'uniform pale blue-ash' in colour, a deep chest, long legs and small, semi-erect ears. It was such an imposing animal that, when one was taken 'down the streets, all the house curs slunk away'.

In earlier days, some of these dogs were caught, trained and then employed to track down human fugitives. In this role they were greatly feared because, unlike Bloodhounds, they could not be prevented from attacking the victim once he was found.

It is not clear whether during the 20th century these St Domingo Dogs became extinct, but it seems likely. There may be a few, managing to cling on in remote country districts, but the chances are that they were all killed off long ago by local farmers, because of the damage they were causing to the livestock. Some puppies, however, were taken and reared by the farmers as guard dogs, and it is just possible that the descendants of some of those dogs may still exist in Haiti or the Dominican Republic. If Hamilton Smith's colour plate is reasonably accurate, this was a handsome breed, and if a few survivors could be found, it could easily become a strongly supported pedigree show dog.

WORLDWIDE

MONGREL   WORLDWIDE

This word has been in use since the 15th century to refer to any dog of mixed parentage. In earlier days the name was sometimes given as mengrell, mungerell, mangrel or mungrill. It is useful to make a distinction between the accidental cross-matings of different breeds, and deliberately planned cross-matings of carefully selected breeds when new types of dog are being created. The former give rise to mongrels of unknown parentage, while the latter give rise to cross-breeds of known parentage.

The mongrel is not a true breed, but it is certainly a common category of domestic dog. It has been estimated that, worldwide, there are 150 million of them. Many are much loved pets, but the majority are strays that must somehow struggle to survive without human help. Indeed, in some places they must survive despite repeated human attempts to destroy them. Their stubborn persistence in the face of deprivation and stern opposition is a remarkable testimony to the resilience of the domestic dog.

The mongrel is endlessly variable in its anatomy and appearance, but possesses a lively energy that has been described as 'hybrid vigour'. Veterinary officials have often voiced their approval of this type of dog. The well-known London vet Dr Bruce Fogle has issued a challenge to the Kennel Clubs of the world with his recent statement that mongrels 'have never been bred for an exclusive purpose and are therefore far less likely to suffer from the wide range of inherited medical problems, such as blindness, heart disease, and hip dysplasia, that occur with distressing frequency in certain pure-bred dogs'.

The famous Austrian naturalist Konrad Lorenz added his voice to the assault on extended pure-breeding of dogs, saying: 'It is a sad but undeniable fact that breeding to a strict standard of physical points is incompatible with breeding for mental qualities.'

In defence of the hundreds of pure breeds, it should, however, be pointed out that in the majority of cases these problems of physical and mental health do not arise. Where they do so, they are now under close scrutiny and every effort is being made to correct some of the extremes of exaggerated breeding that have occurred in the past. It has to be admitted, however, that mongrels do have the benefit of a rich genetic mixing that undeniably gives them a stronger constitution, both physically and mentally. If only it also gave them the appeal that would ensure that they all found friendly owners, instead of ending up in their thousands, either on the streets, or in animal shelters waiting to be put down because no homes can be found for them.

References

1954. Riddle, Maxwell. *Lovable Mongrel*. All-Pets, Fond du Lac, Wisconsin.
1981. Cooper, Jilly. *Intelligent and Loyal, a Celebration of the Mongrel*. Eyre Methuen, London.
1985. Patmore, Angela. *The Mongrel*. Popular Dogs, London.
1997. White, Kay. *Book of the Mongrel*. HarperCollins.

OBSCURE BREEDS

While preparing this dictionary I have from time to time come across references to breeds about which little or nothing is known. It is hoped that in the future further information will become available, but for the moment they are listed here alphabetically, simply to record the fact that they exist and merit investigation. It is possible that, in some cases, the names used are early alternatives for breeds that have already been described in this book.

Please note that the presence of a dog on this list is not to be taken as an endorsement of its status as a true breed. There is not enough information to make such a decision at present. Dogs are included here simply because someone, at some point in the past, has, rightly or wrongly, recorded each one as a named breed, and it is hoped that their inclusion here will encourage closer scrutiny in the future; 278 breeds are listed.

ABYSSINIAN SHEEP DOG Registered at the London Zoo in 1841.

AFGHAN SPANIEL A small spaniel, two of which were imported into England in 1929, when they were shown at Cruft's. The long coat was red-and-white.

AGASSAEI An ancient, extinct breed – a small, shaggy dog mentioned by a third-century Greek author as 'a strong breed of dog... used for tracking... which the wild tribes of painted Britons are accustomed to breed... In power of scent... easily the superior of all other dogs, and the very best in the world for tracking.'

AICHI An extinct spitz-type breed from the central region of Japan.

ALASKAN TERRIER No information. Listed without comment by Dutch compiler, Christoph Bouthillier.

ALUBULL No information. Listed without comment by Dutch compiler, Christoph Bouthillier.

AMERICAN MASTIFF A recent breed, created by Fredericka Wagner of Piketon, Ohio. It is a huge dog, weighing up to 195 lb (88 kg). In colour it is fawn or brindle, with a black face mask. It should not be confused with the Swinford Bandog, which has also sometimes been given the name of American Mastiff.

AM TONG No information. Listed without comment by Dutch compiler, Christoph Bouthillier.

ANATOLIAN MASTIFF A massive dog from Turkey, weighing up to 200 lb (91 kg). In colour it is fawn or brindle, with a black mask. It is 50 lb (23 kg) heavier than the two Turkish flock guards, the Anatolian Shepherd Dog and the Kangal Dog.

ANDALUSIAN DOG A breed described in 1864 as having 'the short muzzle of the pug, with the long hair of the spaniel'. It was also called the Alicant Dog.

ANHUI DOG Not to be confused with the Ainu Dog, this Chinese breed from the Anhui district appears to have been developed from greyhounds/mastiff crosses. It has drooped ears and a long, thin tail.

AQUALATE SPANIEL An extinct breed of English Spaniel.

ARIKARA DOG An American breed named after the Arikara Indians of the Missouri River region in what are now North and South Dakota.

ARTOIS DOG Described in 1864 as a small dog with a 'short, flat muzzle... a produce of the shock-dog and the pug'. Not to be confused with the Basset Hound, which has sometimes been called the Artois Dog because it originated in that district of France.

ASO Listed as a native Philippines breed by PADS (the Primitive and Aboriginal Dogs Society).

BAGANDA DOG A long-legged African pack dog from Uganda, also called the Baganda Hunting Dog. Employed in the pursuit of gazelle, buffalo, hippo, and elephant. In appearance it is more like a Lurcher than a Basenji. Each pack has a 'King Dog' who wears a bell on its collar.

BAGIRMI DOG A large, powerful, pied dog from Africa.

BALI DOG Listed as a native Balinese breed by PADS (the Primitive and Aboriginal Dogs Society).

BAND KAEW DOG No information. Listed without comment by Dutch compiler, Christoph Bouthillier.

BARBARY DOG A breed registered at the London Zoo in 1839.

BARDINO MAJERO The ancient, indigenous dog of the Canary Islands which disappeared as a pure breed in the 19th century when English Mastiffs and Bulldogs were imported and crossed with it.

BASHKIR LAIKA A little-known Siberian hunting dog.

BASKETMAKER DOG An extinct North American Indian dog that once inhabited the south-eastern region of what is now the United States.

BASS-A-POO A new American breed based on a Basset Hound x Poodle cross.

BASSIM FISHING DOG No information. Listed without comment by Dutch compiler, Christoph Bouthillier.

BAUX-HOUND Described as 'a kind of hunting dog, mentioned in Holme's Academy of Armoury'. Judging by its name, this was probably a French hound associated with the medieval citadel of Les Baux-de-Provence, near Arles in southern France.

BEAG-A-POO A new American breed based on a Beagle x Poodle cross.

BELGRADE TERRIER No information. Listed without comment by Dutch compiler, Christoph Bouthillier.

BI-TZU A new American breed based on a Bichon Frisé x Shih Tzu cross.

BLACK-AND-FAWN RUSSIAN HOUND A thick-set Russian pack-hound with a long body, a blunt muzzle and a long tail, created by crossing imported foxhounds with local Russian hounds.

BLACK BOBTAIL An extinct breed of Australian cattle dog. The first type to be employed as a controller of herds in Australia, it was unable to stand the heat and was soon replaced.

BLACK POINTER Also known as the Arkwright Pointer, after William Arkwright who championed it in the 1890s. It was little more than a colour variant of the English Pointer, but has been recorded as a separate breed by some authors.

BLACK ST HUBERT An early form of St Hubert Hound called a separate breed by their owners, rather than a mere colour form.

BLACK WOLF DOG An early breed from Florida, believed by Charles Hamilton Smith to be the result of crosses between the Newfoundland and the local native Indian dogs.

BLUE SHAG SHEEPDOG An early form of rough-coated English sheepdog found in Devon and Dorset, but now extinct.

BOLONKA ZWETNA A recently developed breed of lapdog, related to the Bolognese. It appears in any colour variation or combination except the Bolognese's pure white. Established as a separate breed in 1988, it is described as ideal for the living room and with children. Its height is 8–11 in (20–28 cm).

BOLTON GREY An early form of Scottish setter, with a black-speckled grey coat described as having 'the hue of a Scotch mist'.

BORDEL Described as a terrier from India.

BRAHNI SHEEPDOG Herds sheep in the district of Nuski, in the Baluchistan region of Pakistan, just south of the border with Afghanistan. Height 24 in (61 cm).

BRAQUE POITOU An extinct French pointer.

BREVIPILIS A fashionable lapdog of the Middle Ages, based on a cross between the Pug and the Italian Greyhound. Black or brindle, with white markings. Height 13 in (33 cm); weight 16 lb (7 kg).

BUCCIRISCU A local variant of the Cane Corso, found only in Calabria, at the southernmost tip of mainland Italy. It is sometimes called the Calabrian Cane Corso and is slightly smaller than the typical form.

BULLPUG Developed from a Bulldog/Pug cross.

CALHOUN HOUND No information. Listed without comment by Dutch compiler, Christoph Bouthillier.

CAMBODIAN SPITZ DOG Two versions exist: the Cambodian Particoloured Spitz and the Cambodian Solid-coloured Spitz.

CAMEROONS DOG A primitive West African hunting dog. It is of medium size and is prick-eared, long-legged and short-coated. Its coat pattern is usually pied or variegated.

CANE CUR A local variety of the Cane Corso, found around Naples, in Italy. Also known as the Cane di Presa, it has a heavier build than the Cane Corso. It is employed mainly as a property guard.

CANE DI MANERRA A large 'molosser' or mastiff-type dog from Sicily.

CASTILIAN GREYHOUND A breed registered at the London Zoo in 1829.

CAYGOTTE A breed of native dog belonging to Mexican Indians.

CELTIC GREYHOUND An ancient sighthound, also referred to in the second century as the Vertraha, Vertregusi or Vertragus. The coat was 'fine, close and soft'.

CÉRIS An extinct French hound created by Monsieur de Céris, from crosses between the 'King's White Hound' and Swiss hounds. It was one of the three ancestors of the Billy.

CERVEIRO No information. Listed without comment by Dutch compiler, Christoph Bouthillier.

CHEREMISS LAIKA A little-known Russian hunting dog.

CHIEN DES GARRIGUES An extinct, white or grey, smooth-coated breed of French livestock dog. It was a close relative of the Berger du Languedoc.

CHILEAN TERRIER A southern relative of the Brazilian Terrier, known in the rural districts of Chile for over 100 years.

CHINCHA DOG A breed of fighting dog.

CHINCHILLA HOUND A Russian Hound, grey-coated with black points. Used in the pursuit of small game.

CHINESE COOLIE DOG A white dog with lemon or biscuit-markings on the head, a coarse coat, drooping ears and a sickle-shaped tail. A spitz-type breed looking like a cross between the Chow Chow and the Akita. Some were imported into England in the 1920s by a Colonel P. T. Etherington.

CHINESE FLOWERED DOG No information.

CHINESE HAIRLESS DOG A relative of the Chinese Crested Dog, but without its tufts of hair on the head, feet and tail. Last figured by W. D. Drury in his British Dogs in 1903.

CHODSKY PES A little-known breed from the Czech Republic.

CHOOTCH LAIKA A little-known Siberian hunting dog.

CHORCINO-INOK No information.

COCK-A-SHEL A new American breed based on a Cocker Spaniel x Shetland Sheepdog cross.

COCKER-CHON A new American breed based on a Cocker Spaniel x Bichon Frisé cross.

CONEY DOG A small breed of Lurcher created from crosses between Whippet and Border Terrier, or Whippet and Bedlington Terrier. Used for hunting rabbits.

COPOI HUNTING DOG No information. Listed without comment by Dutch compiler, Christoph Bouthillier.

CORNISH GREYHOUND A now extinct local breed of greyhound, from the extreme south-west of England.

CORSAND No information. Listed without comment by Dutch compiler, Christoph Bouthillier.

COWLEY TERRIER An extinct English terrier breed created and developed by John Cowley of King's Langley, Hertfordshire. It was a white, wire-haired, short-legged dog, marked like a Fox Terrier, and described as 'exceedingly game' and 'extremely varmint-looking'.

CREVASSEAU No information. Listed without comment by Dutch compiler, Christoph Bouthillier.

CRIMEAN SIGHTHOUND No information.

CRYNJAK No information. Listed without comment by Dutch compiler, Christoph Bouthillier.

CUBAN BLOODHOUND A breed registered at the London Zoo in 1842. (Not to be confused with the Cuban Mastiff, which arrived at the London Zoo in 1830.)

CYPRUS GREYHOUND An unusual local breed of greyhound. Employed in the 19th century to catch rather than kill hares. Once taken, the live hare is brought back to the hunter and presented to him by the hound.

DALMANER Probably a new American breed based on a Dalmatian x Weimaraner cross.

DANISH SWEDISH GUARD DOG A medium-sized, short-coated, Scandinavian property guard, similar in appearance to the Jack Russell Terrier. Known locally as the Dansk Svensk Gardshund.

DARTMOOR TERRIER A local, 19th-century breed related to the Fox Terrier and ancestral to the Jack Russell Terrier, found in the extreme south-west of England.

DAYAK DOG A Bornean native breed, intermediate in appearance between the African Basenji and the Australian Dingo. It is used by Dayak tribesmen to assist them in their forest hunts for wild pigs.

DECKER GIANT TERRIER No information. Listed without comment by Dutch compiler, Christoph Bouthillier.

DEVONSHIRE POINTER A local form of gun dog, distinguished by its 'total freedom from anything approaching a hound cross'. Also known as the Devon Pointer.

DEVONSHIRE SPANIEL A local variant of the Cocker Spaniel, most closely resembling the Welsh Cocker. It was a dark brown dog and was also known as the Devonshire Cocker.

DEVONSHIRE TERRIER A localized and now extinct breed of working terrier that was absorbed into, and eventually superseded by, the Jack Russell Terrier.

DOGO SARDO A Sardinian breed described as 'a small molosser' used for the protection of sheep and as a guarding dog. Their owners refuse to sell them to people from outside Sardinia. Also called the Dogo Sardesco.

DOGUE DE MIDA A large, 'molossan' breed also known as the Bouledogue de Mida, which may now be extinct.

DOSA A large, 'molossan' breed from Korea.

DOXIE-POO A new American breed based on a Poodle cross.

DROK-KYI No information. Listed without comment by Dutch compiler, Christoph Bouthillier.

DURMITORKSI HERDING DOG A large breed from Serbia.

DUTCH MASTIFF A large, extinct breed from Holland. The Pug was once called the Dutch Mastiff, but it appears that this title may have been applied to two distinct breeds.

DWARF TYROLEAN HOUND A reduced version of the Tyrolean Hound, with a height of only 12–15 in (30–39 cm), compared with 18–23 in (46–58 cm) for its larger relative.

EAST AFRICAN DOG A large, powerful Kenyan breed used as a hunting dog.

EDIBLE HAIRLESS DOG A naked dog from Laos.

ELOSCHABORO A new breed created by Heinz Szobries of Hannover, Germany, in the 1990s. By mixing together the Bobtail, Chow Chow, Eurasier and German Spitz, it is his aim to develop the perfect urban family dog.

ELTERWATER TERRIER An extinct English terrier breed, similar to the Border Terrier. It still existed at the start of the 20th century but vanished soon after that. It was found in the Lake District in north-west England and was worked in the field with the West Cumberland Otterhounds.

EPIRUS MASTIFF An ancient breed of Greek molossan which, according to certain Roman authors, was no match for the larger, more ferocious English Mastiff. Also known as the Grecian Mastiff.

FAULKNER TERRIER No information. Listed without comment by Dutch compiler, Christoph Bouthillier.

FINNO LAIKA A little-known European-Russian hunting dog.

FLORIDA CUR A combination of hound and bulldog, from the extreme south-east of the United States. It is used to hunt wild boar and also to herd cattle. When employed to control cattle, it is sometimes referred to as the Florida Cur Cowdog.

FOX-BEAGLE An extinct breed of small foxhound, admired for its intelligence by owners such as the Duke of Cumberland.

FOX COLLIE An extinct, medium-sized sheepdog that existed for centuries in northern Scotland. It is sometimes referred to as the Fox Shepherd.

FRIESLAND HOUND No information. (Also called the Friesland Greyhound.)

FUNLUN MOUNTAIN DOG A large breed from northern China. Two little-known breeds called the South Funlun Dog and North Funlun Dog are probably no more than variants of this one.

GALAPAGOS DOG Some of the dogs arriving on the Galapagos Islands in the Pacific aboard visiting ships remained there and bred, developing into a local breed. Uniquely they developed the amazing ability to drink sea-water. They thrived by gorging on the unique fauna of the islands, a crime for which they were completely exterminated by conservationists.

GARPEHUND A large, extinct breed from Norway.

GAUCHEN HOUND No information. Listed without comment by Dutch compiler, Christoph Bouthillier.

GAWI A large, extinct breed from Afghanistan which was also known as the Afghan Bulldog.

GLADAKKER No information. Listed without comment by Dutch compiler, Christoph Bouthillier.

GLENWHERRY COLLIE A rough-coated sheepdog from the glens of County Antrim in north-eastern Ireland. The coat is blue-and-white and may have tan markings. It was known from before the middle of the 19th century and still existed in the 1940s. Present status unknown. Also recorded as the Glengarry Collie.

GOODMAN HOUND No information. Listed without comment by Dutch compiler, Christoph Bouthillier.

GORSKAJA An extinct Russian breed, recorded as one of the ancestors of the Chortai.

GRECIAN GREYHOUND Described in the 19th century as a breed 'somewhat smaller than the English dog and the hair… longer and slightly wavy'. Appears to be a different breed from the Greek Greyhound, which is larger than the English Greyhound.

GRIFFON DE BRESSES The ancestor of the Otterhound. An ancient breed dating from at least the ninth century, and identified by one author as 'the oldest hound in Europe'.

GUJAE DOG A Korean breed, originally found on Gujae Island, it was completely exterminated during the Japanese occupation between 1910 and 1931.

HAENAM DOG Originally found in the Haenam region in the south-west of Korea, this breed was completely exterminated during the Japanese occupation between 1910 and 1931.

HATZRÜDE An early form of German mastiff.

HUDESPETH HOUND No information. Listed without comment by Dutch compiler, Christoph Bouthillier.

HUNGARIAN WOLF DOG A breed registered at the London Zoo in 1828.

HÜTESPITZ A medium-sized German flock guard. Also known as the Shepherd Spitz, it has a long, harsh, thick coat, usually white but often with some fawn markings. A thick mane and bushy tail. Erect ears. Height: 20–23 in (51–58 cm).

HYRCANIAN DOG An ancient form of mastiff, renowned for its ferocity.

INDIAN TAILLESS DOG A small Indian breed described as like a fox, but 'heavier in bone, more stoutly built, and shorter in the body'. Also said to 'resemble the Pomeranian, except that they have no tail'. A pair belonging to the Prince of Wales was exhibited in England in 1876.

INN KWE A Burmese fishing dog.

INU NUS'TO A medium-sized Japanese breed. A short-coated dog similar in appearance to a Bull Terrier.

ISTRIAN POINTER A gun dog from Istria, a peninsula protruding into the Adriatic Sea in the north-west corner of what used to be Yugoslavia, but which is now shared by the separate states of Slovenia and Croatia. The rough or smooth coat is white, with tan, red or black markings. The ears are drooped.

JACKAWAWA Probably a new American breed based on a Jack Russell x Chihuahua cross.

JAGDGRIFFON Despites its name, which means, literally, 'a wire-haired hunter', this is reported to have been a large livestock herder from Austria, similar to the Briard. Now extinct, it is thought to have been one of the ancestors of the Leonberger.

JAHASZ No information. Listed without comment by Dutch compiler, Christoph Bouthillier.

JAVANESE DOG Not to be confused with the feral Javanese Dingo, this sighthound was kept in packs by high-status Javanese for hunting the local muntjac deer.

JELLY HOUND An early type of black-and-tan Welsh scenthound, with a heavy body and a good voice.

JUAN FERNANDEZ SHEEPDOG A Chilean breed found only on the South Pacific islands of the Juan Fernandez archipelago (one of which is famous as 'Robinson Crusoe's island'), situated 400 miles (650 km) to the west of the Chilean capital, Santiago. This is a voiceless dog supposedly descended from the Patagonian Sheepdog.

KACHIN KWE A Burmese spitz dog found near the Chinese border.

KALAGH A close relative of the Afghan Hound which differs in having short hair on the body and long hair only on the head.

KAMA KWE A Burmese dog. (Its name is also given as Kame Kwe.)

KAMCHATKA DOG Writing in 1790, Thomas Bewick described a large breed of sled dog from the remote east Siberian peninsula of Kamchatka. Its coat was either black or white. It was a powerful dog, 'strong, nimble and active'. A team of them was reported to have pulled a sled a distance of 270 miles (435 km) in four days. (Note: Bewick misspelled the name as Kamschatka.)

KANNI DOG No information. Listed without comment by Dutch compiler, Christoph Bouthillier.

KENTUCKY SHELL HEAP DOG An extinct North American Indian dog that once inhabited the south-eastern region of what is now the United States. Known only from fossils.

KHAMPAS HOUND No information. Listed without comment by Dutch compiler, Christoph Bouthillier. This may be an alternative name for the Tibetan Hound (see separate entry).

KHONCH NOKHOI A Mongolian sheepdog, also known as the Mongolian Ovtcharka. This may be no more than a Mongolian version of the Central Asian Shepherd Dog. It may also be the same animal as the Mongolian Four-eyed Dog, although that may be a larger flock-guarding breed.

KOMAINU A hairy Japanese breed employed as a guardian of the nobility.

KOREL LAIKA A little-known European-Russian hunting dog.

KRYMSKAJA An extinct Russian breed, recorded as one of the ancestors of the Chortai. Listed by Dutch compiler, Christoph Bouthillier, as the Krymakaja.

LANE BASSET A local breed of basset developed by Charles Lane of Franqueville, Baos, Seine-Inférieur, France. Compared with the typical basset, it was longer-legged and lighter-boned and had a broader head and shorter ears. The dog referred to as the Lane Hound, 'a smooth-coated type of Basset Hound developed by Charles Lane', appears to be the same breed.

LANGEHREN A small, extinct, medieval breed thought to have been the ancestor of the Talbot.

LAOS EDIBLE DOG A hairless breed that became extinct in the 1940s, when the Japanese overran Laos.

LAOTIAN SPITZ DOG No information.

LAPLAND LAIKA A little-known European-Russian hunting dog.

LARYE An extinct French hound created by the Marquis François de Larye (sometimes spelled Larrye). One of the three ancestors of the Billy.

LEBANESE MOUNTAIN DOG No information. Listed without comment by Dutch compiler, Christoph Bouthillier.

LECOURS DOG No information. Listed without comment by Dutch compiler, Christoph Bouthillier.

LHASA-CHON A new American breed based on a Lhasa Apso x Bichon Frisé cross.

LHASA-POO A new American breed based on a Lhasa Apso x Poodle cross.

LIBERIAN DOG A small, compact, reddish-brown, terrier-like West African Dog. Also referred to as the Liberian Terrier.

LO-CHIANG DOG Also known as the Lo-chiang-sze or Lo-sze, this ancient Chinese breed from the western province of Szechuan is believed to be the ancestor of the Pug.

LO-LO GAU A Chinese spitz dog.

LONG-HAIRED PUG An extinct variant of the Pug, also known as the Carlin à Poil Long.

LOONG CHUA An extinct feathered version of the Pug.

LUCHAK A short-haired Afghan Hound, considered by some to be a separate breed.

MADAGASCAR HUNTING DOG A local sporting breed.

MADEIRA HOUND A little-known breed from the small Atlantic island of Madeira.

MAGELLANIC A breed registered at the London Zoo in 1833.

MAHRATTA GREYHOUND An Indian sighthound, also known as the Mahratta Dog. It is a small, smooth-coated greyhound breed, usually white with slate blue and tan markings. Height 22 in (56 cm).

MALCHOWER A large 'molosser-type' German breed.

MALTESE BULLDOG No information. Listed as an extinct breed from the small Mediterranean island of Malta.

MALTESE LITTLE LION-DOG A specially created breed that has replaced the pure white of the typical Maltese with a tan-coloured coat. It does not appear to have been a popular innovation.

MALTESE POCKET DOG Said to be the ancestor of the Chihuahua by those who believe that the latter originated on the Maltese islands.

MALTI-POO A new American breed based on a Maltese x Toy Poodle cross.

MALTOODLE A new American breed based on a Maltese x Poodle cross.

MANCHURIAN SNOW DOG A large, white Poodle-like dog with a heavy fleece.

MAUPIN DOG A special American breed of foxhound championed by General Maupin in Kentucky, and named after him. The importance of this mid-19th century dog was its ancestral role in the development of later American foxhound breeds. (See entries for Trigg Hound and Walker Hound.)

MEZZOANGUE An Italian breed created by crossing the Cane Corso and the Segugio (the Italian Hound), with the aim of combining the tracking abilities of the Segugio with the killing power of the Cane Corso, to create a dual-purpose hunting dog.

MEZZOCORSO An Italian breed created by crossing the Cane Corso and the Mastino Abruzzese, to create a better herding dog than the Cane Corso and a better flock-guard than the Mastino Abruzzese.

MEZZOLEVRIERO An Italian hunting breed created by crossing the Cane Corso with the Levriero (Greyhound). It was bred to create a faster dog than the Cane Corso.

MHA SI SAVAT A spitz dog from Thailand.

MIKAWA DOG A Japanese breed, also known as the Mikawa Inu. It is a comparatively recent breed, created from crosses between the Nippon Inu and the Smooth-coated Chow Chow.

MISTABELLA An extinct European farm dog, dating from the Middle Ages, and believed to be the ancestor of the spitz breeds.

MOGADORE A breed registered at the London Zoo in 1831.

MONGOLIAN DOG A Poodle-shaped luxury dog, with a very thick and closely packed coat that is 'as dense and deep as that of a Leicestershire sheep'. It has a long head, drop ears and a square muzzle, and is high on the leg. Taken up by French breeders and exhibited in Paris in the early part of the 20th century. Present status unknown.

MONGOLIAN FOUR-EYED DOG Mongolian equivalent of the Tibetan Mastiff. Also known as the Mongolian Mastiff. This is the largest of all the mastiffs, being 30 in (76 cm) in height. The coat is black or black-and-tan.

MONGOLIAN HAIRLESS DOG A relative of the Manchurian Hairless Dog.

MONTEMBOEUF An extinct French hound created by Monsieur de Montemboeuf (sometimes spelled Montainboeuf or Montaimboeuf). One of the three ancestors of the Billy.

MOSCOW MASTIFF No information. A large Russian breed.

MOSCOW VODOLAZ No information. A large Russian breed.

MOUNTAIN BORZOI A Russian highland coursing hound.

MUCUCHÍES A large 'molosser-type' Venezuelan breed.

NEJDI Described as a 'smooth-coated Saluki'.

NEPALESE MASTIFF This appears to have been the Nepalese equivalent of the Tibetan Mastiff. In the 19th century it was recorded as a separate breed, but this requires confirmation. It was sometimes referred to as the Nepalese Hound.

NEW GUINEA COASTAL DOG A native Papuan dog, distinct from the feral breed called the New Guinea Singing Dog. This breed is highly valued by the local people, who perform rituals in which their dogs' droppings are ceremonially placed in the sea, to the accompaniment of special chants. This is done to enhance the success of the dog as a fisherman's aid. The short, smooth coat is red-and-white. Also known as the Papuan Dog.

NEW GUINEA HILL DOG A native Papuan dog, distinct from the feral breed called the New Guinea Singing Dog. This is an inland dog, larger than the coastal, fisherman's dog, and used solely as a guardian. Its short, smooth coat is black, marked with white. It has a curled tail and small, erect ears.

NEW IRELAND DOG A close relative of the New Zealand Native Dog, enjoyed by the South Pacific islanders of New Ireland both as a companion and as a food delicacy. It has a pied coat.

NIVERNAIS DE PETITE TAILLE A smaller version of the Griffon Nivernais, now said to be extinct.

NORFOLK LURCHER A special kind of lurcher traditionally created from crosses between collies and greyhounds.

NORFOLK RETRIEVER A local breed of retriever popular in the marshy districts of East

Anglia, created from crosses between field spaniels and some kind of retriever. A coarse, hardy breed well suited to its habitat, but now apparently extinct.

NORTH CAUCASIAN STEPPE OVTCHARKA A little-known Russian guard dog. It is a smaller relative of the Transcaucasian Ovtcharka. Colours: white, grey, pied or dappled.

NORTHERN HOUND In earlier days the foxhounds from the extreme north-east of England were considered as a separate type and were then known by this name.

OLD ENGLISH BIRD DOG No information.

PANNONIAN HOUND An extinct Hungarian dog, thought to have contributed to the ancestry of the Vizsla. Also referred to as the Pannonian Dog.

PARDOG A new computer-designed breed conceived by Italian Luigi Langella in 1986. After a visit to Australia, he employed complex theoretical bio-mechanics to produce a blueprint for a breed that would be the ideal defender of Australian sheep against attacks from Dingoes. He decided that it must consist of precise percentages of Staffordshire Bull Terrier; German Shepherd Dog, Bull Terrier, Neapolitan Mastiff, Argentinian Mastiff, Dogo Argentino and Dingo. It is not clear how far his complex breeding programme has progressed at the present time.

PASTORE FONNESE Also known as the Mastino Fonnese, this breed is confined to the Mediterranean island of Sardinia. It is a dual-purpose livestock dog, acting as both a sheep-herder and a flock guard.

PASTORE SILANO A large, black-coated shepherd dog found only in Calabria, in the extreme south of Italy.

PEK-A-POM A new American breed based on a Pekingese x Pomeranian cross.

PEN-LO The name given to the tiniest version of the Pekingese, smaller even than the Sleeve or Miniature Peke. It was also known as the Pa-Erh or the Pen-Lo Pah-Erh. Its height was as little as 3.5 in (9 cm) and its weight no more than 2.5 lb (1.1 kg). It came into fashion in China in 1900, replacing the sleeve dog.

PERSIAN SHEEP DOG A breed registered at the London Zoo in 1840.

PIEBALD SHEPHERD Possibly a variant of GSD. No information.

PILA DOG An Argentinian version of the Peruvian Inca Orchid. It was recorded in Buenos Aires as early as the 15th century. Today it is rare but is still being bred. It may be dark-coloured or pale with dark spots.

PLUMIN DOG An incipient breed created on a farm in southern England in the early 1990s.

POLISH WATER DOG A medium-sized Polish gun dog which is now extinct.

POMERANIAN SHEEPDOG Also known as the Pommerscher Hütehund, this all-white breed is a native sheepdog of north-eastern Germany. In the early part of the 20th century some were imported into England and worked on farms in Devonshire.

POMERANIAN WOLF-DOG A large, wolf-like livestock-guard employed to protect sheep from the attacks of wolves. Long muzzle, short pricked ears and a long, silky coat. Colours: black, white, grey or yellow. The tail was described as 'long and spirally curled'.

POM-POO A new American breed based on a Pomeranian x Poodle cross.

PREDDA MALLORQUIN A little-known Spanish breed from the Balearic island of Mallorca.

PWAYLEE A Burmese hunting dog.

QUEBEC HUSKY A local breed of sled dog from eastern Canada.

RAFEIRO MONTANO A large Portuguese dog also known as the Rafeiro Transmontano.

REZNICKY PES A large breed from the Czech Republic, it is thought to have become extinct in the 1950s.

RINGERIKE HOUND An extinct Norwegian breed.

ROSENEATH TERRIER An extinct breed of white terrier from Scotland. It was absorbed into the West Highland White Terrier.

ROTT-A-DOR A new American breed based on a Rottweiler x Labrador cross.

RUNNING WALKER COONHOUND A smaller, faster version of the Treeing Walker Coonhound, also called the Running Treeing Walker, which some authorities describe as a separate breed, rather than as a minor variant.

RUSSIAN BULLDOG An extinct breed also known as the Mordashka.

RUSSIAN RETRIEVER A large Russian gun dog, reminiscent of the Golden Retriever, and now thought to be extinct.

RUSSO-FINNISH LAIKA Closely related to the Finnish Laika, but with a fawn instead of a golden-red coat. This breed has been listed separately from the Karelo-Finnish Laika, but it may emerge that this distinction is not justified.

RYUKYU DOG A Japanese breed employed to hunt wild pigs and other game.

SAMOS ISLAND HOUND No information. Listed without comment by Dutch compiler, Christoph Bouthillier.

SANTHAL A scenthound from eastern India. Also known as the Santal Hound.

SARAILA An Indian terrier, from the Assam region, employed as a house dog.

SEIDENSPITZ A small Toy dog from Germany, intermediate in appearance between a Pomeranian and a Maltese. It is now extinct.

SHAN KWE A Burmese spitz dog found near the Chinese border.

SHANTUNG GREYHOUND A rare form of Chinese greyhound. It was smaller than the typical greyhound breeds, and was similar to the Long-haired Whippet. It had a short, wiry coat, showing medium feathering.

SHELTIE-POO A new American breed based on a Shetland Sheepdog x Poodle cross.

SHIH-POO A new American breed based on a Shih Tzu x Poodle cross.

SHORT-NOSED INDIAN DOG A breed known only from mummified specimens found in the southern parts of the United States and the northern parts of South America, down to Peru. It was a small dog with a short muzzle, a shaggy coat, a long hairy tail and erect ears.

SHOWER OF HAIL SETTER Sometimes known simply as the 'Hail', this breed was found in the extreme north-west of Ireland and displayed a red coat sprinkled with small white spots. It is thought by many to be extinct, although a single example was observed as recently as 1998.

SIBERIAN SHEEPDOG Also known as the Tooroochan Sheepdog, this hardy livestock dog is of the spitz type, with erect ears and curled tail. Its coat is black, pied or white with tan ears. Height up to 26 in (66 cm).

SIMAKU A southern African breed used for controlling house rats and cleaning up homesteads by scavenging on discarded scraps and refuse. It originated from crosses between Pariah Dogs and terriers.

SKIOKU A little-known Japanese spitz breed with a short, harsh coat in either brindle or red. Height: 17–22 in (44–56 cm).

SMALLTESE Probably a recent American breed involving the Maltese.

SOJENICKI An Asian breed, sometimes given as the Soyenicki, thought to be one of the ancestors of the Croatian Sheepdog.

SONKUTTA A terrier from India.

SPARTIATE A smaller version of the Greek Sheepdog, considered by some to be a separate breed. Also known as the Greek Herder.

STEENBRAK A Dutch farm dog, descended from 17th-century crosses between local hound-like farm dogs and German hounds. Sometimes called the Dutch Steenbrak. Height: under 18 in (46 cm).

STRAVIERE TOSCANO A large, 'molosser-type' dog from Italy.

SUDAN GREYHOUND A small coursing hound from the Sudan which is now believed to be extinct.

TARTARY HOUND No information. Listed without comment by Dutch compiler, Christoph Bouthillier.

TEACUP POODLE Also called the Tiny Toy Poodle, this minute breed has been developed from crosses between the smallest of the Toy Poodles. Its greatly reduced size has led to health and breeding difficulties.

TEMPLE HAIRLESS DOG A naked dog from Laos.

TERMINO HOUND An extinct type of basset hound dating from the end of the 19th century in England. It had a more domed head, a more Roman nose and slightly longer legs than other basset hounds.

TERRI-POO A new American breed based on a terrier x Poodle cross.

TERRY An extinct terrier from western Scotland, similar to the Fox Terrier, but with a shorter and rounder head. Ears semi-erect or pricked. Coat colour: sandy.

THAMBAI A hare-coursing Indian sighthound.

THAMIN KWE A Burmese hunting dog.

THORNTON TERRIER An extinct breed of terrier developed by Colonel Thomas Thornton.

TIMMON'S BITER An extinct Australian sheepdog developed in the 19th century from crosses between European collies and native Dingoes.

TRAILHOUND A local breed of scenthound developed for hill-racing over a long, man-made, aniseed trail. Found only in the west Cumberland region of north-west England. This lively, intelligent dog is essentially a faster, longer-legged version of the foxhound.

TRESETNI An Asian breed, considered to be one of the ancestors of the Croatian Sheepdog.

TUNGUSE LAIKA A little-known Siberian hunting dog.

TURKISH YELLOW DOG A breed thought to have contributed to the ancestry of the Vizsla.

TYROLEAN SHEEPDOG An Austrian breed from the Tyrol that is similar in appearance to the Welsh Sheepdog or the old British working collie.

UBANJI No information. Listed without comment by Dutch compiler, Christoph Bouthillier.

UKRANIAN SHEEPDOG A common sheepdog in the Ukraine, with a long, rough, thick coat, long ears and a plumed tail. Used in the past by the Russian military as an army messenger dog. Closely related to the Hungarian Komondor.

UTCHAK SHEEPDOG Described as 'a notoriously aggressive dog', this breed was used to increase the size and ferocity of the Russo-European Laika.

VIETNAMESE SPITZ DOG No information.

VOGOOL LAIKA A little-known European-Russian hunting dog.

VUCCERISCO A butcher's dog from Sicily, looking like a slightly smaller version of the Cane Corso. It was thought to be extinct, but a recent survey has revealed that there are still a few hundred left on the island.

WALLIS SHEEPDOG An extinct European breed of livestock guardian.

WEST AFRICAN MOUSE DOG A rare breed about which little is known. It is said that only a single example has ever been seen in England. It had a short, smooth red coat, and looked like a small version of a Dobermann. Its height was 14 in (36 cm).

WEST RUSSIAN COURSING HOUND A Russian sighthound with a thick, smooth coat. It is not clear whether this is a separate breed, or an alternative name for one of the other Russian sighthounds, such as the Chortai or Tazi.

WHITE TOY TERRIER A dwarf version of the English White Terrier. Both are now extinct. The miniature breed weighed only 3–4 lb (1.5–2 kg).

WOLD GREYHOUND A large, long-haired, curly-tailed breed of greyhound developed in the 18th century to course hares on the difficult terrain of England's Yorkshire moors. It was prepared to take a hare even in the middle of a thorn-bush. Now extinct.

YAK HOUND No information.

YAKKI DOG Icelandic breed taken to the Shetland islands by whalers.

YORKIE-POO A new American breed based on a Yorkshire Terrier x Poodle cross.

YORKI-HUAHUA A new American breed based on a Yorkshire Terrier x Chihuahua cross.

YORKSHIRE BUCKHOUND An extinct breed of Staghound, from north-east England.

YORKSHIRE HEELER No information.

YORKTESE A new American breed based on a Yorkshire Terrier x Maltese cross.

ZORIAN LAIKA A little-known European-Russian hunting dog.

ZULU DOG A small, strong, square-muzzled, fawn-coated African dog used as both a guard and a hunter. It should not be confused with the Zulu Sand Dog, which is hairless.

WILD DOGS

This is a dictionary of domestic dogs, but for the sake of completeness, the following very brief details of the seven wild species of the genus *Canis* are included:

WOLF (*CANIS LUPUS*)   EUROPE/ASIA/NORTH AMERICA/ARCTIC

This species has also been called the grey wolf, the Eurasian wolf, the northern wolf or the timber wolf.

The wolf is the ancestor of all domestic dogs. Until the last few centuries it was an immensely successful and widespread predator, but has been ruthlessly destroyed both as a pest and for its valuable fur. Wherever human agriculture has spread, the wolf has become an enemy of the farmers, and its attacks on their livestock have led to its complete extermination in many regions. It survives today only in remote areas or in densely forested districts. It was extinct in England by the 16th century and in Scotland and Ireland by the 18th. Tiny populations still survive in some European countries. There are about 700 in Spain and Portugal, about 300 in Italy, and small groups in Finland, Norway, Sweden, Greece, Bulgaria, Slovakia, the Czech Republic, Yugoslavia, Rumania and Poland. It has fared better in Russia, where it is estimated that about 100,000 exist even today. In North America wolves were once common over the whole region, from the extreme north to as far south as Mexico. Today they have been exterminated almost everywhere except the frozen north, where they are now protected. The only New World regions where they are still found living naturally in the wild are Canada, Alaska and northern Minnesota. It is estimated that there is now a total of about 60,000 wolves in these areas. In the 1990s a very small number were reintroduced into Yellowstone National Park by conservationists, against strong opposition from local ranchers.

Wolves are pack-hunters that pursue large prey, and in their behaviour it is possible to see all the elements that have been exaggerated in different breeds of dogs. When they set off together on a hunt, the first one to catch the scent of the prey stops in its tracks and stays very still, facing the direction of the scent. This is the action that has been emphasized during the development of the modern pointers. When the pack comes closer to the prey they fan out and encircle it. This is what has been accentuated in the development of modern herding dogs. As they cautiously close in on the prey, they often lie down to conceal themselves as they wait, aiming their body in the direction of the unsuspecting victim. This is the action that has been emphazised in the development of modern setters. When they finally rush in for the kill, they leap at the prey, drag it to the ground and kill it. This is what has been focused upon in the development of modern sighthounds and scenthounds. The biting at the legs of the fleeing prey has been emphasized in the development of modern cattle-droving dogs. Smaller prey may be driven into trees or dug out of their burrows — leading today to the treeing dogs and to earth dogs like the terriers. Adult hunting wolves often bring home a food surplus for their cubs — the basis of the actions of modern retrievers.

References

There is a huge amount of literature on the wolf. The following is a small selection:

1944. Young, Stanley P. and Goldman, Edward A. *The Wolves of North America.* American Wildlife Institute, Washington.
1958. Crisler, Lois. *Arctic Wild.* Curtis, New York.
1963. Mowat, F. *Never Cry Wolf.* Little, Brown, Boston.
1968. Rutter, R. J. and Pimlott, D. H. *The World of the Wolf.* Lippincott, Philadelphia.
1970. Mech, L. David. *The Wolf: The Ecology and Behavior of an Endangered Species.* Natural History Press, New York.
1976. Fiennes, Richard. *The Order of Wolves.* Bobbs-Merrill, Indianapolis.
1978. Hall, Roberta L. and Sharp, Henry S. (Editors). *Wolf and Man. Evolution in Parallel.* Academic Press, London.
1978. Lopez, Barry Holstun. *Of Wolves and Men.* Dent, London.
1980. Fox, Michael W. *The Soul of the Wolf.* Lyons & Burford, New York.
1981. Zimen, Erik. *The Wolf. His Place in the Natural World.* Souvenir Press, London.
1988. Mech, L. David. *The Arctic Wolf. Living with the Pack.* Voyageur Press, Stillwater, Minnesota.
1992. Mech, L. David. *The Way of the Wolf.* Swan Hill Press, Shropshire.
1996. Rue, Leonard Lee, III. *Wolves: a Portrait of the Animal World.* Todtri, New York.

RED WOLF (*CANIS RUFUS*)   UNITED STATES

A close relative of the typical wolf *(Canis lupus)*, this species is almost extinct, with only about 250 individuals surviving. It used to inhabit much of the south-eastern region of North America in what is today North Carolina, South Carolina, Missouri, Oklahoma and Texas.

In the 1970s the US Fish and Wildlife Service began a project to capture the few remaining wild specimens. Only 14 suitable animals were obtained and these were used as the foundation stock for a captive breeding programme. This project proved a success and today there are about 200 red wolves alive in captivity, at 22 locations. In addition, some have been released back into the wild, in specially protected areas. There are about 30 at the Alligator River National Wildlife Refuge in North Carolina, 16 in the Great Smoky Mountains National Park in Tennessee, and seven on three islands managed as propagation projects.

As its name suggests, this species has a reddish tinge to its fur. It also has longer legs, larger ears and a shorter coat than the typical wolf. Weighing 45–80 lb (20–36 kg), it is intermediate in size between the typical, northern wolf and the coyote. Its natural food consists largely of deer, raccoons, rabbits and rodents.

References

1975. Carley, C. J. *Activities and Findings of the Red Wolf Recovery Program from Late 1973 to 1 July 1975.* United States Fish and Wildlife Service.

1987. Parker, W. T. *A Plan for Re-establishing the Red Wolf on Alligator River National Wildlife Refuge.* United States Fish and Wildlife Service.

1990. Parker, W. T. *A Proposal to Reintroduce the Red Wolf into the Great Smoky Mountains National Park.* United States Fish and Wildlife Service.

COYOTE (*CANIS LATRANS*)   NORTH AMERICA/CENTRAL AMERICA

The coyote is the New World equivalent of the Old World jackal. It has also been known as the prairie wolf.

Similar in appearance and colouring to the wolf, but on a smaller scale, this species stands about 24 in (61 cm) in height and weighs about 55 lb (25 kg), roughly the size of a collie. In earlier days it was found only on the prairie and the drier regions of the western parts of North America, but the widespread persecution of the wolf and the destruction of forests allowed the coyote to spread further east. Today it is encountered from the Pacific to the Atlantic coasts and from the Arctic Circle down as far as Costa Rica in Central America. The coyote is now the most widely distributed, and arguably the most successful, wild carnivore in North America. It is a food opportunist, eating almost anything that is available, from mammals and birds to fish and fruits.

References

1939. Hoyt, Vance. *Song Dog – the Story of a Coyote.* Winston, New York.

1950. Dobie, J. Frank. *The Voice of the Coyote.* Hammond, London.

1964. Wormer, Joe Van. *The World of the Coyote.* Lippincott, Philadelphia.

1975. Ryden, Hope. *God's Dog, a Celebration of the North American Coyote.* Coward, New York.

1978. Young, Stanley P. and Jackson, Hartley, H. T. *The Clever Coyote.* Bison Books, University of Nebraska Press, Lincoln, Nebraska.

1988. Leydet, Francois. *The Coyote, Defiant Songdog of the West.* University of Oklahoma, Norman, Oklahoma.

1991. Mitchell, Webster. *God's Dog – Conversations with Coyote.* Skinner House.

1994. Grady, Wayne. *The World of the Coyote.* Sierra Club Books, San Francisco.

1995. Meinzer, Wyman. *Coyote.* Texas Tech., Press, Lubbock, Texas.

1999. Swinburne, Stephen R. *Coyote: North America's Dog.* Boyds Mills Press, Honesdale, Pennsylvania.

Ellis, Mel. *Sad Song of the Coyote.* Holt Rinehart Winston, New York.

GOLDEN JACKAL (*CANIS AUREUS*) AFRICA/EUROPE/ASIA

This species has also been called the common jackal, the wolf-like jackal, the oriental jackal, the North African jackal, the chacal commun (in French), the Goldsschakal (in German), or the bweha wa mbuga (in Swahili).

This sandy-coloured jackal has a black-tipped tail. Its back is slightly darker than its underside. Its height is 15–20 in (38–50 cm).

A versatile and adaptable animal, this is the most common of the four jackal species, with a wide distribution from northern and eastern Africa, to south-eastern Europe, and across southern Asia as far as Burma and Thailand. It was once thought to have been an ancestor of the domestic dog, but careful analysis of its vocalizations and behaviour patterns has since shown that this is not the case.

Food is obtained both by scavenging and by hunting. The diet includes young gazelles, rabbits, hares, rodents, ground birds, fish, insects and fruit. Unlike the pack-living wolf, this species tends to form pairs and to exist in family groups.

Where the golden jackal has come into conflict with growing human populations in the Middle East, local extermination schemes have sometimes been implemented, with surprising results. After the jackals had been removed, the incidence of human deaths from snakebite quickly doubled. When the jackals were allowed to recolonize the region, the situation returned to normal, venomous snakes being an important part of their wild diet.

BLACK-BACKED JACKAL (*CANIS MESOMELAS*) EASTERN & SOUTHERN AFRICA

This species has sometimes been called the silver-backed jackal. It is also known as the chacal à chabraque (in French), the Schabrackenschakal (in German) or the bweha nyekundu (in Swahili).

This slender-bodied, long-legged, large-eared jackal exists today in two separate populations, one occurring in southern Africa and the other in east-central Africa. It is slightly bolder and more assertive than other jackals, with parents prepared to defend their young against powerful intruders. It is also more adventurous when feeding. When larger carnivores, such as lions or hyenas, have made a kill, the black-backed jackals will often dart in to snatch pieces of meat before the bigger animals have finished their meal. Like the golden jackals, they often hunt in pairs, especially when tackling heavier prey. They have even been known to take newborn wildebeest and to invade beached seal colonies during their breeding season, attacking the newborn seal pups.

In southern Africa the black-backed jackal is facing mounting difficulties. The widespread destruction of lions had reduced its opportunities for scavenging at major kills; the introduction of poisons to kill off rodent pests has robbed it of its smaller prey; and the spread of sheep-farming has thrown it into conflict with the rural human populations. Inevitably its numbers are falling.

SIDE-STRIPED JACKAL *(CANIS ADUSTUS)* TROPICAL AFRICA

This is also known as the chacal à flancs rayés (in French), the Streifenschakal (in German) or the bweha (in Swahili). In South Africa it used to be called the ashy jackal.

This species is very similar to the black-backed jackal but can be distinguished by its white tail-tip and a white stripe on its flank. It has shorter legs and smaller ears than other jackal species. The omnivorous diet includes small mammals, small birds, fish, insects, fruit and carrion.

Being confined to tropical Africa, it is less persecuted than the golden or the black-backed jackal, but in some regions it is killed by local tribes who believe that some parts of its body, such as its heart, skin and nails, are of magical or medicinal value.

SIMIEN JACKAL *(CANIS SIMENSIS)* ETHIOPIA

This is also sometimes known as the Ethiopian wolf or the simien fox.

A reddish-coloured jackal found only in the highlands of Ethiopia, this species is now extremely rare. It is estimated that there are only about 500–700 left alive in the wild. There are none in captivity.

It is slightly larger than the typical jackals, being 23 in (60 cm) in height. The tail is black-tipped and the predominantly red coat has white underparts. This is a daytime hunter of rabbits, hares and rodents, although it will sometimes scavenge on large carcasses. When food is plentiful it hoards its kills in 'larders'.

――――――――――

To complete this section on the wild dog species, the table shown opposite summarizes the classification of the entire dog family.

Family CANIDAE

	SCIENTIFIC NAME	COMMON NAME	DISTRIBUTION
1	*Canis lupus*	Wolf	Europe, Asia, N. America, Arctic
2	*Canis rufus*	Red wolf	N. America
3	*Canis latrans*	Coyote	N. and Central America
4	*Canis aureus*	Golden jackal	Europe, S. Asia and N. Africa
5	*Canis mesomelas*	Black-backed jackal	Africa
6	*Canis adustus*	Side-striped jackal	Africa
7	*Canis simensis*	Simien jackal	N. E. Africa
8	*Alopex lagopus*	Arctic fox	Arctic
9	*Vulpes velox*	Kit fox	N. America
10	*Vulpes vulpes*	Red fox	N. Hemisphere
11	*Vulpes corsac*	Corsac fox	Central Asia
12	*Vulpes bengalensis*	Bengal fox	Central Asia
13	*Vulpes rueppelli*	Sand fox	N. Africa and S.W. Asia
14	*Vulpes pallida*	Pale fox	N. Africa
15	*Vulpes cana*	Blanford's fox	W. Asia
16	*Vulpes chama*	Cape fox	S. Africa
17	*Vulpes ferrilata*	Tibetan fox	Central Asia
18	*Fennecus zerda*	Fennec fox	N. Africa & S. W. Asia
19	*Urocyon cinereoargenteus*	Grey fox	N. & S. America
20	*Urocyon littoralis*	Island grey fox	Santa Barbara Island, America
21	*Nyctereutes procyonoides*	Raccoon dog	E. Asia
22	*Dusicyon australis*	Falkland Island wolf	Falkland Islands (extinct)
23	*Dusicyon culpaeus*	Colpeo fox	S. America
24	*Dusicyon griseus*	Argentine grey fox	S. America
25	*Dusicyon gymnocercus*	Pampas fox	S. America
26	*Dusicyon sechurae*	Secura fox	S. America
27	*Dusicyon vetulus*	Hoary fox	S. America
28	*Atelocynus microtis*	Small-eared zorro	S. America
29	*Cerdocyon thous*	Crab-eating fox	S. America
30	*Chrysocyon brachyurus*	Maned wolf	S. America
31	*Speothos venaticus*	Bush dog	S. and Cen. America
32	*Cuon alpinus*	Asiatic wild dog	Asia, Sumatra, Java
33	*Lycaon pictus*	Hunting dog	Africa
34	*Otocyon megalotis*	Bat-eared fox	Africa

Dog Bibliography

Books about individual breeds are listed with their entries throughout the dictionary. For reasons of space, articles in magazines and periodicals are not included, except in rare cases where they are of special importance.

Below are more general references. First, there is a list of all the most important dog books, arranged historically. These are restricted to reference volumes that treat dog breeds systematically. Second, there are regional breed books, arranged country by country. Third, there are reference works that treat one particular group of breeds.

GENERAL BREED REFERENCE WORKS

1576. CAIUS, JOHANNES. *Of Englishe Dogges, the diversities, the names, the natures, and the properties.* **Rychard Johnes, London.**
This slim volume is the first book in English on the subject of dog breeds. It was originally written in Latin, in 1570, by English doctor John Keys at the request of the Swiss naturalist Konrad Gesner, who wished to include it as a section of his great *Historia Animalium.* It appeared in an English edition six years later.

1790. BEWICK, THOMAS. *A General History of Quadrupeds.* **Robinson & Dilly, London.**
Although domestic dogs form only a part of this work, its 18th-century descriptions of no fewer than 36 different canine breeds give it an important role in understanding their early history. This book was so successful that by 1824 it had already reached its 8th edition.

1801. EDWARDS, SYDENHAM. *Cynographia Britannica: Consisting of coloured engravings of the various breeds of dogs existing in Great Britain; drawn from the life, with observations on their properties and uses.* **Privately published, London.**
One of the most valued of all canine reference works, the *Cynographia* was the first dog book to be illustrated with hand-coloured plates. It was never completed and only covered 23 of the breeds. A facsimile edition was issued in 1992.

1803. TAPLIN, WILLIAM. *The Sportsman's Cabinet; or, a correct delineation of the various dogs used in the sports of the field: including the canine race in general. Consisting of a series of engravings of every distinct breed, from original paintings, taken from life. Interspersed with beautiful vignettes engraved on wood. Illustrated by a comprehensive, historical and systematic description of the different species, with a review of the various diseases to which they are subject, and the most approved and efficacious modes of treatment and cure. To which is added, a scientific disquisition upon the distemper, canine madness, and the hydrophobia.* **2 vols. Cundee, London.**
Although there are many early works on hunting or natural history which include sections on dog breeds, this two-volume work is the first lengthy study devoted entirely to the subject.

1809. BINGLEY, THE REVD W. *Memoirs of British Quadrupeds. Illustrative principally of their habits of life, instincts, sagacity, and uses to mankind.* **Darton & Harvey, London.**
A similar volume to Bewick's more famous (1790) work, this one describes only 21 different breeds of domestic dog.

1826. SCOTT, JOHN. *The Sportsman's Repository; comprising a series of highly finished engravings representing the horse and the dog in all their varieties; accompanied with a comprehensive historical and systematic description of the different species of each, their appropriate uses, management, and improvement.* Sherwood, Neely & Jones, London.
Only one third of this volume deals with horses, so that it remains primarily a book about dogs and presents details of 24 sporting breeds.

1829. BROWN, CAPTAIN THOMAS. *Biographical Sketches & Authentic Anecdotes of Dogs, exhibiting instances of instinct, sagacity and social disposition of this faithful animal: illustrated by representations of the most striking varieties.* Oliver & Boyd, Edinburgh.
With over 400 pages of breed descriptions, covering no fewer than 68 breeds of domestic dog, this was the most comprehensive treatment available at the time of its publication.

1837. BELL, THOMAS. *A History of British Quadrupeds.* Jan van Voorst, London.
Another general study that includes a long section on domestic dogs, in this case describing 22 different breeds.

1839. HAMILTON SMITH, CHARLES. *The Natural History of Dogs. Canidae or genus Canis of authors.* (Vol. IX and X of the Naturalist's Library conducted by Sir William Jardine) Lizars, Edinburgh. These two volumes cover all the wild species of the dog family as well as 78 breeds of domestic dogs.

1858. JESSE, EDWARD. *Anecdotes of Dogs.* Bohn, London.
Although it covers only 24 breeds, this book of nearly 500 pages provides greater detail on those which it does include.

1859. 'STONEHENGE' (JOHN HENRY WALSH). *The Dog in Health and Disease. Comprising the various modes of breaking and using him, for hunting, coursing, shooting etc., and including the points or characteristics of toy dogs.* Longman's, London.
A general treatment of dogs, including descriptions of 63 breeds, both sporting and non-sporting.

1866. JESSE, GEORGE R. *Researches into the History of the British Dog, from ancient laws, charters and historical records. With original anecdotes, and illustrations of the nature and attributes of the dog.* Hardwicke, London.
This detailed, two-volume work of over 800 pages covers the various dog breeds historically and anecdotally rather than listing them systematically.

1867. 'STONEHENGE' (JOHN HENRY WALSH). *The Dogs of the British Islands, being a series of articles on the points of their various breeds, and the treatment of the diseases to which they are subject.* Horace Cox, London.
A popular book by the editor of *The Field* magazine, which ran into five editions between 1867 and 1886. It contained sections on 52 breeds.

1872. 'IDSTONE' (THOMAS PEARCE). *The Dog; with simple directions for his treatment, and notices of the best dogs of the day and their breeders or exhibitors.* Cassell, London.
Another popular Victorian dog book, running to six editions. The text covers 41 breeds.

1872. WEBB, HENRY (Editor). *Dogs: Their Points, Whims, Instincts, and Peculiarities. With a retrospection of dog shows. Illustrated with over sixty photographs of champion and other prize dogs.* Dean & Son, London.
The first canine reference work to illustrate the various breeds with photographs.

1880. DALZIEL, HUGH. *British Dogs: their varieties, history, characteristics, breeding, management and exhibition.* The Bazaar Office, London.
An important, systematic treatment of dog breeds, arranging them according to their particular function.

1881. SHAW, VERO. *The Illustrated Book of the Dog.* Cassell, London.
The first true Canine Encyclopedia, covering 79 species, heavily illustrated, and with more than 600 pages. It was the major dog book of its time and was reissued in 1984 as *The Classic Encyclopedia of the Dog.*

1883. STABLES, GORDON. *Our Friend the Dog. A complete practical guide to all that is known about every breed of dog in the world.* Dean, London.
The special feature of this volume is its inclusion of 'the standard of points of the different breeds as recognized by judges'. It covers 71 breeds.

1887. 'STONEHENGE' (JOHN HENRY WALSH). *The Dogs of Great Britain, America, & Other Countries. Their breeding, training and management in health and disease. Comprising all the essential parts on the two standard works on the dog by Stonehenge. Together with chapter by American authors. With over one hundred illustrations.* Judd, New York.
This is the rarely encountered American edition of Stonehenge's classic studies, published in New York. It was produced to satisfy a growing interest in pedigree dogs in the United States. Importing Stonehenge's British volumes was too expensive for most American readers, so this modified, combined text was produced to be sold at 'less than one fifth the cost'.

1888–97. DALZIEL, HUGH. *British Dogs: describing the history, characteristics, breeding, management, and exhibition of the various breeds of dogs established in Great Britain. 3 vols.* Upcott Gill, London.
A greatly enlarged, heavily illustrated, three-volume, second edition of Dalziel's 1880 one-volume work, covering 85 breeds.

1890. MIVART, ST GEORGE. *Dogs, Jackals, Wolves, and Foxes: a Monograph of the Canidae.* Porter, London.
One of the most beautiful of all the early dog books, with 45 full-page colour plates by Keulemans, covering all the wild species and with a short section on domestic dogs.

1891. SHIELDS, G. O. (Editor). *The American Book of the Dog. The origin, development, special characteristics, utility, breeding, training, points of judging, diseases and kennel management of all breeds of dogs.* Rand McNally, Chicago.
The first American encyclopedia of canine information, covering 45 breeds in its 700 pages.

1893. LEE, RAWDON B. *A History and Description of the Modern Dogs of Great Britain and Ireland (sporting division).* Horace Cox, London.

1894. LEE, RAWDON B. *A History and Description of the Modern Dogs of Great Britain and Ireland (non-sporting division).* Horace Cox, London.

1894. LEE, RAWDON B. *A History and Description of the Modern Dogs of Great Britain and Ireland. (The Terriers.)* Horace Cox, London.
Three detailed, illustrated breed surveys by the kennel editor of *The Field* magazine, covering 62 breeds in a total of 1,386 pages.

1897. BEILBY, WALTER. *The Dog in Australasia.* Robertson, Melbourne.
The first major study of pedigree show dogs in Australia, covering 58 different breeds.

1898. MILLS, WESLEY. *The Dog Book. A manual on the dog: his origin, history, varieties, breeding, education, and general management in health and disease.* Fisher Unwin, London.
A general text on dog breeds and dog care, covering 54 breeds. This is the last of the 19th century, Victorian volumes on the subject.

1900. LANE, CHARLES HENRY. *All About Dogs. A book for doggy people. with eighty-seven illustrations of the most celebrated champions of our time drawn from life.* John Lane, London.
The author describes himself as 'Breeder, Exhibitor, Judge', and his survey of over 50 breeds focuses mainly on show dogs and the show-ring. Two years later he developed this theme in a work entitled 'Dog Shows and Doggy People', in which the dogs take second place to their celebrated owners.

1903. BARTON, FRANK TOWNEND. *The Kennel Encyclopedia.* Virtue, London.
A general canine encyclopedia that remained in print for over half a century. The seventh edition, revised by Leo Wilson, appeared in the mid 1950s.

1903. DRURY, W. D. *British Dogs. Their points, selection, and show preparation.* **Upcott Gill, London.**
A major study of British breeds, running to nearly 700 pages and providing detailed information on the breed standards laid down by the early breed clubs.

1904. COMPTON, HERBERT. *The Twentieth Century Dog. Compiled from the contributions of over 500 experts. Vol. 1. Non-sporting. Vol. 2. Sporting.* **Grant Richards, London.**
The author submitted a questionnaire to 2,000 dog-show experts and used their replies to form the basis of this work. Together the two volumes cover 82 breeds.

1904. DE BYLANDT, COUNT HENRY. *Dogs of all Nations. Their varieties, characteristics, points, etc.* **Kegan Paul, London.**
Perhaps the most amazing of all dog-breed books, this huge two-volume work runs to over 1,700 pages, with over 1,000 illustrations of 2,150 dogs. What makes it so extraordinary is that each breed is fully described in four languages: French, English, German and Dutch.

1906. WATSON, JAMES. *The Dog Book. A popular history of the dog, with practical information as to care and management of house, kennel, and exhibition dogs; and descriptions of all the important breeds.* **2 vols. Doubleday Page, New York.**
An ambitious work, well illustrated with photographs and reproductions of earlier plates, it covered 64 breeds in 750 pages.

1907. FREEMAN LLOYD, FREDERICK (Senior Editor). *Dogs.* **Library Supply Company, New York.**
This impressive American volume, edited by an international dog judge and breeder, covers only the 52 major breeds, but it does so in a spectacular way in a luxury format which, at 14 x 11 in (36 x 28 cm), defeats any normal bookcase. Published as part of 'Melbourne's Sporting Library', it is often referred to as 'Melbourne's Dogs'.

1907. LEIGHTON, ROBERT. *Cassell's New Book of the Dog. A comprehensive natural history of British dogs and their foreign relatives, with chapters on law, breeding, kennel management, and veterinary treatment.* **4 vols. Cassell, London.**
Illustrated with 21 colour plates and a large number of photographs, this was another ambitious canine work from the Edwardian period. It covers 84 major breeds.

1910. NOBLE, EDWIN. *The Dog Lover's Book.* **Wells, Gardner, Darton, London.**
Both written and illustrated by the author, with 24 colour plates and 57 black-and-white vignettes.

1925. JUDY, WILL. *Dog Encyclopedia. A complete reference work on dogs. Presenting the origin, development, history and standards of all breeds of the world; also all general subjects concerning the care, breeding, kenneling, training and exhibiting of the dog: together with interesting lore on the dog thruout the centuries.* **Judy, Chicago.**
Despite its modest size this is a true encyclopedia, its 460 densely packed pages offering a text of 325,000 words, with 375 illustrations. Written by the editor of *Dog World* magazine in the United States, its popularity led to a second, enlarged edition in 1936.

1927. SANDERSON, C. C. *Pedigree Dogs as recognized by the Kennel Club.* **Werner Laurie, London.**
An important early record presenting a complete survey of all the 74 breeds that were, at that date, officially recognized by the Kennel Club, including details of the breed standards.

1927. ASH, EDWARD C. *Dogs: Their History and Development.* **Benn, London.**
This monumental, two-volume work on the history of dog breeds remains to this day the most wide-ranging and scholarly treatment of the subject ever published.

1930. ASH, EDWARD C. *The Practical Dog Book. With chapters on the authentic history of all varieties hitherto unpublished, and a veterinary guide and dosage section, and information on advertising and on exporting to all parts of the world. A comprehensive work dealing with the buying, selling, breeding, showing, care, and feeding of the dog.* **Simpkin, Marshall, London.**
Following the success of his 1927 *magnum opus*, the author produced a sequel that followed a breed-by-breed approach.

1931. CROXTON-SMITH, A. *About Our Dogs. The breeds and their management.* **Ward Lock, London.**
Yet another breed-by-breed account. Its 450 pages cover all the popular breeds, providing information about origin, history and breed standards in each case.

1932. CROXTON-SMITH, A. and others. *Hounds & Dogs. Their care, training & working; for hunting, shooting, coursing, hawking, police purposes etc.* **Seeley Service, London.**
As a sequel to his 1931 general treatment, the author, with the help of many breed specialists, presented another breed-by-breed study, but this time focussing on their roles in the hunting field.

1934–35. HUTCHINSON, WALTER (Editor). *Hutchinson's Dog Encyclopedia. An invaluable work of international importance (alphabetically arranged for easy reference) on breeds of dogs of every country, with full veterinary advice in cases of accidents or ailments, etc., on their care and home treatment, contributed by the most eminent authorities.* **3 vols. Hutchinson, London.**
Despite the boastfulness of subtitling his own work as 'invaluable', one has to admire the editor of this huge three-volume compilation for the grand scope of his undertaking and its copious illustrations. At 2,000 pages it remains to this day the longest work on dog breeds ever published. Each breed is dealt with in great detail. To take one at random, the entry for the British Bulldog runs to 32 pages with no fewer than 44 illustrations.

1945. HUBBARD, CLIFFORD L. B. *The Observer's Book of Dogs.* **Warne, London.**
For many English-speaking people, this superb little volume was the only dog-breed book they ever possessed. Tiny in size but vast in information, it was a publishing paradox. Although it was inexpensive and would slip easily into a pocket, it contained descriptions of no fewer than 300 breeds and was illustrated with 147 photographs.

1947. HUBBARD, CLIFFORD L. B. *Working Dogs of the World.* **Sidgwick & Jackson, London.**
The excellent text, covering 85 working dog breeds in rewarding detail, compensates for the poor production qualities imposed on book publications in the years immediately following World War II.

1948. HUBBARD, CLIFFORD L. B. *Dogs in Britain. A description of all native breeds and most foreign breeds in Britain.* **Macmillan, London.**
An erudite text by one of the world's greatest experts on the subject.

1948. VESEY-FITZGERALD, BRIAN (Editor). *The Book of the Dog.* **Nicholson & Watson, London.**
Interest in pedigree dogs and dog shows returned after the savage interruption of World War II, and this impressive volume of over 1,000 pages was published to herald the new era. The entries were written by a wide range of canine specialists and covered 119 breeds in addition to general topics.

1953. DAVIS, HENRY P. (Editor). *The Modern Dog Encyclopedia.* **Stackpole & Heck, Harrisburg, Pennsylvania.**
Although poorly produced on inferior paper, this 600-page American encyclopedia, with its densely packed text, is a mine of information, culled from a wide variety of specialists. It contains a survey of all the breeds recognized, at the time, by the American Kennel Club, including details of breed standards and points. A much enlarged, second edition, called *The New Dog Encyclopedia*, appeared in 1970, printed on better paper and with over 100 additional pages.

1960. SCHNEIDER-LEYER, ERICH. *Dogs of the World.* **Fitch Daglish, London.**
Translated from the German, this was an interesting attempt to classify the breeds of dog according to their function and country of origin.

1968. HART, ERNEST H. *Encyclopedia of Dog Breeds. Histories and official standards. Evolution, geneology, genetics, breeding, feeding, husbandry, training, medical care, showing.* **TFH, New Jersey.**
This lengthy text devotes more than 650 of its nearly 800 pages to the sections on breed histories and standards. It covers 145 of the most important breeds. A second edition appeared in 1975.

1971. DANGERFIELD, STANLEY and HOWELL, ELSWORTH (Editors). *The International Encyclopedia of Dogs.* **Pelham Books, London.**

A well-presented general encyclopedia, with colour plates of 125 major breeds, this volume has the advantage of an editorship that combines a well-known British authority (Dangerfield) with a leading American one (Howell), giving it a transatlantic flavour.

1971. GWYNNE JONES, E. *A Bibliography of the Dog. Books Published in the English Language 1570–1965.* **The Library Association, London.**
An indispensable guide to the nearly 4,000 books written on dogs over the centuries, including a long section on breed monographs arranged on a breed-by-breed basis.

1971. HAMILTON, FERELITH. *The World Encyclopedia of Dogs.* **New English Library, London.**
Yet another general canine encyclopedia, this one is by the Editor of *Dog World* and describes over 280 of the world's important breeds. There are over 1,000 black-and-white illustrations.

1973. FIORIONE, FIORENZO (Editor). *The Encyclopedia of Dogs.* **Granada, London.**
Compiled with the help of 35 specialists, this major work was prepared with the cooperation of the Fédération Cynologique Internationale and includes details of all the 308 internationally recognized breeds. (It was originally published in Italian in 1970.)

1974. BROWNE, A. GONDREXON-IVES. *Guide to the Dogs of the World.* **Treasure Press, London.**
A useful, if somewhat utilitarian, small guidebook, describing and illustrating over 340 dog breeds, arranged three to a page,

1977. GLOVER, HARRY. *A Standard Guide to Pure-Bred Dogs.* **Macmillan, London.**
For those who wish to check the details of any official breed standard, this work provides the most detailed and best laid-out information, including explanatory diagrams. The author, who served as chairman of the Kennel Club's Stud Book and Registration Committee, covers some 350 different breeds, including a number which were not, at the time, officially recognized.

1980. SUTTON, CATHERINE G. *Dog Shows and Show Dogs. A definitive study.* **K & R Books, Lincolnshire.**
The ultimate volume for all those involved in showing pedigree dogs, with a mass of factual reference material on the Kennel Club. All officially recognized breeds are described and detailed breed standards are given, but there is nothing on breed history.

1980. ANON. *The Complete Dog Book. Golden Anniversary Edition. Official publication of the American Kennel Club.* **Howell, New York.**
This is a special (16th) edition of the AKC offical breed survey, the first of which appeared in 1929. It includes a photograph, history and the official standard of every one of the 124 breeds currently admitted to AKC registration.

1981. BARKER, A. J. and BARKER, H. A. *The Complete Book of Dogs.* **Bison Books, London.**
A well-produced general study by two appropriately named dog breeders who present a richly illustrated survey of a large number of breeds including some rarities.

1983. ANON. *The Macdonald Encyclopedia of Dogs. Over 320 breeds, each illustrated in full colour, with information on physical characteristics and temperament, uses and care, such as gentle dog, watchdog or guard dog, needs clipping, and many more...* **Macdonald, London.**
Undoubtedly the best of the small, modern pocket-guides to dog breeds, and invaluable for quick reference. Despite its small size, it packs in 450 pages of well-organized canine information.

1983. BONGIANNI, MAURIZIO and MORI, CONCETTA. *Dogs of the World.* **W H Allen, London.**
Originally an Italian work, this survey of 260 dog breeds is lavishly illustrated with meticulouly life-like paintings of dogs by illustrator Peiro Cozzaglio.

1984 (?). ALDERTON, DAVID. *The Dog. The most complete, illustrated, practical guide to dogs and their world.* **New Burlington Books, London.**
Although with only 200 pages this cannot support its claim to be the most complete guide to dogs, it does manage to cover, succinctly, over 350 different breeds.

1984. SYLVESTER, PATRICIA (Editor). *The Reader's Digest Illustrated Book of Dogs.* Reader's Digest, Montreal.
This is perhaps the best-designed, easiest-to-use dog-breed reference work ever published. It covers only the 170 most popular breeds, but it does so in such an efficient way that it tends to be the first book one reaches for in a shelf of dog books, when seeking a quick answer to a breed question.

1985. CARAS, ROGER (Editor). *Harper's Illustrated Handbook of Dogs. Every dog breed recognized in America.* Harper & Row, New York.
A useful, small guidebook covering 160 breeds with valuable charts giving practical information such as the suitability of a pet and potential health problems of each breed.

1985. SCANZIANI, PIERO. *The British Encyclopedia of Dogs. With a full-colour key to breeds recognized by the Kennel Club.* Orbis, London.
A useful general encycopedia translated from the original Italian edition of 1981, complete with details of breed standards.

1986. FLAMHOLTZ, CATHY J. *A Celebration of Rare Breeds. Vol. I.* OTR, Alabama.
The author has collected together an impressive amount of information on the rarer breeds of dogs. Together with Vol. II, which followed in 1991, a total of 88 rare breeds are surveyed in detail in more than 400 pages of text.

1988. ANON. *The Canadian Kennel Club Book of Dogs. Centennial Edition.* Stoddard, Toronto.
This bible of the Canadian Kennel Club includes meticulous details, including breed standards, of all the 140 dog breeds recognized by that club.

1989. WILCOX, BONNIE and WALKOWICZ, CHRIS. *The Atlas of Dog Breeds of the World.* TFH, New Jersey.
Claiming to be 'the most comprehensive fully illustrated volume on dogs ever published', this monumental work weighs more than a family bible. It is so heavy that it has been provided with a specially reinforced binding to prevent it disintegrating. With over 1,100 colour photographs and a huge variety of breeds represented, it is an impressively glossy volume of over 900 pages. It soon appeared in revised, enlarged versions and by 1995 had already reached its fifth edition.

1990. GANNON, DEE. *The Rare Breed Handbook.* 2nd edition. Golden Boy Press, New Jersey.
A curious, loose-leaf book from America that gathers together all the rare breeds that are currently seeking promotion to the ranks of the 'officially recognized'. A valuable source of information about the lesser known breeds.

1993. DE PRISCO, ANDREW and JOHNSON, JAMES B. Canine Lexicon. TFH, New Jersey.
A massive, 900-page canine encyclopedia with 3,500 entries, illustrated with 1,300 colour photographs. It surveys over 500 dog breeds from around the world.

1995. CLARK, ANNE ROGERS and BRACE, ANDREW H. (Editors). *The International Encyclopedia of Dogs.* Howell, New York.
Although the title of this volume has been used before (see 1971), this work, described as 'the ultimate reference to the global canine family', has some important new features. All breeds, alphabetically arranged, are illustrated by high-quality colour photographs, and the editors can boast that their book 'presents every breed currently recognized by the American and Canadian Kennel Clubs, the Kennel Club (England) and the Fédération Cynologique Internationale'. As with the 1971 volume, one of the editors (Clark) is American and one (Brace) is British.

1995. FOGLE, BRUCE. *The Encyclopedia of the Dog. The most comprehensive illustrated guide to the canine world, featuring over 400 breeds and varieties.* Dorling Kindersley, London.
This book of 300 pages covering 400 breeds claims to be 'the most comprehensive exploration of the dog world ever published', despite that fact that two years earlier a rival publication of 900 pages covered 500 breeds. A second complaint is that this is a packager's book first and an author's book second. It is so relentlessly over-illustrated that the extremely well-written text is pushed into

corners and wrapped around the endless photographs, reducing it to little more than a series of captions. Despite this, it is a beautifully produced and visually stunning volume.

1995. JACKSON, FRANK. *Dictionary of Canine Terms.* **Crowood Press, Wiltshire.**
Although much more modest in size than the 1993 Canine Lexicon, this is the most comprehensive dictionary of canine terms ever published. Containing 15,000 concise entries, it includes the names of most dog breeds and provides a brief description in each case.

1995. YAMAZAKI, TETSU. *Legacy of the Dog. The Ultimate Illustrated Guide to over 200 Breeds.* **Chronicle Books, San Francisco.**
Almost identical in visual treatment to *The Encyclopedia of the Dog* (1995), this book, translated from the Japanese, makes no pretence at giving its text any priority. This is confirmed by the fact that the 'author's' name on the title page is in reality that of the superb photographer who has supplied all the illustrations. The author of the text, Toyoharu Kojima, is relegated to small print on the next page. Having said that, the quality of the photographs is truly outstanding.

1997. LARKIN, PETER and STOCKMAN, MIKE. *The Ultimate Encyclopedia of Dogs, Dog Breeds and Dog Care.* **Select Editions, Oxford.**
A well-produced volume with excellent illustrations of about 180 breeds. As often happens in recent dog books, the all-too-brief breed texts take second place to the photographs.

1998. ANON. *The Kennel Club's Illustrated Breed Standards.* **Ebury Press, London.**
A sumptuously produced collection of the official breed standards of the 157 breeds recognized by the Kennel Club.

1998. RICE, DAN. *Dogs from A to Z. A Dictionary of Canine Terms.* **Barron, New York.**
The American equivalent of Frank Jackson's 1995 *Dictionary of Canine Terms* (see above), although on a more modest scale, including only 6,000 entries.

1999. CUNLIFFE, JULIETTE. *The Encyclopedia of Dog Breeds.* **Dempsey Parr, Bath.**
A well-organized, illustrated survey of nearly 400 dog breeds by a dedicated canine expert whose breed-by-breed texts are too short to do justice to her extensive knowledge of her subject. She has also been badly served editorially, but this remains a highly readable and extremely valuable general reference work.

REGIONAL BREED REFERENCE WORKS

BRITAIN

1866. Jesse, George R. *Researches into the History of the British Dog.* Hardwicke, London. 2 vols.
1867. 'Stonehenge' (John Henry Walsh). *The Dogs of the British Islands.* Horace Cox, London.
1888–97. Dalziel, Hugh. *British Dogs.* Upcott Gill, London. 3 vols.
1893. Lee, Rawdon B. *A History and Description of the Modern Dogs of Great Britain and Ireland (sporting division).* Horace Cox, London.
1894. Lee, Rawdon B. *A History and Description of the Modern Dogs of Great Britain and Ireland (non-sporting division).* Horace Cox, London.
1903. Drury, W. D. *British Dogs.* Upcott Gill, London.
1945. Smith, A. Croxton. *British Dogs.* Collins, London.
1948. Hubbard, Clifford L. B. *Dogs in Britain.* Macmillan, London.
1949. Hubbard, Clifford L. B. *Literature of British Dogs.* Hubbard, Ponterwyd.
1981. Ritchie, Carson I. A. *The British Dog: Its History from Earliest Times.* Hale, London.
1986. Wigan, Felicity. *The English Dog at Home.* Chatto & Windus, London.

SCOTLAND

1891. Gray, D. J. Thomson. *The Dogs of Scotland; their Varieties, History, Characteristics and Exhibition Points.* Mathew, Dundee. (Reissued in 1989)

IRELAND

1949. Redlich, Anna. *The Dogs of Ireland.* Dundalgan Press.
1984. Osborn, Catherine (Editor). *The Native Dogs of Ireland. Their Origin – Development – Standards.* Irish Kennel Club, Dublin.

BELGIUM

1997. Comstock, Sallyann. *Belgians from Start to Finish.* (All Belgian breeds)

HUNGARY

1977. Sarkany, Pal and Ocsag, Imre. *Dogs of Hungary.* Corvina Press.

ASIA

1921 Collier, V. W. F. *Dogs of China and Japan in Nature and Art.* Stokes, New York.
1963. Soman, W. V. *The Indian Dog.* Bhatkal, Bombay.
1970. Apso Committee. *A Brief Account of Tibetan Dogs.* Tibet House, New Delhi.
1971. Epstein, H. *Domestic Animals of China.* Africana, New York.
1977. Epstein, H. *Domestic Animals of Nepal.* Holmes & Meier, New York.
1978. Legl-Jacobsson, Elisabeth. *East Asiatic Breeds.* Tryck Produktion, Sweden.
1982. Wynyard, Anne Lindsay. *Dogs of Tibet and the History of the Tibetan Spaniel.* Book World, Rugby.
1991. Mitchell, Elsie P. *The Lion-Dog of Buddhist Asia.* Fugaisha, New York.
1992–98. Cunliffe, Juliette. *Tibetan Breeds International magazine.* (Later called: *Tibetan and Oriental Breeds International*). Issues 1–12.

AUSTRALIA

1897. Beilby, Walter. *The Dog in Australasia.* Robertson, Melbourne.
1914. Kaleski, Robert. *Australian Barkers and Biters.* NSW Book Selling Co, Sydney.
1948. McGorien, Tom. *The Australian Dog Book.* The Shakespeare Head, London.
1981. Sanderson, Angela. *The Complete Book of Australian Dogs.* The Currawong Press, New South Wales.

NORTH AMERICA

1948. Connett, Eugene V. (Editor). *American Sporting Dogs.* Van Nostrand, London.
1964. Griffen, Jeff. *The Hunting Dogs of America.* Doubleday, New York.
1987. Pferd, William, III. *Dogs of the American Indians.* Denlinger's, Virginia.

BREED GROUP REFERENCE WORKS

SIGHTHOUNDS

1976. Russell, Joanna. *All About Gazehounds.* Pelham Books, London.
1977. Salmon, M. H. *Gazehounds and Coursing.* High Lonesome Books, New Mexico.
1988. Miller, Constance O. *Gazehounds: the Search for Truth.* Hoflin, Colorado.
1992. Cunliffe, Juliette. *Popular Sight Hounds.* Popular Dogs, London.
1994. Beaman, Arthur. *Lure Coursing, Field Training for Sighthounds.* Howell, New York.

SCENTHOUNDS

1913. Barton, Frank Townend. *Hounds. Their Points and Management.* John Long, London.

1928. Thomas, Joseph. *Hounds and Hunting Through the Ages.* Derrydale Press, New York.
1937. Buchanan-Jardine, John. *Hounds of the World.* Methuen, London.
1939. Acton, C. R. *Hounds. An Account of the Kennels of Great Britain.* Heath Cranton, London.
1964. Wimhurst, C. G. E. *The Book of the Hound.* Muller, London.
1972. Duffey, David Michael. *Hunting Hounds.* Winchester Press, New York.
1979. Gilbey, Walter. *Hounds in the Old Days.* Spur, Surrey.
1979. Johnston, George and Ericson, Maria. *Hounds of France.* Spur, Surrey.
1987. Macgregor, J. and Johnston, J.*The Illustrated Guide to Hound Breeds.* Kelso Graphics,Scotland.
1988. Cummins, John. *The Hound and Hawk. The Art of Medieval Hunting.* Weidenfeld & Nicolson, London.
2000. Alderton, David. *Hounds of the World.* Swan Hill Press, Shrewsbury.

TERRIERS
1873. James, Ed. *Terrier Dogs.*
1894. Lee, Rawdon B. *The Terriers.* Horace Cox, London.
1907. Barton, Frank Townend. *Terriers. Their Points and Management.* John Long, London.
1909. Maxtee, John. *British Terriers: their breeding, management and training for show or work.* Upcott Gill, London. (2 vols)
1922. Matheson, Darley. *Terriers.* John Lane, London.
1925. Bristow-Noble, J. C. *Working Terriers, Their Management and Training.*
1925. O'Conor, Pierce. *Sporting Terriers.*
1931. Lucas, Jocelyn. *Hunt and Working Terriers.* Chapman & Hall, London.
1937. Smith, A. Croxton. *Terriers, Their Training, Working and Management.* Lonsdale Library.
1948. Russell, Dan. *Working Terriers.*
1964. Marvin, John T. *The Book of All Terriers.* Howell, New York.
1968. Wimhurst, G. E. *The Book of Terriers.* Frederick Muller, London.
1984. Delaney, Ronald. *Hounds and Terriers.* Blandford Press, Dorset.
1984. Horner, Tom. *Terriers of the World; their History and Characteristics.* Faber & Faber, London.
1988. Kern, Kerry. *The New Terrier Handbook.* Barron, New York.
1992. Plummer, Brian D. *The Sporting Terrier.* Boydell Press, Suffolk.

TREEING DOGS
1911. Williams, J. E. *Night Hunting.* The Southern Farm Coon Hound Kennels.
1924. Legare, Robert. *The Coonhound.* Hunter-Trapper-Trader Co., Columbus, Ohio.
1952. Whitney, Leon F. and Underwood, Acil B. *The Coon Hunter's Handbook.* Holt, Rinehart & Winston, New York.
1964. Henschel, Stan. *How to Raise and Train a Coonhound.* TFH, New Jersey.
1965. Long, T. A. *The Rugged Breed: True Adventures of Coon Hunters and Their Dogs.* Exposition Press, NY.
1983. Grewell, B. *The Modern World of Coon Hunting.* BHP Books, Johnson City, Tennessee.
1985. Wick, J. *Walk with Wick: the Tree Dog Encyclopedia.* Privately published.
1999. Osborn, David A. *Squirrel Dog Basics. A Guide to Hunting Squirrels with Dogs.* Treetop Publications, Watkinsville, Georgia.

GUN DOGS
1814. Dobson, William. *Kunopaedia.* Whittingham & Arliss, London.
1819. Johnson, T. B. *The Shooter's Companion.* Longman, London,
1890. 'H. H.' *The Scientific Education of Dogs for the Gun.* Sampson Low, London.
1890. Mercer, F. H. F. *The Spaniel and Its Training.* The Forest and Stream Publishing Co, New York.
1906. Bruette, William A. *Modern Breaking: a Treatise on the Rearing, Breaking and Handling of Setters and Pointers.* Privately published, Chicago.
1906. Phillips, C. A. and Cane, R. Claude. *The Sporting Spaniel.* Our Dogs, Manchester.
1913. Barton, Frank Townend. *Gun Dogs.* John Long, London.

1915. Carlton. *Spaniels. Their Breaking for Sport and Field Trials.*

1922. Hochwalt, A. F. *Bird Dogs.* Sportsman's Digest, Ohio.

1922. Sanderson, C. M. *The Practical Breaking and Training of Gundogs.* Our Dogs, Manchester.

1923. Hochwalt, A. F. *The Modern Setter.* Hochwalt.

1923. Lytle, Horace. *Breaking a Bird Dog.* Fenno, New York.

1924. Young, Eugene. *Dog and Gun.* Crocker, Waterford, Eire.

1926. Lytle, Horace. *Bird Dog Days.* Appleton, New York.

1926. Ripley, Ozark. *Bird Dog Training Made Easy.* Sportsman's Digest, Cincinnati.

1926. Sprake, Leslie C., et al. *The Popular Retrievers.* Popular Dogs, London.

1927. Phillips C. A. and Caine, R. Claude. *The Sporting Spaniel.* Our Dogs, Manchester.

1928. Whitford, C. B. *Training the Bird Dog.* Macmillan, New York.

1929. Holland, Ray P. *My Gun Dogs.* Houghton Mifflin, New York.

1930. Hardy, H. F. H. *Good Gun Dogs.* Country Life, London.

1930. Lloyd, Freeman. *All Spaniels. Their Breeding, Rearing and Training.* Privately published, New York.

1931. Badcock, G. H. *The Early Life and Training of a Gun Dog.* Watmoughs, Bradford, Yorkshire.

1931. Chalmers, Patrick R. *Gun Dogs.* Eyre & Spottiswoode, London.

1934. Lytle, Horace. *How to Train Your Bird Dog.* Hochwalt, Dayton, Ohio.

1935. Clark, Atwood. *Gun Dogs and their Training.* A & C Black, London.

1936. Bruette, W. *Modern Breaking. Rearing, Breaking, Handling Bird Dogs.* Nessmuk Library, New York.

1936. Smith, Lawrence Breese. *Modern Gun Dogs; their Uses and Care.* Scribner's, New York.

1937. Freeman, Lloyd. *All Setters: Their Histories, Rearing and Training.* Privately published.

1937. Moffit, Ella B. *Elias Vail Trains Gun Dogs.* Orange Judd, New York.

1938. Riviere, B. B. *Retrievers: Some Hints on Breaking and Handling for Amateurs.* Faber & Faber, London.

1942. Brown, William. *How to Train Hunting Dogs.* Barnes, New York.

1942. Lytle, Horace. *Gun Dogs Afield.* Putnam's, New York.

1945. Brown, William F. *Retriever Gun Dogs — History, Breed Standards and Training.* Barnes, New York.

1947. Moxon, P. R. A. *Gundogs. Modern Methods of Training.* The Shooting Times.

1947. Pfaffenberger, Clarence. *Training Your Spaniel.* Putnam's, New York.

1947. Shelley, E. M. *Bird Dog Training Today and Tomorrow.* Putnam's, New York.

1948. Bennett, Logan Johnson. *Training Grouse and Woodcock Dogs.* Putnam's, New York.

1948. Davis, Henry P. *Training Your Own Bird Dog.* Putnam's, New York.

1948. Yeatter, Ralph E. *Bird Dogs in Sport and Conservation.* INHS, Illinois.

1949. Taber, Gladys. *Especially Spaniels.*

1951. Badcock, G. H. *The Handling of Gun Dogs, during and after Training.* Gamekeeper and Countryside, Hertford.

1952. Elliot, David, D. *Training Gun Dogs to Retrieve.* Holt, New York.

1952. Moxon, P. R. A. *Gundogs. Training and Field Trials.* Popular Dogs, London.

1956. Lytle, Horace. *Point! a Book about Bird Dogs.* Derrydale, New York.

1957. Anon. *The Rough Shooter's Dog.* MacGibbon & Kee, London.

1959. Cofield, Thomas R. *Training the Hunting Retriever.* Van Nostrand, New Jersey.

1961. Wolters, Richard A. *Gun Dog; Revolutionary Rapid Training Method.* Dutton, New York.

1962. Leclerc, Maurice J. *The Retriever Trainer's Manual.* Ronald Press, New York.

1963. Brander, Michael. *Gundogs. Their Care and Training.* A & C Black, London.

1963. Coykendall, Ralf W., Jnr. *You and Your Retriever.* Doubleday, New York.

1963. Marr, W. *Pointers and Setters.* Privately published, Ireland.

1964. Garton, R. V. *Dogs and Guns.* Bles, London.

1964. Wehle, Robert G. *Wing and Shot, Gun Dog Training.* Country Press, New York.

1965. Stetson, Joe. *The Hunter's Handbook of Gundogs.* TFH, New Jersey.

1967. Gordon, John F. *The Spaniel Owner's Encyclopedia.* Pelham Books, London.

1969. Monk, John. *Gun Dogs. A Training Guide for Australia and New Zealand.* Reed, Sydney.

1969. Radcliffe, Talbot. *Spaniels for Sport.* Faber & Faber, London.

1972. Burnell, Roy. *Gundogs for Field or Trial.* Pollard Publishing, Australia.

1973. Unkelbach, Kurt. *Those Lovable Retrievers.* McGraw Hill, New York.

1974. Jackson, Tony (Editor). *The Complete Book of Gundogs in Britain.* Barrie & Jenkins, London.

1974. Knap, Jerome and Knap, Alison. *Training the Versatile Gun Dog.* Scribners, New York.

1975. Duffey, Dave. *Dave Duffey Trains Gun Dogs.* Spencerport, New York.

1975. Maurice, J. B. *Training Pointers and Setters.* Barnes, New York.

1975. Moreau, L. *Les Épagneuls.* Éditions Bornemann, Paris.

1976. Burnell, Roy. *Gun Dogs for Field or Trial.* Pollard Publishing.

1976. Scales, Susan. *Retriever Training. The Modern Way.* David & Charles, Newton Abbot, Devon.

1977. Duffey, David Michael. *Expert Advice on Gun Dog Training.* Winchester, New York.

1978. Goodall, Charles. *How to Train Your own Gun Dog.* Howell, New York.

1978. Luedke, Jacky. *Les Pointers.* Solar.

1980. Irving, J. *Training Spaniels.* David & Charles, Newton Abbot, Devon.

1980. Johnston, James. *The Illustrated Guide to Gundog Breeds.* Kelso, Scotland.

1980. McCarty, Diane (Editor). *German Shorthaired Pointer.* TFH, New Jersey.

1980. Osbourn, H. J. I. *Working Gundogs and their Training.* Country Life Books.

1982. Roebuck, Kenneth C. *Gundog Training: Spaniels and Retrievers.* Stackpole Books.

1983. Irving, Joe. *Gundogs: Their Learning Chain.* Swan Hill Press, Shrewsbury.

1984. Bishop, Gerald. *Spaniels.* David & Charles, Newton Abbot, Devon.

1984. Tarrant, Bill and Samson, Jack. *Best Way to Train Your Gun Dog; the Delmar Smith Method.* David McKay.

1985. Duffey, David Michael. *Expert Advice on Gun Dog Training.* New Win Publishing.

1987. Dumand, Michel. *Le Cocker et les Autres Spaniels.* Éditions de Vecchi, Paris.

1987. Mueller, Larry. *Speed Train Your Own Retriever: The Quick, Efficient, Proven System for Training a Finished Dog.*

1988. Goodall, Charles S. *How to Train your own Gun Dog.* IDG Books Worldwide.

1989. Smith, Stanley W. C. *Bird Dogs of the World.* Nimrod Press, Alton, Hamshire.

1991. Free, James Lamb. *Training Your Retriever.*

1991. Mohn, Ronald D. *Shortcuts in Gun Dog Training.* RDM Enterprises.

1991. Tarrant, Bill. *Training the Hunting Retriever: The New Program.*

1992. Fergus, Charles. *Gun Dog Breeds. A Guide to Spaniels, Retrievers, and Pointing Dogs.* Lyons & Burford, NY.

1992. Hooper, Johnson Jones. *Dog and Gun.* University of Alabama Press, Alabama.

1993. Hobson, J. C. Jeremy. *Gundog Training – Your Problems Solved!* Batsford, London.

1994. Jenkins, Len. *Gun Dog Training.* CJ Publishing.

1995. Hudson. *The Shooting Man's Dog.* Swan-Hill.

1995. Wolters, Richard A. *Game Dog: The Hunter's Retriever for Upland Birds and Waterfowl: A Concise New Training Method.*

1996. Tarrant, Bill. *Gun Dog Training; New Strategies from Today's Top Trainers.* Voyageur Press.

1996. Tarrant, Bill. *Training the Versatile Retriever to Hunt Upland Birds.* Wilderness Adventures Press, Montana.

1997. Averis, Gillian. *Veterinary Advice for Gundog Owners.* Howell, New York.

1997. Falk, J. *Master Training Series. Gun Dogs.* Voyageur Press, Stillwater, Minnesota.

1998. Smith, Steve. *Just Setters.* Just Series.

1998. Spencer, James B. *Training Retrievers for the Marshes and Meadows.*

1999. Robinson, Jerome B. *Training the Hunting Retriever.*

2000. Arnette, Joe. *Training Retrievers and Spaniels to Hunt 'Em Up!*

Bailey, Joan. *The Griffon – Gun Dog Supreme.* Doral Publishing.

Gagniard, André. *L'Épagneul Breton, Chien d'Arrêt Idéal.* Crépin-Leblond, Paris.

Little, Crawford. *The Dog and the Gun.*

Knap, Jerome J. *Training the Versatile Gun Dog.*

Kersley, J. A. *Training the Mind of your Gun Dog.*

Roebuck, Kenneth C. *Gundog Training: Pointing Dogs.* Stackpole Books.

FIGHTING DOGS

1935. Armitage, George. *Thirty Years With Fighting Dogs.*

1984. Semencic, Carl. *The World of Fighting Dogs.* TFH, New Jersey.

1996. Fleig, Dieter. *Fighting Dog Breeds.* TFH, New Jersey. (Translation of German book, *Kampfhunde II*, published by Kynos Verlag.)

1996. Fleig, Dieter. *History of Fighting Dogs.* TFH, New Jersey. (Translation of German book, *Kampfhunde I*, published by Kynos Verlag.)

1998. Semencic, Carl. *Gladiator Dogs.* TFH, New Jersey.

2000. Homan, Mike. *A Complete History of Fighting Dogs.* IDG Books Worldwide.

HERDING DOGS

1892. Jones, Edward W. H. *Sheep-dog Trials and the Sheep-Dog.* Edwin Poole, Brecon.

1911. Gosset, Adelaide L. J. *Shepherds of Britain.* Constable, London.

1927. Whyte, William. *The Sheepdog.* Whitcombe and Tombs, Auklland, New Zealand.

1929. Moore, James L. *The Canine King: the Working Sheepdog.* Standard, Cheltenham.

1938. McCulloch, John Herries. *Sheep Dogs and Their Masters.* Moray Press.

1942. Kelly, R. B. *Sheep Dogs.* Angus & Robertson, London.

1948. Puxley, W. Lavallin. *Collies and Sheep-dogs.* Williams & Norgate, London.

1950. Moorhouse, Sydney. *The British Sheep Dog.* Witherby, London.

1951. Hartley, WC, W. G. *The Shepherd's Dogs.* Whitcombe and Tombs, Christchurch, New Zealand.

1954. Day, J. Wentworth. *The Wisest Dogs in the World.* Ward, Derbyshire.

1960. Holmes, John. *The Farmer's Dog.* Popular Dogs, London.

1976. Longton, Tim and Hart, Edward. *The Sheep Dog – Its Work and Training.* David & Charles, Newton Abbot, Devon.

1977. Ederer, Bernard Francis. *Bingo. Gallant Reindeer Dog.* Exposition Press, Hicksville. (An account of life among Eskimo reindeer herders and their dogs, on Richards Island in the Northwest Territory of the Canadian Arctic.)

1978. Drabble, Phil. *One Man and His Dog.* Michael Joseph, London.

1978. Iley, Tony. *Sheepdogs at Work.* Dalesman Books.

1980. Halsall, Eric. *Sheepdogs. My Faithful Friend.* Stephens, Wellingborough.

1980. Philip, Ron. *Training Sheepdogs.* South African Sheepdog Association.

1982. Halsall, Eric. *Sheepdog Trials.* Stephens, Wellingborough.

1982. Luquet, Maurice. *Les Chiens de Berger Français.* (French Sheepdogs). Éditions de Vecchi, Paris.

1983. Combe, Iris. *Shepherds, Sheep and Sheepdogs.* Dalesman Books.

1983. Hunter, R. G. *Sheep Dog Training Explained.* Hereford.

1984. Billingham, Viv. *One Woman and Her Dog.* Stephens, Wellingborough.

1986. Taggart, Mari. *Sheepdog Training – an All-Breed Approach.* Alpine, Colorado.

1987. Combe, Iris. *Herding Dogs. Their Origins and Development in Britain.* Faber & Faber, London.

1988. Templeton, John and Mundell, Matt. *Working Sheep Dogs.* Crowood Press, Wiltshire.

1994. Holland, Vergil S. *Herding Dogs: Progressive Training.* Howell, New York.

1997. Starkweather, Pat. *The Magnificent Collie.*

GUARD DOGS

1923. Richardson, Edwin Hautonville. *Watch-dogs: Their Training and Management.* Hutchinson, London.

1949. MacInnes, John Watson. *Guard Dogs.* Williams & Norgate, London.

1955. Lampson, S. M. (Editor). *Training Guard Dogs.* Ernest Benn, London.

1991. Anon. *Pit Bulls & Tenacious Guard Dogs.* TFH, New Jersey.

SLED DOGS

1871. Bush, Richard J. *Reindeer, Dogs and Snow-shoes.* Sampson Low, London.

1873. Butler, W. F. *The Wild North Land.* Sampson Low, London.

1902. Young, Egerton Ryerson. *My Dogs in the Northland.* Revell, New York.

1925. Hutton, S. K. *By Eskimo Dog-Sled and Kayak.* Service, Seeley.

1928. Walden, Arthur Treadwell. *A Dog-Puncher in Yukon.* Werner Laurie, London.

1931. O'Brien, John S. *By Dog Sled for Byrd*. Rockwell, Chicago.
1939. Machetanz, Frederick. *Panuck – Eskimo Sled Dog*. Charles Scribners, New York.
1945. Caldwell, Elsie Noble. *Alaska Trail Dogs*. Richard R. Smith. New York.
1957. Howarth, David. *The Sledge Patrol*. Collins, London.
1960. Taylor, Phyllis M. *Dog-Team and School Desk*. Herbert Jenkins, London.
1995. Paulsen. *Winterdance: The Fine Madness of Alaskan Dog Training*.

HAIRLESS DOGS
1987. Gorwill, S. G. *Hairless Dogs of the World*. Gorwill, Bonvilston, Glamorgan.
1999. Fernandez, Amy and Rhae, Kelly. *Hairless Dogs – The Naked Truth*. (Chinese Crested, Xoloitzcuintli, and Peruvian Inca Orchid)

TOY DOGS
1879. Stables, Gordon. *Ladies' Dogs as Companions*. Dean, London.
1899. Diehl, John E. *The Toy Dog*. Associated Fanciers, Philadelphia.
1902. Spicer, Muriel Handley. *Toy Dogs*. Black, London.
1904. Barton, Frank T. *Toy Dogs*. Everett, London.
1904. Williams, Mrs Leslie. *A Manual of Toy Dogs and their Treatment*. Appleton, London.
1907. Raymond-Mallock, Lillian C. *Toy Dogs*. Dogdom, Battle Creek, Michigan.
1910. Megnin, Pierre and Lussigney, Jacques. *Toy Dogs*. Vincennes, Paris.
1911. Barton, Frank T. *My Book of Little Dogs*. Jarrold, London.
1911. Lytton, Mrs Neville. *Toy Dogs and Their Ancestors*. Duckworth, London.
1922. Maxtee, John. *Popular Toy Dogs*. The Bazaar, London.
1924. Milner, Ada. *Les chiens d'agrément. Toy Dogs*. Lapina Imp, Paris.
1930. Valdes, André. *Le Chien de Luxe*. Paris.
1933. Rine, Joseph Z. *Toy Dogs*. Orange Judd, New York.
1935. American Kennel Club. *Toy Dogs*. Watt, New York.
1964. De Kock, Henri. *Les Petits Chiens*. de Vresse, Paris.
1965. Ricketts, Viva Leone. *All about Toy Dogs*. Howell, New York.
1965. Wimhurst, C. G. E. *The Book of Toy Dogs*. Muller, London.
1967. Dangerfield, Stanley. *Dogs: Toy and Miniature Breeds*. Arco, London.
1970. Sheldon, Margaret and Lockwood, Barbara. *The Toy Breeds*. Pelham Books, London.
1976. Hogg, Peggy G. and Berndt, R. J. *Grooming and Showing Toy Dogs*. Denlinger's, USA.
1976. Kalstone, Shirley. *The Kalstone Guide to Grooming all Toy Dogs*. Howell, New York.
1977. Glover, Harry. *Toydogs*. David & Charles, Newton Abbot, Devon.
1980. Möckesch, Eduard. *Des Kleinhundebuch*. Kosmo-Verlag, Germany.
1989. Waud, Clarice and Hutchings, Mark. *Toy Dogs*. Nimrod, Hampshire.
1994. Waud, Clarice and Hutchings, Mark. *A Bibliography of Toy Dogs*. Waud & Hutchings, Surrey.
1996. Jester, Terry. *Living with Small and Toy Dogs*. Alpine Productions.

WILD DOGS
1965. Colby, C. B. *Wild Dogs*. Duell, Sloan & Pearce, New York.
1971. Fox, Michael W. *Behaviour of Wolves, Dogs and Related Canids*. Jonathan Cape, London.
1974. Bueler, Lois E. *Wild Dogs of the World*. Constable, London.
1979. Riddle, Maxwell. *The Wild Dogs in Life and Legend*. Howell, New York.
1983. Fox, Michael W. (Editor). *The Wild Canids*. Krieger, Florida.
1992. Sheldon, Jennifer W. *Wild Dogs. The Natural History of Nondomestic Canidae*. Academic Press, London.
1994. Alderton, David. *Foxes, Wolves and Wild Dogs of the World*. Blandford, London.
1996. Biel, Timothy L. *Wild Dogs*. Mankato, Minnesota.
2000. Reid, Mary E. *Wolves and other Wild Dogs*. World Book's Animals of the World.

INDEX OF BREEDS

Pachon de Vitoria 261
Pachon Iberico 261
Pa-Erh 708
Paisley Skye 181
Paisley Terrier 181
Palace Dog 537
Pannonian Dog 708
PANNONIAN HOUND 708
PAPILLON 512
Papuan Dog 707
PARDOG 708
PARIAH DOG 686
PARSON JACK RUSSELL TERRIER 171
Particoloured Setter 246
PARTRIDGE DOG (DUTCH) 312
Pashmi Hound 47
Pastore Abruzzese 380
PASTORE FONNESE 708
Pastore Maremmano 380
Pastore Maremmano-Abruzzese 380
PASTORE SILANO 708
PATAGONIAN DOG 337
PATAGONIAN SHEEPDOG 456
Patched Fighting Terrier 346
PATTERDALE TERRIER 172
Patterdale Terrier (Lakeland Terrier) 165
PATTI 404
Peerie 412
Peiching Kou 451
Peintinger 96
Peintinger Bracke 96
PEK-A-POM 708
Pek-a-Poo 566
PEKEPOO 565
Pekinese 541
Pekinese Spaniel 541
PEKINGESE 541
Peking Palace Dog 541
Peking Palasthund 541
Pekin Spaniel 541
Pelo Encaracolado 490
Pelon 592
Pembrokeshire Terrier 189
PEMBROKE WELSH CORGI 464
PEN-LO 708
Pen-Lo Pa-Erh 708
Pepper and Mustard Terrier 182
Perdiguero Burgalés 262
Perdiguero De Burgos 262
Perdiguero Navarro 261
Perdigueiro Portugueso 262
PERRO CIMARRON 635
Perro Criollo 635
Perro de Agua de Español 293
Perro de Pastor Catalan 431
Perro de Pastor Catalan de Pelo Corto 432
Perro de Pastor Catalan de Pelo Largo 431
Perro de Pastor Mallorquin 375
Perro de Presa Canario 351

Perro de Presa España 352
Perro de Presa Mallorquin 351
Perro Flora 594
Perro Gaucho 635
Perro Jorobado 590
Perro Mastin del Pireneo 376
Perro sin Pelo del Peru 594
Persian Greyhound 34
PERSIAN SHEEP DOG 708
Peruaanse Haarloze Hond 594
Peruanischer Nackthund 594
Perunkarvatonkoira 594
PERUVIAN HAIRLESS DOG 594
PERUVIAN INCA ORCHID 594
PERUVIAN PUG-NOSED DOG 595
Petit Anglo-Français 72
PETIT BASSET GRIFFON VENDÉEN 133
Petit Berger 423
PETIT BLEU DE GASCOGNE 76
PETIT BRABANÇON 198
Petit Braque Français 257
Petit Chien Lion 511
PETIT GASCON-SAINTONGEOIS 80
PETIT GRIFFON BLEU DE GASCOGNE 76
PHALÈNE 518
PHARAOH HOUND 33
PHILIPPINES EDIBLE DOG 585
Philippines Islands Dog 585
Philippines Native Dog 585
PHU QUOC DOG 633
Pic 466
Picardy Setter 310
PICARDY SHEPHERD 422
PICARDY SPANIEL 310
Piccolo Brabantino 198
Piccolo Levriero Italiano 517
Pi-Dog 686
PIEBALD SHEPHERD 708
Pie-Dog 686
PILA DOG 708
Pillow Dog 570
PINSCHER 207
PINSCHER (AUSTRIAN SHORT-HAIRED) 200
Pinscher (German) 207
PINSCHER (HARLEQUIN) 524
Pinscher (Medium) 207
PINSCHER (MINIATURE) 208
Pinscher (Reh) 207
Pinscher (Standard) 207
Pit Bull 363
PIT BULLMASTIFF 368
PIT BULL TERRIER (AMERICAN) 363
Pit-dog 346, 363
PITTENWEEM TERRIER 184
PLAINS-INDIAN DOG 662
Plantation Dog 359
Plizeilich Soldatenhund 611
Plott Cur 237

PLOTT HOUND 233
PLUMIN DOG 708
PLUMMER TERRIER 173
Plum Pudding Dog 673
Poacher's Dog 17
Pocadan 69
POCKET BEAGLE 127
PODENCO (ANDALUSIAN) 26
Podenco Andaluz 26
Podenco Canario 27
PODENCO (CANARY ISLANDS) 27
Podenco Español 26
Podenco Ibérico 26
Podenco Ibicenco 28
Podenco Mallorquin 28
Podengo de Mastra 262
PODENGO (LARGE PORTUGUESE) 29
PODENGO (MEDIUM PORTUGUESE) 30
PODENGO (SMALL PORTUGUESE) 199
Podengo Pequeno 199
Podengo Portuguesa Grande 29
Podengo Portuguesa Medio 30
Podengo Portuguesa Pequeno 199
Pohjanpystykorva 315
POI DOG 588
POINTER (ARIÈGE) 253
Pointer (Arkwright) 700
POINTER (AUVERGNE) 254
Pointer (Belgian) 259
POINTER (BELGIAN SHORT-HAIRED) 259
POINTER (BLACK) 700
POINTER (BOURBONNAIS) 254
POINTER (CHARLES X) 255
POINTER (CZECH) 275
POINTER (DUPUY) 255
POINTER (ENGLISH) 252
POINTER (GASCONY) 257
POINTER (GERMAN BROKEN-COATED) 265
POINTER (GERMAN LONG-HAIRED) 265
POINTER (GERMAN SHORT-HAIRED) 266
POINTER (GERMAN WIRE-HAIRED) 267
POINTER (HERTHA) 273
POINTER (ITALIAN) 263
POINTER (OLD DANISH) 273
POINTER (OLD SPANISH) 261
POINTER (PORTUGUESE) 262
POINTER (PYRENEES) 257
POINTER (SAINT-GERMAIN) 258
POINTER (SHORT-HAIRED BELGIAN) 259
POINTER (SLOVENSKY) 275
POINTER (SPANISH) 261
POINTER (WÜRTEMBERG) 272
Pointing Wire-haired Griffon 260
POITEVIN 84

Index of Breeds